2016 Wiley CPAexcel® EXAM REVIEW STUDY GUIDE JANUARY 2016

2016

Wiley

CPAexcel®
EXAM REVIEW
STUDY GUIDE
JANUARY 2016

BUSINESS ENVIRONMENT
AND CONCEPTS

O. Ray Whittington, CPA, PhD

WILEY

CONTENTS

PREFACE

Passing the CPA exam upon your first attempt is possible! The *Wiley CPAexcel® Exam Review 2016 Study Guide January: Business Environment and Concepts* preparation materials provide you with the necessary materials (visit our website at www.wiley.com/cpa for more information). It's up to you to add the hard work and commitment. Together we can beat the pass rate on each section of about 50%. All Wiley CPAexcel® products are continuously updated to provide you with the most comprehensive and complete knowledge base. Choose your products from the Wiley preparation materials and you can proceed confidently. You can select support materials that are exam-based and user-friendly. You can select products that will help you pass!

Remaining current is one of the keys to examination success. Here is a list of what's new in this edition of the *Wiley CPAexcel® Exam Review 2016 Study Guide January: Business Environment and Concepts* text.

- The new AICPA Content Specification Outlines on Business Environment and Concepts for the Computerized CPA Examination beginning in 2014
- New task-based simulations involving communication
- AICPA questions released in 2015

The objective of this work is to provide you with the knowledge to pass the Business Environment and Concepts portion of the Uniform Certified Public Accounting (CPA) Exam. The text is divided up into eight areas of study called modules. Each module contains written text with discussion, examples, and demonstrations of the key exam concepts. Following each text area, actual American Institute of Certified Public Accountants (AICPA) unofficial questions and answers are presented to test your knowledge. We are indebted to the AICPA for permission to reproduce and adapt examination materials from past examinations. Author-constructed questions are provided for new areas or areas that require updating. All author constructed questions are modeled after AICPA question formats. The multiple-choice questions are grouped into topical areas, giving candidates a chance to assess their areas of strength and weakness. Selection and inclusion of topical content is based upon current AICPA Content Specification Outlines. Only testable topics are presented. If the CPA exam does not test it, this text does not present it.

The CPA exam is one of the toughest exams you will ever take. It will not be easy. But if you follow our guidelines and focus on your goal, you will be thrilled with what you can accomplish.

Ray Whittington
January 2016

DON'T FORGET TO VISIT OUR WEBSITE AT WILEY.COM/GO/CPAERRATA FOR SUPPLEMENTS AND UPDATES.

ABOUT THE AUTHOR

Ray Whittington, PhD, CPA, CMA, CIA, is the dean of the Driehaus College of Business at DePaul University. Prior to joining the faculty at DePaul, Professor Whittington was the Director of Accountancy at San Diego State University. From 1989 through 1991, he was the Director of Auditing Research for the American Institute of Certified Public Accountants (AICPA), and he previously was on the audit staff of KPMG. He previously served as a member of the Auditing Standards Board of the AICPA and as a member of the Accounting and Review Services Committee and the Board of Regents of the Institute of Internal Auditors. Professor Whittington has published numerous textbooks, articles, monographs, and continuing education courses.

ABOUT THE CONTRIBUTOR

Kurt Pany, PhD, CPA, is a Professor of Accounting at Arizona State University. His basic and advanced auditing courses provided the basis on which he received the Arizona Society of CPAs' Excellence in Teaching Award and an Arizona CPA Foundation Award for Innovation in the Classroom for the integration of computer and professional ethics applications. His professional experience includes serving for four years on the AICPA's Auditing Standards Board, serving as an academic fellow in the Auditing Division of the AICPA, and, prior to entering academe, working as a staff auditor for Deloitte and Touche.

INTRODUCTION

To maximize the efficiency of your review program, begin by studying (not merely reading) Chapters 1 through 5 of this volume. They have been carefully organized and written to provide you with important information to assist you in successfully completing the Business Environment and Concepts (BEC) section of the CPA exam. Beyond providing a comprehensive outline to help you organize the material tested on the BEC exam, these chapters will assist you in organizing a study program to prepare for the exam. Self-discipline is essential.

Chapter 1: Beginning Your CPA Review Program

GENERAL COMMENTS ON THE EXAMINATION

The Uniform CPA Examination is delivered using computer-based testing (CBT). CBT has several advantages. You may take the exam one section at a time. As a result, your studies can be focused on that one section, improving your chances for success. In addition, you may take the exam on your schedule, eight months of the year, six days a week, and in the morning or in the afternoon.

Successful completion of the BEC section of the CPA Examination is an attainable goal. Keep this point foremost in your mind as you study the first five chapters in this volume and develop your study plan.

Purpose of the Examination[1]

The Uniform CPA Examination is designed to test the entry-level knowledge and skills necessary to protect the public interest. These knowledge and skills were identified through a Practice Analysis performed in 2008, which served as a basis for the development of the content specifications for the exam beginning in 2013.

The CPA examination is one of many screening devices to assure the competence of those licensed to perform the attest function and to render professional accounting services. Other screening devices include educational requirements, ethics examinations, and work experience.

The examination appears to test the material covered in accounting programs of the better business schools. It also appears to be based upon the body of knowledge essential for the practice of public accounting and the audit of a medium-sized client. Since the examination is primarily a textbook or academic examination, you should plan on taking it as soon as possible after completing your required accounting education.

Examination Content

Specific guidance concerning topical content of the computer-based exam in BEC can be found in *Content and Skills Specifications for the Uniform CPA Exam*. We have included the detailed content and skills outline for BEC at the beginning of Chapter 5. The outline should be used as an indication of the topics' relative emphasis on the exam.

The Board's objective in preparing this detailed listing of topics tested on the exam is to help "in assuring the continuing validity and reliability of the Uniform CPA Examination." These outlines are an excellent source of guidance concerning the areas and the emphasis to be given each area on future exams.

The new Content and Skill Specification Outlines for the CPA examination went into effect January 1, 2014. In addition, the AICPA adopted CBT-e, which is a new computer platform. All questions that test writing skills have been moved to the BEC exam.

New accounting, auditing, and ethics pronouncements, including those in the governmental and not-for-profit areas, are tested in the testing window starting six months after the pronouncement's *effective* date. If early application is permitted, a pronouncement is tested six months after the *issuance* date; candidates are responsible for the old pronouncement also until it is superseded. For the BEC section, federal laws are tested six months following their *effective* date and for uniform acts one year after their adoption by a simple majority of jurisdictions. If there is no federal or uniform law on a topic, the questions are intended to test knowledge of the law of the majority of jurisdictions. The AICPA posts content changes regularly on its Internet site. The address is www.cpa-exam.org.

Nondisclosure and Computerization of Examination

Beginning in May 1996, the Uniform CPA Examination became nondisclosed. For each exam section, candidates are required to agree to a *Statement of Confidentiality*, which states that they will not divulge the nature and content of any exam question. The CPA exam is computer-based, and candidates take the exam at Prometric sites in the 55 jurisdictions in which the exam is offered. The CPA exam is offered continually during the testing windows shown next.

---

[1]More information may be obtained from the AICPA's *Uniform CPA Examination Candidate Bulletin*, which you can find on the AICPA's website at www.cpa-exam.org.

Testing Window (Exam Available)	January through February	April through May	July through August	October through November
AICPA Review and Update (Exam Unavailable)	March	June	September	December

One or more exam sections may be taken during any exam window, and the sections may be taken in any desired order. **However, no candidate will be allowed to sit for the same section more than once during any given testing window.** In addition, a candidate must pass all four sections of the CPA exam within a "rolling" eighteen-month period, which begins on the date he or she passes a section. In other words, you must pass the other three sections of the exam within eighteen months of when you pass the first section. If you do not pass all sections within the eighteen-month period, credit for any section(s) passed outside the eighteen-month period will expire and the section(s) must be retaken.

Types of Questions

The computer-based Uniform CPA Examination consists of two basic question formats.

1. Multiple-Choice—questions requiring the selection of one of four responses to a short scenario.
2. Task-Based Simulations—short case studies that are used to assess knowledge and skills in a context approximating that found on the job, through the use of realistic scenarios and tasks, and access to normally available and familiar resources. On the BEC exam the task-based simulations test writing skills.

The multiple-choice questions are much like the ones that have constituted a majority of the CPA examination for years. **And the good news is that these types of questions constitute 85% of the BEC section. The BEC section has three simulations testing a candidate's writing skills.**

Process for Sitting for the Examination

While there are some variations in the process from state to state, the basic process for sitting for the CPA examination may be described as follows:

1. Apply to take the examination (request, complete, and submit an application).
2. Pay the examination fees.
3. Review the tutorial and sample tests.
4. Receive your Notice to Schedule (NTS).
5. Schedule your examination.
6. Take your examination(s).
7. Receive your Score Report(s).

Applying to Take the Examination

The right to practice public accounting as a CPA is governed by individual state statutes. While some rules regarding the practice of public accounting vary from jurisdiction to jurisdiction, all State Boards of Accountancy use the Uniform CPA Examination and AICPA advisory grading service as one of the requirements to practice public accounting. The State Boards of Accountancy determine the requirements to sit for the exam (e.g., education requirements). For comparisons of requirements for various state boards and those policies that are uniform across jurisdictions you should refer to the website of the National Association of State Boards of Accountancy (NASBA) at www.nasba.org.

A frequent problem candidates encounter is failure to apply by the deadline. **Apply to sit for the examination early. Also, you should use extreme care in filling out the application and mailing required materials to your State Board of Accountancy.** If possible, have a friend review your completed application before mailing with your check and other documentation. Candidates may miss a particular CPA examination window simply because of minor technical details that were overlooked (check not signed, items not enclosed, question not answered on application, etc.). **Because of the very high volume of applications received in the more populous states, the administrative staff does not have time to call or write to correct minor details and will simply reject your application.**

The NASBA website has links to the registration information for all 55 jurisdictions. It is possible for candidates to sit for the examination at a Prometric site in any state or territory. Candidates desiring to do so should refer to the registration information for the applicable State Board of Accountancy.

International Applicants

International administration of the CPA Exam is currently offered in Brazil, Japan, Bahrain, Kuwait, Lebanon, and the United Arab Emirates. If you live in one of these testing locations, or other select countries, you may be able to take the Exam without traveling to the U.S. The Exam is only offered in English, and is the same computerized test as the one administered in the U.S. You are required to meet the same eligibility requirements and complete the same licensure requirements as your U.S. counterparts.

Applicants from countries other than the U.S. must follow the same basic steps as U.S. applicants. This means they must select the jurisdiction in which they wish to qualify and file an application with the board of accountancy (or its designated agent) in that jurisdiction. Any special instructions for candidates who have completed their education outside the U.S. are included in the board of accountancy requirements. For more information on the international administration of the CPA Examination, visit the International section of the NASBA website.

Obtaining the Notice to Schedule

Once your application has been processed and you have paid all fees, you will receive a Notice to Schedule (NTS) from NASBA. The NTS will list the section(s) of the examination that you are approved to take. When you receive the NTS, verify that all information is correct. **Be certain that the name appearing on the NTS matches EXACTLY the name on the identification documents that you will use during check-in at the testing center. If the information is incorrect or the name does not match, immediately contact your board of accountancy or its designated agent to request a correction. You must bring your NTS with you to the examination.**

Exam Scheduling

Once you have been cleared to take the exam by the applicable state board, you will receive by mail a Notice to Schedule (NTS) and may then schedule to sit for one or more sections of the exam. **Make sure that your name is exactly correct on the NTS.**

You have the following two options for scheduling your examination:

1. **Visit www.prometric.com/cpa on the Internet**
   This is the easiest and quickest way to schedule an examination appointment (or cancel and reschedule an appointment, if necessary). Simply go to the website, select "Schedule your test," and follow the directions. It is advised that you print and keep for your records the confirmation number for your appointment.

2. **Call 800-580-9648 (Candidate Services Call Center)**
   Before you call, you must have your NTS in front of you, and have in mind several times, dates, and locations that would work for you. You will not receive written confirmation of your appointment. Be sure to write down the date, time, location, and confirmation number for each of your appointments.

You should also be aware that if you have to cancel or reschedule your appointment, you may be subject to a cancellation/rescheduling fee. The AICPA's *Uniform CPA Examination Candidate Bulletin* lists the rescheduling and cancellation fees.

To assure that you get your desired location and time period it is imperative that you schedule early. To get your first choice of dates, you are advised to schedule at least 45 days in advance. You will not be scheduled for an exam fewer than 5 days before testing.

ATTRIBUTES OF EXAMINATION SUCCESS

Your primary objective in preparing for the BEC section is to pass. Other objectives such as learning new and reviewing old material should be considered secondary. The six attributes of examination success discussed below are **essential**. You should study the attributes and work toward achieving/developing each of them **before** taking the examination.

1. **Knowledge of Material**
   Two points are relevant to "knowledge of material" as an attribute of examination success. **First,** there is a distinct difference between being familiar with material and knowing the material. Frequently candidates confuse familiarity with knowledge. Can you remember when you just could not answer an examination question or did poorly on an examination, but maintained to yourself or your instructor that you knew the material? You probably were only familiar with the material. On the CPA examination, familiarity is insufficient; you

must know the material. Remember, the exam will test your ability to analyze data, make judgments, and demonstrate understanding of the material. For example, you may be familiar with the concepts of strategic performance measurement, but you may have difficulty linking measures to particular strategies in a balanced scorecard framework. Once again, a major concern must be to know the material rather than just being familiar with it. **Second,** the BEC exam tests a literally overwhelming amount of material at a rigorous level. From an undergraduate point of view, the CPA examination in BEC includes material from the following courses:

Economics	Management Information systems
Finance	Managerial/Cost Accounting
Business Law	Corporate Governance

2. **Commitment to Exam Preparation**

Your preparation for the CPA exam should begin at least two months prior to the date you plan to schedule your seating for an exam section. If you plan to take more than one section, you should start earlier. Over the course of your preparation, you will experience many peaks and valleys. There will be days when you feel completely prepared and there will also be days when you feel totally overwhelmed. This is not unusual and, in fact, should be expected.

The CPA exam is a very difficult and challenging exam. How many times in your college career did you study months for an exam? Probably not too many. Therefore, candidates need to remain focused on the objective—succeeding on the CPA exam.

Develop a personal study plan so that you are reviewing material daily. Of course, you should schedule an occasional study break to help you relax, but don't schedule too many breaks. Candidates who dedicate themselves to studying have a much greater chance of going through this process only one time. On the other hand, a lack of focus and piecemeal preparation will only extend the process over a number of exam sittings.

3. **Solutions Approach**

The solutions approach is a systematic approach to solving the multiple-choice questions found on the CPA examination. Many candidates know the material fairly well when they sit for the CPA exam, but they do not know how to take the examination. Candidates generally neither work nor answer questions efficiently in terms of time or grades. The solutions approach permits you to avoid drawing "blanks" on CPA exam questions; using the solutions approach coupled with grading insights (see below) allows you to pick up a sizable number of points on test material with which you are not familiar. Chapter 3 outlines the solutions approach for multiple-choice questions and the task-based simulations.

4. **Grading Insights**

The multiple-choice questions within each section are organized into three groups which are referred to as testlets. Each multiple-choice testlet is comprised of approximately 24 multiple-choice questions. The multiple-choice testlets vary in overall difficulty. A testlet is labeled either "medium difficult" or "difficult" based on its makeup. A "difficult" testlet has a higher percentage of hard questions than a "medium difficult" testlet. Every candidate's first multiple-choice testlet in each section will be a "medium difficult" testlet. If a candidate scores well on the first testlet, he or she will receive a "difficult" second testlet. Candidates that do not perform well on the first testlet receive a second "medium difficult" testlet. Because the scoring procedure takes the difficulty of the testlet into account, candidates are scored fairly regardless of the type of testlets they receive.

Task-based simulations on the BEC exam test a candidate's writing skills. Each candidate receives a fourth testlet that includes three task-based simulation writing assignments. These assignments are graded solely for writing skills and not for technical accuracy. Refer to Chapter 3 for a discussion of how to maximize your score on these simulations.

The AICPA includes a tutorial and sample examinations on its website that allow you to get experience with the use of the actual computer tools used on the CPA exam. Also, more experience with computer testing can be obtained by using the *Wiley CPAexcel® Exam Review Test Bank*.

5. **Examination Strategy**

Prior to sitting for the examination, it is important to develop an examination strategy (i.e., an approach to working efficiently throughout the exam). Your ability to cope successfully with 3 hours of examination can be improved by

a. Recognizing the importance and usefulness of an examination strategy
b. Using Chapter 4, Taking the Examination, and previous examination experience to develop a "personal strategy" for the exam
c. Testing your "personal strategy" on example examinations under conditions similar to those at the testing centers

6. **Examination Confidence**

You need confidence to endure the physical and mental demands of 3 hours of test-taking under tremendous pressure. Examination confidence results from proper preparation for the exam which includes mastering the first four attributes of examination success. Examination confidence is necessary to enable you to overcome the initial frustration with questions for which you may not be specifically prepared.

This study manual, when properly used, contributes to your examination confidence. Build confidence by completing the questions contained herein.

Common Candidate Mistakes

The CPA Exam is a formidable hurdle in your accounting career. With a pass rate of about 45% on each section, the level of difficulty is obvious. The good news, though, is that about 75% of all candidates (first-time and re-exam) sitting for each examination eventually pass. The authors believe that the first-time pass rate could be higher if candidates would be more careful. Eight common mistakes that many candidates make are

1. Failure to understand the exam question requirements
2. Misunderstanding the supporting text of the question
3. Lack of knowledge of material tested, especially recently issued pronouncements
4. Failure to develop proficiency with computer-based testing and practice tools such as electronic research databases and spreadsheets
5. Inability to apply the solutions approach
6. Lack of an exam strategy (e.g., allocation of time)
7. Sloppiness and computational errors
8. Failure to proofread and edit

These mistakes are not mutually exclusive. Candidates may commit one or more of the above items. Remind yourself that when you decrease the number of common mistakes, you increase your chances of successfully becoming a CPA. Take the time to read carefully the exam question requirements. Do not jump into a quick start, only to later find out that you didn't understand what information the examiners were asking for. Read slowly and carefully. Take time to recall your knowledge. Respond to the question asked. Apply an exam strategy such as allocating your time among all testlets. Answer questions quickly but precisely, avoid common mistakes, and increase your score.

PURPOSE AND ORGANIZATION OF THIS REVIEW TEXTBOOK

This book is designed to help you prepare adequately for the BEC Examination. There is no easy way to prepare for the successful completion of the CPA Examination; however, through the use of this manual, your approach will be systematic and logical.

The objective of this book is to provide study materials supportive to CPA candidates. While no guarantees are made concerning the success of those using this text, this book promotes efficient preparation by

1. Explaining how to **maximize your score** through analysis of examination grading and illustration of the solutions approach.
2. **Defining areas tested** through the use of the content specification outlines. Note that predictions of future exams are not made. You should prepare yourself for all possible topics rather than gambling on the appearance of certain questions.
3. **Organizing your study program** by comprehensively outlining all of the subject matter tested on the examination in eight easy-to-use study modules. Each study module is a manageable task which facilitates your exam preparation. Turn to Chapter 5 and peruse the contents to get a feel for the organization of this book.
4. **Providing CPA candidates with previous examination questions** organized by topic (e.g., cost measurement, planning, control and analysis, etc.) Since a significant amount of this examination content is material not previously tested, questions have been developed for new areas. Some have been adapted from other professional exams, (i.e., the Certified Management Accountants and Certified Internal Auditors exams).
5. **Explaining the AICPA unofficial answers** to the examination questions included in this text. The AICPA publishes unofficial answers for all questions from exams administered prior to 1996 and for any released questions from exams administered on or after May 1996. However, no explanation is made of the approach that should have been applied to the examination questions to obtain these unofficial answers. Relatedly, the AICPA unofficial answers to multiple-choice questions provide no justification and/or explanation.

As you read the next few paragraphs which describe the contents of this book, flip through the chapters to gain a general familiarity with the book's organization and contents. Chapters 2, 3, and 4 are to help you "maximize your score."

Chapter 2   Examination Grading
Chapter 3   The Solutions Approach
Chapter 4   Taking the Examination

Chapters 2, 3, and 4 contain material that should be kept in mind throughout your study program. Refer to them frequently. Reread them for a final time just before you sit for the exam.

BEC Modules contain

1. AICPA Content Specification Outlines of material tested on the BEC Examination
2. Multiple-choice questions
3. Task-based simulation problems
4. AICPA unofficial answers with the author's explanations for the multiple-choice questions
5. Author answers to task-based simulations

Also included at the end of this text in Appendix A is a complete Sample BEC Examination. The sample exam is included to enable candidates to gain experience in taking a "realistic" exam. While studying the modules, the candidate can become accustomed to concentrating on fairly narrow topics. By working through the sample examination near the end of their study programs, candidates will be better prepared for taking the actual examination.

Other Textbooks

This text is a comprehensive compilation of study guides and outlines; it should not be necessary to supplement them with accounting textbooks and other materials for most topics. You probably already have economics, cost accounting, finance, and information systems textbooks. In such a case, you must make the decision whether to replace them and trade familiarity (including notes therein, etc.), with the cost and inconvenience of obtaining the newer texts containing a more updated presentation.

Before spending time and money acquiring a new book, begin your study program with the *Wiley CPAexcel® Exam Review 2016 Study Guide January: Business Environment and Concepts* to determine your need for a supplemental text.

Ordering Other Textual Materials

If you want to order AICPA materials, locate an AICPA educator member to order your materials, since educator members are entitled to a discount and may place website or telephone orders.

AICPA (CPA2Biz)
    Telephone: 888-777-7077
    Website: www.CPA2Biz.com

A variety of supplemental CPA products is available from John Wiley & Sons, Inc. By using a variety of learning techniques, such as software, computer-based learning, and audio CDs, the candidate is more likely to remain focused during the study process and to retain information for a longer period of time. Visit our website at **www.wiley.com/cpa** for other products, supplements, and updates.

Working CPA Questions

The AICPA content outlines, study outlines, etc., will be used to acquire and assimilate the knowledge tested on the examination. This, however, should be only **one-half** of your preparation program. The other half should be spent practicing how to work questions. Some candidates probably spend over 90% of their time reviewing material tested on the CPA exam. Much more time should be allocated to working examination questions **under exam conditions**. Working examination questions serves two functions. First, it helps you develop a solutions approach that will maximize your score. Second, it provides the best test of your knowledge of the material.

The multiple-choice questions and answer explanations can be used in many ways. First, they may be used as a diagnostic evaluation of your knowledge. For example, before beginning to review financial management you may wish to answer 10 to 15 multiple-choice questions to determine your ability to answer CPA examination questions on financial management. The apparent difficulty of the questions and the correctness of your answers will allow you to determine the necessary breadth and depth of your review. Additionally, exposure to examination questions prior to review and study of the material should provide motivation. You will develop a feel for your level of proficiency and an understanding of the scope and difficulty of past examination questions. Moreover, your review materials will explain concepts encountered in the diagnostic multiple-choice questions.

Second, the multiple-choice questions can be used as a poststudy or postreview evaluation. You should attempt to understand all concepts mentioned (even in incorrect answers) as you answer the questions. Refer to the explanation of the answer for discussion of the alternatives even though you selected the correct response. Thus, you should read the explanation of the answer unless you completely understand the question and all of the alternative answers.

Third, you may wish to use the multiple-choice questions as a primary study vehicle. This is probably the quickest but least thorough approach in preparing for the exam. Make a sincere effort to understand the question and to select the correct response before referring to the answer and explanation. In many cases, the explanations will appear inadequate because of your lack of familiarity with the topic. Always refer back to an appropriate study source, such as the outlines and text in this volume, your economics, information systems, finance and cost accounting textbooks, etc.

Since the task-based simulations in BEC solely test writing skills, you can use a focused approach to studying for these simulations. Chapter 3 contains material that can help you review the principles for proper written communications.

After you have reviewed for the BEC section of the exam, work the complete BEC Sample Exam provided in Appendix A.

SELF-STUDY PROGRAM

CPA candidates generally find it difficult to organize and complete their own self-study programs. A major problem is determining **what** and **how** to study. Another major problem is developing the self-discipline to stick to a study program. Relatedly, it is often difficult for CPA candidates to determine how much to study (i.e., determining when they are sufficiently prepared.) The following suggestions will assist you in developing a **systematic**, **comprehensive**, and **successful** self-study program to help you complete the BEC exam.

Remember that these are only suggestions. You should modify them to suit your personality, available study time, and other constraints. Some of the suggestions may appear trivial, but CPA candidates generally need all the assistance they can get to systemize their study programs.

Study Facilities and Available Time

Locate study facilities that will be conducive to concentrated study. Factors that you should consider include

1. Noise distraction
2. Interruptions
3. Lighting
4. Availability (e.g., a local library is not available at 5:00 A.M.)
5. Accessibility (e.g., your kitchen table vs. your local library)
6. Desk or table space

You will probably find different study facilities optimal for different times (e.g., your kitchen table during early morning hours and local libraries during early evening hours).

Next review your personal and professional commitments from now until the exam to determine regularly available study time. Formalize a schedule to which you can reasonably commit yourself. At the end of this chapter, you will find a detailed approach to managing your time available for the exam preparation program.

Self-Evaluation

The *Wiley CPAexcel® Exam Review 2016 Study Guide January: Business Environment and Concepts* self-study program is partitioned into eight topics or modules. Since each module is clearly defined and should be studied separately, you have the task of preparing for the CPA BEC exam by tackling eight manageable tasks. Partitioning the overall project into eight modules makes preparation psychologically easier, since you sense yourself completing one small step at a time rather than seemingly never completing one or a few large steps.

By completing the following "Preliminary Estimate of Your Present Knowledge of Subject" inventory below, organized by the eight modules in this program, you will tabulate your strong and weak areas at the beginning of your study program. This will help you budget your limited study time. Note that you should begin studying the material in each module by answering up to ¼ of the total multiple-choice questions covering that module's topics (see step 4.A in the next section). This "mini-exam" should constitute a diagnostic evaluation as to the amount of review and study you need.

PRELIMINARY ESTIMATE OF YOUR PRESENT KNOWLEDGE OF SUBJECT

No.	Module	Proficient	Fairly Proficient	Generally Familiar	Not Familiar
40	Corporate Governance, Internal Control, and Enterprise Risk Management				
41	Information Technology				
42	Economics, Strategy, and Globalization				
43	Financial Risk Management and Capital Budgeting				
44	Financial Management				
45	Performance Measures and Management Techniques				
46	Cost Measurement and Assignment				
47	Planning, Control, and Analysis				

NOTE: The numbering of modules in this text commences with number 40 to correspond with the numbering system used in our two-volume set.

Time Allocation

The study program below entails an average of 60 hours (Step 5 below) of study time. The breakdown of total hours is indicated in the left margin.

[1 hr.]   1. Study Chapters 2–5 in this volume. These chapters are essential to your efficient preparation program. (Time estimate includes candidate's review of the examples of the solutions approach in Chapter 3.)

[5 hrs.]   2. Begin by studying the introductory material at the beginning of Chapter 5.

             3. Spend as much time as necessary reviewing the characteristics of a good memorandum and the principles of proper grammar.

             4. Study one module at a time. The modules are listed above in the self-evaluation section.

             5. For each module:

[5 hrs.]   A. First, review the listing of key terms at the end of the module. Then, work ¼ of the multiple-choice questions (e.g., if there are 40 multiple-choice questions in a module, you should work every 4th question, 10 total questions). Score yourself.

                   This diagnostic routine will provide you with an index of your proficiency and familiarity with the type and difficulty of questions.

                   The outlines for each module are broken into smaller sections that refer you to multiple-choice questions to test your comprehension of the material. You may find this organization useful in breaking your study into smaller bites.

                   Time estimate: 3 minutes each, not to exceed 1 hour total.

[27 hrs.]   B. Study the outlines and illustrations. Where necessary, refer to your economics, information systems, finance, and cost accounting textbooks. (This will occur more frequently for topics in which you have a weak background.)

                   Time estimate: 2 hour minimum per module with more time devoted to topics less familiar to you.

[12 hrs.]   C. Work the remaining multiple-choice questions. Study the explanations of the multiple-choice questions you missed or had trouble answering.

                   Time estimate: 3 minutes to answer each question and 2 minutes to study the answer explanation of each question missed.

[6 hrs.]   D.   Spend time reviewing the principles of good written communication. Practice with several simulations.

[4 hrs.]   E.   Work through the sample CPA examination presented in Appendix A.

> Take the examination under simulated exam conditions (i.e., in a strange place with other people present [your local municipal library or a computer lab]). Apply your solutions approach to each question and your exam strategy to the overall exam.
>
> You should limit yourself to the time you will have when taking the actual CPA exam section (3 hours for the BEC section). Spend time afterwards grading your work and reviewing your effort.
>
> Time estimate: To take the exam and review it later, approximately 4 hours.

5.   The total suggested time of 60 hours is only an average. Allocation of time will vary candidate by candidate. Time requirements vary due to the diverse backgrounds and abilities of CPA candidates. Allocate your time so you gain the most proficiency in the least time. Remember that while 60 hours will be required, you should break the overall project down into eight more manageable tasks. Do not study more than one module during each study session.

Using Notecards

Below are one candidate's notecards on BEC topics which illustrate how key definitions, lists, etc., can be summarized on index cards for quick review. Since candidates can take these anywhere they go, they are a very efficient review tool.

Calculation of Labor Variances

$AH \times AR$ $AH \times SR$ $SH \times SR$

Rate variance

Efficiency variance

Components of an Enterprise Risk Management System (COSO framework)

- Internal environment
- Objective setting
- Event identification
- Risk assessment
- Risk response
- Control activities
- Information and communication
- Monitoring

Level of Proficiency Required

What level of proficiency must you develop with respect to each of the topics to pass the exam? You should work toward a minimum correct rate on the multiple-choice questions of 80%. Working toward a correct rate of 80% or higher will give you a margin.

Multiple-Choice Feedback

One of the benefits of working through exam questions is that it helps you to identify your weak areas. Once you have graded your answers, your strong areas and weak areas should be clearly evident. Yet, the important point here is that you should not stop at a simple percentage evaluation. The percentage only provides general feedback about your knowledge of the material contained within that particular module. The percentage **does not** give you any specific feedback regarding the concepts which were tested. In order to get this feedback, you should look at the questions missed on an individual basis because this will help you gain a better understanding of **why** you missed the question.

This feedback process has been facilitated by the fact that within each module where the multiple-choice answer key appears, two blank lines have been inserted next to the multiple-choice answers. As you grade the multiple-choice questions, mark those questions which you have missed. However, instead of just marking the questions right and wrong, you should now focus on marking the questions in a manner which identifies **why** you missed the question. As an example, a candidate could mark the questions in the following manner: ✓ for math mistakes, x for conceptual mistakes, and ? for areas which the candidate was unfamiliar with. The candidate should then correct these mistakes by reworking through the marked questions.

The objective of this marking technique is to help you identify your weak areas and thus, the concepts which you should be focusing on. While it is still important for you to get between 75% and 80% correct when working multiple-choice questions, it is more important for you to understand the concepts. This understanding applies to both the questions answered correctly and those answered incorrectly. Remember, questions on the CPA exam will be different from the questions in the book; however, the concepts will be the same. Therefore, your preparation should focus on understanding concepts, not just getting the correct answer.

Conditional Candidates

If you have received conditional status on the examination, you must concentrate on the remaining section(s). Unfortunately, many candidates do not study after conditioning the exam, relying on luck to get them through the remaining section(s). Conditional candidates will find that material contained in Chapters 1–5 and the information contained in the appropriate modules will benefit them in preparing for the remaining section(s) of the examination.

PLANNING FOR THE EXAMINATION

Overall Strategy

An overriding concern should be an orderly, systematic approach toward both your preparation program and your examination strategy. A major objective should be to avoid any surprises or anything else that would rattle you during the examination. In other words, you want to be in complete control as much as possible. Control is of paramount importance from both positive and negative viewpoints. The presence of control on your part will add to your confidence and your ability to prepare for and take the exam. Moreover, the presence of control will make your preparation program more enjoyable (or at least less distasteful). On the other hand, a lack of organization will result in inefficiency in preparing for and taking the examination, with a highly predictable outcome. Likewise, distractions during the examination (e.g., inadequate lodging, long drive) are generally disastrous.

In summary, establishing a systematic, orderly approach to taking the examination is of paramount importance.

1. Develop an overall strategy at the beginning of your preparation program (see below)
2. Supplement your overall strategy with outlines of material tested on the BEC exam
3. Supplement your overall strategy with an explicitly stated set of question-and problem solving-procedures—the solutions approach
4. Supplement your overall strategy with an explicitly stated approach to each examination session (see Chapter 4)
5. Evaluate your preparation progress on a regular basis and prepare lists of things "to do." (See Weekly Review of Preparation Program Progress below.)
6. RELAX: You can pass the exam. About 40 to 45% of the candidates taking a section of the CPA examination pass. But if you take out the individuals that did not adequately prepare, these percentages increase substantially. You will be one of those who pass if you complete an efficient preparation program and execute well (i.e., solutions approach and exam strategy) while taking the exam.

The following outline is designed to provide you with a general framework of the tasks before you. You should tailor the outline to your needs by adding specific items and comments.

A. **Preparation Program (refer to Self-Study Program discussed previously)**

1. Obtain and organize study materials.
2. Locate facilities conducive for studying and block out study time.
3. Develop your solutions approach.
4. Prepare an examination strategy.
5. Study the material tested recently and prepare answers to actual exam questions on these topics under examination conditions.
6. Periodically evaluate your progress.

B. **Physical Arrangements**

1. Apply to and obtain acceptance from your state board.
2. Schedule your test location and time.

C. **Taking the Examination (covered in detail in Chapter 4)**

1. Become familiar with location of the test center and procedures.
2. Implement examination strategies and the solutions approach.

Weekly Review of Preparation Program Progress

The following pages contain a hypothetical weekly review of program progress. You should prepare a similar progress chart. This procedure, taking only 5 minutes per week, will help you proceed through a more efficient, complete preparation program.

Make notes of materials and topics

1. That you have studied
2. That you have completed
3. That need additional study

Weeks to go	Comments on progress, "to do" items, etc.
12	1) Read Corporate Governance, Internal Control and Enterprise Risk Management Module 2) Made notecards 3) Worked MC questions 4) Reviewed principles of good written communications (Chapter 3) 5) Need to use solutions approach
11	1) Read Information Technology Module 2) Made notecards 3) Worked some MC questions 4) Need to finish Corporate Governance MC
10	1) Read Economics, Strategy, and Globalization Module 2) Made notecards 3) Worked the MC questions 4) Need to work more questions on types of markets
9	1) Read Financial Risk Management and Capital Budgeting Module 2) Made notecards 3) Worked some MC questions 4) Need to work more on probability analysis
8	1) Read Financial Management Module 2) Made notecards 3) Worked some MC questions 4) Need to work more capital asset pricing questions
7	1) Read Performance Measures and Management Techniques Module 2) Made notecards 3) Worked the MC questions 4) Need to study the balanced scorecard 5) Practiced writing using simulations
6	1) Reviewed Cost Measurement and Assignment Module 2) Completed MC for prior Modules 3) Made notecards 4) Worked some MC questions 5) Practiced writing using simulations
5	1) Read Planning, Control, and Analysis Module 2) Made notecards 3) Worked the MC questions 4) Need to review standard costing 5) Practiced writing using simulations
4	1) Reviewed all Modules 2) Completed all MC questions
3	1) Reviewed principles of good written communications (Chapter 3) 2) Practiced writing using simulations

2	1)	*Took BEC Sample Exam*
	2)	*Wrote down topics I still do not feel confident in*
	3)	*Worked variance analysis, working capital management, and balanced scorecard questions—Am now finally confident in these areas*
1	1)	*Reviewed the Economics, Strategy and Globalization and Financial Management Modules and worked all the MC again*
	2)	*Reviewed all notecards*
0	1)	*Tried to relax and review topics*

Time Management of Your Preparation

As you begin your CPA exam preparation, you obviously realize that there is a large amount of material to cover over the course of the next two to three months. Therefore, it is very important for you to organize your calendar, and maybe even your daily routine, so that you can allocate sufficient time to studying. An organized approach to your preparation is much more effective than a final-week cram session. An organized approach also builds up the confidence necessary to succeed on the CPA exam.

An approach which we have already suggested is to develop weekly "to do" lists. This technique helps you to establish intermediate objectives and goals as you progress through your study plan. You can then focus your efforts on small tasks and not feel overwhelmed by the entire process. And as you accomplish these tasks you will see yourself moving one step closer to realizing the overall goal, succeeding on the CPA exam.

Note, however, that the underlying assumption of this approach is that you have found the time during the week to study and thus accomplish the different tasks. Although this is an obvious step, it is still a very important step. Your exam preparation should be of a continuous nature and not one that jumps around the calendar. Therefore, you should strive to find available study time within your daily schedule, which can be utilized on a consistent basis. For example, everyone has certain hours of the day which are already committed for activities such as jobs, classes, and, of course, sleep. There is also going to be the time you spend relaxing because CPA candidates should try to maintain some balance in their lives. Sometimes too much studying can be counterproductive. But there will be some time available to you for studying and working through the questions. Block off this available time and use it only for exam prep. Use the time to accomplish your weekly tasks and to keep yourself committed to the process. After a while your preparation will develop into a habit and the preparation will not seem as overwhelming as it once did.

NOW IS THE TIME TO MAKE YOUR COMMITMENT

Chapter 2: Examination Grading

All State Boards of Accountancy use the AICPA advisory grading service. As your grade is to be determined by this process, it is very important that you understand the AICPA grading process and its implications for your preparation program and for the solution techniques you will use during the examination.

The AICPA has a full-time staff of CPA examination personnel under the supervision of the AICPA Board of Examiners, which has responsibility for the CPA examination.

This chapter contains a description of the AICPA grading process including a determination of the passing standard.

Setting the Passing Standard of the Uniform CPA Examination

As a part of the development of any licensing process, the passing score on the licensing examination must be established. This passing score must be set to distinguish candidates who are qualified to practice from those who are not. After conducting a number of studies of methods to determine passing scores, the Board of Examiners decided to use candidate-centered methods to set passing scores for the computer-based Uniform CPA Examination. In candidate-centered methods, the focus is on looking at actual candidate answers and making judgments about which sets of answers represent the answers of qualified entry-level CPAs. To make these determinations, the AICPA convened panels of CPAs to examine candidate responses and set the passing scores for multiple-choice questions and simulations. The data from these panels provide the basis for the development of question and problem points (relative weightings). **A passing score on the computer-based examination is 75%.**

Grading the Examination

The Business Environment and Concepts (BEC) section consists of multiple-choice questions and task-based simulations that test written communications. The AICPA pretests multiple-choice questions; a few of the questions in each testlet of the exam are pretest questions that are not considered in the candidate's score.

Multiple-Choice Grading

BEC exams contain three multiple-choice testlets of 24 questions each. The possible score on a question and on a testlet will vary based on the difficulty of the questions. You will receive more raw points for hard and medium questions than for easy questions.

Task-Based Simulation Grading

BEC exams contain one testlet of three task-based simulations that test written communication skills on BEC topics. The responses to these simulations are scored by hand based on the following criteria:

1. Organization: structure, ordering of ideas, and linking one idea to another

   - Overview/thesis statement
   - Unified paragraphs (topic and supporting sentences)
   - Transitions and connectives

2. Development: supporting evidence/information to clarify thoughts

   - Details
   - Definitions
   - Examples
   - Rephrasing

3. Expression: use of standard business English

   - Grammar
   - Punctuation
   - Word usage
   - Capitalization
   - Spelling

A communication response is not graded for technical accuracy. However, it must be on point to be graded at all. For example, if the requirement is to write a memorandum to describe the components of internal control, the response must describe a group of components although the group does not have to be complete or technically accurate.

Requesting a Score Review

For an additional fee, you may request a score review. A score review is a verification of your score making certain that the approved answer key was used. Because the AICPA grades your exam twice as a part of its normal process, it is unlikely that you will get an adjustment to your score. You should contact the applicable board of accountancy to request a score review.

NOW IS THE TIME TO MAKE YOUR COMMITMENT

Chapter 3: The Solutions Approach

The **solutions approach** is a systematic problem-solving methodology. The purpose is to assure efficient, complete solutions to CPA exam questions, some of which are complex and confusing relative to most undergraduate accounting problems. This is especially true with regard to the new simulation type problems. Unfortunately, there appears to be a widespread lack of emphasis on problem-solving techniques in accounting courses. Most accounting books and courses merely provide solutions to specific types of problems. Memorization of these solutions for examinations and preparation of homework problems from examples is "cookbooking." "Cookbooking" is perhaps a necessary step in the learning process, but it is certainly not sufficient training for the complexities of the business world. Professional accountants need to be adaptive to a rapidly changing complex environment. For example, CPAs have been called on to interpret and issue reports on new concepts such as price controls, energy allocations, and new taxes. These CPAs rely on their problem-solving expertise to understand these problems and to formulate solutions to them.

The steps outlined below are only one of many possible series of solution steps. Admittedly, the procedures suggested are **very** structured; thus, you should adapt the suggestions to your needs. You may find that some steps are occasionally unnecessary, or that certain additional procedures increase your own problem-solving efficiency. Whatever the case, substantial time should be allocated to developing an efficient solutions approach before taking the examination. You should develop your solutions approach by working questions.

As discussed in Chapter 1, the Business Environment and Concepts (BEC) section of the exam includes multiple-choice questions and task-based simulations that test writing skills. The steps below relate to these types of questions; overall examination or section strategies are discussed in Chapter 4.

Multiple-Choice Screen Layout

The following is a computer screenshot that illustrates the manner in which multiple-choice questions will be presented:

Characteristics of the computerized testlets of multiple-choice questions include the following:

1. You may move freely within a particular testlet from one question to the next or back to previous questions until you click the "Exit" button. Once you have indicated that you have finished the testlet by clicking on the "Exit" button, you can never return to that set of questions.
2. A button on the screen will allow you to "flag" a question for review if you wish to come back to it later.
3. A four-function computer calculator with an electronic tape is available as a tool.
4. The time remaining for the entire exam section is shown on the screen.
5. The number of the questions out of the total in the testlet is shown on the screen.
6. The "Help" button will provide you with help in navigating and completing the testlet.

The previous screenshot was obtained from the AICPA's tutorial at www.cpa-exam.org. Candidates are urged to complete the tutorial and other example questions on the AICPA's website to obtain additional experience with the computer-based testing.

Multiple-Choice Question Solutions Approach

1. **Work individual questions in order.**

   a. If a question appears lengthy or difficult, skip it until you can determine that extra time is available. **Mark it for review** to remind you to return to a question that you have skipped or need to review.

2. **Read the stem of the question without looking at the answers.**

   a. The answers are sometimes misleading and may cause you to misread or misinterpret the question.

3. **Read each question *carefully* to determine the topical area.**

   a. Study the requirements **first** so you know which data are important.
   b. Note keywords and important data.
   c. Identify pertinent information with notations in the margin of the exam.
   d. Be especially careful to note when the requirement is an **exception** (e.g., "Which of the following is **not** included in gross income?").
   e. If a set of data is the basis for two or more questions, read the requirements of each of the questions first before beginning to work the first question (sometimes it is more efficient to work the questions out of order or simultaneously).
   f. Be alert to read questions as they are, not as you would like them to be. You may encounter a familiar looking item; do not jump to the conclusion that you know what the answer is without reading the question completely.
   g. For comprehensive questions, prepare intermediary solutions as you read the question.

4. **Anticipate the answer before looking at the alternative answers.**

   a. Recall the applicable principle (e.g., job order costing) and the applicable model (e.g., net present value), or the applicable law section (e.g., Chapter 7 of the US Bankruptcy Law).
   b. If a question deals with a complex area like standard costing, set up full-blown diagrams on the scratch paper provided, if necessary, using abbreviations that enable you to follow your work.

5. **Read the answers and select the *best* alternative.**

   a. If the answer you have computed is not among the choices, quickly check the logic of your solution. If you do not arrive at one of the given answers in the time you have allotted for that particular problem, make an educated guess or mark it for review.

6. **Click on the correct answer (or your educated guess).**
7. **After completing all of the questions including the ones flagged for review click on the "Exit" button to close out the testlet. Remember once you have closed out the testlet you can never return to it.**

Multiple-Choice Question Solutions Approach Example

A good example of the multiple-choice solutions approach is provided, using an actual multiple-choice question from a previous CPA examination.

Step 3:

Topical area? Job **order costing**

Step 4A:

Production costs include direct materials used, direct labor, and manufacturing overhead applied. Since there is no ending WIP inventory, all production costs are for jobs completed.

Under Pick Co.'s job order costing system manufacturing overhead is applied to work in process using a predetermined annual overhead rate. During January 2010, Pick's transactions included the following:

Direct materials issued to production	$90,000
Indirect materials issued to production	8,000
Manufacturing overhead incurred	125,000
Manufacturing overhead applied	113,000
Direct labor costs	107,000

Pick had <u>neither beginning nor ending work in process inventory</u>. What was the cost of jobs completed in January 2010?

a. $302,000
b. $310,000
c. $322,000
d. $330,000

WIP

90	
107	310
113	
0	

Currently, all multiple-choice questions are scored based on the number correct, weighted by a difficulty rating (i.e., there is no penalty for guessing). The rationale is that a "good guess" indicates knowledge. Thus, you should answer all multiple-choice questions.

Task-Based Communication Simulations

Communication simulations will involve some real-world writing assignment that a CPA might have to perform, such as a memorandum to a client explaining a management technique. The subject of the communication will be a BEC topic.

It is essential for the communication to be in your own words. In addition, the communication will not be graded for technical accuracy. If it is on point, it will only be graded for usefulness to the intended user and writing skills. The following screenshot illustrates a task-based simulation requiring the composition of a memorandum to a company president.

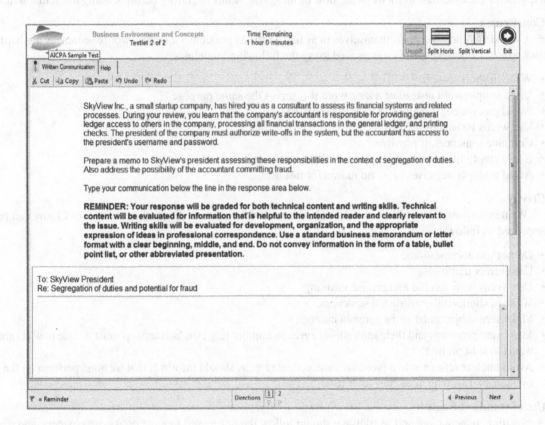

Candidates' writing skills will be graded according to the following criteria:

1. **Coherent organization**

    Candidates should organize their responses in a manner that is logical and easy to follow. Jumbled paragraphs and disorderly sentences will only confuse the grader and make his/her job more difficult. The following techniques will help improve written coherence.[1]

    - Use short paragraphs composed of short sentences.
    - Indent paragraphs to set off lists, equations, key ideas, etc. when appropriate.
    - Maintain coherence **within** paragraphs.
    - Use a topic sentence at the beginning of each paragraph.

---

[1] Adapted from *Writing for Accountants* by Aletha S. Hendrickson (Cincinnati, OH: Southwestern Publishing Co., 1993) pp. 128–209.

- Develop and support this topic throughout the rest of the paragraph.
- Present old or given information before discussing new information.
- Discuss ideas in chronological order.
- Use parallel grammatical structure.
- Be consistent in person, verb tense, and number.
- Substitute pronouns or synonyms for previously used keywords.
- Use transitions (e.g., therefore, finally).

  - Maintain coherence **between** paragraphs

    - Repeat keywords from previous paragraph.
    - Use transitions.

Candidates are strongly advised to keyword outline their responses **before** writing their communications. This technique helps the candidate to focus on the flow of ideas s/he wants to convey before starting the actual writing task.

2. **Conciseness**

   Candidates should express themselves in as few words as possible. Complex, wordy sentences are hard to understand. Conciseness can be improved using the following guidelines.

- Write in short sentences.
- Use a simple word instead of a long word if it serves the same purpose.
- Avoid passive constructions (e.g., **was** evalua**ted**).
- Use words instead of phrases.
- Combine sentences, if possible.
- Avoid empty fillers (e.g., **it is** apparent; **there seems to be**).
- Avoid multiple negatives (e.g., **no** reason for **not** using).

3. **Clarity**

   Written responses should leave no doubt in the reader's mind as to the meaning intended. Clarity can be improved as follows:

- Do **not** use abbreviations.
- Use correct terminology.
- Use words with specific and precise meanings.
- Write in short, well-constructed sentences.
- Make sure subjects and verbs agree in number.
- Make sure pronouns and their antecedents agree in number (e.g., the partnership must decide how **it** (not **they**) wants to split profits).
- Avoid unclear reference to a pronoun's antecedent (e.g., A should inform B that **he** must perform on the contract by January 1.—Who does "he" refer to?).

4. **Use of standard English**

   Spelling, punctuation, and word usage should follow the norm used in most books, newspapers, and magazines. Note the following common mistakes:

- Confusion of its/it's

  - The firm issued **its** stock.
  - **It's** (it is) the stock of that firm.

- Confusion of there/their/they're

  - **There** will be a contract.
  - **Their** contract was signed last week.
  - **They're** (they are) signing the contract.

- Spelling errors

  - Separate not seperate
  - Receivable not recievable

The word processing software that you will use to write the communication on the exam will likely have a spell-check function. Use it.

5. **Appropriateness for the reader**

Candidates will be asked to prepare a communication for a certain reader (e.g., a memorandum for a client). Writing that is appropriate for the reader will take into account the reader's background, knowledge of the subject, interests, and concerns. (When the intended reader is not specified, the candidate should write for a knowledgeable CPA.)

Intended readers may include those who are unfamiliar with most terms and concepts, and who seek financial information because of self-interest (i.e., clients, stockholders). Try the following techniques for these readers:

- Avoid jargon, if possible (e.g., HDC, etc.)
- Use parenthetical definitions

  - Limited partner (liable only to the extent of contributed capital)
  - Marketable equity securities (short-term investments in stock)

- Set off definitions as appositives

  - A note, a two-party negotiable instrument, may become uncollectible.

- Incorporate a "you" attitude

The requirement of a question may also specify that the response should be directed to professionals who are knowledgeable of most terms and concepts. Employ the following techniques with these readers:

- Use jargon
- Refer to authoritative sources (i.e., Code section 543)
- Incorporate a "we" attitude

Again, preparing a keyword outline will assist you in meeting many of these requirements. You should also reread each written communication in its entirety. Writing errors are common during the exam, so take your time to proofread and edit your answers. Again, make use of the spell-check function of the word processing software if it is available.

Methods for Improving Your Writing Skills

1. **Organization**

Logical organization is very important. Again, this is where the keyword outline helps.

2. **Syntax, grammar, and style**

By the time you sit for the CPA exam, you have at your disposal various grammatical constructs from which you may form sentences. Believe it or not, you know quite a bit of English grammar; if you did not, you would never have made it this far in your studies. So in terms of your grammar, relax! You already know it.

A frequent problem with writing occurs with the syntactic structure of sentences. Although the Board of Examiners does not expect the rhetoric of Cicero, it does expect to read and understand your answer. The way in which the graders will assess writing skills further indicates that they are looking more for writing skills at the micro level (sentence level) than at the macro level (organizational level).

a. Basic syntactic structure (transitive and intransitive action verbs)

Most English sentences are based on this simple dynamic: that someone or something (the subject) does some action (the predicate). These sentences involve action verbs and are grouped in the following categories:

(1) Subject-Verb

(a) The TAXPAYER WAITED for 3 weeks to get a refund.

(2) Subject-Verb-Direct Object (The object receives the action of the verb.)

(a) The TAXPAYER SIGNED the CONTRACT.

(3) Subject-Verb-Indirect Object-Direct Object (The direct object receives the action of the verb, but the indirect object is also affected by this action, though not in the same way as the direct object.)

(a) The IRS GAVE US a DEFINITE DECISION well beyond our expectations.

b. Syntactic structure (linking verbs)

Linking verbs are verbs which, rather than expressing action, say something about the subject's state of being. In sentences with linking verbs, the subject is linked to a work which describes it or renames it.

(1) Subject-Linking Verb-Nominative (The nominative renames the subject.)

 (a) In the field of Accounting, the FASB IS the standard-setting BOARD.

(2) Subject-Linking Verb-Adjective (The adjective describes the subject.)

 (a) Evidence of SCIENTER IS always HELPFUL in proving fraud.

c. Subordinate clauses

(1) Adverbial clauses (subordinating connector + sentence). These clauses modify the action of the main clause.

 (a) When amounts are not substantiated, a nondeductible expense is incurred.

(2) Noun clauses (nominal connectors + sentence). These clauses function as nouns in the main sentence.

 (a) When a tax return is not signed, we know that the return is not filed.

(3) Adjective clauses [relative pronoun + verb + (object/nominative/adjective)]. These clauses function as noun modifiers.

 (a) The court with the highest authority is the one that sets the precedent.

d. The above are patterns which form basic clauses (both dependent and independent). In addition, numerous phrases may function as modifiers of the basic sentence elements.

(1) Prepositional (a preposition + an object)

 (a) of the FASB
 (b) on the data
 (c) about a new type of depreciation

(2) Verbal

 (a) Verb + ing + a modifier (noun, verb, adverb, prepositional phrase)

  1] Used as an adjective

   a] the expense requiring substantiation
   b] the alternative minimizing taxes

  2] Used as a noun (gerund)

   a] Performing all of the duties required by a contract is necessary to avoid breach.

 (b) Verb + ed + modifier (noun, adverb, prepositional phrase)

  1] Used as an adjective

   a] The basis used when historical cost cannot be determined is estimated value.

 (c) Infinitive (to + verb + object)

  1] Used as a noun

   a] The company needs to respond by filing an amended tax return.

3. **Sentence clarity**

a. When constructing your sentences, do not separate basic sentence elements with too many phrases.

(1) The liability for partnership losses exceeding capital contributions is another characteristic of a general partnership.
(2) **Better:** One characteristic of a general partnership is the liability for partnership losses which exceed capital contributions.

b. Refrain from lumping prepositional and infinitive phrases together.

(1) The delegation of authority by a corporate director of day-to-day or routine matters to officers and agents of that corporation is a power and a duty of the director.

(2) **Better:** Delegating authority for routine matters to officers and agents is a power and a duty of corporations' directors.

c. Make sure that your pronouns have a clear and obvious referent.

(1) When an accountant contracts with a client for the primary benefit of a third party, they are in privity of contract.

(2) **Better:** When known to be a primary beneficiary of an accountant-client contract, a third party is in privity of contract with the accountant.

d. Make sure that any adjectival verbal phrase clearly modifies a noun stated in the sentence.

(1) To avoid incurring a penalty, each return was prepared exactly as required.

(2) **Better:** To avoid incurring a penalty, we prepared each return exactly as required.

Time Requirements for the Solutions Approach

Many candidates bypass the solutions approach, because they feel it is too time-consuming. Actually, the solutions approach is a time-saver and, more importantly, it helps you prepare better solutions to all questions.

Without committing yourself to using the solutions approach, try it step-by-step on several multiple-choice questions. After you conscientiously go through the step-by-step routine a few times, you will begin to adopt and modify aspects of the technique which will benefit you. Subsequent usage will become subconscious and painless. The important point is that you must try the solutions approach several times to accrue any benefits.

Efficiency of the Solutions Approach

The mark of an inefficient solution is one wherein the candidate immediately selects an answer. Remember, the final solution is one of the last steps in the solutions approach. You should have the solution under complete control before you decide on your final answer.

While the large amount of intermediary work in the solutions approach may appear burdensome and time-consuming, this technique results in better answers in less time than do haphazard approaches. Moreover, the solutions approach really allows you to work out problems that you feel unfamiliar with at first reading. The solutions approach, however, must be mastered prior to sitting for the CPA examination. In other words, the candidate must be willing to invest a reasonable amount of time into perfecting the solutions approach.

In summary, the solutions approach may appear foreign and somewhat cumbersome. At the same time, if you have worked through the material in this chapter, you should have some appreciation for it. Develop the solutions approach by writing down the steps in the solutions approach at the beginning of this chapter, and keep them before you as you work CPA exam questions. Remember that even though the suggested procedures appear **very structured** and **time-consuming,** integration of these procedures into your own style of problem solving will help improve **your** solutions approach. The next chapter discusses strategies for the overall examination.

NOW IS THE TIME TO MAKE YOUR COMMITMENT

Chapter 4: Taking the Examination

This chapter is concerned with developing an examination strategy (e.g., how to cope with the environment at the examination site, the way in which to work problems, etc.).

EXAMINATION STRATEGIES

Your performance during the examination is final and not subject to revision. While you may sit for the examination again if you are unsuccessful, the majority of your preparation will have to be repeated, requiring substantial, additional amounts of time. Thus, examination strategies (discussed in this chapter) that maximize your exam-taking efficiency are very important.

Getting "Psyched Up"

The CPA exam is quite challenging and worthy of your best effort. Explicitly develop your own psychological strategy to get yourself "up" for the exam. Pace your study program such that you will be able to operate at peak performance when you are actually taking the exam. A good aspect of the computerized exam is that if you have scheduled early in a testing window and do not feel well, you can reschedule your sitting. However, once you start the exam, you cannot retake it in the same testing window, so do not leave the exam early. Do the best you can.

Lodging, Meals, Exercise

If you must travel to the test center, make advance reservations for comfortable lodging convenient to the test center. Do not stay with friends, relatives, etc. Both uninterrupted sleep and total concentration on the exam are a must. Consider the following in making your lodging plans:

1. Proximity to the test center
2. Availability of meals and snacks
3. Recreational facilities

Plan your meal schedule to provide maximum energy and alertness during the day and maximum rest at night. Do not experiment with new foods, drinks, etc., around your scheduled date. Within reasonable limits, observe your normal eating and drinking habits. Recognize that overconsumption of coffee during the exam could lead to a hyperactive state and disaster. Likewise, overindulgence in alcohol to overcome nervousness and to induce sleep the night before might contribute to other difficulties the following morning.

Tenseness should be expected before and during the examination. Rely on a regular exercise program to unwind at the end of the day. As you select your lodging for the examination, try to accommodate your exercise pleasure (e.g., running, swimming etc.). Continue to indulge in your exercise program on the days of the examination.

To relieve tension or stress while studying, try breathing or stretching exercises. Use these exercises before and during the examination to start and to keep your adrenaline flowing. Remain determined not to go through another sitting for the Business Environment and Concepts (BEC) section to obtain your certificate.

In summary, the examination is likely to be both rigorous and fatiguing. Expect it and prepare for it by getting in shape, planning methods of relaxation during the exam and the evening before, and finally, building the confidence and competence to complete the exam (successfully).

Test Center and Procedures

If possible, visit the test center before the examination to assure knowledge of the location. Remember: no surprises. Having a general familiarity with the facilities will lessen anxiety prior to the examination. Talking to a recent veteran of the examination will give you background for the general examination procedures. **You must arrive at the testing center 30 minutes before your scheduled time.**

Upon completion of check-in at the test location, the candidate

- Is seated at a designated workstation
- Begins the exam after the proctor launches the session
- Is monitored by a Test Center Administrator
- Is videotaped

If you have any remaining questions regarding examination procedure, call or write your state board or go to Prometric's website at www.prometric.com/cpa.

Allocation of Time

Budget your time. Time should be carefully allocated in an attempt to maximize points per minute. While you must develop your own strategy with respect to time allocation, some suggestions may be useful. Allocate 5 minutes to reading the instructions. When you begin the exam you will be given an inventory of the total number of testlets and suggested times. Budget your time based on this inventory. Plan on spending 1½ to 2 minutes per individual multiple-choice question. Plan to spend about ¾ to 1 hour on the simulations testlet.

Techniques for Time Management

The Business Environment and Concepts (BEC) exam will have three testlets of multiple-choice questions with 24 questions each. Referring to the above guidelines, note that the maximum time you should take to complete a testlet of 24 questions is about 36 to 48 minutes. As you complete each testlet keep track of how you performed in relation to this standard. The exam will also include one testlet containing three task-based simulations requiring written communication.

Examination Rules

1. Prior to the start of the examination, you will be required to accept a Confidentiality and Break Policy Statement.
2. You must not bring any personal/unauthorized items into the testing room. Such items include but are not limited to outerwear, hats, food, drinks, purses, briefcases, notebooks, pagers, watches, cellular telephones, recording devices, and photographic equipment. You will be asked to empty and turn your pockets inside out prior to every entry into the test room to confirm that you have no prohibited items. Lockers are provided for storage of personal items.
3. Breaks may be taken at any time between testlets. **However, your exam time continues to run while you take the break.**
4. If you need access to an item stored in the test center during a break such as food or medicine, you must inform the Test Center Administrator before you retrieve the item. You are not allowed to access a prohibited item.
5. Any reference during the examination to books or other materials or the exchange of information with other persons shall be considered misconduct sufficient to bar you from further participation in the examination.
6. Penalties will be imposed on any candidate who is caught cheating before, during, or after the examination. These penalties may include expulsion from the examination, denial of applications for future examinations, and civil or criminal penalties.
7. You may not leave the examination room with any notes about the examination.

Refer to the brochure *CPA Candidate Bulletin* for other rules.

CPA EXAM CHECKLIST

One week before you are scheduled to sit

___ 1. Review outlines (your own or those in this volume) underlining buzzwords.

___ 2. If time permits, work through a few questions in your weakest areas so that techniques/concepts are fresh in your mind.

___ 3. Assemble notecards and key outlines of major topical areas into a manageable "last review" notebook to be taken with you to the exam.

What to bring

___ 1. *Notice to Schedule (NTS)*—You must bring the proper NTS with you.

___ 2. *Identification*—Bring two valid forms of ID. One must be government issued. The name on the ID must match exactly the name on the NTS. The *CPA Candidate Bulletin* lists valid primary and secondary IDs.

___ 3. *Hotel confirmation*—(if you must travel).

___ 4. *Cash*—Payment for anything by personal check is rarely accepted.

___ 5. *Major credit card*—American Express, Master-Card, Visa, etc.

___ 6. *Alarm clock*—This is too important an event to trust to a hotel wake-up call that might be overlooked.

___ 7. *Clothing*—Should be comfortable and layered to suit the possible temperature range in the testing room.

___ 8. *Earplugs*—Even though examinations are being given, there may be constant activity in the testing room (e.g., people walking around, rustling of paper, clicking of keyboards, people coughing, etc.). The use of earplugs may block out some of this distraction and help you concentrate better.

___ 9. *Other*—Any "last review" materials.

Evenings before exams

1. Reviewing the evening before the exam could earn you the extra points needed to pass a section. Just keep this last-minute effort in perspective and do **not** panic yourself into staying up all night trying to cover every possible point. This could lead to disaster by sapping your body of the endurance needed to attack questions creatively during the next day.

2. Reread key outlines or notecards, reviewing important topics in which you feel deficient.

3. Go over mnemonics and acronyms you have developed as study aids. Test yourself by writing out the letters on paper while verbally giving a brief explanation of what the letters stand for.

4. **Set your alarm and get a good night's rest!** Being well rested will permit you to meet each day's challenge with a fresh burst of creative energy. **You must arrive 30 minutes before your scheduled time.**

Exam-taking strategy

1. Do not spend an excess amount of time on the introductory screens. If you take longer than 10 minutes on these screens, the test session will automatically terminate. If the exam session terminates, it will not be possible to restart the examination and you will have to reapply to take the section.

2. Report equipment/software issues to the test center staff immediately. Do not attempt to correct the problem yourself and do not use examination time thinking about it before reporting it. Remind the test center staff to file a report describing the problem. The test center staff should be able to handle any equipment or software problems. However, if you believe the problem was not handled appropriately, contact NASBA at candidatecare@nasba.org.

3. Report any concerns about test questions to test center staff after you have completed the session. The members of the test center staff know nothing about the CPA Examination content. The test center staff can report the issues to the AICPA. You should also report concerns about the questions in writing to the AICPA (FAX to [609] 671-2922). If possible, the question and testlet numbers should be included in the FAX.

4. In the event of a power outage or incident requiring a restart, the computer clock will stop and you will not lose examination time. Your responses up to the time of the restart will not be lost as responses are saved at frequent intervals throughout the examination.

5. If you have questions about the examination software functions, you should read the instructions and "Help" tab information. The test center staff is not familiar with the functioning of the examination software and, therefore, will not be able to help you.

6. The crucial technique to use for multiple-choice questions is to read through each question stem **carefully,** nothing keywords such as "oral," "without disclosing," "qualified pension plan," etc. Then **read each choice** carefully before you start eliminating inappropriate answers. Often the first or second answer may **sound** correct, but a later answer may be **more correct.** Be discriminating! Reread the question and choose the best answer.

7. If you are struggling with questions beyond a minute or two, use the strategy of dividing multiple-choice questions into two categories.

   a. Questions for which you **know** you lack knowledge to answer: Drawing from any responses you have, narrow answers down to as few as possible, then make an **educated guess.**

   b. Questions for which you feel you should be getting the correct answer: Mark the question for review. Your mental block may clear, or you may spot a simple error in logic that will be corrected when you rereview the question.

8. Remember: **Never** change a first-impulse answer later unless you are absolutely certain you are right.

It is a proven fact that your subconscious often guides you to the correct answer.

9. Constantly compare your progress with the time remaining. **Never** spend an excessive amount of time on one testlet or one simulation.

10. Remember not to spend time getting a communication requirement technically correct. Communication requirements are not graded for technical accuracy. As long as your communication addresses the issue, it will be graded for demonstrated writing skills.

11. The cardinal rule is **never,** but **never,** leave an answer blank.

After taking the examination

1. Retain the Confirmation of Attendance form issued after the examination because it provides valuable contact information.

2. Report any examination incidents/concerns in writing, even if the issues were already reported to test center staff.

3. If you feel that the circumstances surrounding your test administration prevented you from performing at a level consistent with your knowledge and skills, immediately contact NASBA at candidatecare@ nasba.org

HAVE YOU MADE YOUR COMMITMENT?

Chapter 5: Exam Content Overview

The content of the Business Environment and Concepts (BEC) examination includes a number of general business and accounting topics. The areas are covered as shown below.

Topic	Percentage
Corporate Governance	16–20
Economic Concepts and Analysis	16–20
Financial Management	19–23
Information Systems and Communication	15–19
Strategic Planning	10–14
Operations Management	12–16

The BEC section of the exam tests knowledge and skills using multiple-choice questions and written communication skills using task-based simulations.

The basic concepts for preparation are the same as for other sections of the exam. You need to have the skills and knowledge necessary to solve both **how** (number crunching) and **why** (conceptual) type questions. In addition, you must be prepared for the simulations that require written communication.

First, become acquainted with the nature of the BEC exam itself. With the computerization of the exam, the AICPA has issued a set of content specifications. These content specifications are printed below.

Relatedly, you should evaluate your competence by working 10 to 20 multiple-choice questions from each of the modules (40–47). This diagnostic routine will acquaint you with the specific nature of the questions tested on each topic as well as indicate the amount of study required per topic. However, do not get discouraged. Remember, more difficult questions are more heavily weighted in determining your score. See discussion of self-study programs (Chapter 1) and examination grading (Chapter 2).

Second, study the content of modules 40–47, emphasizing the mechanics of each topic such as economic concepts, strategic performance measurement, working capital management, etc. Use simple examples, journal entries, and diagrams to get a handle on the basic concepts underlying each topic. You may have to refer to your textbooks, etc., for topics to which you have had no previous exposure.

Third, work as many multiple-choice questions as time allows and take the sample examination in Appendix A of this manual.

Fourth, prepare for the simulations by studying the methods to improve your writing skills presented in Chapter 3 of this manual, and **practice**, **practice**, **practice** writing short memos.

AICPA CONTENT AND SKILLS SPECIFICATIONS

The AICPA Content and Skills Specifications for the Uniform CPA Exam set forth the coverage of topics on the BEC exam. This outline was issued by the AICPA and is effective beginning in 2014. The first part of the outline describes the topical coverage of the BEC exam, and the second part provides some insights into the skills tested on all sections of the Uniform CPA exam.

Content Specification Outlines (CSOs)

The BEC section tests knowledge and skills necessary to demonstrate an understanding of the general business environment and business concepts. The topics in this section include knowledge of corporate governance; economic concepts essential to understanding the global business environment and its impact on an entity's business strategy; financial risk management; financial management processes; information systems and communications; strategic planning, and operations management. In addition to demonstrating knowledge and understanding of these topics, candidates are required to apply that knowledge in performing audit, attest, financial reporting, tax preparation, and other professional responsibilities as certified public accountants. To demonstrate such knowledge and skills, candidates will be expected to perform the following tasks:

- Demonstrate an understanding of globalization on the business environment.
- Distinguish between appropriate and inappropriate governance structures within an organization (e.g., tone at the top, policies, steering committees, strategies, oversight, etc.).

- Assess the impact of business cycles on an entity's industry or business operations.
- Apply knowledge of changes in the global economic markets in identifying the impact on an entity in determining its business strategy and financial management policies, including managing the risks of inflation, deflation, commodity costs, credit defaults, interest rate variations, currency fluctuation, and regulation.
- Assess the factors influencing a company's capital structure, including risk, leverage, cost of capital, growth rate, profitability, asset structure, and loan covenants.
- Evaluate assumptions used in financial valuations to determine their reasonableness (e.g., investment return assumptions, discount rates, etc.).
- Determine the business reasons for and explain the underlying economic substance of transactions and their accounting implications.
- Identify the information systems within a business that are used to process and accumulate transactional data, as well as provide monitoring and financial reporting information.
- Distinguish between appropriate and inappropriate internal control systems, including system design, controls over data, transaction flow, wireless technology, and internet transmissions.
- Evaluate whether there is appropriate segregation of duties, levels of authorization, and data security in an organization to maintain an appropriate internal control structure.
- Obtain and document information about an organization's strategic planning processes to identify key components of the business strategy and market risks.
- Develop a time-phased project plan showing required activities, task dependencies, and required resources to achieve a specific deliverable.
- Identify the business and operational risks inherent in an entity's disaster recovery/business continuity plan.
- Evaluate business operations and quality control initiatives to understand its use of best practices and the ways to measure and manage performance and costs.

The outline below specifies the knowledge in which candidates are required to demonstrate proficiency:

I. Corporate Governance (16%–20%)

A. Rights, Duties, Responsibilities, and Authority of the Board of Directors, Officers, and Other Employees

1. Financial reporting
2. Internal control (including COSO or similar framework)
3. Enterprise risk management (including COSO or similar framework)

B. Control Environment

1. Tone at the top—establishing control environment
2. Monitoring control effectiveness
3. Change control process

II. Economic Concepts and Analysis (16%–20%)

A. Changes in Economic and Business Cycle—Economic Measures/Indicators
B. Globalization and Local Economies

1. Impacts of globalization on companies
2. Shifts in economic balance of power (e.g., capital) to/from developed from/to emerging markets

C. Market Influences on Business Strategies
D. Financial Risk Management

1. Market, interest rate, currency, liquidity, credit, price, and other risks
2. Means for mitigating/controlling financial risks

III. Financial Management (19%–23%)

A. Financial Modeling, Projections, and Analysis

1. Forecasting and trends
2. Financial and risk analysis
3. Impact of inflation/deflation

B. Financial Decisions

1. Debt, equity, leasing
2. Asset and investment management

C. Capital Management, including Working Capital

1. Capital structure
2. Short-term and long-term financing
3. Asset effectiveness and/or efficiency

D. Financial Valuations (e.g., Fair Value)

1. Methods for calculating valuations
2. Evaluating assumptions used in valuations

E. Financial Transaction Processes and Controls

IV. Information Systems and Communications (15%–19%)

A. Organizational Needs Assessment

1. Data capture
2. Processing
3. Reporting
4. Role of information technology in business strategy

B. Systems Design and Other Elements

1. Business process design (integrated systems, automated, and manual interfaces)
2. Information technology (IT) control objectives
3. Role of technology systems in control monitoring
4. Operational effectiveness
5. Segregation of duties
6. Policies

C. Security

1. Technologies and security management features
2. Policies

D. Internet—Implications for Business

1. Electronic commerce
2. Opportunities for business process reengineering
3. Roles of internet evolution on business operations and organization cultures

E. Types of Information System and Technology Risks

F. Disaster Recovery and Business Continuity

V. Strategic Planning (10%–14%)

A. Market and Risk Analysis
B. Strategy Development, Implementation, and Monitoring

C. Planning Techniques

1. Budget and analysis
2. Forecasting and projection

3. Coordinating information from various sources for integrated planning

VI. Operations Management (12%–16%)

A. Performance Management and Impact of Measures on Behavior

1. Financial and nonfinancial measures
2. Impact of marketing practices on performance
3. Incentive compensation

B. Cost Measurement Methods and Techniques
C. Process Management

1. Approaches, techniques, measures, and benefits to process-management-driven businesses
2. Roles of shared services, outsourcing, and off-shore operations, and their implications on business risks and controls
3. Selecting and implementing improvement initiatives
4. Business process reengineering
5. Management philosophies and techniques for performance improvement such as Just in Time (JIT), Quality, Lean, Demand Flow, Theory of Constraints, and Six Sigma

D. Project Management

1. Project planning, implementation, and monitoring
2. Roles of project managers, project members, and oversight or steering groups
3. Project risks, including resource, scope, cost, and deliverables

References—Business Environment and Concepts

- The Committee of Sponsoring Organizations of the Treadway Commission (COSO):

  - Internal Control—Integrated Framework
  - Enterprise Risk Management

- Sarbanes-Oxley Act of 2002:

  - Title III, Corporate Responsibility
  - Title IV, Enhanced Financial Disclosures
  - Title VIII, Corporate and Criminal Fraud Accountability
  - Title IX, White-Collar Crime Penalty Enhancements
  - Title XI, Corporate Fraud Accountability

- Current Business Periodicals
- Current Textbooks on

  - Accounting Information Systems
  - Budgeting and Measurement
  - Corporate Governance
  - Economics
  - Enterprise Risk Management
  - Finance

- Management
- Management Information Systems
- Managerial Accounting
- Production Operations
- Project Management

- International Standards for the Professional Practice of Internal Auditing
- COBIT (Control OBjectives for Information and related Technology)

Skill Specification Outlines (SSOs)

The Skill Specification Outlines (SSOs) identify the skills to be tested on the Uniform CPA Examination. There are three categories of skills, and the weightings will be implemented through the use of different question formats in the exam. For each of the question formats, a different set of tools will be available as resources to the candidates, who will need to use those tools to demonstrate proficiency in the applicable skills categories.

Weights

The percentage range assigned to each skill category will be used to determine the quantity of each type of question, as described below. The percentage range assigned to each skill category represents the approximate percentage to which that category of skills will be used in the different sections of the CPA Examination to assess proficiency. The ranges are designed to provide flexibility in building the examination, and the midpoints of the ranges for each section total 100%. No percentages are given for the bulleted descriptions included in these definitions. The presence of several groups within an area or several topics within a group does not imply equal importance or weight will be given to these bullets on an examination.

Skills category	Weights (FAR, REG, AUD)	Weights (BEC)
Knowledge and Understanding	50%–60%	80%–90%
Application of the Body of Knowledge	40%–50%	–
Written Communication	–	10%–20%

Knowledge and Understanding. Multiple-choice questions will be used as the proxy for assessing knowledge and understanding, and will be based upon the content topics as outlined in the CSOs. Candidates will not have access to the authoritative literature, spreadsheets, or database tools while answering these questions. A calculator will be accessible for the candidates to use in performing calculations to demonstrate their understanding of the principles or subject matter.

Application of the Body of Knowledge. Task-based simulations will be used as the proxy for assessing application of the body of knowledge and will be based upon the content topics as outlined in the CSOs. Candidates will have access to the authoritative literature, a calculator, spreadsheets, and other resources and tools which they will use to demonstrate proficiency in applying the body of knowledge.

Written Communication will be assessed through the use of responses to essay questions, which will be based upon the content topics as outlined in the CSOs. Candidates will have access to a word processor, which includes a spell-check feature.

Outlines

The outlines below provide additional descriptions of the skills that are represented in each category.

Knowledge and Understanding. Expertise and skills developed through learning processes, recall, and reading comprehension. Knowledge is acquired through experience or education and is the theoretical or practical understanding of a subject; knowledge is also represented through awareness or familiarity with information gained by experience of a fact or situation. Understanding represents a higher level than simple knowledge and is the process of using concepts to deal adequately with given situations, facts, or circumstances. Understanding is the ability to recognize and comprehend the meaning of a particular concept.

Application of the Body of Knowledge, Including Analysis, Judgment, Synthesis, Evaluation, and Research. Higher-level cognitive skills that require individuals to act or transform knowledge in some fashion. These skills are inextricably intertwined and thus are grouped into this single skill area.

- Assess the Business Environment

  - Business Process Evaluation: Assessing and integrating information regarding a business's operational structure, functions, processes, and procedures to develop a broad operational perspective; identify the need for new systems or changes to existing systems and/or processes.
  - Contextual Evaluation: Assessing and integrating information regarding client's type of business or industry.
  - Strategic Analysis: Understanding the business: Obtaining, assessing and integrating information on the entity's strategic objectives, strategic management process, business environment, the nature of and value to customers, its products and services, extent of competition within its market space, etc.).
  - Business Risk Assessment: Obtaining, assessing and integrating information on conditions and events that could impede the entity's ability to achieve strategic objectives.
  - Visualize Abstract Descriptions: Organizing and processing symbols, pictures, graphs, objects, and other information.

- Research

  - Identify the appropriate research question.
  - Identify key search terms for use in performing electronic searches through large volumes of data.
  - Search through large volumes of electronic data to find required information.
  - Organize information or data from multiple sources.
  - Integrate diverse sources of information to reach conclusions or make decisions.
  - Identify the appropriate authoritative guidance in applicable financial reporting frameworks and auditing standards for the accounting issue being evaluated.

- Application of Technology

  - Using electronic spreadsheets to perform calculations, financial analysis, or other functions to analyze data.
  - Integration of technological applications and resources into work processes.
  - Using a variety of computer software and hardware systems to structure, utilize, and manage data.

- Analysis

  - Review information to determine compliance with specified standards or criteria.
  - Use expectations, empirical data, and analytical methods to determine trends and variances.
  - Perform appropriate calculations on financial and nonfinancial data.
  - Recognize patterns of activity when reviewing large amounts of data or recognize breaks in patterns.
  - Interpretation of financial statement data for a given evaluation purpose.
  - Forecasting future financial statement data from historical financial statement data and other information.
  - Integrating primary financial statements: using data from all primary financial statements to uncover financial transactions, inconsistencies, or other information.

- Complex Problem Solving and Judgment

  - Develop and understand goals, objectives, and strategies for dealing with potential issues, obstacles, or opportunities.
  - Analyze patterns of information and contextual factors to identify potential problems and their implications.
  - Devise and implement a plan of action appropriate for a given problem.
  - Apply professional skepticism, which is an attitude that includes a questioning mind and a critical assessment of information or evidence obtained.
  - Adapt strategies or planned actions in response to changing circumstances.
  - Identify and solve unstructured problems.
  - Develop reasonable hypotheses to answer a question or resolve a problem.
  - Formulate and examine alternative solutions in terms of their relative strengths and weaknesses, level of risk, and appropriateness for a given situation.
  - Develop creative ways of thinking about situations, problems, and opportunities to create insightful and sound solutions.
  - Develop logical conclusions through the use of inductive and deductive reasoning.
  - Apply knowledge of professional standards and laws, as well as legal, ethical, and regulatory issues.
  - Assess the need for consultations with other professionals when gray areas, or areas requiring specialized knowledge, are encountered.

- Decision Making

  - Specify goals and constraints.
  - Generate alternatives.
  - Consider risks.
  - Evaluate and select the best alternative.

- Organization, Efficiency, and Effectiveness

  - Use time effectively and efficiently.
  - Develop detailed work plans, schedule tasks and meetings, and delegate assignments and tasks.
  - Set priorities by determining the relevant urgency or importance of tasks and deciding the order in which they should be performed.
  - File and store information so that it can be found easily and used effectively.

Written Communication. The various skills involved in preparing written communication, including

- Basic writing mechanics, such as grammar, spelling, word usage, punctuation, and sentence structure.
- Effective business writing principles, including organization, clarity, and conciseness.
- Exchange technical information and ideas with coworkers and other professionals to meet goals of job assignment.
- Documentation

  - Prepare documents and presentations that are concise, accurate, and supportive of the subject matter.
  - Document and cross-reference work performed and conclusions reached in a complete and accurate manner.

- Assist client to recognize and understand implications of critical business issues by providing recommendations and informed opinions.
- Persuade others to take recommended courses of action.
- Follow directions.

BUSINESS ENVIRONMENT AND CONCEPTS

As indicated previously, this manual consists of eight modules designed to facilitate your study for the Business Environment and Concepts section of the Uniform CPA Examination. The table of contents at the right describes the content of each module

Module 40: Corporate Governance, Internal Control, and Enterprise Risk Management

Overview

This module focuses on the related topics of corporate governance, internal control, and enterprise risk management. Corporate governance is designed to compensate for the agency problem resulting from the fact that corporations are managed by professional management that may not operate them in the best interest of the shareholders. Corporate governance includes the policies, procedures, and mechanisms that are established to control management. The major controls over management include compensation systems, boards of directors (including major committees), external auditors, internal auditors, attorneys, regulators, creditors, securities analysts, and internal control systems.

Internal control is defined by COSO (2013 revision) as a process, effected by the entity's board of directors, managements, and other personnel designed to provide reasonable assurance regarding the achievement of objectives relating to operations, reporting, and compliance. It can be viewed as including five components: (1) the control environment, (2) risk assessment, (3) control activities, (4) information and communication, and (5) monitoring activities. It is important to realize that internal control is not perfect. It has a number of limitations, including management can override internal control, controls that rely on segregation of duties can be circumvented with collusion, internal control can break down due to bad judgment or misunderstanding of duties, and internal control cannot be perfect because its cost cannot exceed its benefits.

COSO has also developed a framework for enterprise risk management. Enterprise risk management is a process designed to identify potential events that may affect the entity, and manage risk to be within its risk appetite, to provide reasonable assurance regarding the achievement of entity objectives. It consists of eight interrelated components, including (1) internal environment, (2) objective setting, (3) event identification, (4) risk assessment, (5) risk response, (6) control activities, (7) information and communication, and (8) monitoring. All of these components work together to allow an organization to identify risks to achieving the organization's objectives and appropriately manage those risks. Before beginning the reading you should review the key terms at the end of the module.

A. Corporate Governance

In the corporate form of organization, owners (shareholders) are separated from operations (management) of the firm. This creates an agency problem in that management (the agents) may not act in the best interest of the shareholders (the principals). Managers may be tempted to engage in self-serving activities, such as shirking, taking too little or too much risk, or consuming excessive perks. Effective corporate governance involves developing an appropriate legal structure, and establishing appropriate incentives (i.e., forms of compensation) and monitoring devices to prevent this inappropriate activity.

Shareholders are a major stakeholder of the corporation, but there are others, including employees, customers, suppliers, government regulators, and society.

1. Legal Structure of Corporations

   a. **Articles of incorporation.** Corporations are almost universally incorporated under the laws and regulations of one of the states. A corporation is formed with the filing of **articles of incorporation** with the secretary of state who issues a certificate of incorporation. The articles of incorporation include

   (1) Proposed name of the corporation and initial address
   (2) Purpose of the corporation
   (3) The powers of the corporation

37

(4) The name of the registered agent of the corporation

(5) Name and address of each incorporator

(6) Number of authorized shares of stock and types of stock

The articles of incorporation may be subsequently amended by approval of shareholders (often a majority vote but sometimes two-thirds vote required). Shareholders dissenting from the amendments may assert their right to sell their shares to the corporation for fair value before the vote. The **bylaws** of the corporation set forth how the directors and/or officers are elected/selected, how meetings are conducted, the types and duties of officers, and the required meetings. In addition, the bylaws should prescribe the process for bylaw amendment. For good governance all officers and directors should be provided with a copy of the corporation's bylaws.

b. **Shareholders.** Common shareholders provide the basic capital of the corporation and elect the board of directors. Annual meetings of shareholders are required as set forth in the bylaws. Certain matters require vote of the shareholders, such as amendment of the articles of incorporation and fundamental changes affecting the corporation, such as mergers and liquidations. Sarbanes-Oxley, which is discussed later in this module, also prescribes certain matters that must be voted on by shareholders. The common shareholders are the last to receive their capital in the event of liquidation of the corporation. Other rights of the common shareholders include

(1) Right to receive dividends if declared by the board of directors

(2) Right to subscribe to stock issues so that their ownership is not diluted as set forth in the Articles of Incorporation (preemptive right)

(3) Right to inspect books and records in good faith and for a proper purpose

(4) Right to sue on behalf of the corporation if officers and directors do not for reasons such as director violation of fiduciary duty, illegal declaration of dividends, or fraud by an officer (referred to as a derivative suit)

Shareholders have no right to manage the corporation unless they are also officers or directors. Preferred shareholders generally have no voting rights but they have preference as to dividends and receipt of capital upon liquidation of the company.

In many cases common shareholders have **cumulative voting rights** in the election of directors allowing them to cast 1 vote for each director of the corporation for each share of stock they own. This allows minority shareholders to have an opportunity to elect directors by voting all their votes for one or two directors.

c. **Boards of directors.** The board of directors is charged with running the corporation on behalf of the shareholders and other stakeholders. It is responsible for providing strategic direction and guidance about the establishment of the key business objectives of the corporation. Examples of duties of the board include

(1) Determining the mission of the corporation

(2) Selection and removal of the chief executive officer

(3) Amending the bylaws, unless this is a responsibility of the shareholders

(4) Determining management compensation

(5) Decisions regarding declaration and payment of dividends

(6) Decisions regarding major acquisitions and capital structure

(7) Advising management

(8) Providing governance oversight, with the assistance of internal and external auditors

(9) Ensuring accurate financial reporting by the corporation

(10) Risk management

Directors are elected by the common shareholders and have no individual power to bind the corporation. The power resides in the board collectively. A majority vote of directors present is needed for most business decisions providing a quorum is present. Actions may be taken with no meeting if allowed by the corporation's articles of incorporation or bylaws. However, there must be unanimous written consent by board members for action to be taken without a meeting.

Directors must exercise ordinary care and due diligence in performing their duties, and act in a manner that they believe is in the best interest of the corporation. In addition, they must disclose any conflicts of interest. The **business judgment rule** is a case law-derived concept that provides that a corporate director may not be held liable for errors in judgment providing the director acted with good faith, loyalty, and due care. Directors, however, may be held personally liable for approving and paying dividends that are illegal. Directors are also responsible for their own torts (wrongful acts) even if they are acting on behalf of the corporation.

The directors' **duty of loyalty** means that they must put the interest of the corporation before their personal interest.

EXAMPLE

Assume a director is approached with a business opportunity that would be of interest to and benefit the corporation. However, the director is also interested in the opportunity. The director must first offer the opportunity to the corporation before pursuing it on his or her own behalf.

---

  d. **Officers.** Officers operate the company based on the authority delegated to them by the board of directors. An officer of the corporation is an agent that can bind the corporation within the scope of his or her authority. A corporation is not bound by acts of an officer acting beyond the scope of his or her authority. The officers of the corporation are responsible for the fair presentation of the corporation's financial reports, including the financial statements. Sarbanes-Oxley requires the chief financial officer and chief executive officer to certify to financial statements. Officers have a fiduciary duty to the corporation and are liable for their own torts. Finally, the Sarbanes-Oxley Act generally prohibits personal loans to officers or directors of a public company.

2. **Forms of Executive Compensation**

Various types of compensation are used to attempt to align management behavior with the objectives of the shareholders. A key objective in setting executive compensation is to align management's decisions and actions with the long-term interests of shareholders (e.g., long-term stock price). If managers are given too much fixed compensation, they may become too complacent and not take appropriate risks to increase share price. If managers are given too much incentive compensation based on operating profit or short-term stock price, they have incentives to manage profit or take excessive risks to maximize their compensation. Common types of management compensation are described below.

  a. **Base salary and bonuses**—Using this system, managers are compensated based on performance which is typically measured by accounting profit. Compensation systems based on accounting measures of profit are problematic because accounting profit can be manipulated or managed. For example, the timing of research and development and maintenance expenditures may be altered to manage profit and maximize bonuses. Managers may put too much focus on short-term profits instead of focusing on maximizing the long-term wealth of shareholders.

  b. **Stock options**—The use of stock options as a form of compensation provides managers with an incentive to manage the corporation to increase the stock price, which is consistent with the goal of shareholders. A disadvantage of stock options is that managers may have an incentive to increase the stock price in the short-term at the expense of long-term stock value, even by manipulating accounting income to increase stock price. In addition, stock options may encourage management to take on risks that are that are in excess of shareholders' risk appetite. Finally, if the stock price falls substantially, the stock options may be so underwater that they no longer provide an incentive to management.

  c. **Stock grants**—Stock grants involve issuing shares of stock as part of management's compensation. Two common types of stock grants are

  (1) Restricted stock—The issuance of stock that cannot be sold by the manager for a specific period of time, usually 10 years. This form of compensation is effective because it encourages managers to undertake operations that increase the long-term value of the corporation's stock price.

  (2) Performance shares—The issuance of stock to management if certain levels of performance are met. If the price of the corporation's stock increases, the value of the manager's compensation increases.

  d. **Executive perquisites (perks)**—Management also may get various perquisites such as retirement benefits, use of corporate assets, golden parachutes, and corporate loans.

  e. **The best forms of executive compensation**—It is generally believed that the best compensation systems include a combination of fixed compensation and incentive compensation that is related to long-term stock price.

> **EXAMPLE**
>
> A company may establish incentive compensation in the form of stock options or stock that can be exercised or sold only after being held for a long period of time (e.g., 5 to 10 years).

Bonuses are effective if they are based on a composite of performance measures in addition to net profit, such as the amount of research and development expenditures, the corporation's market share, the number of new products developed, and/or the percentage of stock held by institutional investors (who tend to hold the stock for the long term). Such performance systems are often referred to as a balanced scorecard.

3. Monitoring Devices

Various devices exist in the United States to monitor management behavior. Some of the devices are internal (e.g., the board of directors and internal auditors), while others are external (e.g., external auditors, analysts, credit agencies, attorneys, the SEC, and the IRS).

a. **Board oversight.** To be effective at providing governance oversight, board members must be competent and a majority of the board members should be independent. Independence means the board member is not part of management of the corporation and does not receive significant benefit from the corporation other than compensation as a board member. Directors also must be adequately trained and be provided with complete and accurate information to carry out the board's functions. Officers, employees or major stockholders who are on the board of directors are referred to as **inside directors**. The **Wall Street Reform and Consumer Protection (Dodd-Frank) Act of 2010** requires public corporations to disclose why or why not the chairman of the board is also the chief executive officer.

Boards of directors should have a set of governance guidelines that are reviewed and revised annually. These guidelines will set forth the board organization, which will include its various committees and subcommittees. Committees that are particularly important to effective corporate governance include (1) the nominating/corporate governance committee, (2) the compensation committee, and (3) the audit committee.

(1) The nominating/corporate governance committee (1) oversees board organization, including committee assignments, (2) determines director qualifications and training, (3) develops corporate governance principles, and (4) oversees CEO succession.

(2) The audit committee plays a critical role in corporate governance. The Sarbanes-Oxley Act defines the audit committee as a "committee established by and amongst the board of directors of an issuer for the purpose of overseeing the accounting and financial reporting processes of the issuer; and audits of the financial statements of the issuer." A major responsibility of the audit committee is the appointment, compensation and oversight of the corporation's external auditor, including the resolution of any disagreements between management and the external auditor. An independent audit committee is mandated by the Sarbanes-Oxley Act and regulations of the NYSE and NASDAQ. Other important characteristics of an audit committee include

(a) The Sarbanes-Oxley Act provides that at least one member should be a "financial expert." The names of the financial experts must be disclosed. If the firm does not have a financial expert, it must provide an explanation. A financial expert is one that possesses all of the following attributes:

1] An understanding of generally accepted accounting principles and financial statements;
2] Experience in preparing, auditing, analyzing, or evaluating financial statements of the breadth and complexity expected to be encountered with the company;
3] An understanding of internal controls and procedures for financial reporting; and
4] An understanding of audit committee functions.

These attributes may be acquired through (1) education and experience as a principal financial officer, controller, public accountant, or equivalent, (2) experience supervising an individual in one of the positions in (1), (3) experience overseeing or assessing the performance of companies or public accountants with respect to preparing, auditing or evaluating financial statements, or (4) other relevant experience.

(b) The audit committee should appoint, determine compensation of, and oversee the work of the corporation's external auditor.

(c) External auditors must report directly to the audit committee.

      (d)   Internal auditors should have direct access to the audit committee.

      (e)   The audit committee should establish procedures for the receipt and treatment of complaints regarding accounting or auditing matters, including submission of concerns by employees (whistle-blowers). The Dodd-Frank Act provides for civil actions by whistle-blowers who are retaliated against by the company.

      (f)   Section 302 of the Sarbanes-Oxley Act requires certification that the CEO and CFO (1) have reviewed the quarterly and annual financial reports filed with the SEC and they believe they are fairly stated and contain no material misstatements, (2) are responsible for establishing and maintaining internal controls that are designed to assure that relevant information is made known to them, and (3) have evaluated internal controls and believe controls are effective as indicated in management's report on internal control. They must also certify that they have reported to the auditors and the audit committee all significant deficiencies in internal control, and are not aware of any postevaluation changes that could significantly affect controls.

  (3)   The compensation committee (1) reviews and approves CEO compensation based on meeting performance goals, (2) makes recommendations to the board with respect to incentive and equity-based compensation plans, and (3) attempts to align incentives with shareholder objectives and risk appetite. The **Dodd-Frank Act** established a requirement that all members of the compensation committee of public companies must be independent. In addition, shareholders must be allowed a nonbinding vote on executive compensation at least every three years, and a vote at least every six years as to whether the vote on compensation should be held more often. Finally, the act also requires a nonbinding vote by shareholders on "golden parachutes" to be provided to executives as a result of major transactions.

b. **New York Stock Exchange (NYSE) and NASDAQ Rules Related to Corporate Governance and Director Independence.** Among other items, the NYSE and NASDAQ require listed corporations to

  (1)   Have a majority of independent directors on their boards.

  (2)   Make determination of independence of members and provide information to investors about the determination. Specific NYSE and NASDAQ rules that make a director not independent include

      (a)   A director is not independent if s/he has been an employee of the corporation or an affiliate in the last five years (three years for NASDAQ).

      (b)   A director is not independent if a family member has been an officer of the corporation or affiliate in the last five years (three years for NASDAQ).

      (c)   A director is not independent if s/he was a former partner or employee of the corporation's external auditor in the last five years (three years for NASDAQ).

      (d)   A director is not independent if s/he or a family member in the last three years received more than $120,000 (for a twelve-month period) in payments from the corporation other than for director compensation.

      (e)   A director is not independent if s/he is an executive of another entity that receives significant amounts of revenue from the corporation.

  (3)   Identify certain relationships that automatically preclude a board member from being independent.

  (4)   Have nonmanagement directors meet at regularly scheduled executive sessions.

  (5)   Adopt a comprehensive code of conduct applicable to all directors, officers, and employees, and disclose any waivers of the code for directors or executive officers. The code should be distributed to employees, officers, and directors, and reinforced in training sessions. The code should be periodically acknowledged by all employees.

  (6)   Have an independent audit committee. In addition, nominating/corporate governance and compensation decisions must be made by independent committees (or a majority of independent directors for NASDAQ).

> **NOTE:** It is important to remember that judgment must be used to determine whether a director is independent. For example, based on the facts and circumstances it may be concluded that a director is not independent even though s/he receives less than $120,000 in payments (other than director compensation).

c. **Internal auditors.** Internal auditors perform audits of the risk management activities, internal control, and other governance processes for the corporation. Such audits are often referred to as assurance services. The results of these audits should be communicated directly to the audit committee of the board of directors. The NYSE requires its listed companies to maintain an internal audit function to provide management and the audit committee with ongoing assessments of the company's risk management processes and system of internal control.

The Institute of Internal Auditors (IIA) is a professional organization of internal auditors. Among other activities, the IIA has issued International Standards for the Professional Practice of Internal Auditing and a Code of Ethics for internal auditors. This organization also administers the Certified Internal Auditor (CIA) program. To become a CIA an individual must pass a multipart exam and have a minimum of two years of internal audit experience (or its equivalent). The CIA designation helps to demonstrate that the individual is competent to perform internal audits.

The International Standards for the Professional Practice of Internal Auditing, much like generally accepted auditing standards, include rules and interpretations. They cover the two types of services that internal auditors perform, assurance services and consulting services. Assurance services involve providing an independent assessment of governance, risk management or control processes of an organization. Examples include assurance about financial presentation, compliance, performance, and system security. Consulting services involve advisory-related services to improve an organization's governance, risk management or control processes. Examples of consulting services include training, advising, and facilitating. The internal auditing standards are broken down into attribute standards (related to the characteristics of the internal audit activity) and performance standards (related to the quality of internal audit activities). The International Standards also include implementation standards that expand upon the attribute and performance standards. Aspects of the International Standards for the Professional Practice of Internal Auditing that relate particularly to corporate governance include

(1) The purpose, authority, and responsibility of the internal audit activity should be formally defined in the internal audit charter. The internal audit charter should recognize the need to adhere to the Code of Ethics and International Standards for the Professional Practice of Internal Auditing. The Standards apply to individual internal auditors and internal audit activities.

(2) The internal audit activity must be independent and internal auditors must be objective in performing their work. Independence for the internal auditor activity is achieved by organizational independence, which means auditors cannot be influenced by the management of the functional areas that they audit. Accordingly, the chief audit executive should report to a level within the organization that allows the internal audit activity to fulfill its responsibilities. For effective organizational independence, the chief audit executive ideally should report functionally to the audit committee and administratively to the chief executive officer of the corporation. Examples of functional reporting to the board include board approvals of the internal audit charter; budget and resource plan; risk-based audit plan; remuneration of the chief audit executive; and decisions regarding appointment and discharge of the chief audit executive. This helps to prevent the auditor's work from being influenced by management of the corporation. In addition, individual internal auditors must have an impartial, unbiased attitude and avoid conflicts of interest. If independence is impaired, the details of the impairment should be disclosed to appropriate parties.

EXAMPLE

Assume that an internal auditor managed the shipping department of the business before transferring to the internal audit department. That auditor should not be charged with auditing activities in the shipping department for the period he served as manager because independence could be impaired.

---

(3) Internal audit engagements must be performed with proficiency and due professional care. Proficiency means that the internal auditors must possess the knowledge, skills, and competencies needed to perform their individual responsibilities. This includes a sufficient knowledge of key IT risks and controls, and IT audit techniques, and a sufficient knowledge to evaluate fraud risk.

(4) Internal auditors must enhance their knowledge and skills with continuing professional development, and the chief audit executive must develop and maintain a quality assurance and improvement program.
Quality assurance and improvement programs should include

(a) Internal assessments that include ongoing monitoring of performance and periodic reviews through self-assessment or review by other qualified individuals within the organization.

(b) External assessments at least once every five years by qualified independent assessors.

The chief audit executive should communicate the results of the quality assurance and improvement program to senior management and the board.

(5) The internal audit activity must evaluate the effectiveness and contribute to the improvement of the corporation's risk management processes, and assist the management in maintaining effective controls by evaluating their effectiveness and efficiency and promoting continuous improvement.

(6) The chief audit executive must establish risk-based plans to determine audit priorities. He or she must also effectively deploy internal audit resources to achieve the plan, and establish effective policies and procedures to guide audit activities.

(7) The chief audit executive should share information and coordinate work with other internal auditors and external auditors.

(8) The chief audit executive should periodically report to senior executives and the board on the internal audit activity's purpose, authority, responsibility, and performance relative to its plan. Reporting must also include significant risk exposures and control issues, including fraud risks, and governance issues.

(9) The internal audit activity must assess and make appropriate recommendations for improving the governance process in its accomplishment of the following objectives:

    (a) Promoting appropriate ethics and values within the organization;

    (b) Ensuring effective organizational performance management and accountability;

    (c) Communicating risk and control information to appropriate areas of the organization; and

    (d) Coordinating the activities of and communicating information among the board, external and internal auditors, and management.

(10) The internal audit activity must evaluate the effectiveness and contribute to the improvement of risk management processes.

(11) The internal audit activity must assist the organization in maintaining effective controls by evaluating their effectiveness and efficiency and by promoting continuous improvement.

(12) Audit engagements should be adequately planned, including appropriate identification of objectives and scope. Audit work programs should be developed, and audit work should be adequately supervised. Engagements should be assigned adequate resources, and sufficient information should be collected and analyzed to achieve the audit objectives. Finally, results should be effectively communicated.

(13) The chief audit executive must establish and maintain a system to monitor the disposition of audit results communicated to management.

  d. **External auditors.** The external auditor is responsible for performing an audit of the corporation's financial statements and internal control in accordance with standards of the Public Company Accounting Oversight Board (PCAOB). The external auditor is a major external corporate governance monitoring device for a corporation. The external audit helps assure that corporation financial reports are accurate and management is not engaging in fraudulent financial reporting.

      Section 404 of the Sarbanes-Oxley Act requires that management acknowledge its responsibility for establishing adequate internal control over financial reporting and provide an assessment in the annual report of the effectiveness of internal control. For large public corporations (accelerated filers), it also requires that external auditors attest to management's report on internal control as part of the audit of the financial statements.

      External auditors are required to communicate to the audit committee information that will help the committee perform its oversight function, including the following matters:

    (1) Auditor responsibility to form and express an opinion.

    (2) An audit does not relieve management or the audit committee with their responsibilities for governance.

    (3) Planned scope and timing of the audit.

    (4) Significant audit findings, including:

        (a) Auditor views of qualitative aspects of significant accounting practices.

        (b) Significant difficulties encountered during the audit.

        (c) Disagreements with management.

        (d) Other findings or issues which the auditor believes are significant and relevant.

        (e) Uncorrected misstatements other than those that are trivial.

    (5) Material corrected misstatements.

    (6) Significant issues discussed with management.

(7) Auditor's views about significant matters on which management consulted with other accountants.

(8) Written representations the auditor is requesting.

(9) Significant deficiencies and material weaknesses in internal control.

Section 802 prohibits a person from knowingly destroying, mutilating, or concealing records or documents to impede or influence the investigation of any department or agency of the United States. The penalty is a fine or imprisonment for not more than 20 years, or both.

e. **Investment banks and securities analysts.** Investment bankers help corporations issue equity and debt offerings. Therefore, they represent an external monitoring device because they must evaluate the company prior to becoming involved in selling the securities.

Securities analysts analyze companies to attempt to develop recommendations to "buy," "hold," or "sell" a particular corporation's stock. Therefore, securities analysts act as an external monitoring device because they use financial and nonfinancial information, including information about corporate management to make their recommendations. An issue with considering the recommendations of analysts is potential conflicts of interest. For example, analysts may be employed by firms that also perform investment banking activities, and the analyst's recommendations may be influenced by the fees received from the corporation for investment banking services. Regulations adopted by the SEC attempt to control these conflicts of interest by, among other requirements, requiring analysts to certify that their compensation will not be impacted by their recommendations.

f. **Creditors.** Creditors also act as an external monitoring device. Debt agreements contain covenants (requirements) that must be complied with to prevent the creditor from taking actions such as accelerating payment terms. Creditors monitor compliance by the corporation with the covenants of these agreements. One limitation of creditors as a monitoring device is that they monitor largely based on information provided by management. However, they do often engage external auditors to perform procedures to provide assurance about the corporation's compliance with certain covenants of the loan agreements.

g. **Credit rating agencies.** Credit rating agencies rate the creditworthiness of corporate bonds. Credit rating agencies are an external corporate monitoring device much like securities analysts. The biggest criticism of credit rating agencies is that they may improperly set the initial rating and are slow to downgrade the rating once the corporation gets in financial difficulty.

> **NOTE:** The Dodd-Frank Act has provisions that help prevent conflicts of interests and increase transparency by credit rating agencies.

h. **Attorneys.** Corporate legal counsel provide another external monitoring device in that they review securities filings and provide management advice on legal matters.

i. **The Securities and Exchange Commission (SEC).** The SEC is responsible for protecting investors; maintaining fair, orderly, and efficient markets; and facilitating capital formation. In achieving these responsibilities, the SEC enforces the US securities laws. The SEC consists of five presidentially appointed Commissioners. The SEC's activities act as an important external monitoring device for corporate government. The divisions and offices of the SEC that are particularly relevant to corporate governance include

(1) Division of Corporate Finance—This division reviews documents of publicly held companies that are filed with the SEC. Through the review process, the Division checks to see if companies are meeting disclosure requirements and seeks to improve the quality of the disclosures by companies.

(2) Division of Enforcement—This division assists the SEC in executing its law enforcement function by recommending the commencement of investigations of securities law violations, recommending which cases to take to court, and prosecuting these cases on behalf of the Commission.

(3) The Office of the Chief Accountant—The Chief Accountant advises the Commission on accounting and auditing, oversees the development of accounting principles, and approves the auditing rules put forward by the Public Company Accounting Oversight Board (PCAOB).

Several provisions of the Sarbanes-Oxley Act improved the SEC's power as an external monitoring device, including:

(1) Section 906 of the Sarbanes-Oxley Act requires the chief executive officer (CEO) and the chief financial officer (CFO) to certify the accuracy and truthfulness of periodic financial reports filed with the SEC. If the certification of the reports is later found to be inaccurate, the CEO and CFO can be found criminally liable and face imprisonment of 10 to 20 years. Also, civil penalties can involve fines of up to $5 million.

(2) Sarbanes-Oxley requires public companies to disclose in their filings whether they have established a code of ethics for senior financial officers.

(3) Under Sarbanes-Oxley, any person who knowingly perpetrates or attempts a scheme to defraud any other person by misrepresenting or making false claims in connection with the purchase or sale of securities can be fined or imprisoned for up to 25 years, or both. While securities fraud has long been an offense under the other securities acts, Sarbanes-Oxley made prosecution much easier.

(4) The destruction, mutilation, alteration, concealment, or falsification of documentation with the intent to obstruct or influence an investigation that is ongoing or being considered can result in fines or imprisonment of up to 20 years.

(5) Sarbanes-Oxley prohibits any acts of retaliation against employees who alert the government to possible violations of securities laws (whistle-blowers). The punishment for a violation of this provision can include fines or imprisonment of up to 10 years or both.

The Dodd-Frank act provides that the SEC will pay awards to whistle-blowers for providing information about violations of securities laws that result in aggregate monetary sanctions in excess of $1 million. The Act and related rules provide that

(1) A whistle-blower is eligible to receive 10 to 30% of the monetary sanction if the information is derived from independent knowledge or analysis of the whistle-blower and not known to the government from any other source.

(2) Tips can be made anonymously (through an attorney) with the whistle-blower only being identified to the SEC after determination that an award will be given.

(3) A broad group of individuals are eligible including employees, customers, and suppliers. Individuals that are generally excluded from eligibility include

  (a) Officers, directors, trustees, or partners of an entity, when those individuals learned of information about the misconduct from another person or in connection with the company's processes for identifying potential illegal conduct.

  (b) Employees whose main job functions involve compliance or internal audit, or persons who are employed by a firm hired to perform audit or compliance functions or to investigate possible violations of the law.

  (c) Employees of public accounting firms performing an engagement required by the securities laws.

  However, the above individuals may be still eligible if it appears that the company is attempting to behave in a way that would harm investors or inhibit an investigation, or 120 days have passed since they notified the company of the violation.

(4) Whistle-blowers are encourage to report the information through the normal internal corporate governance system of the company by an indication that doing so may increase the amount of the award.

(5) Sarbanes-Oxley includes provisions to discourage retaliation against whistle-blowers, which were strengthened by Dodd-Frank.

The Jumpstart Our Business Startups (JOBS) Act exempted "emerging growth companies" for a maximum of five years from the date of their initial public offering from certain requirements that apply to larger public companies, including

(1) Certain disclosure requirements.

(2) The requirement for an integrated audit of internal control.

(3) The requirements regarding shareholder votes on executive compensation.

j. **The Internal Revenue Service (IRS).** The IRS acts as an external governance device by requiring certain accounting information on the corporation's income tax return. The IRS also audits corporations' tax returns, and enforces penalties for filing false tax returns.

k. **Corporate takeovers.** Takeovers also act as a corporate governance device. If management is performing poorly, the corporation may be subject to takeover by a firm that believes it can more efficiently utilize the corporation's resources. This provides an incentive for management to operate the corporation consistent with the interests of the shareholders. Corporations sometime engage in strategies to prevent a takeover, such as **a poison pill** defense. A poison pill defense triggers an option for the shareholders to purchase additional shares at a discount if someone attempts to acquire a controlling interest in the corporation. Such defenses are controversial because they inhibit an active market for corporate control.

> ## NOW REVIEW MULTIPLE-CHOICE QUESTIONS 1 THROUGH 28

B. Internal Controls

There are a number of internal control frameworks used as benchmarks. The most commonly used framework in the US is *Internal Control—Integrated Framework* developed by COSO. According to COSO internal control is

A process, effected by the entity's board of directors, management, and other personnel designed to provide reasonable assurance regarding the achievement of objectives relating to operations, reporting, and compliance.

As can be seen from the definition, internal control has three objectives: (1) reliability of reporting, (2) efficiency and effectiveness of operations, and (3) compliance with applicable laws and regulations. When internal control is determined to be effective, senior management and the board of directors have the following reasonable assurance with respect to the objectives:

(1) Operations objectives—the organization achieves effective and efficient operations when significant external events can be predicted and their potential effects mitigated, or the organization understands the extent to which operations can be managed when the effects of significant events cannot be mitigated. The operations category of objectives also includes safeguarding of assets.

(2) Reporting objectives—the organization prepares internal and external financial and nonfinancial reports in conformity with applicable laws, rules, regulations, standards, and internal policies.

(3) Compliance objectives—the organization complies with applicable laws, rules and regulations.

Under the COSO framework internal control can be viewed as including five components: (1) the control environment, (2) risk assessment, (3) control activities, (4) information and communication, and (5) monitoring activities. Seventeen principles are incorporated within the five components.

1. The Control Environment

The control environment is the set of standards, processes, and structures that provide the basis for carrying out internal control across the organization. It may be viewed as the foundation for the other components of internal control. The control environment comprises the integrity and ethical values of the organization; the parameters enabling the board of directors to carry out its oversight responsibilities; the organizational structure and assignment of authority and responsibility; the process for attracting, developing, and retaining competent individuals; and the rigor around performance measures, incentives, and rewards to drive accountability for performance.

a. The principles relating to the control environment component include:

(1) The organization demonstrates a commitment to integrity and ethical values.

(2) The board of directors demonstrates independence from management and exercises oversight of the development and performance of internal control.

(3) Management establishes, with board oversight, structures, reporting lines, and appropriate authorities and responsibilities in the pursuit of objectives.

(4) The organization demonstrates a commitment to attract, develop and retain competent individuals in alignment with objectives.

(5) The organization holds individuals accountable for their internal control responsibilities in the pursuit of objectives.

b. **Demonstrate commitment to integrity and ethical values**. The effectiveness of internal control depends on the communication and enforcement of integrity and ethical values. Management should establish a tone at the top of the organization through directives, actions, and behavior that encourages appropriate behavior. Top management should communicate these values through standards (codes) of conduct, official policies, directives, and by example. Individuals should be evaluated for adherence to standards, and deviations should be addressed in a timely manner.

c. **Exercise oversight responsibility.** It is essential that the board of directors establishes appropriate oversight of management and the system of internal control. To do so, the board must collectively possess appropriate expertise and have sufficient members that are independent from management.

d. **Establish structure, authority, and responsibility.** Management should establish with board oversight, structures, reporting lines, and appropriate authorities and responsibilities. Organizations are structured along various dimensions, such as by product or service, legal entity, or geographic market. Relationships with outsourced service providers may also affect the organization's structure. Organizations delegate authority and responsibility to enable management and other personnel to make decisions according to management's directives. Delegating authority increases risks. Therefore, management should establish appropriate limitations of authority.

e. **Demonstrate commitment to competence.** Management adopts policies and practices that reflect expectations of stakeholders, and provide the foundation for defining competence needed within an organization, and the basis for executing and evaluating performance. Commitment to competence is supported by human resource management processes for attracting, developing, and retaining the right fit of management, other personnel, and outsourced service providers. Succession planning for key managers as well as contingency plans for assignment of internal control responsibilities are also important aspects of this area.

f. **Enforce accountability.** The board of directors should hold the chief executive officer responsible for establishing the requisite system of internal control to support the achievement of organizational objectives. Accountability for internal control should be established at all levels of the organization and it should be supported by appropriate performance measures, incentives, and rewards. The board and senior management must be cognizant of the effects that undue pressure can have on behavior. Undue pressure may cause individuals to circumvent processes or engage in fraudulent activities.

2. **Risk Assessment**

Risk is defined as the possibility that an event will occur and adversely affect the achievement of objectives in the areas of operations, reporting, or compliance. Effective internal control requires that management have a system of risk assessment. Risk assessment is management's process for identifying, analyzing, and responding to risks. The principles related to risk assessment include:

a. The organization specifies objectives with sufficient clarity to enable the identification and assessment of risks relating to objectives.

b. The organization identifies risks to the achievement of its objectives across the entity and analyzes risks as a basis for determining how the risks should be managed.

c. The organization considers the potential for fraud in assessing risks to the achievement of objectives.

d. The organization identifies and assesses changes that could significantly impact the system of internal control.

As a part of this process, management must determine how much risk may be prudently accepted, strive to maintain risk within these levels, and understand how much tolerance it has for exceeding the targeted risk levels. A precondition to risk assessment is establishment of objectives that are clear and linked through the organization.

After risks have been identified at both the entity and transaction-level, a risk analysis is performed, which involves assessing the likelihood of the risk occurring and estimating its impact. Based on this analysis, management determines which risks require a response. Risk responses may involve acceptance, avoidance, reduction or sharing. The risk assessment and response processes are described more fully in the section on enterprise risk management.

3. **Control Activities**

Control activities are policies and procedures that help ensure that management directives are carried out. Principles related to the control activities component include:

a. The organization selects and develops control activities that contribute to the mitigation of risks to the achievement of objectives to acceptable levels.

b. The organization selects and develops general control activities over technology to support the achievement of objectives.

c. The organization deploys control activities through policies that establish what is expected and in procedures that put policies into action.

Management develops various types of control activities to mitigate risks, including:

a.   Authorizations and approvals—manual or computerized review of the validity of transactions.
b.   Verifications—comparison of two or more items with each other or with a policy to determine validity or conformance with a policy.
c.   Physical controls—restriction of access to physical assets and performing periodic inventories.
d.   Controls over standing data—controls over data that is used in transaction processing, such as controls over the processes used to populate, update and maintain the accuracy, completeness, and validity of data in a price master file used to record sales transactions.
e.   Reconciliations—comparisons of two or more data elements and if differences are identified taking action to resolve the differences.
f.   Supervisory controls—high level controls to help ensure that other control activities are operating, e.g., a review of reconciliation by the supervisor of the individual that performed the reconciliation.

In designing control activities, management should consider whether duties are appropriately segregated among different people to reduce the risk of error or fraud. Segregation of duties generally entails dividing the responsibility for recording, authorizing, and approving transactions, and handling the related asset. Segregation of duties helps assure that an individual cannot both perpetrate an error or fraud and also conceal it.

Control activities may be also be categorized as general controls over technology and transactions (application) controls.

(1)   General controls over technology—control activities that support the reliability of two or more types of transactions or processes. General controls over technology encompass control activities (1) over technology infrastructure which are designed to ensure the completeness, accuracy, and availability of technology processing, (2) over access to technology to restrict access to authorized users, and (3) over the acquisition, development, and maintenance of technology and its infrastructure.

(2)   Transaction (application) controls—control activities designed to ensure that particular transactions (e.g., payroll) are accurate, complete, and valid (authorized). Transaction controls are further segregated into:

(a)   Input controls—Controls to ensure that data are input accurately and completely, and transactions are (valid) authorized.
(b)   Processing controls—Controls to ensure that data is processed accurately.
(c)   Output controls—Controls over the distribution of and accuracy of output.

4. **Information and Communication**

The information and communication component of internal control supports all of the other components. The principles related to the information and communication component include:

a.   The organization obtains or generates and uses relevant, quality information to support the functioning of internal control.
b.   The organization internally communicates information, including objectives and responsibilities for internal control, necessary to support the functioning of internal control.
c.   The organization communicates with external parties regarding matters affecting the functioning of internal control.

Internal communication is essential to the effective functioning of internal control. Management must design an effective information system, considering the requirements of the users, that reliably captures internal and external sources of data, processes the data into information, and maintains quality throughout processing. Maintaining the quality of information is essential. The quality of information depends on whether it is accessible, correct, current, protected, retained, sufficient, timely, valid, and verifiable. To be effective, the information must be communicated through appropriate methods to management, other personnel, and the board of directors. For example, an anonymous whistle-blower hotline should be established to ensure that employees and other parties can report inappropriate activity.

The organization must also periodically communicate to external parties. Therefore, processes and channels must be established to facilitate communication to parties such as regulators, owners, financial analysts, and customers. The processes and channels should also provide for appropriate communication from external parties such as customers, suppliers, auditors, and regulators to the management and the board of directors.

5. Monitoring

Monitoring activities assess whether each of the five components are present and functioning. Monitoring may be achieved by performing ongoing activities or by separate evaluations. Ongoing monitoring activities include regularly performed supervisory and management activities, such as continuous monitoring of customer complaints, or reviewing the reasonableness of management reports. Continuous monitoring is often performed with the use of technology, such as embedded software. Separate evaluations are monitoring activities that are performed on a nonroutine basis, such as periodic audits by the internal auditors. The two principles related to the monitoring component include:

a. The organization selects, develops, and performs ongoing and/or separate evaluations to ascertain whether the components of internal control are present and functioning.

b. The organization evaluates and communicates internal control deficiencies in a timely manner to those parties responsible for taking corrective action, including senior management and the board of directors, as appropriate.

In 2009 COSO issued guidance on monitoring internal control systems that elaborates on the monitoring component of internal control. Individuals that monitor controls within an organization are referred to as evaluators.

a. Characteristics of evaluators—Evaluators should be competent and objective in the particular circumstances. Competence refers to the evaluator's knowledge of internal control and related processes, including how controls should operate and what constitutes a deficiency. The evaluator's objectivity refers to whether that person can evaluate the controls without concern about possible consequences of discovering deficiencies.

b. Internal control systems fail because

(1) They are not designed or implemented properly;

(2) They are properly designed and implemented but environment changes have occurred making the controls ineffective; or

(3) They are properly designed and implemented but the way they operate has changed making the controls ineffective.

c. A baseline understanding of an internal control system's effectiveness in an area serves as the starting point for monitoring. This baseline understanding allows organizations to design ongoing and separate monitoring procedures. Monitoring may be considered as consisting of the following sequence of activities (monitoring-for-change control continuum):

(1) Control baseline—Establishing a starting point that includes a supported understanding of the existing internal control system.

(2) Change identification—Identifying through monitoring changes in internal control that are necessary because changes in the operating environment have taken place, such as changes in regulations or changes in the economic environment.

(3) Change management—Evaluating the design and implementation of the changes, and establishing a new baseline. An effective change management process enables management to control (1) change requests, (2) change analyses, (3) change decisions, and (4) change planning, implementation, and tracking. When a change occurs in an organization, it often has an effect on other areas of the organization. It is important that the change management process considers these effects and incorporates them into the analysis, planning, and implementation phases of the change. Also, a system of documentation should be established to ensure that changes are authorized, communicated, and documented. Finally, changes should be thoroughly tested before being implemented. If employees are not adequately trained on new processes, control may break down.

(4) Control revalidation/update—Periodically revalidating control operation when no known changes have occurred.

d. It is important to understand that this entire sequence does not reside solely in the monitoring component of internal control. For example, changes in the operating environment might be identified through risk assessment.

e. The effectiveness and efficiency of monitoring can be enhanced by linking it to the results of the risk assessment component of internal control. This allows evaluators to focus monitoring attention on controls that address meaningful risks (referred to as key controls). Key controls often have the following characteristics:

    (1) Their failure could materially affect the area's objectives, and other controls would not be expected to detect the failure on a timely basis; and

    (2) Their operation might prevent or detect other control failures before they had an opportunity to become material to the organization's objectives.

  f. For key controls the evaluator should determine what constitutes sufficient suitable evidence that the control is operating as designed. This evidence is of two types:

    (1) Direct evidence—Evidence obtained from observing the control and reperforming it.

    (2) Indirect evidence—Evidence that identifies anomalies that may signal control change or failure (e.g., evidence derived from operating statistics, key risk indicators (forward-looking metrics that serve to identify problems), performance indicators (metrics that reflect critical success factors), and comparative industry data).

  g. Ongoing monitoring is generally better than separate monitoring because ongoing monitoring operates continuously and can offer the first opportunity to identify and correct control deficiencies.

  h. Technology has enhanced an organization's ability to monitor internal controls and risk. Internal control systems can have embedded modules that look for unusual or suspicious transactions or relationships. This makes it more efficient and effective for management to perform ongoing monitoring.

  i. Separate evaluations may be performed by internal auditors, objective evaluators, cross-functional evaluators, or through benchmarking/peer against comparable organizations. Self-assessment by individuals within a department may also be used if suitably supervised. In all cases, consideration should be given to the competence and objectivity of the individuals performing the evaluations.

  j. Monitoring includes reporting deficiencies to appropriate personnel both within and outside of the organization so that corrective action may be taken. Management should track whether corrective action is taken on timely basis.

6. Classifications of Internal Controls

Various classifications of internal controls have been developed to help in the evaluation process, including

  a. Preventive, detective, and corrective controls

    (1) **Preventive controls** serve to prevent misstatements from occurring in the first place.

    (2) **Detective controls** serve to detect misstatements after they have occurred.

    (3) **Corrective controls** serve to correct misstatements after they have been detected.

  b. Feedback and feed-forward controls

    (1) **Feedback controls** evaluate the results of a process and adjust the process if the results indicate the process is not operating effectively.

    (2) **Feed-forward controls** project results into the future and make changes to alter the projected results.

7. Limitations of Internal Control

As we indicated previously, internal control provides reasonable, but not absolute, assurance that specific entity objectives will be achieved. Even the best internal control may break down because

  a. Human judgment in decision making can be faulty.

  b. Breakdowns can occur because of human failures such as simple errors or mistakes.

  c. Controls, whether manual or automated, can be circumvented by collusion.

  d. Management has the ability to override internal control.

  e. Cost constraints (the cost of internal control should not exceed the benefits expected to be derived).

  f. Custom, culture, and the corporate governance system may inhibit fraud, but they are not absolute deterrents.

8. Controls over Business Processes

Organizations use various approaches to executing and controlling financial transactions. Some are still very manual in nature. However, more and more transactions are being processed completely by the technology through private links within and between companies, or over the Internet. All transactions have risks that must be controlled.

A fundamental control over transactions is segregation of duties. For each transaction cycle, the functions of authorization, approval (for certain types of transactions), execution (custody of assets), and recordkeeping should be segregated. In a manual accounting system, segregation of duties is achieved by having different individuals physically performing the functions. In a technology-based system, the computer performs many of these processes and segregation of duties is achieved by controlling access to terminals and through the use of passwords. Of course in a technology-based system control is achieved over processing and data by appropriate information technology controls as discussed in Module 41.

The tables below presents two major processes (transaction cycles) including the risks and examples of controls that might be used to mitigate those risks.

SALES AND COLLECTIONS BUSINESS PROCESS

Risk	Nature of the Process	Example Controls
Inaccurate or incomplete sales data and lack of security over sales order information	Sales orders inputted manually	Password control over terminals to assure that sales are authorized by sales department; accuracy and completeness controls over inputs*; physical controls over terminals and files
	Sales over the Internet	Encryption of transmitted data; accuracy and completeness controls over inputs; password control over access to information to maintain a segregation of duties; data controls to ensure that sales prices are accurately inputted and updated
Sales to customers that are not creditworthy	Outsource credit to credit card company	Protect credit card information with password control and physical security over terminals and files
	Organization has credit department that extends credit	Credit department should be independent of sales function and approve credit limits; effective practices for collecting credit information to make evaluations to grant credit
Maintaining too much or too little inventory	Inventory control and management	Use of a perpetual inventory system; use of techniques such as just-in-time, economic order quantity, and reorder points as methods of managing inventory; heavy reliance on technology to determine when and how much to order
Inaccurate filling of orders	Manual filling of orders	Have an individual not involved in filling the order check it for accuracy
	Technology used to fill orders	Input controls to assure information is correct in computer fulfillment process; use technology such as bar code scanners to pack goods
Inaccurate billing of customers	Manual billing process	Individual doing billing should match sales order to shipping document to assure the accuracy of billing invoice; use of prenumbered documents and accounting for all documents; invoice checked for clerical accuracy by an individual not involved in preparation; billing department is independent of individuals maintaining receivables records; account for numerical sequence of documents
	Technology used for billing	Accuracy and completeness input controls to assure billing information is accurate and based on accurate shipping information input by shipping personnel; accuracy and completeness controls to assure that pricing information is accurate and based on authorization from the sales department; password control over terminals to insure segregation of duties
Failure to bill for shipment	Manual billing process	Accounting for all prenumbered shipping documents
	Technology used for billing	Accuracy and completeness input controls to assure that all shipping information is entered to the system for billing
Errors or fraud in processing and depositing cash receipts	Cash receipts received through the mail	Segregation of cash handling from accounts receivable records or use of a lockbox at a financial institution
	Electronic funds transfer system	Control over access to the system through the use of a password system; use of accuracy and completeness controls over input of cash receipt information
Accounts may be written off without authorization	Manual	Individual independent of sales and cash receipts should be authorized to write off accounts; use of prenumbered authorization forms; accounting for all forms
	Technology-based system	Access to terminal for authorization by independent individual should be restricted by password system

* Accuracy and completeness controls include controls such as validity checks, missing data checks, logic checks, limit tests, etc.

ACQUISITIONS AND PAYMENTS PROCESS

Risk	Nature of the Process	Example Controls
Ordering unneeded goods	Manual or technology-based system	Use of a perpetual inventory system; ordering based on inventory management techniques, such as just-in-time, economic order quantity, and reorder points
Purchasing goods from unauthorized vendors	Manual or technology-based system	Establish preferred vendor relationships; establish criteria for authorized vendors
		Creation of purchase orders; accuracy and completeness controls over inputting purchasing information into the computer; password control over terminals
Receiving goods that were not ordered	Manual system	Matching of purchase order to goods received
	Technology-based system	Computer comparison of purchase information input by the purchasing department with information on goods received inputted by the receiving department
Receiving goods that are damaged or inferior	Manual or technology-based system	Inspect goods received
Payment for goods not received	Manual system	Matching of purchase orders with receiving reports; accounting for all prenumbered documents; individual authorized to sign checks is independent of those maintaining records and receiving goods; check signer cancels supporting documentation
	Computer generation of payments based on purchase and receiving information	Accuracy and completeness input controls for purchase and receiving information; segregation of those maintaining records and processing payments from those authorized to make payments; password control to ensure segregation of duties
Payment for purchase twice	Manual system	Cancel supporting documents for all payments
	Technology-based system	Control access to receiving and purchasing information by use of passwords and appropriate segregation of duties
Unauthorized cash payments	Manual system	Segregation of duties of accounting and authorized check signers; reconciliation of bank account by individual independent of individuals preparing and signing checks
	Technology-based system	Passwords and controls over terminals prevent issuance of unauthorized payments; reconciliation of bank account by computer or independent individual
Loss or theft of assets	Manual or technology-based system	Periodic reconciliations of physical assets to accounting records by individuals independent of individuals having custody of the assets and individuals maintaining the accounting records for the assets; examples include reconciliations of bank accounts, taking physical inventories, and inventories of supplies and equipment

a. **Additional controls over inventories**

    (1) Perpetual inventory records for large dollar items

    (2) Prenumbered receiving reports prepared when inventory received; receiving reports accounted for

    (3) Adequate standard cost system to cost inventory items

    (4) Physical controls against theft

    (5) Written inventory requisitions used

    (6) Proper authorization of purchases and use of prenumbered purchase orders

b. **Controls over payrolls**

    (1) Segregate: Timekeeping

                          Payroll preparation

                          Personnel

                          Paycheck distribution

      (2) Time clocks used where possible

      (3) Job time tickets reconciled to time clock cards

      (4) Time clock cards approved by supervisors (overtime and regular hours)

      (5) Treasurer signs paychecks

      (6) Unclaimed paychecks controlled by someone otherwise independent of the payroll function (locked up and eventually destroyed if not claimed). In cases in which employees are paid cash (as opposed to checks) unclaimed pay should be deposited into a special bank account.

      (7) Personnel department promptly sends termination notices to the payroll department.

  c. **Controls over fixed assets**

      (1) Major asset acquisitions are properly approved by the firm's board of directors and properly controlled through capital budgeting techniques.

      (2) Detailed records are available for property assets and accumulated depreciation.

      (3) Written policies exist for capitalization vs. expensing decisions.

      (4) Depreciation properly calculated.

      (5) Retirements approved by an appropriate level of management.

      (6) Physical control over assets to prevent theft.

      (7) Periodic physical inspection of plant and equipment by individuals who are otherwise independent of property, plant, and equipment (e.g., internal auditors).

9. **Reporting on Internal Control**

    Section 404 of the Sarbanes-Oxley Act requires management to establish and maintain effective internal control over financial reporting and document the system. In addition, it requires management to provide a report on the effectiveness of the system. Management's report should include the following:

  a. A statement of management's responsibility for establishing and maintaining adequate internal control over financial reporting for the corporation.

  b. A statement identifying the framework used by management to conduct the required assessment of the effectiveness of the corporation's internal control over financial reporting (e.g., COSO).

  c. An assessment of the effectiveness of the corporation's internal control over financial reporting as of the end of the company's most recent fiscal year, including an explicit statement as to whether the internal control over financial reporting is effective. If there are any material weaknesses, they should be disclosed.

  d. If applicable, a statement that the corporation's registered public accounting firm that audited the financial statements included in the annual report has issued an attestation report on management's assessment of the company's internal control over financial reporting. Larger public corporations (accelerated filers) are required to have their external auditors attest to, and report on, the effectiveness of internal control over financial reporting. The Dodd-Frank Act permanently exempted small corporations from this requirement.

NOW REVIEW MULTIPLE-CHOICE QUESTIONS 29 THROUGH 43

C. **Enterprise Risk Management**

    In addition to an internal control framework, COSO has also developed a framework for enterprise risk management (ERM). The framework defines ERM as follows:

> *Enterprise risk management is a process, effected by an entity's board of directors, management and other personnel, applied in a strategy setting and across the enterprise, designed to identify potential events that may affect the entity, and manage risk to be within its risk appetite, to provide reasonable assurance regarding the achievement of entity objectives.*

    ERM helps align the risk appetite of the organization with its strategy, enhances risk response decisions, reduces operational surprises and losses, identifies and manages cross-enterprise risks, provides integrated responses to multiple risks, helps the organization seize opportunities, and improves the deployment of capital.

    A key aspect of ERM is the identification and management of events that have a negative impact, positive impact, or both. Events with negative impact represent risks. Events with positive impact may offset negative impacts or represent opportunities. The risk management process involves (1) identifying risks, assessing risks, prioritizing risks, determining risk responses, and monitoring risk responses.

    Everyone in the organization has some responsibility for ERM. The best run organizations have a culture of risk management that is understood by every employee. Many organizations assign a risk officer, financial officer, and/

or internal auditor with key support responsibilities. The internal control of the organization is an integral part of the organization's ERM system.

1. Components of ERM

According to COSO, ERM consists of eight interrelated components, including (1) internal environment, (2) objective setting, (3) event identification, (4) risk assessment, (5) risk response, (6) control activities, (7) information and communication, and (8) monitoring.

a.   Internal environment

The internal environment is the basis for all other components of ERM, providing discipline and structure. It encompasses the tone of the organization, and sets the basis for how risk is viewed and addressed by an organization's people, including risk management philosophy and risk appetite, and integrity and ethical values.

The board of directors is a critical part of the internal environment. The board provides oversight over management's implementation of ERM, helping to make sure that it is effective.

Integrity and ethical values help insure that management and other individuals within the organization are not inclined to engage in unethical or illegal activities. Management sets an ethical tone by action and example, and communicates the tone through codes of conduct and established policies. Management also should avoid the use of incentives and temptations to engage in unethical behavior, unless effective controls are established to prevent such behavior.

Other factors that contribute to an effective internal environment include competent, well-trained employees, an appropriate organizational structure, properly assigned authority and responsibility, and effective human resource policies and procedures.

An important aspect of the organization's internal environment is its risk appetite. **Risk appetite** is the amount of risk an organization is willing to accept to achieve its goals. It reflects the organization's culture and operating style and is directly related to the organization's strategy. Some organizations consider risk appetite qualitatively (e.g., low, moderate, high) while others consider risk quantitatively (e.g. in percentages). **Risk tolerance** relates to the organization's objectives. It is the acceptable variation with respect to a particular objective.

EXAMPLE

Assume a company has an objective of 97% customer satisfaction rating. However, the company may tolerate as low as a 94% customer satisfaction rating. The difference between 97% and 94% represents the company's risk tolerance with respect to the customer satisfaction rating.

---

b.   Objective setting

Objectives must exist before management can identify potential events affecting their achievement. Enterprise risk management ensures that management has in place a process to set objectives and that the chosen objectives support and align with the organization's mission and are consistent with its risk appetite. The organization's mission sets forth in broad terms what the organization aspires to achieve. Strategic objectives are high-level goals aligned with the organization's mission. These high-level objectives are linked and integrated with the specific objectives established for various activities. By setting objectives the organization can identify critical risk factors, which are the key things that must go right for the objectives to be met.

Objectives may be divided into three categories: (a) operations objectives, which relate to the effectiveness and efficiency of operations, (b) reporting objectives, which relate to reliable reporting of internal and external, financial and nonfinancial information, and (c) compliance objectives which relate to adherence to laws and regulations.

c.   Event identification

Potential internal and external events affecting achievement of an organization's objectives must be identified, distinguishing between risks and opportunities. An event is an incident that occurs or might occur that affects implementation of strategy or achievement of objectives. Events may be negative (risks), positive (opportunities) or both. Risks require a response while opportunities should be channeled back to management's strategy or objective-setting processes. Some events may be external in nature, such as those resulting from economic, natural environment, political, social, or technological factors. Other events result from internal factors such as the organization's infrastructure, personnel, processes, or technology.

Event identification techniques include

(1) Event inventories. Developing a detailed listing of potential events.
(2) Internal analysis. This may be done at regular staff meetings. It may involve using information from other stakeholders, such as customers, suppliers, etc.
(3) Escalation or threshold triggers. Management predetermines limits that cause an event to be further assessed.

EXAMPLE

A company may identify a potential pricing issue when competitor sales prices change by a predetermined percentage.

---

(4) Facilitated workshops or interviews. This technique involves soliciting information about events from management and staff. For example, a facilitator may lead a discussion of events that might affect achieving an organization's objectives.
(5) Process flow analysis. Involves breaking processes down into inputs, tasks, responsibilities, and outputs to identify events that might adversely affect the process.
(6) Leading event indicators. This technique involves monitoring data correlated to events, to identify when the event is likely to occur.
(7) Loss event data methodologies. By developing repositories of data on past loss events, management can identify event trends and the root causes of events. Management can also perform **black swan analysis** which involves evaluating the occurrence of events that had negative effects and were unanticipated or viewed as highly unlikely.

d. **Risk assessment**

Risks are analyzed, considering likelihood and impact, as a basis for determining how they should be managed. Management should assess both inherent risk and residual risk for an event. Inherent risk is the risk to the organization if management does nothing to alter its likelihood or impact. Residual risk is the risk of the event after considering management's response. Risks are assessed in terms of their likelihood of occurring and their impact (e.g., financial effect). Management often uses qualitative techniques to assess risk when risks do not lend themselves to quantification or when sufficient reliable data is not available to use a quantitative model. Probabilistic or nonprobabilistic models may be used to quantify risk. Probabilistic models associate a range of events and the resulting impact with the likelihood of those events based on certain assumptions. Examples of probabilistic models include value at risk, cash flow at risk, earnings at risk, and development of credit and operational loss distributions. Nonprobabilistic models use subjective assumptions in estimating the impact of events without quantifying an associated likelihood. Examples of nonprobabilistic models include sensitivity measures, stress tests, and scenario analysis.

e. **Risk response**

In this aspect of ERM, management selects risk responses that are consistent with the risk appetite of the organization including

(1) Avoidance. This response involves exiting the activity that gives rise to the risk.
(2) Reduction. This response involves taking action to reduce risk likelihood or impact, or both. For example, this might involve managing the risk or adding additional controls to processes.
(3) Sharing. This response involves reducing risk likelihood or impact by transferring or sharing a portion of the risk. Techniques for sharing include insurance, hedging, and outsourcing.
(4) Acceptance (retention). No action is taken because the risk is consistent with the risk appetite of the organization.

All risk responses must be assessed in terms of their costs and benefits to select the responses that should be implemented. The position that is best suited to devise and execute risk procedures for a particular department is the manager of the department.

f. **Control activities**

Policies and procedures should be established and implemented to help ensure the risk responses are effectively carried out.

g. **Information and communication**

Relevant information is identified, captured, and communicated to enable people to carry out their responsibilities. Information is needed at all levels of the organization to identify, assess and respond to risks. Communication should effectively convey the importance and relevance of effective ERM, the organization's objectives, the organization's risk appetite and risk tolerances, a common risk language, and the roles and responsibilities of personnel in effecting and supporting the components of ERM.

h. **Monitoring**

The entire ERM process should be monitored to make needed modifications. Monitoring is accomplished by ongoing management activities, and separate evaluations, such as those performed by internal auditors.

2. **Limitations of ERM**

In considering limitations of ERM, three distinct concepts must be recognized:

a. Risk relates to the future which is uncertain,

b. ERM provides information about risks of achieving objectives but it cannot provide even reasonable assurance that objectives will be achieved, and

c. ERM cannot provide absolute assurance with respect to any of the objective categories. Specific limitations include the following:

(1) The effectiveness of ERM is subject to the limitations of the ability of humans to make judgments about risk and impact.

(2) Well-designed ERM can break down.

(3) Collusion among two or more individuals can result in ERM failures.

(4) ERM systems can never be perfect due to cost-benefit constraints.

(5) ERM is subject to management override.

NOW REVIEW MULTIPLE-CHOICE QUESTIONS 44 THROUGH 51

KEY TERMS

Articles of incorporation. The document filed with the secretary of the state to obtain a certificate of incorporation.

Audit committee. The committee of the board of directors that oversees the accounting and financial reporting processes of the company and oversees the audits of the financial statements of the company. The Sarbanes-Oxley Act requires all members to be independent.

Black swan analysis. Evaluating the occurrence of events that had negative effects and were unanticipated or viewed is highly unlikely.

Board of directors. The body charged with running the corporation on behalf of the shareholders.

Business judgment rule. A case law–derived concept that provides that a corporate director may not be held liable for errors in judgment providing the director acted with good faith, loyalty, and due care.

Compensation committee. The committee of the board of directors that reviews and approves executive compensation, makes recommendations to the board regarding incentive-based compensation, and attempts to align incentives with shareholder objectives and risk appetite. The Dodd-Frank Act requires all members to be independent and provides that in setting compensation, the members may request the company to engage compensation advisors that are independent of management.

Corporate bylaws. Set forth how the directors and/or officers are selected, how meetings are conducted, the types and duties of officers, and the required meetings.

Duty of loyalty. A concept that provides that directors and officers must put the interest of the corporation before their personal interest. Accordingly, if a director is approached with a business opportunity that would be of interest to and benefit the corporation, he or she must first offer the opportunity to the corporation before pursuing it on his or her own behalf.

Enterprise risk management. A process designed to identify potential events that may affect the organization, and manage risk to be within its risk appetite, to provide reasonable assurance regarding the achievement of organizational objectives.

Evaluator. An individual that monitors internal control within an organization.

Executive perquisites. Executive benefits other than compensation, such as retirement, use of corporate assets, golden parachutes, and corporate loans.

Inherent risk. The risk to the organization if management does nothing to alter its likelihood or impact.

Residual risk. The risk of the event after considering management's response.

Risk appetite. The amount of risk an organization is will to accept to achieve its objectives.

Risk assessment. Analyzing the potential (likelihood and impact) effects of a risk.

Risk tolerance. The acceptable variation with respect to achieving a particular objective.

Multiple-Choice Questions (1–51)

A. Corporate Governance

1. Which of the following is **not** generally a power of the board of directors of a corporation?

a. Selecting officers.
b. Declaring dividends.
c. Determining management compensation.
d. Amending the Articles of Incorporation.

2. Which of the following is **not** true concerning corporations?

a. Directors owe a fiduciary duty to the corporation.
b. All shareholders owe a fiduciary duty to the corporation.
c. Officers owe a fiduciary duty to the corporation.
d. Directors who act in good faith may use the business judgment rule as a defense.

3. Which of the following is **not** a right of the shareholder of a corporation?

a. Right to inspect the books and records.
b. Right to share in dividends if declared.
c. Right to determine the mission of the corporation.
d. Right to sue on behalf of the corporation if the officers and directors fail to uphold corporate rights.

4. Which of the following actions normally requires shareholder approval?

a. Appointing the chief executive officer.
b. Issuing a dividend.
c. The corporate strategic plan.
d. Changing the nature of the corporation.

5. To which of the following rights is a stockholder of a public corporation entitled?

a. The right to have annual dividends declared and paid.
b. The right to vote for the election of officers.
c. The right to a reasonable inspection of corporate records.
d. The right to have the corporation issue a new class of stock.

6. Which of the following is correct with respect to the rights of stockholders in a corporation?

a. Stockholders have no right to manage their corporation unless they are also directors or officers.
b. Stockholders have a right to receive dividends.
c. Stockholders have no right to inspect the books and records of their corporation.
d. Stockholders have a right to get a list of their corporation's customers to use for a business mailing list.

7. A corporate stockholder is entitled to which of the following rights?

a. Elect officers.
b. Receive annual dividends.
c. Approve dissolution.
d. Prevent corporate borrowing.

8. Which of the following **best** identifies the reason that effective corporate governance is important?

a. The separation of ownership from management.
b. The goal of profit maximization.
c. Excess management compensation.
d. Lack of oversight by boards of directors.

9. The articles of incorporation and bylaws of a corporation serve as a basis for the governance structure of a corporation. Which of the following items are normally included in the bylaws of the corporation as opposed to the articles of incorporation?

a. Purpose of the corporation.
b. Number of authorized shares of stock.
c. Procedure for electing directors.
d. Powers of the corporation.

10. Which of the following forms of compensation would **most** likely align management's behavior with the interests of the shareholders?

a. A fixed salary.
b. A salary plus a bonus based on current period net income.
c. A salary plus stock options that cannot be exercised for 10 years.
d. A salary plus stock.

11. Which of the following forms of compensation would encourage management to take on excessive risk?

a. A fixed salary.
b. A salary and bonuses based on current period net income.
c. A salary plus stock options that cannot be exercised for 10 years.
d. A salary plus restricted stock.

12. Which of the following is **not** a duty that is typically reserved for the board of directors of a corporation?

a. Selection and removal of the chief executive officer.
b. Determining executive compensation.
c. Amending the articles of incorporation.
d. Decisions regarding declaration of dividends.

13. Which of the following is a legal rule that prevents directors from being held liable for making bad decisions if they act with good faith, loyalty, and due care?

    a. The good faith rule.
    b. The business judgment rule.
    c. The due care rule.
    d. The director liability rule.

14. Which of the following is **not** a requirement of the New York Stock Exchange regarding corporate governance of companies listed on the exchange?

    a. Have a majority of independent directors of the corporate board.
    b. Adopt and make publicly available a code of conduct.
    c. Prohibit the chief financial officer from serving on the board of directors.
    d. Have an independent audit committee.

15. Which of the following does **not** act as an external corporate governance mechanism?

    a. External auditors.
    b. The SEC.
    c. Credit analysts.
    d. Independent boards of directors.

16. The Sarbanes-Oxley Act provides that at least one member of the audit committee should be

    a. Independent.
    b. The chief financial officer of the company.
    c. A financial expert.
    d. A CPA.

17. Which of the following is **not** a statutory requirement regarding the committees of the board of directors of publicly held corporations registered with the SEC?

    a. All members of the compensation committee must be independent.
    b. At least one member of the compensation committee must be a "compensation expert."
    c. All members of the audit committee must be independent.
    d. At least one member of the audit committee must be a "financial expert."

18. Which of the following is necessary to be an audit committee financial expert according to the criteria specified in the Sarbanes-Oxley Act of 2002?

    a. An understanding of income tax law.
    b. An understanding of generally accepted accounting principles and financial statements.
    c. An understanding of corporate law.
    d. An understanding of corporate governance rules and procedures.

19. Which of the following is **not** a requirement of the Wall Street Reform and Consumer Protection (Dodd-Frank) Act for publicly held corporations registered with the SEC?

    a. If it is decided that the CEO should also be appointed chairman of the board, the corporation must disclose why this decision was made.
    b. The members of the compensation committee of the board must be independent.
    c. Shareholders must be allowed a nonbinding vote on officer compensation at least every three years.
    d. All members of the audit committee of the board must be financial experts.

20. Which of the following is most effective as an external monitoring device for a publicly held corporation than the others?

    a. Internal auditors.
    b. External auditors.
    c. The SEC.
    d. Attorneys.

21. An important corporate governance mechanism is the internal audit function. For good corporate governance, the chief internal audit executive should have direct communication to the audit committee and report to

    a. The chief financial officer.
    b. The chief executive officer.
    c. The controller.
    d. The external auditors.

22. In setting priorities for internal audit activities, the chief audit executive should

    a. Use a risk-based approach.
    b. Use management's priorities.
    c. Use an approach that cycles audit areas each year.
    d. Use a random approach to more likely detect fraud.

23. The Institute of Internal Auditors' *International Standards for the Professional Practice of Internal Auditing* cover what two major types of internal auditing services?

    a. Assurance and consulting.
    b. Financial and operational.
    c. Compliance and taxation.
    d. Audit and review.

24. According to the *International Standards for the Professional Practice of Internal Auditing*

    a. All internal audit seniors must be Certified Internal Auditors.
    b. The internal auditors must establish and maintain a system to monitor the disposition of audit results.
    c. Internal auditors must be assigned to assist the external auditors.
    d. Internal auditors must not have a financial interest in the company.

25. Which of the following is **not** a section of the Institute of Internal Auditors' *International Standards for the Professional Practice of Internal Auditing*?

    a. Performance Standards.
    b. Independence Standards.
    c. Implementation Standards.
    d. Attribute Standards.

26. Securities analysts act as one form of monitoring device from a corporate governance standpoint. What is a limitation that is often identified when considering the effectiveness of securities analysts in this regard?

    a. Conflicts of interest.
    b. Lack of competence.
    c. Use of only nonfinancial information for analyses.
    d. They are employees of the company.

27. Which of the following divisions of the SEC reviews corporate filings?

    a. The Office of the Chief Accountant.
    b. The Division of Enforcement.
    c. The Division of Corporate Disclosure.
    d. The Division of Corporate Finance.

28. According to the Sarbanes-Oxley Act of 2002, which of the following statements is correct regarding an issuer's audit committee financial expert?

    a. The issuer's current outside CPA firm's audit partner must be the audit committee financial expert.
    b. If an issuer does **not** have an audit committee financial expert, the issuer must disclose the reason why the role is **not** filled.
    c. The issuer must fill the role with an individual who has experience in the issuer's industry.
    d. The audit committee financial expert must be the issuer's audit committee chairperson to enhance internal control.

B. Internal Controls

29. Which of the following components is considered the foundation of the internal controls established by an organization?

    a. Control activities.
    b. Monitoring.
    c. The control environment.
    d. The audit committee.

30. Which of the following COSO categories of objectives includes safeguarding of assets?

    a. Operations.
    b. Reporting.
    c. Compliance.
    d. Financing.

31. Which of the following is **not** a principle related to the component of the control environment?

    a. Demonstrate a commitment to integrity and ethical values.
    b. Demonstrate a commitment to attract, develop and retain competent individuals.
    c. Identify and assess changes that could significantly impact the system of internal control.
    d. Hold individuals accountable for their internal control responsibilities.

32. Which of the following is **not** true regarding the information and communication component of internal control?

    a. The information system captures both internal and external sources of data.
    b. The information and communication component involves developing channels for communication from external stakeholders.
    c. A whistle-blower hotline is an important aspect of the information and communication component.
    d. An important aspect of the information and communication component is assessment of information about fraud.

33. According to the COSO framework, evaluators that monitor controls within an organization should have which of the following sets of characteristics?

    a. Competence and objectivity.
    b. Respect and judgment.
    c. Judgment and objectivity.
    d. Authority and responsibility.

34. Which of the following is a general control rather than a transaction control activity?

    a. Technology development policies and procedures.
    b. Reconciliations.
    c. Physical controls over assets.
    d. Controls over standing data.

35. According to COSO, the use of ongoing and separate evaluations to establish a new baseline after changes have been made can **best** be accomplished in which of the following stages of the monitoring-for-change continuum?

    a. Control baseline.
    b. Change identification.
    c. Change management.
    d. Control revalidation/update.

36. Which of the following is **not** a type of control under the control activity component of the COSO framework for internal control?

    a. Supervisory controls.
    b. Physical controls.
    c. Monitoring controls.
    d. Verifications.

37. Which of the following is **not** a control environment factor?

    a. Integrity and ethical values.
    b. Board of directors or audit committee.
    c. Human resources policies and procedures.
    d. Control monitoring.

38. Which of the following components of internal control would encompass the routine controls over business processes and transactions?

    a. The control environment.
    b. Information and communication.
    c. Control activities.
    d. Risk assessment.

39. Which of the following is **not** a component in the COSO framework for internal control?

    a. Control environment.
    b. Segregation of duties.
    c. Risk assessment.
    d. Monitoring.

40. Management of Johnson Company is considering implementing technology to improve the monitoring component of internal control. Which of the following **best** describes how technology may be effective at improving monitoring?

    a. Technology can identify conditions and circumstances that indicate that controls have failed or risks are present.
    b. Technology can assure that items are processed accurately.
    c. Technology can provide information more quickly.
    d. Technology can control access to terminals and data.

41. Which of the following is **not** a limitation of internal control?

    a. Human judgment in decision-making may be faulty.
    b. External forces may attack the system.
    c. Management may override internal control.
    d. Controls may be circumvented by collusion.

42. Which of the following is **not** required to be included in management's report on internal control required under Section 404 of the Sarbanes-Oxley Act?

    a. A statement of management's responsibility for establishing and maintaining adequate internal control over financial reporting.
    b. A statement indicating that the board of directors has approved the system of internal control over financial reporting.
    c. A statement indentifying the framework used to assess internal control over financial reporting.
    d. An assessment of the effectiveness of the corporation's internal control over financial reporting.

43. Which of the following would generally be entitled to a reward for whistle-blowing under the Dodd-Frank Act?

    a. An external auditor who discovers a violation while performing an audit of a company's financial statement and internal control under SEC requirements.
    b. A customer of a company who discovers a violation in the course of doing business with the company.
    c. A director of a company who discovers a violation while performing her duties as a director.
    d. An internal auditor of a company who discovers a violation while performing an audit of compliance.

C. Enterprise Risk Management

44. According to COSO, which of the following components of enterprise risk management addresses an entity's integrity and ethical values?

    a. Information and communication.
    b. Internal environment.

    c. Risk assessment.
    d. Control activities.

45. Jarrett Corporation is considering establishing an enterprise risk management system. Which of the following is **not** a benefit of enterprise risk management?

    a. Helps the organization seize opportunities.
    b. Enhances risk response decisions.
    c. Improves the deployment of capital.
    d. Insures that the organization shares all major risks.

46. In the COSO enterprise risk management framework, the term risk tolerance refers to

    a. The level of risk an organization is willing to accept.
    b. The acceptable variation with respect to a particular objective.
    c. The risk of an event after considering management's response.
    d. Events that require no risk response.

47. Management of Warren Company has decided to respond to a particular risk by hedging the risk with futures contracts. This is an example of risk

    a. Avoidance.
    b. Acceptance.
    c. Reduction.
    d. Sharing.

48. Which of the following is **not** a technique for identifying events in an enterprise risk management program?

    a. Process flow analysis.
    b. Facilitated workshops.
    c. Probabilistic models.
    d. Loss event data methodologies.

49. Devon Company is using an enterprise risk management system. Management of the company has set the company's objectives, identified events, and assessed risks. What is the next step in the enterprise risk management process?

    a. Establish control activities to manage the risks.
    b. Monitor the risks.
    c. Determine responses to the risks.
    d. Identify opportunities.

50. Which of the following is **not** an advantage of establishing an enterprise risk management system within an organization?

    a. Reduces operational surprises.
    b. Provides integrated responses to multiple risks.
    c. Eliminates all risks.
    d. Identifies opportunities.

51. Kelly, Inc. is considering establishing an enterprise risk management system. Which of the following is **not** a limitation of such a system?

    a. Business objectives are not usually articulated.
    b. The system may break down.
    c. Collusion among two or more individuals can result in system failure.
    d. Enterprise risk management is subject to management override.

Multiple-Choice Answers and Explanations

Answers

1. d	__ __	12. c	__ __	23. a	__ __	34. a	__ __	45. d	__ __
2. b	__ __	13. b	__ __	24. b	__ __	35. c	__ __	46. b	__ __
3. c	__ __	14. c	__ __	25. b	__ __	36. c	__ __	47. d	__ __
4. d	__ __	15. d	__ __	26. a	__ __	37. d	__ __	48. c	__ __
5. c	__ __	16. c	__ __	27. d	__ __	38. c	__ __	49. c	__ __
6. a	__ __	17. b	__ __	28. b	__ __	39. b	__ __	50. c	__ __
7. c	__ __	18. b	__ __	29. c	__ __	40. a	__ __	51. a	__ __
8. a	__ __	19. d	__ __	30. a	__ __	41. b	__ __		
9. c	__ __	20. b	__ __	31. c	__ __	42. b	__ __		
10. c	__ __	21. b	__ __	32. d	__ __	43. b	__ __	1st: __/51 __%
11. b	__ __	22. a	__ __	33. a	__ __	44. b	__ __	2nd: __/51 __%

Explanations

1. (d) The requirement is to identify the item that is **not** generally a power of the board of directors of a corporation. Answer (d) is correct because generally only the shareholders have the power to amend the Articles of Incorporation. Answers (a), (b), and (c) are all incorrect because they are normally powers of the board of directors.

2. (b) The requirement is to identify the item that is **not** true concerning corporations. Answer (b) is true because shareholders do not owe a fiduciary duty to the corporation. However, majority shareholders owe a fiduciary duty to minority shareholders. Answers (a), (c) and (d) are all incorrect because all of these statements are true about corporations.

3. (c) The requirement is to identify the item that is **not** a right of a shareholder. Answer (c) is correct because the board of directors determines the mission of the corporation. Answers (a), (b), and (d) are incorrect because they are all rights of the shareholder.

4. (d) The requirement is to identify the action that normally requires shareholder approval. Answer (d) is correct because changing the nature of the corporation requires approval by the shareholders. Answers (a), (b), and (c) are incorrect because they are all actions that can be taken by the board of directors without shareholder approval.

5. (c) The requirement is to identify the right of the shareholder. Shareholders have the right to inspect the corporate records if done in good faith for a proper purpose. Answer (a) is incorrect because shareholders do not have a right to dividends. It is the decision of the board of directors whether or not to declare dividends. Answer (b) is incorrect because although at least one class of stock must have voting

rights to elect the board of directors, the officers may be selected by the board of directors. Answer (d) is incorrect because a shareholder cannot force an issuance of a new class of stock.

6. (a) The requirement is to identify the correct statement regarding the rights of stockholders. Stockholders do not have the right to manage their corporation. However, stockholders who are also directors or officers do have the right to manage as part of their rights as directors and officers. Answer (b) is incorrect because stockholders generally have no right to receive dividends unless the board of directors declares such dividends. Answer (c) is incorrect because stockholders are given the right to inspect the books and records of their corporation under certain circumstances. Answer (d) is incorrect because the stockholders may demand a list of shareholders for a proper purpose such as to help wage a proxy fight; however, they may not require the corporation to give them a list of its customers to use for a mailing list.

7. (c) The requirement is to identify the right of a shareholder. Shareholders have the right to vote on the dissolution of the corporation. Stockholders also have the right to elect the directors of the corporation, who in turn elect the officers. Answer (b) is incorrect, as shareholders do not have the right to receive dividends unless they are declared by the board of directors. Answer (d) is incorrect, as shareholders are not necessarily involved in the management of the corporation and cannot prevent corporate borrowing.

8. (a) The requirement is to identify the reason that effective corporate governance is important. Answer (a) is correct because the separation of ownership and management creates an agency problem in that management may not act in the best interest of the shareholders. Answer (b) is incorrect because profit maximization is an appropriate goal of management. Answer (c) is incorrect because while corporate governance is designed to prevent excess management compensation, that is not the only reason it is important. Answer (d) is incorrect because oversight by boards of directors is a part of corporate governance.

9. (c) The requirement is to identify the item that is normally included in the bylaws of the corporation. Answer (c) is correct because the procedure for electing directors is normally included in the bylaws. Answers (a), (b), and (d) are incorrect because they are normally included in the articles of incorporation.

10. (c) The requirement is to identify the form of compensation that would most likely align management's behavior with the interests of the shareholders. Answer (c) is correct because stock options that cannot be exercised for 10 years provide an incentive to manage the firm to maximize long-term stock value. Answer (a) is incorrect because a fixed salary does not provide an incentive to maximize shareholder value. Answers (b) and (d) are incorrect because they provide an incentive to maximize short-term profit of the firm. This may not be consistent with long-term profitability.

11. (b) The requirement is to identify the form of compensation that would encourage management to take on excess risk. Answer (b) is correct because with a bonus based on current period net income, management has an incentive to take on excessive risk to maximize its bonuses. Answer (a) is incorrect because a fixed salary encourages management to take on little risk. Answers (c) and (d) are incorrect because stock options that cannot be exercised for 10 years and restricted stock encourage management to be concerned about the long-term viability of the firm.

12. (c) The requirement is to identify the item that is typically a duty reserved for the board of directors. Answer (c) is correct because this duty is typically reserved for the shareholders. Answers (a), (b), and (d) are incorrect because these are all typically duties of the board of directors.

13. (b) The requirement is to identify the legal rule that prevents directors from being held liable for making bad decisions if they act with good faith, loyalty, and due care. Answer (b) is correct because this is referred to as the business judgment rule. Answers (a), (c), and (d) are incorrect because they are not terms used to describe this legal rule.

14. (c) The requirement is to identify the item that is **not** a requirement of the NYSE regarding corporate governance of listed companies. Answer (c) is correct because the rules do not prohibit the CFO from serving on the board of directors. Answers (a), (b) and (d) are all requirements of the NYSE.

15. (d) The requirement is to identify the organization or group that does **not** act as an external corporate governance mechanism. Answer (d) is correct because directors are internal corporate governance mechanisms regardless of whether or not they are independent. Answers (a), (b), and

(c) are incorrect because they all act as external corporate governance mechanisms.

16. (c) The requirement is to identify the characteristic that must apply to at least one member of the audit committee. Answer (c) is correct because Sarbanes-Oxley requires that at least one member of the audit committee be a financial expert. Answer (a) is incorrect because all audit committee members should be independent. Answer (b) is incorrect because the chief financial officer is not independent and should not be on the audit committee. Answer (d) is incorrect because while a CPA would generally qualify as a financial expert, it is not required that the financial expert be a CPA.

17. (b) The requirement is to identify the item that is **not** a statutory requirement for publicly held corporations registered with the SEC. Answer (b) is correct because there is no requirement to have a compensation expert on the compensation committee. Answers (c) and (d) are incorrect because they are requirements of the Sarbanes-Oxley Act. Answer (a) is incorrect because it is a requirement of the Dodd-Frank Act.

18. (b) The requirement is to identify the understanding that is a necessary to be an audit committee financial expert according to the criteria specified in the Sarbanes-Oxley Act of 2002. Answer (b) is correct because it is one of the items required to meet the criteria. Answers (a), (c), and (d) are incorrect because they are not part of the criteria.

19. (d) The requirement is to identify the item that is **not** a requirement of the Wall Street Reform and Consumer Protection Act. Answer (d) is correct because the Act does not require all members of the audit committee to be financial experts. The Sarbanes-Oxley Act requires one member of the audit committee to be a financial expert. Answers (a), (b), and (c) are incorrect because they are all requirements of the Wall Street Reform and Consumer Protection Act.

20. (b) The requirement is to identify the most effective external monitoring device. Answer (b) is correct because external auditors audit the financial statements and internal controls of a publicly held corporation. Answer (a) is incorrect because internal auditors are an internal monitoring device. Answer (c) is incorrect because the SEC relies upon external auditors to audit the corporation's financial statements and internal controls. Answer (d) is incorrect because attorneys only advise management on legal issues. They cannot take action if management does not take their advice.

21. (b) The requirement is to identify to whom the chief audit executive should report. Answer (b) is correct because ideally the chief audit executive should report to the chief executive officer. Answers (a) and (c) are incorrect because reporting to financial personnel may compromise the internal auditor's effectiveness in assessing financial reporting and controls. Answer (d) is incorrect because the external auditors are not part of the organization.

22. (a) The requirement is to identify the approach the chief audit executive should use to set audit priorities. Answer (a) is correct because a risk-based approach is required. Answers (b), (c), and (d) are incorrect because they do not describe appropriate overall approaches to setting priorities.

23. (a) The requirement is to identify the two major types of internal audit services as set forth in the Standards for the Professional Practice of Internal Auditing. Answer (a) is correct because the two major types of services include assurance and consulting. Answers (b), (c) and (d) are incorrect because they do not present the two major types of services.

24. (b) The requirement is to identify the requirement of the *International Standards for the Professional Practice of Internal Auditing*. Answer (b) is correct because it is a requirement of the standards. Answers (a), (c) and (d) are incorrect because they are not required by the standards.

25. (b) The requirement is to identify the item that is not a section of the Institute of Internal Auditors' *International Standards for the Professional Practice of Internal Auditing*. Answer (b) is correct because independence standards are not a section of the IIA standards. Answers (a), (c) and (d) are incorrect because they are all sections of the IIA standards.

26. (a) The requirement is to identify the limitation that is often attributed to securities analysts regarding their value as an external monitoring device. Answer (a) is correct because occasionally the analyst's firm has a vested interest in the welfare of the company. Answer (b) is incorrect because while some analysts may lack competence, it is not a common trait. Answer (c) is incorrect because analysts use all types of information to make evaluations. Answer (d) is incorrect because analysts are not employees of the company.

27. (d) The requirement is to identify the division of the SEC that reviews corporate filings. Answer (d) is correct because the Division of Corporate Finance reviews filings. Answer (a) is incorrect because the Office of the Chief Accountant advises the SEC on accounting and auditing matters and approves the rules of the PCAOB. Answer (b) is incorrect because the Division of Enforcement assists the SEC in executing its law enforcement function. Answer (c) is incorrect because the Division of Corporate Disclosure is not a division of the SEC.

28. (b) The requirement is to identify the correct statement regarding a financial expert. Answer (b) is correct because an issuer is required to disclose the names of the financial experts, or the reason that the issuer does not have a financial expert on the audit committee.

29. (c) The requirement is to identify the component that is considered the foundation of a company's internal control. Answer (c) is correct because the control environment is considered the foundation of all of the other components of internal control. Answers (a) and (b) are incorrect. While they are both components of internal control, neither is considered the foundation. Answer (d) is incorrect because the audit committee is one aspect of the control environment.

30. (a) The requirement is to identify the category of objectives that includes safeguarding of assets. Answer (a) is correct because safeguarding assets is included in the operations objective. Answers (b), (c), and (d) are incorrect because safeguarding of assets is an aspect of the operations objective.

31. (c) The requirement is to identify the principle that is **not** related to the control environment component. Answer (c) is correct because identify and assess changes that could significantly impact the system of internal control is a principle of the risk assessment component. Answers (a), (b), and (d) are incorrect because they are all principles of the control environment component.

32. (d) The requirement is to identify the item that is **not** true regarding the information and communication component of internal control. Answer (d) is correct because it is related to the risk assessment component. Answers (a), (b), and (c) are incorrect because they are all true of the information and communication component.

33. (a) The requirement is to identify the characteristics of an evaluator. Answer (a) is correct because COSO indicates that the evaluator must have competence and objectivity. Answers (b), (c), and (d) are incorrect because they do not describe the desired characteristics.

34. (a) The requirement is to identify the item that is a general control rather than a transaction control activity. Answer (a) is correct because technology development policies and procedures are part of the general controls. Answers (b), (c), and (d) are incorrect because they are all transaction control activities.

35. (c) The requirement is to identify the stage in which monitoring is used to establish a new baseline after changes have been made. Answer (c) is correct because the change management stage involves evaluating the design and implementation of changes and establishing a new baseline. Answer (a) is incorrect because control baseline involves developing the initial understanding of the control system. Answer (b) is incorrect because change identification involves identifying necessary changes. Answer (d) is incorrect because control revalidation/update involves revalidating the understanding periodically.

36. (c) The requirement is to identify the item that is **not** a type of control activity under the COSO framework. Answer (c) is correct because monitoring is a separate component of internal control. Answers (a), (b), and (d) are incorrect because they are all types of control activities.

37. (d) The requirement is to identify the item that is **not** a control environment factor. Answer (d) is correct because control monitoring is a separate component of internal control. Answers (a), (b), and (c) are all incorrect because they are all aspects of the control environment.

38. (c) The requirement is to identify the component of internal control that encompasses the routine controls over processes and transaction cycles. Answer (c) is correct because control activities, policies and procedures are designed to assure that management's directives are followed. Answer (a) is incorrect because the control environment is a high-level control. Answer (b) is incorrect because information and communication encompass the controls to assure that management and employees have the information to perform their functions. Answer (d) is incorrect because risk assessment encompasses the organization's processes to identify, assess, and control risks.

39. (b) The requirement is to identify the item that is **not** a component of the COSO framework for internal controls. Answer (b) is correct because segregation of duties is an aspect of control activities, which is the component. Answers (a), (c), and (d) are all incorrect because they are components of internal control.

40. (a) The requirement is to identify the statement that best describes how technology can improve the monitoring component of internal control. Answer (a) is correct because monitoring involves collecting information to determine that controls are working. Answers (b), (c), and (d) are incorrect because while they represent control advantages to the use of technology, they do not relate as directly to the monitoring component.

41. (b) The requirement is to identify the item that is **not** considered a limitation of internal control. Answer (b) is correct because this is a business risk; it is not a limitation of internal control. Answers (a), (c), and (d) are incorrect because they all represent limitations of internal control.

42. (b) The requirement is to identify the item that is **not** required to be included in management's report on internal control. Answer (b) is correct because a statement of the board of directors' approval of the system is not required. Answers (a), (c), and (d) are incorrect because they are all required aspects of management's report on internal control.

43. (b) The requirement is to identify the party that would generally be entitled to a reward under the whistle-blowing provision of the Dodd-Frank Act. Answer (b) is correct because a customer would be entitled to receive a reward. Answer (a) is incorrect because an external auditor performing an audit would generally not be eligible for a reward. Answer (c) is incorrect because a director who discovers a violation in the course of performing her duties would generally not be eligible for a reward. Answer (d) is incorrect because an internal auditor who discovers a violation while performing an audit would generally not be eligible for a reward.

44. (b) The requirement is to identify the component that addresses an entity's integrity and ethical values. Answer (b) is correct because integrity and ethical values are part of the internal environment. Answer (a) is incorrect because information and communication is the way information is identified, captured, and communicated to enable people to carry out their responsibilities. Answer (c) is incorrect because risk assessment is the process of analyzing risks. Answer (d) is incorrect because control activities are policies and procedures to help ensure the risk responses are carried out.

45. (d) The requirement is to identify the item that is not a benefit of enterprise risk management. Answer (d) is correct because sharing risk is only one way of responding, and this technique cannot be used for all risks, nor should it be. Answer (a) is incorrect because ERM involves identifying events with positive effects (i.e., opportunities). Answer (b) is incorrect because ERM involves designing appropriate responses to risks. Answer (c) is incorrect because with ERM capital is deployed to opportunities that are consistent with the organization's risk appetite.

46. (b) The requirement is to identify the item that defines the term risk tolerance. Answer (b) is correct because the COSO ERM framework defines risk tolerance as the acceptable variation with respect to a particular organizational objective. Answer (a) is incorrect because it defines risk appetite. Answer (c) is incorrect because it defines residual risk. Answer (d) is incorrect because it defines risks that are accepted.

47. (d) The requirement is to decide what type of response is illustrated by hedging a risk. Answer (d) is correct because hedging involves sharing the risk with another party. Answer (a) is incorrect because avoidance involves exiting the activity that gives rise to the risk. Answer (b) is incorrect because acceptance involves no response to the risk. Answer (c) is incorrect because reduction involves managing the risk to reduce its likelihood or impact.

48. (c) The requirement is to identify the item that is **not** a technique for identifying risks. Answer (c) is correct because probabilistic models are used for risk assessment. Answers (a), (b) and (d) are incorrect because they are all methods used for event identification.

49. (c) The requirement is to identify the next step in the ERM process. Answer (c) is correct because the next step in the process is to determine the risk responses to the assessed risks. Answers (a) and (b) are incorrect because they are subsequent steps in the process. Answer (d) is incorrect because it is part of the event identification process.

50. (c) The requirement is to identify the item that does **not** represent an advantage of enterprise risk management. Answer (c) is correct because an enterprise risk management system does not seek to eliminate all risks. Risks are avoided, reduced, shifted, or accepted based on the risk appetite of the organization. Answers (a), (b), and (d) are incorrect because they all represent advantages of enterprise risk management.

51. (a) The requirement is to identify the item that is **not** a limitation of an enterprise risk management system. Answer (a) is correct because an enterprise risk management system assumes that objectives have been set as a part of the strategic planning process. Answers (b), (c), and (d) are incorrect because they all represent limitations of enterprise risk management systems.

Written Communication Tasks

Written Communication Task 1

Written Communication	
	Help

Skyview, Inc., a small start-up company, has hired you as a consultant to assess its financial systems and related processes. During your review, you learned that the company accountant is responsible for providing general ledger access to others in the company, processing of transactions in the general ledger, and printing checks. The president of the company must authorize write-offs in the system, but the accountant has access to the president's user name and password.

Prepare a memorandum to Skyview's president assessing these responsibilities in the context of segregation of duties. Also assess the possibility of the accountant committing fraud.

REMINDER: Your response will be graded for both technical content and writing skills. Technical content will be evaluated for information that is helpful to the intended user and clearly relevant to the issue. Writing skills will be evaluated for development, organization, and the appropriate expression of ideas in professional correspondence. Use a standard business memorandum or letter format with a clear beginning, middle, and end. Do not convey the information in the form of a table, bullet point list, or other abbreviated presentation.

To: Skyview President
Re: Segregation of duties and potential for fraud

Written Communication Task 2

Written Communication	
	Help

Assume that you are acting as a consultant for Winston Co. The president of the company is considering implementing an enterprise risk management system. To evaluate whether to go forward with the project, the president has asked you to describe the limitations of an enterprise risk management system.

Prepare a memorandum to Winston's president describing the purpose and limitations of an enterprise risk management system.

REMINDER: Your response will be graded for both technical content and writing skills. Technical content will be evaluated for information that is helpful to the intended user and clearly relevant to the issue. Writing skills will be evaluated for development, organization, and the appropriate expression of ideas in professional correspondence. Use a standard business memorandum or letter format with a clear beginning, middle, and end. Do not convey the information in the form of a table, bullet point list, or other abbreviated presentation.

To: Winston Co. President
Re: Limitations of an enterprise risk management system

Written Communication Task 3

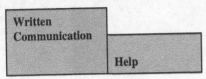

Carolyn Johnson, the chairman of the compensation committee of the board of directors of York Corporation, is concerned about the incentives that exist in the current compensation system for management of the company. Currently, the compensation system provides for a base salary plus a bonus that may amount to as much as 100% of the executive's base salary. The bonus is based on accounting net income.

Prepare a memorandum explaining the risks in the company's compensation system and describing one or more other systems that might be better.

> **REMINDER:** Your response will be graded for both technical content and writing skills. Technical content will be evaluated for information that is helpful to the intended reader and clearly relevant to the issue. Writing skills will be evaluated for development, organization, and the appropriate expression of ideas in professional correspondence. Use a standard business memo or letter format with a clear beginning, middle, and end. Do not convey information in the form of a table, bullet point list, or other abbreviated presentation.

To: Ms. Carolyn Johnson, Chairman
        Compensation Committee
        York Corporation
From: CPA Candidate

Written Communication Task 4

The chairman of the board of Hanover Corporation, Jack Vu, is in the process of evaluating the effectiveness of the board's audit committee. Prepare a memorandum to explain the nature and responsibilities of an effective audit committee.

> **REMINDER:** Your response will be graded for both technical content and writing skills. Technical content will be evaluated for information that is helpful to the intended reader and clearly relevant to the issue. Writing skills will be evaluated for development, organization, and the appropriate expression of ideas in professional correspondence. Use a standard business memo or letter format with a clear beginning, middle, and end. Do not convey information in the form of a table, bullet point list, or other abbreviated presentation.

To: Mr. Jack Vu, Chairman of the Board
        Hanover Corporation
From: CPA Candidate

Written Communication Task Solutions

Written Communication Task 1

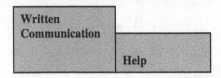

To: Skyview President
Re: Segregation of duties and potential for fraud

You have requested that I perform an independent assessment of Skyview's financial systems and related processes. In a properly controlled financial system the duties of authorization of transactions, approval of transactions, custody of assets, and record keeping should all be segregated. In other words, these functions should all be performed by different individuals. Your current financial system and processes do not include this proper segregation of duties. Skyview's accountant has incompatible duties that would allow him to make an error or perpetrate a fraud and prevent its detection. He processes transactions and has access to assets (printed checks). As an example, he could process fictitious purchase transactions to his own shell companies and cause payments to be made for goods or services that were not received by Skyview.

In addition, the fact that the accountant has access to your user name and password allows him to circumvent the control provided by your being the only individual authorized to write off accounts. This would allow the accountant to process an unauthorized sales transaction to his own shell company and use your user name and password to write off the account.

I would recommend that you develop a new financial system that would include appropriate segregation of duties to ensure that no individual in the organization has the ability to perpetrate errors or fraud without it being detected in the normal course of operations. In addition, you should establish polices regarding the maintenance and confidentiality of user names and passwords to ensure that the controls cannot be circumvented.

If you have any questions, please contact me.

Written Communication Task 2

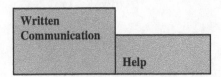

To: Winston Co. President
Re: Limitations of an enterprise risk management system

You have requested that I provide you with information about an enterprise risk management system. You are particularly concerned with the limitations of such a system. The primary purpose of an enterprise risk management system is to provide processes to identify potential risks to achieving a company's objectives and to manage those risks to be within the company's risk appetite.

In considering implementation of an enterprise risk management system, it is important to recognize that these systems have limitations. All enterprise risk management systems rely on judgments about future events that may or may not occur. Also, while an enterprise risk management system provides information about risks to achieving the company's objectives, it does not even provide reasonable assurance that the objectives will be achieved. The company may have a well-established enterprise risk management system and still fail. Finally, as with all control systems, an enterprise risk management system can break down for a number of reasons, including bad judgments about risks and their impact, collusion among two or more individuals, or override by management. Also, due to cost-benefit constraints, no enterprise risk management system can be perfect.

If you have any additional questions about enterprise risk management systems, please contact me.

Written Communication Task 3

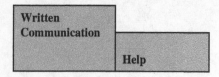

To: Ms. Carolyn Johnson, Chairman
           Compensation Committee
           York Corporation
From: CPA Candidate

This memorandum is designed to describe the factors that should be considered in evaluating and selecting a management compensation system.

Effective management compensation systems are those that are successful at aligning management behavior with the objectives of the shareholders. Your current compensation provides for a base salary plus a large potential bonus based on accounting income. This motivates managers to attempt to maximize accounting income. While this may result in behavior that also benefits the shareholders, it may not. Accounting income can be manipulated in the short run by making uneconomic decisions, such as postponing research and development and maintenance projects. In addition, such a compensation system provides management with an incentive to manipulate accounting income and perhaps even commit fraud.

Compensation systems that are tied to the long-term value of the company's stock tend to be more effective. They clearly align management's incentives with those of the shareholders of the firm. I would suggest that the compensation committee consider creating a compensation system that includes deferred stock options or stock grants. Such a system should motivate management to maximize the long-term stock price of the corporation.

I believe that a management compensation system that is tied to long-term stock price would be superior to the company's current method. I would be delighted to assist in your discussions regarding the selection of an appropriate method.

Written Communication Task 4

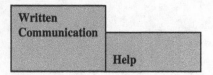

To: Mr. Jack Vu, Chairman of the Board
           Hanover Corporation
From: CPA Candidate

This memorandum is designed to provide you with information about the role and responsibilities of an effective audit committee of the board of directors. The audit committee plays a critical role in corporate governance of a corporation. A major responsibility of the audit committee is the appointment, compensation and oversight of the corporation's external auditor, including the resolution of any disagreements between management and the external auditor. Other responsibilities include interaction with the internal auditors, receipt and treatment of complaints regarding accounting or auditing matters, and investigation of issues that impact reliable financial reporting and internal control. To be effective, it is important that the audit committee actively question management and the auditors about the reliability of the financial reporting process and the effectiveness of internal controls. In addition, it is important that the members of the audit committee are independent and competent. In fact, the Sarbanes-Oxley Act provides that at least one member should be a "financial expert."

By effectively discharging these responsibilities, the audit committee can help ensure the reliability of the financial reporting process and prevent management fraud. I am available to help you develop criteria to be used to evaluate the effectiveness of Hanover's audit committee.

Module 41: Information Technology

Overview

Computers have become the primary means used to process financial accounting information and have resulted in a situation in which auditors must be able to use and understand current information technology. Accordingly, knowledge of information technology implications is included in the Business Environment and Concepts section of the CPA exam. In addition, auditing procedures relating to information technology (IT) are included in the Auditing and Attestation portion of the CPA exam.

This module describes various types of information technology and describes the major types of controls that are used to assure the accuracy, completeness, and integrity of technology-processed information.

Ideally, to effectively reply to technology-related questions, you should have previously studied or worked in computerized business environments. However, if you do not have this background, we believe that the information in this module should prepare you to perform reasonably well on a typical exam. Keep in mind that the review of these materials cannot make you an expert, and a module such as this cannot cover all possible topics related to information technology. However, this material should help you to understand the complexities introduced by computers in sufficient detail to answer most questions.

A. Information Systems Within a Business

1. **Definition**—An information system processes data and transactions to provide users with the information they need to plan, control and operate an organization, including

    a. Collecting transaction and other data
    b. Entering it into the information system
    c. Processing the data
    d. Providing users with the information needed
    e. Controlling the process

2. **Manual vs. Computer Systems**

    a. On an overall basis, manual accounting systems have in most circumstances been replaced by computerized accounting information systems of various types, although portions of many systems remain manual.
    b. Computer processing tends to reduce or eliminate processing time, and prevent computational errors and errors in processing routine transactions (when fraud is not involved).

3. **General Types of IT Systems**

    a. **Office automation systems**—Designed to improve productivity by supporting daily work of employees (e.g., word processing, spreadsheets, presentation tools, e-mail, electronic calendars, contact management software)
    b. **Transaction processing systems**—Involve the daily processing of transactions (e.g., airplane reservation systems, payroll recording, cash receipts, cash disbursements)
    c. **Management reporting systems**—Designed to help with the decision-making process by providing access to computer data

(1) **Management information systems**—Systems designed to provide past, present and future information for planning, organizing and controlling the operations of the organization
(2) **Decision support systems**—Computer-based information systems that combine models and data to resolve nonstructured problems with extensive user involvement
(3) **Expert systems**—Computer systems that apply reasoning methods to data in a specific relatively structured area to render advice or recommendations, much like a human expert
(4) **Executive information systems**—Computerized systems that are specifically designed to support executive work

> **NOTE:** It is helpful to consider these two distinct roles for systems—that is, (a) recording transactions of various types versus (b) providing support for decision making. These topics are discussed in detail under Section B.2. (Methods of Processing).

4. Systems Design and Process Improvement

Designing and implementing a new information and control system provides an opportunity to reexamine business processes, especially if the new system is an enterprise resource planning (ERP) system. Management can take advantage of the capabilities of the technology to redesign business processes making them more efficient and effective. The traditional methodology for developing information systems is the systems development lifecycle (SDLC). This methodology is characterized by its phases, each representing a specific set of development activities. Typically, the SDLC phases include: planning, analysis, design, development, testing, implementation, and maintenance.

a. The Planning Phase

Major activities in the planning phase include

(1) Identify the problem(s) the proposed system will solve.
(2) Define the system to be developed. This involves identifying and selecting the system to be developed based on the strategic goals of the organization.
(3) Determine the project scope. This activity sets the project's boundaries by providing a clear understanding of what the new system will do and how it will be evaluated. A project scope document is used to describe the project scope. During the process of systems design, the scope of the project may be revisited and revised.
(4) Develop a project plan. The project plan defines the activities that will be performed, and the individuals and resources that will be used. A project manager is the individual who develops the plan and tracks its progress. The plan establishes project milestones which set forth dates by which certain activities need to be performed.
(5) Evaluate the initial feasibility of the project. Feasibility analysis may involve multiple measures including determining the project's technical, organizational, and economic feasibility.

b. The Analysis Phase

This phase involves teams including end users, information technology specialists, systems analysts, and process design specialists to understand the requirements for the proposed system. Typically, processing, data, and logic models are produced during this phase to help determine the system requirements. A needs assessment may also be performed. A needs assessment involves determining the requirements for the system in terms of processes, data capture, information and reporting. Next, an analysis is performed on the existing system along the same dimensions. Then, a gap analysis is performed to examine the differences (gaps) between the required system and the existing system. Finally priorities will be established for the gaps (requirements) which will be documented in a requirements definition document, which will receive sign-off from the end users. It is during this phase that a company can take advantage of the processes inherent in the new system to improve existing processes. System specification documents contain information on basic requirements which include

(1) Performance levels
(2) Reliability
(3) Quality
(4) Interfaces
(5) Security and privacy
(6) Constraints and limitations
(7) Functional capabilities
(8) Data structures and elements

c.   **The Design Phase**

The primary goal of the design phase is to build a technical blueprint of how the proposed system will work. The components that are typically designed during this phase include

(1)   Databases
(2)   User interfaces for input and output
(3)   Required reports
(4)   Programs
(5)   Infrastructure and controls

d.   **The Development Phase**

During the development phase the documents from the design phase are transformed into the actual system. In the design phase the platform on which the system is to operate is built or purchased off-the-shelf and customized and databases are developed.

e.   **The Testing Phase**

The testing phase involves verifying that the system works and meets the business requirements as set forth in the analysis phase. The testing phase is obviously critical. The following types of test should be performed:

(1)   *Unit testing.* Unit testing involves testing the units or pieces of code.
(2)   *System testing.* System testing involves testing of the integration of the units or pieces of code into a system.
(3)   *Integration testing.* Integration testing involves testing whether the separate systems can work together.
(4)   *User acceptance testing.* User acceptance testing determines whether the system meets the business requirements and enables users to perform their jobs efficiently and effectively.

f.   **The Implementation Phase**

The implementation phase involves putting the system in operation by the users. In order to effectively implement the system detailed user documentation must be provided to the users, and the users must be adequately trained. An organization may choose from a number of implementation methods including:

(1)   *Parallel implementation.* This method uses both systems until it is determined that the new system is operating properly. This has the advantage of a full operational test of the new system with less risk of a system disaster. The disadvantage of this method is the additional work and cost during the period in which both systems are operating.
(2)   *Plunge implementation.* Using this method the organization ceases using the old system and begins using the new system immediately. This method is less costly than the parallel method but it has higher risk of a system breakdown.
(3)   *Pilot implementation.* This method involves having a small group of individuals using the new system until it is seen to be working properly. This has the advantage of providing a partial operational test of the new system at a lower cost than parallel implementation.
(4)   *Phased implementation.* This method involves installing the system in a series of phases.

g.   **The Maintenance Phase**

This phase involves monitoring and supporting the new system. In this phase the organization provides ongoing training, help desk resources, and a system for making authorized and tested changes to the system.

NOW REVIEW MULTIPLE-CHOICE QUESTIONS 1 THROUGH 14

B.   **Characteristics of IT Systems—General**

1. **Types of Computers, Hardware, and Software**

a.   **Types of computers (in order of size and power)**

(1)   **Supercomputers**—Extremely powerful, high-speed computers used for extremely high-volume and/or complex processing needs.
(2)   **Mainframe computers**—Large, powerful, high-speed computers. While less powerful than supercomputers, they have traditionally been used for high-volume transaction processing. Clusters of lower cost, less powerful "servers" are increasingly taking over the processing chores of mainframe computers.

(3) **Servers**—High-powered microcomputers that "serve" applications and data to clients that are connected via a network (e.g., web servers, database servers). Servers typically have greater capacity (faster processors, more RAM, more storage capacity) than their clients (microcomputers) and often act as a central repository for organizational data. Servers today are often configured as a "virtual machine," meaning multiple operating systems can coexist and operate simultaneously on the same machine. Virtual machines are appealing because they lower hardware costs and they create energy savings.

(4) **Microcomputers** (e.g., desktop computers, laptop computers)—Designed to be used by one person at a time, they are often called personal computers. Typically used for word processing, e-mail, spreadsheets, surfing the web, creating and editing graphics, playing music, and gaming.

(5) **Tablets/Smart Phones/Personal Digital Assistants** (e.g., iPad, iPhone, Android, Blackberry)—These are typically smaller, handheld wireless devices that depend on WiFi and/or cellular technology for communication. Many of these devices support touch screen input.

b. **Hardware—Physical equipment**

(1) **Central processing unit (CPU)**—The principal hardware components of a computer. It contains an arithmetic/logic unit, primary memory, and a control unit. The major function of the CPU is to fetch stored instructions and data, decode the instructions, and carry out the instructions.

(a) **Arithmetic/logic unit**—Performs mathematical operations and logical comparisons.

(b) **Primary memory (storage)**—Active data and program steps that are being processed by the CPU. It may be divided into RAM (random-access memory) and ROM (read-only memory). Application programs and data are stored in the RAM at execution time.

(c) **Control unit**—Interprets program instructions and coordinates input, output, and storage devices.

(2) **Secondary storage**

(a) **Storage devices**

1] **Magnetic tape**—Slowest type of storage available because data is stored sequentially. Primarily used for archiving purposes today.

2] **Magnetic disks**—The most common storage medium in use on computers today. Magnetic disks are also called "hard disks" or "hard disk drives" (HDD). Data can be accessed directly.

3] **RAID (Redundant array of independent [previously, inexpensive] disks)**—A way of storing the same data redundantly on multiple magnetic disks

a] When originally recorded, data is written to multiple disks to decrease the likelihood of loss of data.

b] If a disk fails, at least one of the other disks has the information and continues operation.

4] **Compact Discs**—Discs (CDs) and Digital Video Discs (DVDs)—Both are the same physical size and both use optical technology to read and write data to the disc.

5] **Solid State Drives (SSDs)**—Use microchips to store data and require no moving parts for read/write operations. SSDs are faster and more expensive per gigabyte than CDs, DVDs, and HDDs. SSDs are increasingly being used in place of HDDs in microcomputers but cost and limited capacity have constrained their adoption as a primary storage device. SSDs are more commonly used for auxiliary storage. SSDs that are "pluggable" are often called "thumb drives," "flash drives," or "USB drives" (because they use a USB interface to "plug" into other devices).

6] **Cloud-Based Storage**—Also called "Storage as a Service" (SaaS). This type of storage is hosted offsite, typically by third parties, and is accessed via the Internet.

(b) **Manner in which information is represented in a computer**

1] **Digital**—A series of binary digits (0s and 1s). One binary digit is called a "bit." A series of 8 bits is referred to as a "byte." One byte can form a letter, a number, or a special character (e.g., 00000111 is the binary equivalent of the decimal number 7).

2] **Analog**—The representation that is produced by the fluctuations of a continuous signal (e.g., speech, temperature, weight, speed, etc.). Rather than using 0s and 1s to represent information, analog signals use electrical, mechanical, hydraulic or pneumatic devices to transmit the fluctuations in the signal itself to represent information.

(c) **Related computer terms**

   1] **Online**—Equipment in direct communication with, and under the control of, the CPU. Online also refers to having a connection to the Internet.

   2] **Off-line**—Equipment not in direct communication with the CPU; the operator generally must intervene to connect off-line equipment or data to the CPU (e.g., mount a magnetic tape of archival data). Off-line also refers to the absence of an Internet connection.

   3] **Console**—A terminal used for communication between the operator and the computer (e.g., the operator of a mainframe computer)

   4] **Peripheral equipment**—All non-CPU hardware that may be placed under the control of the central processor. Classified as online or off-line, this equipment consists of input, storage, output, and communication.

   5] **Controllers**—Hardware units designed to operate specific input-output units

   6] **Buffer**—A temporary storage unit used to hold data during computer operations

   7] **MIPS**—Millions of instructions per second; a unit for measuring the execution speed of computers

(3) **Input devices**

  (a) **Keying data—Data entry devices**

    1] **Key-to-tape** and **key-to-disk** in which data is entered on magnetic tape and/or disk respectively, and then read into a computer

  (b) **Online entry**

    1] **Visual display terminal/monitors**—Uses keyboard to directly enter data into computer

      a] **Input interface**—A program that controls the display for the user (usually on a computer monitor) and that allows the user to interact with the system

      b] **Graphical user interface (GUI)** uses icons, pictures, and menus instead of text for inputs (e.g., Windows).

      c] **Command line interface**—Uses text-type commands

    2] **Mouse, joystick, light pens**—Familiar devices that allow data entry

    3] **Touch-sensitive screen**—Allows users to enter data from a menu of items by touching the surface of the monitor

  (c) **Turnaround documents**—Documents that are sent to the customer and returned as inputs (e.g., utility bills)

  (d) **Automated source data input devices**

    1] **Magnetic tape reader**—A device capable of sensing information recorded as magnetic spots on magnetic tape

    2] **Magnetic ink character reader (MICR)**—Device that reads characters that have been encoded with a magnetic ink (e.g., bank check readers)

    3] **Scanner**—A device that reads characters on printed pages

    4] **Automatic teller machine (ATM)**—A machine used to execute and record transactions with financial institutions

    5] **Radio Frequency Identification (RFID)**—Uses radio waves to track and input data. Increasingly used for inventory and contactless payment systems. RFID tags can be read wirelessly by RFID readers; does not require line-of-sight access like bar code technology (e.g., Mobil's Speedpass® payment systems, FasTrak® toll collection system).

    6] **Point-of-sale (POS) recorders**—Devices that read price and product code data (e.g., recall purchasing groceries—items are frequently passed over a POS recorder). POS recorders ordinarily function as both a terminal and a cash register.

      a] POS processing allows one to record and track customer orders, process credit and debit cards, connect to other systems in a network, and manage inventory. Generally, a POS terminal has as its core a personal computer, which is provided with application-specific programs and input/output devices for the particular environment in which it will serve.

      b] POS terminals are used in most industries that have a point of sale such as a service desk, including restaurants, lodging, entertainment, and museums. For example, a POS system for a restaurant is likely to have all menu items stored in a database that can be queried for information in a number of ways.

c] Increasingly, POS terminals are also Web-enabled, which makes remote training and operation possible, as well as inventory tracking across geographically dispersed locations.

7] **Voice recognition**—A system that understands spoken words and transmits them into a computer.

(e) **Electronic commerce** and **electronic data interchange**—Involves one company's computer communicating with another's computer. For example, a buyer electronically sending a purchase order to a supplier. Discussed in further detail in Section C.5. of this module.

(4) **Output devices**

(a) Many automated source data input devices and electronic commerce/electronic data interchange devices [(3)(d) and (e) above] are capable of outputting data ("writing" in addition to "reading") and therefore become output devices as well as input devices.

(b) **Monitors**—Visually display output

(c) **Printers**—Produce paper output

(d) **Plotters**—Produce paper output of graphs

(e) **Computer output to microfilm or microfiche (COM)**—Makes use of photographic process to store output

c. **Software**—Computer programs that control hardware

(1) **Systems software**

(a) **Operating system**—Manages the input, output, processing and storage devices and operations of a computer (e.g., Windows, Linux, Unix)

1] Performs scheduling, resource allocation, and data retrieval based on instructions provided in job control language

(b) **Utility programs**—Handle common file, data manipulation and "housekeeping" tasks

(c) **Communications software**—Controls and supports transmission between computers, computers and monitors, and accesses various databases

(2) **Applications software**—Programs designed for specific uses, or "applications," such as

(a) Word processing, graphics, spreadsheets, email, and database systems

(b) Accounting software

1] **Low-end**—All in one package, designed for small organizations

2] **High-end**—Ordinarily in modules (e.g., general ledger, receivables)

3] **Enterprise Resource Planning (ERP)**—Designed as relatively complete information system "suites" for large and medium size organizations (e.g., human resources, financial applications, manufacturing, distribution). Major vendors are well known—SAP, PeopleSoft, Oracle, and J.D. Edwards.

a] Advantages of ERP systems—Integration of various portions of the information system, direct electronic communication with suppliers and customers, increased responsiveness to information requests for decision-making

b] Disadvantages of ERP systems—Complexity, costs, integration with supplier and customer systems may be more difficult than anticipated

(3) **Software terms**

(a) **Compiler**—Produces a machine language object program from a source program language

(b) **Multiprocessing**—Simultaneous execution of two or more tasks, usually by two or more CPUs that are part of the same system

(c) **Multitasking**—The simultaneous processing of several jobs on a computer

(d) **Object program**—The converted source program that was changed using a compiler to create a set of machine readable instructions that the CPU understands

(e) **Source program**—A program written in a language from which statements are translated into machine language; computer programming has developed in "generations"

1] Machine language (composed of combinations of 1's and 0's that are meaningful to the computer).

2] Assembly language—A low-level programming language that uses words (mnemonics) instead of numbers to perform an operation. Assembly language must be translated to machine language by a utility program called an *assembler*. Generally, an assembly language is specific to a computer architecture and is therefore not portable like most high-level languages.

3] "High-level" programming languages such as COBOL, Basic, Fortran, C++, and Java.

    a] C++ and Java are considered object-oriented programs (OOPs) in that they are based on the concept of an "object" which is a data structure that uses a set of routines, called "methods," which operate on the data. The "objects" are efficient in that they often are reusable in other programs.

    b] Object-oriented programs keep together data structures and procedures (methods) through a procedure referred to as encapsulation. Basic to object-oriented programs are the concepts of a class (a set of objects with similar structures) and inheritance (the ability to create new classes from existing classes).

4] An "application-specific" language usually built around database systems. These programs are ordinarily closer to human languages than the first three generations (e.g., SQL, Structured Query Language: an instruction to create a report might be *Extract all Customers where "Name" is Jones*).

5] A relatively new and developing form that includes visual or graphical interfaces used to create source language that is usually compiled with a 3rd or 4th generation language compiler.

    (f) **Virtual memory (storage)**—Online secondary memory that is used as an extension of primary memory, thus giving the appearance of larger, virtually unlimited internal memory

    (g) **Protocol**—Rules determining the required format and methods for transmission of data

(4) **Programming terms**

    (a) **Desk checking**—Review of a program by the programmer for errors before the program is run and debugged on the computer

    (b) **Debug**—To find and eliminate errors in a computer program. Many compilers assist debugging by listing errors such as invalid commands in the program.

    (c) **Edit**—To correct input data prior to processing

    (d) **Loop**—A set of program instructions performed repetitively a predetermined number of times, or until all of a particular type of data has been processed

    (e) **Memory dump**—A listing of the contents of storage

    (f) **Patch**—A section of coding inserted into a program to correct a mistake or to alter a routine

    (g) **Run**—A complete cycle of a program including input, processing and output

2. Methods of Processing

a. **Batch or online real-time**

(1) **Batch**

    (a) Transactions flow through the system in groups of like transactions (batches). For example, all cash receipts on accounts receivable for a day may be aggregated and run as a batch.

    (b) Ordinarily leaves a relatively easy-to-follow audit trail.

(2) **Online real-time** (also referred to as **direct access processing**)

General: Transactions are processed in the order in which they occur, regardless of type. Data files and programs are stored online so that updating can take place as the edited data flows to the application. System security must be in place to restrict access to programs and data to authorized persons. Online systems are often categorized as being either online transaction processing systems or online analytical processing systems.

    (a) **Online transaction processing (OLTP)**

        1] Databases that support day-to-day operations

        2] Examples: airline reservations systems, bank automatic teller systems, and Internet website sales systems

    (b) **Online analytical processing (OLAP)**

        1] A category of software technology that enables the user to query the system (retrieve data), and conduct an analysis, etc., ordinarily while the user is at a PC. The result is generated in seconds. OLAP systems are primarily used for analytical analysis.

> **EXAMPLE**
>
> An airline's management downloads its OLAP reservation information into another database to allow analysis of that reservation information. At a minimum, this will allow analysis without tying up the OLAP system that is used on a continuous basis; the restructuring of the data into another database is also likely to make a more detailed analysis possible.

2] Uses statistical and graphical tools that provide users with various (often multidimensional) views of their data, and allows them to analyze the data in detail.

3] These techniques are used as **decision support systems** (computer-based information systems that combine models and data in an attempt to solve relatively unstructured problems with extensive user involvement).

4] One approach to OLAP is to periodically download and combine operational databases into a **data warehouse** (a subject-oriented, integrated collection of data used to support management decision-making processes) or a **data mart** (a data warehouse that is limited in scope).

    a] **Data mining**—Using sophisticated techniques from statistics, artificial intelligence and computer graphics to explain, confirm and explore relationships among data (which is often stored in a data warehouse or data mart)

    b] **Business intelligence (BI)**—A combination of systems that help aggregate, access, and analyze business data and assist in the business decision-making process.

5] **Artificial intelligence (AI)**—Computer software designed to help humans make decisions. AI may be viewed as an attempt to model aspects of human thought on computers. AI ordinarily deals with decisions that may be made using a relatively structured approach. It frequently involves using a computer to quickly solve a problem that a human could ultimately solve through extremely detailed analysis.

6] **Expert system**—One form of AI. A computerized information system that guides decision processes within a well-defined area and allows decisions comparable to those of an expert. Expert knowledge is modeled into a mathematical system.

> **EXAMPLE**
>
> An expert system may be used by a credit card department to authorize credit card purchases so as to minimize fraud and credit losses.

  b. **Centralized, Decentralized, or Distributed**

    (1) **Centralized**

      (a) Processing occurs at one location.

      (b) Historically, this is the model used in which a mainframe computer processes data submitted to it through terminals.

      (c) Today, centralized vs. decentralized processing is often a matter of degree—how much is processed by a centralized computer vs. how much by decentralized computers.

    (2) **Decentralized**

      (a) Processing (and data) are stored on computers at multiple locations.

      (b) Ordinarily the computers involved are not interconnected by a network, so users at various sites cannot share data.

      (c) May be viewed as a collection of independent databases, rather than a single database.

      (d) End-user computing (Section C.4. below) is relatively decentralized.

    (3) **Distributed**

      (a) Transactions for a single database are processed at various sites.

EXAMPLE

Payroll is processed for Minneapolis employees in Minneapolis, and for Santa Fe employees in Santa Fe. Yet the overall payroll information is in one database.

    (b)   Processing may be on either a batch or online real-time basis.

    (c)   An overall single database is ordinarily updated for these transactions and available at the various sites.

3. **Methods of Data Structure**

  a. **Data organization for computer operations**

     (1) **Bit**—A binary digit (0 or 1) which is the smallest storage unit in a computer.

     (2) **Byte**—A group of adjacent bits (usually 8) that is treated as a single unit, or character, by the computer. Printable alphanumeric characters (e.g., A–Z, a–z, 0–9); special characters (e.g., $, %, !, @, etc.) and unprintable control codes (e.g., those that control peripheral devices such as printers) can be represented by an 8-bit byte. Character-encoding schemes for computers, such as ASCII and UTF-8, ensure universal interpretation of the 8-bit codes.

     (3) **Field**—A group of related characters (e.g., a social security number).

     (4) **Record**—An ordered set of logically related fields. For example, all payroll data (including the social security number field and others) relating to a single employee.

     (5) **File**—a group of related records (e.g., all the weekly pay records year-to-date), which is usually arranged in sequence.

     (6) **Table**—A group of related records in a relational database with a unique identifier (primary key field) in each record.

     (7) **Database**—A group of related files or a group of related tables (if a relational database).

     (8) **Array**—In a programming language, an aggregate that consists of data objects with attributes, each of which may be uniquely referenced by an index (address). For example, an array may be used to request input of various payroll information for a new employee in one step. Thus an array could include employee name, social security number, withholdings, pay rate, etc.—for example (John Jones, 470-44-5044, 2, $18.32, …). Name would be indexed as 1 (or zero), with each succeeding attribute receiving the next higher number as an address. Also arrays may be multidimensional. They are often used with object-oriented programming languages such as C++ and Java.

     (9) **Master file**—A file containing relatively permanent information used as a source of reference and periodically updated with a detail (transaction) file (e.g., permanent payroll records).

    (10) **Detail or transaction file**—A file containing current transaction information used to update the master file (e.g., hours worked by each employee during the current period used to update the payroll master file).

  b. **Data file structure**

     (1) **Traditional file processing systems**—These systems focus upon data processing needs of individual departments. Each application program or system is developed to meet the needs of the particular requesting department or user group. For accounting purposes these systems are often similar to traditional accounting systems, with files set up for operations such as purchasing, sales, cash receipts, cash disbursements, etc.

       (a) **Advantages of traditional processing systems**

          1] Currently operational for many existing (legacy) systems

          2] Often cost effective for simple applications

       (b) **Disadvantages of traditional processing systems**

          1] Data files are dependent upon a particular application program.

          2] In complex business situations there is much duplication of data between data files.

          3] Each application must be developed individually.

          4] Program maintenance is expensive.

          5] Data may be isolated and difficult to share between functional areas.

(2) **Database systems**

    (a) **Definitions**

        1] **Database**—A collection of interrelated files, ordinarily most of which are stored online.

           a] **Normalization**—The process of separating the database into logical tables to avoid certain kinds of updating difficulties (referred to as "anomalies").

        2] **Database system**—Computer hardware and software that enables the database(s) to be implemented.

        3] **Database management system**—Software that provides a facility for communications between various applications programs (e.g., a payroll preparation program) and the database (e.g., a payroll master file containing the earnings records of the employees).

        4] **Data independence**—Basic to database systems is this concept which separates the data from the related application programs.

        5] **Data modeling**—Identifying and organizing a database's data, both logically and physically. A data model determines what information is to be contained in a database, how the information will be used, and how the items in the database will be related to each other.

           a] **Entity-relationship modeling**—An approach to data modeling. The model (called the entity-relationship diagram, or ERD) divides the database in two logical parts—entities (e.g. "customer," "product") and relations ("buys," "pays for").

           b] **Primary key**—The field(s) that make a record in a relational database table unique.

           c] **Foreign key**—The field(s) that are common to two (or more) related tables in a relational database.

           d] **REA data model**—A data model designed for use in designing accounting information databases. REA is an acronym for the model's basic types of objects: **R**esources—Identifiable objects that have economic value, **E**vents—An organization's business activities, **A**gents—People or organizations about which data is collected.

        6] **Data Dictionary** (also referred to as a **data repository** or **data directory** system)—A data structure that stores meta-data.

           a] **Meta-data**—Definitional data that provides information about or documentation of other data managed within an application or environment. For example, data about data elements, records and data structures (length, fields, columns, etc.).

        7] **Structured query language (SQL)**—The most common language used for creating and querying relational databases (see (b)3] below), its commands may be classified into three types.

           a] **Data definition language (DDL)**—Used to define a database, including creating, altering, and deleting tables and establishing various constraints.

           b] **Data manipulation language (DML)**—Commands used to maintain and query a database, including updating, inserting in, modifying, and querying (asking for data). For example, a frequent query involves the joining of information from more than one table.

           c] **Data control language (DCL)**—Commands used to control a database, including controlling which users have various privileges (e.g., who is able to read from and write to various portions of the database).

    (b) **Database structures**

        1] **Hierarchical**—The data elements at one level "own" the data elements at the next lower level (think of an organization chart in which one manager supervises several assistants, who in turn each supervise several lower level employees).

        2] **Networked**—Each data element can have several owners and can own several other elements (think of a matrix-type structure in which various relationships can be supported).

        3] **Relational**—A database with the logical structure of a group of related spreadsheets. Each row represents a record, which is an accumulation of all the fields related to the same identifier or key; each column represents a field common to all of the records. Relational databases have in many situations largely replaced the earlier developed hierarchical and networked databases.

        4] **Object-oriented**—Information (attributes and methods) are included in structures called object classes. This is the newest database management system technology

5] **Object-relational**—Includes both relational and object-oriented features.

6] **Distributed**—A single database that is spread physically across computers in multiple locations that are connected by a data communications link. (The structure of the database is most frequently relational, object-oriented, or object-relational.)

(c) **Database controls**

1] **User department**—Because users directly input data, strict controls over who is authorized to read and/or change the database are necessary.

2] **Access controls**—In addition to the usual controls over terminals and access to the system, database processing also maintains controls within the database itself. These controls limit the user to reading and/or changing (updating) only authorized portions of the database.

   a] **Restricting privileges**—This limits the access of users to the database, as well as operations a particular user may be able to perform. For example, certain employees and customers may have only read, and not write, privileges.

   b] **Logical views**—Users may be provided with authorized *views* of only the portions of the database for which they have a valid need.

3] **Backup and recovery**—A database is updated on a continuous basis during the day. Three methods of backup and recovery are:

   a] **Backup of database and logs of transactions** (sometimes referred to as "systems logs"). The approach is to backup the entire database several times per week, generally to magnetic tape. A log of all transactions is also maintained. If there is extensive damage to a major portion of the database due to catastrophic failure, such as disk crash, the recovery method is to restore the most recent past copy of the database and to reconstruct it to a more current state by reapplying or redoing transactions from the log up to the point of failure.

   b] **Database replication.** To avoid catastrophic failure, another approach is to replicate the database at one or more locations. Thus, all data may be recorded to both sets of the database.

   c] **Backup facility.** Another approach is to maintain a backup facility with a vendor who will process data in case of an emergency.

   Further information on backup and recovery is included under Disaster Recovery—D.11 of this module.

4] **Database administrator (DBA)**—Individual responsible for maintaining the database and restricting access to the database to authorized personnel.

5] **Audit software**—Usually used by auditors to test the database; see Auditing with Technology Module.

(d) **Advantages of database systems**

1] **Data independence**—Data can be used relatively easily by differing applications.

2] **Minimal data redundancy**—The manner in which data is structured results in information being recorded in only one place, thus making updating much easier than is the case with traditional file systems.

3] **Data sharing**—The sharing of data between individuals and applications is relatively easy.

4] Reduced program maintenance.

5] Commercial applications are available for modification to a company's needs.

(e) **Disadvantages of database systems**

1] Need for specialized personnel with database expertise

2] Installation of database is costly

3] Conversion of traditional file systems (legacy systems) is costly

4] Comprehensive backup and recovery procedures are necessary.

NOW REVIEW MULTIPLE-CHOICE QUESTIONS 15 THROUGH 52

C. Characteristics of IT Systems—Specific

  1. **Types of Networks**

    a. **Background**

      (1) A network is a group of interconnected computers and terminals.

      (2) The development of **telecommunications**—The electronic transmission of information by radio, fiber optics, wire, microwave, laser, and other electromagnetic systems—has made possible the electronic transfer of information between networks of computers. This topic is discussed in detail later in this module.

    b. **Classified by geographical scope**

      (1) **Personal area network (PAN)**—A computer network that is centered around an individual and the personal communication devices he/she uses. PANs can be associated with both wireless and wired communication devices (e.g., the Bluetooth devices we use with our mobile phones for driving; the USB devices that we connect to our computers).

      (2) **Local area networks (LAN)**—Privately owned networks within a single building or campus of up to a few miles in size. Because this topic has been emphasized in AICPA materials, it is discussed further later in this module.

      (3) **Metropolitan area network (MAN)**—A larger version of a LAN. For example, it might include a group of nearby offices within a city.

      (4) **Wide area networks (WAN)**—Networks that span a large geographical area, often a country or continent. It is composed of a collection of computers and other hardware and software for running user programs.

    c. **Classified by ownership**

      (1) **Private**—One in which network resources are usually dedicated to a small number of applications or a restricted set of users, as in a corporation's network.

        (a) A typical approach is to lease telephone lines that are dedicated to the network's use.

        (b) Also, traditional EDI systems (discussed below) use a private network.

        (c) Advantages: Secure, flexible, performance often exceeds that of public.

        (d) Disadvantage: Costly

      (2) **Public**—Resources are owned by third-party companies and leased to users on a usage basis (also referred to as public-switched networks [PSN]).

        (a) Access is typically through dial-up circuits.

        (b) Example: Applications using the Internet.

        (c) Advantages and disadvantage: In general, the opposite of those for private networks, but certainly a significant disadvantage is that they are less secure.

          1] Improvements in Internet communications will decrease the disadvantages and will lead to a dramatic increase in the use of public networks (e.g., rapid increases in the use of Internet-based electronic commerce).

      (3) **Cloud computing/cloud services**—The use and access of multiple server-based computational resources via a digital network (WAN, Internet connection using the World Wide Web, etc.). A user accesses the server resources using a computer, netbook, tablet computer, smart phone, or other device. With cloud computing, applications are provided and managed by the cloud server and data is stored remotely in the cloud configuration. Users do not download and install applications on their own device or computer; all processing and storage is maintained by the cloud server. Cloud services may be offered by a cloud provider or by a private organization.

        (a) Risks of cloud computing

          1] Information security and privacy—users must rely on the cloud providers' data access controls.

          2] Continuity of services—user problems may occur if the cloud provider has disruptions in service.

          3] Migration—users may have difficulty in changing cloud providers because there are no data standards.

    d. **Classified by use of Internet**
    General: The following all use the Internet. They have in common that data communications are ordinarily through **Hypertext Markup Language (HTML)** and/or **Extensible Markup Language (XML)**—languages

used to create and format documents, link documents to other Web pages, and communicate between Web browsers. XML is increasingly replacing HTML in Internet applications due to its superior ability to tag (i.e., label) and format documents that are communicated among trading partners.

Extensible Business Reporting Language (XBRL) is an XML-based language being developed specifically for the automation of business information requirements, such as the preparation, sharing, and analysis of financial reports, statements, and audit schedules. XBRL is used in filings with the SEC that are made available on EDGAR, the SEC's Electronic Data Gathering and Retrieval database.

(1) **Internet**—An international collection of networks made up of independently owned computers that operate as a large computing network. Internetwork communication requires the use of a common set of rules, or protocols (TCP), and a shared routing system (IP).

    (a) Primary applications of the Internet include

        1] E-mail
        2] News dissemination
        3] Remote log-in of computers
        4] File transfer among computers
        5] Electronic commerce
        6] Videoconferencing
        7] Groupware systems

    (b) The internet has facilitated the advent of social media which can have a significant effect on consumer behavior. As a result, most businesses attempt to monitor and influence their reputations in the social media space.

    (c) Terminology

        1] **Hypertext Transfer Protocol (HTTP)**—The primary Internet protocol for data communication on the World Wide Web.
        2] **Uniform Resource Locator (URL)**—A standard for finding a document by typing in an address (e.g., www.azdiamondbacks.com). URLs work in much the same way as addresses on mail processed by the postal department.
        3] **World Wide Web (the web or WWW)**—A framework for accessing linked resources (e.g., documents, pictures, music files, videos, etc.) spread out over the millions of machines all over the Internet.
        4] **Web browser**—Client software (e.g., Internet explorer, Firefox, Chrome, Mosaic, etc.) that provides the user with the ability to locate and display web resources.
        5] **Web servers**—The software that "serves," (i.e., makes available) web resources to software clients. web servers (e.g., Apache and Internet Information Server [IIS]) typically run on "server" hardware. However, many computing devices today support their own web server software.
        6] **Firewall**—A method for protecting an organization's computers and computer information from outsiders. A firewall consists of security algorithms and router communications protocols that prevent outsiders from tapping into corporate database and e-mail systems.
        7] **Router**—A communications interface device that connects two networks and determines the best way for data packets to move forward to their destinations.
        8] **Bridge**—A device that divides a LAN into two segments, selectively forwarding traffic across the network boundary it defines; similar to a switch.
        9] **Switch**—A device that channels incoming data from any of multiple input ports to the specific output port that will take the data toward its intended destination.
        10] **Gateway**—A combination of hardware and software that links to different types of networks. For examples, gateways between e-mail systems allow users of differing e-mail systems to exchange messages.
        11] **Proxy server**—A server that saves and serves copies of web pages to those who request them (e.g., potential customers). When a web page is requested, the proxy server is able to access that page either through its cache (reserve of web pages already sent or loaded) or by obtaining it through the original server. A proxy server can both increase efficiency of Internet operations and help assure data security.
        12] **Web 2.0**—2nd generation of the web. Refers to era of web-based collaboration and community-generated content via web-based software tools such as

a] **Blog**—An asynchronous discussion, or web log, led by a moderator that typically focuses on a single topic. Similar to an electronic bulletin board. Blogs are an efficient way to share information, views, and opinions.

b] **Wiki**—An information-gathering and knowledge-sharing website that is developed collaboratively by a community or group, all of whom can freely add, modify, or delete content.

c] **Twitter**—A micro-variation of a blog. Restricts input (tweets) to 140 characters. Commonly used to "follow" friends and celebrities. Increasingly companies are using Twitter to inform followers.

d] **RSS (Really Simple Syndication)/ATOM Feeds**—An XML application that facilitates the sharing and syndication of website content by subscription. RSS feeds are automatically checked by RSS-enabled client software (including most browsers and RSS readers) for new website content on a regular basis.

13] **TCP/IP (Transmission Control Protocol/Internet Protocol)**—The basic communication language or protocol of the Internet. It has two layers. The higher layer assembles messages or files into smaller packets that are transmitted over the Internet. The lower layer assigns IP addresses and insures that messages are delivered to the appropriate computer.

14] **IP address**—The number that identifies a machine as unique on the Internet.

15] **ISP (Internet Service Provider)**—An entity that provides access to the Internet.

(d) The nature of the Internet has resulted in the spread of a series of malicious programs (often through email) that may adversely affect computer operations, including

1] **Virus**—A program (or piece of code) that requests the computer operating system to perform certain activities not authorized by the computer user. Viruses can be easily transmitted through use of files that contain macros that are sent as attachment to e-mail messages.

a] **Macro**—A stored set of instructions and functions that are organized to perform a repetitive task and can be easily activated, often by a simple keystroke combination. Most macros serve valid purposes, but those associated with viruses cause problems.

b] Unexpected changes in, or losses of, data may be an indication of the existence of a virus on one's computer.

c] E-mail attachments and public domain software (generally downloadable from the Internet at no cost to users) are notorious sources of viruses.

2] **Trojan horse**—A malicious, security-breaking program that is disguised as something benign, such as a game, but actually is intended to cause IT damage.

3] **Worm**—A program that propagates itself over a network, reproducing itself as it goes.

4] **Antivirus software**—Is used to attempt to avoid the above types of problems. But the rapid development of new forms of viruses, Trojan horses, and worms results in a situation in which antivirus software developers are always behind the developers.

5] **Botnet**—A network of computers that are controlled by computer code, called a "bot," that is designed to perform a repetitive task such as sending spam, spreading a virus, or creating a distributed denial of service attack.

(2) **Intranet**—A local network, usually limited to an organization, that uses internet-based technology to communicate within the organization.

(3) **Extranet**—Similar to an intranet, but includes an organization's external customers and/or suppliers in the network.

e. **Database client-server architecture**
General: When considering networks, it is helpful to consider their architecture (design). Bear in mind that the architecture must divide the following responsibilities (1) input, (2) processing, and (3) storage. In general, the client-server model may be viewed as one in which communications ordinarily take the form of a request message from the client to the server asking for some service to be performed. A "client" may be viewed as the computer or **workstation** of an individual user. The server is a high-capacity computer that contains the network software and may provide a variety of services ranging from simply "serving" files to a client to performing analyses.

(1) **Overall client-server systems**—A networked computing model (usually a LAN) in which database software on a server performs database commands sent to it from client computers

Illustration of Client/Server Architecture

(2) **Subtypes of client/server architectures**

(a) **File servers**—The file server manages file operations and is shared by each of the client PCs (ordinarily attached to a LAN). The three responsibilities (input/output, processing, and storage) are divided in a manner in which most input/output, and processing occurs on client computers rather than on the server. The file server acts simply as a shared data storage device, with all data manipulations performed by client PCs.

(b) **Database servers**—Similar to file servers, but the server here contains the database management system and thus performs more of the processing.

NOTE: The above two architectures are referred to as "two-tier" architecture—client tier and server database tier.

(c) **Three-tier architectures**—A client/server configuration that includes three tiers. The change from the above systems is that this architecture includes another server layer in addition to the two tiers discussed above. For example, application programs (e.g., a transaction processing monitor that controls the input of transactions to the database) may reside on the additional server rather than on the individual clients. This system of adding additional servers may generalize to additional tiers and thus become **n-tier** architecture. Examples of other servers that may be added are as follows:

1] **Print server**—Make shared printers available to various clients.
2] **Communications server**—May serve a variety of tasks, such as acting as a gateway (i.e., means of entrance) to the internet or to the corporate intranet.
3] **Fax server**—Allow clients on the network to share the hardware for incoming and outgoing fax transmissions.
4] **Web server**—Stores and serves web pages on request.

(3) **Distributed systems**—These systems connect all company locations to form a distributed network in which each location has its own input/output, processing, and storage capabilities. These local computers also pass data among themselves and possibly to a server (often referred to as a "host" in this context) for further processing. An illustration of this type of system is presented in the database section of this outline.

2. **Local Area Networks (LANs)**—Privately owned networks within a single building or campus of up to a few miles in size.

a. **Software**

(1) Software allows devices to function cooperatively and share network resources such as printers and disk storage space.

(2)　Common services

    (a)　Network server
    (b)　File server
    (c)　Print server
    (d)　Communications server

b.　**Hardware components**

(1)　**Workstations**—Ordinarily microcomputers.
(2)　**Peripherals**—For example, printers, network attached storage (NAS) devices, optical scanners, fax board.
(3)　**Transmission media**—Physical path that connect components of LAN, ordinarily twisted-pair wire, coaxial cable, or optical fiber. LANs that are connected wirelessly are called WLANs or WiFi networks.
(4)　**Network interface cards**—Connect workstation and transmission media.

c.　**Control implications**

(1)　General controls are often weak (e.g., controls over development and modification of programs, access and computer operations).
(2)　Controls often rely upon end users, who may not be control conscious.
(3)　Often users may not be provided adequate resources for problem resolution, troubleshooting and recovery support.
(4)　Controlling access and gaining accountability through logging of transactions enforces a segregation of duties.
(5)　Good management controls are essential—for example, access codes, passwords.
(6)　LAN software ordinarily does not provide security features available in larger scale environments.

NOTE: Tests of controls may address whether controls related to the above are effective.

d.　LANs generally make possible the computer audit techniques that may be performed either by internal auditors or external auditors.

3.　**Microcomputers and Portable Computing Devices**

a.　The proliferation of microcomputers (e.g., personal computers [PCs], laptop computers) has had a profound effect on information systems. A small-business client will probably use a PC to run a commercially purchased general ledger package (off-the-shelf software). Segregation of duties becomes especially difficult in such an environment because one individual may perform all recordkeeping (processing) as well as maintain other nonrecordkeeping responsibilities.

b.　A larger client may use a network of PCs that may or may not be linked to a large corporate mainframe computer. In all systems, management policies should be in place regarding the development and modification of programs and data files.

c.　Regardless of the system, the control objectives remain the same. When small computers are involved, the following points need to be considered:

(1)　**Security**—Security over small computers, while still important, may not be as critical as security over the data and any in-house developed software. Most companies can easily replace the hardware, but may suffer a severe setback if the data and/or in-house developed software is lost. Access to the software installation files should be controlled and backup copies should be made. Access to the hard drive must be restricted since anyone turning on the power switch can read the data stored on those files. Also, a control problem may exist because the computer operator often understands the system and also has access to the input data. The management of the company may need to become more directly involved in supervision when a lack of segregation of duties exists in data processing.
(2)　**Verification of processing**—Periodically, an independent verification of the applications being processed on the small computer system should be made to prevent the system from being used for personal projects. Also, verification helps prevent errors in internally developed software from going undetected. Controls should be in operation to assure the accuracy of in-house created spreadsheets and databases.

(3) **Personnel**—Centralized authorization to purchase hardware and software should be required to ensure that appropriate purchasing decisions are made, including decisions that minimize software and hardware compatibility difficulties. Software piracy and viruses may be controlled by prohibiting the loading of unauthorized software and data on company-owned computers.

    (a) Software is copyrighted, and violation of copyright laws may result in litigation against the company.

    (b) A company may control possible software piracy (the use of unlicensed software) by employees with procedures such as:

        1] Establishing a corporate software policy
        2] Maintaining a log of all software purchase
        3] Auditing individual computers to identify installed software

    (c) Portable computing devices—Portable computing devices (e.g., laptop computers, tablets, smart phones, etc.) often contain sensitive information that must be secured. Accordingly, access to the devices should be secured with passwords and/or biometrics. Disk drives should be encrypted and particularly sensitive data should not be allowed to be downloaded on portable devices.

4. **End-User Computing (EUC)**—The end user is responsible for the development and execution of the computer application that generates the information used by that same end user.

  a. User substantially eliminates many of the services offered by an MIS department.

  b. Risks include

    (1) End-user applications are not always adequately tested before implemented.
    (2) More client personnel need to understand control concepts.
    (3) Management often does not review the results of applications appropriately.
    (4) Old or existing applications may not be updated for current applicability and accuracy.

  c. Overall physical access controls become more difficult when companies leave a controlled MIS environment and become more dependent upon individual users for controls.

  d. Control implications

    (1) Require applications to be adequately tested before they are implemented
    (2) Require adequate documentation
    (3) Physical access controls, including

        (a) Clamps or chains to prevent removal of hard disks or internal boards
        (b) Diskless workstations that require download of files
        (c) Regular backup
        (d) Security software to limit access to those who know user ID and password
        (e) Control over access from outside
        (f) Commitment to security matters written into job descriptions, employee contracts, and personnel evaluation procedures

    (4) Control access to appropriate users

        (a) Passwords and user IDs
        (b) Menus for EUC access to database
        (c) Protect system by restricting user ability to load data
        (d) When end user uploads data, require appropriate validation, authorization, and reporting control
        (e) Independent review of transactions
        (f) Record access to company databases by EUC applications.

    (5) Control use of incorrect versions of data files.

        (a) Use control totals for batch processing of uploaded data.

    (6) Require backup of files.
    (7) Provide applications controls (e.g., edit checks, range tests, reasonableness checks).
    (8) Support programmed or user reconciliations to provide assurance that processing is correct.

NOTE: Since end-user computing relies upon microcomputers, the controls here required for microcomputers and EUC are similar. Also, tests of controls may address whether controls related to the above are effective.

5. **Electronic Commerce**

   a. **General:** Electronic commerce involves individuals and organizations engaging in a variety of electronic transactions with computers and telecommunication networks. The networks involved may be publicly available (e.g., the Internet) or private to the individuals and organizations involved (e.g., through telephone lines privately leased by the parties involved). Wide acceptance of the Internet (more specifically, that portion of the Internet referred to as the World Wide Web, or the web) is currently leading to a great expansion in electronic commerce.

   b. Five areas of risk associated with electronic commerce IT systems (as well as to varying degrees with other IT systems) are (1) security, (2) availability, (3) processing integrity, (4) online privacy, and (5) confidentiality. See Section E.1 of this module for a discussion.

   c. Use of the web is growing rapidly as both the number and types of electronic transactions increase. However, many believe that risks such as those listed above are currently impairing its growth.

      (1) As discussed further in the Reporting Module, the AICPA and the Canadian Institute of Chartered Accountants have developed a form of assurance referred to as the "WebTrust Seal of Assurance" that tells potential customers that the firm has evaluated a website's business practices and controls to determine whether they are in conformity with WebTrust principles.

      (2) Digital certificates, also referred to as digital IDs, are a means of assuring data integrity.

         (a) A digital certificate (signature) allows an individual to digitally sign a message so the recipient knows that it actually came from that individual and was not modified in any manner.

         (b) Ordinarily the message is encrypted and the recipient decrypts it and is able to read the contents.

      (3) **Encryption**—The conversion of data into a form called a cipher text, that cannot be easily understood by unauthorized people. **Decryption** is the process of converting encrypted data back into its original form so it can be understood. The conversion is performed using an algorithm and key which only the users control.

         (a) **Algorithm**—A detailed sequence of actions to perform to accomplish some task (in this case to encrypt and/or decode data).

         (b) **Key**—In the content of encryption, a value that must be fed into the algorithm used to decode an encrypted message in order to reproduce the original plain text.

         (c) **Private key system**—An encryption system in which both the sender and receiver have access to the electronic key, but do not allow others access. The primary disadvantage is that both parties must have the key.

         (d) Encryption is important in a variety of contexts, including any time two or more computers are used to communicate with one another, and even to keep private information on one computer.

         (e) The machine instructions necessary to encrypt and decrypt data constitute **system overhead;** that is, they slow down the rate of processing.

      (4) To assure continuity in the event of a natural disaster, firms should establish off-site mirrored Web servers.

   d. **Electronic funds transfer (EFT)**—Making cash payments between two or more organizations or individuals electronically rather than by using checks (or cash).

      (1) Banks first became heavily involved with EFT; it is now a major part of most types of electronic commerce.

      (2) EFT systems are vulnerable to the risk of unauthorized access to proprietary data and to the risk of fraudulent fund transfers; controls include

         (a) Control of physical access to network facilities.

         (b) Electronic identification should be required for all network terminals authorized to use EFT.

         (c) Access should be controlled through passwords.

         (d) Encryption should be used to secure stored data and data being transmitted. See Section C.5.c.(3) for more information on encryption.

   e. **Electronic data interchange (EDI)**—The electronic exchange of business transactions, in a standard format, from one entity's computer to another entity's computer through an electronic communications network.

      (1) Traditionally, the definition of electronic commerce has focused on EDI. Currently, web-based commerce is replacing a portion of these EDI systems.

      (2) Risks related to EDI

(a) EDI is commonly used for sales and purchasing, and related accounts. The speed at which transactions occur often reduces amounts receivable (payables) due to electronic processing of receipts (payments). Another effect is to make preventive controls particularly desirable, since detective controls may be too late.

(b) In these systems, documents such as purchase orders, invoices, shipping forms, bills of lading, and checks are replaced by electronic transactions.

    1] For example, in electronic funds transfer systems, a form of EDI, electronic transactions replace checks as a means of payment. As discussed below, EDI is often conducted on private networks.

    2] To determine that transactions are properly processed, effective audit trails for both internal auditors and external auditors include activity logs, including processed and failed transactions, network and sender/recipient acknowledgment of receipt of transactions, and proper time sequence of processing.

    3] In some EDI applications, portions of the documentation of transactions are retained for only a short period of time; this may require auditors to pay particular attention to controls over the transactions and to test controls on a timely basis when records remain available.

(3) Methods of communication between trading partners

    (a) **Point-to-point**—A direct computer-to-computer private network link

        1] Automakers and governments have traditionally used this method.

        2] Advantages

            a] No reliance on third parties for computer processing.

            b] Organization controls who has access to the network.

            c] Organization can enforce proprietary (its own) software standard in dealings with all trading partners.

            d] Timeliness of delivery may be improved since no third party is involved.

        3] Disadvantages

            a] Must establish connection with each trading partner

            b] High initial cost

            c] Computer scheduling issues

            d] Need for common protocols between partners

            e] Need for hardware and software compatibility

    (b) **Value-added network (VAN)**

        1] A VAN is a privately owned network that routes the EDI transactions between trading partners and in many cases provides translation, storage, and other processing. It is designed and maintained by an independent company that offers specialized support to improve the transmission effectiveness of a network. It alleviates problems related to interorganizational communication that results from the use of differing hardware and software.

        2] A VAN receives data from the sender, determines the intended recipient, and places data in the recipient's electronic mailbox.

        3] Advantages

            a] Reduces communication and data protocol problems since VANs can deal with differing protocols (eliminating need for trading partners to agree on them).

            b] Partners do not have to establish the numerous point-to-point connections.

            c] Reduces scheduling problems since receiver can request delivery of transactions when it wishes.

            d] In some cases, VAN translates application to a standard format the partner does not have to reformat.

            e] VAN can provide increased security.

        4] Disadvantages

            a] Cost of VAN

            b] Dependence upon VAN's systems and controls

            c] Possible loss of data confidentiality

      (c) **Public networks**—For example, the Internet-based commerce solutions described earlier

         1] Advantages

           a] Avoids cost of proprietary lines
           b] Avoids cost of VAN
           c] Directly communicates transactions to trading partners
           d] Software is being developed which allows communication between differing systems.

         2] Disadvantages

           a] Possible loss of data confidentiality on the Internet
           b] Computer or transmission disruption
           c] Hackers and viruses
           d] Attempted electronic frauds

      (d) **Proprietary networks**—In some circumstances (e.g., health care, banking) organizations have developed their own network for their own transactions. These systems are costly to develop and operate (because of proprietary lines), although they are often extremely reliable.

   (4) Controls required for other network systems are required for EDI systems. In addition, disappearance of "paper transactions" and the direct interrelationship with another organization's computer makes various authentication and encryption controls particularly important for these transactions.

      (a) **Authentication**—Controls must exist over the origin, proper submission, and proper delivery of EDI communications. Receiver of the message must have proof of the origin of the message, as well as its proper submission and delivery.

      (b) **Packets**—A block of data that is transmitted from one computer to another. It contains data and authentication information.

      (c) **Encryption**—The conversion of plain text data into cipher text data used by an algorithm and key which only the users control. See Section C.5.c.(3) for more information on encryption.

   (5) The AICPA Auditing Procedures Study, *Audit Implications of EDI*, lists the following benefits and exposures of EDI:

      (a) Benefits

         1] Quick response and access to information
         2] Cost efficiency
         3] Reduced paperwork
         4] Accuracy and reduced errors and error-correction costs
         5] Better communications and customer service
         6] Necessary to remain competitive

      (b) Exposures

         1] Total dependence upon computer system for operation
         2] Possible loss of confidentiality of sensitive information
         3] Increased opportunity for unauthorized transactions and fraud
         4] Concentration of control among a few people involved in EDI
         5] Reliance on third parties (trading partners, VAN)
         6] Data processing, application and communications errors
         7] Potential legal liability due to errors
         8] Potential loss of audit trails and information needed by management due to limited retention policies
         9] Reliance on trading partner's system

6. **Telecommunications**—The electronic transmission of information by radio, wire, fiber optic, coaxial cable, microwave, laser, or other electromagnetic system.

  a. Transmitted information—Voice, data, video, fax, other
  b. Hardware involved:

    (1) Computers for communications control and switching
    (2) Transmission facilities such as copper wire, fiber optic cables, microwave stations and communications satellites
    (3) Modems may be used to provide compatibility of format, speed, etc.

c. Software controls and monitors the hardware, formats information, adds appropriate control information, performs switching operations, provides security, and supports the management of communications.

d. While telecommunications is **not** an end in itself, it enables technologies such as the following:

   (1) Electronic data interchange
   (2) Electronic funds transfer
   (3) Point of sale systems
   (4) Commercial databases
   (5) Airline reservation systems

e. Controls needed

   (1) System integrity at remote sites
   (2) Data entry
   (3) Central computer security
   (4) Dial-in security
   (5) Transmission accuracy and completeness
   (6) Physical security over telecommunications facilities

> **NOTE:** Tests of controls may address whether controls related to the above are effective.

7. **Computer Service Organizations (Bureaus, Centers)**—Computer service organizations record and process data for companies. These organizations allow companies (users) to do away with part of the data-processing function. While many computer service organizations simply record and process relatively routine transactions for a client (e.g., prepare payroll journals and payroll checks), a VAN is a service organization that takes a broader role of providing network, storing, and forwarding (mailbox) services for the companies involved in an EDI system.

> **NOW REVIEW MULTIPLE-CHOICE QUESTIONS 53 THROUGH 95**

D. Control Objectives for Information and Related Technology (COBIT)

1. The Information Systems Audit and Control Association (ISACA) has developed a framework to assist enterprises in achieving their objectives for governance and management of enterprise IT. The current version of the framework (COBIT 5) is business-oriented in that it provides a systematic way of integrating IT with business strategy and governance. COBIT 5 takes a stakeholder approach to addressing information needs and incorporates the following five principles:

   a. Meeting stakeholder needs.
   b. Covering the enterprise end-to-end.
   c. Applying a single integrated framework.
   d. Enabling a holistic approach.
   e. Separating governance from management.

   The factors that individually and collectively influence whether something will work in an organization are referred to as the COBIT 5 enablers. They include:

   a. Processes—an organized set of practices and activities to achieve certain objectives.
   b. Organizational structures—the key decision-making entities in an organization.
   c. Culture, ethics, and behavior of individuals and the organization.
   d. Principles, policies and frameworks—the vehicle to translate the desired behavior into guidance for day-to-day management.
   e. Information produced and used by the enterprise.
   f. Services, infrastructure and applications—the infrastructure, technology, and applications that provide the enterprise with information technology processing and servicers.
   g. People, skills, and competencies required for successful completion of all activities and for making correct decisions.

E. IT Risks and Internal Control

> **NOTE:** We have already discussed the effect of a computer on internal control of several systems under C. (microcomputers, end-user computing, and electronic commerce). In this section we discuss the effect in general terms as presented in the AICPA Audit Guide, *Consideration of Internal Control in a Financial Statement Audit*. This section presents information on controls a company may have. We begin by discussing overall principles of a reliable system and overall risks. We then consider the effect of a computer on internal control using the five components of internal control—control environment, risk assessment, information and communication, monitoring, and control activities.

1. **Principles of a Reliable System and Examples of Overall Risks**

   a. A reliable system is one that is capable of operating without material error, fault, or failure during a specified period in a specified environment.

   b. One framework for analyzing a reliable system is presented by the AICPA's Trust Services. Trust Services, which provide assurance on information systems, use a framework with five principles of a reliable system—(1) security, (2) availability, (3) processing integrity, (4) online privacy, and (5) confidentiality. Accordingly, when a principle is not met a risk exists.

Principle	Examples of Risks
1. *Security.* The system is protected against unauthorized access (both physical and logical)	Physical access—A lack of physical security allows damage or other loss (e.g., theft) to the system • Weather • Acts of war • Disgruntled employees or others Logical access—A lack of security over access to the system allows • Malicious (or accidental) alteration of, or damage to, files and/or the system • Computer-based fraud • Unauthorized access to confidential data
2. *Availability.* The system is available for operation and use as committed or agreed. The system is available for operation and use in conformity with the entity's availability policies.	System failure results in • Interruption of business operations • Loss of data
3. *Processing Integrity.* System processing is complete, accurate, timely, and authorized.	Invalid, incomplete, or inaccurate • Input data • Data processing • Updating of master files • Creation of output
4. *Online Privacy.* Personal information obtained as a result of e-commerce is collected, used, disclosed, and retained as committed or agreed.	Disclosure of customer information (or that of others) such as • Social security numbers • Credit card numbers • Credit rating • Medical conditions
5. *Confidentiality.* Information designated as confidential is protected as committed or agreed.	Examples of confidential data that might be disclosed: • Transaction details • Engineering details of products • Business plans • Banking information • Legal documents • Inventory or other account information • Customer lists • Confidential details of operations

> **NOTE:** Make certain that you are familiar not only with the above principles, but are familiar with the nature of the various risks relating to computer processing.

2. Control Environment

a. Recall the principles of the control environment:

    (1) Commitment to integrity and ethical values
    (2) Board demonstrates independence and exercises oversight
    (3) Appropriate structures, reporting lines, and authorities and responsibilities
    (4) Commitment to attract, develop, and retain competent personnel
    (5) Hold individuals accountable for internal control responsibilities

b. Although all five principles may be affected by computer processing, the organizational structure is modified to include an information systems department (EDP department). It is helpful to keep in mind that the information systems department is involved with two distinct functions—systems development and data processing.

c. Steps in the *system development lifecycle:*

    (1) Software concept—identify the need for the new system.
    (2) Requirements analysis—determine the needs of the users.
    (3) Architectural design—determining the hardware, software, people, etc. needed.
    (4) Coding and debugging—acquiring and testing the software.
    (5) System testing—testing and evaluating the functionality of the system.

d. Organizational structure

    (1) **Segregation controls**

        (a) Segregate functions between information systems department and user departments.

            1] User departments are the other departments of the company that utilize the data prepared by the information systems department.

        (b) Do not allow the information systems department to initiate or authorize transactions.

        (c) At a minimum, segregate programming, data entry, operations, and the library function within the information systems department.

        (d) A more complete segregation of key functions within the information systems department may be possible; one way to separate key functions is as follows:

            1] **Systems analysis**—The systems analyst analyzes the present user environment and requirements and may (1) recommend specific changes, (2) recommend the purchase of a new system, or (3) design a new information system. The analyst is in constant contact with user departments and programming staff to ensure the users' actual and ongoing needs are being met. A system flowchart is a tool used by the analyst to define the systems requirements.

2] **Systems programming**—The systems programmer is responsible for implementing, modifying, and debugging the software necessary for making the hardware work (such as the operating system, telecommunications monitor, and the database management system). For some companies the term "software engineer" is viewed as similar or identical to that of systems programmer. For others, the software engineer is involved with the creation of designs used by programmers.

3] **Applications programming**—The applications programmer is responsible for writing, testing, and debugging the application programs from the specifications (whether general or specific) provided by the systems analyst. A program flowchart is one tool used by the applications programmer to define the program logic.

4] **Database administration**—In a database environment, a database administrator (DBA) is responsible for maintaining the database and restricting access to the database to authorized personnel.

5] **Data preparation**—Data may be prepared by user departments and input by key to storage devices.

6] **Operations**—The operator is responsible for the daily computer operations of both the hardware and the software. The operator supervises operations on the operator's console, accepts any required input, and distributes any generated output. The operator should have adequate documentation available to run the program (a run manual), but should not have detailed program information.

    a] Help desks are usually a responsibility of operations because of the operational nature of their functions (for example, assisting users with systems problems and obtaining technical support/vendor assistance).

7] **Data library**—The librarian is responsible for custody of the removable media (i.e., magnetic tapes or disks) and for the maintenance of program and system documentation. In many systems, much of the library function is maintained and performed electronically by the computer.

8] **Data control**—The control group acts as liaison between users and the processing center. This group records input data in a control log, follows the progress of processing, distributes output, and ensures compliance with control totals.

    Ideally, in a large system, all of the above key functions should be segregated; in a small computer environment, many of the key functions are concentrated in a small number of employees. For purposes of the CPA exam remember that, at a minimum, an attempt should be made to segregate *programming, operations,* and the *library* functions. Large organizations typically have a chief information officer (CIO) that oversees all information technology and activities.

(e) Electronic commerce has resulted in a number of new web-related positions, including

1] **Web administrator (web manager)**—Responsible for overseeing the development, planning, and the implementation of a website. Ordinarily a managerial position.

2] **Web master**—Responsible for providing expertise and leadership in the development of a website, including the design, analysis, security, maintenance, content development, and updates.

3] **Web designer**—Responsible for creating the visual content of the website.

4] **Web coordinator**—Responsible for the daily operations of the website.

5] **Internet developer**—Responsible for writing programs for commercial use. Similar to a software engineer or systems programmer.

6] **Intranet/Extranet developer**—Responsible for writing programs based on the needs of the company.

3. **Risk Assessment**

  a. Changes in computerized information systems and in operations may increase the risk of improper financial reporting.

4. **Information and Communication**

  a. The computerized accounting system is affected by whether the company uses small computers and/or a complex mainframe system.

    (1) For small computer systems, purchased commercial "off-the-shelf" software may be used.

      (a) Controls within the software may be well known.

      (b) Analysis of "exception reports" generated during processing is important to determine that exceptions are properly handled.

(2) For complex mainframe systems a significant portion of the software is ordinarily developed within the company by information systems personnel.

    (a) Controls within the software are unknown to the auditor prior to testing.

    (b) As with small computer systems, analysis of exception reports is important, but controls over the generation of such reports must ordinarily be tested to a greater extent.

5. Monitoring

a. Proper monitoring of a computerized system will require adequate computer skills to evaluate the propriety of processing of computerized applications.

b. A common method of monitoring for inappropriate access is review of system-access log.

c. IT can also facilitate monitoring.

    (1) IT can constantly evaluate data and transactions based on established criteria and highlight items that appear to be inconsistent or unusual.

    (2) IT can capture samples of items for audit by internal auditors.

6. Control Activities—Overall

a. Control activities in which a computer is involved may be divided into the following categories:

    (1) Computer **general** control activities.

    (2) Computer **application** control activities.
       Programmed application control activities.
       Manual follow-up of computer exception reports.

    (3) **User** control activities to test the completeness and accuracy of computer processed controls.

The following illustration, adapted from the AICPA Audit Guide, *Consideration of Internal Control in a Financial Statement Audit*, summarizes the relationships among the controls.

COMPUTER CONTROL ACTIVITIES

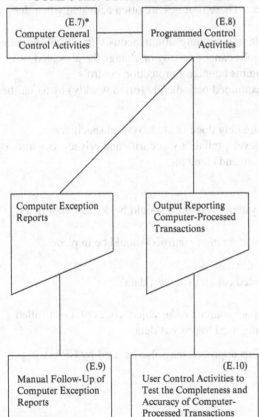

EXPLANATION OF COMPUTER CONTROL ACTIVITIES

Computer General Control Activities control program development, program changes, computer operations, and access to programs and data. These control activities increase the assurance that programmed control activities operate effectively during the period.

Computer Application Control Activities

Programmed Control Activities relate to specific computer applications and are embedded in the computer program used in the financial reporting system. The concepts presented here related to programmed control activities may also apply to other activities within the computer accounting system.

Manual Follow-Up of Computer Exception Reports involves employee follow-up of items listed on computer exception reports. The effectiveness of application control activities that involve manual follow-up of computer reports depends on the effectiveness of both the programmed control activities that produce the exception report and the manual follow-up activities.

User Control Activities to Test the Completeness and Accuracy of Computer Processed Transactions represent manual checks of computer output against source document or other input, and thus provide assurance that programmed aspects of the accounting system and control activities have operated effectively.

---

* Section below in which control discussion is presented.

7. **Computer General Control Activities**

> **NOTE:** General control activities affect all computer applications. There are four types of general controls— (a) developing new programs and systems, (b) changing existing programs and systems, (c) controlling access to programs and data, and (d) controlling computer operations.

a. **Developing new programs and systems**

(1) **Segregation controls**

(a) User departments participate in systems design.

(b) Both users and information systems personnel test new systems.

(c) Management, users, and information systems personnel approve new systems before they are placed into operation.

(d) All master and transaction file conversions should be controlled to prevent unauthorized changes and to verify the accuracy of the results.

(e) Programs and systems should be properly documented (see Section F).

(2) **Computer hardware is extremely reliable.** This is primarily due to the chip technology. However, it is also due to the controls built into the hardware and systems software to provide for a self-diagnostic mechanism to detect and prevent equipment failures. The following are examples of such controls:

(a) **Parity check**—A special bit is added to each character that can detect if the hardware loses a bit during the internal movement of a character.

(b) **Echo check**—Primarily used in telecommunications transmissions. During the sending and receiving of characters, the receiving hardware repeats back to the sending hardware what it received and the sending hardware automatically resends any characters that were received incorrectly.

(c) **Diagnostic routines**—Hardware or software supplied by the manufacturer to check the internal operations and devices within the computer system. These routines are often activated when the system is booted up.

(d) **Boundary protection**—Most CPUs have multiple jobs running simultaneously (multiprogramming environment). To ensure that these simultaneous jobs cannot destroy or change the allocated memory of another job, the systems software contains boundary protection controls.

(e) **Periodic maintenance**—The system should be examined periodically (often weekly) by a qualified service technician.

(3) **Documentation.** Systems and programs should be adequately documented. System specification documents should detail such matters as performance levels, reliability, security and privacy, constraints and limitations, functional capabilities, and data structure and elements.

b. **Changing existing programs and systems**

(1) Suggestions for changes (from users and information system personnel) should be documented in a change request log.

(2) Proper *change control* procedures (also referred to as *modification controls*) should be in place.

(a) The information systems manager should review all changes.

(b) The modified program should be appropriately tested (often using test data).

(c) Details of all changes should be documented.

(d) A code comparison program may be used to compare source and/or object codes of a controlled copy of a program with the program currently being used to process data.

1] This will identify any unauthorized changes (this approach may also be used by CPAs).

c. **Controlling access to programs and data**

(1) **Segregation controls**

(a) Access to program documentation should be limited to those persons who require it in the performance of their duties.

(b) Access to data files and programs should be limited to those individuals authorized to process data.

(c) Access to computer hardware should be limited to authorized individuals such as computer operators and their supervisors.

(2) **Physical access to computer facility**

(a) **Limited physical access**—The physical facility that houses the computer equipment, files, and documentation should have controls to limit access only to authorized individuals. Possible controls include using a guard, automated key cards, and manual key locks, as well as the new access devices that permit access through fingerprints or palm prints.

(b) **Visitor entry logs**—Used to document those who have had access to the area.

(3) **Hardware and software access controls**

(a) **Access control software** (user identification)—The most used control is a combination of a unique *identification code* and a confidential *password*.

1] Passwords should be made up of a combination of alphabetic, numeric, and symbol elements.
2] Passwords should be changed periodically.
3] Passwords should be disabled promptly when an employee leaves the company.

(b) **Call back**—Call back is a specialized form of user identification in which the user dials the system, identifies him/herself, and is disconnected from the system. Then either (1) an individual manually finds the authorized telephone number or (2) the system automatically finds the authorized telephone number of the individual and calls back.

(c) **Encryption**—Data is encoded when stored in computer files and/or before transmission to or from remote locations (e.g., through use of modems and telephone lines). This coding protects data, since to use the data unauthorized users must not only obtain access, but must also translate the coded form of the data. Encryption performed by physically secure hardware (often special-purpose computers) is ordinarily more secure, but more costly than that performed by software. See Section C.5.c.(3) for more information on encryption.

d. **Controlling computer operations**

(1) **Segregation controls**

(a) Operators should have access to an operations manual that contains the instructions for processing programs and solving routine operational program issues, but not with detailed program documentation.

(b) The control group should monitor the operator's activities and jobs should be scheduled.

(2) **Other controls**

(a) **Backup and recovery**—Discussed in Section D.11 in this module

(b) **Contingency processing**—Detailed contingency processing plans should be developed to prepare for system failures. The plans should detail the responsibilities of individuals, as well as the alternate processing sites that should be utilized. Backup facilities with a vendor may be used to provide contingent sites in case of an emergency. This topic is discussed further in Section D.11 of this module.

(c) **Internal and external labels**—External labels are gummed-paper labels attached to storage media which identify the file. Internal labels perform the same function through the use of machine readable identification in the first record of a file. The use of labels allows the computer operator to determine whether the correct file has been selected for processing.

8. **Computer Application Control Activities**—Programmed Control Activities

NOTE: Programmed application controls apply to a specific application rather than multiple applications. These controls operate to assure the proper input and processing of data. The input step converts human-readable data into computer-readable data. Ensuring the integrity of the data in the computer is critical during processing. The candidate should be prepared to identify the following common controls in a multiple-choice question.

a. **Input controls**

(1) **Overall controls**

    (a) Inputs should be properly authorized and approved.

    (b) The system should verify all significant data fields used to record information (editing the data).

    (c) Conversion of data into machine-readable form should be controlled and verified for accuracy.

(2) **Input validation (edit) controls**

    (a) **Preprinted form**—Information is preassigned a place and a format on the input form.

    (b) **Check digit**—An extra digit added to an identification number to detect certain types of data transmission errors. For example, a bank may add a check digit to individuals' 7-digit account numbers. The computer will calculate the correct check digit based on performing predetermined mathematical operations on the 7-digit account number and will then compare it to the check digit.

    (c) **Control, batch, or proof total**—A total of one numerical field for all the records of a batch that normally would be added, (e.g., total sales dollars).

    (d) **Hash total**—A control total where the total is meaningless for financial purposes (e.g., a mathematical sum of employee social security numbers).

    (e) **Record count**—A control total of the total records processed.

    (f) **Limit (reasonableness) test**—A test of the reasonableness of a field of data, given a predetermined upper and/or lower limit (e.g., for a field that indicates auditing exam scores, a limit check would test for scores over 100).

    (g) **Menu driven input**—As input is entered, the operator responds to a menu prompting the proper response (e.g., What score did you get on the Auditing part of the CPA Exam [75–100]?).

    (h) **Field check**—A control that limits the types of characters accepted into a specific data field (e.g., a pay rate should include only numerical data).

    (i) **Validity check**—A control that allows only "valid" transactions or data to be entered into the system (e.g., a field indicating sex of an individual where 1 = female and 2 = male—if the field is coded in any other manner it would not be accepted).

    (j) **Missing data check**—A control that searches for blanks inappropriately existing in input data (e.g., if an employee's division number were left blank an error message would result).

    (k) **Field size check**—A control of an exact number of characters to be input (e.g., if part numbers all have 6 digits, an error message would result if more or less than 6 characters were input).

    (l) **Logic check**—Ensures that illogical combinations of input are not accepted (e.g., if the Tuba City branch has no company officers, an error message would result if two fields for a specified employee indicated that the employee worked as an officer in Tuba City).

    (m) **Redundant data check**—Uses two identifiers in each transaction record (e.g., customer account number and the first five letters of customer's name) to confirm that the correct master file record is being updated.

    (n) **Closed-loop verification**—A control that allows data entry personnel to check the accuracy of input data. For example, the system might retrieve an account name of a record that is being updated, and display it on the operator's terminal. This control may be used instead of a redundant data check.

(3) **Processing controls**

Overall: When the input has been accepted by the computer, it usually is processed through multiple steps. Processing controls are essential to ensure the integrity of data. Essentially all of the controls listed for input may also be incorporated during processing. For example, processed information should include limit tests, record counts, and control totals. In addition, external labels should be used on removable media, with internal header and trailer labels used to determine that all information on a file has been read.

NOTE: Previously, the professional standards divided application controls into three categories—input, processing, and output. The current categories of application controls (programmed and manual) and user controls have replaced that breakdown. As an aid to discussing controls we distinguish between input and processing above. User control activities include the essentials of the previous "output" controls.

9. **Application Controls**—Manual Follow-Up of Computer Exception Reports

   a.   These controls involve employee (operator and/or control group) follow-up of items listed on computer exception reports. Their effectiveness depends on the effectiveness of both the programmed control activities that produce the reports and the manual follow-up activities.

10. **User Control Activities to Test the Completeness and Accuracy of Computer-Processed Controls**

   a.   These manual controls, previously referred to as *output controls,* include

   (1)   Checks of computer output against source documents, control totals, or other input to provide assurance that programmed aspects of the financial reporting system and control activities have operated effectively.

   (2)   Reviewing computer processing logs to determine that all of the correct computer jobs executed properly.

   (3)   Maintaining proper procedures and communications specifying authorized recipients of output.

   b.   These procedures are often performed by both the control group and users.

   c.   In some systems, user departments evaluate the reliability of output from the computer by extensive review and testing; in others, users merely test the overall reasonableness of the output.

11. **Disaster Recovery and Business Continuity**

   a.   A plan should allow the firm to

   (1)   Minimize the extent of disruption, damage, and loss.

   (2)   Establish an alternate (temporary) method for processing information.

   (3)   Resume normal operations as quickly as possible.

   (4)   Train and familiarize personnel to perform emergency operations.

   b.   A plan should include priorities, insurance, backup approaches, specific assignments, period testing and updating, and documentation, as described below.

   (1)   **Priorities**—Which applications are most critical?

   (2)   **Insurance to defer costs**

   (3)   **Backup approaches**

   (a)   Batch systems—The most common approach is the grandfather-father-son method. A master file (e.g., accounts receivable) is updated with the day's transaction files (e.g., files of cash receipts and credit sales). After the update, the new file master file is the son. The file from which the father was developed with the transaction files of the appropriate day is the grandfather. The grandfather and son files are stored in different locations. If the son were destroyed, for example, it could be reconstructed by rerunning the father file and the related transaction files.

   (b)   Online databases and master file systems

   1]   **Checkpoint**—Similar to grandfather-father-son, but at certain points, "checkpoints," the system makes a copy of the database and this "checkpoint" file is stored on a separate disk or tape. If a problem occurs the system is restarted at the last checkpoint and updated with subsequent transactions.

    2] **Rollback**—As a part of recovery, to undo changes made to a database to a point at which it was functioning properly

    3] **Backup facilities**

        a] **Reciprocal agreement**—An agreement between two or more organizations (with compatible computer facilities) to aid each other with their data processing needs in the event of a disaster. This is sometimes referred to as a mutual aid pact.

        b] **Hot site**—A commercial disaster recovery service that allows a business to continue computer operations in the event of computer disaster. For example, if a company's data processing center becomes inoperable, that enterprise can move all processing to a hot site that has all the equipment needed to continue operation. This is also referred to as a recovery operations center (ROC) approach.

        c] **Cold site**—Similar to a hot site, but the customer provides and installs the equipment needed to continue operations. A cold site is less expensive, but takes longer to get in full operation after a disaster. This is sometimes referred to as an "empty shell" in that the "shell" is available and ready to receive whatever hardware the temporary user needs.

        d] **Internal site**—Large organizations with multiple data processing centers sometimes rely upon their own sites for backup in the event of a disaster.

NOTE: Be aware that most approaches to control for catastrophic failures rely upon backup of the entire system in one form or another. Also, various combinations of the above approaches may be used.

        e] **Mirrored web server**—An exact copy of a website, which is the best way to back up the website.

  (4) **Specific assignments, including having individuals involved with**

    (a) Arranging for new facilities.
    (b) Computer operations.
    (c) Installing software.
    (d) Establishing data communications facilities.
    (e) Recovering vital records.
    (f) Arranging for forms and supplies.

  (5) **Periodic testing and updating of plan**
  (6) **Documentation of plan**

NOW REVIEW MULTIPLE-CHOICE QUESTIONS 96 THROUGH 139

F. Flowcharting

General: Flowcharts analytically describe some aspect of an information system. Flowcharting is a procedure to graphically show the sequential flow of data and/or operations. The data and operations portrayed include document preparation, authorization, storage, and decision making. The more common flowcharting symbols are illustrated below. Knowledge of them would help with occasional multiple-choice questions and with problems that present a detailed flowchart that must be analyzed.

1. Common Flowcharting Symbols

Symbol	Name	Description
	Document	This can be a manual form or a computer printout
	Computer Operation	Computer process which transforms input data into useful information
	Manual Operation	Manual (human) process to prepare documents, make entries, check output, etc.
	Decision	Determines which alternative path is followed (IF/THEN/ELSE Conditions)
	Input/Output	General input or output to a process. Often used to represent accounting journals and ledgers on document flowcharts
	Online Storage	Refers to direct access computer storage connected directly to the CPU. Data is available on a random access basis
	Disc Storage	Refers to data stored on a magnetic disk
	Off-Line Storage	Refers to a file or indicates the mailing of a document (i.e., invoices or statements to customers). A letter in the symbol below the line indicates the order in which the file is stored. (N—Numerical, C—Chronological, A—Alphabetical)
	Display	Visual display of data and/or output on a terminal screen
	Batch Total Tape	Manually computed total before processing (such as the number of records to be processed). This total is recomputed by the computer and compared after processing is completed.
	Magnetic Tape	Used for reading, writing, or storage on sequential storage media
	Manual Data Entry	Refers to data entered through a terminal keyboard or key-to-tape or key-to-disk device
	Annotation	Provides additional description or information connected to symbol to which it annotates by a dotted line (not a flowline)
	Flowline	Shows direction of data flow, operations, and documents
	Communication Link	Telecommunication line linking computer system to remote locations
	Start/Termination	Used to begin or end a flowchart. (Not always used or shown in flowcharts on the CPA exam.) May be used to show connections to other procedures or receipt/ sending of documents to/from outsiders
	On Page Connector	Connects parts of flowchart on the same page
	Off Page Connector	Connects parts of flowchart on separate pages

2. **Types and Definitions**

   a. **System flowchart**—A graphic representation of a data-processing application that depicts the interaction of all the computer programs for a given system, rather than the logic for an individual computer program.

   b. **Program flowchart**—A graphic representation of the logic (processing steps) of a computer program.

   c. **Internal control (audit) flowchart** or **document flowchart**—A graphic representation of the flow of documents from one department to another, showing the source flow and final disposition of the various copies of all documents. Most flowcharts on the CPA exam have been of this type.

3. **Other Documentation Charting Techniques**

   a. **Decision table**—Decision tables use a matrix format that lists sets of conditions, and the actions that result from various combinations of these conditions. See Module 3 on internal control in the Auditing and Attestation volume for an example of a decision table.

   b. **Data flow diagram (DFD)**—Presents logical flows of data and functions in a system. For example, a data flow diagram for the delivery of goods to a customer would include a symbol for the warehouse from which the goods are shipped and a symbol representing the customer. It would not emphasize details such as computer processing and paper outputs.

NOW REVIEW MULTIPLE-CHOICE QUESTIONS 140 THROUGH 147

KEY TERMS

Because the content of this module is largely terminology, a set of key terms is not provided.

Multiple-Choice Questions (1–147)

A. Information Systems within a Business

1. A software package that is used with a large set of organized data that presents the computer as an expert on a particular topic is referred to as a(n)

    a. Data mining.
    b. Expert system.
    c. Artificial intelligence.
    d. Virtual reality.

2. Computer memory which is used to store programs that must be accessed immediately by the central processing unit is

    a. Primary storage.
    b. Secondary storage.
    c. Tertiary storage.
    d. Tape storage.

3. The most common output device is a(n)

    a. Mouse.
    b. Printer.
    c. Expert system.
    d. Keyboard.

4. The part of the computer that does most of the data processing is referred to as the

    a. Analyzer.
    b. Compiler.
    c. CPU.
    d. Printer.

5. An "office suite" of software is **least** likely to include a(n)

    a. Database.
    b. Operating system.
    c. Spreadsheet.
    d. Word processing.

6. Software that performs a variety of general technical computer-controlling operations is a(n)

    a. Integrated "suite."
    b. Shareware.
    c. Database.
    d. Operating system.

7. Which of the following is **not** a part of the central processing unit?

    a. Control unit.
    b. Arithmetic unit.
    c. Logic unit.
    d. Printer unit.

8. MIPS stands for

    a. Memory in protocol standards.
    b. Millions of instructions per second.
    c. Mitigating individualistic personnel standards.
    d. Multiple input physical savings.

9. Which of the following is an example of application software that a large client is **most** likely to use?

    a. Enterprise resource planning.
    b. Operating system.
    c. Central processing unit.
    d. Value-added network.

10. Which of the following characteristics distinguishes computer processing from manual processing?

    a. Computer processing virtually eliminates the occurrence of computational error normally associated with manual processing.
    b. Errors or fraud in computer processing will be detected soon after their occurrences.
    c. The potential for systematic error is ordinarily greater in manual processing than in computerized processing.
    d. Most computer systems are designed so that transaction trails useful for audit purposes do not exist.

11. A general type of IT system that is designed to improve the productivity of daily office work is referred to as a(n)

    a. Office automation system.
    b. Transaction processing system.
    c. Decision support system.
    d. Executive information system.

12. The Systems Development Life Cycle (SDLC) is the traditional methodology for developing information systems. In which phase of the SDLC would the activity of identifying the problem(s) that need to be solved **most** likely occur?

    a. Analysis.
    b. Implementaion.
    c. Planning.
    d. Development.

13. Samco Inc. is in the process of designing a new customer relations system. In which phase of the development life-cycle would a needs assessment **most** likely be performed?

    a. Analysis.
    b. Design.
    c. Development.
    d. Testing.

14. Which of the following system implementation models has the advantage of achieving a full operational test of the new system before it is implemented?

    a. Parallel implementation.
    b. Plunge implementation.
    c. Pilot implementation.
    d. Phased implementation.

B. Characteristics of IT Systems—General

15. Which computer application is most frequently used on mainframe computers?

    a. Databases.
    b. Graphics.
    c. Spreadsheets.
    d. Word processing.

16. Which computer application is most frequently used to analyze numbers and financial information?

    a. Computer graphics programs.
    b. WAN applications.
    c. Spreadsheets.
    d. Word processing programs.

17. Analysis of data in a database using tools which look for trends or anomalies without knowledge in advance of the meaning of the data is referred to as

    a. Artificial intelligence.
    b. Data mining.
    c. Virtual reality.
    d. Transitory analysis.

18. The most common type of primary storage in a computer is referred to as

    a. CMAN.
    b. RAM.
    c. ROM.
    d. Flash memory.

19. A set of step-by-step procedures used to accomplish a task is a(n)

    a. Algorithm.
    b. Compilation master.
    c. Linux.
    d. Transistor.

20. Which of the following compiles a complete translation of a program in a high-level computer language before the program is run for the first time?

    a. Visual Basic.
    b. Java.
    c. Algorithm.
    d. Compiler.

21. GUI is the abbreviation for

    a. Grandfather, Uncle, Individual.
    b. Graphical User Interface.
    c. Graphics Utilization Institutes.
    d. Grand Union Internet.

22. Unix is a(n)

    a. Operating system.
    b. Singular disk drive.
    c. Central processing unit.
    d. Logic unit.

23. In a spreadsheet, each specific cell may be identified by a specific

    a. Address.
    b. Column.
    c. Row.
    d. Diagonal.

24. In a spreadsheet, which of the following is correct concerning rows and columns?

	Rows	Columns
a.	Numbered	Numbered
b.	Numbered	Lettered
c.	Lettered	Numbered
d.	Lettered	Lettered

25. Which of the following is **least** likely to be considered an advantage of a database?

    a. Easy to store large quantities of information.
    b. Easy to retrieve information quickly.
    c. Easy to organize and reorganize information.
    d. Easy to distribute information to every possible user.

26. Most current computers process data using which of the following formats?

    a. Analog.
    b. Digital.
    c. Memory enhanced.
    d. Organic.

27. Which term below describes the technology that allows multiple operating systems to run simultaneously on a single computer?

    a. Client.
    b. Mainframe.
    c. Linux.
    d. Virtualization.

28. What type of secondary storage device requires no moving parts for read/write operations?

    a. Magnetic tape.
    b. Compact discs.
    c. Solid State drives.
    d. RAID.

29. Another term for cloud-based storage is

    a. RAID.
    b. Solid state storage.
    c. Analog.
    d. Storage-as-a-Service.

30. The wireless input device that is used for inventory control and similar to bar-codes technology but does **not** require line-of sight access is

    a. MICR.
    b. RFID.
    c. Touch screen.
    d. Point-of-sale recorders.

31. The 2nd generation programming language that is generally specific to a computer architecture (i.e., it is not portable) is

a. Binary.
b. Assembly language.
c. COBOL.
d. C++.

32. The online analytical processing term that represents a combination of systems that help aggregate, access, and analyze business data and assist in the business decision-making process is

a. Artificial intelligence.
b. Data mart.
c. Decision support system.
d. Business intelligence.

33. What is the hierarchy of data organization, from smallest to largest unit, for a relational database?

a. Bit, byte, field, record, table, database.
b. Byte, bit, record, field, table, database.
c. Byte, bit, table, field, record, database.
d. Database, table, field, record, byte, bit.

34. A current day instruction to a computer such as "*Extract all Customers where 'Name' is Smith*" would **most** likely relate to a

a. First generation programming language.
b. Fourth generation programming language.
c. Seventh generation programming language.
d. Ninth generation programming language.

35. Several language interfaces exist in a database management system. These typically include a data definition language (DDL), a data control language (DCL), a data manipulation language (DML), and a database query language (DQL). What language interface would a database administrator use to establish the structure of database tables?

a. DDL.
b. DCL.
c. DML.
d. DQL.

36. Users making database queries often need to combine several tables to get the information they want. One approach to combining tables is known as

a. Joining.
b. Merging.
c. Projecting.
d. Pointing.

37. User acceptance testing is more important in an object-oriented development process than in a traditional environment because of the implications of the

a. Absence of traditional design documents.
b. Lack of a tracking system for changes.
c. Potential for continuous monitoring.
d. Inheritance of properties in hierarchies.

38. A company's management has expressed concern over the varied system architectures that the organization uses. Potential security and control concerns would include all of the following **except:**

a. Users may have different user ID codes and passwords to remember for the several systems that they use.
b. There are difficulties in developing uniform security standards for the various platforms.
c. Backup file storage administration is often decentralized.
d. Having data distributed across many computers throughout the organization increases the risk that a single disaster would destroy large portions of the organization's data.

39. All of the following are methods for distributing a relational database across multiple servers **except:**

a. Snapshot (making a copy of the database for distribution).
b. Replication (creating and maintaining replica copies at multiple locations).
c. Normalization (separating the database into logical tables for easier user processing).
d. Fragmentation (separating the database into parts and distributing where they are needed).

40. Client/server architecture may potentially involve a variety of hardware, systems software, and application software from many vendors. The **best** way to protect a client/server system from unauthorized access is through

a. A combination of application and general access control techniques.
b. Use of a commercially available authentication system.
c. Encryption of all network traffic.
d. Thorough testing and evaluation of remote procedure calls.

41. What technology is needed in order to convert a paper document into a computer file?

a. Optical character recognition.
b. Electronic data interchange.
c. Bar-coding scanning.
d. Joining and merging.

42. Unauthorized alteration of online records can be prevented by employing

a. Key verification.
b. Computer sequence checks.
c. Computer matching.
d. Database access controls.

43. A manufacturer of complex electronic equipment such as oscilloscopes and microscopes has been shipping its products with thick paper manuals but wants to reduce the cost of producing and shipping this documentation. Of the following, the **best** medium for the manufacturer to use to accomplish this is

a. Write-once-read-many.
b. Digital audio tape.

c. Compact disc/read-only memory.
d. Computer-output-to-microform.

44. Misstatements in a batch computer system caused by incorrect programs or data may **not** be detected immediately because

a. Errors in some transactions may cause rejection of other transactions in the batch.
b. The identification of errors in input data typically is **not** part of the program.
c. There are time delays in processing transactions in a batch system.
d. The processing of transactions in a batch system is **not** uniform.

45. Which of the following is **not** a characteristic of a batch processed computer system?

a. The collection of like transactions which are sorted and processed sequentially against a master file.
b. Keypunching of transactions, followed by machine processing.
c. The production of numerous printouts.
d. The posting of a transaction, as it occurs, to several files, without intermediate printouts.

46. Able Co. uses an online sales order processing system to process its sales transactions. Able's sales data are electronically sorted and subjected to edit checks. A direct output of the edit checks **most** likely would be a

a. Report of all missing sales invoices.
b. File of all rejected sales transactions.
c. Printout of all user code numbers and passwords.
d. List of all voided shipping documents.

47. First Federal S & L has an online real-time system, with terminals installed in all of its branches. This system will not accept a customer's cash withdrawal instructions in excess of $1,000 without the use of a "terminal audit key." After the transaction is authorized by a supervisor, the bank teller then processes the transaction with the audit key. This control can be strengthened by

a. Online recording of the transaction on an audit override sheet.
b. Increasing the dollar amount to $1,500.
c. Requiring manual, rather than online, recording of all such transactions.
d. Using parallel simulation.

48. Mill Co. uses a batch processing method to process its sales transactions. Data on Mill's sales transaction tape are electronically sorted by customer number and are subjected to programmed edit checks in preparing its invoices, sales journals, and updated customer account balances. One of the direct outputs of the creation of this tape **most** likely would be a

a. Report showing exceptions and control totals.
b. Printout of the updated inventory records.

c. Report showing overdue accounts receivable.
d. Printout of the sales price master file.

49. Where disk files are used, the grandfather-father-son updating backup concept is relatively difficult to implement because the

a. Location of information points on disks is an extremely time-consuming task.
b. Magnetic fields and other environmental factors cause off-site storage to be impractical.
c. Information must be dumped in the form of hard copy if it is to be reviewed before used in updating.
d. Process of updating old records is destructive.

**50. In a computerized system, procedure or problem-oriented language is converted to machine language through a(n)

a. Interpreter.
b. Verifier.
c. Compiler.
d. Converter.

51. What type of computer system is characterized by data that is assembled from more than one location and records that are updated immediately?

a. Microcomputer system.
b. Minicomputer system.
c. Batch processing system.
d. Online real-time system.

52. Which of the following characteristics distinguishes electronic data interchange (EDI) from other forms of electronic commerce?

a. EDI transactions are formatted using the standards that are uniform worldwide.
b. EDI transactions need **not** comply with generally accepted accounting principles.
c. EDI transactions ordinarily are processed without the Internet.
d. EDI transactions are usually recorded without security and privacy concerns.

C. Characteristics of IT Systems—Specific

53. LAN is the abbreviation for

a. Large Area Network.
b. Local Area Network.
c. Longitudinal Analogue Network.
d. Low Analytical Nets.

54. A computer that is designed to provide software and other applications to other computers is referred to as a

a. Microcomputer.
b. Network computer.
c. Server.
d. Supercomputer.

**CMA adapted

55. Which is **least** likely to be considered a component of a computer network?

    a. Applications programs.
    b. Computers.
    c. Software.
    d. Routers.

56. The network most frequently used for private operations designed to link computers within widely separated portions of an organization is referred to as a(n)

    a. Bulletin board service.
    b. Local area network.
    c. Wide area network.
    d. Zero base network.

57. A set of rules for exchanging data between two computers is a

    a. Communicator.
    b. Operating system.
    c. Protocol.
    d. Transmission speed.

58. A web page is most frequently created using

    a. Java or C++.
    b. Visual Basic.
    c. SQL.
    d. HTML or XML.

59. Laptop computers provide automation outside of the normal office location. Which of the following would provide the **least** security for sensitive data stored on a laptop computer?

    a. Encryption of data files on the laptop computer.
    b. Setting up a password for the screensaver program on the laptop computer.
    c. Using a laptop computer with a removable hard disk drive.
    d. Using a locking device that can secure the laptop computer to an immovable object.

60. When developing a new computer system that will handle customer orders and process customer payments, a high-level systems design phase would include determination of which of the following?

    a. How the new system will affect current inventory and general ledger systems.
    b. How the file layouts will be structured for the customer order records.
    c. Whether to purchase a turn-key system or modify an existing system.
    d. Whether formal approval by top management is needed for the new system.

**61. A company using EDI made it a practice to track the functional acknowledgments from trading partners and to issue warning messages if acknowledgments did not occur within a reasonable length of time. What risk was the company attempting to address by this practice?

a. Transactions that have not originated from a legitimate trading partner may be inserted into the EDI network.
b. Transmission of EDI transactions to trading partners may sometimes fail.
c. There may be disagreement between the parties as to whether the EDI transactions form a legal contract.
d. EDI data may not be accurately and completely processed by the EDI software.

62. Management is concerned that data uploaded from a microcomputer to the company's mainframe system in batch processing may be erroneous. Which of the following controls would **best** address this issue?

    a. The mainframe computer should be backed up on a regular basis.
    b. Two persons should be present at the microcomputer when it is uploading data.
    c. The mainframe computer should subject the data to the same edits and validation routines that online data entry would require.
    d. The users should be required to review a random sample of processed data.

Items 63 and 64 are based on the following information:

One major category of computer viruses is programs that attach themselves to other programs, thus infecting the other programs. While many of these viruses are relatively harmless, some have the potential to cause significant damage.

63. Which of the following is an indication that a computer virus of this category is present?

    a. Frequent power surges that harm computer equipment.
    b. Unexplainable losses of or changes to data.
    c. Inadequate backup, recovery, and contingency plans.
    d. Numerous copyright violations due to unauthorized use of purchased software.

64. Which of the following operating procedures increases an organization's exposure to computer viruses?

    a. Encryption of data files.
    b. Frequent backup of files.
    c. Downloading public-domain software from electronic bulletin boards.
    d. Installing original copies of purchased software on hard disk drives.

65. Which of the following is a risk that is higher when an electronic funds transfer (EFT) system is used?

    a. Improper change control procedures.
    b. Unauthorized access and activity.
    c. Insufficient online edit checks.
    d. Inadequate backups and disaster recovery procedures.

66. The use of message encryption software

    a. Guarantees the secrecy of data.
    b. Requires manual distribution of keys.

** CMA adapted

c. Increases system overhead.

d. Reduces the need for periodic password changes.

**67. A company's management is concerned about computer data eavesdropping and wants to maintain the confidentiality of its information as it is transmitted. The company should utilize

a. Data encryption.

b. Dial-back systems.

c. Message acknowledgement procedures.

d. Password codes.

68. Which of the following is likely to be a benefit of electronic data interchange (EDI)?

a. Increased transmission speed of actual documents.

b. Improved business relationships with trading partners.

c. Decreased liability related to protection of proprietary business data.

d. Decreased requirements for backup and contingency planning.

69. The internal auditor is reviewing a new policy on electronic mail. Appropriate elements of such a policy would include all of the following **except:**

a. Erasing all employee's electronic mail immediately upon employment termination.

b. Encrypting electronic mail messages when transmitted over phone lines.

c. Limiting the number of electronic mail packages adopted by the organization.

d. Directing that personnel do not send highly sensitive or confidential messages using electronic mail.

70. Which of the following risks is **most** likely to be encountered in an end-user computing (EUC) environment as compared to a mainframe computer system?

a. Inability to afford adequate uninterruptible power supply systems.

b. User input screens without a graphical user interface (GUI).

c. Applications that are difficult to integrate with other information systems.

d. Lack of adequate utility programs.

71. Which of the following risks is **not** greater in an electronic funds transfer (EFT) environment than in a manual system using paper transactions?

a. Unauthorized access and activity.

b. Duplicate transaction processing.

c. Higher cost per transaction.

d. Inadequate backup and recovery capabilities.

72. Methods to minimize the installation of unlicensed microcomputer software include all of the following **except:**

a. Employee awareness programs.

b. Regular audits for unlicensed software.

c. Regular monitoring of network access and start-up scripts.

d. An organizational policy that includes software licensing requirements.

73. In traditional information systems, computer operators are generally responsible for backing up software and data files on a regular basis. In distributed or cooperative systems, ensuring that adequate backups are taken is the responsibility of

a. User management.

b. Systems programmers.

c. Data entry clerks.

d. Tape librarians.

74. An auditor is **least** likely to find that a client's data is input through

a. Magnetic tape reader.

b. Dynamic linking character reader.

c. Point-of-sale recorders.

d. Touch sensitive screens.

75. End-user computing is an example of which of the following?

a. Client/server processing.

b. A distributed system.

c. Data mining.

d. Decentralized processing.

76. End-user computing is **most** likely to occur on which of the following types of computers?

a. Mainframe.

b. Minicomputers.

c. Personal computers.

d. Personal reference assistants.

77. Which of the following statements is correct regarding the Internet as a commercially viable network?

a. Organizations must use firewalls if they wish to maintain security over internal data.

b. Companies must apply to the Internet to gain permission to create a homepage to engage in electronic commerce.

c. Companies that wish to engage in electronic commerce on the Internet must meet required security standards established by the coalition of Internet providers.

d. All of the above.

78. To reduce security exposure when transmitting proprietary data over communication lines, a company should use

a. Asynchronous modems.

b. Authentic techniques.

c. Call-back procedures.

d. Cryptographic devices.

79. Securing client/server systems is a complex task because of all of the following factors **except:**

a. The use of relational databases.

b. The number of access points.

c. Concurrent operation of multiple user sessions.

d. Widespread data access and update capabilities.

80. Which of the following would an auditor ordinarily consider the greatest risk regarding an entity's use of electronic data interchange (EDI)?

a. Authorization of EDI transactions.

b. Duplication of EDI transmissions.

c. Improper distribution of EDI transactions.

d. Elimination of paper documents.

81. Which of the following characteristics distinguish electronic data interchange (EDI) from other forms of electronic commerce?

a. The cost of sending EDI transactions using a value-added network (VAN) is less than the cost of using the Internet.

b. Software maintenance contracts are unnecessary because translation software for EDI transactions need not be updated.

c. EDI commerce is ordinarily conducted without establishing legally binding contracts between trading partners.

d. EDI transactions are formatted using strict standards that have been agreed to worldwide.

82. Which of the following is considered a component of a local area network?

a. Program flowchart.

b. Loop verification.

c. Transmission media.

d. Input routine.

83. Which of the following represents an additional cost of transmitting business transactions by means of electronic data interchange (EDI) rather than in a traditional paper environment?

a. Redundant data checks are needed to verify that individual EDI transactions are **not** recorded twice.

b. Internal audit work is needed because the potential for random data entry errors is increased.

c. Translation software is needed to convert transactions from the entity's internal format to a standard EDI format.

d. More supervisory personnel are needed because the amount of data entry is greater in an EDI system.

84. Which of the following is **not** considered an exposure involved with electronic data interchange (EDI) systems as compared to other systems?

a. Increased reliance upon computer systems.

b. Delayed transaction processing time.

c. Possible loss of confidentiality of information.

d. Increased reliance upon third parties.

85. Which of the following statements is correct concerning internal control when a client is using an electronic data interchange system for its sales?

a. Controls should be established over determining that all suppliers are included in the system.

b. Encryption controls may help to assure that messages are unreadable to unauthorized persons.

c. A value-added-network (VAN) must be used to assure proper control.

d. Attention must be paid to both the electronic and "paper" versions of transactions.

86. Which of the following statements **most** likely represents a disadvantage for an entity that keeps microcomputer-prepared data files rather than manually prepared files?

a. Random error associated with processing similar transactions in different ways is usually greater.

b. It is usually more difficult to compare recorded accountability with physical count of assets.

c. Attention is focused on the accuracy of the programming process rather than errors in individual transactions.

d. It is usually easier for unauthorized persons to access and alter the files.

87. Which of the following is usually a benefit of transmitting transactions in an electronic data interchange (EDI) environment?

a. A compressed business cycle with lower year-end receivables balances.

b. A reduced need to test computer controls related to sales and collections transactions.

c. An increased opportunity to apply statistical sampling techniques to account balances.

d. No need to rely on third-party service providers to ensure security.

88. Which of the following is a network node that is used to improve network traffic and to set up as a boundary that prevents traffic from one segment to cross over to another?

a. Router.

b. Gateway.

c. Firewall.

d. Heuristic.

89. Which of the following is an example of how specific controls in a database environment may differ from controls in a nondatabase environment?

a. Controls should exist to ensure that users have access to and can update only the data elements that they have been authorized to access.

b. Controls over data sharing by diverse users within an entity should be the same for every user.

c. The employee who manages the computer hardware should also develop and debug the computer programs.

d. Controls can provide assurance that all processed transactions are authorized, but **cannot** verify that all authorized transactions are processed.

90. A retail entity uses electronic data interchange (EDI) in executing and recording most of its purchase transactions. The entity's auditor recognized that the documentation of the transactions will be retained for only a short period of time. To compensate for this limitation, the auditor **most** likely would

a. Increase the sample of EDI transactions to be selected for cutoff tests.

b. Perform tests several times during the year, rather than only at year-end.

c. Plan to make a 100% count of the entity's inventory at or near the year-end.

d. Decrease the assessed level of control risk for the existence or occurrence assertion.

91. Which of the following is an encryption feature that can be used to authenticate the originator of a document and ensure that the message is intact and has **not** been tampered with?

a. Heuristic terminal.
b. Perimeter switch.
c. Default settings.
d. Digital signatures.

92. In building an electronic data interchange (EDI) system, what process is used to determine which elements in the entity's computer system correspond to the standard data elements?

a. Mapping.
b. Translation.
c. Encryption.
d. Decoding.

93. Which of the following passwords would be most difficult to crack?

a. OrCa!FlSi
b. language
c. 12 HOUSE 24
d. pass56word

94. Which of the following is a password security problem?

a. Users are assigned passwords when accounts are created, but do **not** change them.
b. Users have accounts on several systems with different passwords.
c. Users copy their passwords on note paper, which is kept in their wallets.
d. Users select passwords that are **not** listed in any online dictionary.

95. Many of the Web 2.0 applications rely on an XML-based application that facilitates the sharing and syndication of web content, by subscription, Which of the applications below represents this XML application?

a. Wiki.
b. Blog.
c. RSS/Atom Feeds.
d. Twitter.

D. Control Objectives for Information and Related Technology (COBIT)

96. Which of the following is not one of the five principles of COBIT 5?

a. Meeting stakeholder needs.
b. Business processes.
c. Covering the enterprise end-to-end.
d. Applying a single integrated framework.

97. The Control Objectives for Information and Related Technology (COBIT) framework has been established by:

a. The American Institute of Certified Public Accountants.
b. The Information Technology Institute.
c. The Information Systems Audit and Control Association.
d. The Committee of Sponsoring Organizations.

E. IT Risk and Internal Control

98. Which of the following procedures would an entity **most** likely include in its computer disaster recovery plan?

a. Develop an auxiliary power supply to provide uninterrupted electricity.
b. Store duplicate copies of critical files in a location away from the computer center.
c. Maintain a listing of entity passwords with the network manager.
d. Translate data for storage purposes with a cryptographic secret code.

99. A company is concerned that a power outage or disaster could impair the computer hardware's ability to function as designed. The company desires off-site backup hardware facilities that are fully configured and ready to operate within several hours. The company **most** likely should consider a

a. Cold site.
b. Cool site.
c. Warm site.
d. Hot site.

100. Which of the following procedures would an entity **most** likely include in its disaster recovery plan?

a. Convert all data from EDI format to an internal company format.
b. Maintain a Trojan horse program to prevent illicit activity.
c. Develop an auxiliary power supply to provide uninterrupted electricity.
d. Store duplicate copies of files in a location away from the computer center.

101. Almost all commercially marketed software is

	Copyrighted	Copy protected
a.	Yes	Yes
b.	Yes	No
c.	No	Yes
d.	No	No

102. A widely used disaster recovery approach includes

a. Encryption.
b. Firewalls.
c. Regular backups.
d. Surge protectors.

103. A "hot site" is most frequently associated with

    a. Disaster recovery.
    b. Online relational database design.
    c. Source programs.
    d. Temperature control for computer.

104. Output controls ensure that the results of computer processing are accurate, complete, and properly distributed. Which of the following is **not** a typical output control?

    a. Reviewing the computer processing logs to determine that all of the correct computer jobs executed properly.
    b. Matching input data with information on master files and placing unmatched items in a suspense file.
    c. Periodically reconciling output reports to make sure that totals, formats, and critical details are correct and agree with input.
    d. Maintaining formal procedures and documentation specifying authorized recipients of output reports, checks, or other critical documents.

105. Minimizing the likelihood of unauthorized editing of production programs, job control language, and operating system software can **best** be accomplished by

    a. Database access reviews.
    b. Compliance reviews.
    c. Good change-control procedures.
    d. Effective network security software.

106. Some companies have replaced mainframe computers with microcomputers and networks because the smaller computers could do the same work at less cost. Assuming that management of a company decided to launch a downsizing project, what should be done with respect to mainframe applications such as the general ledger system?

    a. Plan for rapid conversion of all mainframe applications to run on a microcomputer network.
    b. Consider the general ledger system as an initial candidate for conversion.
    c. Defer any modification of the general ledger system until it is clearly inadequate.
    d. Integrate downsized applications with stable mainframe applications.

107. A corporation receives the majority of its revenue from top-secret military contracts with the government. Which of the following would be of greatest concern to an auditor reviewing a policy about selling the company's used microcomputers to outside parties?

    a. Whether deleted files on the hard disk drive have been completely erased.
    b. Whether the computer has viruses.
    c. Whether all software on the computer is properly licensed.
    d. Whether the computer has terminal emulation software on it.

108. A manufacturer is considering using bar-code identification for recording information on parts used by the manufacturer. A reason to use bar codes rather than other means of identification is to ensure that

    a. The movement of all parts is recorded.
    b. The movement of parts is easily and quickly recorded.
    c. Vendors use the same part numbers.
    d. Vendors use the same identification methods.

109. A company often revises its production processes. The changes may entail revisions to processing programs. Ensuring that changes have a minimal impact on processing and result in minimal risk to the system is a function of

    a. Security administration.
    b. Change control.
    c. Problem tracking.
    d. Problem-escalation procedures.

110. Pirated software obtained through the Internet may lead to civil lawsuits or criminal prosecution. Of the following, which would reduce an organization's risk in this area?

  I. Maintain a log of all software purchases.
  II. Audit individual computers to identify software on the computers.
  III. Establish a corporate software policy.
  IV. Provide original software diskettes to each user.

    a. I and IV only.
    b. I, II, and III only.
    c. II and IV only.
    d. II and III only.

111. Good planning will help an organization restore computer operations after a processing outage. Good recovery planning should ensure that

    a. Backup/restart procedures have been built into job streams and programs.
    b. Change control procedures cannot be bypassed by operating personnel.
    c. Planned changes in equipment capacities are compatible with projected workloads.
    d. Service level agreements with owners of applications are documented.

112. In a large organization, the biggest risk in not having an adequately staffed information center help desk is

    a. Increased difficulty in performing application audits.
    b. Inadequate documentation for application systems.
    c. Increased likelihood of use of unauthorized program code.
    d. Persistent errors in user interaction with systems.

113. To properly control the improper access to accounting database files, the database administrator should ensure that database system features are in place to permit

    a. Read-only access to the database files.
    b. Updating from privileged utilities.
    c. Access only to authorized logical views.
    d. User updates of their access profiles.

114. When evaluating internal control of an entity that processes sales transactions on the Internet, an auditor would be most concerned about the

    a. Lack of sales invoice documents as an audit trail.
    b. Potential for computer disruptions in recording sales.
    c. Inability to establish an integrated test facility.
    d. Frequency of archiving and data retention.

115. Which of the following statements is correct concerning internal control in an electronic data interchange (EDI) system?

    a. Preventive controls generally are more important than detective controls in EDI systems.
    b. Control objectives for EDI systems generally are different from the objectives for other information systems.
    c. Internal controls in EDI systems rarely permit control risk to be assessed at below the maximum.
    d. Internal controls related to the segregation of duties generally are the most important controls in EDI systems.

116. Which of the following statements is correct concerning the security of messages in an electronic data interchange (EDI) system?

    a. When the confidentiality of data is the primary risk, message authentication is the preferred control rather than encryption.
    b. Encryption performed by physically secure hardware devices is more secure than encryption performed by software.
    c. Message authentication in EDI systems performs the same function as segregation of duties in other information systems.
    d. Security at the transaction phase in EDI systems is **not** necessary because problems at that level will usually be identified by the service provider.

117. Which of the following is an essential element of the audit trail in an electronic data interchange (EDI) system?

    a. Disaster recovery plans that ensure proper backup of files.
    b. Encrypted hash totals that authenticate messages.
    c. Activity logs that indicate failed transactions.
    d. Hardware security modules that store sensitive data.

118. Which of the following are essential elements of the audit trail in an electronic data interchange (EDI) system?

    a. Network and sender/recipient acknowledgments.
    b. Message directories and header segments.
    c. Contingency and disaster recovery plans.
    d. Trading partner security and mailbox codes.

119. To avoid invalid data input, a bank added an extra number at the end of each account number and subjected the new number to an algorithm. This technique is known as

    a. Optical character recognition.
    b. A check digit.
    c. A dependency check.
    d. A format check.

120. Preventing someone with sufficient technical skill from circumventing security procedures and making changes to production programs is **best** accomplished by

    a. Reviewing reports of jobs completed.
    b. Comparing production programs with independently controlled copies.
    c. Running test data periodically.
    d. Providing suitable segregation of duties.

121. Computer program libraries can **best** be kept secure by

    a. Installing a logging system for program access.
    b. Monitoring physical access to program library media.
    c. Restricting physical and logical access.
    d. Denying access from remote terminals.

122. Which of the following security controls would **best** prevent unauthorized access to sensitive data through an unattended data terminal directly connected to a mainframe?

    a. Use of a screen saver with a password.
    b. Use of workstation scripts.
    c. Encryption of data files.
    d. Automatic log-off of inactive users.

123. An entity has the following invoices in a batch:

Invoice #	Product	Quantity	Unit price
201	F10	150	$5.00
202	G15	200	$10.00
203	H20	250	$25.00
204	K35	300	$30.00

Which of the following **most** likely represents a hash total?

    a. FGHK80
    b. 4
    c. 204
    d. 810

124. A customer intended to order 100 units of product Z96014, but incorrectly ordered nonexistent product Z96015. Which of the following controls **most** likely would detect this error?

    a. Check digit verification.
    b. Record count.
    c. Hash total.
    d. Redundant data check.

125. In entering the billing address for a new client in Emil Company's computerized database, a clerk erroneously entered a nonexistent zip code. As a result, the first month's bill mailed to the new client was returned to Emil Company. Which one of the following would **most** likely have led to discovery of the error at the time of entry into Emil Company's computerized database?

    a. Limit test.
    b. Validity test.
    c. Parity test.
    d. Record count test.

126. Which of the following controls is a processing control designed to ensure the reliability and accuracy of data processing?

	Limit test	Validity check test
a.	Yes	Yes
b.	No	No
c.	No	Yes
d.	Yes	No

127. Which of the following activities would **most** likely be performed in the information systems department?

- a. Initiation of changes to master records.
- b. Conversion of information to machine-readable form.
- c. Correction of transactional errors.
- d. Initiation of changes to existing applications.

128. The use of a header label in conjunction with magnetic tape is **most** likely to prevent errors by the

- a. Computer operator.
- b. Keypunch operator.
- c. Computer programmer.
- d. Maintenance technician.

129. For the accounting system of Acme Company, the amounts of cash disbursements entered into a terminal are transmitted to the computer that immediately transmits the amounts back to the terminal for display on the terminal screen. This display enables the operator to

- a. Establish the validity of the account number.
- b. Verify the amount was entered accurately.
- c. Verify the authorization of the disbursement.
- d. Prevent the overpayment of the account.

130. When computer programs or files can be accessed from terminals, users should be required to enter a(n)

- a. Parity check.
- b. Personal identification code.
- c. Self-diagnosis test.
- d. Echo check.

131. The possibility of erasing a large amount of information stored on magnetic tape **most** likely would be reduced by the use of

- a. File protection rings.
- b. Check digits.
- c. Completeness tests.
- d. Conversion verification.

132. Which of the following controls **most** likely would assure that an entity can reconstruct its financial records?

- a. Hardware controls are built into the computer by the computer manufacturer.
- b. Backup diskettes or tapes of files are stored away from originals.
- c. Personnel who are independent of data input perform parallel simulations.
- d. System flowcharts provide accurate descriptions of input and output operations.

133. Which of the following input controls is a numeric value computed to provide assurance that the original value has **not** been altered in construction or transmission?

- a. Hash total.
- b. Parity check.
- c. Encryption.
- d. Check digit.

134. Which of the following is an example of a validity check?

- a. The computer ensures that a numerical amount in a record does **not** exceed some predetermined amount.
- b. As the computer corrects errors and data are successfully resubmitted to the system, the causes of the errors are printed out.
- c. The computer flags any transmission for which the control field value did **not** match that of an existing file record.
- d. After data for a transaction are entered, the computer sends certain data back to the terminal for comparison with data originally sent.

135. Which of the following is a computer test made to ascertain whether a given characteristic belongs to the group?

- a. Parity check.
- b. Validity check.
- c. Echo check.
- d. Limit check.

136. A control feature in an electronic data processing system requires the central processing unit (CPU) to send signals to the printer to activate the print mechanism for each character. The print mechanism, just prior to printing, sends a signal back to the CPU verifying that the proper print position has been activated. This type of hardware control is referred to as

- a. Echo control.
- b. Validity control.
- c. Signal control.
- d. Check digit control.

137. Which of the following is an example of a check digit?

- a. An agreement of the total number of employees to the total number of checks printed by the computer.
- b. An algebraically determined number produced by the other digits of the employee number.
- c. A logic test that ensures all employee numbers are nine digits.
- d. A limit check that an employee's hours do not exceed fifty hours per workweek.

138. Which of the following **most** likely represents a significant deficiency in internal control?

- a. The systems analyst reviews applications of data processing and maintains systems documentation.
- b. The systems programmer designs systems for computerized applications and maintains output controls.
- c. The control clerk establishes control over data received by the information systems department and reconciles control totals after processing.
- d. The accounts payable clerk prepares data for computer processing and enters the data into the computer.

139. Internal control is ineffective when computer department personnel

    a. Participate in computer software acquisition decisions.

    b. Design documentation for computerized systems.

    c. Originate changes in master files.

    d. Provide physical security for program files.

F. Flowcharting

140. Which of the following tools would **best** give a graphical representation of a sequence of activities and decisions?

    a. Flowchart.

    b. Control chart.

    c. Histogram.

    d. Run chart.

Items 141 and 142 are based on the following flowchart of a client's revenue cycle:

141. Symbol A most likely represents the

    a. Remittance advice file.

    b. Receiving report file.

    c. Accounts receivable master file.

    d. Cash disbursements transaction file.

142. Symbol B **most** likely represents

    a. Customer orders.

    b. Receiving reports.

    c. Customer checks.

    d. Sales invoices.

143. An auditor's flowchart of a client's accounting system is a diagrammatic representation that depicts the auditor's

    a. Assessment of control risk.

    b. Identification of weaknesses in the system.

    c. Assessment of the control environment's effectiveness.

    d. Understanding of the system.

Item 144 is based on the following flowchart:

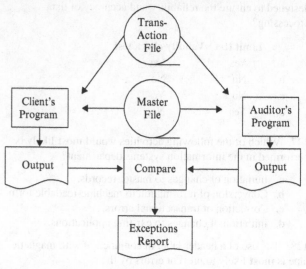

144. The above flowchart depicts

    a. Program code checking.

    b. Parallel simulation.

    c. Integrated test facility.

    d. Controlled reprocessing.

Item 145 is based on the following flowchart:

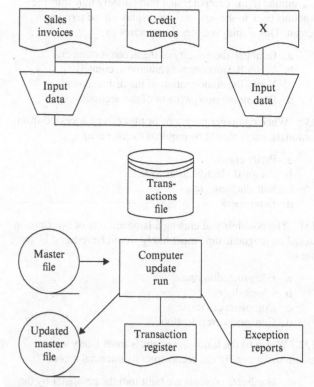

145. In a credit sales and cash receipts system flowchart, symbol X could represent

    a. Auditor's test data.

    b. Remittance advices.

    c. Error reports.

    d. Credit authorization forms.

146. Which of the following symbolic representations indicate that a file has been consulted?

147. A well-prepared flowchart should make it easier for the auditor to

    a. Prepare audit procedure manuals.
    b. Prepare detailed job descriptions.
    c. Trace the origin and disposition of documents.
    d. Assess the degree of accuracy of financial data.

Multiple-Choice Answers and Explanations

Answers

1. b	__ __	32. d	__ __	63. b	__ __	94. a	__ __	125. b	__ __
2. a	__ __	33. a	__ __	64. c	__ __	95. c	__ __	126. a	__ __
3. b	__ __	34. b	__ __	65. b	__ __	96. b	__ __	127. b	__ __
4. c	__ __	35. a	__ __	66. c	__ __	97. c	__ __	128. a	__ __
5. b	__ __	36. a	__ __	67. a	__ __	98. b	__ __	129. b	__ __
6. d	__ __	37. d	__ __	68. b	__ __	99. d	__ __	130. b	__ __
7. d	__ __	38. d	__ __	69. a	__ __	100. d	__ __	131. a	__ __
8. b	__ __	39. c	__ __	70. c	__ __	101. b	__ __	132. b	__ __
9. a	__ __	40. a	__ __	71. b	__ __	102. c	__ __	133. d	__ __
10. a	__ __	41. a	__ __	72. c	__ __	103. a	__ __	134. c	__ __
11. a	__ __	42. d	__ __	73. a	__ __	104. b	__ __	135. b	__ __
12. c	__ __	43. c	__ __	74. b	__ __	105. c	__ __	136. a	__ __
13. a	__ __	44. c	__ __	75. d	__ __	106. d	__ __	137. b	__ __
14. a	__ __	45. d	__ __	76. c	__ __	107. a	__ __	138. b	__ __
15. a	__ __	46. b	__ __	77. a	__ __	108. b	__ __	139. c	__ __
16. c	__ __	47. a	__ __	78. d	__ __	109. b	__ __	140. a	__ __
17. b	__ __	48. a	__ __	79. a	__ __	110. b	__ __	141. c	__ __
18. b	__ __	49. d	__ __	80. c	__ __	111. a	__ __	142. d	__ __
19. a	__ __	50. c	__ __	81. d	__ __	112. d	__ __	143. d	__ __
20. d	__ __	51. d	__ __	82. c	__ __	113. c	__ __	144. b	__ __
21. b	__ __	52. a	__ __	83. c	__ __	114. b	__ __	145. b	__ __
22. a	__ __	53. b	__ __	84. b	__ __	115. a	__ __	146. d	__ __
23. a	__ __	54. c	__ __	85. b	__ __	116. b	__ __	147. c	__ __
24. b	__ __	55. a	__ __	86. d	__ __	117. c	__ __		
25. d	__ __	56. c	__ __	87. a	__ __	118. a	__ __		
26. b	__ __	57. c	__ __	88. c	__ __	119. b	__ __		
27. d	__ __	58. d	__ __	89. a	__ __	120. d	__ __		
28. c	__ __	59. b	__ __	90. b	__ __	121. c	__ __		
29. d	__ __	60. c	__ __	91. d	__ __	122. d	__ __		
30. b	__ __	61. b	__ __	92. a	__ __	123. d	__ __	1st: __/147 __%
31. b	__ __	62. c	__ __	93. a	__ __	124. a	__ __	2nd: __/147 __%

Explanations

1. (b) The requirement is to identify a type of software package that uses a large set of organized data that presents the computer as an expert on a particular topic. Answer (b) is correct because an expert system presents the computer as such an expert. Answer (a) is incorrect because data mining uses tools which look for trends or anomalies without advance knowledge of the meaning of the data. Answer (c) is incorrect because artificial intelligence is a branch of computer science that involves computer programs that can solve specific problems creatively. Answer (d) is incorrect because virtual reality involves computer creation of an artificial, three-dimension world that may be interacted with.

2. (a) The requirement is to identify the type of computer memory used to store programs that must be accessed immediately by the central processing unit. Answer (a) is correct because primary memory is quickly accessed and generally used to store programs that must be accessed immediately. Answer (b) is incorrect because secondary storage is accessed less quickly. Answer (c) is incorrect because the term tertiary storage has no meaning in information technology. Answer (d) is incorrect because tape storage requires relatively long access times.

3. (b) The requirement is to identify the most common output device. Answer (b) is correct because a printer is a common output device and because the other replies represent input, not output devices.

4. (c) The requirement is to identify the part of the computer that does most of the data processing. Answer (c) is correct because the CPU, the central processing unit, does the primary processing for a computer. Answer (a) is incorrect because the word "analyter" has no meaning in information technology. Answer (b) is incorrect because a compiler is used to compile a particular type of computer program. Answer (d) is incorrect because a printer is an output device.

5. (b) The requirement is to identify the software **least** likely to be included in an "office suite" of software. Answer (b), operating systems, (e.g., Windows, Linux, Unix) is not ordinarily included in an office suite. Answers (a), (c) and (d) are all incorrect because databases, spreadsheets, and word processing software are often included.

6. (d) The requirement is to identify the software that performs a variety of technical operations. Answer (d) is correct because an operating system controls the execution of computer programs and may provide various services. Answer (a) is incorrect because an integrated "suite" (e.g., Microsoft Office) is a series of applications such as a word processor, database, and spreadsheet. Answer (b) is incorrect because shareware is generally considered to be software made available at a low, or no, cost to users. Answer (c) is incorrect because a database system deals with more specific technical processing.

7. (d) The requirement is to identify the part listed that is **not** considered a part of the central processing unit. Answer (d) is correct because the printer is a separate output device. Answers (a), (b), and (c) are all incorrect because a computer includes control, arithmetic, and logic units.

8. (b) The requirement is to identify the meaning of MIPS. Answer (b) is correct because MIPS is an abbreviation for millions of instructions per second, a unit for measuring the execution speed of computers. Answers (a), (c), and (d) all include combinations of words with no particular meaning in information technology.

9. (a) The requirement is to identify the type of applications software that a large client is most likely to use. Answer (a) is correct because enterprise resource planning (ERP) software is a form of applications software that provides relatively complete information systems for large and medium size organizations. Answer (b) is incorrect because a computer operating system is considered systems software, not applications software. Answer (c) is incorrect because the central processing unit is the principal hardware component of a computer, not software. Answer (d) is incorrect because a value-added network is a privately owned network whose services are sold to the public.

10. (a) The requirement is to identify a characteristic that distinguishes computer processing from manual processing. Answer (a) is correct because the high degree of accuracy of computer computation virtually eliminates the occurrence of computational errors. Answer (b) is incorrect because errors or fraud in computer processing may or may not be detected, depending upon the effectiveness of an entity's internal control. Answer (c) is incorrect because a programming error will result in a high level of systematic error in a computerized system and therefore, such errors may occur in either a manual or a computerized system. Answer (d) is incorrect because most computer systems are designed to include transaction trails.

11. (a) The requirement is to identify the type of general IT system that is designed to improve productivity by supporting the daily work of employees. Answer (a) is correct because office automation systems include the software tools of daily work, including word processing programs, spreadsheets, email, and electronic calendars. Answer (b) is incorrect because transaction processing systems are designed to improve the efficiency of processing transactions. Answer (c) is incorrect because decision support systems are used to solve nonstructured problems. Answer (d) is incorrect because executive information systems are specifically designed to support executive work.

12. (c) The requirement is to identify the phase of the SDLC where analysts identify the problem(s) of an existing information system. Answer (c) is correct because planning is the first phase of the SDLC and this information is needed before most of the analysis phase activities can be initiated. Answer (a) is incorrect because analysis phase activities are generally dependent on knowing exactly what problem(s) need to be solved before an effort is made to determine the requirements of a new system. Answer (b) is incorrect because implementation is the phase where the new system is put into operation. Answer (d) is incorrect because development is the phase of the SDLC where the new system design is transformed into an actual system.

13. (a) The requirement is to identify the phase in which a needs assessment is most likely to be performed. Answer (a) is correct because in the analysis phase the team attempts to get an understanding of the requirements of the system. Answers (b), (c) and (d) are incorrect because these phases occur after the requirements have been determined.

14. (a) The requirement is to identify the implementation model that has the advantage of a full operational test of the system before it is implemented. Answer (a) is correct because with parallel implementation both systems are operated until it is determined that the new system is operating properly. Answer (b) is incorrect because with the plunge model the new system is put into operation without a full operational test. Answer (c) is incorrect because with pilot implementation the system is only tested with a pilot group. Answer (d) is incorrect because with the phased implementation the system is phased in over time.

15. (a) The requirement is to identify the most frequently used mainframe computer application. Answer (a) is correct because mainframe computers (the largest and most powerful computers available at a particular point in time) are generally used to store and process extremely large computer databases. Answers (b), (c), and (d) are all incorrect because they are less frequent mainframe computer applications.

16. (c) The requirement is to identify the computer application most frequently used to analyze numbers and financial information. Answer (c) is correct because the purpose of a spreadsheet is generally to process numbers and financial information; for example, spreadsheets are often used to perform "what if" analysis which makes various assumptions with respect to a particular situation. Answer (a) is incorrect because while computer graphics programs may present numbers and financial information, they do not in general process them to the extent of spreadsheets. Answer (b) is incorrect because a WAN is a wide area network, and not an application used to analyze numbers and financial information. Answer (d) is incorrect because the emphasis of word processing programs is not ordinarily on processing numbers and financial information.

17. (b) The requirement is to identify the type of analysis that uses a database and tools to look for trends or anomalies, without knowledge in advance of the meaning of the data. Answer (b) is correct because data mining uses tools which look for trends or anomalies without such advance knowledge. Answer (a) is incorrect because artificial intelligence is a branch of computer science that involves computer programs that can solve specific problems creatively. Answer (c) is incorrect because virtual reality involves computer creation of an artificial, three-dimension world that may be interacted with. Answer (d) is incorrect because the term transitory analysis has no meaning relating to information technology.

18. (b) The requirement is to identify the most common type of primary storage in a computer. Answer (b) is correct because RAM (Random Access Memory) is the most common computer memory which can be used by programs to perform necessary tasks; RAM allows information to be stored or accessed in any order and all storage locations are equally accessible. Answer (a) is incorrect because CMAN has no meaning in information technology. Answer (c) is incorrect because ROM (Read Only Memory) is memory whose contents can be accessed and read but cannot be changed. Answer (d) is incorrect because it is a nonvolatile storage that can be electrically erased and programmed anew that is less common than RAM.

19. (a) The requirement is to identify a set of step-by-step procedures that are used to accomplish a task. Answer (a) is correct because an algorithm uses a step-by-step approach to accomplish a task. Answer (b) is incorrect because the term "compilation master" has no meaning in information technology. Answer (c) is incorrect because Linux is a form of operating system. Answer (d) is incorrect because the term "transitor" has no meaning in information technology.

20. (d) The requirement is to identify the item that compiles a complex translation of a program in a high-level computer language before the program is run for the first time. Answer (d) is correct because a compiler decodes instructions written in a higher order language and produces an assembly language program. Answers (a) and (b) are incorrect because Visual Basic and JAVA are programming languages. Answer (c) is incorrect because an algorithm is a "step-by-step" approach used to accomplish a particular task.

21. (b) The requirement is to identify the meaning of the abbreviation GUI. Answer (b), graphical user interface, is correct. The other replies all represent combinations of words with no meaning in information technology.

22. (a) The requirement is to identify the nature of Unix. Answer (a) is correct because Unix is a powerful operating system, originally developed by AT&T Bell Labs, that is used by many users of high-end computing hardware. Answers (b), (c), and (d) are all incorrect because Unix is not a singular disk drive, a central processing unit, or a logic unit.

23. (a) The requirement is to identify how each specific cell within a spreadsheet is identified. Answer (a) is correct because each cell has an address, composed of a combination of its column and row in the spreadsheet. Answer (b) is incorrect because the column portion of the address is not specific to the cell. Answer (c) is incorrect because the row portion of the address is not specific to the cell. Answer (d) is incorrect because no diagonal is ordinarily used to identify a particular cell.

24. (b) The requirement is to identify whether rows and columns of a spreadsheet are numbered or lettered. Answer (b) is correct because rows are numbered and columns are lettered. The other replies are all incorrect because they include incorrect combinations of "numbered" and "lettered."

25. (d) The requirement is to identify what is **least** likely to be considered an advantage of a database. Answer (d) is correct because a database itself does not make it easy to distribute information to every possible user—information must still be distributed either electronically or physically. Answer (a) is incorrect because a database is used to store large quantities of information. Answer (b) is incorrect because information may ordinarily be required quickly from a database. Answer (c) is incorrect because specific normalization rules have been identified for organizing information within a database.

26. (b) The requirement is to identify the most frequent current format for computer processing of data. Answer (b) is correct because most current computers process data using a digital approach in that they represent information by numerical (binary) digits. Answer (a) is incorrect because analog computers, which represent information by variable quantities (e.g., positions or voltages), are less frequent in practice than digital computers. Answer (c) is incorrect because "memory enhanced" is not a format for processing information. Answer (d) is incorrect because "organic" is not a format for processing information.

27. (d) The requirement is to identify the computer technology that is being widely adopted by organizations to lower computer hardware costs and to reduce energy costs by allowing multiple operating systems to coexist and operate simultaneously on the same machine. Answer (d) is correct because virtualization software allows a single computer to run multiple operating systems simultaneously. Answer (a) is incorrect because a client is a computing device that connects to a server or mainframe. Answer (b) is incorrect because a mainframe typically runs a single operating system but serves clients. Answer (c) is incorrect because Linux is an operating system, not a hardware device.

28. (c) The requirement is to identify the secondary storage technology that essentially has no moving parts. Answer (c) is correct because solid state devices store data on microchips and not a medium that must move to write or read data. Answer (a) is incorrect as the magnetic tape drive must spin for read/write operations. Answer (b) is incorrect as CDs and DVDs must also spin and use a moveable read/write head for operation. Answer (d) is incorrect as RAID devices are typically hard disk drives that must also spin and use a moveable read/write head for operations.

29. (d) The requirement is to identify another term for cloud-based storage. Answer (d) is correct because Storage-as-a-Service is another term for cloud-based storage. Answer (a) is incorrect as RAID is disk storage that is directly attached to a computing device. Answer (b) is incorrect as solid state storage is usually associated with a storage device that is directly attached to a computing device. Answer (c) is incorrect as analog refers to the representation of data.

30. (b) The requirement is to identify the wireless technology that is being used for inventory control that does **not** require line-of-sight access to the inventory. Answer (b) is the correct answer as Radio Frequency Identification (RFID) tags do not need to be seen by RFID readers to work. Answer (a) is incorrect as MICR technology requires items (documents) to pass through a read/write device. Answer (c) is incorrect as touch screen technology is not considered a wireless technology. Answer (d) is incorrect as current point-of-sale scanners must "see" the barcode to read it.

31. (b) The requirement is to distinguish between the various generations of programming languages. Answer (b) is correct as it is the only 2nd generation language listed. Answer (a) is incorrect as binary is considered machine language, the 1st generation programming language. Answer (c) is incorrect as COBOL is a 3rd generation programming language. Answer (d) is incorrect as it is also considered a higher-level, or 3rd generation programming language.

32. (d) The requirement is to distinguish among the OLAP technologies. Answer (d) is correct as business intelligence is the combination of systems that help aggregate, access, and analyze business data. Answer (a) is incorrect as artificial intelligence deals with relatively structured decision making in many areas, not specifically business. Answer (b) is incorrect as a data mart may be used in the process of business intelligence. Answer (c) is incorrect as decision support systems are used in a variety of business and nonbusiness decision-making situations.

33. (a) The requirement here is to identify the hierarchy of data with respect to relational databases. Answer (a) is the correct representation of data, from smallest to largest, for relational databases.

34. (b) The requirement is to identify the generation of programming language most likely to include an instruction such as *"Extract all Customers where 'Name' is Smith."* Answer (b) is correct because fourth generation programs ordinarily include instructions relatively close to human languages—such as the instruction in this question. Answer (a) is incorrect because first generation instructions are in terms of "1's" and "0's." Answers (c) and (d) are incorrect because seventh and ninth generation programming languages have not yet been developed (a few fifth generation languages with extensive visual and graphic interfaces are currently in process).

35. (a) The requirement is to identify the language interface used to establish the structure of database tables. Answer (a)

is correct because DDL is used to define (i.e., determine) the database. Answer (b) is incorrect because DCL is used to specify privileges and security rules. Answer (c) is incorrect because DML provides programmers with a facility to update the database. Answer (d) is incorrect because DQL is used for ad hoc queries.

36. (a) The requirement is to identify the function used in a database query to combine several tables. Answer (a) is correct because joining is the combining of one or more tables based on matching criteria. For example, if a supplier table contains information about suppliers and a parts table contains information about parts, the two tables could be joined on supplier number (assuming both tables contained this attribute) to give information about the supplier of particular parts. Answers (b), (c), and (d) are all incorrect.

37. (d) The requirement is to identify a reason that user acceptance testing is more important in an object-oriented development process than in a traditional environment. Answer (d) is correct because user acceptance testing is more important in object-oriented development because of the fact that all objects in a class inherit the properties of the hierarchy, which means that changes to one object may affect other objects, which increases the importance of user acceptance testing to verify correct functioning of the whole system. Answer (a) is incorrect because instead of traditional design documents, items such as the business model, narratives of process functions, iterative development screens, computer processes and reports, and product description guides are produced in object-oriented development, but the existence of specific documents does not affect the importance of user acceptance testing. Answer (b) is incorrect because in general, object-oriented development systems do include tracking systems for changes made to objects and hierarchies. Answer (c) is incorrect; because object-oriented systems are usually developed in client/server environments there is the potential for continuous monitoring of system use, but continuous monitoring typically occurs during system operation, not during development.

38. (d) The requirement is to identify the reply that does **not** represent a potential security and control concern. Answer (d) is correct because the distribution of data actually decreases this risk so this would not cause a control concern; it is a potential advantage to distributed systems of various architectures versus centralized data in a single mainframe computer. Answer (a) is incorrect because password proliferation is a considerable security concern because users will be tempted to write their passwords down or make them overly simplistic. Answer (b) is incorrect because consistent security across varied platforms is often challenging because of the different security features of the various systems and the decentralized nature of those controlling security administration. Answer (c) is incorrect because under centralized control, management can feel more confident that backup file storage is being uniformly controlled. Decentralization of this function may lead to lack of consistency and difficulty in monitoring compliance.

39. (c) The requirement is to determine which answer is **not** a method for distributing a relational database across multiple servers. Answer (c) is correct because normalization is a process of database design, not distribution. Answer (a) is incorrect because making a copy of the database for distribution is a viable method for the described distribution. Answer (b) is incorrect because creating and maintaining replica copies at multiple locations is a viable method for the described distribution. Answer (d) is incorrect because separating the database into parts and distributing where they are needed is a viable method for the described distribution.

40. **(a)** The requirement is to identify the best way to protect a client/server system from unauthorized access. Answer (a) is correct because since there is no perfect solution, this is the best way. Answer (b) is incorrect because authentication systems, such as Kerberos, are only a part of the solution. Answer (c) is incorrect because this only affects general access control techniques. Answer (d) is incorrect because testing and evaluation of remote procedure calls may be a small part of an overall security review.

41. **(a)** The requirement is to identify the technology needed to convert a paper document into a computer file. Answer (a) is correct because optical character recognition (OCR) software converts images of paper documents, as read by a scanning device, into text document computer files. Answer (b) is incorrect because electronic data interchange involves electronic transactions between trading partners. Answer (c) is incorrect because bar-code scanning reads price and item information, but does not convert a paper document into a computer file. Answer (d) is incorrect because joining and merging are processes applied to computer files.

42. **(d)** The requirement is to identify the best method for preventing unauthorized alteration of online records. Answer (d) is correct because users can gain access to databases from terminals only through established recognition and authorization procedures, thus unauthorized access is prevented. Answer (a) is incorrect because key verification ensures the accuracy of selected fields by requiring a second keying of them, ordinarily by another individual. Answer (b) is incorrect because sequence checks are used to ensure the completeness of input or update data by checking the use of preassigned document serial numbers. Answer (c) is incorrect because computer matching entails checking selected fields of input data with information held in a suspense master file.

43. **(c)** The requirement is to identify a way of eliminating thick paper manuals and reducing costs. Answer (c) is correct since a compact disc/read-only memory (CD-ROM) would be cheaper to produce and ship than the existing paper, yet would permit large volumes of text and images to be reproduced. Answer (a) is incorrect because write-once-read-many (WORM) is an optical storage technique often used as an archival medium. Answer (b) is incorrect because digital audio tape is primarily used as a backup medium in imaging systems and as a master for CD-ROM. Answer (d) is incorrect because computer-output-to-microform is used for frequent access to archived documents such as canceled checks in banking applications.

44. **(c)** The requirement is to identify a reason that misstatements in a batch computer system may **not** be detected

immediately. Answer (c) is correct because batch programs are run periodically and thereby result in delays in processing; accordingly, detection of misstatements may be delayed. Answer (a) is incorrect because errors will be detected in the batch. Answer (b) is incorrect because the identification of errors in input data is typically included as a part of a batch program. Answer (d) is incorrect because a batch system will ordinarily process transactions in a uniform manner.

45. **(d)** The requirement is to determine which answer is **not** a characteristic of a batch processed computer system. Simultaneous posting to several files is most frequently related to an online real-time system, not a batch system. Answer (a) is incorrect since a batch system may process sequentially against a master file. Answer (b) is incorrect because keypunching is followed by machine processing in batch systems. Answer (c) is incorrect because the numerous batches ordinarily result in numerous printouts.

46. **(b)** The requirement is to identify the most likely direct output of an edit check included in an online sales order processing system. Edit checks are used to screen incoming data against established standards of validity, with data that pass all edit checks viewed as "valid" and then processed. Answer (b) is correct because an edit check will ordinarily create an output file of rejected transactions. Answer (a) is incorrect because sales invoices may not have been prepared at the point of the sales order processing and because the answer is much less complete than answer (b). Answer (c) is incorrect because while periodic printouts of user code numbers and passwords should be prepared, this is not a primary purpose of an edit check. Answer (d) is incorrect because shipping documents will not ordinarily be prepared at this point and because the answer is much less complete than answer (b).

47. **(a)** The requirement is to determine a control which will strengthen an online real-time cash withdrawal system. Answer (a) is correct because documentation of all situations in which the "terminal audit key" has been used will improve the audit trail. Answer (b) is incorrect because increasing the dollar amount required for use of the key will simply reduce the number of times it is used (and allow larger withdrawals to be made without any required special authorization). Answer (c) is incorrect because there is no reason to believe that a manual system will be more effective than an online system. Answer (d) is incorrect because parallel simulation, running the data through alternate software, would seem to have no particular advantage for processing these large withdrawals.

48. **(a)** The requirement is to identify a direct output of a sorting, editing, and updating program. Answer (a) is correct because the program will output both exceptions and control totals to determine whether all transactions have been processed properly. Answers (b), (c), and (d) are all incorrect because while a program such as this may output such schedules, this will occur after exceptions are cleared and control totals are reconciled.

49. **(d)** The requirement is to determine why the grandfather-father-son updating backup concept is relatively difficult to implement for disk files. Answer (d) is correct because updating destroys the old records. Answer (a) is incorrect because the location of information points on disks is not an extremely time consuming task if the disks have been properly organized and maintained. Answer (b) is incorrect because off-site storage through disks is possible, though costly. Answer (c) is incorrect because information need not be dumped in the form of hard copy.

50. (c) The requirement is to determine the item which converts problem-oriented language to machine language. A compiler produces a machine-language object program from a source-program (i.e., problem oriented) language. Answer (a) is incorrect because an interpreter is used to make punched cards easily readable to people. Answer (b) is incorrect because a verifier is used to test whether key punching errors exist on punched cards. Answer (d) is incorrect because a converter changes a program from one form of problem oriented language to another, related form (e.g., from one form of COBOL to another form of COBOL).

51. (d) The requirement is to determine the type of computer system characterized by more than one location and records that are updated immediately. Answer (d) is correct because online real-time systems typically allow access from multiple locations, and always have the immediate update of records. Answers (a) and (b) are incorrect because small computers often are limited to one location, and they may or may not allow immediate updating for particular applications. Answer (c) is incorrect because batch processing is a method which does not update records immediately (e.g., processing the "batch" of the firm's daily sales each evening, not at the moment they occur).

52. (a) The requirement is to identify a characteristic that distinguishes electronic data interchange (EDI) from other forms of electronic commerce. Answer (a) is correct because EDI transactions are ordinarily formatted using one of the available uniform worldwide sets of standards. Answer (b) is incorrect because, when financial statements are prepared, EDI transactions must follow generally accepted accounting principles. Answer (c) is incorrect because EDI transactions may or may not be processed using the Internet. Answer (d) is incorrect because security and privacy are considered when recording EDI transactions. See the Auditing Procedure Study *Audit Implications of EDI* for more information on electronic data interchange.

53. (b) The requirement is to identify the meaning of the abbreviation LAN. Answer (b) is correct because LAN is the abbreviation for local area network. A local area network is a computer network for communication between computers. For example, a local area network may connect computers, word processors and other electronic office equipment to create a communication system within an office. Answers (a), (c) and (d) are all incorrect because they are combinations of words that have no specific meaning in information technology.

54. (c) The requirement is to identify the type of computer that is designed to provide software and other applications to other computers. Answer (c) is correct because a server provides other computers ("clients") with access to files and printers as shared resources to a computer network. Answer

(a) is incorrect because a microcomputer is a small digital computer based on a microprocessor and designed to be used by one person at a time. Answer (b) is incorrect because a network computer is a low-cost personal computer for business networks that is configured with only essential equipment. Answer (d) is incorrect because a supercomputer is a mainframe computer that is one of the most powerful available at a given time.

55. (a) The requirement is to identify the item **least** likely to be considered a component of a computer network. Answer (a) is least likely because application program is a program that gives a computer instructions that provide the user with tools to accomplish a specific task (e.g., a word processing application). Answer (b) is incorrect because computers are an integral part of a computer network. Answer (c) is incorrect because software is required for operation of the network. Answer (d) is incorrect because routers are used to forward data within a computer network.

56. (c) The requirement is to identify the type of network used to link widely separated portions of an organization. Answer (c) is correct because a wide area network is used to span a wide geographical space to link together portions of an organization. Answer (a) is incorrect because a bulletin board is a computer that is running software that allows users to leave messages and access information of general interest. Answer (b) is incorrect because a local area network's coverage is restricted to a relatively small geographical area. Answer (d) is incorrect because the term "zero base network" has no meaning in information technology.

57. (c) The requirement is to identify a set of rules for exchanging data between two computers. Answer (c) is correct because a protocol is such a set of rules. Answer (a) is incorrect because the term "communicator" is very general and has no specific meaning in this context. Answer (b) is incorrect because while an operating system controls the execution of computer programs and may provide various services related to computers, it is not a set of rules for exchanging data. Answer (d) is incorrect because transmission speed is the speed at which computer processing occurs.

58. (d) The requirement is to identify the approach most frequently used to create a webpage. Answer (d) is correct because HTML (hypertext markup language) or XML (extensible markup language) are used to develop hypertext documents such as webpages. Answers (a), (b), and (c) are all incorrect because while such tools may be used on webpage creation, they are not as fundamentally related as are HTML or XML.

59. (b) The requirement is to identify the reply that would provide the **least** security for sensitive data stored on a laptop computer. Answer (b) is correct because password protection for a screensaver program can be easily bypassed. Answer (a) is incorrect because data encryption provides adequate security for laptop computers. Answer (c) is incorrect because removable hard drives would provide adequate security. Answer (d) is incorrect because security is promoted by physically locking the laptop computer to an immovable object.

60. (c) The requirement is to identify the most likely procedure to be included in the high-level systems design phase of a computer system that will handle customer orders and process customer payments. Answer (c) is correct because the determination of what type of system to obtain is made during the high-level design phase. Answer (a) is incorrect because the effect of the new system would be part of the feasibility study. Answer (b) is incorrect because the file layouts are part of the detailed design phase. Answer (d) is incorrect because formal approval is made during the request for the systems design phase.

61. (b) The requirement is to identify the risk being controlled when a company using EDI makes it a practice to track the functional acknowledgments from trading partners. Answer (b) is correct because tracking of customers' functional acknowledgments, when required, will help to ensure successful transmission of EDI transactions. Answer (a) is incorrect because to address this issue, unauthorized access to the EDI system should be prevented, procedures should be in place to ensure the effective use of passwords, and data integrity and privacy should be maintained through the use of encryption and authentication measures. Answer (c) is incorrect because contractual agreements should exist between the company and the EDI trading partners. Answer (d) is incorrect because the risk that EDI data may not be completely and accurately processed is primarily controlled by the system.

62. (c) The requirement is to identify the best control to assure that data uploaded from a microcomputer to the company's mainframe system in batch processing is properly handled. Answer (c) is correct because this could help prevent data errors. Answer (a) is incorrect because while this practice is a wise control, it does not address the issue of upload-data integrity. Backups cannot prevent or detect data-upload problems, but can only help correct data errors that a poor upload caused. Answer (b) is incorrect because this control may be somewhat helpful in preventing fraud in data uploads, but it is of little use in preventing errors. Answer (d) is incorrect because this control is detective in nature, but the error could have already caused erroneous reports and management decisions. Having users try to find errors in uploaded data would be costly.

63. (b) The requirement is to identify the most likely indication that a computer virus is present. Answer (b) is correct because unexplainable losses of or changes to data files are symptomatic of a virus attack. Answer (a) is incorrect because power surges are symptomatic of hardware or environmental (power supply) problems. Answer (c) is incorrect because inadequate backup, recovery, and contingency plans are symptomatic of operating policy and/ or compliance problems. Answer (d) is incorrect because copyright violations are symptomatic of operating policy and/ or compliance problems.

64. (c) The requirement is to identify the operating procedure most likely to increase an organization's exposure to computer viruses. Answer (c) is correct because there is a risk that downloaded public-domain software may be contaminated with a virus. Answers (a) and (b) are incorrect because viruses are spread through the distribution of computer programs.

Answer (d) is incorrect because original copies of purchased software should be virus-free and cannot legally be shared.

65. (b) The requirement is to identify the risk that increases when an EFT system is used. Answer (b) is correct because unauthorized access is a risk which is higher in an EFT environment. Answers (a), (c), and (d) are all incorrect because this is a risk which is common to each IT environment.

66. (c) The requirement is to identify the statement that is correct concerning message encryption software. Answer (c) is correct because the machine instructions necessary to encrypt and decrypt data constitute system overhead, which means that processing may be slowed down. Answer (a) is incorrect because no encryption approach absolutely guarantees the secrecy of data in transmission although encryption approaches are considered to be less amenable to being broken than others. Answer (b) is incorrect because keys may be distributed manually, but they may also be distributed electronically via secure key transporters. Answer (d) is incorrect because using encryption software does not reduce the need for periodic password changes because passwords are the typical means of validating users' access to unencrypted data.

67. (a) The requirement is to identify the method to prevent data eavesdropping. Answer (a) is correct because data encryption prevents eavesdropping by using codes to ensure that data transmissions are protected from unauthorized tampering or electronic eavesdropping. Answer (b) is incorrect because dial back systems ensure that data are received from a valid source. Answer (c) is incorrect because message acknowledgment procedures help ensure that data were received by the intended party. Answer (d) is incorrect because password codes are designed to prevent unauthorized access to terminals or systems.

68. (b) The requirement is to identify a likely benefit of EDI. Answer (b) is correct because improved business relationships with trading partners is a benefit of EDI. Answer (a) is incorrect because EDI transmits document data, not the actual document. Answer (c) is incorrect because liability issues related to protection of proprietary business data are a major legal implication of EDI. Answer (d) is incorrect because EDI backup and contingency planning requirements are not diminished.

69. (a) The requirement is to identify the **least** likely part of a company's policy on electronic mail. Answer (a) is correct because the company should have access to the business-related e-mail that is left behind. Access to e-mail can also be critical in business or possible criminal investigations. The privacy concerns of the individual case must be mitigated by compelling business interests: the need to follow up on business e-mail and to assist in investigations. Answer (b) is incorrect because encryption helps prevent eavesdropping by unauthorized persons trying to compromise e-mail messages. Answer (c) is incorrect because limiting the number of packages would decrease the number of administrators who might have access to all messages. Answer (d) is incorrect because controlling the transmission of confidential information by e-mail will help avoid theft of information through intrusion by outsiders.

70. (c) The requirement is to identify the most likely risk relating to end-user computing as compared to a mainframe computer system. Answer (c) is correct because this risk is considered unique to end-user computing (EUC) system development. Answer (a) is incorrect because this risk relates to both traditional information systems and end-user computing (EUC) environments. Answer (b) is incorrect because this risk relates to both traditional information systems and end-user computing (EUC) environments. Answer (d) is incorrect because this risk relates to all computing environments.

71. (c) The requirement is to identify the risk that is **not** greater in an EFT environment as compared to a manual system using paper transactions. Answer (c) is correct because per transaction costs are lower with electronic funds transfer. Answer (a) is incorrect because this is a major risk factor inherent to electronic funds transfer (EFT). Answer (b) is incorrect because this is another inherent risk factor. Answer (d) is incorrect because this is a critical risk factor.

72. (c) The requirement is to identify the reply that is **not** a method to minimize the risk of installation of unlicensed microcomputer software. Answer (c) is correct because this technique will not affect introduction of unlicensed software. Answer (a) is incorrect because this technique works. Answer (b) is incorrect because such audits are a must to test the other controls that should be in place. Answer (d) is incorrect because the basis for all good controls is a written policy.

73. (a) The requirement is to determine whose responsibility it is to back up software and data files in distributed or cooperative systems. Answer (a) is correct because in distributed or cooperative systems, the responsibility for ensuring that adequate backups are taken is the responsibility of user management because the systems are under the control of users. Answer (b) is incorrect because in distributed environments, there will be no systems programmers comparable to those at central sites for traditional systems. Answer (c) is incorrect because in distributed environments, there may be no data entry clerks because users are typically performing their own data entry. Answer (d) is incorrect because in distributed environments, there are no tape librarians.

74. (b) The requirement is to identify the **least** likely way that a client's data will be input. Answer (b) is correct because the term "dynamic linking character reader" is a combination of terms that has no real meaning. The other three terms all represent methods of data input.

75. (d) The requirement is to identify what end-user computing is an example of. Answer (d) is correct because end-user computing involves individual users performing the development and execution of computer applications in a decentralized manner. Answer (a) is incorrect because client/server processing involves a networked model, rather than an end-user approach. Answer (b) is incorrect because a distributed system involves networked computers processing transactions for a single (or related) database. Answer (c)

is incorrect because using sophisticated techniques from statistics, artificial intelligence, and computer graphics to explain, confirm, and explore relationships among data may be performed in many environments.

76. (c) The requirement is to identify the type of computer that end-user computing is most likely to occur on. Answer (c) is correct because end-user computing involves individual users performing the development and execution of computer applications in a decentralized manner and these individuals are most likely to be using personal computers. Answers (a) and (b) are incorrect because they represent computers less frequently used by end users. Answer (d) is incorrect because "personal reference assistants" is a term not used in information technology.

77. (a) The requirement is to identify the correct statement regarding the Internet as a commercially viable network. Answer (a) is correct because companies that wish to maintain adequate security must use firewalls to protect data from being accessed by unauthorized users. Answer (b) is incorrect because anyone can establish a homepage on the Internet without obtaining permission. Answer (c) is incorrect because there are no such security standards for connecting to the Internet.

78. (d) The requirement is to identify a method of reducing security exposure when transmitting proprietary data over communication lines. Answer (d) is correct because cryptographic devices protect data in transmission over communication lines. Answer (a) is incorrect because asynchronous modems handle data streams from peripheral devices to a central processor. Answer (b) is incorrect because authentication techniques confirm that valid users have access to the system. Answer (c) is incorrect because callback procedures are used to ensure incoming calls are from authorized locations.

79. (a) The requirement is to identify the reply which is **not** a reason that securing client/server systems is a complex task. Answer (a) is correct because client/server implementation does not necessarily use relational databases. Answers (b), (c), and (d) are all incorrect because the number of access points, concurrent operation by multiple users, and widespread data access and update capabilities make securing such systems complex.

80. (c) The requirement is to identify what an auditor would ordinarily consider the greatest risk regarding an entity's use of electronic data interchange (EDI). Answer (c) is correct because an EDI system must include controls to make certain that EDI transactions are processed by the proper entity, using the proper accounts. Answers (a) and (b) are incorrect because authorization of EDI transactions and duplication of EDI transmissions ordinarily pose no greater risk than for other systems. Answer (d) is incorrect because the elimination of paper documents in and of itself does not propose a great risk.

81. (d) The requirement is to identify the characteristic that distinguishes electronic data interchange (EDI) from other forms of electronic commerce. Answer (d) is correct because standards for EDI transactions, within any one group of trading partners, have been agreed upon so as to allow the system to function efficiently. Answer (a) is incorrect because the cost of EDI transaction using a VAN will often exceed the cost of using the Internet. Answer (b) is incorrect because software maintenance contracts are often necessary. Answer (c) is incorrect because EDI commerce involves legally binding contracts between trading partners.

82. (c) The requirement is to identify a component of a local area network. Answer (c) is correct because a local area network requires that data be transmitted from one computer to another through some form of transmission media. Answers (a), (b), and (d) are all general replies that are not requirements of a local area network.

83. (c) The requirement is to identify an additional cost of transmitting business transactions by means of electronic data interchange (EDI) rather than in a traditional paper environment. Answer (c) is correct because such transactions must be translated to allow transmission. Answer (a) is incorrect because no particular controls are required for redundant data checks under EDI as compared to a traditional paper environment. Answer (b) is incorrect because there need be no increase in random data entry errors under EDI. Answer (d) is incorrect because since computer controls are ordinarily heavily relied upon under EDI, often fewer supervisory personnel are needed.

84. (b) The requirement is to identify the statement which does not represent an exposure involved with electronic data interchange (EDI) systems. Answer (b) is correct because EDI ordinarily decreases transaction processing time; it does not delay transaction processing time. Answer (a) is incorrect because increased reliance upon both one's own computers and those of other parties are involved in EDI. Answer (c) is incorrect because involvement with other parties in EDI systems may result in the loss of confidentiality of information. Answer (d) is incorrect because EDI systems involve third parties such as customers, suppliers, and those involved with the computer network, and accordingly result in increased reliance upon their proper performance of their functions.

85. (b) The requirement is to identify the correct statement concerning internal control when a client uses an electronic data interchange system for processing its sales. Answer (b) is correct because encryption controls are designed to assure that messages are unreadable to unauthorized persons and to thereby control the transactions. Answer (a) is incorrect because suppliers are not ordinarily included in a company's sales controls and because even in a purchasing EDI system all suppliers need not be included. Answer (c) is incorrect because a value-added-network that provides network services may or may not be used in an EDI system. Answer (d) is incorrect because "paper" versions of transactions typically disappear in an EDI system.

86. (d) The requirement is to identify the statement that represents a disadvantage for an entity that keeps microcomputer-prepared data files rather than manually prepared files. Answer (d) is correct because persons with computer skills may be able to improperly access and alter microcomputer files. When a system is prepared manually

such manipulations may be more obvious. Answer (a) is incorrect because random error is more closely associated with manual processing than with computer processing. Answer (b) is incorrect because comparing recorded accountability with the physical count of assets should not be affected by whether a manual or a microcomputer system is being used. Answer (c) is incorrect because the accuracy of the programming process is not generally tested when microcomputers are used.

87. (a) The requirement is to identify a benefit of transmitting transactions in an electronic data interchange (EDI) environment. Answer (a) is correct because the speed at which transactions can occur and be processed electronically results in lower year-end receivables since payments occur so quickly. Answer (b) is incorrect because an EDI environment requires many controls related to sales and collections. Answer (c) is incorrect because sampling may or may not be used in such circumstances. Answer (d) is incorrect because third-party service providers are often involved in such transactions—accordingly they are relied upon. See Auditing Procedure Study *Audit Implications of EDI* for information on electronic data interchange systems.

88. (c) The requirement is to identify the network node that is used to improve network traffic and to set up as a boundary that prevents traffic from one segment to cross over to another. Answer (c) is correct because a firewall is a computer that provides a defense between one network (inside the firewall) and another network (outside the firewall) that could pose a threat to the inside network. Answer (a) is incorrect because a router is a computer that determines the best way for data to move forward to their destination. Answer (b) is incorrect because a gateway is a communications interface device that allows a local area network to be connected to external networks and to communicate with external computers and databases. Answer (d) is incorrect because a heuristic is a simplified rule to help an individual make decisions.

89. (a) The requirement is to identify the best example of how specific controls in a database environment may differ from controls in a nondatabase environment. Answer (a) is correct because a primary control within a database environment is to appropriately control access and updating by the many users; in most nondatabase environments there are ordinarily far fewer users who are able to directly access and update data. Answer (b) is incorrect because controls over data sharing differ among users for both database and nondatabase environments. Answer (c) is incorrect because under both database and nondatabase systems, the programmer should debug the program. Answer (d) is incorrect because controls can verify that authorized transactions are processed under either a database or nondatabase environment.

90. (b) The requirement is to identify an effective audit approach in an EDI environment in which documentation of transactions will be retained for only a short period of time. Answer (b) is correct because performing tests throughout the year will allow the auditor to examine transaction documentation before the transactions are destroyed. Answer (a) is incorrect because if documentation relating to the transactions is not maintained, it will be impossible to perform such cutoff tests. Answer (d) is incorrect because such a situation need not lead to a 100% count of inventory at or near year-end. Answer (d) is incorrect because an increase in the assessed level of control risk rather than a decrease is more likely.

91. (d) The requirement is to identify the encryption feature that can be used to authenticate the originator of a document and to ensure that the message is intact and has not been tampered with. Answer (d) is correct because digital signatures are used in electronic commerce to authenticate the originator and to ensure that the message has not been tampered with. Answers (a), (b), and (c) are all incorrect because they do not directly deal with such authentication.

92. (a) The requirement is to identify the process used in building an electronic data interchange (EDI) system to determine that elements in the entity's computer system correspond to the standard data elements. Answer (a) is correct because mapping, or "data mapping," is the processes of selecting the appropriate data fields from the various application databases and passing them to the EDI translation software. Answer (b) is incorrect because translation involves the actual modification of the data into a standard format that is used by the EDI system. Answer (c) is incorrect because encryption is a technique for protecting information within a computer system in which an algorithm transforms that data to render it unintelligible; the process can be reversed to regenerate the original data for further processing. Answer (d) is incorrect because decoding is the process of making data intelligible. See the Auditing Procedure Study *Audit Implications of EDI* for more information on electronic data interchange.

93. (a) The requirement is to identify the password that would be most difficult to crack. A password is a secret series of characters that enables a user to access a file, computer, or program; ideally, the password should be something nobody could guess. Answer (a) is correct because OrCA!FlSi does not seem like a password that one would guess or even recall if seen briefly. Answers (b), (c), and (d) are all incorrect because they represent passwords that would be easier to identify.

94. (a) The requirement is to determine which reply represents a password security problem. A password is a secret series of characters that enables a user to access a file, computer, or program; ideally the password should be something that nobody could guess. Answer (a) is correct because individuals have a tendency to not change passwords, and over time, others may be able to identify them. Answer (b) is incorrect because using different passwords for different accounts on several systems represents a control (assuming the user can remember them). Answer (c) is incorrect because copying of passwords to a secure location (e.g., a wallet) does not ordinarily represent a security problem. Answer (d) is incorrect because passwords should be kept secret and not listed in an online dictionary.

95. (c) The requirement is to distinguish between the Web 2.0 applications. Answer (c) is correct because RSS feeds (and Atom feeds) are XML applications that are designed specifically for sharing and syndication of web content. The acronym RSS refers to Really Simple Syndication. (Atom

feeds are similar to RSS feeds). Answer (a) is incorrect because a wiki is a collaboratively-developed information sharing website. Answer (b) is incorrect because a blog is a moderator-led electronic discussion. Answer (d) is incorrect because Twitter is similar to a blog but restricts input to 140 characters per entry.

96. (b) The requirement is to identify the item that is **not** a COBIT 5 principle. Answer (b) is correct because business processes is not one of the five principles of COBIT 5. The five principles include: (1) Meeting stakeholder needs, (2) Covering the enterprise end-to-end, (3) Applying a single integrated framework, (4) Enabling a holistic approach, and (5) Separating governance from management.

97. (c) The requirement is to identify the organization that developed the COBIT framework. Answer (c) is correct because the COBIT framework was created by The Information Systems Audit and Control Association.

98. (b) The requirement is to identify the most likely procedure to be included in a computer disaster recovery plan. Answer (b) is correct because duplicate copies of critical files will allow an entity to reconstruct the data whose original files have been lost or damaged. Answer (a) is incorrect because an auxiliary power supply will provide uninterrupted electricity to avoid the need for a recovery since it may reduce the likelihood of such a disaster. Answer (c) is incorrect because simply maintaining passwords will not allow the entity to reconstruct data after a disaster has occurred. Answer (d) is incorrect because while cryptography will enhance the security of files from unintended uses, it is not a primary method to recover from a computer disaster.

99. (d) The requirement is to identify the type of backup site a company would most likely consider when there is concern about a power outage and desires for a fully configured and ready to operate system. Answer (d) is correct because a hot site is a site that is already configured to meet a user's requirements. Answer (a) is incorrect because a cold site is a facility that provides everything necessary to quickly install computer equipment but doesn't have the computers installed. Answers (b) and (c) are incorrect because they represent terms not frequently used in such circumstances.

100. (d) The requirement is to identify the procedure an entity would most likely include in its disaster recovery plan. Answer (d) is correct because storing duplicate copies of files in a different location will allow recovery of contaminated original files. Answer (a) is incorrect because converting all data from EDI format to an internal company format is ordinarily inefficient, and not a disaster recovery plan. Answer (b) is incorrect because a Trojan horse program (one which masquerades as a benign application but actually causes damage) ordinarily causes illicit activity, it does not prevent illicit activity. Answer (c) is incorrect because an auxiliary power supply is meant to prevent disaster, not recover from disaster.

101. (b) The requirement is to determine whether almost all commercially marketed software is copyrighted, copy protected, or both. Answer (b) is correct because while almost all such software is copyrighted, much of it is not copy protected. Answer (a) is incorrect because it suggests that almost all such software is copy protected. Answer (c) is incorrect both because it suggests that such software is not copyrighted and that it is copy protected. Answer (d) is incorrect because it suggests that such software is not copyrighted.

102. (c) The requirement is to identify a widely used disaster recovery approach. Answer (c) is correct because regular backups (copying) of data allows recovery when original records are damaged. Answer (a) is incorrect because encryption is used with a goal of making files impossible to read by those other than the intended users. Answer (b) is incorrect because firewalls are designed to control any possible inappropriate communication between computers within one system and those on the outside. Answer (d) is incorrect because surge protectors are electrical devices inserted in a power line to protect equipment from sudden fluctuations in current, and thereby prevent disasters, not recover from them.

103. (a) The requirement is to identify what a "hot site" is most frequently associated with. Answer (a) is correct because a hot site is a commercial disaster recovery service that allows a business to continue computer operations in the event of computer disaster. For example, if a company's data processing center become inoperable, that enterprise can move all processing to a hot site that has all the equipment needed to continue operation. Answer (b) is incorrect because a hot site is not frequently associated with online relational database design. Answer (c) is incorrect because source programs (programs written in a language from which statements are translated into machine language) are not directly related to a hot site. Answer (d) is incorrect because when used in information technology, the term hot site is not directly related to temperature control for computers.

104. (b) The requirement is to determine which reply is **not** a typical output control. Answer (b) is correct because matching the input data with information held on master or suspense files is a processing control, not an output control, to ensure that data are complete and accurate during updating. Answer (a) is incorrect because a review of the computer processing logs is an output control to ensure that data are accurate and complete. Answer (c) is incorrect because periodic reconciliation of output reports is an output control to ensure that data are accurate and complete. Answer (d) is incorrect because maintaining formal procedures and documentation specifying authorized recipients is an output control to ensure proper distribution.

105. (c) The requirement is to identify the best way to minimize the likelihood of unauthorized editing of production programs, job control language, and operating system software. Answer (c) is correct because program change control comprises: (1) maintaining records of change authorizations, code changes, and test results; (2) adhering to a systems development methodology (including documentation; (3) authorizing changeovers of subsidiary and headquarters' interfaces; and (4) restricting access to authorized source and executable codes. Answer (a) is incorrect because the purpose of database reviews is to determine if (1) users have gained access to database areas

for which they have no authorization; and (2) authorized users can access the database using programs that provide them with unauthorized privileges to view and/or change information. Answer (b) is incorrect because the purpose of compliance reviews is to determine whether an organization has complied with applicable internal and external procedures and regulations. Answer (d) is incorrect because the purpose of network security software is to provide logical controls over the network.

106. (d) The requirement is to determine the most likely actions relating to mainframe applications when a company decides to launch a downsizing project. Answer (d) is correct because mainframe applications represent a significant investment and may still provide adequate service. The fact that mainframes can provide a stable platform for enterprise applications may be an advantage while exploring other nonmainframe options. Answer (a) is incorrect because the costs of converting mainframe applications to a microcomputer network and retraining the personnel who would rewrite and maintain them preclude any rapid transition. Answer (b) is incorrect because general ledger programs that aggregate business data on a regular basis will be among the last to be converted. Answer (c) is incorrect because incremental modifications may have high paybacks.

107. (a) The requirement is to identify the greatest concern relating to a client's setting of used microcomputers when that corporation receives the majority of its revenue from top-secret military contracts with the government. Answer (a) is correct because while most delete programs erase file pointers, they do not remove the underlying data. The company must use special utilities that fully erase the data; this is especially important because of the potential for top-secret data on the microcomputers. This risk is the largest because it could cause them to lose military contract business. Answer (b) is incorrect because while it could create a liability for the company if a virus destroyed the purchasing party's data or programs the purchasing party should use antiviral software to detect and eliminate any viruses. This concern, while important, is not as serious as the one in answer (a). Answer (c) is incorrect because the purchasing party has a responsibility to insure that all their software is properly licensed. If the company represented that all the software was properly licensed, this could create a liability. However, this liability is not as serious as the implication from answer (a). Answer (d) is incorrect because terminal emulation software is widely available.

108. (b) The requirement is to identify a reason to use bar codes rather than other means of identifying information on parts. Answer (b) is correct because a reason to use bar codes rather than other means of identification is to record the movement of parts with minimal labor costs. Answer (a) is incorrect because the movement of parts can escape being recorded with any identification method. Answer (c) is incorrect because each vendor has its own part-numbering scheme, which is unlikely to correspond to the buyer's scheme. Answer (d) is incorrect because each vendor has its own identification method, although vendors in the same industry often cooperate to minimize the number of bar code systems they use.

109. **(b)** The requirement is to identify the function that ensures that changes in processing programs have a minimal impact on processing and result in minimal risk to the system. Answer (b) is correct because change control is the process of authorizing, developing, testing, and installing coded changes so as to minimize the impact on processing and the risk to the system. Answer (a) is incorrect because security administration is not involved as directly applicable as is change control. Answer (c) is incorrect because problem tracking is the process of collecting operational data about processes so that they can be analyzed for corrective action. Answer (d) is incorrect because problem-escalation procedures are a means of categorizing problems or unusual circumstances so that the least skilled person can address them.

110. **(b)** The requirement is to identify the approach(es) that may reduce an organization's risk of civil lawsuit due to the use of pirated software. Answer (b) is correct because: (I) Maintaining a log protects an organization since a log documents software purchases. (II) Auditing individual computers will discourage illegal software usage. (III) Establishing a corporate software policy will discourage illegal software usage. (IV) Allowing users to keep original diskettes increases both the likelihood of illegal copies being made and the loss of diskettes. Answers (a), (c), and (d) are all incorrect.

111. **(a)** The requirement is to identify a benefit of good recovery planning. Answer (a) is correct because an essential component of a disaster recovery plan is that the need for backup/restart has been anticipated and provided for in the application systems. Answer (b) is incorrect because change control procedures should not be bypassed by operating personnel, but that is not generally a consideration in disaster recovery planning. Answer (c) is incorrect because planned changes in equipment capacities should be compatible with projected workloads, but that is not generally a consideration in disaster recovery planning. Answer (d) is incorrect because service level agreements with owners of critical applications should be adequate, but that is not generally a consideration in disaster recovery planning.

112. **(d)** The requirement is to identify the biggest risk in not having an adequately staffed information center help desk. Answer (d) is correct because not having such a help desk may lead to a situation in which users will unknowingly persist in making errors in their interaction with the information systems. Answer (a) is incorrect because application audits should be about the same difficulty with or without an adequately staffed help desk. Answer (b) is incorrect because the preparation of documentation is a development function, not a help desk function. Answer (c) is incorrect because the likelihood of use of unauthorized program code is a function of change control, not of a help desk.

113. **(c)** The requirement is to determine how a database administrator should ensure that the database system properly controls access to accounting database files. Answer (c) is correct because one security feature in database systems is their ability to let the database administrator restrict access on a logical view basis for each user. Answer (a) is incorrect because if the only access permitted is read-only, then there could no updating of database files Answer (b) is

incorrect because permitting catalog updating from privileged software would be a breach of security, which might permit unauthorized access. Answer (d) is incorrect because updating of users' access profiles should be a function of a security officer, not the user.

114. **(b)** The requirement is to identify a major auditor concern when a client processes sales transactions on the Internet. Answer (b) is correct because computer disruptions may result in the incorrect recording of sales. Answer (a) is incorrect because electronic sales invoices may replace sales invoice documents in such an environment. Answer (c) is incorrect because there may or may not be a need to establish an integrated test facility in such circumstances. Answer (d) is incorrect because the frequency of archiving and data retention is not as important as is ensuring that such policies appropriately control system backup.

115. **(a)** The requirement is to identify the correct statement concerning internal control in an electronic data interchange (EDI) system. Answer (a) is correct because preventive controls are important and often cost-effective in an EDI environment so as to not allow the error to occur, and because detective controls may detect misstatements too late to allow proper correction. Answer (b) is incorrect because the control objectives under EDI systems generally remain the same as for other information systems. Answer (c) is incorrect because a well-controlled EDI system may allow control risk to be assessed below the maximum. Answer (d) is incorrect because the programmed nature of most EDI controls limits the possible segregation of duties within the system. See Auditing Procedure Study *Audit Implications of EDI* for information on electronic data interchange systems.

116. **(b)** The requirement is to identify the correct statement relating to the security of messages in an electronic data interchange (EDI) system. Answer (b) is correct because both the physical security of the hardware and the hardware itself create a situation in which the encryption is ordinarily more secure than encryption performed by software. Answer (a) is incorrect because message authentication deals with whether the message received is the same as that sent, and not as directly with confidentiality. Answer (c) is incorrect because message authentication deals most directly with whether changes have been made in the message sent, and not with the variety of other potential problems addressed by segregation of duties. Answer (d) is incorrect because security is necessary at the transaction phase in EDI systems. See Auditing Procedure Study *Audit Implications of EDI* for information on electronic data interchange systems.

117. **(c)** The requirement is to identify an essential element of the audit trail in an electronic data interchange (EDI) system. Answer (c) is correct because effective audit trails need to include activity logs, including processed and failed transactions, network and sender/recipient acknowledgments, and time sequence of processing. Answer (a) is incorrect because disaster recovery plans, while essential to the overall system, are not an essential element of the audit trail. Answer (b) is incorrect because encrypted hash totals deal less directly with the audit trail than do activity logs. Answer (d) is incorrect because hardware security modules that store sensitive data do not deal directly with the audit trail. See Auditing Procedure Study *Audit Implications of EDI* for information on electronic data interchange systems.

118. (a) The requirement is to identify an essential element of the audit trail in an electronic data interchange (EDI) system. Answer (a) is correct because effective audit trails need to include activity logs, including processed and failed transactions, network and sender/recipient acknowledgments, and time sequence of processing. Answer (b) is incorrect because neither message directories nor header segments directly affect the audit trial. Answer (c) is incorrect because contingency and disaster recovery plans, while important, are not as directly related to the audit trail as are the acknowledgments suggested in answer (a). Answer (d) is incorrect because while knowing trading partner security and mailbox codes is essential, it is more closely related to overall security than is answer (a). See Auditing Procedure Study *Audit Implications of EDI* for information on electronic data interchange systems.

119. (b) The requirement is to identify the type of control that involves adding an extra number at the end of an account number and subjecting the new number to an algorithm. Answer (b) is correct because a check digit is an extra reference number that follows an identification code and bears a mathematical relationship to the other digits. Answer (a) is incorrect because optical character recognition involves a computer being able to "read in" printed data. Answer (c) is incorrect because a dependency check involves some form of check between differing related pieces of data. Answer (d) is incorrect because a format check involves determining whether the proper type of data has been input or processed (e.g., numerical data input under account withdrawal amount).

120. (d) The requirement is to identify the best control for preventing someone with sufficient technical skill from circumventing security procedures and making changes to production programs. Answer (d) is correct because a suitable segregation of duties will make such alteration impossible since when duties are separated, users cannot obtain the detailed knowledge of programs and computer operators cannot gain unsupervised access to production programs. Answers (a), (b), and (c) are all incorrect because the reviews of jobs processed, comparing programs with copies, and running attest data will all potentially disclose such alteration, but will not prevent it.

121. (c) The requirement is to identify the best method of keeping computer program libraries secure. Answer (c) is correct because restricting physical and logical access secures program libraries from unauthorized use in person or remotely via terminals. Answers (a) and (b) are incorrect because installing a logging system for program access or monitoring physical access would permit detection of unauthorized access but would not prevent it. Answer (d) is incorrect because denying all remote access via terminals would likely be inefficient and would not secure program libraries against physical access.

122. (d) The requirement is to identify the security control that would best prevent unauthorized access to sensitive data

through an unattended data terminal directly connected to a mainframe. Answer (d) is correct because automatic log-off of inactive users may prevent the viewing of sensitive data on an unattended data terminal. Answer (a) is incorrect because data terminals do not normally use screen-saver protection, and because a screen saver would not prevent access. Answer (b) is incorrect because scripting is the use of a program to automate a process such as startup. Answer (c) is incorrect because encryption of data files will not prevent viewing of data on an unattended data terminal.

123. (d) The requirement is to identify the reply that most likely represents a hash total. A hash total is a control total where the total is meaningless for financial purposes, but has some meaning for processing purposes. Answer (d) is correct because 810 represents the sum of the invoice numbers. Answer (a) is incorrect because it appears to be an accumulation of all letters, plus a sum of the numbers. Answer (b) is more likely to be considered a record count. Answer (c) is incorrect because it is simply the invoice number of the last invoice in the batch.

124. (a) The requirement is to determine the type of control that would detect a miscoding of a product number on an order from a customer. Answer (a) is correct because a check digit is an extra digit added to an identification number to verify that the number is authorized and to thereby detect such coding errors. Answer (b) is incorrect because a record count involves a count of the number of records processed which is not being considered here. Answer (c) is incorrect because the term "hash total" ordinarily relates to a total of items and is meaningless for financial purposes (e.g., the total of the invoice numbers for a particular day's sales), but has some meaning for processing purposes. Answer (d) is incorrect because a redundant data check uses two identifiers in each transaction record to confirm that the correct master file record has been updated (e.g., the client account number and first several letters of the customer's name can be used to retrieve the correct customer master record from the accounts receivable file).

125. (b) The requirement is to identify the technique that would most likely detect a nonexistent zip code. Answer (b) is correct because a zip code that is nonexistent would not pass a validity test. It would not be a valid item. Answer (a) is incorrect because a limit test restricts the amount of a transaction that will be processed. Answer (c) is incorrect because a parity test prevents loss of digits in processing. Answer (d) is incorrect because a record count test helps prevent the loss of records.

126. (a) The requirement is to determine whether limit tests and validity check tests are processing controls designed to ensure the reliability and accuracy of data processing. Answer (a) is correct because both a limit test and a validity check test may serve as a control over either inputs or processing in an accounting system. A limit test will establish an upper and/or lower limit as reasonable, with results outside of those limits indicated (e.g., after net pay is calculated, an "error message" is printed for any employee with a weekly salary in excess of a certain amount). A validity check test allows only "valid" transactions or data to be processed in the system (e.g., during the processing of payroll, a control determines whether a paycheck is improperly issued to an ex-employee).

127. (b) The requirement is to identify the activity most likely to be performed in the information systems department. Answer (b) is correct because the conversion of information into machine-readable form is essential to the inputting of data; computer equipment is generally used to perform this function. Answer (a) is incorrect because under good internal control, the initiation of changes to master records should be authorized by functions independent of those which process the records. Answer (c) is incorrect because a separate function should exist to correct transactional errors. Answer (d) is incorrect because changes to computer applications should be initiated by the appropriate user group.

128. (a) The requirement is to determine the errors which a header label is likely to prevent. Since the header label is actually on the magnetic tape, it is the computer operator whose errors will be prevented. Answer (b) is incorrect because the keypunch operator deals with punch cards. Answer (c) is incorrect because the programmer will write the programs and not run them under good internal control. Answer (d) is incorrect because the maintenance technician will not run the magnetic tape.

129. (b) The requirement is to determine the purpose of programming computer to immediately transmit back to the terminal for display information that has been input on cash disbursements. Answer (b) is correct because the entry of disbursement amounts and the subsequent display of the amounts on the terminal screen will allow the operator to visually verify that the data provided to be input was entered accurately. Answer (a) is incorrect because displaying on the screen the data entered does not ensure the validity of the data, only that the data was entered correctly. Answer (c) is incorrect because no evidence has been provided as to whether the disbursement was authorized. Answer (d) is incorrect because the display of the amount will not be compared to a "correct" amount—only to the amount that was to be input.

130. (b) The requirement is to identify a useful control when computer programs or files can be accessed from terminals. Answer (b) is correct because use of personal identification codes (passwords) will limit access to the programs or files on the terminal to those who know the codes. Answers (a), (c), and (d) are all incorrect because while they list valid controls used in computer systems, none of them require entry of data by the user. A parity check control is a special bit added to each character stored in memory to help detect whether the hardware has lost a bit during the internal movement of that character. A self-diagnosis test is run on a computer to check the internal operations and devices within the computer system. An echo check is primarily used in telecommunications transmissions to determine whether the receiving hardware has received the information sent by the sending hardware.

131. (a) The requirement is to identify the item which would reduce the possibility of erasing a large amount of information stored on magnetic tape. Answer (a) is correct

because a file protection ring is a control that ensures that an operator does not erase important information on a magnetic tape. Answer (b) is incorrect because a check digit is a digit added to an identification number to detect entry errors. Answer (c) is incorrect because a completeness test would generally be used to test whether all data were processed. Answer (d) is incorrect because conversion verification would address whether the conversion of data from one form to another (e.g., disk to magnetic tape) was complete.

132. (b) The requirement is to identify the controls most likely to assure that an entity can reconstruct its financial records. Answer (b) is correct because backup diskettes or tapes may be maintained that will provide the information needed to reconstruct financial records. Answer (a) is incorrect because while hardware controls are meant to assure the proper processing of data, when reconstruction is needed, hardware controls will not have the data necessary to reconstruct the financial records. Answer (c) is incorrect because parallel simulations will only occasionally be run and will not maintain adequate data to reconstruct records. Answer (d) is incorrect because while systems flowcharts will provide information on the design of the overall system, they will not assure the reconstruction of financial records.

133. (d) The requirement is to identify the type of input control that is a numeric value computed to provide assurance that the original value has not been altered in construction or transmission. Answer (d) is correct because a check digit is an extra digit added to an identification number to detect such errors. Answer (a) is incorrect because the term "hash total" ordinarily relates to a total of items and is meaningless for financial purposes (e.g., the total of the invoice numbers for a particular day's sales), but has some meaning for processing purposes. Answer (b) is incorrect because a parity check is a process in which a computer reads or receives a set of characters and simultaneously sums the number of 1 bits in each character to verify that it is an even (or alternatively, odd) number. Answer (c) is incorrect because encryption involves a coding of data, ordinarily for purposes of ensuring privacy and accuracy of transmission.

134. (c) The requirement is to identify the best example of a validity check. A validity test compares data (for example, employee, vendor, and other codes) against a master file for authenticity. Answer (c) is correct because the computer flagging of inappropriate transactions due to data in a control field that did not match that of an existing file record is such a test. Answer (a) is incorrect because a limit test ensures that a numerical amount in a record does not exceed some predetermined amount. Answer (b) is incorrect because the resubmission of data is not a validity check. Answer (d) is incorrect because the reading back of data to the terminal is an echo check.

135. (b) The requirement is to identify the type of computer test made to ascertain whether a given characteristic belongs to a group. Answer (b) is correct because a validity check determines whether a character is legitimate per the given character set. Note the validity check determines whether a given character is within the desired group. Answer (a) is incorrect because a parity check is a summation check in which the binary digits of a character are added to determine whether the sum is odd or even. Another bit, the parity bit, is turned on or off so the total number of bits will be odd or even as required. Answer (c) is incorrect because an echo check is a hardware control wherein data is transmitted back to its source and compared to the original data to verify the transmission correctness. Answer (d) is incorrect because a limit or reasonableness check is a programmed control based on specified limits. For example, a calendar month cannot be numbered higher than twelve, or a week cannot have more than 168 hours.

136. (a) The requirement is to identify the type of hardware control that requires the CPU to send signals to the printer to activate the print mechanism for each character. Answer (a) is correct because an echo check or control consists of transmitting data back to the source unit for comparison with the original data that were transmitted. In this case, the print command is sent to the printer and then returned to the CPU to verify that the proper command was received. A validity check [answer (b)] consists of the examination of a bit pattern to determine that the combination is legitimate for the system character set (i.e., that the character represented by the bit combination is valid per the system). Answer (c), a signal control or signal check, appears to be a nonsense term. Answer (d), check digit control, is a programmed control wherein the last character or digit can be calculated from the previous digits.

137. (b) The requirement is to identify an example of a check digit. Answer (b) is correct because a check digit is an extra digit in an identification number, algebraically determined, that detects specified types of data input, transmission, or conversion errors. Answer (a) is incorrect because the agreement of the total number of employees to the checks printed is an example of a control total. Answer (c) is incorrect because ensuring that all employee numbers are nine digits could be considered a logic check, a field size check, or a missing data check. Answer (d) is incorrect because determining that no employee has more than fifty hours per workweek is a limit check.

138. (b) The requirement is to determine the most likely significant deficiency in internal control. Answer (b) is correct because the systems programmer should not maintain custody of output in a computerized system. At a minimum, the programming, operating, and library functions should be segregated in such computer systems.

139. (c) The requirement is to identify the weakness in internal control relating to a function performed by computer department personnel. Answer (c) is correct because individuals outside of the computer department should originate changes in master files; this separates the authorization of changes from the actual processing of records. Answer (a) is incorrect because participation of computer department personnel in making computer software acquisition decisions is often appropriate and desirable given their expertise in the area. Answer (b) is incorrect for similar reasons as (a). In addition, computer department personnel will often be able to effectively design the required documentation for computerized systems. Answer (d) is incorrect because

the physical security for program files may appropriately be assigned to a library function within the computer department.

140. (a) The requirement is to identify the tool that would best give a graphical representation of a sequence of activities and decisions. Answer (a) is correct because a flowchart is a graphical representation of a sequence of activities and decisions. Answer (b) is incorrect because a control chart is used to monitor actual versus desired quality measurements during repetition operation. Answer (c) is incorrect because a histogram is a bar chart showing conformance to a standard bell curve. Answer (d) is incorrect because a run chart tracks the frequency or amount of a given variable over time.

141. (c) The requirement is to determine what the symbol A represents in the flowchart of a client's revenue cycle. Answer (c) is correct because the accounts receivable master file will be accessed during the revenue cycle and does not appear elsewhere on the flowchart. Answers (a), (b), and (d) are all incorrect because remittance advices, receiving reports, and cash disbursements transaction files are not a primary transaction file accessed during the revenue cycle.

142. (d) The requirement is to determine what the symbol B represents in the flowchart of a client's revenue cycle. Answer (d) is correct because it represents the only major document of the revenue cycle that is not presented elsewhere on the flowchart and because one would expect generation of a sales invoice in the cycle. Answer (a) is incorrect because the customer order appears in the top left portion of the flowchart. Answer (b) is incorrect because no receiving report is being generated during the revenue cycle. Answer (c) is incorrect because the customer's check (remittance) is represented on the top portion of the flowchart.

143. (d) The requirement is to identify the correct statement concerning an auditor's flowchart of a client's accounting system. Answer (d) is correct because a flowchart is a diagrammatic representation that depicts the auditor's understanding of the system. See AU 319 for various procedures auditors use to document their understanding of internal control. Answer (a) is incorrect because the flowchart depicts the auditor's understanding of the system, not the assessment of control risk. Answer (b) is incorrect because while the flowchart may be used to identify weaknesses, it depicts the entire system—strengths as well as weaknesses. Answer (c) is incorrect because the flowchart is of the accounting system, not of the control environment.

144. (b) The requirement is to determine the approach illustrated in the flowchart. Answer (b) is correct because parallel simulation involves processing actual client data through an auditor's program. Answer (a) is incorrect because program code checking involves an analysis of the client's actual program. Answer (c) is incorrect because an integrated test facility approach introduces dummy transactions into a system in the midst of live transaction processing and is usually built into the system during the original design. Answer (d) is incorrect because controlled reprocessing often includes using the auditor's copy of a client program, rather than the auditor's program.

145. (b) The requirement is to identify the item represented by the "X" on the flowchart. Answer (b) is correct because the existence of a credit memo, in addition to a sales invoice, would indicate that this portion of the flowchart deals with cash receipts; therefore, the "X" would represent the remittance advices. Thus, the receipt transactions are credited to the accounts receivable master file, and an updated master file, a register of receipts, and exception reports are generated. Answer (a) is incorrect because an auditor's test data will not result in an input into the transactions file. Answer (c) is incorrect because since no processing has occurred at the point in question—an error report is unlikely. Answer (d) is incorrect because credit authorization will generally occur prior to the preparation of credit memos.

146. (d) The requirement is to determine the symbolic representations that indicate that a file has been consulted. Answer (d) indicates that a manual operation (the trapezoid symbol) is accessing data from a file and returning the data to the file (i.e., "consulting" the file). Answer (a) is incorrect because it represents a processing step (the rectangle) being followed by a manual operation. Answer (b) is incorrect because it represents a document being filed. Answer (c) is incorrect because the diamond symbol represents a decision process.

147. (c) The requirement is to determine a benefit of a well-prepared flowchart. Answer (c) is correct because a flowchart may be used to document the auditor's understanding of the flow of transactions and documents. Answer (a) is incorrect because while an audit procedures manual may suggest the use of flowcharts, flowcharts will not in general be used to prepare such a manual. Answer (b) is less accurate than (c) because while it may be possible to obtain general information on various jobs, the flowchart will not allow one to obtain a **detailed** job description. Answer (d) is incorrect because a flowchart does not directly address the actual accuracy of financial data within a system.

Written Communication Task

Written Communication Task 1

Written
Communication

Help

Tintco, Inc. is a distributor of auto supplies. Currently, the corporation has a batch processing system for processing all transactions and maintaining its inventory records. Batches are processed monthly. George Wilson, the chief information officer for the corporation, is considering adopting an online, real-time processing system. He has asked you (a consultant) to prepare a memorandum describing the advantages of adopting such a system for the corporation.

REMINDER: Your response will be graded for both technical content and writing skills. Technical content will be evaluated for information that is helpful to the intended reader and clearly relevant to the issue. Writing skills will be evaluated for development, organization, and the appropriate expression of ideas in professional correspondence. Use a standard business memo or letter format with a clear beginning, middle, and end. Do not convey information in the form of a table, bullet point list, or other abbreviated presentation.

To: Mr. George Wilson, CIO
        Tintco, Inc.
From: CPA Candidate

Written Communication Task Solution

Written Communication Task 1

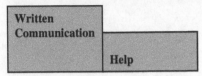

To: Mr. George Wilson, CIO
        Tintco, Inc.
From: CPA Candidate

As you requested, this memorandum describes the advantages of implementing an online, real-time processing system for inventory. As you are aware, the firm currently uses a batch processing system that processes transactions monthly. The primary advantage of an online, real-time processing system is that it provides timely information for decision making. With your batch system you have current and accurate information about inventory only monthly when the records are updated. Therefore, decisions about ordering inventory, valuation of inventory, and company profitability are not based on timely information. As a result, management cannot do a very good job of managing inventory. If the company implements an online, real-time system, information about inventory levels, inventory investment, and cost of goods sold would be available on a continuous basis. As a result, business decisions will be based on accurate and timely information. This should result in much better decisions and better financial performance.

It is clear that an online, real-time inventory system is superior to your current batch processing system. If you would like to have additional information about implementation of a new inventory processing system, please contact me.

Module 42: Economics, Strategy, and Globalization

Overview

This module covers three interrelated topics: economics, business strategy, and globalization. The module begins with a discussion of microeconomic and macroeconomic concepts. These concepts are important in determining effective strategies for a business. It is important to understand the effects of the macroeconomic factors on the business, including actions by governments that impact global markets. Business managers must also understand the nature of the markets that the company purchases and sells in. These factors provide inputs into strategy formulation for the firm. Because business is truly global, managers must understand the global economy and how global factors provide opportunities and risks for their companies. Before you begin the reading, you should review the key terms at the end of the module.

MICROECONOMICS

A. Focus

Microeconomics focuses on the behavior and purchasing decisions of individuals and firms. In a market economy goods and services are distributed through a system of prices. Goods and services are sold to those willing and able to pay the market price. The market price is determined based on demand and supply.

B. Demand

Demand is the quantity of a good or service that consumers are willing and able to purchase at a range of prices at a particular time. Therefore, market demand for a product is actually a schedule of the amount that would be purchased at various prices, with all other variables that affect demand being held constant. Graphically a demand curve shows an inverse relationship between the price and quantity demanded. That is, fewer products are demanded at higher prices. Illustrated below is the demand schedule and demand curve for Product X.

MARKET DEMAND FOR PRODUCT X

Price per unit	Quantity Demanded
$70	2,000
60	2,500
50	3,000
40	4,000
30	6,000
20	10,000

DEMAND CURVE

As illustrated, at a price of $50, 3,000 units of Product X will be bought. If the price of Product X changes, more or less will be bought.

1. **Demand curve shift.** A demand curve shifts when demand variables other than price change. For example, if the price of substitute products for Product X increase in price, the demand for Product X would shift upward and to the right. A demand curve shift is illustrated in the graph below.

2. Variables that may cause a demand curve shift include changes in the price of other goods and services, consumer tastes, spendable income, wealth, and the size of the market. The table below summarizes the effects of these factors on the demand for a particular product.

FACTORS AFFECTING THE DEMAND FOR A PRODUCT OTHER THAN ITS PRICE

Factor	Effect
Price of other goods and services (e.g. substitute goods)	**Direct relationship.** As goods that may be purchased instead go up in price the demand for the product goes up. As an example, if the price of pork increases the demand for beef may increase.
Price of complement products (i.e., products that must be used with the product or enhance its usefulness)	**Inverse relationship.** As the prices of complement goods go up, the demand for the product goes down. As an example, if the price of hamburger increases the demand for hamburger buns decreases.
Expectations of price increase	**Direct relationship.** If the price of the good is expected to increase in the future, there will be an increase in demand.
Consumer income and wealth	**Generally a direct relationship.** As consumer income (wealth) goes up the demand for many products (normal goods) goes up. However, there are certain **goods that are inferior** (e.g., bread, potatoes, etc.) and the demand for such goods actually goes up as consumer income (wealth) goes down. This is because consumers buy more inferior goods when they are short of money.
Consumer tastes	**Indeterminate relationship.** The effect depends on whether the shift is towards or away from the product.
Size of the market	**Direct relationship.** As the size of the market increases, the demand for the product will increase.
Group boycott	**Inverse relationship.** If a group of consumers boycott a product, demand will be decreased.

3. **Price elasticity of demand.** The elasticity of demand measures the sensitivity of demand to a change in price. It is calculated as follows:

$$E_D = \frac{\text{Percentage change in quantity demanded}}{\text{Percentage change in price}}$$

To make results the same regardless of whether there is an increase or decrease in price, the amount is usually calculated using the *arc method* as shown below.

$$E_D = \frac{\text{Change in quantity demanded}}{\text{Average quantity}} \div \frac{\text{Change in price}}{\text{Average price}}$$

EXAMPLE

Assume that you are operating a hot dog stand and sell hot dogs for $2.50. Your usual demand for hot dogs is 200 per day. To increase sales, you decide to run a $1.50 hot dog special and you sell 400 hot dogs for the day. The price elasticity of hot dogs is calculated as follows:

The change in quantity demanded = 200 (400 − 200)
The change in price = $1.00 ($2.50 − $1.50)
The average quantity = 300 [(200 + 400) ÷ 2]
The average price = $2.00 [($2.50 + $1.50) ÷ 2]

$$E_D = \frac{\text{Change in quantity demanded}}{\text{Average quantity}} \div \frac{\text{Change in price}}{\text{Average price}}$$

$$= \frac{200}{300} \div \frac{\$1.00}{\$2.00}$$

$$= .667 \div .5$$

$$= 1.334$$

Interpretation of the demand elasticity coefficient. If ED is greater than 1, demand is said to be elastic (sensitive to price changes). If ED is equal to 1, demand is said to be unitary (not sensitive or insensitive to price changes). If ED is less than 1, demand is said to be inelastic (not sensitive to price changes).

The price elasticity of demand coefficient allows management to calculate the effect of a price change on demand for the product. In the example above, a 10% decrease in the price of a hot dog results in a 13.34% (10% × 1.334) increase in demand. The elasticity of demand is greater for a product when there are more substitutes for the good, a larger proportion of income is spent on the good, or a longer period of time is considered.

> **NOTE:** The demand for luxury goods tends to be more elastic than for necessities.

4. **Relationship between price elasticity and total revenue.** Total revenue from the sale of a good is equal to the price times the quantity. Price elasticity is an important concept because if demand is elastic an increase in sales price results in a decrease in total revenue for all producers. If demand is unitary total revenue remains the same if price changes, and total revenue increases if price is increased when demand is inelastic. These relationships are shown in the following table:

EFFECT OF PRICE CHANGES ON VARIOUS TYPES OF GOODS

Price Change	Elastic Demand E > 1	Inelastic Demand E < 1	Unitary Demand E = 1
Price increase	Total revenue decreases	Total revenue increases	Total revenue does not change
Price decrease	Total revenue increases	Total revenue decreases	Total revenue does not change

In the example of the hot dog stand above, we calculated price elasticity to be 1.334. Therefore, demand is elastic and, as expected, we find that the price decline resulted in an increase in total revenue, $600 ($1.50 × 400) versus $500 ($2.50 × 200).

Price elasticity is an important concept because it reveals whether the firm is likely to be able to pass on cost increases to its customers. Obviously, when demand is inelastic the firm can increase its price with less of a negative impact.

5. **Income elasticity of demand.** Income elasticity of demand measures the change in the quantity demanded of a product given a change in income. Income elasticity is calculated as follows:

$$E_I = \frac{\text{Percentage change in quantity demanded}}{\text{Percentage change in income}}$$

The income elasticity of demand can be used to describe the nature of the product. The demand for normal products increases as consumer income increases. For example, the demand for **normal goods,** such as beefsteaks, increases as consumer income increases. Therefore, EI for beefsteaks is positive. The demand for **inferior goods,** such as beans, decreases as income increases; EI is negative. The demand for inferior goods increases as income declines, because when individuals have less money they substitute these less expensive goods for normal goods.

6. **Cross-elasticity of demand.** Cross-elasticity of demand measures the change in demand for a good when the price of a related or competing product is changed. For example, Coca Cola Company would be interested in knowing how an increase in the price of Pepsi would affect the sales of Coca Cola. The coefficient of cross-elasticity is calculated as follows:

$$E_{XY} = \frac{\text{Percentage change in the quantity demanded of Product X}}{\text{Percentage change in the price of Product Y}}$$

In our case Pepsi would be Product Y, the competing product with the price change, and Coca Cola would be Product X. The coefficient describes the relationship between the two products. If the coefficient is positive, the products are substitutes (like Pepsi and Coca Cola). If the coefficient is negative, the products are complements (like hamburger and hamburger buns) and if the coefficient is zero, the products are unrelated. The table below illustrates these relationships.

CROSS-ELASTICITY OF DEMAND

Coefficient	Relationship between goods
Coefficient of cross-elasticity positive ($E_{xy} > 0$)	Substitutes
Coefficient of cross-elasticity negative ($E_{xy} < 0$)	Complements
Coefficient of cross-elasticity zero ($E_{xy} = 0$)	Unrelated

EXAMPLE

Assume that the cross-elasticity of demand for Product X in relation to Product Y is calculated to be 2.00. If the price of Product Y increases by 5%, then the demand for Product X would increase by 10% (5% × 2.00).

7. **Consumer demand and utility**

   a. As illustrated previously, the demand curve for a particular good is downward sloping. As the price of the good declines, consumers will purchase more because of substitution and income effects. The **substitution effect** refers to the fact that as the price of a good falls, consumers will use it to replace similar goods. As an example, as the price of pork falls, consumers will purchase more pork than other types of meat. The **income effect** refers to the fact that as the price of a good falls, consumers can purchase more with a given level of income.

   b. An individual demands a particular good because of the utility (satisfaction) he or she receives from consuming it. The more goods an individual consumes the more total utility the individual receives. However, the marginal (additional) utility from consuming each additional unit decreases. This is referred to as the **law of diminishing marginal utility**.

   c. A consumer maximizes utility from spending his or her income when the marginal utility of the last dollar spent on each commodity is the same. Utility maximization may be presented mathematically as shown below.

   $$\frac{\text{Marginal Utility of A}}{\text{Price of A}} = \frac{\text{Marginal Utility of B}}{\text{Price of B}} = \frac{\text{Marginal Utility of Z}}{\text{Price of Z}}$$

   d. To simplify this concept most economics books illustrate marginal utility with only two types of goods (e.g., chocolate bars and cans of soda). They construct a series of **indifference curves** which illustrate the combinations of chocolate bars and soda that provide equal utility. The optimal level of consumption of the two goods is then found where the individual's **budget constraint** line intersects the highest possible utility curve. At this point the individual receives the greatest amount of utility for the amount of money available. This relationship is illustrated below.

           As illustrated, the individual gets the greatest satisfaction for the funds available at point A.

e.   Consumption decisions depend on many factors but the main one is **personal disposable income**. This is the amount of income consumers have after receiving transfer payments from the government (e.g., welfare payments) and paying their taxes. When their personal disposable income goes up, consumers buy more. They buy less when it goes down.

f.   The relationship between changes in personal disposable income and consumption is described by a **consumption function**. The function is typically described as follows:

$$C = c_0 + c_1 Y_D$$

Where

C = Consumption for a period
Y_D = Disposable income for the period
c_0 = The constant
c_1 = The slope of the consumption function

      The important factor from the above function is the slope, c1. It measures the consumer's **marginal propensity to consume (MPC)** describing how much of each additional dollar in personal disposable income that the consumer will spend. A consumption function is shown graphically below.

g.   The **marginal propensity to save (MPS)** is the percentage of additional income that is saved. Since a consumer can either spend or save money, the marginal propensity to consume plus the marginal propensity to save is equal to one as shown below.

$$MPC + MPS = 1$$

h.   Certain nonincome factors may also affect consumption, including

     (1)   Expectations about future prices of goods
     (2)   Quantity of consumer liquid assets
     (3)   Amount of consumer debt
     (4)   Stock of consumer durable goods
     (5)   Attitudes about saving money
     (6)   Interest rates

C. Supply

A supply curve shows the amount of a product that would be supplied at various prices. Graphically a supply curve shows a direct relationship between price and quantity sold. The higher the price the more products that would be supplied. A supply schedule and supply curve for Product X are presented below.

MARKET SUPPLY FOR PRODUCT X

Price per unit	Quantity supplied
$70	10,000
60	6,000
50	4,000
40	1,800
30	1,000
20	500

SUPPLY CURVE

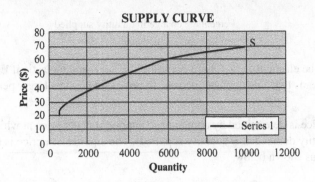

A change in the market price of the product results in a shift along the existing supply curve. For example, at $50, the market would supply 4,000 units but if the price changes to $60, the amount supplied will increase to 6,000.

1. **Supply curve shift.** A supply curve shift occurs when supply variables other than price change. As an example, if the costs to produce the product increase, the supply curve would shift upward and to the left. A shift in the supply curve is illustrated below.

SHIFT IN SUPPLY FOR BEER

2. Variables that cause a supply curve shift include changes in the number or size of producers, changes in various production costs (wages, rents, raw materials), technological advances, and government actions. The effects of these variables are shown in the table below.

FACTORS AFFECTING THE SUPPLY OF A PRODUCT OTHER THAN ITS PRICE

Factor	Effect
Number of producers	**Direct relationship.** Generally an increase in the number of producers will cause an increase in the amount of goods supplied at a given price.
Change in production costs or technological advances	**Inverse relationship.** As production costs go up fewer products will be supplied at a given price. If costs go down, more products will be produced.
Government subsidies	**Direct relationship.** Subsidies in effect reduce the production cost of goods and, therefore, increase the goods supplied at a given price.
Government price controls	Price controls would tend to limit the amount of goods supplied by holding the price artificially low.
Prices of other goods	**Inverse relationship.** If other products can be produced with greater returns, producers will produce those goods.
Price expectations	**Direct relationship.** If it is expected that prices will be higher for the good in the future, production of the good will increase.

3. **Elasticity of supply.** The elasticity of supply measures the percentage change in the quantity supplied of a product resulting from a change in the product price. The elasticity of supply is calculated as follows:

$$E_s = \frac{\text{Percentage change in quantity supplied}}{\text{Percentage change in price}}$$

- Supply is said to be elastic if $E_s > 1$, unitary elastic if $E_s = 1$, and inelastic if $E_s < 1$.
- Elastic supply means that a percentage increase in price will create a larger percentage increase in supply.

D. Market Equilibrium

A product's equilibrium price is determined by demand and supply; it is the price at which all the goods offered for sale will be sold (i.e., quantity demanded = quantity supplied). The equilibrium price is the price at which the demand and supply curve intersect as shown below.

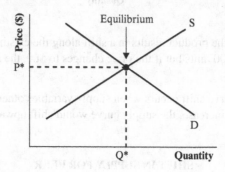

1. **Government intervention.** Government actions may change market equilibrium through taxes, subsidies, and rationing. For example, a subsidy paid to farmers will reduce the cost of producing a particular farm product and, therefore, cause the equilibrium price to be lower than it would be without the subsidy. Import taxes, on the other hand, would increase the cost of an imported product causing the equilibrium price to be higher.

   a. **Price ceiling.** A price ceiling is a specified maximum price that may be charged for a good. If the price ceiling is set for a good below the equilibrium price, it will cause good shortages because suppliers will devote their production facilities to producing other goods.

   b. **Price floor.** A price floor is a minimum specified price that may be charged for a good. If the price floor is set for a good above the equilibrium price, it will cause overproduction and surpluses will develop.

   Therefore, we see that government intervention in terms of taxes, subsidies, or price controls interfere with the free market and can result in an inefficient allocation of resources. Too many resources are devoted to certain sectors of the economy at the expense of other sectors.

2. **Externalities.** Another factor that causes inefficiencies in the pricing of goods in the market is the existence of externalities. **Externalities** is the term used to describe damage to common areas that is caused by the production of certain goods. A prominent example of an externality is pollution. Because these externalities are not included in the production costs of the goods, the supply is higher and the price is lower than is appropriate. Government laws and regulations (e.g., Environmental Protection Agency regulations) attempt to force firms to change their production methods to make externalities part of the cost of production. This causes the market price of these products to be a more accurate reflection of the cost of the goods to society.

3. **The effects of shifts in demand and supply.** The effects on equilibrium of shifts in demand and supply are shown in the following graphs.

INCREASE IN DEMAND AND NEW EQUILIBRIUM

INCREASE IN SUPPLY AND NEW EQUILIBRIUM

The effects of shifts in demand and supply can be complex especially when both shift simultaneously. The following table describes the effects of these changes:

Change in demand or supply	Effect
1. Increase (decrease) in demand, no change in supply	Equilibrium price will increase (decrease) and quantity purchased will increase (decrease)
2. Increase (decrease) in supply, no change in demand	Equilibrium price will decrease (increase) and quantity purchased will increase (decrease)
3. Both demand and supply increase (decrease)	Quantity purchased will increase (decrease) and the new equilibrium price is indeterminate
4. Demand increases and supply decreases	Equilibrium price will increase and quantity purchased is indeterminate.
5. Demand decreases and supply increases	Equilibrium price will decrease and quantity purchased is indeterminate

E. Costs of Production

1. **Short-run total costs**

   a. In the short run, firms have both fixed and variable costs. Total fixed costs are those that are committed and will not change with different levels of production. An example of a fixed cost is the rent paid on a long-term lease for a factory. Variable costs are the costs of variable inputs, such as raw materials, variable labor costs, and variable overhead. These costs are directly related to the level of production for the period. In the short run, costs behave as follows:

      - **Average fixed cost (AFC)**—Fixed cost per unit of production. It goes down consistently as more units are produced.
      - **Average variable cost (AVC)**—Total variable costs divided by the number of units produced. It initially stays constant until the inefficiencies of producing in a fixed-size facility cause variable costs to begin to rise.
      - **Marginal cost (MC)**—The added cost of producing one extra unit. It initially decreases but then begins to increase due to inefficiencies.
      - **Average total cost (ATC)**—Total costs divided by the number of units produced. Its behavior depends on the makeup of fixed and variable costs.

   b. The cause of the inefficiencies described above is referred to as the **law of diminishing returns**. This law states that as we try to produce more and more output with a fixed productive capacity, marginal productivity will decline. The graph below illustrates the relationships between various short-run costs.

2. **Long-run total costs**

a. In the long run all inputs are variable because additional plant capacity can be built. If in the long run a firm increases all production factors by a given proportion, there are the following three possible outcomes:

- **Constant returns to scale**—Output increases in same proportion.
- **Increasing returns to scale**—Output increases by a greater proportion.
- **Decreasing returns to scale**—Output increases by a smaller proportion.

b. In many industries, especially those that are capital intensive, increasing returns to scale occur up to a point, generally as a result of division of labor and specialization in production. However, beyond a certain size, management has problems controlling production and decreasing returns to scale arise. The following graph illustrates a long-run average total cost (ATC) curve which begins with increasing returns to scale (A), and proceeds to constant returns to scale (B), and eventually decreasing returns to scale (C) as the firm grows.

3. **Profits.** Economists refer to two different types of profit.

a. **Normal profit**—The amount of profit necessary to compensate the owners for their capital and/or managerial skills. It is just enough profit to keep the firm in business in the long run.

b. **Economic profit**—The amount of profit in excess of normal profit. In a perfectly competitive market, economic profit cannot be experienced in the long run.

F. **Production**

1. Management makes production decisions based on the relationship between marginal revenue and marginal cost. **Marginal revenue** is the additional revenue received from the sale of one additional unit of product. A good should be produced and sold as long as the marginal cost (MC) of producing the good is less than or equal to the marginal revenue (MR) from sale of that good. This relationship is shown in the following graph.

2. The price of input resources (e.g., labor, raw materials, etc.) is determined by demand and supply. If the price of an input increases, demand will decline. On the other hand, demand will increase if the price declines. In making decisions about the employment of resources, management considers the marginal product for each input resource. The **marginal product** is the additional output obtained from employing one additional unit of a resource. The change in total revenue from employing one additional unit of a resource is referred to as the **marginal revenue product**.

EXAMPLE

Thorp Corporation produces Product G and has developed the following chart illustrating relationships between number of workers producing the product, the number of units produced, and the revenue generated.

Number of workers	Products produced	Revenue generated
4	100	$200,000
5	120	$240,000
6	139	$275,000
7	157	$300,000

The marginal product of employing the 6th worker is equal to 19 (139 – 120), and the marginal revenue product is equal to $35,000 ($275,000 – $240,000).

---

3. The **marginal revenue per-unit** is calculated by dividing the marginal revenue product by the increase in products produced by employing one additional unit of resource. Using the above example of employing a 6th worker, the marginal revenue per-unit is equal to $1,842.11 [$35,000 (marginal revenue product) ÷ 19 (139 – 120) increase in products produced].

4. To be competitive management must produce the optimal output in the most efficient manner. The cost of production in the long run is minimized when the marginal product (MP) per dollar of every input (resource) is the same. Similar to utility maximization for a consumer, the least cost formula is

$$\frac{\text{MP of input A}}{\text{Price of input A}} = \frac{\text{MP of input B}}{\text{Price of input B}} = \frac{\text{MP of input C}}{\text{Price of input C}} = \frac{\text{MP of input Z}}{\text{Price of input Z}}$$

G. Market Structure

1. Industries are often classified by their market structure as perfect competition, pure monopoly, monopolistic competition, and oligopoly.

a. **Perfect (pure) competition**

(1) An industry is perfectly competitive if

(a) It is composed of a large number of sellers, each of which is too small to affect the price of the product or service

    (b) The firms sell a virtually identical product

    (c) Firms can enter or leave the market easily (i.e., no barriers to entry)

There are few perfectly competitive markets; common examples include the commodity markets, such as markets for wheat, soybeans, and corn.

  (2) In this market, the **firm's demand curve** is perfectly elastic (horizontal). The firm can sell as many goods as it can produce at the equilibrium price but no goods at a higher price. The firm is a price taker. The **market demand curve** is downwards sloping. Therefore, demand will increase if all suppliers lower prices and will decrease if all suppliers raise their prices.

  (3) In a perfectly competitive market a firm will continue to produce and sell products until the margin cost is greater than marginal revenue.

  (4) Theoretically, no economic profits can be generated in the long run. The price will reflect the costs plus the normal profit of the most efficient producers.

  (5) In a perfectly competitive market there is no product differentiation and the key to being successful is being the lowest cost producer in the marketplace. Innovation is restricted to attempting to make production, distribution, and sales processes more efficient.

b. **Pure monopoly**

  (1) A pure monopoly is a market in which there is a single seller of a product or service for which there are no close substitutes. A monopoly may exist for one or more of the following reasons:

    (a) Increasing returns to scale

    (b) Control over the supply of raw materials

    (c) Patents (e.g., a drug manufacturer)

    (d) Government franchise (e.g., a public utility)

  (2) Monopolies that exist when economic or technical conditions permit only one efficient supplier are called **natural monopolies**.

  (3) The monopolist sets the price for the product (unless it is set by regulation). The demand curve for the firm is negatively sloping; the company must reduce price to sell more output. The firm will continue to produce and sell products as long as the marginal revenue is greater than average variable cost.

  (4) Entry barriers make it possible for the firm to make economic profit in the long run.

  (5) In a pure monopoly, the company has little market incentive to innovate or control costs. The company has no market control on the price it charges. As a result pure monopolies are generally subject to government regulation. Price boards generally review the company's prices and costs. From a strategic standpoint monopolistic firms want to create a positive image with the public to forestall additional regulation. Therefore any advertising expenditures they incur tend to be for public relations. These firms also spend a lot of effort attempting to influence laws and regulations. They can increase total revenue if they can engage in price discrimination by market segment (e.g., charging business customers more than individual customers).

  (6) The US government has passed legislation to discourage the development of monopolies because prices are higher and output less in such markets as compared to competitive markets. These laws include the Sherman Act of 1890, the Clayton Act of 1914, the Robinson-Patman Act of 1936, and the Celler-Kefauver Anti-Merger Act of 1950.

c. **Monopolistic competition**

  (1) Monopolistic competition is characterized by many firms selling a differentiated product or service. The differentiation may be real or only created by advertising, and there is relatively easy entry to the market but not as easy as in a perfectly competitive market. This type of market is prevalent in retailing, including the markets for groceries, detergents, and breakfast cereals.

  (2) The demand curve in a monopolistic competitive market is negatively sloped and firms tend to produce and sell products until the marginal revenue is less than average variable cost. Therefore, goods tend to be priced somewhat higher than in a perfectly competitive market but less than in a monopoly. Also, there tends to be underproduction as compared to a perfectly competitive market.

  (3) The strategies of firms in monopolistic competitive markets tend to focus on product or service innovation. Companies may spend heavily on product development. Customer relations and advertising necessarily are important to firm strategies.

d. **Oligopoly**

(1) Oligopoly is a form of market characterized by significant barriers to entry. As a result there are few (generally large) sellers of a product. Because there are few sellers the actions of one affect the others. As a result, game theory is often used to analyze the behavior of the firms. An example of an oligopoly is the automobile industry. Other examples are found in the production of steel, aluminum, cigarettes, personal computers, and many electrical appliances.

(2) Oligopolists often attempt to engage in nonprice competition (e.g., by product differentiation or providing high levels of service). However, during economic downturns and periods of overcapacity, price competition in an oligopolistic market can turn fierce.

(3) The kinked-demand-curve model seeks to explain the price rigidity in oligopolistic markets. This model holds that the demand curve is kinked down at the market price because other oligopolists will not match price increases but will match price decreases. Generally, in the oligopolistic market there is a price leader that determines the pricing policy for the other producers.

(4) If left unregulated, ologopolists tend to establish cartels that engage in price fixing. Regulations in the US prohibit collusion by firms to set prices.

> ## NOW REVIEW MULTIPLE-CHOICE QUESTIONS 1 THROUGH 58

MACROECONOMICS

A. Focus

Macroeconomics looks at the economy as a whole. It focuses on measures of economic output, employment, inflation, and trade surpluses or deficits. It also examines the spending of the three major segments of the economy, consumers, business, and government. The levels of economic activity is measured using a number of benchmarks, including

- **Nominal Gross Domestic Product (GDP)**—The price of all goods and services produced by a domestic economy for a year at current market prices.
- **Real GDP**—The price of all goods and services produced by the economy at price level adjusted (constant) prices. Price level adjustment eliminates the effect of inflation on the measure.
- **Potential GDP**—The maximum amount of production that could take place in an economy without putting pressure on the general level of prices. The difference between **potential GDP** and **real GDP** is called the GDP gap. When it is positive, it indicates that there are unemployed resources in the economy and we would expect unemployment. Alternatively, when it is negative, it indicates that the economy is running above normal capacity and prices should begin to rise.
- **Net Domestic Product (NDP)**—GDP minus depreciation.
- **Gross National Product (GNP)**—The price of all goods and services produced by labor and property supplied by the nation's residents.

1. There are two ways to calculate GDP: the income approach and the expenditure approach.

   a. The income (output) approach adds up all incomes earned in the production of final goods and services, such as wages, interest, rents, dividends, etc.

   b. The expenditure (input) approach adds up all expenditures to purchase final goods and services by households, businesses, and the government. Specifically, it includes personal consumption expenditures, gross private investment in capital goods (e.g., machinery). It also includes the country's net exports. The tables below illustrate these computations.

THE INCOME SIDE OF GDP

Compensation to employees	6,010
Corporate profits	767
Net interest	554
Proprietor's income	743
Rental income of persons	143
National income	8,217
Plus: indirect taxes	794

Minus: other, including statutory discrepancy	(160)
Net national product	8,851
Plus: consumption of fixed capital	1,351
Gross national product	10,202
Plus: payments of factor income to other countries	341
Minus: receipts of labor income from other countries	(335)
Gross domestic product	10,208

THE PRODUCT SIDE OF GDP

Personal consumption expenditures	7,065
Gross private domestic fixed investment	
Business	1,246
Residential	446
Government purchases	
Federal	616
State and local	1,223
Net exports	(330)
Changes in business inventories	(58)
Gross domestic product	10,208

B. Aggregate Demand and Supply

1. An aggregate demand curve depicts the demand of consumers, businesses, and government as well as foreign purchasers for the goods and services of the economy at different price levels. The aggregate demand curve looks like the demand curve for a single product (presented above); it is inversely related to price level. The price level affects aggregate demand for several reasons.

    a. **Interest rate effect**—As price levels increase (inflation increases) nominal interest rates increase causing a decrease in interest sensitive spending. Interest sensitive spending includes spending for items such as houses, automobiles, and appliances.

    b. **Wealth effect**—When price levels increase, the market value of certain financial assets decreases (e.g., fixed rate bonds) causing individuals to have less wealth and therefore they reduce their consumption.

    c. **International purchasing power effect**—When domestic price levels increase relative to foreign currencies, foreign products become less expensive causing an increase in imported goods and a decrease in exported goods. This decreases the aggregate demand for domestic products.

2. An aggregate demand curve shifts when consumers, businesses, or governments are willing to spend more or less, or when there is an increase or decrease in the demand for domestic products abroad (i.e., an increase or decrease in net exports). Government can affect aggregate demand through its own spending levels, taxes, and monetary policy. For example, a reduction in individual or corporate taxes increases the spendable income of consumers or businesses. This would be expected to increase spending.

3. An aggregate supply (output) schedule presents the relationship between goods and services supplied and the price level, assuming that all other variables that affect supply are held constant. While there is not complete agreement on the shape of the aggregate supply curve, it is generally depicted as shown below.

Aggregate Supply Curve

As shown, prices remain relatively constant until the economy reaches near capacity, at which time prices begin to increase at a significant rate. Shifts in the aggregate supply curve may be caused by technology improvements, changes in resource availability, or changes in resource costs.

4. Equilibrium GDP occurs when the output level of the economy creates just enough spending to purchase the entire output.

5. **The multiplier.** The multiplier refers to the fact than an increase in spending by consumers, businesses, or the government has a multiplied effect on equilibrium GDP. The reason for this is that increased spending generates increases in income to businesses and consumers which in turn increases their spending, which again increases the income of other consumers and businesses, etc. Therefore, the increased spending ripples through the economy increasing GDP by much more than the original increase in spending. The effect of the multiplier can be estimated by examining an economy's **marginal propensity to consume (MPC)** and **marginal propensity to save (MPS)**. From our previous discussion we know that additional income is either spent or saved as shown below.

$$MPS + MPC = 1$$

The multiplier may be calculated from the following formula:

$$\frac{1}{MPS} \times \text{Change in spending}$$

EXAMPLE

If MPS is .25 (MPC = .75) and spending increases by $1,000,000, the increase in equilibrium GDP is calculated below.

$$\frac{1}{.25} \times \$1,000,000 = \$4,000,000$$

C. Business Cycles

1. A business cycle is a fluctuation in aggregate economic output that lasts for several years. Business cycles are recurring but vary in terms of both length and intensity. They are depicted as a series of peaks and troughs. A peak marks the end of a period of economic expansion and the beginning of a recession (contraction) while a trough marks the end of a recession and the beginning of an economic recovery (expansion). The chart below illustrates the nature of the business cycle.

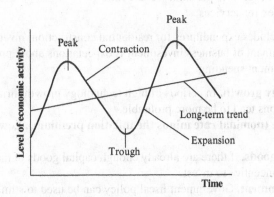

2. Economic contractions are characterized by a decrease in real gross domestic product (GDP) due to reduced spending. In a period of expansion, real GDP is increasing. At the peak real GDP generally surpasses potential GDP causing a scarcity of labor and materials. These shortages generally cause inflation.

3. **Unemployment and Output**—In most cases, there is a clear relationship between the change in unemployment and GDP growth, as explained by Okum's law. High output growth is generally associated with a decrease in the unemployment rate. This makes perfect sense because when output increases less.

4. A **recession** is a period of negative GDP growth. Usually, recession refers to at least two consecutive quarters of negative GDP growth. A deep and long-lasting recession is referred to as a **depression**.

5. There are a number of explanations for the occurrence of business cycles but they generally relate to the level of investment spending by businesses, or the level of consumer spending for durable goods (e.g., automobiles and appliances). The effects of a business cycle vary by business sector. For obvious reasons, heavy manufacturing is one of the sectors that is most affected. Such businesses are referred to as **cyclical** businesses because they perform better in periods of expansion and worse in periods of recession. Some business sectors are called **defensive** because they are affected little by business cycles and some may actually perform better in periods of recession.

6. Economists attempt to predict business cycles using economic indicators. Some indicators lead future economic trends, others coincide with economic trends, and still others lag economic trends. The Conference Board, a private research group, has developed the following list of indicators:

   a. Leading indicators

      * Average weekly hours, manufacturing
      * Average weekly initial claims for unemployment insurance
      * Manufacturer's new orders, consumer goods and materials
      * Vendor performance, slower deliveries diffusion index
      * Manufacturer's new orders, nondefense capital goods
      * Building permits, new private housing units
      * Stock prices, 500 common stocks
      * Money supply, M2
      * Interest rate spread, 10-year Treasury bonds less federal funds
      * Index of consumer expectations

   b. Coincident indicators

      * Employees on nonagricultural payrolls
      * Personal income less transfer payments
      * Industrial production
      * Manufacturing and trade sales

   c. Lagging indicators

      * Average duration of unemployment
      * Inventories to sales ratio, manufacturing and trade
      * Labor cost per unit of output, manufacturing
      * Average prime rate
      * Commercial and industrial loans
      * Consumer installment credit to personal income ratio
      * Consumer price index for services

7. **Investment.** Investment includes expenditures for residential construction, inventories, and plant and equipment. The most important determinant of business investment is expectations about profitability. Accordingly, the following factors affect investment spending:

   a. **The rate of technology growth.** In periods of high technology growth, firms tend to invest more because new products and innovations tend to be more profitable.

   b. **The real interest rate (nominal rate minus the inflation premium).** Lower real interest rates reduce the cost of investment.

   c. **The stock of capital goods.** If there are already enough capital goods in the economy to meet aggregate demand there is little incentive to invest.

   d. **Actions by the government.** Government fiscal policy can be used to stimulate investment spending (e.g., reductions in taxes, tax incentives, or increased government spending).

   e. **The acquisition and operating cost of capital goods.** As the purchase price or operating cost of plant and equipment decreases, firms will invest more.

Investment spending is the most volatile portion of GDP. **Autonomous investment** includes expenditures made by businesses based on expected profitability that are independent of the level of national income. That is, they are constant regardless of whether the economy is expanding or contracting. **Induced investment** is incremental spending based on an increased level of economic activity.

8. **Accelerator theory.** Accelerator theory states that as economic activity increases, capital investment must be made to meet the level of increased demand. The increased capital investment in turn creates additional economic demand which further feeds the economic expansion.

D. Economic Measures

Previously we described several important measures of economic activity: GDP, GNP, etc. In this section we will describe other economic measures, such as rates of unemployment, inflation, and personal disposable income.

1. **Unemployment**

   The unemployment rate is the percent of the total labor force that is unemployed at a given time. Individuals may be unemployed because of frictional, structural, or cyclical causes.

   a. **Frictional unemployment** occurs because individuals are forced or voluntarily change jobs. At any point in time some individuals will be temporarily unemployed while they look for a job. New entrants into the workforce also fall into this category.

   b. **Structural unemployment** occurs due to changes in demand for products or services, or technological advances causing not as many individuals with a particular skill to be needed. Structural unemployment is reduced by retraining programs.

   c. **Cyclical unemployment** is caused by the condition in which real GDP is less than potential GDP. Therefore, such unemployment increases during recessions and decreases during expansions.

2. **Inflation**

   a. **Inflation** is the rate of increase in the price level of goods and services, usually measured on an annual basis. Hyperinflation is a very high, unusually increasing level of inflation.

   b. **Deflation** is a term used to describe a decrease in the price levels. While Japan has experienced deflation in prices recently, the US has not experienced an annual rate of decrease in price level since the 1930s. Deflation is very damaging because businesses do not want to borrow money and pay it back with money that has more purchasing power, and they do not want to invest in plant and equipment given that the cost of plant and equipment is declining.

   c. High rates of inflation are not good for the economy either. Inflation generally causes economic activity to contract and redistributes income and wealth.

   d. A price index measures the prices of a basket of goods and/or services at a point in time in relation to the prices in a base period.

      (1) **The consumer price index** (CPI) measures the price that urban consumers paid for a fixed basket of goods and services in relation to the price of the same goods and services purchased in some base period.

      (2) **The producer price index** (PPI) measures the prices of finished goods and materials at the wholesale level.

      (3) **The GDP deflator** measures the prices for net exports, investment, government expenditures, and consumer spending. It is the most comprehensive measure of price level.

3. **Causes of inflation.** There are generally two causes for inflation that are commonly referred to as demand-pull and cost-push.

   a. **Demand-pull** inflation occurs when aggregate spending exceeds the economy's normal full-employment output capacity. It generally occurs at the peak of a business cycle and is characterized by real GDP exceeding potential GDP. Because labor is short companies bid up the price and inflation occurs.

   b. **Cost-push** inflation occurs from an increase in the cost of producing goods and services. It is usually characterized by decreases in aggregate output and unemployment because consumers are not willing to pay the inflated prices.

   There is an inverse relationship between inflation and unemployment. When the unemployment rate is low, inflation tends to increase. Inflation tends to decrease when the unemployment rate is high. This relationship is depicted by the **Phillips curve**.

4. **Personal disposable income** is the amount of income that individuals receive and have available to purchase goods and services. Personal disposable income has a significant effect on the economy because it is a large determinant of consumer demand. Personal disposable income is equal to **personal income** minus personal taxes.

5. **Interest rates.** Interest is the price paid for the use of money. Economists typically focus on the risk-free or pure rate of interest. In practice, interest rates are also affected by credit risk, maturity, and administrative costs. As with other commodities, interest rates are determined by demand and supply. The intersection of the demand and supply

curves for money determines the equilibrium price or interest rate. On the demand side, firms borrow money to make investments in assets and will continue to borrow as long as investment return exceeds the interest rate at which the funds are borrowed. The supply of funds is affected by the past and current savings of individuals and firms, but it is also affected by the monetary policy of the government. Interest rates are often quoted as

a.　**Real interest rate**—Interest rate in terms of goods. These rates are adjusted for inflation.

b.　**Nominal interest rate**—Interest rate in terms of the nation's currency. These are the rates that are quoted by financial institutions and in the financial pages of newspapers. The difference between the real rate and the nominal rate is the inflation premium, which represents the expected inflation rate. The higher the expected inflation rate the larger the inflation premium. The interest rate charged to a particular business or individual will be higher than the nominal rate due to **credit risk,** which is the risk that the firm will not pay the interest or principal of the loan.

6.　**Government budget surplus (deficit)**—The excess (deficit) of government taxes in relation to government transfer payments and purchases. To finance a deficit the government issues debt (e.g., Treasury bonds).

7.　**Money.** Money in an economy serves three major purposes—a medium of exchange; a common denominator to measure prices, revenue, expenses, and income; and a store of value allowing individuals and firms to save. Economists use three basic measures of money, M1, M2, and M3. M1 includes only currency and demand deposits, M2 is equal to M1 plus savings accounts and small-time deposits (less $100,000), and M3 is equal to M2 plus other (larger) time deposits. In regulating the economy the Federal Reserve focuses on M2.

E.　Monetary Policy

Depository institutions (banks, savings and loans, and credit unions, etc.) borrow savers' money and lend the money to consumers, businesses, and governments. The Federal Reserve (the US central bank), through its open market controls the actions of depository institutions and can affect the supply of money in the following ways:

1.　**Reserve requirements.** When a bank lends money, it gives the borrower a check drawn on the bank itself. The Federal Reserve controls a bank's ability to issue check-writing deposits by imposing a reserve requirement on checking deposits. The institution must hold in reserve (much of which is on deposit at a Federal Reserve Bank) a certain percentage of their total checking deposits. The Federal Reserve can influence interest rates by changing the reserve requirements and therefore increasing or decreasing the supply of money. However, making changes in reserve requirements is rarely done.

2.　**Open-market operations.** A more common instrument of monetary policy is open-market operations (by the **Federal Open-Market Committee**), which involves the purchase or sale of government securities using the Federal Reserve Bank deposits. If the Federal Reserve purchases government securities, they are able to increase the monetary supply and, therefore, put downward pressure on interest rates. When a central bank is purchasing government securities and expanding the money supply, it is called an **expansionary open-market operation**. If a central bank is selling government securities it is said to be pursuing a **contractionary open-market operation,** because this reduces the money supply.

3.　**The discount rate.** When a bank has a reserve deficiency it may borrow funds from a Federal Reserve Bank. By setting the discount rate for such borrowing, the Federal Reserve can influence interest rates in the economy.

4.　**Economic analysis.** In making its monetary decisions, the Federal Open-Market Committee does extensive economic analysis. In speeches by the members and when providing the basis for its decisions insights are provided into the state of the economy. This information also may have an effect on economic factors such as interest rates, business spending, and the stock prices.

5.　The Federal Reserve uses monetary policy to attempt to sustain economic growth while keeping inflation under control. Monetary policy works on the principle that a decrease in interest rates will stimulate the economy, and an increase in interest rates will slow the economy. Lower interest rates tend to encourage consumer and business spending because finance charges are lower. Higher interest rates tend to discourage spending because finance charges are higher. It also encourages saving because the return on savings is higher.

6.　The effects of monetary policy depend on their effects on the expectations of investors, businesses, and consumers. If monetary expansion leads the financial markets to revise their expectations about inflation, interest rates and output, the effect on output will be dramatic. On the other hand, if expectations remain unchanged, the effects will be minimal.

7.　**Rational expectations** assume that investors, firms, and consumers develop expectations about inflation, interest rates, and output based on a consideration of all available information. This is contrasted to adaptive expectations in which investors, firms and consumers adjust their expectations based on new information. As an example, if they find that inflation is higher than expected, they adjust their expectation upward.

F. Fiscal Policy

Fiscal policy is government actions, such as taxes, subsidies, and government spending, designed to achieve economic goals. As an example, a reduction of taxes increases personal disposable income, which will serve to stimulate economic activity. The economy may also be stimulated through increased government spending. An increase in deficit, either due to an increase in government spending or to a decrease in taxes, is called a fiscal expansion. On the other hand, increases in taxes to reduce a deficit is called fiscal contraction.

1. **Taxes.** Taxes are levied by a government based on two general principles: (1) the ability to pay (e.g., progressive income taxes), and (2) derived benefit (e.g., gasoline taxes used to pay for roads). The following are the major types of taxes:

   a. **Income tax.** Income taxes are levied on taxable income. In the US the rate structure is generally progressive. However, there are a number of social and economic incentives built into the system that dilute its progressive structure.

   b. **Property tax.** Property taxes are levied based on wealth. They generally are progressive based on the value of the property.

   c. **Sales tax.** Sales taxes are levied based on the amount of income spent. Sales taxes are viewed as regressive because low-income individuals pay the same percentage rate as high-income individuals.

   d. **Wage taxes.** The most significant wage tax in the US is the social security tax. This tax is borne both directly (the employee's share) and indirectly (the employer's share) by employees because without the tax, wages would be higher.

   e. **Value-added tax.** A tax commonly used in other industrial nations is the value-added tax (VAT). Value-added taxes are levied on the increase in value of each product as it proceeds through production and distribution processes. Ultimately, the tax is paid by the final consumer. The VAT is thought to encourage savings because it taxes consumption instead of earnings.

2. Both monetary and fiscal policy take time to have the desired effects for a number of reasons, including

   a. Consumers take time to adjust their consumption based on changes in personal disposal income
   b. Firms take time to adjust investment based on changes in sales
   c. Firms take time to adjust spending based on changes in interest rates
   d. Firms take time to adjust production based on changes in sales

3. Fiscal policies can have a large effect on the size of budget deficits. In the long and medium run, a budget deficit reduction is likely to be beneficial to the economy. Lower budget deficits usually mean more savings and investment, and therefore, more output. In the short run, a reduction in budget deficit leads to reductions in spending and therefore less output.

G. Economic Theories

1. **Classical economic theory**—This theory holds that market equilibrium will eventually result in full employment over the long run without government intervention. This theory does not support the use of fiscal policy to stimulate the economy.

2. **Keynesian theory**—This theory holds that the economy does not necessarily move towards full employment on its own. It focuses on the use of fiscal policy (e.g., reductions in taxes and government spending) to stimulate the economy.

3. **Monetarist theory**—This theory holds that fiscal policy is too crude a tool for control of the economy. It focuses on the use of monetary policy to control economic growth.

4. **Supply-side theory**—This theory holds that bolstering an economy's ability to supply more goods is the most effective way to stimulate growth. A decrease in taxes (especially for businesses and individuals with high income) increases employment, savings, and investments and is an effective way to stimulate the economy. The tax revenue lost from the reduction in taxes is more than offset by the increase in taxes from increased economic activity. However, this predicted effect only occurs when rates are too high. The **Laffer Curve** attempts to explain how consumers react to changes in rates of income tax. The curve illustrates that if taxes are already too low decreasing them will result in less tax revenue.

5. **Neo-Keynesian theory**—This theory combines Keynesian and monetarist theories. It focuses on using a combination of fiscal and monetary policy to stimulate the economy and control inflation.

NOW REVIEW MULTIPLE-CHOICE QUESTIONS 59 THROUGH 90

H. The Global Economy and International Trade

Economic globalization refers to the increasing economic interdependence of national economies across the world through a rapid increase in cross-border movement of goods, service, technology and capital. It has led to a single world market in which developed economies have integrated with less developed countries by means of foreign direct investment, the reduction of trade barriers, and the modernization of the developing countries. The comparative advantages of natural resources or low-cost labor attract businesses and capital to developing (emerging) economies.

International trade is very important to almost every business. If a country has an **absolute advantage** (e.g., low-cost labor, technology) in the production of a particular good, there is an incentive for that country to produce more than its citizens need to export the good to countries with higher production costs. This is especially true if it also has a comparative advantage to producing the good. A **comparative advantage** means that country has no alternate uses of its resources that would involve a higher return (i.e., the **opportunity costs** are less). In the long term, production of specific goods and services will migrate to countries that have a **comparative advantage**. By exploiting its comparative advantages and exporting goods and services, a nation can import the goods for which it has a comparative disadvantage. In this manner all nations will be better off.

Michael Porter developed a "diamond of national advantage" to explain how a country can create new advanced factor endowments that contribute to the country's comparative advantage. The four points of the diamond can be described as

- **Factor Conditions**—A country can create its own important factors such as skilled resources and technology infrastructure. The stock of factors at a given time is less important than the country's potential. A country can overcome shortages of factors through innovation.
- **Demand Conditions**—A country has a comparative advantage for a particular product when it has a strong domestic market because the firms in the country devote more attention to the product than in other countries.
- **Related and Supporting Industries**—A country has a comparative advantage for a product when the supporting industries are strong because of the cost effective and innovative inputs that result.
- **Firm Strategy, Structure, and Rivalry**—Different types of comparative advantages accrue from different business organizational structures (e.g., hierarchal, matrix, extended family structures). Also, intense rivalry of an industry in a country tends to lead to a competitive advantage for that country's industry globally.

1. **Obstacles to free trade.** Even though trade can be a source of major gains, many nations restrict free trade by various means, for example by imposing tariffs and quotas. That is, they engage in protectionism. An import **tariff** is a tax on an imported product. Tariffs are designed to discourage the consumption of goods from foreign companies or to raise revenue, or both. A trigger price mechanism automatically imposes a tariff barrier against cheap imports by imposing a duty on all imports below a trigger price. An import **quota** is a restriction on the amount of a good that may be imported during a period. Finally, an **embargo** is a total ban on the importation of specific goods.

   An exporting country may elect to establish a **voluntary export restraint** to limit the quality of goods that can be exported to appease importing countries and keep them from imposing stiffer import restrictions.

   Another barrier to trade that a country may impose is a **foreign-exchange control**. A foreign exchange control is a control imposed by a government on the purchase or sale of foreign currencies by residents, or on the purchase or sale of local currency by nonresidents. Examples of such controls include

   a. Banning the use of foreign currency in the country.
   b. Banning possession of foreign currency by citizens.
   c. Restricting currency exchange to government-approved exchangers.
   d. Fixed exchange rates.

   Trade restrictions are advocated by labor unions and firms making products that are more inexpensively produced in other nations. Thus, trade restrictions generally impose a burden on society as a whole because they reduce the availability of goods and increase their prices. Arguments in favor of trade restrictions include

   a. To protect domestic labor against inexpensive foreign labor
   b. To reduce domestic unemployment
   c. To protect young or infant industries
   d. To protect industries important to the nation's defense

   Other arguments against unrestricted trade include the fact that the businesses of developed nations are disadvantaged by social laws in their countries that do not exist in developing countries (e.g., laws restricting pollution, child labor, minimum wage, etc.), and by disproportionate taxing of domestic manufacturing.

Trade restrictions in the US are advocated by labor and firms in the US in industries that have lost their competitive advantage, such as producers of shoes, textiles, and steel. Some firms and industries in the US have been able to regain their competitive advantage through the introduction of new technology.

Most of the arguments for trade restrictions are not valid. Trade restrictions generally have negative effects in that economic activity is inappropriately shifted to less-productive protected industries, resulting in a decline in total world output.

2. **Dumping.** A **dumping** pricing policy is a form of predatory pricing in which a manufacturer in one country exports a product at a price that is lower than the price charged in its home market or below the company's cost of production. Under the World Trade Organization (WTO) Agreement, dumping is condemned (not prohibited) if it causes material injury to a domestic industry in the importing country. US firms can file an antidumping petition with the International Trade Organization when products are being sold at less than "fair value," as defined by Department of Commerce regulations. If the firm's case is proved, antidumping duties may be imposed on goods imported from the dumper's country.

3. **Export subsidies** are payments made by a government to encourage the production and export of specific products. Such payments may be made in various ways, including special tax benefits. **Countervailing duties** are duties imposed by an importing country to neutralize the negative effects of export subsidies.

4. The **World Trade Organization (WTO)** is an organization of countries designed to supervise and liberalize trade among participating countries. It facilitates trade agreements among participants and provides a resolution process to enforce the agreements. Under the WTO provisions, members afford all other members favored nation status, which means a member country will not establish trade barriers that discriminate against other members.

5. **North American Free Trade Agreement (NAFTA)**

   a.   NAFTA is a free trade agreement between the countries of Canada, Mexico, and the US. It was adopted by the US Congress in 1993. NAFTA offers a number of advantages for US businesses including

   (1)   The ability to take advantage of the lower labor costs in Mexico for such functions as manufacturing and assembly.

   (2)   The opening of new markets for goods of US industries that have a comparative advantage, such as technology.

   b.   Disadvantages to US businesses and labor markets include

   (1)   Some US industries, such as producers of shoes and apparel, are concerned that the firms will be hurt by the availability of less expensive products from Mexico.

   (2)   Certain jobs in the US will be lost because of the availability of lower-cost labor in Mexico combined with more lax environmental laws and regulations.

6. **Balance of payments.** The balance of payments is an account summary of a nation's transactions with other nations. It has three major sections: the current account, the capital account, and the official reserve account.

   a.   **Current account**—Shows the flow of goods and services and government grants for a period of time.

   (1)   The **balance of trade** for a period is the difference between the total goods exported and the total goods imported.

   (2)   The balance on goods and services is the difference between the total value of goods and services exported and the total value of goods and services imported.

   (3)   When a nation exports more than it imports a **trade surplus** occurs.

   (4)   When a nation imports more than it exports a **trade deficit** occurs.

   b.   **Capital account**—Shows the flow of investments in fixed and financial assets for a period of time.

   c.   The **balance of payments** surplus or deficit is the amount that nets the current and capital accounts. In other words, when the sum of the outflows exceeds the inflows a deficit in balance of payment occurs. The deficit is settled in currency of other nations, or by an increase in the holdings of the nation's currency by other nations. A deficit is an unfavorable balance of payments while a surplus is a favorable balance of payments.

   d.   **Official reserve account**—Shows the changes in the nation's reserves (e.g., gold and foreign currency).

7. The **G-20** is a group of finance ministers and central bank governors from 20 economies (the European Union and 19 countries). It studies, reviews, and promotes discussion of policy issues affecting global financial stability, and seeks to address issues that go beyond the responsibilities of its individual members.

8. The **European Union (EU)** is an economic and political union of 27 countries primarily in Europe. The EU has developed a single market through a standardized system of laws that apply to all member countries. An economic

and monetary union known as the **eurozone** (officially the euro area) is composed of 17 member countries that use the euro currency. The European Central Bank establishes monetary policy for the members of the eurozone.

9. Globalization has been facilitated by a number of factors, including the development of global financial institutions, reductions in trade and investment barriers, and technology. The major global institutions include

     a.   The **World Bank** has the objective of promoting world-wide economic development.

     b.   The **International Monetary Fund** has the objective of maintaining order in the international monetary system by preventing currency, banking, and financial debt crises.

10. Reduction in Trade and Investment Barriers

     a.   Reduction in trade barriers can be traced to the establishment of the General Agreement on Tariffs and Trade (GATT).

     b.   Reduction by countries on foreign direct investment (FDI).

11. Technology advances—improvements in information technology and transportation make global communication and movement of goods more economical.

I. Foreign Exchange Rates

Firms that do business internationally must be concerned with exchange rates, which are the relationships among the values of currencies. For example, a US firm selling products in Europe is very interested in the relationship of the euro to the US dollar.

1. **Factors influencing exchange rates.** As with any other market, the exchange rate between two currencies is determined by the supply of, and the demand for, those currencies. However, these rates are also subject to intervention by the central banks of countries. Therefore, exchange rates are often said to be determined by **managed float**. In general, the following factors will affect the exchange rate of a particular currency:

     a.   **Inflation.** Inflation tends to deflate the value of a currency because holding the currency results in reduced purchasing power.

     b.   **Interest rates.** If interest returns in a particular country are higher relative to other countries, individuals and companies will be enticed to invest in that country. As a result there will be increased demand for the country's currency.

     c.   **Balance of payments.** Balance of payments is used to refer to a system of accounts that catalogs the flow of goods between the residents of two countries. If country X is a net exporter of goods and therefore has a surplus balance of trade, countries purchasing the goods must use country X's currency. This increases the demand for the currency and therefore its relative value.

     d.   **Government intervention.** Through intervention (e.g., buying or selling the currency in the foreign exchange markets), the central bank of a country may support or depress the value of its currency.

     e.   **Other factors.** Other factors that may affect exchange rates are political and economic stability, extended stock market rallies, or significant declines in the demand for major exports.

2. The **exchange rate regime** is the way a country manages its currency in respect to currencies of other countries. The basic types of exchange rate regimes include

     a.   **Floating exchange rate**—One in which the exchange rate is dictated by market factors as described previously.

     b.   **Pegged exchange rate**—One in which the country's central bank keeps the rate from deviating too far from a target band or value.

     c.   **Fixed exchange rate**—One in which the rate is tied to the value of another currency, such as the US dollar or the euro.

     d.   **Managed exchange rate**—One in which the country's central bank attempts to control the movement in currency value.

3. **Spot rates and forward rates.** The spot rate for a currency is the exchange rate of the currency for immediate delivery. On the other hand, the forward rate is the exchange rate for a currency for future delivery. For example, a forward contract might obligate a company to purchase or sell euros at a specific exchange rate three months hence. The difference between the spot rate and the forward rate is referred to as the discount or premium. If the forward rate is less (greater) than the spot rate, the market believes that the value of the currency is going to decline (increase).

EXAMPLE

Assume that a multinational company sells products to a French company for a receivable payable in 60 days in the amount of 10,000 euros. If at the time of the sale the exchange rate is 1.25 US dollars to the euro, the sale is equal to $12,500 (1.25 × 10,000). If the euro depreciates by 2% against the US dollar in the 60-day period between the sale and collection, the firm has experienced a loss. The 2% depreciation would mean that the new exchange rate is 1.225 (1.25 × 98%) euros to the US dollar. Therefore, the firm has lost $12,500 – $12,250 (1.225 × 10,000) = $250.

---

4. The forward premium or discount of one currency with respect to another is calculated using the following formula:

$$\frac{\text{Forward rate} - \text{Spot rate}}{\text{Spot rate}} \times \frac{\text{Month (or days) in year}}{\text{Months (or days) in forward period}}$$

EXAMPLE

Assume the 180-day forward rate for the British Pound is $1.612 and the spot rate is $1.610. The forward premium is calculated to be 0.5% {[($1.612 – $1.610) / $1.610] × (360 days/180 days)}. Note that the result is a premium because the forward rate is higher than the spot rate.

---

5. The foreign exchange risk for a multinational company is divided into two types: **translation (accounting) risk** and **transaction risk**. Translation risk is the exposure that a multinational company has because its financial statements must be converted to its functional currency.
6. Transaction risk relates to the possibility of gains and losses resulting from income transactions occurring during the year. The example above involving the sale of goods for a receivable in euros illustrates transaction risk. Transaction risk can cause volatility in reported earnings that motivates management to use strategies to minimize the company's exposure. Companies can use various forms of contracts to hedge foreign currency risk, including

   a. **Options**—Allow, but do not require, the holder to buy (call) or sell (put) a specific or standard commodity or financial instrument, at a specified price during a specified period of time (American option) or at a specified date (European option).
   b. **Forwards**—Negotiated contracts to purchase and sell a specific quantity of a financial instrument, foreign currency, or commodity at a price specified at origination of the contract, with delivery and payment at a specified future date.

EXAMPLE

Assume that Company X has agreed to deliver 20,000 units of product in six months to a Japanese company who will pay for the product in yen. To mitigate the risk of losses from devaluation of the yen, Company X could enter into a forward contract to sell the yen for delivery in six months. This contract in effect locks in the price for the sale in terms of US dollars. Alternatively, Company X could purchase a put option allowing them to put the yen up for sale at a specific price in six months.

---

   c. **Futures**—Forward-based standardized contracts to take delivery of a specified financial instrument, foreign currency, or commodity at a specified future date or during a specified period generally at the then-market price.
   d. **Currency swaps**—Forward-based contracts in which two parties agree to exchange an obligation to pay cash flows in one currency for an obligation to pay in another currency.

    e. **Money market hedge**—A second way to eliminate the transaction risk described in b. is to borrow money in yen when the agreement is executed. This strategy immediately converts the yen to US dollars. Then, when the yen are collected from the sale, the loan can be repaid, resulting in no foreign exchange loss or gain over the six-month period.

J. Foreign Investment

1. Foreign direct investments are usually quite large and many are exposed to **political risk** (country risk). Repatriation (transfer) of a foreign subsidiary's profits may be blocked. In the extreme case a foreign government may even expropriate (take) the firm's assets. Strategies to reduce risk include the use of joint ventures, financing with local-country capital, and the purchase of insurance. An emerging country experiences certain advantages to allowing foreign investment, including less stock market volatility, increased investment, and reduced cost of capital.

2. **Transfer pricing.** Transfer pricing is the price at which services or products are bought and sold across international borders between related parties. As an example, if a US parent company purchases products from its French subsidiary, a transfer price must be established for the products. Because the transfer price affects the parent and subsidiary's net income, it affects the taxes that the firm pays in the US and France. Multinational companies can minimize their overall tax burden by using transfer prices to minimize net income in jurisdictions with higher income tax rates, and maximizing net income in jurisdictions with lower income tax rates. However, there are other reasons for setting transfer prices, including avoiding foreign withholding of taxes on cash payments, avoiding import duties, and circumventing profit repatriation restrictions. However, many governments have established tax regulations that are designed to help ensure that transfer prices estimate market prices. In the US, guidance of the appropriate allocation of income (including transfer pricing) is included in the Internal Revenue Code that provides that income should be allocated between entities under common control based on the functions performed and the risks assumed by each of the entities involved in arm's-length transactions. Methods used to determine transfer prices generally include

    a.   The cost method—the price is determined based on the cost of producing the item. This method is commonly used when a market price for the product is not available.

    b.   The market price method—the price is determined based on the external market for the item.

    c.   The negotiated price method—the price is determined based on a negotiated agreement.

> **NOW REVIEW MULTIPLE-CHOICE QUESTIONS 91 THROUGH 109**

THE EFFECTS OF THE GLOBAL ECONOMIC ENVIRONMENT ON STRATEGY

A firm's objectives are the overall plans for the firm as defined by management. Management attempts to achieve these objectives by developing strategies (operational actions). However, achieving management's objectives is always subject to business risks faced by the firm. **Business risks** are conditions that threaten management's ability to execute strategies and achieve the firm's objectives. A comprehensive understanding of the firm's internal and external environments is necessary for management to understand the firm's present condition and its business risks. This understanding includes comprehension of both the general and industry environments.

A. The general environment includes the following factors:

- Economic—Inflation rates, interest rates, budget deficits, personal saving rate, gross domestic product, etc.
- Demographic—Population size, workforce, ethnic mix, income distribution, geographic distribution, etc.
- Political and legal—Antitrust laws, tax laws, deregulation philosophies, etc.
- Sociocultural—Workforce diversity, environmental concerns, shifts in consumer preferences, etc.
- Technological segment—Societal innovations in technology and products, focus of the economy on research and development, etc.
- Global—Important global political events, developments in global markets, etc.

    The general aspects of the environment are out of the control of management of the firm. Management must adapt to its general environment.

B. The **industry environment** is the set of factors that influence the firm's competitive actions. Michael Porter developed a model for industry analyses that focuses on five forces: (1) competitors, (2) potential entrants into the market, (3) equivalent products, (4) bargaining power of customers, and (5) bargaining power of input suppliers.[1]

Entry Barriers
Economies of scale
Proprietary product of differences
Brand identity
Switching costs
Capital requirements
Access to distribution
Absolute cost advantages
   Proprietary learning curve
   Access to necessary inputs
   Proprietary low-cost product design
Government policy
Expected retaliation

Rivalry Determinants
Industry growth
Fixed (or storgae) costs/value added
Intermittent overcapacity
Product differences
Brand identity
Switching costs
Concentration and balance
Informational complexity
Diversity of competitors
Corporate stakes
Exit barriers

New Entrants

Threat of new entrants

Bargaining power of suppliers

Industry Competitors

Intensity of Rivalry

Bargaining power of buyers

Suppliers

Buyers

Threat of substitutes

Substitutes

Determinants of Supplier Power
Differentiation of inputs
Switching cost of suppliers and firms in the industry
Presence of substitute inputs
Supplier concentration
Importance of volume to supplier
Cost relative to total purchases in the industry
Impact of inputs on cost or differentiation
Threat of forward integration relative to threat of
   backward integration by firms in the industry

Determinants of Buyer Power

Bargaining Leverage	**Price Sensitivity**
Buyer concentration versus firm concentration	Price/total purchases
	Product differences
	Brand identity
Buyer volume	Impact on quality/ performance
Buyer switching costs relative to firm switching costs	Buyer profits
	Decision makers' incentives
Buyer information	
Ability to backward integrate	
Substitute products	
Pull-through	

Determinants of Substitution Threat
Relative price performance of substitutes
Switching costs
Buyer propensity to substitute

1. The industry environment directly affects the firm and the types of strategies it must develop to compete. It is most relevant to the firm's profit potential. Management attempts to position the firm where it can influence the industry factors and successfully defend against their influence. **Remember, management has little or no control over the general environment factors but through its actions may have significant influence over industry factors.** Generally, the larger the firm's market share the more influence it can have on its industry environment.

2. Since firms must make strategic decisions that involve long-term commitments (e.g., investments in technology, plant, etc.), management must not only deal with the current environment, it must forecast the future. Effective management must analyze and forecast the general environment to identify opportunities and threats to the firm. In doing so, the following techniques are used:

   a. **Scanning**—A study of all segments in the general environment. The objective is to predict the effects of the general environment on the firm's industry. Management can use this information to modify its strategies and operating plans. Scanning of the general environment is critical to firms in volatile industries. Sources of information for scanning include trade publications, newspapers, business publications, public polls, government publications, etc.

   b. **Monitoring**—A study of environmental changes identified by scanning to spot important trends. As an example, the trend in aging of the population in this country would definitely be important to firms that provide services to retired individuals. Effective monitoring involves identifying the firm's major stakeholders (e.g., customers, investors, employees, etc.).

   c. **Forecasting**—Developing probable projections of what might happen and its timing. As an example, management might attempt to forecast changes in personal disposable income or the timing of introduction of a major technological development.

   d. **Assessing**—Determining changes in the firm's strategy that are necessary as a result of the information obtained from scanning, monitoring, and forecasting. It is the process of evaluating the implications of changes in the general environment on the firm.

---

[1]M. Porter, *Competitive Strategy*, New York Free Press (1980).

C. Industry Analysis

1. An industry is a group of firms that produce products that are substitutes or close substitutes. Industries are often classified by their fundamental economics as perfect competition, pure monopoly, monopolistic competition, and oligopoly.

2. The competitive market of the firm determines the intensity of competition and threats to new entrants to the industry. However, the firm must also consider the threat of substitute products, bargaining power of suppliers, and bargaining power of its customers.

3. **Threat of substitute products.** Substitute products are goods or services from outside a given industry that perform similar functions. As an example, plastic containers constrain the price of glass containers.

4. **Bargaining power of suppliers.**

   a. The power of suppliers affects a firm's ability to negotiate price or quality concessions. When suppliers have a good deal of power, they will be able to increase prices, and the firm purchasing those supplies may or may not be able to pass the cost on to its customers. Suppliers have power, for example, when the market is dominated by a few large companies, the industry firms are not significant customers for suppliers, or there are large costs to switching to another supplier.

   b. The supplier market also includes the firm's labor market. The firm's ability to influence wage rate will depend on the other firms that are competing for the labor, and actions of the government and labor unions.

   c. A **monopsony** is a market where only one buyer exists for all sellers. A monopsonist has monopoly power in the purchase of a resource. The marginal cost curve for a monopsonist is different from other firms' in that each time it purchases an additional unit of product or labor it increases the cost of all of the resource.

5. **Bargaining power of customers.** The power of customers determines the firm's ability to increase prices or lower quality of their products. When customers are powerful, the firm has difficulty passing cost increase on to them. Therefore the firm must concentrate on controlling costs. Customers are powerful, for example, when they purchase a large percentage of the industry output, they could switch to another product with little cost, the industry's products are standardized and the customers pose a threat to integrate backward into the firm's market.

6. **Techniques for industry analysis.** Firms use a variety of techniques to analyze their industries. In this section we will describe three of those techniques, competitor analysis, price elasticity analysis, and target market analysis.

   a. **Competitor analysis.** In formulating strategy, management must consider the strategies of the firm's competitors. Competitor analysis is of vital importance to devising strategies in concentrated industries. Competitor analysis involves two major activities: (1) gathering information about competitors' capabilities, objectives, strategies, and assumptions (competitor intelligence), and (2) using the information to understand the competitors' behavior. Management uses a number of sources of information for competitor analysis including the competitor's

   • Annual reports and SEC filings
   • Interviews with analysts
   • Press releases

   However, management must also consider information derived from the actions of the competitor such as the following:

   • Research and development projects
   • Capital investments
   • Promotional campaigns
   • Strategic partnerships
   • Mergers and acquisitions
   • Hiring practices

   In a competitor analysis, management seeks to understand

   • What are the competitor's objectives?
   • What can and is the competitor doing based on its current strategy?
   • What does the competitor assume about the industry?
   • What are the competitor's strengths and weaknesses?

   Information from the analysis of the competitor's objectives, assumptions, strategy and capabilities can be developed into a **response profile** of possible actions that may be taken by the competitor under varying circumstances. This will allow management to anticipate or influence the competitor's actions to the firm's advantage.

b. **Price elasticity analysis.** Recall that the price elasticity of demand measures the effect of a change in price on the demand for the product. It is calculated with the following equation:

$$E_D = \frac{\text{Change in quantity demanded}}{\text{Average quantity}} \div \frac{\text{Change in price}}{\text{Average price}}$$

In order to develop a pricing strategy, management may perform price elasticity analysis of product or service. By observing the effects of price changes management can obtain a better understanding of the relationship. Regression analysis may be used to perform a more sophisticated analysis.

EXAMPLE

Assume that Carlton Corp. manufactures Product X, a commodity-type product. Management is attempting to understand the price elasticity of the product to assist in planning production levels. Management has collected the following historical data regarding the price and aggregate demand for Product X. The prices have been price-level adjusted to take out the effects of inflation.

Date	Price	Quantity Sold	Date	Price	Quantity Sold
1/1/X1	$5.00	10,000	3/31/X2	$4.00	14,500
3/31/X1	4.50	13,000	6/30/X2	4.25	13,000
6/30/X1	4.00	15,000	9/30/X2	5.00	10,500
9/30/X1	5.50	9,000	1/1/X3	5.50	9,000
1/1/X2	5.25	10,000	3/31/X3	6.00	7,500

Management decides to use regression analysis on a spreadsheet program to assist with estimating the relationship between price and quantity demanded. The results of the analysis are illustrated below.

	A	B	C	D	E	F	G	
1	**SUMMARY OUTPUT**							
2								
3								
4	**Regression Statistics**							
5	Multiple R	0.986247						
6	R Square	0.972684						
7	Adjusted R							
8	Square	0.969269						
9	Standard Error	447.0297						
10	Observations	10						
11								
12	**ANOVA**							
13		df	SS	MS	F	Significance F		
14	Regression	1	56926316	56926316	284.8658	1.54E-07		
15	Residual	8	1598684	199835.5				
16	Total	9	58525000					
17								
18		Coefficients	Standard error	t Stat	P-value	Lower 95%	Upper 95%	
19	Intercept	29030.7	1068.801	27.16194	3.64E-09	26566.04	31495.36	
20	X variable 1	–3649.12	216.2063	–16.878	1.54E-07	–4147.7	–3150.55	

As expected, the results indicate that there is a very significant relationship between price and aggregate demand for the product. The adjusted R Squared indicates that about 97% of the variance in quantity demanded is explained by price. The equation for simple regression is as follows:

$$y = a + bx$$

Where

y = the dependent variable—in this case demand volume
a = the y-axis intercept
b = the slope of the line
x = the independent variable—in this case price

Assuming that management wants to predict aggregate demand if the price was set at $5.75, we can use the equation that was developed from the analysis. Under the column Coefficients we see Intercept of 29030.7 and X variable 1 (price) of –3649.12. The equation to predict aggregate demand would be

Demand	=	$a + (b)$Price
	=	$29030.7 + (-3649.12 \times \text{Price})$
	=	$29030.7 + (-3649.12 \times 5.75)$
	=	$8{,}048$

At a price of $5.75, the firm should expect aggregate demand to be about 8,048. Notice that the slope of the line (b) is negative indicating a negative relationship between demand and price, which is what we would expect. Regression analysis is explained in detail in Module 47.

D. Strategic Planning

Strategic planning involves identifying an organization's long-term goals and determining the best approaches to achieving those goals. To facilitate strategic planning an organization may establish a planning department, committee, or planning officer. Strategic planning should include involvement from decision makers at all company levels—the corporate, business, and functional levels. It is important to get as many stakeholders as possible involved in the process. Because strategic decisions have a huge impact on the company and require large commitments of financial resources, top management must approve and embrace the strategic plan.

Strategic planning begins with the development or review of the organization's mission. The **mission** sets forth the purpose of the organization, including its distinguishing characteristics. The organization may also develop a **vision** which sets forth where the organization would like to be in the future.

Next, a situational analysis will be performed which involves collection and evaluation of past and present economical, political, social, and technology data (an **environmental scan**) to (1) identify internal and external forces that may affect the organization's performance and choice of strategies, and (2) to assess the organization's strengths, weaknesses, opportunities, and threats (a **SWOT analysis**).

The SWOT analysis is then used to develop strategies to minimize risks and take advantage of major opportunities. This analysis is usually displayed in a SWOT matrix.

SWOT Matrix

	Strengths	**Weaknesses**
Opportunities	*Strength-opportunity strategies*	*Weakness-opportunity strategies*
For example, unfilled customer need, new technologies, etc.	Strategies to pursue opportunities that are a good fit for the firm's strengths.	Strategies to overcome weaknesses to pursue opportunities.
Threats	*Strength-threat strategies*	*Weakness-threat strategies*
For example, shifts in consumer tastes away from the firm's product, new regulations, etc.	Strategies to use strengths to overcome threats.	Defensive strategies to prevent the firm's weaknesses from making it highly vulnerable to threats.

After performing the situational analysis, specific strategies will be developed consistent with the mission and vision of the organization. Then, the strategies will be implemented within the organization. Effective implementation requires communication of the strategies throughout the organization and establishment of incentives and performance expectations that are consistent with the strategies. Finally, controls and outcome measures should be developed and monitored to provide feedback on whether the strategies are effectively implemented and achieving the desired results.

1. **Generic Business Strategies.** Generic business strategies are generally classified as being product differentiation or cost leadership. These two strategies have been broken down by Michael Porter into industry-wide or market segment strategy as illustrated below.

Target Scope	Advantage	
	Low Cost	Product Uniqueness
Broad (Industry-Wide)	Cost Leadership Strategy	Differentiation Strategy
Narrow (Market Segment)	Focus Strategy (low cost)	Focus Strategy (differentiation)

a. **Product differentiation.** Product differentiation involves development of a unique product to make it more attractive to the target market or to differentiate it from competitors' products. Products may be differentiated in the following ways:

   (1) Physical characteristics (e.g., aesthetics, durability, reliability, performance, serviceability, features, etc.)
   (2) Perceived differences (e.g., advertising, brand name, etc.)
   (3) Support service differences (e.g., exchange policies, assistance, after-sale support, etc.)

   By differentiating its products, the firm may be able to charge higher prices than its competitors or higher prices for the same products sold in different market segments.

b. **Cost leadership.** Striving for cost leadership fundamentally involves focusing on reducing the costs and time to produce, sell, and distribute a product or service. A number of techniques are used to attempt to reduce costs and time, including process reengineering, lean manufacturing (production), supply chain management, strategic alliances, and outsourcing.

   (1) **Process reengineering** involves a critical evaluation and major redesign of existing processes to achieve breakthrough improvements in performance. Process reengineering differs from total quality management (TQM) in that TQM involves gradual improvement of processes, while reengineering often involves radical redesign and drastic improvement in processes. Many of the significant improvements in processes over the last few years have been facilitated with innovations in information technology.

   (2) **Lean manufacturing** is a management technique that involves the identification and elimination of all types of waste in the production function. Operations are reviewed for those components, processes, or products that add cost rather than value. A basic premise underlying lean manufacturing is by focusing on improving design, increasing flexibility, and reducing time, defects, and inventory, costs can be minimized.

   (3) **Supply chain management**

       (a) The term supply chain describes the flow of goods, services, and information from basic raw materials through the manufacturing and distribution process to delivery of the product to the consumer, regardless of whether those activities occur in one or many firms.

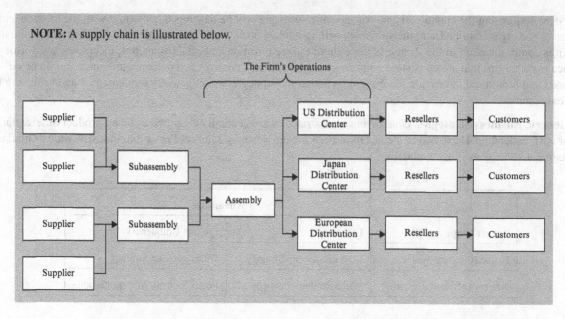

NOTE: A supply chain is illustrated below.

As shown, the firm's operations include only the assembly and distribution processes. Other firms supply raw materials, perform subassembly, and are the resellers of the final product. In viewing the supply chain, it is critical to go beyond the firm's immediate suppliers and customers to encompass the entire chain.

(b) To improve operations and manage the relationships with their suppliers many firms use a process known as supply chain management. A key aspect of supply chain management is the sharing of key information from the point of sale to the final consumer back to the manufacturer, the manufacturer's suppliers, and the suppliers' suppliers. As an example, if a manufacturer/distributor shares its sales forecasts with its suppliers and they in turn share their sales forecasts with their suppliers, the need for inventories for all firms is significantly decreased. The manufacturer/distributor, for example, needs far less raw materials inventory than normally would be the case because its suppliers are aware of the manufacture's projected needs and is prepared to have the materials available when needed. Specialized software facilitates this process of information sharing along the supply chain network.

(c) Supply chain management also focuses on improving processes to reduce time, defects, and costs all along the supply chain. By focusing on the entire supply chain, management may evaluate the full cost of inefficient processes, defective materials, and inaccurate forecasts of sales.

(d) However, supply chain management presents the company with a number of problems and risks including those arising from

1]Incompatible information systems
2]Refusal of some companies to share information
3]Failure of suppliers or customers to meet their obligations

2. **Target market analysis**

a. In implementing a generic strategy a firm will often use target market analysis. A firm's target market is a market in which the firm actually sells or plans to sell its product or services. A thorough understanding of the market is key to accurate sales forecasts. Just defining the market in geographic terms is not enough. Management should perform target market analysis to understand exactly who the firm's customers are. Management needs to understand why customers purchase the firm's product or service. For an individual customer the purpose might be to satisfy a basic need, to make things easier, or for entertainment. Target market analysis generally involves market segmentation, which involves breaking the market into groups that have different levels of demand for the firm's product or service. For example, a clothing store like GAP, that sells clothing primarily for teens, is interested in the size of the segment of the market—the number of teens in the geographical area that the store serves. Segmentation may be performed along any dimension that defines the firm's market, including

   (1) Demographics (e.g., sex, education, income, etc.)
   (2) Psychographics (e.g., lifestyle, social class, opinions, activities, attitudes, etc.)

b. If the firm's customers are businesses, segmentation might be performed in terms of other relevant dimensions including

   (1) Industry
   (2) Size (in terms of sales, total employees, etc.)
   (3) Location
   (4) How they purchase (e.g., seasonality, volume, who makes the purchasing decision)

   Unlike individuals, businesses purchase products to increase revenue, decrease costs, or maintain status quo.

c. Target market analysis may be essential to the firm's success. The greater the understanding management has of the firm's market, the more effective it can be at making marketing decisions. Advertising, for example, can be tailored to particular market segments. The firm may even be able to use differential pricing in which they charge different prices to different market segments. As an example, airlines have long attempted to develop fare schedules and restrictions that segment the business traveler from the vacation traveler because the business traveler will generally pay more for a ticket.

3. **Strategic alliances** involve collaborative agreements between two or more firms. They may be organized as joint ventures, equity ventures, equity investments, or simple agreements (such as comarketing or codevelopment agreements). Firms enter into strategic alliances for a number of reasons, including to

a. Refocus the firm's efforts on its core competencies and value creation activities
b. Speed innovation
c. Compensate for limited resources
d. Reduce risk

4. **Globalization involves developing strategies to deal with, and capitalize on, markets in other countries.** Companies in developed countries are able to compete with companies in developing countries in a number of ways, including

   • Use of sophisticated technology to reduce costs
   • Effective process management
   • Innovation in products or services
   • Product quality
   • Customer service
   • Adopting a global strategy

   In operating in a global economy, it is important that executives understand the cultural differences among countries. Differences in customs, values, and behavior result in problems that can only be managed by cross-cultural communication and interaction. These cultural differences affect negotiations, personnel management, and commerce.

   Multinational companies generally pursue a global strategy in which they locate and consolidate operations in countries with the greatest strategic advantages. Organizations that pursue a global strategy can benefit in a number of ways, including

   • Pooling international production to one or a few locations can achieve increased economies of scale
   • Manufacturing costs can be cut by moving production to low-cost countries
   • A firm that can switch production among different countries has increased bargaining power over labor, suppliers, and host governments
   • Worldwide access to resources, labor, suppliers and customers

5. **Outsourcing** involves contracting for the performance of processes by other firms. Outsourcing provides a way for firms to focus on their core competencies and value creation activities. Any processes, such as information technology, human resources, product service, etc., for which the firm does not have a competitive advantage may be outsourced to other firms that can perform the process more effectively or efficiently. In doing so, the firm may

be able to decrease its costs. Outsourcing may provide the following advantages to a firm: (1) cost savings, (2) higher quality, (3) reduced time to delivery, and (4) scalability.

Outsourcing can present a firm with new risks. For example, agreements must be appropriately structured to allow the firm to control performance, quality, and ethical employment practices of the other firm. Also, the firm may face risks to its reputation due to low quality or for outsourcing jobs, especially if the work is outsourced to another country. Finally, outsourcing may present the firm with legal risk and foreign currency risk.

E.   Estimating the Effects of Economic Changes

1. Successful management involves being able to anticipate changes in economic conditions and competitor actions and devising strategies and plans to react to those changes. To begin with, management must thoroughly understand the effects of economic changes on the firm. "How will demand for the firm's products or services be affected?" and "How will the change affect the firm's costs?" are key questions. In order to estimate the effects, management will collect and analyze historical data. Quantitative techniques such as regression analysis may be used. Management will also examine the effects of any competitor analysis that has been performed. The following table illustrates the process.

Economic change	Estimated effects	Response
1. Management of an airline predicts an economic downturn that will cause a significant decline in business travel.	• Revenue from business travel will decline. • The firm is in an oligopolistic market, and competitors will react to the economic downturn by reducing fares.	• Execute a preemptive price decrease in the vacation travel segment of the business. • Disguise the price decrease by selling the fares with travel packages and through Priceline.
2. A financial institution predicts a significant increase in interest rates.	• The increase will increase the institution's cost of capital and therefore increase its interest expense. Based on historical data, the estimated effect is an increase in interest expense of 15%. • Because the institution has a significant amount of long-term loans at fixed rates, the increase cannot be passed on to a significant segment of its customers.	• Management decides to use interest rate swaps to minimize the effects of the projected interest rate increase.
3. Management of an appliance manufacturer expects an upturn in economic activity resulting in an increase in demand for the firm's products. The upturn is expected to increase the cost of raw materials.	• Revenue will increase due to increased sales and costs will increase.	• The increase in demand is built into the firm's forecasts to assure that products will be available. • Management decides to purchase futures contracts to hedge the cost of raw materials.

2. On the CPA exam you can expect questions that will require you to determine the effects of economic changes and competitor actions on the firm's financial results. If no data to predict the effect of the change are provided, the solution to the question will merely require you to predict the direction of the change. For example, if personal disposable income increases, how are sales for a chain of jewelry stores affected? Obviously, the effect will be an increase in sales. However, without historical data on the effect of changes in personal disposable income on jewelry sales there would be no way to determine the extent of the effect. Other questions may provide you with indications of the effects of economic changes allowing the determination of a more precise answer. For example, if you were provided with the price elasticity of demand for a product, say 1.5, and told that the price was to be increased by 10% you could estimate the effects of the price increase on demand using the formula for price elasticity as shown below.

$$E_D = \frac{\text{Percentage change in quantity demanded}}{\text{Percentage change in price}}$$

We know that the percentage change in quantity demanded can be calculated as follows:

$$\text{Percentage change in quantity demanded} = E_D \times \text{Percentage change in price}$$
$$= 1.5 \times 10\%$$
$$= 15\%$$

Still other questions might provide you with historical data on the effect of changes in economic variables on the firm's results, and ask you to estimate the impact of some anticipated change in economic conditions on the firm's future financial results.

NOW REVIEW MULTIPLE-CHOICE QUESTIONS 110 THROUGH 126

KEY TERMS

Absolute advantage. An advantage a country has over other countries in the production of a good or service.

Business cycle. A fluctuation in aggregate economic output that lasts for several years.

Comparative advantage. An advantage a country has in producing a good or service because it has no alternative users of its resources that would involve a higher return.

Consumption function. Depicts the relationship between changes in personal disposable income and consumption.

Cost leadership. A strategy that involves focusing on reducing the costs and time to produce, sell, and distribute a product or service.

Demand. The quantity of a good or service that a consumer is willing and able to purchase at a given price.

Deflation. The rate of decline in the price level of goods and services.

Depression. A deep and long-lasting recession.

Dumping. A form of predatory pricing in which a manufacturer in one country exports a product at a price that is lower than the priced charged in its home country.

Economic profit. The amount of profit in excess of normal profit.

Export subsidies. Payments made by a government to encourage the production and export of specific products.

Government budget surplus (deficit). The excess (deficit) of government taxes in relation to government transfer payments and purchases.

Inflation. The rate of increase in the price level of goods and services.

Marginal product. The additional output obtained from employing one additional unit of resource (e.g., one additional worker).

Marginal revenue. The additional revenue received from the sale of one additional unit of a product.

Marginal revenue product. The change in total revenue from employing one additional unit of a resource.

Market equilibrium. The price at which all the goods offered for sale will be sold.

Monopolistic competition. A market characterized by many firms selling a differentiated product or service.

Nominal gross domestic product. The price of all goods and services produced by a domestic economy for a year at current market prices.

Nominal interest rate. The interest rate in terms of the nation's currency.

Normal profit. The amount of profit necessary to compensate the owners for their capital and/or managerial skills.

Oligopoly. A market characterized by significant barriers to entry. As a result there are few sellers of the product.

Personal disposable income. The amount of income that individuals receive and have available to purchase goods and services.

Potential gross domestic product. The maximum amount of production that could take place in an economy without putting pressure on the general level of prices.

Price ceiling. A specified maximum price that may be charged for a good, usually established by a government. A price ceiling will cause goods shortages.

Price floor. A specified minimum price that may be charged for a good, usually established by a government. A price floor will cause overproduction of the good.

Product differentiation. A strategy that involves modification of a product to make it more attractive to the target market or to differentiate it from competitors' products.

Pure competition. An industry in which there are a large number of sellers of virtually identical products or services. No individual seller is able to affect the market price.

Pure monopoly. A market in which there is a single seller of a product or service for which there are no close substitutes.

Real gross domestic product. The price of all goods and services produced by a domestic economy at price level adjusted (constant) prices.

Real interest rate. The interest rate adjusted for inflation.

Recession. A period of negative gross domestic product growth.

Substitution effect. The fact that as the price of a good or service falls, consumers will use it to replace similar goods or services.

Supply. The quantity of a good or service that will be supplied by producers at a given price.

Unemployment rate. The percentage of the total labor force that is unemployed at a given time.

Multiple-Choice Questions (1–126)

Demand, Supply, and Market Equilibrium

**1. If both the supply and the demand for a good increase, the market price will

    a. Rise only in the case of an inelastic supply function.
    b. Fall only in the case of an inelastic supply function.
    c. Not be predictable with only these facts.
    d. Rise only in the case of an inelastic demand function.

**2. A supply curve illustrates the relationship between

    a. Price and quantity supplied.
    b. Price and consumer tastes.
    c. Price and quantity demanded.
    d. Supply and demand.

3. As a business owner you have determined that the demand for your product is inelastic. Based upon this assessment you understand that

    a. Increasing the price of your product will increase total revenue.
    b. Decreasing the price of your product will increase total revenue.
    c. Increasing the price of your product will have no effect on total revenue.
    d. Increasing the price of your product will increase competition.

Items 4 and 5 are based on the following information:

Assume that demand for a particular product changed as shown below from D1 to D2.

4. Which of the following could cause the change shown in the graph?

    a. A decrease in the price of the product.
    b. An increase in supply of the product.
    c. A change in consumer tastes.
    d. A decrease in the price of a substitute for the product.

5. What will be the result on the equilibrium price for the product?

    a. Increase.
    b. Decrease.

    c. Remain the same.
    d. Cannot be determined.

**6. Which one of the following has an inverse relationship with the demand for money?

    a. Aggregate income.
    b. Price levels.
    c. Interest rates.
    d. Flow of funds.

7. An improvement in technology that in turn leads to improved worker productivity would **most likely result in

    a. A shift to the right in the supply curve and a lowering of the price of the output.
    b. A shift to the left in the supply curve and a lowering of the price of the output.
    c. An increase in the price of the output if demand is unchanged.
    d. Wage increases.

8. Which of the following market features is likely to cause a surplus of a particular product?

    a. A monopoly.
    b. A price floor.
    c. A price ceiling.
    d. A perfect market.

**9. A decrease in the price of a complementary good will

    a. Shift the demand curve of the joint commodity to the left.
    b. Increase the price paid for a substitute good.
    c. Shift the supply curve of the joint commodity to the left.
    d. Shift the demand curve of the joint commodity to the right.

**10. Demand for a product tends to be price inelastic if

    a. The product is considered a luxury item.
    b. People spend a large percentage of their income on the product.
    c. The population in the market area is large.
    d. Few good substitutes for the product are available.

11. Which of the following has the highest price elasticity coefficient?

    a. Milk.
    b. Macaroni and cheese.
    c. Bread.
    d. Ski boats.

**12. The local video store's business increased by 12% after the movie theater raised its prices from $6.50 to $7.00. Thus, relative to movie theater admissions, videos are

---

** CMA adapted

a. Substitute goods.
b. Superior goods.
c. Complementary goods.
d. Public goods.

*13. An individual receives an income of $3,000 per month, and spends $2,500. An increase in income of $500 per month occurs, and the individual spends $2,800. The individual's marginal propensity to save is

a. 0.2
b. 0.4
c. 0.6
d. 0.8

**14. In any competitive market, an equal increase in both demand and supply can be expected to always

a. Increase both price and market-clearing quantity.
b. Decrease both price and market-clearing quantity.
c. Increase market-clearing quantity.
d. Increase price.

**15. Given the following data, what is the marginal propensity to consume?

Level of	
Disposable income	Consumption
$40,000	$38,000
48,000	44,000

a. 1.33
b. 1.16
c. 0.95
d. 0.75

*16. Which of the following will cause a shift in the supply curve of a product?

a. Changes in the price of the product.
b. Changes in production taxes.
c. Changes in consumer tastes.
d. Changes in the number of buyers in the market.

17. When the federal government imposes health and safety regulations on certain products, one of the **most likely results is

a. Greater consumption of the product.
b. Lower prices for the product.
c. Greater tax revenues for the federal government.
d. Higher prices for the product.

18. In which of the following situations would there be inelastic demand?

a. A 5% price increase results in 3% decrease in the quantity demanded.
b. A 4% price increase results in a 6% decrease in the quantity demanded.
c. A 4% price increase results in a 4% decrease in the quantity demanded.
d. A 3% price decrease results in a 5% increase in the quantity demanded.

**19. In a competitive market for labor in which demand is stable, if workers try to increase their wage

a. Employment must fall.
b. Government must set a maximum wage below the equilibrium wage.
c. Firms in the industry must become smaller.
d. Product supply must decrease.

*20. A polluting manufacturing firm tends, from the societal viewpoint, to

a. Price its products too low.
b. Produce too little output.
c. Report too little profitability.
d. Employ too little equity financing.

**21. If the federal government regulates a product or service in a competitive market by setting a maximum price below the equilibrium price, what is the long-run effect?

a. A surplus.
b. A shortage.
c. A decrease in demand.
d. No effect on the market.

**22. A valid reason for the government to intervene in the wholesale electrical power market would include which one of the following?

a. A price increase that is more than expected.
b. Electricity is an essential resource and the wholesale market is not competitive.
c. The electricity distribution companies are losing money.
d. Foreign power generators have contracts with the local government at very high prices.

23. If the income elasticity of demand coefficient for a particular product is 3.00, the good is likely

a. A luxury good.
b. A complementary good.
c. An inferior good.
d. A necessity.

**24. Long Lake Golf Course has raised greens fees for a nine-hole game due to an increase in demand.

	Previous rate	New rate	Average games played at previous rate	Average games played at new rate
Regular weekday	$10	$11	80	70
Senior citizen	6	8	150	82
Weekend	15	20	221	223

---

* CIA adapted
** CMA adapted

Which one of the following is correct?

   a. The regular weekday and weekend demand is inelastic.
   b. The regular weekday and weekend demand is elastic.
   c. The senior citizen demand is elastic, and weekend demand is inelastic.
   d. The regular weekday demand is inelastic, and weekend demand is elastic.

**25. Which one of the following would cause the demand curve for a commodity to shift to the left?

   a. A rise in the price of a substitute product.
   b. A rise in average household income.
   c. A rise in the price of a complementary commodity.
   d. A rise in the population.

**26. Price ceilings

   a. Are illustrated by government price support programs in agriculture.
   b. Create prices greater than equilibrium prices.
   c. Create prices below equilibrium prices.
   d. Result in persistent surpluses.

*27. X and Y are substitute products. If the price of product Y increases, the immediate impact on product X is

   a. Price will increase.
   b. Quantity demanded will increase.
   c. Quantity supplied will increase.
   d. Price, quantity demanded, and supply will increase.

28. Wilson Corporation has a major competitor that produces a product that is a close substitute for Wilson's good. If the coefficient of cross-elasticity of demand for Wilson's product with respect to the competitor's product is 2.00 and the competitor decreases its price by 5%, what is the expected effect on demand for Wilson's product?

   a. A 5% increase in demand.
   b. A 5% decrease in demand.
   c. A 10% increase in demand.
   d. A 10% decrease in demand.

¹**29. As the price for a particular product changes, the quantity of the product demanded changes according to the following schedule:

Total quantity demanded	Price per unit
100	$50
150	45
200	40
225	35
230	30
232	25

Using the arc method, the price elasticity of demand for this product when the price decreases from $50 to $45 is

   a. 0.20
   b. 10.00
   c. 0.10
   d. 3.80

**30. As the price for a particular product changes, the quantity of the product demanded changes according to the following schedule:

Total quantity demanded	Price per unit
100	$50
150	45
200	40
225	35
230	30
232	25

Using the arc method, the price elasticity of demand for this product when the price decreases from $40 to $35 is

   a. 0.20
   b. 0.88
   c. 10.00
   d. 5.00

**31. If a group of consumers decide to boycott a particular product, the expected result would be

   a. An increase in the product price to make up lost revenue.
   b. A decrease in the demand for the product.
   c. An increase in product supply because of increased availability.
   d. That demand for the product would become completely inelastic.

32. Which of the following is **not** likely to affect the supply of a particular good?

   a. Changes in government subsidies.
   b. Changes in technology.
   c. Changes in consumer income.
   d. Changes in production costs.

**33. If a product's demand is elastic and there is a decrease in price, the effect will be

   a. A decrease in total revenue.
   b. No change in total revenue.
   c. A decrease in total revenue and the demand curve shifts to the left.
   d. An increase in total revenue.

---

*CIA adapted
**CMA adapted

34. All of the following are complementary goods **except

    a. Margarine and butter.
    b. Cameras and rolls of film.
    c. VCRs and video cassettes.
    d. Razors and razor blades.

**35. The law of diminishing marginal utility states that

    a. Marginal utility will decline as a consumer acquires additional units of a specific product.
    b. Total utility will decline as a consumer acquires additional units of a specific product.
    c. Declining utilities causes the demand curve to slope upward.
    d. Consumers' wants will diminish with the passage of time.

36. In the pharmaceutical industry where a diabetic must have insulin no matter the cost and where there is no other substitute, the diabetic's demand curve is **best described as

    a. Perfectly elastic.
    b. Perfectly inelastic.
    c. Elastic.
    d. Inelastic.

Costs of Production

**37. Because of the existence of economies of scale, business firms may find that

    a. Each additional unit of labor is less efficient than the previous unit.
    b. As more labor is added to a factory, increases in output will diminish in the short run.
    c. Increasing the size of a factory will result in lower average costs.
    d. Increasing the size of a factory will result in lower total costs.

**38. In the long run, a firm may experience increasing returns due to

    a. Law of diminishing returns.
    b. Opportunity costs.
    c. Comparative advantage.
    d. Economies of scale.

**39. The measurement of the benefit lost by using resources for a given purpose is

    a. Economic efficiency.
    b. Opportunity cost.
    c. Comparative advantage.
    d. Absolute advantage.

Items 40 and 41 are based on the following information:

Total units of product	Average fixed cost	Average variable cost	Average total cost
6	$15.00	$25.00	$40.00
7	12.86	24.00	36.86
8	11.25	23.50	34.75
9	10.00	23.75	33.75

**40. The total cost of producing seven units is

    a. $90.02
    b. $168.00
    c. $258.02
    d. $280.00

**41. The marginal cost of producing the ninth unit is

    a. $23.50
    b. $23.75
    c. $25.75
    d. $33.75

**42. Daily costs for Kelso Manufacturing include $1,000 of fixed costs and total variable costs are shown below.

Unit output	10	11	12	13	14	15
Cost	$125	$250	$400	$525	$700	$825

The average total cost at an output level of 11 units is

    a. $113.64
    b. $125.00
    c. $215.91
    d. $250.00

Items 43 through 45 are based on the following information:

Number of workers	Total product units	Average selling price
10	20	$50.00
11	25	49.00
12	28	47.50

**43. The marginal physical product when one worker is added to a team of 10 workers is

    a. 1 unit.
    b. 8 units.
    c. 5 units.
    d. 25 units.

**44. The marginal revenue per unit when one worker is added to a team of 11 workers is

    a. $105.00
    b. $225.00
    c. $35.00
    d. $47.50

**45. The marginal revenue product when one worker is added to a team of 11 workers is

    a. $42.00
    b. $225.00
    c. $105.00
    d. $47.50

**46. Marginal revenue is

    a. Equal to price in monopolistic competition.
    b. The change in total revenue associated with increasing prices.
    c. Greater than price in pure competition.
    d. The change in total revenue associated with producing and selling one more unit.

** CMA adapted

**47. In microeconomics, the distinguishing characteristic of the long run on the supply side is that

    a. Only supply factors determine price and output.
    b. Only demand factors determine price and output.
    c. Firms are not allowed to enter or exit the industry.
    d. All inputs are variable.

48. What is the main factor that differentiates the short-run cost function from the long-run cost function?

    a. Nothing, the two functions are identical.
    b. The level of technology.
    c. Changes in government subsidies.
    d. The nature of the costs.

Items 49 and 50 are based on the following information:

Karen Parker wants to establish an environmental testing company that would specialize in evaluating the quality of water found in rivers and streams. However, Parker has discovered that she needs either certification or approval from five separate local and state agencies before she can commence business. Also, the necessary equipment to begin would cost several million dollars. Nevertheless, Parker believes that if she is able to obtain capital resources, she can gain market share from the two major competitors.

**49. The large capital outlay necessary for the equipment is an example of a(n)

    a. Entry barrier.
    b. Minimum efficient scale.
    c. Created barrier.
    d. Production possibility boundary.

50. The market structure Karen Parker is attempting to enter is **best described as

    a. A natural monopoly.
    b. A cartel.
    c. An oligopoly.
    d. Monopolistic competition.

**51. The distinguishing characteristic of oligopolistic markets is

    a. A single seller of a homogeneous product with no close substitutes.
    b. A single seller of a heterogeneous product with no close substitutes.
    c. Lack of entry and exit barriers in the industry.
    d. Mutual interdependence of firm pricing and output decisions.

52. Economic markets that are characterized by monopolistic competition have all of the following characteristics **except

    a. One seller of the product.
    b. Economies or diseconomies of scale.
    c. Advertising.
    d. Heterogeneous products.

53. Which type of economic market structure is characterized by a few large sellers of a product or service, engaging primarily in nonprice competition?

    a. Monopoly.
    b. Oligopoly.
    c. Perfect competition.
    d. Monopolistic competition.

54. Which type of economic market structure is composed of a large number of sellers, each producing an identical product, and with no significant barriers to entry and exit?

    a. Monopoly.
    b. Oligopoly.
    c. Perfect competition
    d. Monopolistic competition.

**55. A natural monopoly exists because

    a. The firm owns natural resources.
    b. The firms holds patents.
    c. Economic and technical conditions permit only one efficient supplier.
    d. The government is the only supplier.

56. A market with many independent firms, low barriers to entry, and product differentiation is **best classified as

    a. A monopoly.
    b. A natural monopoly.
    c. Monopolistic competition.
    d. An oligopoly.

57. Which of the following is **not a key assumption of perfect competition?

    a. Firms sell a homogeneous product.
    b. Customers are indifferent about which firm they buy from.
    c. The level of a firm's output is small relative to the industry's total output.
    d. Each firm can price its product above the industry price.

**58. An oligopolist faces a "kinked" demand curve. This terminology indicates that

    a. When an oligopolist lowers its price, the other firms in the oligopoly will match the price reduction, but if the oligopolist raises its price, the other firms will ignore the price change.
    b. An oligopolist faces a nonlinear demand for its product, and price changes will have little effect on demand for that product.
    c. An oligopolist can sell its product at any price, but after the "saturation point" another oligopolist will lower its price and, therefore, shift the demand curve to the left.
    d. Consumers have no effect on the demand curve, and an oligopolist can shape the curve to optimize its own efficiency.

** CMA adapted

Aggregate Demand and Business Cycles

59. If consumer confidence falls, the impact upon the economy is

     a. A downturn.
     b. An upturn.
     c. No change.
     d. Consumer confidence does not have an impact upon the economy.

**60. If an increase in government purchases of goods and services of $20 billion causes equilibrium GDP to rise by $80 billion, and if total taxes and investment are constant, the marginal propensity to consume out of disposable income is

     a. 0.75
     b. 0.25
     c. 1.25
     d. 4.00

**61. During the recessionary phase of a business cycle

     a. The purchasing power of money is likely to decline rapidly.
     b. The natural rate of unemployment will increase dramatically.
     c. Potential national income will exceed actual national income.
     d. Actual national income will exceed potential national income.

*62. For a given level of tax collections, prices, and interest rates, a decrease in governmental purchases will result in a(n)

     a. Increase in aggregate demand.
     b. Increase in aggregate supply.
     c. Decrease in aggregate demand.
     d. Decrease in aggregate supply.

**63. In macroeconomic terms, aggregate demand is the

     a. Demand for money by the community in a period of full employment.
     b. Total expenditure on capital goods by entrepreneurs during a period of full employment.
     c. Demand that is needed if a country's economy is to operate at optimum level and the level of investment is to be raised.
     d. Total expenditures on consumer goods and investment, including government and foreign expenditures, during a given period.

*64. Which one of the following would not be included in the calculation of the gross domestic product (GDP)?

     a. Purchase of a new home.
     b. An automotive worker's wages.
     c. A doctor's fee.
     d. Purchase of common stock.

65. An upturn in economic activity is indicated by all of the following, **except**

     a. Increased housing starts.
     b. Reduction in the quantity of unemployment claims.
     c. Increase in personal travel.
     d. Reduction in the amount of luxury purchases.

66. Which of the following may provide a leading indicator of a future increase in gross domestic product?

     a. A reduction in the money supply.
     b. A decrease in the issuance of building permits.
     c. An increase in the timeliness of delivery by vendors.
     d. An increase in the average hours worked per week of production workers.

*67. Disposable income is calculated as

     a. Gross domestic product minus the capital cost allowance.
     b. Net domestic product minus indirect business taxes plus net income earned abroad.
     c. Personal income minus transfer payments.
     d. Personal income minus personal taxes.

*68. The primary reason for allowing legal immigration into industrial nations is the immigrants' potential for

     a. Reducing a trade deficit.
     b. Fulfilling a trade agreement.
     c. Contributing to economic growth.
     d. Fulfilling a political agreement.

*69. Some economic indicators lead the economy into a recovery or recession, and some lag it. An example of a lagging indicator is

     a. Chronic unemployment.
     b. Orders for consumer and producer goods.
     c. Housing starts.
     d. Consumer expectations.

**70. Government borrowing to finance large deficits increases the demand for lendable funds and

     a. Increases the supply of lendable funds.
     b. Exerts downward pressure on interest rates.
     c. Has no impact on interest rates.
     d. Puts upward pressure on interest rates.

Economic Measures and Policy

**71. A period of rising inflation

     a. Increases the price level, which benefits those who are entitled to receive specific amounts of money.
     b. Enhances the positive relationship between the price level and the purchasing power of money.
     c. Will not be affected by contracts that include the indexing of payments.
     d. Increases the price level, which is negatively related to the purchasing power of money.

---

* CIA adapted
** CMA adapted

**72. The most effective fiscal policy program to help reduce demand-pull inflation would be to

a. Decrease the rate of growth of the money supply.
b. Increase both taxes and government spending.
c. Decrease taxes and increase government spending.
d. Increase taxes and decrease government spending.

*73. The money supply in a nation's economy will decrease following

a. Open-market purchases by the nation's central bank.
b. A decrease in the discount rate.
c. An increase in the reserve ratio.
d. A decrease in the margin requirement.

**74. The Federal Reserve Board most directly influences a corporation's decision of whether or not to issue debt or equity financing when it revises the

a. Corporate income tax rate.
b. Prime rate at which the Federal Reserve Bank lends money to member banks.
c. Discount rate at which the Federal Reserve Bank lends money to member banks.
d. Discount rate at which member banks lend money to their customers.

**75. According to fiscal policy principles, a tax increase will

a. Increase spending and increase aggregate demand.
b. Increase spending and reduce aggregate demand.
c. Reduce spending and increase aggregate demand.
d. Reduce spending and reduce aggregate demand.

**76. If the Federal Reserve Board wanted to implement an expansionary monetary policy, which one of the following actions would the Federal Reserve Board take?

a. Raise the reserve requirement and the discount rate.
b. Purchase additional US government securities and lower the discount rate.
c. Reduce the reserve requirement and raise the discount rate.
d. Raise the discount rate and sell US government securities.

**77. The Federal Reserve System's reserve ratio is

a. The specified percentage of a commercial bank's deposit liabilities that must be deposited in the central bank or held as cash in the bank's vault.
b. The rate that the central bank charges for loans granted to commercial banks.
c. The ratio of excess reserves to legal reserves that are deposited in the central bank.
d. The specified percentage of a commercial bank's demand deposits to total liabilities.

*78. Which of the following instruments of monetary policy is the most important means by which the money supply is controlled?

a. Changing the reserve ratio.
b. Open-market operations.
c. Manipulation of government spending.
d. Changing the discount rate.

*79. If a government were to use only fiscal policy to stimulate the economy from a recession, it would

a. Raise consumer taxes and increase government spending.
b. Lower business taxes and government spending.
c. Increase the money supply and increase government spending.
d. Lower consumer taxes and increase government spending.

**80. The federal budget deficit is the

a. Total accumulation of the federal government's surpluses and deficits.
b. Excess state, local, and federal spending over their revenues.
c. Amount by which the federal government's expenditures exceed its revenues in a given year.
d. Amount by which liabilities exceed assets on the federal government's balance sheet.

*81. Which of the following is a tool of monetary policy that a nation's central bank could use to stabilize the economy during an inflationary period?

a. Selling government securities.
b. Lowering bank reserve requirements.
c. Lowering bank discount rates.
d. Encouraging higher tax rates.

**82. Economists and economic policy makers are interested in the multiplier effect because the multiplier explains why

a. A small change in investment can have a much larger impact on gross domestic product.
b. Consumption is always a multiple of savings.
c. The money supply increases when deposits in the banking system increase.
d. The velocity of money is less than one.

83. Assume that the United States Congress passes a tax law that provides for a "rebate" to taxpayers. One of the goals of the rebate is

a. Increase consumer disposable income and expand the economy.
b. Increase consumer disposable income and contract the economy.
c. Decrease consumer disposable income and expand the economy
d. Decrease consumer disposable income and contract the economy.

_____

* CIA adapted
** CMA adapted

84. The rate of unemployment caused by changes in the composition of unemployment opportunities over time is referred to as the

a. Frictional unemployment rate.
b. Cyclical unemployment rate.
c. Structural unemployment rate.
d. Full-employment unemployment rate.

85. The producer price index measures

a. The price of a basket of commodities at the point of the first commercial sale.
b. Price changes for all products sold by domestic producers to foreigners.
c. Price changes of goods purchased from other countries.
d. The price of a fixed market basket of goods and services purchased by a typical urban consumer.

86. The formula for calculating a price index for the year 2013, using the year 2008 as a reference period is

a.
$$\frac{\text{Price of 2013 market basket in 2013}}{\text{Price of 2013 market basket in 2008}} \times 100$$

b.
$$\frac{\text{Price of 2008 market basket in 2013}}{\text{Price of 2008 market basket in 2008}} \times 100$$

c.
$$\frac{\text{Price of 2013 market basket in 2008}}{\text{Price of 2008 market basket in 2008}} \times 100$$

d.
$$\frac{\text{Price of 2008 market basket in 2008}}{\text{Price of 2008 market basket in 2013}} \times 100$$

**87. The discount rate set by the Federal Reserve System is the

a. Required percentage of reserves deposited at the central bank.
b. Rate that commercial banks charge for loans to each other.
c. Rate that commercial banks charge for loans to the general public.
d. Rate that the central bank charges for loans to commercial banks.

88. Which of the following is true about deflation?

a. It motivates consumers to borrow money.
b. It motivates businesses to make investments.
c. It results in very low interest rates.
d. It results in economic expansion.

89. Economies often experience inflation but seldom experience long periods of deflation. Which of the following is true about a deflationary economy?

a. Companies are hesitant to make investments.
b. The lower prices encourage consumers to make major purchases.
c. Interest rates tend to be high.
d. Actual GDP is above potential GDP.

90. What factor explains the difference between real and nominal interest rates?

a. Inflation risk.
b. Credit risk.
c. Default risk.
d. Market risk.

Global Economics

91. All of the following are true about international trade **except that

a. The gains from international trade depend on specialization with comparative advantage.
b. Absolute advantage without comparative advantage does not result in gains from international trade.
c. Absolute advantage is defined as the ability of one nation to produce a product at a relatively lower opportunity cost than another nation.
d. Where there is reciprocal absolute advantage between two countries, specialization will make it possible to produce more of each product.

92. If the central bank of a country raises interest rates sharply, the country's currency will **most likely

a. Increase in relative value.
b. Remain unchanged in value.
c. Decrease in relative value.
d. Decrease sharply in value at first and then return to its initial value.

93. Which one of the following groups would be the **primary beneficiary of a tariff?

a. Domestic producers of export goods.
b. Domestic producers of goods protected by the tariff.
c. Domestic consumers of goods protected by the tariff.
d. Foreign producers of goods protected by the tariff.

94. In the law of comparative advantage, the country which should produce a specific product is determined by

a. Opportunity costs.
b. Profit margins.
c. Economic order quantities.
d. Tariffs.

**95. Assuming exchange rates are allowed to fluctuate freely, which one of the following factors would likely cause a nation's currency to appreciate on the foreign exchange market?

a. A relatively rapid rate of growth in income that stimulates imports.
b. A high rate of inflation relative to other countries.
c. A slower rate of growth in income than in other countries, which causes imports to lag behind exports.
d. Domestic real interest rates that are lower than real interest rates abroad.

** CMA adapted

**96. If the US dollar declines in value relative to the currencies of many of its trading partners, the likely result is that

    a. Foreign currencies will depreciate against the dollar.
    b. The US balance of payments deficit will become worse.
    c. US exports will tend to increase.
    d. US imports will tend to increase.

**97. Exchange rates are determined by

    a. Each industrial country's government.
    b. The International Monetary Fund.
    c. Supply and demand in the foreign currency market.
    d. Exporters and importers of manufactured goods.

**98. If the value of the US dollar in foreign currency markets changes from $1 = 3 Brazilian real to $1 = 2 Brazilian real

    a. The Brazilian real has depreciated against the dollar.
    b. Brazilian imported products in the US will become more expensive.
    c. US tourists in Brazil will find their dollars will buy more German products.
    d. US exports to Brazil should decrease.

*99. Which of the following measures creates the **most** restrictive barrier to exporting to a country?

    a. Tariffs.
    b. Quotas.
    c. Embargoes.
    d. Exchange controls.

100. Which of the following is not a foreign exchange control that may be implemented by a country?

    a. Banning possession of foreign currency by citizens.
    b. Fixed exchange rates.
    c. Restricting currency exchange to government approved exchangers.
    d. Requiring a floating exchange rate.

101. Which of the following accurately describes a dumping pricing policy?

    a. Selling goods domestically at a price less than cost.
    b. Selling goods in another country at a price less than cost.
    c. Selling goods in another country at an excessive price.
    d. Selling goods domestically at an excessive price.

102. What is an appropriate response by an importing country for the payment of export subsidies by an exporting country?

    a. Countervailing duties.
    b. Foreign exchange controls.
    c. Trade embargo.
    d. A dumping pricing policy.

103. Which of the following describes a pegged exchange rate?

    a. A currency rate that is tied to the US dollar.
    b. A currency rate with its value determined by market factors.
    c. A currency market in which the country's central bank keeps the rate from deviating too far from a target band or value.
    d. A currency rate that is tied to the prime rate.

104. Assume that the three-month forward rate for the euro is $1.367 and the spot rate is $1.364. What is the forward premium or discount on the euro?

    a. 0.88% premium.
    b. 0.88% discount.
    c. 0.23% premium.
    d. 0.23% discount.

**105. When net exports are negative, there is a net flow of

    a. Goods from firms in foreign countries to the domestic country.
    b. Money from foreign countries to the firms of the domestic country.
    c. Goods from the firms of the domestic country to foreign countries.
    d. Goods and services which result in a trade surplus.

106. Which of the following factors is **least** likely to affect a country's currency foreign exchange rates?

    a. Interest rates in the country.
    b. Political stability in the country.
    c. Inflation in the country.
    d. The tax rate in the country.

107. Assume that the exchange rate of US dollars to euros is $1.80 to 1 euro. How much would a US company gain or lose if the company has a 10,000 euro receivable and the exchange rate went to $1.75 to 1 euro?

    a. $10,000 loss.
    b. $10,000 gain.
    c. $500 loss.
    d. $500 gain.

108. Simon Corp., a US company, has made a large sale to a French company on a 120-day account payable in euros. If management of Simon wants to hedge the transaction risk related to a decline in the value of the euro, which of the following strategies would be appropriate?

    a. Lend euros to another company for payment in 120 days.
    b. Enter into a forward exchange contract to purchase euros for delivery in 120 days.
    c. Enter into a futures contract to sell euros for delivery in the future.
    d. Purchase euros on the spot market.

---

* CIA adapted
** CMA adapted

109. Which of the following is **not** a means by which a firm might hedge the political risk of an investment in another country?

    a. Insurance.
    b. Buy futures contracts for future delivery of the country's currency.
    c. Finance the operations with local-country capital.
    d. Enter into joint ventures with local-country firms.

Economics and Strategy

**110. Patents are granted in order to encourage firms to invest in the research and development of new products. Patents are an example of

    a. Vertical integration.
    b. Market concentration.
    c. Entry barriers.
    d. Collusion.

111. The market for product RK-25 is perfectly competitive. The current market price is $30, and the quantity demanded is 4 million. Due to changes in consumer tastes, a permanent increase in demand for RK-25 is expected in the near term. If nothing else changes in this market, which of the following would be the **most feasible levels of short-term and long-term prices?

	Short-term	Long-term
a.	$39	$35
b.	$35	$39
c.	$35	$30
d.	$30	$35

112. The ultimate purpose of competitor analysis is to

    a. Identify the competition.
    b. Determine the competition's strength and weaknesses.
    c. Identify the competition's major customers.
    d. Understand and predict the behavior of the competition.

113. Which of the following is **not** an important aspect of supply chain management?

    a. Information technology.
    b. Accurate forecasts.
    c. Customer relations.
    d. Communications.

114. Which of the following types of organizations would **most** likely engage in public relations type advertising?

    a. An airline.
    b. A hotel chain.
    c. A toy manufacturer.
    d. An electric utility company.

115. Target marketing analysis involves

    a. Analyzing the firm's input markets.
    b. Understanding and segmenting the firm's customer markets.
    c. Analyzing the firm's market structure.
    d. Deciding on whether to offer a new product line.

116. If a firm's customers are businesses, market segmentation might be performed along all of the following dimensions, **except**

    a. Industry.
    b. Location.
    c. Lifestyle.
    d. Size.

Items 117 and 118 are based on the following information:

Yeager Corporation has used regression analysis to perform price elasticity analysis. In doing so management regressed the quantity demanded (y variable) against price (x variable) with the following results:

Multiple R	.86798
Adjusted R squared	.72458
Standard error	542.33
Intercept	56400.50
Price coefficient	−4598.20

117. What percentage of the variation in quantity demanded is explained by price?

    a. 86.798%
    b. 72.458%
    c. 56.4%
    d. 54.233%

118. Calculate the predicted quantity demanded if price is set at $7.00.

    a. 24,213
    b. 88,588
    c. 31,234
    d. 18,454

119. Which of the following is **not** one of the five forces in Porter's model for industry analysis?

    a. Competitors.
    b. Bargaining power of customers.
    c. Bargaining power of suppliers.
    d. General economic conditions.

120. Which of the following is a defining characteristic of supply chain management?

    a. Focuses on the sharing of information with suppliers and customers.
    b. Focuses on redesigning processes.
    c. Focuses on improving quality.
    d. Focuses on strategic alliances.

121. Which of the following is **not** a likely strategy for a firm in a purely competitive market?

    a. Lean manufacturing.
    b. Supply chain management.
    c. Process reengineering.
    d. Development of a brand name.

** CMA adapted

122. What is the purpose of a response profile in competitor analysis?

    a. To develop an understanding of the firm's industry.
    b. To analyze the firm's strengths in relation to its competitors.
    c. To identify possible actions by competitors.
    d. To understand the nature of the firm's major markets.

**123. The process of dividing all potential consumers into smaller groups of buyers with distinct needs, characteristics, or behaviors, who might require a similar product or service mix, is called

    a. Strategic planning.
    b. Market segmentation.
    c. Product positioning.
    d. Objective setting.

124. Which of the following measures of unemployment would be of **least** importance to management when trying to predict the future state of the economy?

    a. Structural unemployment.
    b. Cyclical unemployment.
    c. Frictional unemployment.
    d. Overall unemployment.

** CMA adapted

125. Which of the following **best** describes the steps involved in performing competitor analysis?

    a. Gathering information about the competitor and using it to predict the competitor' behavior.
    b. Determining the type of market structure and the number of competitors.
    c. Assessing the general environment and determining how that affects competition.
    d. Assessing the market structure to predict when new competitors will enter the market.

126. All of the following are ways that companies in developed countries generally may compete with companies in developing countries **except**

    a. Technology.
    b. Customer service.
    c. Quality.
    d. Low-cost resources.

Multiple-Choice Answers and Explanations

Answers

1. c __ __	27. b __ __	53. b __ __	79. d __ __	105. a __ __
2. a __ __	28. d __ __	54. c __ __	80. c __ __	106. d __ __
3. a __ __	29. d __ __	55. c __ __	81. a __ __	107. c __ __
4. c __ __	30. b __ __	56. c __ __	82. a __ __	108. c __ __
5. a __ __	31. b __ __	57. d __ __	83. a __ __	109. b __ __
6. c __ __	32. c __ __	58. a __ __	84. c __ __	110. c __ __
7. a __ __	33. d __ __	59. a __ __	85. a __ __	111. c __ __
8. b __ __	34. a __ __	60. a __ __	86. a __ __	112. d __ __
9. d __ __	35. a __ __	61. c __ __	87. d __ __	113. c __ __
10. d __ __	36. b __ __	62. c __ __	88. c __ __	114. d __ __
11. d __ __	37. c __ __	63. d __ __	89. a __ __	115. b __ __
12. a __ __	38. d __ __	64. d __ __	90. a __ __	116. c __ __
13. b __ __	39. b __ __	65. d __ __	91. c __ __	117. b __ __
14. c __ __	40. c __ __	66. d __ __	92. a __ __	118. a __ __
15. d __ __	41. c __ __	67. d __ __	93. b __ __	119. c __ __
16. b __ __	42. a __ __	68. c __ __	94. a __ __	120. a __ __
17. d __ __	43. c __ __	69. a __ __	95. c __ __	121. d __ __
18. a __ __	44. c __ __	70. d __ __	96. c __ __	122. c __ __
19. a __ __	45. c __ __	71. d __ __	97. c __ __	123. b __ __
20. a __ __	46. d __ __	72. d __ __	98. b __ __	124. c __ __
21. b __ __	47. d __ __	73. c __ __	99. c __ __	125. a __ __
22. b __ __	48. d __ __	74. c __ __	100. d __ __	126. d __ __
23. a __ __	49. a __ __	75. d __ __	101. b __ __	
24. c __ __	50. c __ __	76. b __ __	102. a __ __	
25. c __ __	51. d __ __	77. a __ __	103. c __ __	1st: __/126 __%
26. c __ __	52. a __ __	78. b __ __	104. a __ __	2nd: __/126 __%

Explanations

1. (c) The requirement is to predict the market price based on an increase in both supply and demand. The correct answer is (c) because without additional information about the extent of the change, the effect on price is not determinable. Answers (a), (b), and (d) are incorrect because the price elasticity of the demand or supply function does not provide enough information to determine the effect.

2. (a) The requirement is to describe the relationship shown by a supply curve. A supply curve illustrates the quantity supplied at varying prices at a point in time. Therefore, the correct answer is (a). Answers (b) and (c) are incorrect because they deal with demand. Answer (d) is incorrect because it deals with demand-supply equilibrium.

3. (a) The requirement is to apply the concept of price-elasticity of demand. If demand is inelastic an increase in price will increase total revenue. Answer (a) is correct because it accurately states this rule. Answer (b) is incorrect because if demand is inelastic the quantity demanded will not be affected significantly by a change in price. Answer (c) is incorrect because if the quantity demanded is not significantly affected by an increase in price, total revenue will increase. Answer (d) is incorrect because an increase in price may, or may not, increase competition.

4. (c) The requirement is to identify the reason for the shift in demand. The correct answer is (c) because a shift in demand could result from a change in consumer tastes. Answer (a) is incorrect because this would result in movement along the existing demand curve. Answer (b) is incorrect because a change in supply would not affect the demand function. Answer (d) is incorrect because a decrease in price of a substitute would result in a shift of the curve to the left.

5. (a) The requirement is to determine the effect of the shift in the demand function on the price of the product. The correct answer is (a) because the shift (increase) in demand will increase the price of the product. Answer (b) is incorrect because a shift of the demand curve to the left would have to occur to decrease price. Answers (c) and (d) are incorrect because the effect on price will not be to remain the same and it can be determined.

6. (c) The requirement is to identify the item that has an inverse relationship with the demand for money. The correct answer is (c) because as interest rates increase the demand for money decreases. Answers (a), (b), and (d) are incorrect because they do not have an inverse relationship with the demand for money.

7. (a) The requirement is to describe the effect of an improvement in technology that leads to increased worker productivity. If the cost of producing a good declines, more will be supplied at a given price. Therefore, the supply curve will shift to the right and answer (a) is correct. Answer (b) is incorrect because a shift to the left would result in decreased supplies. Answer (c) is incorrect because price would not increase, and answer (d) is incorrect because wages would not necessarily increase.

8. (b) The requirement is to identify the market feature that is likely to cause a surplus of a particular product. Answer (b) is correct because a price floor, if it is above the equilibrium price, will cause excess production and a surplus. Answer (a) is incorrect because a monopoly market is likely to be characterized by underproduction of the product. Answer (c) is incorrect because a price ceiling, if it is below the equilibrium price, will cause underproduction and shortages. Answer (d) is incorrect because in a perfect market with no intervention demand and supply will be equal.

9. (d) The requirement is to describe the effect on demand for a good if a complementary good decreases in price. If the price of a complementary good decreases, demand for the joint commodity will increase. This is due to the fact that the total cost of using the two products decreases. If demand for a product increases the demand curve will shift to the right. Therefore, answer (d) is correct. Answer (a) is incorrect because a shift in the demand curve to the left depicts a decrease in demand. Answers (b) and (c) deal with supply and are not relevant.

10. (d) The requirement is to identify a characteristic of a product with price inelastic demand. The correct answer is (d) because price inelasticity means that the quantity demanded does not change much with price changes. This would be a characteristic of a good with few substitutes. Answers (a), (b), and (c) are characteristics of goods that have price elastic demand.

11. (d) The requirement is to apply the concept of price elasticity of demand. If substitutes for a good are readily available then the demand for the good is more elastic.

Answer (d) is correct because there are many substitutes for luxury goods. Answers (a), (b), and (c) are all considered to be necessities and demand for them is less elastic.

12. (a) The requirement is to identify the relationship between two products for which one has increased demand when the other's price increases. Answer (a) is correct. Substitute goods are selected by a consumer based on price. When the price of one goes up, demand for the other increases. Answer (b) is incorrect because superior goods are those whose demand is directly influenced by income. Answer (c) is incorrect because complementary goods are used together and when the price of one goes up, demand for the other goes down. Answer (d) is incorrect because a public good is one for which it is difficult to restrict use, such as a national park.

13. (b) The requirement is to calculate the marginal propensity to save. Answer (b) is correct because the marginal propensity to save is the change in savings divided by the change in income [($700 − $500)/($3,500 − $3,000) = .4]. Answer (a) is incorrect because the average propensity to save would be calculated by dividing the new savings by the new income ($700/$3,500 = .2). Answer (c) is incorrect because the marginal propensity to consume is the change in spending divided by the change in income [($2,800 − $2,500)/($3,500 − $3,000) = .6]. Answer (d) is incorrect because the average propensity to consume would be calculated by dividing the new consumption by the new income ($2,800/$3,500 = .8).

14. (c) The requirement is to describe market conditions in a competitive market when both demand and supply increase. In a competitive market, the market will always clear at the equilibrium price. If there is an equal increase in both demand and supply, the equilibrium price may increase, decrease, or remain the same. However, there will be more units sold and, therefore, answer (c) is correct. Answers (a), (b), and (d) are incorrect because the equilibrium price may increase, decrease, or remain the same.

15. (d) The requirement is to calculate the marginal propensity to consume. Answer (d) is correct because the marginal propensity to consume is calculated by dividing the change in consumption by the change in disposable income. Therefore, the marginal propensity to consume would be .75 [($44,000 − $38,000)/($48,000 − $40,000)].

16. (b) The requirement is to determine the item that will cause a shift in the supply curve. A shift in the supply curve may result from (1) changes in production technology, (2) changes or expected changes in resource prices, (3) changes in the prices of other goods, (4) changes in taxes or subsidies, (5) changes in the number of sellers in the market, and (6) expectations about the future price of the product. Answer (b) is correct because it identifies changes in production taxes, which will alter the supply curve. Answer (a) is incorrect because a change in the price of the product involves movement along the existing supply curve, not a shift in the supply curve. Answers (c) and (d) are incorrect because they identify changes that result in a shift in the demand curve.

17. (d) The requirement is to identify the effects of government regulation on a product. Government regulation increases the cost of the product and therefore will most likely result in higher prices. Thus answer (d) is correct. Answer (a) is incorrect because the regulation has no relationship to consumption. Answer (b) is incorrect because an increase in cost is not likely to result in a decrease in price. Answer (c) is incorrect because tax revenue will likely decline due to the added production costs and reduced sales.

18. (a) The requirement is to identify which of the situations indicate inelastic demand. Elasticity of demand is measured by the percentage change in the quantity demanded divided by the percentage change in price. If the quotient is greater than one, demand for product is price elastic, and if it less than one, demand for the product is price inelastic. A quotient of exactly one indicates unitary elasticity. Answer (a) is correct because the price elasticity quotient is equal to 0.6 (3%/5%). Answer (b) is incorrect because the quotient is 1.5 (6%/4%). Answer (c) is incorrect because the quotient is 1 (4%/4%). Answer (d) is incorrect because the quotient is equal to 1.67 (5%/3%).

19. (a) The requirement is to describe the effect of an increase in wages on demand for labor. Answer (a) is correct because, like any other good or service, if price is increased for labor, the demand will fall and employment will fall. Answer (b) is incorrect because setting a maximum wage will not allow workers to increase wages. Answer (c) is incorrect because firms may or may not change in size. Answer (d) is incorrect because supply will only decrease if the price of the product decreases.

20. (a) The requirement is to identify the market effects of a polluting manufacturer's actions. Answer (a) is correct because a polluting firm calculates its profits without considering the costs of environmental damage and, as a result, prices its products too low. Answer (b) is incorrect because the polluting manufacturer is producing too much, not too little output. Answer (c) is incorrect because the manufacturer reports too much, not too little profitability. Answer (d) is incorrect because there is no direct relationship between the use of equity versus debt financing and the externalities involved in the production activities of the firm.

21. (b) The requirement is to describe the effects of a government-mandated maximum price. If the government mandates a maximum price below the equilibrium price, the product will be selling at an artificially low price resulting in shortages. Thus the correct answer is (b). Answer (a) is incorrect because price floors result in surpluses. Answer (c) is incorrect because price ceilings would probably result in more demand. Answer (d) is incorrect because the market would be affected.

22. (b) The requirement is to identify a valid reason for government intervention in a wholesale market. Answer (b) is correct because a valid reason for government intervention is the lack of a competitive market. Answers (a), (c), and (d) are incorrect because they provide no indication that the market is not competitive.

23. (a) The requirement is to identify the type of good that is likely to have an income elasticity coefficient of 3.00. Answer (a) is correct because an income elasticity coefficient of 3.00 indicates that demand for the good is very sensitive

to income levels. This is a characteristic of a luxury good. Answer (b) is incorrect because while the good may be complementary, it would have to be complementary to a luxury good. Answer (c) is incorrect because an inferior good's coefficient will be negative. Answer (d) is incorrect because demand for a necessity is not sensitive to income levels.

24. (c) The requirement is to calculate the price elasticity of demand for golf. The price elasticity of demand is calculated as the percentage change in quantity divided by the percentage change in price. If the result is greater than one, demand is elastic; if it is less than one, it is inelastic; and if it is equal to one, it is unitary elastic. The regular weekday demand is elastic as calculated below.

$$\frac{(80 - 70) \div [(80 + 70) \div 2]}{(\$11 - \$10) \div [(\$11 + \$10) \div 2]} = 1.4$$

The weekend demand is inelastic as calculated below.

$$\frac{(223 - 221) \div [(223 + 221) \div 2]}{(\$20 - \$15) \div [(\$20 + \$15) \div 2]} = .03$$

The senior citizen demand is elastic as calculated below.

$$\frac{(150 - 82) \div [(150 + 82) \div 2]}{(\$8 - \$6) \div [(\$8 + \$6) \div 2]} = 2.05$$

The only statement that correctly defines these relationships is answer (c).

25. (c) The requirement is to identify the factor that would cause the demand curve for a product to shift to the left. Answer (c) is correct because a shift in the demand curve to the left would be indicative of a decrease in demand for the product, and an increase in the price of a complementary commodity would cause such a shift. Answers (a), (b), and (d) are incorrect because they would all potentially cause an increase in demand, causing the demand curve to shift to the right.

26. (c) The requirement is to describe the effect of price ceilings. Price ceilings cause the price of a product to be artificially low resulting in decreased supply. The price is below the equilibrium price as indicated by answer (c). Answer (a) is incorrect because government price support is an example of a price floor. Answer (b) is incorrect because price ceilings create prices less than equilibrium prices. Answer (d) is incorrect because price ceilings create shortages, not surpluses.

27. (b) The requirement is to determine the immediate effect upon one product of an increase in the price of a substitute good. The demand and price of substitute products are directly related. If the price of a good increases, the demand for its substitute will also increase. Answer (b) is correct because it depicts this relationship. Answer (a) is incorrect because the price of a product will not increase due to an increase in a substitute product's price. Answer (c) is incorrect because the quantity supplied will not be impacted by an increase in price of a substitute product. Answer (d) is incorrect because even though the quantity demanded will increase with an increase in price of a substitute product, the price and supply will not be directly affected.

28. (d) The requirement is to calculate the effect a decrease in the price of a substitute good has on demand for a good. Answer (d) is correct because if the coefficient of cross-elasticity is 2.00, a 5% decrease in price will result in a 10% (5% × 2.00) decrease in the demand for Wilson's product. Answers (a), (b), and (c) are incorrect because they misstate the relationship.

29. (d) The requirement is to calculate the price elasticity of demand for a product. Price elasticity using the arc method is calculated by dividing the percentage change in quantity demanded by the percentage change in price, using the average changes. In this case, price elasticity is calculated below.

$$\frac{(150 - 100) \div [(150 + 100) \div 2]}{(\$50 - \$45) \div [(\$50 + \$45) \div 2]} = 3.8$$

Therefore answer (d) is correct.

30. (b) The requirement is to calculate the price elasticity of demand. Answer (b) is correct because the formula for price elasticity is equal to the percentage change in quantity demanded divided by the percentage change in price. In this case, the percentage change in price is 0.88 as calculated below.

$$\frac{(225 - 200) \div [(225 + 200) \div 2]}{(\$40 - \$35) \div [(\$40 + \$35) \div 2]} = .088$$

31. (b) The requirement is to identify the effect of a boycott on demand for a good. Answer (b) is correct because a boycott means less people are purchasing the good. Therefore, demand is decreased. Answer (a) would not occur because, if anything, a decrease in demand would lead to a decrease in price. Answer (c) is incorrect because demand does not affect supply. Answer (d) is incorrect because the elasticity of demand for a good is determined by its nature.

32. (c) The requirement is to identify the factor that is not likely to affect the supply of a good. Answer (c) is correct because changes in consumer income could affect the demand for the good, but not its supply. Answer (a) is incorrect because government subsidies reduce the cost of producing a good, and therefore, affect supply. Answer (b) is incorrect because changes in technology can alter production costs, and therefore, affect supply. Answer (d) is incorrect because changes in production costs affect the supply of a good.

33. (d) The requirement is to identify the effect on total revenue of a decrease in price of a price-elastic product. Answer (d) is correct because if a product's demand is price-elastic, a decrease in price will lead to an even larger percentage increase in quantity demanded. Therefore, total revenue will increase. Answers (a), (b), and (c) are incorrect because they do not describe the appropriate effect.

34. (a) The requirement is to identify the goods that are **not** complementary goods. Complementary goods are those that are used together because they enhance each other's use. Margarine and butter are substitute goods, not complementary goods. Therefore, (a) is correct. Answers (b), (c), and (d) all are pairs of complementary goods.

35. (a) The requirement is to describe the law of diminishing marginal utility. The law states that marginal utility declines as consumers acquire more of a good. Therefore, answer (a) is correct. Answer (b) is incorrect because total utility will not decline as more of a good is acquired. Answer (c) is incorrect because the demand curve slopes downward.

36. (b) The requirement is to identify the price elasticity of an essential product with no substitutes. The correct answer is (b). Demand for the product is perfectly inelastic because the diabetic will purchase the product regardless of the price.

37. (c) The requirement is to define the implications of economies of scale. In the long run firms may experience increasing returns because they operate more efficiently. With growth comes specialization of labor and related production efficiencies related to the law of diminishing returns. This phenomenon is called economies of scale. Answer (c) is correct because it accurately describes this concept. Answers (a) and (b) are incorrect because they describe inefficiencies. Answer (d) is incorrect because total costs do not decline but average costs do.

38. (d) The requirement is to identify the reason for increasing returns. In the long run firms may experience increasing returns because they operate more efficiently. With growth comes specialization of labor and related production efficiencies. This phenomenon is called economies of scale and, therefore, answer (d) is correct. Answer (a) is incorrect because the law of diminishing returns states that at some point firms get too large and diminishing returns occur. Answer (b) is incorrect because opportunity cost is the benefit forgone by the use of a particular resource. Answer (c) is incorrect because comparative advantage deals with the production choices of countries.

39. (b) The requirement is to identify the term used to describe the benefit lost by using resources for a given purpose. The correct answer is (b) because opportunity cost is the benefit given up from not using the resource for another purpose. Answer (a) is incorrect because economic efficiency is a comparison among uses of resources. Answers (c) and (d) are incorrect because they involve comparisons across countries.

40. (c) The requirement is to calculate the total cost of producing seven units. Total cost is equal to average total cost multiplied by the number of units produced. Therefore, the correct answer is (c) because 7 × $36.86 = $258.02.

41. (c) The requirement is to calculate marginal cost. Marginal cost is the additional cost of producing one additional item. To calculate the marginal cost of producing the ninth unit we take the total cost of producing nine units and deduct the total cost of producing eight units. Thus, the correct answer is (c) because (9 × $33.75) – (8 × $34.75) = $25.75.

42. (a) The requirement is to calculate the average total cost at an output level of 11 units. Answer (a) is correct because the average total cost is calculated by dividing total cost by the number of units: [($1,000 fixed cost + $250 variable cost)/11] = $113.64.

43. (c) The requirement is to calculate the marginal physical product. The marginal physical product is the additional output obtained by adding one additional worker. When one worker is added to a team of 10, five (25 – 20) additional units are produced. Therefore, the correct answer is (c).

44. (c) The requirement is to calculate the marginal revenue per unit. The total revenue of adding one additional worker to a team of 11 is equal to the difference between total revenue at 12 workers and total revenue at 11 workers, or [(25 × $49) – (28 × $47.50)]/28 – 25 units = $105/3 units = $35 (marginal revenue per unit). Answer (c) is correct because the marginal revenue per unit is $35 = $105/3. Answer (d) is incorrect because it is the average selling price for one unit.

45. (c) The requirement is to calculate the marginal revenue product when one worker is added. The marginal revenue product is the increase in total revenue received by the addition of one worker. The total revenue from adding one additional worker to a team of 11 is equal to the difference between total revenue at 12 workers and total revenue at 11 workers, or $105 [(25 × $49) – (28 × $47.50)]. Therefore answer (c) is correct.

46. (d) The requirement is to define marginal revenue. The correct answer is (d) because marginal revenue is the change in total revenue associated with the sale of one more unit of output. Answer (a) is incorrect because in a monopolistic competitive market, price is greater than marginal cost. Answer (b) is incorrect because marginal revenue is the increase in revenue associated with the sale of one additional product. Answer (c) is incorrect because in a purely competitive market, marginal revenue is equal to price.

47. (d) The requirement is to identify the distinguishing characteristic of long-run supply. Answer (d) is correct because the distinguishing characteristic of the long-run production function is that all costs are variable. Answers (a) and (b) are incorrect because price and output are determined by demand and supply. Answer (c) is incorrect because firms can enter or exit the industry.

48. (d) The requirement is to identify the main factor that differentiates the short-run cost function from the long-run cost function. Answer (d) is correct because in the short run firms have fixed and variable costs, whereas in the long run all costs are variable. Answer (a) is incorrect because all costs are variable in the long run. Answer (b) is incorrect because the level of technology will affect short-run and long-run cost functions in a similar manner. Answer (c) is incorrect because changes in government subsidies will not affect an industry's cost functions.

49. (a) The requirement is to describe how a large required capital outlay affects a market. The correct answer is (a) because a large capital outlay constitutes a barrier to entry into the market. Answer (b) is incorrect because minimum efficient scale indicates that a company must be of sufficient

size to compete. This is not indicated by the scenario. Answer (c) is incorrect because a created barrier is one created by the competing firms. Answer (d) is incorrect because the production possibility boundary shows the maximum combination of outputs that can be achieved with a given number of inputs.

50. (c) The requirement is to identify the type of economic market. The correct answer is (c) because an oligopoly is characterized by a few firms in the industry. Answer (a) is incorrect because a natural monopoly has only one firm. Answer (b) is incorrect because a cartel is a group of firms that have joined together to fix prices. Answer (d) is incorrect because monopolistic competition is characterized by a large number of firms selling similar but differentiated products.

51. (d) The requirement is to identify the distinguishing characteristics of oligopolistic markets. The correct answer is (d) because of the small number of suppliers in an oligopolistic market, the actions of one affect the others; there is mutual interdependence with regard to pricing and output in an oligopolistic market. Answers (a) and (b) are incorrect because they describe monopolies. Answer (c) is incorrect because oligopolistic markets typically have barriers to entry.

52. (a) The requirement is to identify the characteristic that is not representative of monopolistic competition. The correct answer is (a) because monopolistic competition is a market that has numerous sellers of similar but differentiated products. Answers (b), (c), and (d) are incorrect because they are all characteristic of monopolistic competition.

53. (b) The requirement is to identify the market that is characterized by a few large sellers. Answer (b) is correct because it is the definition of an oligopoly. Answer (a) is incorrect because a monopoly has a single seller of a product or service for which there are no close substitutes. Answer (c) is incorrect because perfect competition is characterized by many firms selling an identical product or service. Answer (d) is incorrect because monopolistic competition is characterized by many firms selling a differentiated product or service.

54. (c) The requirement is to identify the different types of economic markets. Answer (c) is correct because it is the definition of perfect competition. Answer (a) is incorrect because a monopoly has a single seller of a product or service for which there are no close substitutes. Answer (b) is incorrect because an oligopoly is a form of market in which there are few large sellers of the product. Answer (d) is incorrect because monopolistic competition is characterized by many firms selling a differentiated product or service.

55. (c) The requirement is to identify the definition of a natural monopoly. The correct answer is (c) because a natural monopoly exists when, because of economic or technical conditions, only one firm can efficiently supply the product. Answer (a) is incorrect because while owning natural resources may contribute to the establishment of a natural monopoly, the firm would still have to be the best possible producer of the product. Answer (b) is incorrect because a patent establishes a government-created monopoly. Answer (d) is incorrect because if the government is the only provider, the market is a government-created monopoly.

56. (c) The requirement is to identify the market described as one with low barriers to entry and product differentiation. The correct answer is (c) because monopolistic competition is a market that is characterized by a large number of small producers of a differentiated product. Answer (a) is incorrect because a monopoly has only one producer. Answer (b) is incorrect because a natural monopoly is an industry in which there is only one producer based on the economics of the industry. Answer (d) is incorrect because an oligopoly is an industry that has a few large producers with barriers to entry.

57. (d) The requirement is to identify the item that is not characteristic of perfect competition. In a perfectly competitive market there are a large number of small producers selling a standard product. Answer (d) is correct because all sellers must sell at the industry price. Answers (a), (b), and (c) are all characteristics of perfect competition.

58. (a) The requirement is to describe the reason for the kinked demand curve in an oligopolist market. An oligopolist faces a kinked demand curve because competitors will often match price decreases but are hesitant to match price increases. Therefore, answer (a) is correct. Answer (b) is incorrect because an oligopolist does not face a nonlinear demand for its product. Answer (c) is incorrect because an oligopolist cannot sell its product for any price. Answer (d) is incorrect because consumer demand determines the demand curve in all markets.

59. (a) The requirement is to identify the impact of consumer confidence upon the economy. Answer (a) is correct because if consumer confidence falls then consumers will delay spending until the uncertainty is resolved. The end result is a downturn in the economy. Answers (b), (c), and (d) are incorrect because they do not properly state the relationship between consumer confidence and the economy.

60. (a) The requirement is to determine the marginal propensity to consume given the multiplier. The multiplier refers to the fact that an increase in spending has a multiplied effect on GDP. The effect of the multiplier can be estimated using following formula: $ Multiplier Effect = $ Initial Change in Spending $\times [1/(1 - MPC)]$. Substituting values gives: \$80B = \$20B $\times [1/(1 - MPC)]$, therefore: $[1/(1 - MPC)] = 4$. [Proof: \$80B = \$20B $\times 4$]. If $[1/(1 - MPC)] = 4$, and $(1 - MPC) = MPS$, then $(1/MPS) = 4$, or $MPS = 1/4 = .25$, and $MPC = (1.00 - .25) = MPC = .75$.

61. (c) The requirement is to identify a characteristic of the trough of a business cycle. In the trough of a business cycle, actual output and income are below potential output and income. Therefore, the correct answer is (c). Answer (a) is incorrect because purchasing power is not directly related to business cycles. Answer (b) is incorrect because in a recession it is cyclical unemployment that is high, not natural unemployment. Answer (d) is incorrect because potential income will exceed actual income.

62. (c) The requirement is to describe the effect of a decrease in government spending on the economy. The government represents one segment of the economy that demands goods and services. If government spending decreases, aggregate demand decreases. Thus, answer (c) is correct. Answer (a) is incorrect because a decrease in

government spending will result in a decrease in aggregate demand. Answers (b) and (d) are incorrect because a decrease in government spending will not immediately affect supply.

63. (d) The requirement is to define aggregate demand. The correct answer is (d) because aggregate demand is the total amount of expenditures for consumer goods and investment for a period of time. It includes purchases by consumers, businesses, government, and foreign entities.

64. (d) The requirement is to identify an item that would be included in GDP. Gross domestic product is the value of all final goods and services produced by the country by both domestic and foreign-owned sources. Answer (d) is correct because common stock is not a good or service; it is an ownership interest in a company. Answers (a), (b), and (c) are all incorrect because they all represent the value of goods or services produced.

65. (d) The requirement is to identify the indicator of an upturn in economic activity. Answer (d) is correct because a reduction in the amount of luxury purchases is an indicator of a downturn in economic activity. Answers (a), (b), and (c) are all indicators of positive economic changes.

66. (d) The requirement is to identify a leading indicator of economic expansion. Answer (d) is correct because an increase in weekly hours worked by production workers is a favorable leading indicator. Answer (a) is incorrect because a falling money supply is an indicator associated with falling GDP. Answer (b) is incorrect because a decline in the issuance of building permits signals lower expected building activity and a falling GDP. Answer (c) is incorrect because an increase in the timeliness of delivery by vendors indicates slacking business demand and potentially falling GDP.

67. (d) The requirement is to identify the definition of disposable income. Answer (d) is correct because disposable income equals personal income minus personal taxes. It is the portion of income that can be spent by the consumer. Answer (a) is incorrect because gross domestic product less the capital cost allowance is net domestic product. Answer (b) is incorrect because net domestic product minus indirect business taxes plus net income earned abroad is national income. Answer (c) is incorrect because disposable income is not measured by deducting transfer payments from personal income.

68. (c) The requirement is to identify the primary reason for allowing legal immigration into industrial nations. Answer (c) is correct because immigration will increase the supply of labor and lower its equilibrium price. This results in greater domestic and world output and increases income in the country to which workers migrate. Answer (a) is incorrect because the impact on trade deficit is less than that on growth. Answers (b) and (d) are incorrect because trade agreements and political agreements are not primary reasons.

69. (a) The requirement is to identify a lagging economic indicator. Lagging indicators include (1) average duration of unemployment in weeks, (2) the change in the index of labor cost per unit of output, (3) the average prime rate charged by banks, (4) the ratio of manufacturing and trade inventories to sales, (5) commercial and industrial loans outstanding, (6) the ratio of consumer installment credit outstanding to personal income, and (7) the change in the CPI for services. Answer (a) is correct because chronic unemployment is a lagging indicator. Answers (b), (c), and (d) are incorrect because they are all leading indicators.

70. (d) The requirement is to identify the true statement about government borrowing to finance large deficits. The correct answer is (d) because increased borrowing by the government increases the demand for money, which puts upward pressure on interest rates. Answer (a) is incorrect because government borrowing reduces the amount of lendable funds; it does not increases them. Answer (b) is incorrect because government borrowing exerts upward pressure on interest rates not downward pressure. Answer (c) is incorrect because government borrowing puts upward pressure on interest rates.

71. (d) The requirement is to describe the effects of rising inflation. Answer (d) is correct because rising inflation increases the price level of goods, which means that individuals can purchase less. Answer (a) is incorrect because individuals that receive specific amounts of money lose purchasing power. Answer (b) is incorrect because there is an inverse relationship between price level and purchasing power. Answer (c) is incorrect because if the contracts have indexing provisions, the prices will increase.

72. (d) The requirement is to describe the **most** effective fiscal policy for reducing demand-pull inflation. Demand-pull inflation is caused by excess demand that bids up the cost of labor and other resources. The correct answer is (d) because the most effective government policy would involve reducing demand that could be done by taxation and reduced government spending. Answer (a) is incorrect because it involves monetary policy. Answers (b) and (c) are incorrect because increasing government spending would feed demand-pull inflation.

73. (c) The requirement is to identify an action that will cause a decrease in money supply. The correct answer is (c) because an increase in the reserve requirement will leave financial institutions with less money to lend and therefore decrease the money supply. Answers (a), (b), and (d) are incorrect because they would all result in an increase in the money supply.

74. (c) The requirement is to identify how the Federal Reserve Board **most** directly influences the decision of whether or not to issue debt or equity financing. Answer (c) is correct because the Board sets the discount rate at which the Federal Reserve Bank lends money to member banks, which directly influences the rates that commercial banks charge their customers. Answer (a) is incorrect because the Board does not affect the income tax rate. Answers (b) and (d) are incorrect because the Federal Reserve Bank charges member banks the discount rate.

75. (d) The requirement is to identify the effects of a tax increase. Answer (d) is correct because a tax increase reduces household income and, therefore, reduces spending and decreases aggregate demand.

76. (b) The requirement is to describe an expansionary monetary policy. The correct answer is (b) because purchasing US securities would increase the amount of money in the economy. Answer (a) is incorrect because raising the reserve requirement would decrease the amount of money in the economy. Answer (c) is incorrect because raising the discount rate would discourage borrowing by banks and therefore reduce the amount of money in the economy. Answer (d) is incorrect because both of the actions would tend to reduce the money supply.

77. (a) The requirement is to define the reserve ratio. The reserve ratio is the percentage of total checking deposits that a financial institution must hold on reserve in the central bank or held as cash in the bank's vault. Thus, the correct answer is (a). Answer (b) is incorrect because it is the description of the discount rate.

78. (b) The requirement is to identify the most important way that the money supply is controlled. The correct answer is (b). The purchase and sale of government securities (open-market operations) is the most important way that the government controls the money supply. Answers (a) and (d) are incorrect because, while they are instruments of monetary policy, they are not the most important ways of controlling money supply. Answer (c) is incorrect because it describes an instrument of fiscal policy.

79. (d) The requirement is to define how the government uses fiscal policy to stimulate the economy. To stimulate the economy with fiscal policy, the government would lower taxes and/or increase spending. Therefore, the correct answer is (d). Answer (a) is incorrect because raising taxes does not stimulate the economy. Answer (b) is incorrect because decreasing government spending does not stimulate the economy. Answer (c) is incorrect because increasing the money supply involves monetary policy.

80. (c) The requirement is to define the federal budget deficit. The federal budget deficit is the amount by which the government's expenditures exceed its revenues in a given year. Thus, answer (c) is correct. Answer (a) is incorrect because it defines the government debt. Answer (b) is incorrect because state and local government amounts are not included in the federal budget deficit. Answer (d) is incorrect because the deficit does not deal with assets and liabilities of the government.

81. (a) The requirement is to identify the tool that would serve to control inflation. Answer (a) is correct because selling government securities serves to reduce capital available for other investments and, therefore, serves to contract the economy. Answer (b) is incorrect because lowering reserve requirements serves to increase the amount of funds available for investment. Answer (c) is incorrect because lowering the discount rate serves to decrease the cost of funds and increase investment. Answer (d) is incorrect because encouraging higher tax rates is a fiscal policy.

82. (a) The requirement is to determine the reason for the importance of the multiplier. The multiplier provides an indication of the impact of an increase in consumption or investment in GDP. An increase in spending ripples through the economy because individuals and business save only a portion of the increase in income. Therefore, the correct answer is (a).

83. (a) The requirement is to identify the purpose of a tax rebate. Answer (a) is correct because increasing the amount of funds available to the consumer increases disposable income that should stimulate economic activity. Consumers will spend the additional funds and correspondingly expand the economy. Answers (b), (c), and (d) are erroneous statements about the effects of the rebate.

84. (c) The requirement is to identify the definition of structural unemployment. Answer (c) is correct because structural unemployment exists when aggregate demand is sufficient to provide full employment, but the distribution of the demand does not correspond precisely to the composition of the labor force. This form of unemployment arises when the required job skills or the geographic distribution of jobs changes. Answer (a) is incorrect because frictional unemployment results from imperfections in the labor market. It occurs when both jobs and workers to fill them are available. Answer (b) is incorrect because cyclical unemployment is caused by contractions of the economy. Answer (d) is incorrect because the full-employment unemployment rate is the sum of frictional and structural unemployment.

85. (a) The requirement is to identify the nature of the producer price index. Answer (a) is correct because the price index measures the combined price of a selected group of goods and services for a specified period in comparison with the combined price of the same or similar goods for a base period. The US government's producer price index (PPI) is an example. It measures the price of a basket of 3,200 commodities at the point of their first sale by producers. Answer (b) is incorrect because the export price index measures price changes for all products sold by domestic producers to foreigners. Answer (c) is incorrect because the import price index measures price changes of goods purchased from other countries. Answer (d) is incorrect because the consumer price index measures the price of a fixed market basket of goods purchased by a typical urban consumer.

86. (a) The requirement is to identify the formula for calculating a price index. Answer (a) is correct because the 2013 price index using 2008 as a reference period is the price of the 2013 market basket in 2013 relative to the price of the same basket of goods in 2008. The correct formula is

$$\frac{\text{Price of market basket in a given year}}{\text{Price of same market basket in base year}} \times 100$$

Answer (b) is incorrect because the 2008 market basket is used. Answer (c) is incorrect because it uses two different market baskets. Answer (d) is incorrect because it uses the 2008 prices in the numerator and the denominator and different market baskets.

87. (d) The requirement is to describe the discount rate. The correct answer is (d) because the discount rate is the rate the central bank charges commercial banks for loans. Answer (a) is not correct because it describes the reserve requirement.

88. (c) The requirement is to identify which of the statements is true about deflation. Answer (c) is correct because deflation results in very low interest rates. They could even turn negative. Answer (a) is incorrect because consumers are not motivated to borrow money because they will be paying back the debt with money that has greater purchasing power. Answer (b) is incorrect because businesses are hesitant to make investments because prices for capital goods are declining. Answer (d) is incorrect because deflation typically stalls the economy.

89. (a) The requirement is to identify the characteristics of a deflationary economy. The correct answer is (a) because businesses are hesitant to make investments when the prices of assets are declining. Answer (b) is incorrect because consumers are hesitant to make major purchases when prices are declining. Answer (c) is incorrect because interest rates are very low in periods of deflation. Answer (d) is incorrect because when actual GDP exceeds potential GDP inflation will exist.

90. (a) The requirement is to identify the factor that explains the difference between real and nominal interest rates. Real interest rates are in terms of goods; they are adjusted for inflation. The difference between real and nominal rates is the inflation premium. Thus, answer (a) is correct. Answers (b) and (c) are incorrect because credit risk and default risk explain the difference between the nominal rate and the rate a particular borrower receives. Answer (d) is incorrect because market risk explains the difference between the nominal rate and the rate paid in a particular market.

91. (c) The requirement is to identify the statement that is **not** true regarding international trade. Answer (c) is correct because absolute advantage is the ability to produce a product for less than other nations. Comparative advantage is the ability of one nation to produce at a relatively lower opportunity cost than another nation. Answers (a), (b), and (d) are all incorrect because they are true.

92. (a) The requirement is to describe the effect of an increase in the interest rate on a currency's value. The correct answer is (a) because if the interest rate is increased investors will be able to get a larger return on investment in the country. Therefore, demand for the currency will increase for investment purposes, and the relative value of the currency will increase.

93. (b) The requirement is to identify the group that would most benefit from a tariff. The correct answer is (b) because a tariff restricts the amount of imports of a specific good, and the group most benefiting would be the domestic producers of that good. Answers (a), (c), and (d) are incorrect because these groups would not benefit from the tariff.

94. (a) The requirement is to identify the description of comparative advantage. Answer (a) is correct because the respective opportunity costs determine which country will produce which product. Answer (b) is incorrect because profit margins do not enter into the decision. Answer (c) is incorrect because economic order quantity determines optimum inventory levels. Answer (d) is incorrect because tariffs would only come into play after each country produced its respective products.

95. (c) The requirement is to identify the scenario that would result in appreciation in the value of a country's currency. The correct answer is (c) because the lag in imports in relation to exports means that there will be more demand for the currency from other countries to pay for the country's exported goods. Answer (a) is incorrect because if the country is importing goods this will increase demand for other currencies and cause the country's currency to decline in relative value. Answer (b) is incorrect because a higher rate of inflation depresses a country's currency. Answer (d) is incorrect because lower interest rates means there will be less demand for the currency for investment.

96. (c) The requirement is to identify the effect of a decline in the US dollar. The correct answer is (c) because US goods will be cheaper in foreign countries and, therefore, US exports will increase. Answer (a) is incorrect because foreign currencies will appreciate if the dollar depreciates. Answer (b) is incorrect because the US balance of payments should improve due to the increase in exports. Answer (d) is incorrect because US imports will decline because of the increase in cost of foreign goods in dollars.

97. (c) The requirement is to describe how exchange rates are determined. The correct answer is (c) because exchange rates are determined in the same way price is determined for other goods, based on demand and supply. Answers (a), (b), and (d) are incorrect because while they can have a temporary influence on exchange rates, supply and demand is the major determining factor.

98. (b) The requirement is to determine the effect of changes in exchange rates. Answer (b) is correct because the dollar's value has declined against the real and therefore Brazilian goods become more expensive. Answer (a) is incorrect because the Brazilian real has appreciated against the dollar. Answer (c) is incorrect because the dollar will buy less in Brazil. Answer (d) is incorrect because US exports to Brazil should increase because they are less expensive in Brazilian real.

99. (c) The requirement is to identify the most restrictive barrier to an exporting country. The correct answer is (c) because an embargo is a total ban on certain types of imports. Answer (a) is incorrect because a tariff is merely a tax on imports. Answer (b) is incorrect because quotas are merely restrictions on the amounts of imports. Answer (d) is incorrect because exchange controls are limits of the amount of foreign exchange that can be transacted or exchange rates.

100. (d) The requirement is to identify the item that does **not** describe a foreign exchange control. Answer (d) is correct because requiring a market-driven (floating) exchange rate involves no controls on the market. All others describe ways of controlling foreign exchange.

101. (b) The requirement is to identify the item that describes a dumping pricing policy. Answer (b) is correct because a dumping pricing policy involves sales of goods by a company of one country in another country at a price that is lower than

its cost or significantly lower than the price charged in the company's country.

102. (a) The requirement is to identify the item that describes an appropriate response by importing country to export subsidies. Answer (a) is correct because countervailing subsidies is an appropriate response, as they serve to offset the export subsidies.

103. (c) The requirement is to identify the item that describes a pegged exchange rate. Answer (c) is correct because a pegged exchange rate is one that is kept from deviating far from a range or value by the central bank.

104. (a) The requirement is to calculate the forward premium or discount on the euro. Answer (a) is correct because the premium or discount is calculated as follows:

$$
\begin{array}{c}
\text{Premium} \\
\text{or} \\
\text{Discount}
\end{array}
=
\frac{\text{Forward rate} - \text{Spot rate}}{\text{Spot rate}}
\times
\frac{\text{Months (or days) in year}}{\text{Months (or days) in forward period}}
$$

$$
= \frac{\$1.367 - \$1.364}{\$1.364} \times \frac{12}{3}
$$

$$
= 0.88\% \text{ premium}
$$

105. (a) The requirement is to identify the effect of negative net exports. Answer (a) is correct because when a country has negative net exports, it imports more than it exports. Therefore, it results in a net flow of goods from firms in foreign countries to the domestic country.

106. (d) The requirement is to identify the factor that is **least** likely to affect a country's currency foreign exchange rate. Answer (d) is correct because the country's tax rate is least likely to affect the country's currency exchange rate. Answers (a), (b), and (c) are incorrect because they are all factors that affect the value of the country's currency.

107. (c) The requirement is to compute the foreign exchange loss or gain. The correct answer is (c) because before the decline in value, the receivable had a value of $18,000 (10,000 × $1.80), and after the decline in value, the receivable had a value of $17,500 (10,000 × $1.75). Therefore, the loss is equal to $500. Answers (a), (b), and (d) are incorrect because they inaccurately calculate the loss.

108. (c) The requirement is to identify the appropriate hedging strategy. The correct answer is (c) because by selling euros in the futures market, the firm has locked in the exchange rate today. Answer (a) is incorrect because lending euros puts the company at greater risk for changes in value of the euro. It would need to borrow euros to lock in the exchange rate. Answer (b) is incorrect because it involves the purchase of euros; the appropriate strategy would involve the sale of euros. Answer (d) is incorrect because the purchase of euros on the spot market would put the firm more at risk to losses from decline in the value of the euro.

109. (b) The requirement is to identify hedging strategies that are **not** appropriate for political risk. Political risk is the risk related to actions by a foreign government, such as enacting legislation that prevents the repatriation of a foreign subsidiary's profits or seizing a firm's assets. Answer (b) is correct because purchasing or selling futures contracts is designed to hedge transaction risks relating to foreign exchange rates. Answer (a) is incorrect because a firm can purchase insurance to mitigate political risk. Answer (c) is incorrect because if the firm finances the investment with local-country capital, it may not be forced to repay the loans if assets are seized by the government. Answer (d) is incorrect because by entering into joint ventures with local-country firms, the firm can reduce the risk of seizure of the investment by the government.

110. **(c)** The requirement is to describe how patents affect markets. The correct answer is (c) because a patent prevents another firm from coming into a market and selling the same or a very similar product. Therefore, it is a barrier to entry into the market. Answer (a) is incorrect because vertical integration refers to expansion into another phase of producing the same product. Answer (b) is incorrect because market concentration refers to how many firms compete in the market. Answer (d) is incorrect because collusion refers to firms acting collectively to control the market.

111. **(c)** The requirement is to estimate the short-term and long-term effects of an increase in demand in a perfectly competitive market. Answer (c) is correct because in the short term the price of the product will increase but in the long term it will return to the equilibrium price for the market. Answers (a), (b), and (d) are incorrect because the long-term price will not likely increase.

112. **(d)** The requirement is to identify the ultimate purpose of competitor analysis. Answer (d) is correct because the ultimate purpose of competitor analysis is to understand and predict the behavior of a major competitor. Answer (a) is not a part of competitor analysis. Answers (b) and (c) are part of competitor analysis but not the ultimate purpose.

113. **(c)** The requirement is to identify the item that is not an important aspect of supply chain management. Supply chain management is primarily designed to manage the firm's relationships with suppliers by sharing key information all along the supply chain. The correct answer is (c) because the area of customer relations is not a primary focus of supply chain management. Answer (a) is incorrect because information technology is used extensively to share information electronically. Answer (b) is incorrect because accurate forecasts are essential to effective supply chain management. Answer (d) is incorrect because communication is the basis for supply chain management.

114. **(d)** The requirement is to identify the type of organization that would **most** likely engage in public relations-type advertising. Firms that have monopolies are more likely to engage in public relations-type advertising to forestall additional regulation. Therefore, the correct answer is (d).

115. **(b)** The requirement is to identify target market analysis. The correct answer is (b) because target market analysis involves obtaining a thorough understanding of the market in which the firm sells or plans to sell its product or services.

116. **(c)** The requirement is to identify an unlikely market segmentation dimension for business customers. Answer (c) is correct because lifestyle is a possible individual customer market segmentation dimension for individuals, not businesses. Answers (a), (b), and (d) are incorrect because they all represent possible dimensions for business customer segmentation.

117. **(b)** The requirement is to identify the percentage of variance in quantity demanded explained by price. Answer (b) is correct because the adjusted R squared (.72458) measures the percent of the variance in the dependent variable explained by the independent variable. Answer (a) is incorrect because it is the Multiple R that is the coefficient of correlation. Answer (c) is incorrect because it is the intercept that is used in the equation to predict quantity. Answer (d) is incorrect because it is the standard error that measures the standard deviation of the estimate of quantity.

118. **(a)** The requirement is to calculate the predicted quantity demanded. The correct answer is (a) because the formula is

$$\begin{aligned} \text{Quantity demanded} &= a + bx \\ &= 56{,}400.50 + (7.00\,x - 4{,}598.2) \\ &= 24{,}213. \end{aligned}$$

119. **(d)** The requirement is to identify the item that is **not** one of the forces in Porter's model for industry analysis. The correct answer is (d) because consideration of general economic conditions is not part of industry analysis. Answers (a), (b), and (c) are incorrect because the five forces include the threat of new entrants, the bargaining power of customers, the bargaining power of suppliers, the threat of substitute products or services, and the rivalry of the firms in the market.

120. **(a)** The requirement is to identify the defining characteristic of supply chain management. The correct answer is (a) because a key aspect of supply chain management is the sharing of key information from the point of sale to the consumer back to the manufacturer, the manufacturer's suppliers, and the supplier's suppliers. Answer (b) is incorrect because it is the focus of process reengineering. Answer (c) is incorrect because it is the focus of total quality management. Answer (d) is incorrect because strategic alliances involve joint ventures and partnerships.

121. **(d)** The requirement is to identify an unlikely strategy for a firm in a purely competitive market. The correct answer is (d) because in a purely competitive market firms compete based on price, and developing a brand name is a product differentiation strategy. Answers (a), (b), and (c) are all cost leadership strategies and appropriate for a firm in a purely competitive market.

122. **(c)** The requirement is to identify the purpose of a response profile. The correct answer is (c) because a response profile is a description of possible actions that may be taken by a competitor in varying circumstances. Answers (a), (b), and (d) all involve aspects of industry analysis.

123. **(b)** The requirement is to define the process of dividing all potential consumers into smaller groups of buyers with distinct needs, characteristics, or behaviors. Answer (b) is correct because this describes market segmentation. Answer (a) is incorrect because strategic planning involves deciding on the appropriate strategic initiatives for a period. Answer (c) is incorrect because product positioning involves deciding on a strategy for a particular product. Answer (d) is incorrect because objective setting involves establishing short-term goals.

124. **(c)** The requirement is to identify the least important measure of unemployment in predicting the future state of the economy. Answer (c) is the correct answer because frictional unemployment measures the temporary unemployment that always exists as workers change jobs or new workers enter the workforce. Answer (a) is incorrect because structural unemployment measures the workforce that is unemployed due to a mismatch in job skills. Significant amounts of structural unemployment can drag down the economy. Answer (b) is incorrect because cyclical unemployment measures the

workforce that is unemployed due to economic conditions. Answer (d) is incorrect because overall unemployment includes the workforce that is unemployed for all reasons.

125. **(a)** The requirement is to identify the steps involved in performing competitor analysis. Answer (a) is correct because competitor analysis is designed to predict the behavior of major competitors. Answers (b) and (c) are incorrect because they describe aspects of industry analysis. Answer (d) is incorrect because it describes aspects of general environment and industry analyses.

126. **(d)** The requirement is to identify the item that is not a way in which companies in developed countries can generally compete with companies in developing countries. Answer (d) is correct because developing countries typically have low-cost resources. Answers (a), (b) and (c) are incorrect because they all represent ways that a company in a developed country may compete with companies from developing countries.

Written Communication Task

Written Communication Task 1

Written
Communication
Help

The chief executive officer of Urton Corp., Geroge Jones, is preparing for a strategic planning session with the corporation's board of directors. The company has pursued a product differentiation strategy in the past but is having difficulty maintaining margins due to significant competition from domestic and foreign competitors. Write a memorandum describing the product differentiation strategy and another strategy that might be pursued if product differentiation is not working.

REMINDER: Your response will be graded for both technical content and writing skills. Technical content will be evaluated for information that is helpful to the intended reader and clearly relevant to the issue. Writing skills will be evaluated for development, organization, and the appropriate expression of ideas in professional correspondence. Use a standard business memo or letter format with a clear beginning, middle, and end. Do not convey information in the form of a table, bullet point list, or other abbreviated presentation.

To: Mr. George Jones, CEO
        Urton Corp.
From: CPA Candidate

Written Communication Task Solution

Written Communication Task 1

Written Communication	
	Help

To: Mr. George Jones, CEO
        Urton Corp.
From: CPA Candidate

As you requested, this memorandum is designed to discuss some alternative strategies that may be implemented by Urton Corp. Historically, Urton has implemented a product differentiation strategy. This strategy involves providing products that have superior physical characteristics, perceived differences, or support service differences, which allows the products to command higher prices in the market. When effective, this strategy allows the company to effectively compete with companies that sell lower priced products.

For a product differentiation strategy to be successful, the company must continue to invest in the differentiating factor. Since Urton is no longer effectively competing using a product differentiating strategy, the management should consider whether additional investment in product innovation, support services, or brand identity might allow the company to revive the strategy.

On the other hand, if management believes that pursuing a differentiation strategy is no longer feasible, consideration should be given to a cost leadership strategy. Pursuing a cost leadership strategy would involve cutting costs and improving efficiency to allow the company to offer products at lower prices.

To be competitive, it is essential that the company select a strategy and begin to align management's decisions with that strategy. If you need any additional information, please contact me.

Module 43: Financial Risk Management and Capital Budgeting

Overview

This module describes the relationship between risk and return and the use of various techniques to manage financial risk. There is an inverse relationship between risk and return. Companies attempt to maximize return within the risk tolerance level of its owners. There are a number of ways in which management attempts to mitigate risk including diversification and hedging.

This module also covers the concepts of the time value of money. Understanding the topic of the time value of money is essential for successful completion of the BEC exam. You must understand the mechanics as well as the concepts. Specifically, you should understand how present value techniques are used to value financial assets and liabilities.

The concepts of present value provide the basis for the last topic in this module—capital budgeting. Capital budgeting is the term used to describe the process of evaluating and controlling capital investments. The most effective capital budgeting techniques rely on present value techniques. Before beginning the reading you should review the key terms at the end of the module.

A. Risk and Return

There is a trade-off between risk and returns when considering investments—to achieve higher returns an investor must assume greater risk. This relationship is illustrated by the following chart that presents the means and standard deviations of real returns from stocks, bonds, and Treasury bills over a ten-year period. The results are as would be expected: stocks earned significantly higher returns but also with significantly higher risk (variance). The chart can be used to compute the **equity risk premium**. The equity risk premium is equal to the 8.7% real return on stocks minus the risk-free real return as measured by the return on Treasury bills, 1%, or 7.7% (8.7% – 1.0%). The average risk premium on common stock versus bonds over the ten-year period is about 6.6% (8.7% – 2.1%).

REAL RETURNS OF US INVESTMENTS 1900–2000

Assets	Mean return (%)	Standard deviation (%)	Highest year (%)	Lowest Year (%)
Stocks	8.7	20.2	56.8	−38.0
Bonds	2.1	10.0	35.1	−19.3
Bills	1.0	4.7	20.0	−15.1
Inflation	3.3	5.0	20.4	−10.8

Source: Dimson and Marsh, *Triumph of the Optimists*, (Princeton, NJ: Princeton University Press: 2002)

To understand why riskier investments offer a premium, it is necessary to make some assumptions about preferences of investors. Most financial models assume that investors are **risk averse**. Risk aversion does not mean investors will not take risks; it means that they must be compensated for taking risk. Most investors, and the market as a whole, are considered by most analysts to be risk averse. However, certain investors may exhibit different behavior.

1. **Risk-neutral investors**—Investors that prefer investments with higher returns whether or not they have risk. These investors disregard risk.
2. **Risk-seeking investors**—Investors that prefer to take risks and would invest in a higher-risk investment despite the fact that a lower-risk investment might have the same return.

B. **Return on a Single Asset**

1. Investment return is the total gain or loss on an investment for a period of time. It consists of the change in the asset's value (either gain or loss) plus any cash distributions (e.g., cash flow, interest, or dividends). The return is illustrated by the following equation:

$$R_{t+1} = \frac{P_{t+1} - P_t + CF_{t+1}}{P_t}$$

Where

R_{t+1}	=	The investment return from time t to t + 1
P_{t+1}	=	The asset's price (market value) at t + 1
P_t	=	The asset's price (market value) at t
CF_{t+1}	=	Cash flow received from the asset from t to t + 1

This formula measures return on an *ex post* basis (after the fact) and, therefore, does not consider risk. Managers have to evaluate investments on an *ex ante* basis and, therefore, must use **expected returns** and **estimates of risk**.

2. **Estimating Expected Returns**

A common way to estimate expected returns is based on prior history. One could simply calculate the average historical returns on a similar investment to get the expected return. When making this computation two approaches are often used.

a. **Arithmetic average return**—Computed by simply adding the historical returns for a number of periods and dividing by the number of periods.
b. **Geometric average return**—This computation depicts the compound annual return earned by an investor who bought the asset and held it for the number of historical periods examined. If returns vary through time, the geometric average will always fall below the arithmetic average.
c. It is generally recommended that the arithmetic average return be used for assets with short holding periods and the geometric average return be used for assets with longer holding periods.

3. **Estimating Risk**

a. Measures of risk also are often developed from historical returns. Many financial analysts assume that the pattern of historical returns of large numbers of similar investments approximates a **normal distribution** (bell-shaped curve) with the mean being the expected return and the variance, or standard deviation, measuring the dispersion around the expected return. Therefore, the most common estimates of risk come from the variance or standard deviation of historical returns. Remember, if you assume that the distribution is normal, about 95% of the returns will fall within the range created by expected return ± two standard deviations.

b. For many investments, management does not have significant historical data on returns to calculate the mean and variance. In these cases management must resort to **subjective** estimates of risk.

EXAMPLE

Assume that a defense contractor has the possibility of getting a lucrative government contract. The government intends to announce the winner of the contract today. An investor estimates that the probability of the firm getting the contract is 60%, in which case the stock price will increase 20%. If the contractor does not get the contract, the stock price is estimated to decline by 10%. Today's expected return on the stock investment would be computed as follows:

$$\text{Expected return} = 0.60(20\%) + 0.40(-10\%) = 8.0\%$$

The variance of the return is measured by the following formula:

$$\text{Variance} = E\{[R - E(R)]^2\}$$

Where

$\quad R \quad$ = A random possible return
$\quad E(R)$ = The expected value of the return

Therefore to get the variance, we simply sum the squared deviations of the possible returns from the expected return weighted by their probability, as shown below.

$\quad \text{Variance} = 0.60(20\% - 8\%)^2 + 0.40(-10\% - 8\%)^2$
$\quad \text{Variance} = 216\%$

The standard deviation, which is equal to the square root of the variance, is calculated below.

$$\text{Standard deviation} = \sqrt{216\%} = 14.70\%$$

Therefore, the investor can make a decision about whether to invest in the stock knowing that the expected return is 8.0% with a standard deviation of 14.70%.

C. Portfolio Returns and Risk

1. Expected Returns of a Portfolio

When an investor invests in a portfolio of assets, the expected returns are simply the weighted-average of the expected returns of the assets making up the portfolio. The expected return may be calculated with the following formula:

$$E(R_p) = w_1 E(R_1) + w_2 E(R_2) + w_3 E(R_3)\ldots$$

Where

$E(R_p)$	=	The expected return on the portfolio
$w_{1,2,3\ldots}$	=	The weight of each of the assets (1,2,3, etc.) in the portfolio
$E(R_{1,2,3\ldots})$	=	The expected return of each of the assets (1,2,3, etc.) in the portfolio

---

EXAMPLE

Assume that an investor has two assets (or types of assets) in his or her portfolio. Asset 1 is 60% of the portfolio, and it has an expected return of 10%. Asset 2 is 40% of the portfolio, and it has an expected return of 5%. The expected return of the portfolio is calculated below.

$$E(R_p) = 0.60(10\%) + 0.40(5\%) = 8\%$$

---

2. The Variance of Portfolio Returns

a. The variance of portfolio returns depends on three factors

    (1) The percentage of the portfolio invested in each asset (the weight)

    (2) The variance of the returns of each individual asset

    (3) The covariance among the returns of assets in the portfolio. The covariance captures the degree to which the asset returns move together over time. If returns on the individual assets move together, there is little benefit to holding the portfolio. On the other hand, if returns on some assets in the portfolio go up when returns on other assets in the portfolio go down, holding the portfolio reduces overall risk.

b. Portfolios allow investors to diversify away unsystematic risk. **Unsystematic risk** is the risk that exists for one particular investment or a group of like investments (e.g., technology stock). By having a balanced portfolio, investors can theoretically eliminate this risk. **Systematic risk** relates to market factors that cannot be diversified away. All investments are to some degree affected by them. Examples of systematic risk factors include fluctuations in GDP, inflation, interest rates, etc.

3. **Measuring the Systematic Risk of an Individual Investment**

The variance of an individual investment captures the total risk of the investment, both systematic an unsystematic. However, since unsystematic risk can be eliminated by diversification, the variance of a specific investment is not a particularly useful measure when considering a portfolio of investments. A standardized measure that has been developed to estimate an investment's systematic risk is beta.

$$\text{Beta} = B_i = \frac{\sigma_{im}}{\sigma_m^2}$$

The beta of a particular investment equals the covariance of the investment's returns with the returns of the overall portfolio divided by the portfolio's variance. It measures how the value of the investment moves with changes in the value of the total portfolio. Therefore, it can be used to evaluate the effect of an individual investment's risk on the risk of the entire portfolio.

4. An individual investor has a **risk preference function** which describes the investor's trade-off between risk and return. A portfolio that falls on the line described by this function is an **efficient portfolio**.

D. Interest Rates

Interest represents the cost of borrowing funds. Therefore, consideration of interest rates is a critical aspect of financing decisions. In this section, we will review aspects of interest rates that are significant to financing decisions.

1. **Interest Rates and Risk**

As discussed above, risk and return are directly related. Investors and creditors must be paid a premium for assuming higher degrees of risk. In determining the appropriate interest rate to accept, investors and creditors consider the business risks of the loan or investment. The following business risks are relevant:

- **Credit or default risk**—The risk that the firm will default on payment of interest or principal of the loan or bond. This may be divided into two parts: the individual firm's creditworthiness (or risk of default) and **sector risk** (the risk related to economic conditions in the firm's economic sector).
- **Interest rate risk**—The risk that the value of the loan or bond will decline due to an increase in interest rates.
- **Market risk**—The risk that the value of the loan or bond will decline due to a decline in the aggregate value of all the assets in the economy.

Credit risk is an example of an unsystematic (unique) risk. It is unique to the particular loan or investment. Credit risk can be eliminated by diversification (e.g., by investing in a portfolio of loans or bonds). Market and interest rate risks are part of systematic risk that must be accepted by the investor.

2. **Stated Versus Effective Annual Interest Rates**

Management must make objective comparisons of loan costs or investment returns over different compounding periods. In order to put interest rates on a common basis for comparison, management must distinguish between the **stated interest rate** and the **effective annual interest rate**. While the stated rate is the contractual rate charged by the lender, the effective annual rate is the true annual return to the lender. The simple annual rate may vary from the effective annual rate because interest is often compounded more often than annually. The formula for calculating the effective annual rate from the stated rate is presented below.

$$\text{EAR} = \left(1 + \frac{r}{m}\right)^4 - 1$$

Where

r = The stated interest rate

m = Compounding frequency

EXAMPLE

Assume that management is evaluating a loan that has a stated interest rate of 8% with compounding of interest quarterly. Since compounding is quarterly, m is equal to 4 because interest is compounded 4 times each year. Using the following equation, the effective annual rate may be computed as follows:

$$EAR = \left(1 + \frac{.08}{4}\right)^4 - 1$$

$$EAR = .0824 = 8.24\%$$

Management may now compare this 8.24% rate to other options on an effective interest basis.

3. **The Term Structure of Interest Rates**

The term structure of interest rates describes the relationship between long-and short-term rates. These relationships are important in determining whether to use long-term fixed or variable rate financing. A yield curve is used to illustrate the relative level of short-term and long-term interest rates at a point in time. At any point in time a yield curve may take any one of the following three forms:

a. **Normal yield curve**—An upward sloping curve in which short-term rates are less than intermediate-term rates which are less than long-term rates.
b. **Inverted (abnormal) yield curve**—A downward-sloping curve in which short-term rates are greater than intermediate-term rates which are greater than long-term rates.
c. **Flat yield curve**—A curve in which short-term, intermediate-term and long-term rates are all about the same.
d. **Humped yield curve**—A curve in which intermediate-term rates are higher than both short-term and long-term rates.

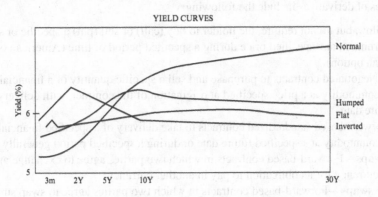

Long-term rates are usually higher (as described by the normal yield curve) because they involve more interest rate risk. Therefore, lenders require higher **maturity risk premiums** for long-term lending. However, market rates are also affected by expectations about the future levels of inflation, defaults, and liquidity, which can vary with the maturity date. These factors cause the relationships depicted by the inverted or humped yield curves.

There are a few theories that attempt to explain the shape of the yield curve, including

(1) **Liquidity preference (premium) theory.** This theory states that long-term rates should be higher than short-term rates, because investors have to be offered a premium to entice them to hold less liquid and more price-sensitive securities. Remember if interest rates increase and an investor holds a fixed-rate long-term security, the value of the security will decline.
(2) **Market segmentation theory.** This theory states that treasury securities are divided into market segments by the various financial institutions investing in the market. Commercial banks prefer short-term securities to match their short-term lending strategies. Savings and loans prefer intermediate-term securities. Finally, life insurance companies prefer long-term securities because of the nature of their commitments to policyholders. The demand for various term securities is therefore dependent on the demands of these segmented groups of investors.

(3) **Expectations theory.** This theory explains yields on long-term securities as a function of short-term rates. Specifically, it states that long-term rates reflect the average of short-term expected rates over the time period that the long-term security will be outstanding. Under this theory long-term rates tell us about market expectations of short-term rates. When long-term rates are lower than short-term rates, the market is expecting short-term rates to fall. Since interest rates are directly tied to inflation rates, long-term rates also tell us about the market's expectations about inflation. If long-term rates are lower than short-term rates, the market is indicating a belief that inflation will decline.

All of the theories and factors described above make it very difficult to predict interest rates, in general, and even moreso for varying maturities. Therefore, sound financial policy calls for using a combination of long- and short-term debt, and equity, to enable the firm to survive in any interest rate environment.

The mix of long- and short-term debt also affects the firm's financial statements. A heavy reliance on short-term or variable-rate debt means that interest expense and, therefore, net income will be more variable. This increases the financial risk of the firm and will cause creditors and investors to demand higher rates to compensate for the increased risk.

> **NOW REVIEW MULTIPLE-CHOICE QUESTIONS 1 THROUGH 18**

DERIVATIVES AND HEDGING

A. The Nature of Derivatives

1. A derivative is a financial instrument or contract whose value is derived from some other financial measure (underlyings, such as commodity prices, stock prices, interest rates, etc.) and includes payment provisions.

2. Common examples of derivatives include the following:

   a. **Options**—Allow, but do not require, the holder to buy (call) or sell (put) a specific or standard commodity or financial instrument, at a specified price during a specified period of time (American option) or at a specified date (European option).

   b. **Forwards**—Negotiated contracts to purchase and sell a specific quantity of a financial instrument, foreign currency, or commodity at a price specified at origination of the contract, with delivery and payment at a specified future date.

   c. **Futures**—Forward-based standardized contracts to take delivery of a specified financial instrument, foreign currency, or commodity at a specified future date or during a specified period generally at the then market price.

   d. **Currency swaps**—Forward-based contracts in which two parties agree to exchange an obligation to pay cash flows in one currency for an obligation to pay in another currency.

   e. **Interest rate swaps**—Forward-based contracts in which two parties agree to swap streams of payments over a specified period of time. An example would be an interest-rate swap in which one party agrees to make payments based on a fixed rate of interest and the other party agrees to make payments based on a variable rate of interest.

   f. **Swaption**—An option of a swap that provides the holder with the right to enter into a swap at a specified future date with specified terms, or to extend or terminate the life of an existing swap. These derivatives have characteristics of an option and an interest rate swap.

3. Forward contracts and swaps are often created and exchanged by **financial intermediaries,** such as

   a. Commercial banks
   b. Insurance companies
   c. Pension funds
   d. Savings and loan associations
   e. Mutual funds
   f. Finance companies
   g. Investment bankers
   h. Money market funds
   i. Credit unions

The other party to the contract or agreement is referred to as the **counterparty**.

B. Risks in Using Derivatives

1. **Credit risk**—The risk of loss as a result of the counterparty to a derivative agreement failing to meet its obligation.
2. **Market risk**—The risk of loss from adverse changes in market factors that affect the fair value of a derivative, such as interest rates, foreign exchange rates, and market indexes for equity securities.
3. **Basis risk**—The risk of loss from ineffective hedging activities. Basis risk is the difference between the fair value (or cash flows) of the hedged item and the fair value (or cash flows) of the hedging derivative. The entity is subject to the risk that fair values (or cash flows) will change so that the hedge will no longer be effective.
4. **Legal risk**—The risk of loss from a legal or regulatory action that invalidates or otherwise precludes performance by one or both parties to the derivative agreement.

C. Uses of Derivatives

1. **Speculation**—As an investment to speculate on price changes in various markets.
2. **Hedging**—To mitigate a business risk that is faced by the firm. Hedging is an activity that protects the entity against the risk of adverse changes in the fair values or cash flows of assets, liabilities, or future transactions. A hedge is a defensive strategy.

D. Financial Statement Effects of Derivative Transactions
The financial statement effects of derivative transactions is governed primarily by Statement of Financial Accounting Standards 133 (SFAS 133), *Accounting for Derivative Instruments and Hedging Activities*. In this section we will briefly review the requirements of that standard.

1. SFAS 133 provides guidance on three types of hedging activities.

   a. **Fair value hedge**—A hedge of the changes in the fair value of a recognized asset or liability, or of an unrecognized firm commitment, that are attributable to a particular risk.
   b. **Cash flow hedge**—A hedge of the variability in the cash flows of a recognized asset or liability, or of a forecasted transaction, that is attributable to a particular risk.
   c. **Foreign currency hedges**

      (1) A fair value hedge of an unrecognized firm commitment or a recognized asset or liability valued in a foreign currency (a foreign currency fair value hedge).
      (2) A cash flow hedge of a forecasted transaction, an unrecognized firm commitment, the forecasted functional-currency-equivalent cash flows associated with a recognized asset or liability, or a forecasted intercompany transaction (a foreign currency cash flow hedge).
      (3) A hedge of a net investment in a foreign operation.

2. In general, SFAS 133 requires an entity to report all derivatives as assets and liabilities in the statement of financial position, measured at fair value. Unrealized gains and losses attributed to changes in a derivative's fair value are accounted for differently, depending on whether the derivative is designated and qualifies as a hedge.

   a. **Accounting for a fair value hedge**—The change in the fair value of a derivative designated and qualifying as a fair value hedge is recognized in earnings and is offset by the portion of the change in the fair value of the hedged asset or liability that is attributable to the risk being hedged. Accordingly, the carrying amount of the hedged asset or liability is adjusted for changes in fair value. If the hedge is completely effective, the change in the derivative's fair value will equal the change in the hedged item's fair value. Therefore, there will be no effect on earnings. However, if the hedge is not completely effective, earnings will be increased or decreased for the difference between the changes in the fair values of the derivative and the hedged item.
   b. **Accounting for a cash flow hedge**—The effective portion of the change in the fair value of a derivative designated and qualifying as a cash flow hedge is reported in other comprehensive income, and the ineffective portion is reported in earnings.
   c. **Accounting for foreign hedges**—The accounting for foreign exchange hedges is very similar to the accounting for fair value and cash flow hedges as describe above.

3. **Valuing Derivatives**
   As indicated above, derivatives are valued on financial statements at fair values, which is the current market price of the derivative. Quoted market prices in active markets are the best source of fair value and may be used for many derivatives. If a quoted market price is not available, valuation techniques are used to estimate the fair value, such as option-pricing models, matrix pricing, option-adjusted spread models, and fundamental analysis. We will briefly describe two commonly used methods.

a. The **Black-Scholes option-pricing model** is a mathematical model for estimating the price of stock options, using the following five variables:

- Time to expiration of the option
- Exercise or strike price
- Risk-free interest rate
- Price of the underlying stock
- Volatility of the price of the underlying stock

Other methods that are used to value options include Monte-Carlo simulation and binomial trees.

b. The **zero-coupon method** is used to determine the fair value of interest rate swaps. The zero-coupon method is a present value model in which the net settlements from the swap are estimated and discounted back to their current value. The key variables in the model include

- Estimated net settlement cash flows (explained in the example below)
- Timing of the cash flows as specified by the contract
- Discount rate

EXAMPLE

Assume that management enters into an agreement to swap payments on a fixed-rate liability for a variable rate. If interest rates decline, the firm will receive a net positive cash flow from the swap because the amount received on the fixed rate will be greater than the amount due on the variable rate. The opposite is true if rates increase. The zero-coupon method estimates future cash flows by calculating the net settlement that would be required if future interest rates are equal to the rates implied by the current yield curve. That amount is discounted to determine the current fair value of the swap for financial reporting purposes.

E. Hedging Examples

EXAMPLE

On January 1, 20X1, a firm forecasts that it will need $10,000,000 in financing December 31, 20X1. Management decides that the appropriate form of financing is a bond issue of 10 years with a fixed interest rate. The market rate at which the firm can issue the debt is based on the Treasury rate, which is the yield on US Treasury bonds. On January 1, 20X1, the Treasury rate is 4%. Since the Treasury rate is the risk-free rate, the firm's actual rate would be higher to compensate the investor for risk of default on the bonds. Assume that based on the firm's credit rating and economic conditions, the credit spread is two basis points. Therefore, the firm's interest rate at January 1, 20X1, is equal to 6% (4% risk free rate + 2% credit spread). Management would like to lock in the risk-free component of interest today to hedge against an increase in rates. The firm hedges the transaction by entering into futures contracts to sell $10,000,000 in 5-year Treasury bonds at the forward rate of 4%. A position such as this, in which the firm is committed to sell something it does not own, is referred to as a **short position**. Around December 31, 20X1, management intends to purchase the contracts to close out its short position. Assume that the interest rate for Treasury bonds increases by one basis point from January 1, 20X1, to December 31, 20X1. If the interest rate on Treasury bonds increases by 1% from the 4% rate at the beginning of the year, the price of the bonds will decrease to allow an investor to earn 5% on the Treasury bonds. Therefore, management can buy futures contracts at much less than the price they were sold at and realize a gain. If the futures contracts for the Treasury bonds can be purchased at $9,400,000 the gain would be $600,000 ($10,000,000 – $9,400,000). Since this is a hedge, the gain would be reported in other comprehensive income rather than ordinary income. Assume that the bond financing that was issued by the firm on December 31, 20X1, was at 7 ½ %, the 5% risk-free rate plus a 2 ½ % credit spread. Hedge accounting would in effect reduce the interest rate on the debt by the 1% increase in the risk-free rate. From an accounting standpoint the gain on the Treasury bond futures contracts would be amortized to reduce interest expense by 1% over the life of the bond. Notice that the credit spread increased from January 1, 20X1, to December 31, 20X1, by ½%. Credit risk cannot be hedged, and therefore, the effective rate (after amortization of the hedging gain) on the bond issue actually increased from the forecasted 6% (4% + 2%) at the beginning of the year to 6 ½% (4% + 2 ½%).

EXAMPLE

Several years ago a firm entered into a $20,000,000, ten-year noncallable debt agreement. The agreement calls for variable interest payments tied to the London Interbank Offered Rate (LIBOR). LIBOR is currently 4.5% but management is concerned about the volatility of current rates and wants to lock in a fixed rate for this debt. The firm enters into an interest rate swap to pay 7% fixed interest for the remaining term of the loan instead of the variable rate. In this way it is able to hedge its interest rate risk. Instead of having a variable interest expense over the life of the loan, the firm will have a fixed rate of 7%. The financial statement effects of this transaction would be recognition of a 7% fixed rate of interest over the life of the loan as opposed to the variable rate.

EXAMPLE

Assume that a firm carries approximately $200,000 in short-term financing at variable interest rates and management is concerned about the current instability of short-term interest rates. To lock in the current rate for a year, management decides to sell on the futures market $200,000 in Treasury notes to be delivered one year from today. Again, this sale gives the firm a **short position.** The futures contracts will sell at approximately the current yield on the short-term Treasury securities. If interest rates rise, the firm will pay more interest on its short-term debt but it will also experience a gain on the futures contract because the price of Treasury notes will decline. Near the end of the year, the firm will purchase Treasury note contracts to close its short position. If the Treasury note contracts can be purchased for $180,000 at the end of the year, the firm's gain on the contract would be calculated as shown below.

Sales price Treasury note contracts (beginning of year)	$200,000
Purchase price of Treasury note contracts (end of year)	180,000
Gain on the contracts	$ 20,000

If the hedge was completely effective, the $20,000 gain on the futures contracts will offset the increase in interest expense experienced by the firm due to the increase in short-term interest rates. From an accounting standpoint, the gain on the contracts would be used to reduce interest expense in operating income.

NOW REVIEW MULTIPLE-CHOICE QUESTIONS 19 THROUGH 27

PRESENT VALUE

This section reviews the basic concepts related to time value of money.

A. The Time Value of Money

On the CPA exam, you do not have to know the complex formulas that are used to compute time value of money factors (TVMF). The factors will be given to you or enough information will be given to you so that you can easily compute them or use a spreadsheet tool to compute them. Your main focus of attention should be centered on understanding which TVMF should be used in a given situation.

> **NOTE:** The following abbreviations are used in the material that follows:
>
> i = interest rate
> n = number of periods or rents

1. **Future Value (FV) of an Amount** (future value of $1)

   The future value of an amount is the amount that will be available at some point in the future if an amount is deposited today and earns compound interest for "n" periods. The most common application is savings deposits. For example, if you deposited $100 today at 10%, you would have $110 [$100 + ($100 × 10%)] at the end of the first year, $121[$100 + ($110 × 10%)] at the end of the second year, etc. The compounding feature allows you to earn interest on interest. In the second year of the example you earn $11 interest: $10 on the original $100 and $1 on the first year's interest of $10.

2. **Present Value (PV) of a Future Amount** (present value of $1)

   The present value of a future amount is the amount you would pay now for an amount to be received "n" periods in the future given an interest rate of "i." A common application would be the money you would lend today for a noninterest-bearing note receivable in the future. For example, if you were lending money at 10%, you would lend $100 for a $110 note due in one year or for a $121 note due in two years.

   The present value of $1 is the inverse of the future value of $1. Thus, given a future value of $1 table, you have a present value of $1 by dividing each value into 1.00. Look at the present value of $1 and future value of $1 tables on the next page. The future value of $1 at 10% in five years is 1.611. Thus, the present value of $1 in five years would be 1.00 ÷ 1.611 which is .621 (check the table). Conversely, the future value of $1 is found by dividing the present value of $1 into 1.00, that is, 1.00 ÷ .621 = 1.611.

3. **Compounding**

   When interest is compounded more than once a year, two extra steps are needed. First, **multiply** "n" by the number of times interest is compounded annually. This will give you the total number of interest periods. Second, **divide** "i" by the number of times interest is compounded annually. This will give you the appropriate interest rate for each interest period. For example, if the 10% was compounded semiannually, the amount of $100 at the end of one year would be $110.25 [$(1.05)^2$] instead of $110.00. The extra $.25 is 5% of the $5.00 interest earned in the first half of the year.

4. **Future Value of an Ordinary Annuity**

   The future value of an ordinary annuity is the amount available "n" periods in the future as a result of the deposit of an amount (A) at the end of every period 1 through "n." Compound interest is earned at the rate of "i" on the deposits. A common application is a bond sinking fund. A deposit is made at the end of the first period and earns compound interest for n–1 periods (not during the first period, because the deposit is made at the end of the first period). The next to the last payment earns one period's interest, that is, n – (n–1) = 1. The last payment earns no interest, because it is deposited at the end of the last (nth) period. Remember that in the FUTURE AMOUNT OF AN ORDINARY ANNUITY TABLE, all of the factors for any "n" row are based on one less interest period than the number of payments.

TIME VALUE OF MONEY FACTOR (TVMF) TABLES

Future Value (Amount) of $1

n	6%	8%	10%	12%	15%
1	1.060	1.080	1.100	1.120	1.150
2	1.124	1.166	1.210	1.254	1.323
3	1.191	1.260	1.331	1.405	1.521
4	1.262	1.360	1.464	1.574	1.749
5	1.338	1.469	1.611	1.762	2.011

Present Value of $1

n	6%	8%	10%	12%	15%
1	.943	.926	.909	.893	.870
2	.890	.857	.826	.797	.756
3	.840	.794	.751	.712	.658
4	.792	.735	.683	.636	.572
5	.747	.681	.621	.567	.497

Future Value (Amount) of an Ordinary Annuity of $1

n	6%	8%	10%	12%	15%
1	1.000	1.000	1.000	1.000	1.000
2	2.060	2.080	2.100	2.120	2.150
3	3.184	3.246	3.310	3.374	3.473
4	4.375	4.506	4.506	4.641	4.993
5	5.637	5.867	6.105	6.353	6.742

Present Value of an Ordinary Annuity of $1

n	6%	8%	10%	12%	15%
1	.943	.926	.909	.893	.870
2	1.833	1.783	1.736	1.690	1.626
3	2.673	2.577	2.487	2.402	2.283
4	3.465	3.312	3.170	3.037	2.855
5	4.212	3.993	3.791	3.605	3.352

5. **Present Value of an Ordinary Annuity**

The present value of an ordinary annuity is the value today, given a discount rate, of a series of future payments. A common application is the capitalization of lease payments by either lessors or lessees. Payments "1" through "n" are assumed to be made at the end of years "1" through "n," and are discounted back to the present.

EXAMPLE

Assume a five-year lease of equipment requiring payments of $1,000 at the end of each of the five years, which is to be capitalized. If the discount rate is 10%, the present value is $3,791 ($1,000 × 3.791). The behavior of the present value of the lease payment stream over the five-year period is shown below. Note that the liability (principal amount) grows by interest in the amount of 10% during each period and decreases by $1,000 at the end of each period.

```
    0              1              2              3              4              5
$3,791 + 380 Int. = $4,171
            - 1,000 Pay
        $3,171 + 320 Int. = $3,491
                    - 1,000 Pay
                $2,491 + 250 Int. = $2,741
                            - 1,000
                        $1,741 + 170 Int. = $1,911
                                    - 1,000
                                $ 911 + 91 Int. =
                                $1,002
                                            - 1,000
                                            2*
```

* Due to rounding

---

6. **Distinguishing a Future Value of an Annuity from a Present Value of an Annuity**

Sometimes confusion arises in distinguishing between the future value (amount) of an annuity and the present value of an annuity. These two may be distinguished by determining whether the total dollar amount in the problem comes at the beginning (e.g., cost of equipment acquired for leasing) or at the end (e.g., the amount needed to retire bonds) of the series of payments as illustrated below.

Remember: if the total amount comes at the end of the series of payments, it is a **future value** of annuity situation. If the total amount comes at the beginning of the series of payments, it is a **present value** of annuity situation. The total dollar amount may be given in the problem or you may have to compute it; either way, it makes no difference in determining whether a problem involves a present value or future value situation.

Some students feel the need to "convert" all time value of money problems into either present value or future value problems, depending on which they're most comfortable with. This process involves more work and more chance for errors, because an additional TVMF equation must be solved in the conversion. This is inefficient, and unnecessary, if you are able to correctly identify between the two initially. Become proficient at determining present value and future value situations, so that you may efficiently select the correct TVMF from the corresponding table.

7. **Annuities Due**

In some cases, the payments or annuities may not conform to the assumptions inherent in the annuity tables. For example, the payments might be made at the beginning of each of the five years instead of at the end of each year. This is an annuity due (annuity in advance) in contrast to an ordinary annuity (annuity in arrears). Both annuity due and ordinary annuity payments are represented by the "x's" in the illustration below.

Periods		1	2	3	4	5
Annuity		x	x	x	x	x
Annuity Due	x	x	x	x	x	

If the payments in the 5-period lease example above were made at the beginning of the period, the present value of the first payment which is made today is $1,000 (i.e., the TVMF is 1.00). The remaining 4 payments comprise an ordinary annuity for 4 periods as you can see on the above diagram. Always use time diagrams to analyze application of annuities.

To convert either a future value of an ordinary annuity or the present value of an ordinary annuity factor to an annuity due factor, multiply the ordinary annuity factor times $(1 + i)$. For the above lease example, you would find the present value of an ordinary annuity factor for n = 5 which is 3.993. Then multiply 3.993 by 1.08 to arrive at the annuity due factor, 4.312. The present value of the payments would be $4,312 (4.312 × $1,000). Notice that the present value of the annuity due in the above example is $319 greater than the present value of the ordinary annuity because the payments are moved closer to the present.

8. **Interest Rates**

Usually, you will be given the interest rate for a time value problem but it is important to remember that the interest rate is generally made up of two components—the expected inflation/deflation rate (which affects the relative value of the currency), and the inflation adjusted return for the particular investment (which is determined by the risk of the investment).

9. **TVMF Applications**

The basic formula to use is

$$FV \text{ or } PV = TVMF \times Amount$$

If an annuity is involved, the amount is the periodic payment or deposit; if not, it is a single sum. Note that FV or PV is determined by three variables: time, interest rate, and payment. TVMF represents two variables: time and interest rate. The tables usually have the interest rate on the horizontal axis and time on the vertical axis. The above formula may also be stated as

$$Amount = \frac{FV \text{ or } PV}{TVMF}$$

For example, if we need to accumulate $12,210 in five years to repay a loan, we could determine the required annual deposit with the above formula. If the savings rate were 10%, we would divide the FV ($12,210) by the TVMF of the future value of annuity, n = 5, i = .10 (6.105) and get $2,000. Thus, $2,000 deposited at the end of each of five years earning 10% will result in $12,210. This formula may also be used to find future values of an amount, present values of amounts, and annuities in the same manner.

Another variation of the formula is

$$TVMF = \frac{FV \text{ or } PV}{Amount}$$

For example, we may be offered a choice between paying $3,312 in cash or $1,000 a year at the end of each of the next four years. We determine the interest rate by dividing the annual payment into the present value of the annuity to obtain the TVMF (3.312) for n = 4. We then find the interest rate which has the same or similar TVMF (in this case 8%).

Alternatively, using the above formula, we may know the interest rate but not know the number of payments. Given the TVMF, we can determine "n" by looking in the TVMF table under the known interest rate. Remember the TVMF reflects two variables: time and interest rate.

B. Valuation of Bonds

Bonds generally provide for periodic fixed interest payments at a coupon (contract) rate of interest. At issuance, or thereafter, the market rate of interest for the particular type of bond may be above, the same, or below the coupon rate. If the market rate exceeds the coupon rate, the book value will be less than the maturity value. The difference (discount) will make up for the coupon rate being below the market rate.

Conversely, when the coupon rate exceeds the market rate, the bond will sell for more than maturity value to bring the effective rate to the market rate. This difference (premium) will make up for the coupon rate being above the market rate. When the coupon rate equals the market rate, the bond will sell for the maturity value.

The market value of a bond is equal to the maturity value and interest payments discounted to the present. You may have to refer to the discussion of time value of money concepts in the previous section before working with the subsequent material. Finally, when solving bond problems, candidates must be careful when determining the number of months to use in the calculation of interest and discount/premium amortization. For example, candidates frequently look at a bond issue with an interest date of September 1 and count three months to December 31. This error is easy to make because candidates focus only on the fact that September is the ninth month instead of also noting whether the date is at the beginning or end of the month.

1. Bond Valuation Example

$10,000 in bonds, semiannual interest at 6% coupon rate, maturing in six years, and market rate of 5%.

a. Find present value of maturity value. Use present value of $1 factor. Discount $10,000 back 12 periods at 2 1/2% interest (Factor = .7436). (Semiannual compounding is going to be required to discount the semiannual payments so it is also assumed here.)

$$\$10,000 \times .7436 = \$7,436$$

b. Find the present value of the annuity of twelve $300 interest payments. Use present value of an ordinary annuity of $1 factor for twelve periods at 2 1/2% interest (Factor = 10.26).

$$\$300 \times 10.26 = \$3,078$$

c. Today's value is $10,514 (7,436 + 3,078)

CAPITAL BUDGETING

A. Stages

Capital budgeting is a technique to evaluate and control long-term investments. There are six stages to capital budgeting.

1. **Identification stage.** Management determines the type of capital projects that are necessary to achieve management's objectives and strategies.
2. **Search stage.** Management attempts to identify alternative capital investments that will achieve management's objectives.
3. **Information-acquisition stage.** Management attempts to revaluate the various investments in terms of their costs and benefits.
4. **Selection stage.** Management chooses the projects that best meet the criteria established.
5. **Financing stage.** Management decides on the best source of funding for the project. This process is described in Module 44.
6. **Implementation and control stage.** Management undertakes the project and monitors the performance of the investment.

This section will focus primarily on the techniques management uses to evaluate various projects. However, these techniques may also be used to monitor their performance. Capital budgeting alternatives are typically evaluated using discounted cash flow techniques. Such techniques involve evaluation of an investment today in terms of the present value of future cash returns from the investment. The objective is to identify the most profitable or best investment alternative. The cash returns can take two forms depending on the nature of the project. If the project will produce revenue, the return is the difference between the cash revenues (inflows) and cash expenses (outflows). Other projects generate cost savings (e.g., cash outflows for labor that are not made because a new machine is more efficient). The latter are, in effect, reductions in outflows, which for simplicity, can be treated as cash inflows. Conceptually, the results of both types of projects are the same. The entity ends up with more cash by making the initial capital investment.

The following terminology is useful to the understanding of capital budgeting analysis:

a. **Sunk, past, or unavoidable costs** are committed costs that are not avoidable and are therefore irrelevant to the decision process.

b. **Avoidable costs** are costs that will **not** continue to be incurred if a department or product is terminated.

c. **Committed costs** arise from a company's basic commitment to open its doors and engage in business (depreciation, property taxes, management salaries).

d. **Discretionary costs** are fixed costs whose level is set by current management decisions (e.g., advertising, research and development).

e. **Relevant costs** are future costs that will change as a result of a specific decision.

f. **Differential (incremental) cost** is the difference in cost between two alternatives.

g. **Opportunity cost** is the maximum income or savings (benefit) forgone by rejecting an alternative.

h. **Outlay (out-of-pocket) cost** is the cash disbursement associated with a specific project.

The choice among alternative investing decisions can be made on the basis of several capital budgeting models: (1) Payback or discounted payback; (2) Accounting rate of return; (3) Net present value; (4) Excess present value index; and (5) Internal (time-adjusted) rate of return.

B. Payback and Discounted Payback

The **payback** method evaluates investments on the length of time until recapture (return) of the investment. For example, if a $10,000 investment were to return a cash flow of $2,500 a year for eight years, the payback period would be four years. If the payback period is to be computed after income taxes, it is necessary to calculate cash flow as shown below, remembering that depreciation itself does not consume cash. Assuming an eight-year life with no salvage value and a 40% income tax rate, the after-tax payback period would be computed as follows:

Cash flow: $2,500 × (1 − 40%) = $1,500
Tax savings from depreciation: $1,250 × 40% = $500
Cash flow after tax: $1,500 + $500 = $2,000
$10,000 ÷ $2,000 = 5 years

The payback method has a number of limitations. First, it ignores total project profitability and therefore has little or no connection to maximization of shareholder value. Second, the method is not really effective in taking into account the time value of money.

The **discounted payback** method is essentially the same as the payback method except that in calculating the payback period, cash flows are first discounted to their present value. This is only a minor improvement over the conventional payback method. It still ignores any cash flows after the cutoff period and therefore does not consider total project profitability.

Using the above example, assume that the cost of capital for the firm is 8%. The discounted payback would be calculated as shown below.

Discounted payback
Cash flow after taxes = $2,000

Year	Cash flow	Present value factor	Present value of cash flow	Cumulative present value
1	$2,000	.926	$1,852	$1,852
2	2,000	.857	1,714	3,566
3	2,000	.794	1,588	5,154
4	2,000	.735	1,470	6,624
5	2,000	.681	1,362	7,986
6	2,000	.630	1,260	9,246
7	2,000	.583	1,166	10,412
8	2,000	.540	1,080	11,492

From the table we see that the discounted payback occurs in year 7. Specifically, it occurs when $754 ($10,000 – $9,246) of cash flow is received in that year. By dividing the $754 needed cash flow by the total $1,166 cash flows in year 7, that we need .65 of year 7 cash flows. Therefore, the discounted payback period is 6.65 years.

C. Accounting Rate of Return

The **accounting rate of return** (ARR) method computes an approximate rate of return which ignores the time value of money. It is computed as follows:

$$\text{ARR} = \text{Annual net income} \div \text{Average (or initial) investment}$$

Using the same example and assuming the annual cash flows approximate annual net income before depreciation and taxes for the project, the ARR before taxes is

$$(\$2,500 - \$1,250) \div (\$10,000 \div 2) = 25\%$$

The ARR after taxes is

$$[(\$2,500 - \$1,250) \times 60\%] \div (\$10,000 \div 2) = 15\%$$

Note that the numerator is the increase in **net income,** not **cash flows,** so depreciation is subtracted. The average investment is one-half the initial investment because the initial investment is depreciated down to 0 by the end of the project. If a problem asked for ARR based on **initial** investment, you would not divide the investment by 2.

The advantage of the accounting rate of return method is that it is simple and intuitive. It also is often the measure that is used to evaluate management. However, it has a number of limitations including

- The results are affected by the depreciation method used
- ARR makes no adjustment for project risk
- ARR makes no adjustment for the time value of money

D. Net Present Value

The **net present value** (NPV) method is a discounted cash flow method which calculates the present value of the future cash flows of a project and compares this with the investment outlay required to implement the project. The net present value of a project is defined as

$$\text{NPV} = \text{(Present value of future cash flows)} - \text{(Required investment)}$$

The calculation of the present value of the future cash flows requires the selection of a discount rate (also referred to as the target or hurdle rate). The rate used should be the minimum rate of return that management is willing to accept on capital investment projects. The rate used should be no less than the cost of capital—the rate management currently must pay to obtain funds. A project which earns exactly the desired rate of return will have a net present value of 0. A positive net present value identifies projects which will earn in excess of the minimum rate. For example, if a company desires a minimum return of 6% on an investment of $10,000 that has an expected return of $2,500 for five years, the present value of the cash flows is $10,530 ($2,500 × 4.212; 4.212 is the TVMF for the present value of an annuity, n = 5, i = 6%; see the previous section on Present Value concepts). The net present value of $530 ($10,530 – $10,000) indicates that the project will earn a return in excess of the 6% minimum desired. If the requirement were for a net-of-tax return of 6%, and the net-of-tax cash flow were $23,000, that amount would be multiplied by 4.212. This would result in a present value of $96,876 for the cash inflows, which is less than the $100,000 initial outlay. Therefore, this investment should not be made.

The NPV method is based on cash flows and would ignore depreciation if taxes were not considered. As shown earlier, however, depreciation results in a tax savings (tax shield) that must be factored into the evaluation. For example, assume that a company is considering the purchase of equipment costing $20,000 for use in a new project. MACRS is used to depreciate equipment for tax purposes, under which the machine has a useful life of seven years.

The required rate of return of the company is 8%. The present value of the tax savings from depreciation would be as follows:

Year	Income tax deduction for depreciation	Income tax savings at 30% tax rate	8% discount factor	Present value at 8%*
1	$2,858	$ 857	.926	$ 794
2	4,898	1,469	.857	1,259
3	3,498	1,049	.794	833
4	2,498	749	.735	551
5	1,786	536	.681	365
6	1,784	535	.630	337
7	1,786	536	.583	312
8	892	268	.540	145
				$4,596

* Tax savings × Discount factor

Therefore, $4,596 would be included in the NPV computation as a cash inflow from the equipment.

The **excess present value (profitability) index** computes the ratio of the present value of the cash inflows to the initial cost of a project. It is used to implement the net present value method when there is a limit on funds available for capital investments. Assuming other factors are equal, this is accomplished by allocating funds to those projects with the highest excess present value indexes.

First, the net present value of each alternative is calculated using the minimum required rate of return. Then the excess present value index is computed

$$\frac{\text{Present value of future net cash inflows}}{\text{Initial investment}} \times 100 = \text{Excess present value index}$$

If the index is equal to or greater than 100%, the project will generate a return equal to or greater than the required rate of return.

Net present value methods are the most widely accepted methods of evaluating a capital expenditure. Their advantages include

- Present results in dollars which are easily understood
- Adjust for the time value of money
- Consider the total profitability of the project
- Provide a straightforward method of controlling for the risk of competing projects—higher-risk cash flows can be discounted at a higher interest rate
- Provide a direct estimate of the change in shareholder wealth resulting from undertaking a project

The limitations of net present value methods include

- May not be considered as simple or intuitive as some other methods
- Do not take into account the management flexibility with respect to a project—management may be able to adjust the amount invested after the first year or two depending on the actual returns

E. Internal Rate of Return

The **internal (time-adjusted) rate of return** (IRR) method is another discounted cash flow method. It determines the rate of discount at which the present value of the future cash flows will exactly equal the investment outlay (i.e., the rate that results in a NPV of zero). This rate is compared with the minimum desired rate of return to determine if the investment should be made. The internal rate of return is determined by setting the investment today equal to the discounted value of future cash flows. The discounting factor (rate of return) is the unknown. The TVMF for the previous example is

$$
\begin{aligned}
\text{PV (investment today)} &= \text{TVMF} \times \text{Cash flows} \\
\$100,000 &= \text{TVMF} \times \$25,000 \\
\text{TVMF} &= 4.00
\end{aligned}
$$

The interest rate of a TVMF of 4.00 where n = 5 is approximately 8%. The after-tax rate of return is determined using the $23,000 after-tax cash inflow amount as follows:

$$\$100,000 = \text{TVMF} \times \$23,000$$
$$\text{TVMF} = 4.35$$

The interest rate of a TVMF of 4.35 where n = 5 is approximately 5%. The answers are worded "less than 5%, but greater than 0%," "less than 7%, but greater than 5%," etc.

The relationship between the NPV method and the IRR method can be summarized as follows:

NPV	IRR
NPV > 0	IRR > Discount rate
NPV = 0	IRR = Discount rate
NPV < 0	IRR < Discount rate

If the firm has sufficient funds to undertake all projects, the calculated internal rate of return on a project is compared to a prespecified **hurdle rate** which is the firm's minimum acceptable rate of return for the project. The hurdle rate is determined based on the market rate of return for projects with similar levels of risk.

1. The advantages of the internal rate of return method include

   a. Adjusts for the time value of money
   b. The hurdle rate is based on market interest rates for similar investments
   c. The results tend to be a little more intuitive than the results of the net present value method

2. Limitations of the internal rate of return method include

   a. Depending on the cash flow pattern there may be no unique internal rate of return for a particular project—there may be multiple returns depending on the assumptions used
   b. Occasionally, there may be no real discount rate that equates the project's NPV to zero
   c. The technique also has limitations when evaluating mutually exclusive investments as described in the next section

F. Mutually Exclusive Projects

1. Until now, we have assumed that management can invest in any project that meets the particular criteria being used. However, at times management must decide on one of several projects that are all acceptable. In other words, management must decide on the best project. This situation is often described as **capital rationing**.
2. To decide on the best investment, management must examine the characteristics of each. One way of summarizing the characteristics of an investment is through the use of the **net present value profile**. The profile allows us to portray the net present value of projects at different discounts rates.

EXAMPLE

Management is considering investment in one of two projects, both of which involve an initial investment of $20,000. Future cash flows from the two projects are shown below.

Year	Investment A	Investment B
1	$3,000	$18,000
2	4,000	6,000
3	5,000	2,400
4	10,000	
5	10,000	

The following graph shows the net present value for the two investments.

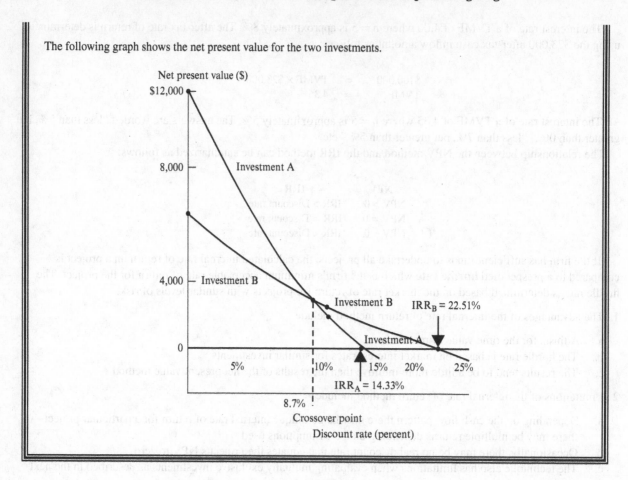

3. Comparing the two investments, we see that at low discount rates Investment A has a higher net present value. Investment B has a higher net present value at higher discount rates. This is because most of the return from Investment B is loaded toward the early years of the investment. The crossover point is at 8.7%, at lower discount rates Investment A should be selected, and at higher rates Investment B should be accepted.

4. Net present value works better than the internal rate of return in a situation in which a choice must be made among a group of investments. The internal rate of return method is based upon an important assumption when comparing investments of different lives and different cash flow patterns. The method implicitly assumes that the cash inflows from an investment can be reinvested at the same internal rate of return. For example, assume a company must choose between two projects, C and D. The IRR on project C is 15% with a life of five years, while the IRR of project D is 13% with a life of ten years. Project C would be the one selected under the IRR criteria. However, the internal rate of return method assumes that the cash inflows from the project can be reinvested at 15%. If the cash inflows can only be reinvested at 9%, then project B may be the better alternative. **Therefore, we see that traditional IRR criteria may not arrive at the best solution in all cases.** As a result, many firms rely on net present value criteria when evaluating competing proposals.

G. Determining Future Cash Flows

1. In evaluating investment alternatives, one of the first challenges is determining the future cash flows that are relevant to the decision. Simply stated, relevant cash flows are those that are expected to differ among the alternatives. Examples of relevant cash flows include

   a. The initial investment in long-term tangible or intangible assets for each investment alternative

   b. Any initial investment in working capital for each investment alternative (e.g., inventories, accounts receivable, etc.)

c. Cash flow from the sale of any assets being replaced
d. Differences in cash flows from operations under the alternatives (e.g., cash inflows from sales and/or cash outflows for operating costs)

- Remember to focus on cash flows not accounting income
- Payments for incremental income taxes should be included
- Depreciation expense does not affect cash flows but the firm receives a tax savings (shield) from depreciation expense. It reduces taxable income and therefore reduces tax payments. Remember it is tax depreciation that generates the tax shield, and book depreciation may differ from tax depreciation.

e. Cash flows at the end of the expected life of the project.

- Terminal disposal price of any long-term tangible or intangible assets. If the tax basis (Initial cost – Tax depreciation taken) is expected to be different from the disposal price, the tax gain or loss will generate a tax inflow or outflow.
- Recovery of any working capital investment—This investment will be recovered at the end of the project by liquidation of inventories, accounts receivable, etc. There are generally no tax implications of this recovery because it is assumed that the cash received will be equal to the book value (tax basis) of the working capital items.

EXAMPLE

Watson Corporation is considering replacing an existing machine with a more efficient model. The existing machine can operate for another five years and will have a terminal value (salvage value) of $0 at the end of five years. The book value and tax basis of the old machine is $30,000, and if it continues in operation, tax and book depreciation will equal $6,000 per year for the next five years. The new machine will not increase revenues but it will reduce operating costs. The required net initial investment for the new machine is $200,000, which consists of $210,000 cost of the new machine plus an additional cash investment in working capital (supplies for the machine) of $10,000, less cash of $20,000 from the disposal of the existing machine ($210,000 + $10,000 – $20,000 = $200,000). The new machine is expected to have a five-year useful life and a terminal value (salvage value) of $20,000. Tax and book depreciation per year on the new machine on a straight-line basis will be $38,000 (($210,000 cost – $20,000 salvage value)/ 5 years). Management expects a cash flow savings in operating costs of $70,000 for the first three years and $60,000 for years four and five. **To simplify computations, operating cash flows are assumed to occur at the end of each year.** The working capital investment of $10,000 is expected to be recovered in full at the end of year five. Watson Corporation's tax rate is 40%. The relevant cash flows are presented below.

Net initial investment		
Purchase price of new machine		$(210,000)
Additional investment in working capital		(10,000)
Cash from disposal of old machine		20,000
Total effect of disposal of old machine:		
Cash from disposal	$20,000	
Less: Tax basis	(30,000)	
Loss on sale of old machine	(10,000)	
Tax rate	40%	
Tax benefit from sale of old machine		4,000
Net initial investment		$(196,000)
Operating cash flow for years 1 through 3		
Cost savings before income taxes		$ 70,000
Less income taxes (40% × $70,000)		(28,000)
Cost savings after taxes		42,000
Tax savings from depreciation:		
Depreciation on new machine	$38,000	

Less depreciation on old machine		6,000
Depreciation differential		$32,000
Tax rate		40%
Tax savings from incremental depreciation		12,800
Cash flow after taxes for years 1 through 3		$ 54,800

Operating cash flow for years 4 and 5

Cost savings before income taxes		$ 60,000
Less income taxes (40% × $60,000)		(24,000)
Cost savings after taxes		36,000
Total savings from depreciation:		
Depreciation on new machine	$38,000	
Less depreciation on old machine	6,000	
Depreciation differential	$32,000	
Tax rate	40%	
Tax savings from incremental depreciation		12,800
Cash flow after taxes for years 4 and 5		$ 48,800

Cash flow at end of year 5

Terminal price of new machine	$ 20,000
Recovery of working capital investment	10,000
Cash flow at end of year 5	$ 30,000

The pattern of relevant cash flows from investment in the new machine is summarized below.

Relevant Cash Flows

	0	1	2	3	4	5
Initial investment	$(196,000)					
Operating cash flow (after tax)		$54,800	$54,800	$54,800	$48,800	$48,800
Terminal price of new machine						20,000
Recovery of working capital						10,000
Total relevant cash flows	$(196,000)	$54,800	$54,800	$54,800	$48,800	$78,800

Assuming that Watson Corporation's cost of capital is 10%, the net present value of purchasing the new machine is calculated below.

Year	Cash flow	Present value factor (10%)	Present value
0	$(196,000)	1.000	$(196,000)
1	54,800	.909	49,813
2	54,800	.826	45,265
3	54,800	.751	41,155
4	48,800	.683	33,330
5	78,800	.621	48,935
Net present value			$22,498

The results indicate that when using the net present value criteria, management should purchase the new machine.

EXAMPLE

Taylor Corporation is considering investing in one of the following two projects. Taylor's marginal tax rate is 25% and its cost of capital is 10%

Investment A		
Initial investment		$150,000
Operating effects for 5-year useful life:		
Cash basis revenues	$200,000	
Cash basis expenses	(160,000)	
Net cash flow from operations (before taxes)		$ 40,000
Tax depreciation on the investment each year		$ 25,000
Terminal value of investment at end of 5 years		$ 25,000
Investment B		
Initial investment		$210,000
Operating effects for 6-year useful life:		
Cash basis revenues	$250,000	
Cash basis expenses	(200,000)	
Net cash flow from operations (before taxes)		$ 50,000
Tax depreciation on the investment each year		$ 35,000
Terminal value of investment at end of 6 years		$ 0

The cash flows from the two projects may be scheduled out as follows:

Investment A

	Relevant Cash Flows				
	0	**1**	**2**	**3**	**4**	**5**
Initial investment	$(150,000)					
Operating cash flow (before taxes)		$40,000	$40,000	$40,000	$40,000	$40,000
Taxes on operating cash flows (25%)		(10,000)	(10,000)	(10,000)	(10,000)	(10,000)
Tax savings from added depreciation (25% × $25,000)		6,250	6,250	6,250	6,250	6,250
Terminal price of investment						25,000
Total relevant cash flows	$(150,000)	$36,250	$36,250	$36,250	$36,250	$61,250

Investment B

	Relevant Cash Flows					
	0	**1**	**2**	**3**	**4**	**5**	**6**
Initial investment	$(210,000)						
Operating cash flow (before taxes)		$50,000	$50,000	$50,000	50,000	$50,000	$50,000
Taxes on operating cash flows (25%)		(12,500)	(12,500)	(12,500)	(12,500)	(12,500)	(12,500)
Tax savings from added depreciation (25% × $35,000)		8,750	8,750	8,750	8,750	8,750	8,750
Terminal value of investment							0
Total relevant cash flows	$(210,000)	$46,250	$46,250	$46,250	$46,250	$46,250	$46,250

Year	Present value factor (10%)	Investment A		Investment B	
		Cash flow	Present value	Cash flow	Present value
0	1.000	$(150,000)	$(150,000)	$(210,000)	$(210,000)
1	.909	36,250	32,951	46,250	42,041
2	.826	36,250	29,943	46,250	38,203
3	.751	36,250	27,224	46,250	34,734
4	.683	36,250	24,759	46,250	31,589
5	.621	61,250	38,036	46,250	28,721
6	.564			46,250	26,085
			$2,913		$(8,627)

The results indicate that when using the net present value criteria, Investment A should be accepted and Investment B rejected.

H. Considering Risk in Capital Budgeting

Risk as applied to capital budgeting is defined in terms of variability of the possible outcomes from a given investment. **Projected cash flows are not known with certainty.** Like individual investors, it is assumed that management is **risk averse**—that is, given the same rate of return they would prefer an investment with less uncertainty. A number of statistical techniques have been developed to measure the extent of risk inherent in a particular situation.

1. Probability Analysis

One way to include risk in the capital budgeting analysis is to assign probabilities to possible outcomes. The probabilities provide a mathematical way of expressing uncertainty about the outcomes. They may be based on past experience, industry ratios and trends, economic forecasts, interviews with executives, or sophisticated simulation techniques.

a. The set of all possible outcomes from an investment with a probability assigned to each outcome is referred to as a **probability distribution**. Probability distributions may be discrete or continuous. A **discrete distribution** identifies a **limited number of potential outcomes** and assigns probabilities to each of the outcomes. **A continuous distribution** theoretically defines an infinite number of possible outcomes. A commonly used continuous distribution is the **normal distribution** (bell-shaped curve). The normal distribution is useful because it approximates many real-world situations and it can be completely described with only two statistics, its mean and its standard deviation. Normal distributions have the following fixed relationships between distance from the mean and area under the curve:

Distance in standard deviations from the mean	Area under the curve
1.00	68.3%
1.64	90.0%
1.96	95.0%
2.00	95.4%
2.57	99.0%

Therefore, by knowing the mean (expected value) and the standard deviation, management can construct a confidence interval for a particular outcome. As an example, 95% of the outcomes will fall within the mean (expected value) plus or minus 1.96 standard deviations. The following chart illustrates this point in graphic form:

b. Once outcomes are determined and probabilities assigned, management can compute two important statistical measures—the expected value and the standard deviation. The following formula can be used to calculate the expected return:

$$\hat{k} = \sum_{i=1}^{n} k_i \, p_i$$

Where

$\hat{k}$ = the expected value of the returns

k = the returns from the various possible outcomes

p = the probabilities assigned to the possible outcomes

The standard deviation can be calculated using the following formula:

$$\sigma = \sum_{i}^{n} \left(\hat{k}_i - k\right)^2 p_i$$

c. The standard deviation provides a rough estimate of how far each outcome falls away from the mean. Generally, the larger the standard deviation, the greater the risk. However, the standard deviation as a measure

---

EXAMPLE

Assume a firm is considering investing in a project with the following possible outcomes and related probabilities.

Outcome (present value of future cash flows)	Probability of outcome	Assumption
$100,000	.2	Pessimistic
$150,000	.6	Most likely
$200,000	.2	Optimistic

The expected return would be $150,000 as calculated below.

k		p		
$100,000	×	.2	=	$20,000
$150,000	×	.6	=	90,000
$200,000	×	.2	=	40,000
$\hat{k}$			=	$150,000

The standard deviation of the expected return would be $31,623 as calculated below.

$$\sigma = \sum_{i}^{n} \left(k_i - \hat{k}\right)^2 p_i$$

$k_i - \hat{k} = (\hat{k}_i - k)$	$(\hat{k}_i - k)^2$	$p_i \times (k_i - \hat{k})^2$	$\sqrt{\text{Square root}}$
100,000 − 150,000 = −50,000	2,500,000,000	500,000,000	$\sqrt{1,000,000,000}$
150,000 − 150,000 = 0	0	0	
		500,000,000	
200,000 − 150,000 = 50,000	2,500,000,000	1,000,000,000	= $31,623

of risk has a significant limitation. Its size depends on the size of the investment. The $31,623 may seem reasonable in relation to these possible outcomes, but what if the expected value of the investment was only $60,000? The standard deviation would be quite large. Therefore, it is difficult to use the standard deviation in comparing risk for investments of different sizes.

d.   To eliminate the size difficulty analysts have developed a preferred measure, the **coefficient of variation,** which is simply the standard deviation divided by the expected value of the investment, as shown below.

$$\text{Coefficient of variation } = \frac{\sigma}{\hat{k}}$$

For the investment described above, the coefficient of variation would equal .2108 as calculated below.

$$\text{Coefficient of variation } = \frac{\$31,623}{\$150,000} = .2108$$

The coefficient of variation provides a measure of risk that is normalized for the size of the investment. Therefore, it allows comparisons across investments of varying size.

2. Risk-Adjusted Discounted Rate

a.   A popular approach to adjust for risk involves using different discount rates for proposals with different levels of risk. Using this technique, management is applying **risk-adjusted discount rates**. A project with a normal level of risk is discounted at the firm's cost of capital and projects with greater levels of risk are discounted at higher rates.

b.   Using the coefficient of variation as a risk measure, management could set different categories of risk with different risk premiums as shown in the following table:

Risk coefficient of variation	Discount rate
0.40 or less	10.0%
0.41 to 0.70	13.0%
0.71 to 1.00	16.0%
1.01 to 1.30	20.0%

Alternatively, management might simply establish qualitative measures of risk as shown below.

Risk (example)	Discount rate
Low risk (replace old equipment)	7.0%
Normal risk (add plant capacity	10.0%
Moderately above normal risk (new market)	15.0%
High risk (new product in foreign market)	20.0%

EXAMPLE

Assume that management is evaluating two alternative projects, Investment A and Investment B. Investment A has a normal level of risk and should be discounted at the firm's cost of capital, 10%. Investment B, on the other hand, has a significantly higher level of risk and management believes that 15% is the appropriate discount rate. Assume that Investment A would require an investment of $30,000, and Investment B would require an investment of $28,000. The table below presents the discounted cash flow for the two projects.

Investment A (10% discount rate)			Investment B (15% discount rate)		
Year			Year		
1	$10,000 × 0.909 =	$ 9,090	1	$5,000 × 0.870 =	$4,350
2	20,000 × 0.826 =	16,520	2	7,000 × 0.756 =	5,292
3	10,000 × 0.751 =	7,510	3	10,000 × 0.658 =	6,580
		$33,120	4	10,000 × 0.572 =	5,720
	Investment	30,000	5	10,000 × 0.497 =	4,970
	Net present value	$ 3,120			$26,912
				Investment	28,000
				Net present value	$(1,088)

As can be seen from the table, Investment A would be acceptable because it has a positive net present value. Project B would be rejected because its net present value is negative.

3. **Time-Adjusted Discount Rates**

   Management's ability to accurately forecast cash flows diminishes as they are forecast further out in time. Therefore, cash flows projected in later years of a project's life are much more uncertain than those forecasted in the early years. Economic conditions, interest rates, inflation rates, etc., may fluctuate very significantly over a number of years in the future. This would imply that the cash flows later in a project's life should be discounted at higher rates than those in the first years. The table below illustrates how this might be done.

Time period	Discount rate
Years 1 through 4	10.0%
Years 5 through 8	13.0%
Years 9 through 12	16.0%

4. **Sensitivity Analysis**

   Most capital budgeting problems require management to make many assumptions before arriving at the investment's net present value. For example, forecasting projected cash flows may require assumptions about demand, costs of production, selling price, etc. When using sensitivity analysis, managers explore the importance of these assumptions. First, managers compute the expected (most likely) results. Then, management allows one variable to change while holding the others constant, and the net present value is recomputed. By repeating the process with all the important variables, management can determine how sensitive the net present value is to changes in each major assumption. Therefore, sensitivity analysis involves exploring "what if" situations to determine the variables to which the outcomes are particularly sensitive. Management can then challenge its assumptions about these sensitive variables.

5. **Scenario Analysis**

   Scenario analysis is a more complex variation of sensitivity analysis. Instead of exploring the effects of a change in one variable, management develops a scenario that might happen if a number of related variables change. As an example, if demand is lower than expected, sales price might have to be reduced, and unit production costs might be higher. Normally, management develops a most likely scenario and one or more pessimistic and optimistic ones. This is useful in illustrating the range of the possible net present values, and therefore the risk of the investment.

6. **Simulation Models**

   Computer simulation software makes it possible to model the effects of even more economic conditions on the results of an investment project. Monte Carlo simulation uses random variables for inputs distributed around the expected means of the economic variables. As an example, management may expect short-term interest rates to be about 4% over the life of the project with a standard deviation of 1.5%. This data would be input and the program would generate simulated results using random interest rates from a probability distribution with a mean of 4% and a standard deviation of 1.5%. Therefore, instead of just developing several possible outcomes for a project, management can generate a range of outcomes with a standard deviation. Some simulation models generate probability acceptance curves for capital budgeting decisions. These curves inform management of the probabilities of having a positive net present value for the project.

7. **Decision Trees**

Most investment decisions are more complex than simply determining the net present value of future cash flows for a period of time and deciding to invest if the project has a positive net present value. Management often faces a series of decisions that may affect the value of the investment. Let's assume that management is deciding whether to introduce a new product. Management is evaluating whether to make an investment in the new product and test market it in a small geographical area. If the product sells well, management will expand the test market to a larger area. Finally, if the product does well in the larger area, management will introduce the product nationally, and there are several possible net present values from the product depending on how well it sells on a national basis. The project may be abandoned based on the results of either marketing test. A decision tree provides a visual representation of these decision points and potential decisions. The value of a decision tree is that it forces

---

EXAMPLE

Assume that a firm is considering a $1,250,000 investment in a new product. Management intends to test-market the product in a small market and if the product hits at least a moderate level of demand, management will expand the test market area. Otherwise, management will abandon the project with no value. Management believes that the probability of meeting a moderate level of sales in the initial test market is 50%. If the product sells at least a moderate level in the expanded test area, management will launch the product nationally. Otherwise, management will abandon the project with no value. Management believes that the probability of the product performing well in the expanded market area is 75%. If the product is launched nationally, management believes the following three outcomes are possible:

Possible outcome	Probability	Net present value of future cash flows
Pessimistic sales	25%	$2,000,000
Most likely sales	50%	$4,000,000
Optimistic sales	25%	$6,000,000

The decision tree below depicts this investment opportunity.

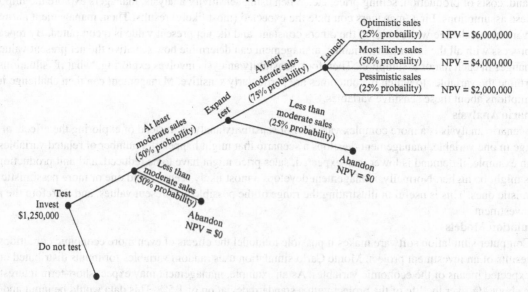

The appropriate way to calculate the expected net present value for the investment using a decision tree is to begin at the end and work backward to the initial decision from one decision point to another.

Expected net present value of future cash flows if the product is launched

Net present value of outcomes	Probability	Expected net present value
$2,000,000	25%	$ 500,000
$4,000,000	50%	2,000,000
$6,000,000	25%	1,500,000
		$4,000,000

The $4,000,000 in expected net present value in the previous step is used to calculate the expected net present value of future cash flows at the point of deciding whether to expand the market test.

Outcome	Net present value of outcomes	Probability	Expected net present value
Moderate sales (launch)	$4,000,000	75%	$3,000,000
Less than moderate sales (abandon)	0	25%	0
			$3,000,000

The $3,000,000 in expected net present value from the previous step is used to calculate the expected net present value of future cash flows at inception.

Outcome	Net present value of outcomes	Probability	Expected net present value
Moderate sales (expand test)	$3,000,000	50%	$1,500,000
Less than moderate sales (abandon)	0	50%	0
			$1,500,000

The final expected net present value after considering the initial investment is calculated below.

Expected net present value of cash flows	$1,500,000
Initial investment	1,250,000
Expected net present value of the investment	$ 250,000

Since the expected net present value is positive, the results indicate that the project should be accepted.

management to think through a series of "if then" scenarios that describe how the firm might react based on future events.

8. **Real Options**

Another technique that takes into account the dynamic nature of an investment decision is one that views an investment as a real option. This technique assumes that once management makes an initial investment, it has an option to take a number of future actions that will change the value of the investment. Therefore, the initial decision can be viewed as purchasing an option. Since net present value ignores the option value of an investment it sometimes does not provide the correct answer.

EXAMPLE

Assume that management is considering bidding on the rights to extract oil from a proven site over the next five years. The extraction costs are expected to be $22 per barrel. Oil is currently selling for $21 per barrel and management does not know whether the price will go up or down over the next five years. Using net present value with an expected price for the oil of $21, management would clearly decide not to make the investment. The expected value of the production costs, $22 per barrel, is greater than the expected sales price of the oil, $21 per barrel.

We get a different answer using the real option approach. Remember, the firm is not obligated to extract the oil, it only has an option to do so. Management knows that oil prices are very volatile and at least some time over the five-year period oil will sell for more than $22 per barrel. Therefore, the investment has value and management may reasonably bid on the rights. The net present value method understates or overstates a project's value depending on whether the investment creates or eliminates options for the firm. To correct this deficiency, the real options approach adds or subtracts an option value for the investment to get a more realistic value for the project.

$$\text{Project value} = \text{NPV} \pm \text{Option value}$$

The option value is estimated much like the option value of a financial instrument is estimated. For a particular investment, the option may be a number of types, including

a. **Expansion options**—Management may receive an option to expand the investment. An example of this option is a new product investment in which management has an option to expand production after the initial investment.
b. **Abandonment options**—Management almost always has an option to abandon a project.
c. **Follow-up investment options**—Management may receive other investment opportunities when investing in the project. The expansion option is really a subset of this type of option, but follow-up investment options are more complex. As an example, investing in a particular research and development project might offer management options for other related projects.
d. **Flexibility options**—Management may be provided with the ability to take advantages of changes in economic circumstances. As an example, an investment in machinery that can be used to produce a number of different products provides management with operating flexibility.

9. **Lease Versus Buy**

In capital budgeting, it is also important to evaluate whether it may be more advantageous to lease the asset rather than purchase it. In making a lease-versus-buy decision, management will often compare the two alternatives using discounted cash flow. Depending on the circumstances, leasing may provide an attractive alternative for a number of reasons, including

• There may be tax advantages to structuring the acquisition as a lease.
• Leasing may require less initial investment.
• Leasing will require less formal borrowing which may be restricted by loan coverants tied to the company's other debt.
• Certain leases do have to be capitalized and therefore will not require recognition of debt on the company's balance sheet.

10. **Portfolio Risk**

a. Theoretically, management should evaluate all possible combinations of investment projects to determine which set will provide the best trade-off between risk and return. This process is very similar to an investor's process of putting together a portfolio of financial investments. Conceptually, the sets of portfolios that meet management's trade-off between risk and return can be visualized as falling on an indifference curve or **risk preference function**. A risk preference function, as presented in the graph below, illustrates the **efficient frontier** for portfolio investments. Any portfolio of investments that falls on the line is an efficient portfolio (e.g., A, B, and C); it meets management's objectives with respect to the trade-off between risk and return. Any portfolio that falls to the right is not efficient.

Return (percent)

Risk level (beta coeffcient of variation)

b. When considering a new investment to be added to an existing portfolio, management must consider the effect of the investment on the overall risk of the portfolio. Whether or not an individual investment will change the overall risk of the firm depends on its relationship to other investments in the portfolio. If a casualty insurance company purchases the casualty insurance division of another firm, there is little risk reduction. Highly correlated investments do nothing to diversify away risk. Investments that are negatively correlated do reduce overall risk. Investments that are negatively correlated are those with performance that moves in opposite directions with changing economic conditions. Simply illustrated, if you match an investment that performs poorly during recessions with one that performs well during recessions, the risk of the two investments combined is much less than the risk of them individually.

c. A measure that is used to express the extent of the correlation between a set of investments is the **coefficient of correlation** from multiple regression analysis. (Multiple regression is illustrated in Module 47.) This measure takes a value of from +1 to –1. The table below illustrates the relationship between the coefficient of correlation and the extent of risk reduction for the portfolio.

Significant risk reduction		Some risk reduction		Little risk reduction	
–1	–.5	0	+.5	+1	

NOW REVIEW MULTIPLE-CHOICE QUESTIONS 28 THROUGH 85

KEY TERMS

Avoidable costs. Costs that will not continue to be incurred if a particular course of action is taken.

Cash flow hedge. A hedge of the variability in the cash flows of a recognized asset or liability or of a forecasted transaction that is attributable to a particular risk.

Committed costs. Costs related to the company's basic commitment to open its doors (e.g., depreciation, property taxes, management salaries, etc.).

Credit (default) risk. The risk that a firm will default on payment of interest or principal of a debt.

Currency swaps. Forward-based contracts in which two parties agree to exchange an obligation to pay cash flows in one currency for an obligation to pay in another currency.

Differential (incremental) cost. The difference in cost between two alternative courses of action.

Discretionary costs. Fixed costs whose level is set by current management decisions (e.g., advertising, research and development, etc.).

Fair value hedge. A hedge of the changes in fair value of a recognized asset or liability, or of an unrecognized firm commitment.

Forwards. Negotiated contracts to purchase and sell a specific quantity of a financial instrument, foreign currency, or commodity at a price specified at the origination of the contract, with delivery and payment at a specified future date.

Futures. Forward-based standardized contracts to take delivery of a specified financial instrument, foreign currency, or commodity at a specified future date or during a specified period generally at the then market price.

Interest rate risk. The risk that the value of a debt instrument will decline due to an increase in prevailing interest rates.

Interest rate swaps. Forward-based contracts in which two parties agree to swap streams of payments over a specified period of time. These contracts are often used to trade variable-rate instruments for fixed-rate instruments.

Internal rate of return method. Uses the rate of return that equates investment with future cash flows to evaluate investment alternatives.

Market risk. The risk that the value of a debt instrument will decline due to a decline in the aggregate value of all assets in the economy.

Net present value method. Uses the present value of future cash flows to evaluate investment alternatives.

Opportunity cost. The maximum income or savings (benefit) forgone by rejecting an alternative.

Options. An instrument that allows, but does not require, the holder to buy (call) or sell (put) a specific or standard commodity or financial instrument, at a specified price during a specified period of time or at a specified date.

Outlay cost. The case disbursement associated with a specific project.

Payback method. Evaluates investment alternatives based on the length of time until the investment is recaptured.

Relevant costs. Future costs that will change as a result of a specific decision.

Sensitivity analysis. Exploring the importance of various assumptions to forecasted results.

Sunk (unavoidable) costs. Committed costs that are not avoidable and are therefore irrelevant to future decisions.

Swaption. An option of a swap that provides the holder with the right to enter into a swap at a specified future date with specified terms.

Systematic risk. The risk related to market factors which cannot be diversified away.

Unsystematic risk. The risk that exists for one particular investment or a group of like investments. This risk can be diversified away.

Risk and Return

1. If an investment is expected to be held for a long period of time the preferred method of calculating the expected return is

   a. Arithmetic average.
   b. Median.
   c. Geometric average.
   d. Subjective estimate.

2. Which of the following expresses the relationship between risk and return?

   a. Inverse relationship.
   b. Direct relationship.
   c. Negative relationship.
   d. No relationship.

Portfolio Returns and Risk

3. The expected return of a portfolio is measured by the

   a. Variance.
   b. Weighted average.
   c. Standard deviation.
   d. Beta.

4. Russell Inc. is evaluating four independent investment proposals. The expected returns and standard deviations for each of these proposals are presented below.

Investment proposal	Expected returns	Standard deviation
I	16%	10%
II	14%	10%
III	20%	11%
IV	22%	15%

Which one of the investment proposals has the **least** relative level of risk?

   a. Investment I.
   b. Investment II.
   c. Investment III.
   d. Investment IV.

Items 5 and 6 are based on the following:

Natco has the following investment portfolio.

	Expected return	Investment	Beta
Investment A	15%	$100,000	1.2
Investment B	10%	$300,000	−0.5
Investment C	8%	$200,000	1.5
Investment D	8%	$100,000	−1.0

---

* CIA adapted
** CMA adapted

5. What is the expected return of the portfolio?

   a. 10.25%
   b. 9.86%
   c. 12.5%
   d. 11.35%

6. If management decided to sell one of the investments, which one should be selected?

   a. Investment A.
   b. Investment B.
   c. Investment C.
   d. Investment D.

7. A market analyst has estimated the equity beta of Modern Homes Inc. to be 1.4. This beta implies that the company's

   a. Systematic risk is lower than that of the market portfolio.
   b. Systematic risk is higher than that of the market portfolio.
   c. Unsystematic risk is higher than that of the market portfolio.
   d. Total risk is higher than that of the market portfolio.

*8. A measure that describes the risk of an investment project relative to other investments in general is the

   a. Coefficient of variation.
   b. Beta coefficient.
   c. Standard deviation.
   d. Expected return.

**9. The expected rate of return for the stock of Cornhusker Enterprises is 20%, with a standard deviation of 15%. The expected rate of return for the stock of Mustang Associates is 10%, with a standard deviation of 9%. The riskier stock is

   a. Cornhusker because its return is higher.
   b. Cornhusker because its standard deviation is higher.
   c. Mustang because its standard deviation is higher.
   d. Mustang because its coefficient of variation is higher.

**10. A US company currently has domestic operations only. It is considering an equal-size investment in either Canada or Britain. The data on expected rate of return and the risk associated with each of these proposed investments are given below.

Proposed investment	Mean return	Standard deviation
British Investment	22%	10%
Canadian Investment	28%	15%

The mean return on the company's current, domestic only, business is 20% with a standard deviation of 15%. Using the above data and the correlation coefficients, the company calculated the following portfolio risk and return (based on a ratio of 50% US domestic operations and 50% international operations).

Proposed investment	Mean return	Standard deviation
US and Britain	21%	3%
US and Canada	24%	15%

The company plans to select the optimal combination of countries based on risk and return for the domestic and international investments taken together. Because the company is new to the international business environment, it is relatively risk averse. Based on the above data, which one of the following alternatives provides the best risk-adjusted return to the firm?

a. Undertake the British investment.
b. Undertake the Canadian investment.
c. Do not undertake either investment.
d. Unable to determine based on data given.

Interest Rates

*11. According to market segmentation theory, long-term interest rates are determined primarily by

a. Commercial banks.
b. Savings institutions.
c. Life insurance companies.
d. Individual investors.

12. Questo borrowed $100,000 from a bank on a one-year 8% term loan, with interest compounded quarterly. What is the effective annual interest rate on the loan?

a. 8%
b. 8.24%
c. 2%
d. 9.12%

13. The yield curve shown below implies that the

Years to maturity

a. Credit risk premium of corporate bonds has increased.
b. Credit risk premium of municipal bonds has increased.
c. Long-term interest rates have a higher annualized yield than short-term rates.
d. Short-term interest rates have a higher annualized yield than long-term rates.

14. Short-term interest rates are

a. Usually lower than long-term rates.
b. Usually higher than long-term rates.
c. Lower than long-term rates during periods of high inflation only.
d. Not significantly related to long-term rates.

* 15. According to the expectations theory, if the yield curve on the New York money market is upward sloping while that on the Tokyo money market is downward sloping, then inflation in

a. The United States is expected to decrease.
b. The United States is expected to remain constant.
c. Japan is expected to decrease.
d. Japan is expected to remain constant.

* 16. According to the expectations theory of the term structure of interest rates, if inflation is expected to increase, the yield curve is

a. Humped, with an upward slope that peaks and then turns downward.
b. Downward sloping.
c. Upward sloping.
d. Flat.

* 17. A curve on a graph with the rate of return on the vertical axis and time on the horizontal axis depicts

a. The internal rate of return on an investment.
b. A yield curve showing the term structure of interest rates.
c. The present value of future returns, discounted at the marginal cost of capital, minus the present value of the cost.
d. A series of payments of a fixed amount for a specified number of years.

** 18. The return paid for the use of borrowed capital is referred to as

a. Cash dividends.
b. Stock dividends.
c. Interest.
d. Principal payment.

Derivatives and Hedging

19. Strobel Company has a large amount of variable rate financing due in one year. Management is concerned about the possibility of increases in short-term rates. Which of the following would be an effective way of hedging this risk?

a. Buy Treasury notes in the futures market.
b. Sell Treasury notes in the futures market.
c. Buy an option to purchase Treasury bonds.
d. Sell an option to purchase Treasury bonds.

20. In valuing interest rate swaps, the zero-coupon method uses all of the following variables **except**

a. Discount rate.
b. Timing of cash flows as specified by the contract.
c. Estimated net settlement cash flows.
d. Underlying assets.

21. Which of the following techniques is used to value stock options?

a. Black-Scholes method.
b. Zero-coupon method.
c. Weighted-average method.
d. Expected earnings method.

22. Which of the following risks relates to the possibility that a derivative might **not** be effective at hedging a particular asset?

a. Credit risk.
b. Legal risk.
c. Market risk.
d. Basis risk.

**23. An American importer of English clothing has contracted to pay an amount fixed in British pounds three months from now. If the importer worries that the US dollar may depreciate sharply against the British pound in the interim, it would be well advised to

a. Buy pounds in the forward exchange market.
b. Sell pounds in the forward exchange market.
c. Buy dollars in the futures market.
d. Sell dollars in the futures market.

**24. When a firm finances each asset with a financial instrument of the same approximate maturity as the life of the asset, it is applying

a. Working capital management.
b. Return maximization.
c. Financial leverage.
d. A hedging approach.

25. Banner Electronics has subsidiaries in several international locations and is concerned about its exposure to foreign exchange risk. In countries where currency values are likely to fall, Banner should encourage all of the following **except

a. Granting trade credit wherever possible.
b. Investing excess cash in inventory or other real assets.
c. Purchasing materials and supplies on a trade credit basis.
d. Borrowing local currency funds if an appropriate interest rate can be obtained.

*26. A company has recently purchased some stock of a competitor as part of a long-term plan to acquire the competitor. However, it is somewhat concerned that the market price of this stock could decrease over the short run. The company could hedge against the possible decline in the stock's market price by

a. Purchasing a call option on that stock.
b. Purchasing a put option on that stock.
c. Selling a put option on that stock.
d. Obtaining a warrant option on that stock.

*27. The risk of loss because of fluctuations in the relative value of foreign currencies is called

a. Expropriation risk.
b. Sovereign risk.
c. Multinational beta.
d. Exchange rate risk.

Present Value

**28. If a $1,000 bond sells for $1,125, which of the following statements are correct?

I. The market rate of interest is greater than the coupon rate on the bond.
II. The coupon rate on the bond is greater than the market rate of interest.
III. The coupon rate and the market rate are equal.
IV. The bond sells at a premium.
V. The bond sells at a discount.

a. I and IV.
b. I and V.
c. II and IV.
d. II and V.

29. Para Co. is reviewing the following data relating to an energy saving investment proposal:

Cost	$50,000
Residual value at the end of 5 years	10,000
Present value of an annuity of 1 at 12% for 5 years	3.60
Present value of 1 due in 5 years at 12%	0.57

What would be the annual savings needed to make the investment realize a 12% yield?

a. $8,189
b. $11,111
c. $12,306
d. $13,889

30. On December 31, 2013, Jet Co. received a $10,000 note receivable from Maxx, Inc. in exchange for services rendered. Interest is calculated on the outstanding balance at the interest rate of 3% compounded annually and payable at maturity. The note from Maxx, Inc. is due in five years. The market interest rate for similar notes on December 31, 2013, was 8%. The compound interest factors are as follows:

Future value of $1 due in nine months at 3%	1.0225
Future value of $1 due in five years at 3%	1.1593
Present value of $1 due in nine months at 8%	.944
Present value of $1 due in five years at 8%	.680

At what amounts should this note receivable be reported in Jet's December 31, 2013 balance sheet?

a. $6,800
b. $7,820
c. $6,200
d. $7,883

---

* CIA adapted

** CMA adapted

31. The market price of a bond issued at a discount is the present value of its principal amount at the market (effective) rate of interest

    a. Less the present value of all future interest payments at the market (effective) rate of interest.

    b. Less the present value of all future interest payments at the rate of interest stated on the bond.

    c. Plus the present value of all future interest payments at the market (effective) rate of interest.

    d. Plus the present value of all future interest payments at the rate of interest stated on the bond.

Capital Budgeting

32. At what stage of the capital budgeting process would management **most** likely apply present value techniques?

    a. Identification stage.

    b. Search stage.

    c. Selection stage.

    d. Financing stage.

Capital Budgeting: Payback and Discounted Payback

33. How is the discounted payback method an improvement over the payback method in evaluating investment projects?

    a. It involves better estimates of cash flows.

    b. It considers the overall profitability of the investment.

    c. It considers the time value of money.

    d. It considers the variability of the return.

34. The capital budgeting technique known as payback period uses

	Depreciation expense	Time value of money
a.	Yes	Yes
b.	Yes	No
c.	No	No
d.	No	Yes

35. Which of the following is a strength of the payback method?

    a. It considers cash flows for all years of the project.

    b. It distinguishes the source of cash inflows.

    c. It considers the time value of money.

    d. It is easy to understand.

36. Tam Co. is negotiating for the purchase of equipment that would cost $100,000, with the expectation that $20,000 per year could be saved in after-tax cash costs if the equipment were acquired. The equipment's estimated useful life is ten years, with no residual value, and would be depreciated by the straight-line method. The payback period is

    a. 4.0 years.

    b. 4.4 years.

    c. 4.5 years.

    d. 5.0 years.

Capital Budgeting: Accounting Rate of Return

37. All of the following capital budgeting analysis techniques use cash flows as the primary basis for the calculation **except for the

    a. Net present value.

    b. Payback period.

    c. Discounted payback period.

    d. Accounting rate of return.

38. Which of the following is an advantage of the accounting rate of return method of evaluating investment returns?

    a. The technique considers depreciation.

    b. The technique corresponds to the measure that is often used to evaluate performance.

    c. The technique considers the time value of money.

    d. The technique considers the risk of the investment.

39. Tam Co. is negotiating for the purchase of equipment that would cost $100,000, with the expectation that $20,000 per year could be saved in after-tax cash costs if the equipment were acquired. The equipment's estimated useful life is ten years, with no residual value, and it would be depreciated by the straight-line method. Tam's predetermined minimum desired rate of return is 12%. The present value of an annuity of 1 at 12% for ten periods is 5.65. The present value of 1 due in ten periods at 12% is .322. Accrual accounting rate of return based on the initial investment is

    a. 30%

    b. 20%

    c. 12%

    d. 10%

40. Lin Co. is buying machinery it expects will increase average annual operating income by $40,000. The initial increase in the required investment is $60,000, and the average increase in required investment is $30,000. To compute the accrual accounting rate of return, what amount should be used as the numerator in the ratio?

    a. $20,000

    b. $30,000

    c. $40,000

    d. $60,000

41. The capital budgeting technique known as accounting rate of return uses

	Revenue over life of project	Depreciation expense
a.	No	Yes
b.	No	No
c.	Yes	No
d.	Yes	Yes

Capital Budgeting: Net Present Value

**42. If an investment project has a profitability index of 1.15, then the

    a. Project's internal rate of return is 15%.

**CMA adapted

b. Project's cost of capital is greater than its internal rate of return.
c. Project's internal rate of return exceeds its net present value.
d. Net present value of the project is positive.

**43. The net present value (NPV) method of investment project analysis assumes that the project's cash flows are reinvested at the

a. Computed internal rate of return.
b. Risk-free interest rate.
c. Discount rate used in the NPV calculation.
d. Firm's accounting rate of return.

44. Kern Co. is planning to invest in a two-year project that is expected to yield cash flows from operations, net of income taxes, of $50,000 in the first year and $80,000 in the second year. Kern requires an internal rate of return of 15%. The present value of $1 for one period at 15% is 0.870 and for two periods at 15% is 0.756. The future value of $1 for one period at 15% is 1.150 and for two periods at 15% is 1.323. The maximum that Kern should invest immediately is

a. $81,670
b. $103,980
c. $130,000
d. $163,340

45. Pole Co. is investing in a machine with a three-year life. The machine is expected to reduce annual cash operating costs by $30,000 in each of the first two years and by $20,000 in year three. Present values of an annuity of $1 at 14% are

Period 1	0.88
2	1.65
3	2.32

Using a 14% cost of capital, what is the present value of these future savings?

a. $59,600
b. $60,800
c. $62,900
d. $69,500

46. For the next two years, a lease is estimated to have an operating net cash inflow of $7,500 per annum, before adjusting for $5,000 per annum tax basis lease amortization, and a 40% tax rate. The present value of an ordinary annuity of $1 per year at 10% for two years is 1.74. What is the lease's after-tax present value using a 10% discount factor?

a. $2,610
b. $4,350
c. $9,570
d. $11,310

47. A project's net present value, ignoring income tax considerations, is normally affected by the

a. Proceeds from the sale of the asset to be replaced.
b. Carrying amount of the asset to be replaced by the project.
c. Amount of annual depreciation on the asset to be replaced.
d. Amount of annual depreciation on fixed assets used directly on the project.

48. The discount rate (hurdle rate of return) must be determined in advance for the

a. Payback period method.
b. Time-adjusted rate of return method.
c. Net present value method.
d. Internal rate of return method.

Capital Budgeting: Internal Rate of Return

**49. The internal rate of return is the

a. Rate of interest that equates the present value of cash outflows and the present value of cash in-flows.
b. Minimum acceptable rate of return for a proposed investment.
c. Risk-adjusted rate of return.
d. Required rate of return.

**50. As used in capital budgeting analysis, the internal rate of return uses which of the following items in its computation?

	Net incremental investment	Incremental average operating income	Net annual cash flows
a.	Yes	No	Yes
b.	Yes	Yes	No
c.	No	No	Yes
d.	No	Yes	Yes

**51. An organization is using capital budgeting techniques to compare two independent projects. It could accept one, both, or neither of the projects. Which of the following statements is true about the use of net present value (NPV) and internal rate of return (IRR) methods for evaluating these two projects?

a. NPV and IRR criteria will always lead to the same accept or reject decision for two independent projects.
b. If the first project's IRR is higher than the organization's cost or capital, the first project will be accepted but the second project will not.
c. If the NPV criterion leads to accepting or rejecting the first project, one cannot predict whether the IRR criterion will lead to accepting or rejecting the first project.
d. If the NPV criterion leads to accepting the first project, the IRR criterion will never lead to accepting the first project.

Items 52 and 53 are based on the following information:

A firm, with an 18% cost of capital, is considering the following projects to begin on January 1, 2011, with a single cash inflow on December 31, 2015:

	Jan. 1, 2011, Cash outflow (000's omitted)	Dec. 31, 2015, Cash inflow (000's omitted)	Project internal rate of return
Project A	$3,500	$7,040	15%
Project B	4,000	9,950	?

Present Value of $1 Due at End of "N" Periods

N	12%	14%	15%	16%	18%	20%	22%
4	.6355	.5921	.5718	.5523	.5158	.4823	.4230
5	.5674	.5194	.4972	.4761	.4371	.4019	.3411
6	.5066	.4556	.4323	.4104	.3704	.3349	.2751

52. Using the net present value method, Project A's net present value is

- a. $316,920
- b. $0
- c. $(265,460)
- d. $(316,920)

53. Project B's internal rate of return is closest to

- a. 15%
- b. 18%
- c. 20%
- d. 22%

Items 54 thru 57 are based on the following information:

An organization has four investment proposals with the following costs and expected cash inflows:

		Expected Cash Inflows		
Project	Cost	End of year 1	End of year 2	End of year 3
A	Unknown	$10,000	$10,000	$10,000
B	$20,000	5,000	10,000	15,000
C	25,000	15,000	10,000	5,000
D	30,000	20,000	Unknown	20,000

Additional information

Discount rate	Number of periods	Present value of $1 due at the end of n periods [PVIF]	Present value of an annuity of $1 per period for n periods [PVIFA]
5%	1	0.9524	0.9524
5%	2	0.9070	1.8594
5%	3	0.8638	2.7232
10%	1	0.9091	0.9091
10%	2	0.8264	1.7355
10%	3	0.7513	2.4869
15%	1	0.8696	0.8696
15%	2	0.7561	1.6257
15%	3	0.6575	2.2832

54. If Project A has an internal rate of return (IRR) of 15%, then it has a cost of

- a. $8,696
- b. $22,832
- c. $24,869
- d. $27,232

55. If the discount rate is 10%, the net present value (NPV) of Project B is

- a. $4,079
- b. $6,789
- c. $9,869
- d. $39,204

56. The payback period of Project C is

- a. 0 years.
- b. 1 year.
- c. 2 years.
- d. 3 years.

57. If the discount rate is 5% and the discounted payback period of Project D is exactly two years, then the year two cash inflow for Project D is

- a. $5,890
- b. $10,000
- c. $12,075
- d. $14,301

58. Tam Co. is negotiating for the purchase of equipment that would cost $100,000, with the expectation that $20,000 per year could be saved in after-tax cash costs if the equipment were acquired. The equipment's estimated useful life is ten years, with no residual value, and would be depreciated by the straight-line method. Tam's predetermined minimum desired rate of return is 12%. Present value of an annuity of 1 at 12% for ten periods is 5.65. Present value of 1 due in ten periods at 12% is .322. In estimating the internal rate of return, the factors in the table of present values of an annuity should be taken from the columns closest to

- a. 0.65
- b. 1.30
- c. 5.00
- d. 5.65

59. How are the following used in the calculation of the internal rate of return of a proposed project? Ignore income tax considerations.

	Residual sales value of project	Depreciation expense
a.	Exclude	Include
b.	Include	Include
c.	Exclude	Exclude
d.	Include	Exclude

60. Neu Co. is considering the purchase of an investment that has a positive net present value based on Neu's 12% hurdle rate. The internal rate of return would be

- a. 0
- b. 12%

c. > 12%

d. < 12%

61. Bennet Inc. uses the net present value method to evaluate capital projects. Bennet's required rate of return is 10%. Bennet is considering two mutually exclusive projects for its manufacturing business. Both projects require an initial outlay of $120,000 and are expected to have a useful life of four years. The projected after-tax cash flows associated with these projects are as follows:

Year	Project X	Project Y
1	$40,000	$10,000
2	40,000	20,000
3	40,000	60,000
4	40,000	80,000
Total	$160,000	$170,000

Assuming adequate funds are available, which of the following project options would you recommend that Bennet's management undertake?

a. Project X only.

b. Project Y only.

c. Projects X and Y.

d. Neither project.

Items 62 thru 64 are based on the following information:

Capital Invest Inc. uses a 12% hurdle rate for all capital expenditures and has done the following analysis for four projects for the upcoming year.

	Project 1	Project 2	Project 3	Project 4
Initial capital outlay	$200,000	$298,000	$248,000	$272,000
Annual net cash inflows				
Year 1	$65,000	$100,000	$80,000	$ 95,000
Year 2	70,000	135,000	95,000	125,000
Year 3	80,000	90,000	90,000	90,000
Year 4	40,000	65,000	80,000	60,000
Net present value	(3,798)	4,276	14,064	14,662
Profitability index	98%	101%	106%	105%
Internal rate of return	11%	13%	14%	15%

** 62. Which project(s) should Capital Invest Inc. undertake during the upcoming year assuming it has no budget restrictions?

a. All of the projects.

b. Projects 1, 2, and 3.

c. Projects 2, 3, and 4.

d. Projects 1, 3, and 4.

** 63. Which project(s) should Capital Invest Inc. undertake during the upcoming year if it has only $600,000 of funds available?

a. Projects 1 and 3.

b. Projects 2, 3, and 4.

c. Projects 2 and 3.

d. Projects 3 and 4.

**64. Which project(s) should Capital Invest Inc. undertake during the upcoming year if it has only $300,000 of capital funds available?

a. Project 1.

b. Projects 2, 3, and 4.

c. Projects 3 and 4.

d. Project 3.

Determining Future Cash Flows

**65. A depreciation tax shield is

a. An after-tax cash outflow.

b. A reduction in income taxes.

c. The cash provided by recording depreciation.

d. The expense caused by depreciation.

**66. Andrew Corporation is evaluating a capital investment that would result in $30,000 higher contribution margin benefit with increased annual personnel costs of $20,000. In calculating the net present value of benefits and costs, income taxes would:

a. Decrease both the amount of the benefits and costs.

b. Have no net effect on either the amount of the benefits or costs.

c. Decrease the amount of the benefits but increase the amount of the costs.

d. Increase the amount of the benefits but decrease the amount of the costs.

67. Buff Co. is considering replacing an old machine with a new machine. Which of the following items is economically relevant to Buff's decision? (Ignore income tax considerations.)

	Carrying amount of old machine	Disposal value of new machine
a.	Yes	No
b.	No	Yes
c.	No	No
d.	Yes	Yes

Items 68 and 69 are based on the following information:

Assume that Straper Industries is considering investing in a project with the following characteristics:

Initial investment	$500,000
Additional investment in working capital	10,000
Cash flows before income taxes for years 1 through 5	140,000
Yearly tax depreciation	90,000
Terminal value of investment	50,000
Cost of capital	10%
Present value of $1 received after 5 years discounted at 10%	.621
Present value of an ordinary annuity of $1 for 5 years at 10%	3.791
Marginal tax rate	30%
Investment life	5 years

Assume that all cash flows come at the end of the year.

*68. What is the amount of the after-tax cash flows in year 2?

a. $140,000
b. $125,000
c. $98,000
d. $70,000

69. What is the net present value of the investment?

a. $175,000
b. $58,000
c. $1,135
d. $(12,340)

Considering Risk in Capital Budgeting

**70. The Madison Company has decided to introduce a new product. The company estimates that there is a 30% probability that the product will contribute $700,000 to profits, a 30% probability that it will contribute $200,000, and a 40% probability that the contribution will be a negative $400,000. The expected contribution of the new product is

a. $500,000
b. $110,000
c. $166,667
d. $380,000

**71. Philip Enterprises, distributor of compact disks (CDs) is developing its budgeted cost of goods sold for 2013. Philip has developed the following range of sales estimates and associated probabilities for the year.

Sales Estimate	Probability
$ 60,000	25%
85,000	40%
100,000	35%

Philip's cost of goods sold averages 80% of sales. What is the expected value of Philip's 2013 budgeted cost of goods sold?

a. $85,000
b. $84,000
c. $68,000
d. $67,200

72. Which of the following capital budgeting techniques would allow management to justify investing in a project that could not be justified currently by using techniques that focus on expected cash flows?

a. Real options.
b. Net present value.
c. Accounting rate of return.
d. Internal rate of return.

Items 73 and 74 are based on the following information:

Assume that Reston Corp. is considering investing in a project. To evaluate the project, management has developed the following cash flow projections and related probabilities.

Present value of future cash flows	Probability of occurrence
$200,000	.4
$500,000	.3
$800,000	.3

73. What is the expected return for the project?

a. $750,000
b. $500,000
c. $470,000
d. $400,000

74. Assume that the standard deviation of the returns for the project is $150,000. What is the coefficient of variation for the project?

a. .2345
b. .3191
c. .4256
d. 1.10

75. Which of the following techniques recognizes that management often faces a series of decisions that may affect the value of an investment?

a. Probability analysis.
b. Risk-adjusted discount rate.
c. Decision tree.
d. Sensitivity analysis.

76. Which of the following is **not** a technique for considering the risk of an investment?

a. Probability analysis.
b. Risk-adjusted discount rate.
c. Simulation techniques.
d. Internal rate of return.

*77. The level of risk that concerns investors who supply capital to a diversified company is

a. Project risk (beta).
b. Pure play risk (beta).
c. The standard deviation of project risk (betas).
d. The weighted-average of project risk (betas).

*78. A company uses portfolio theory to develop its investment portfolio. If the company wishes to obtain optimal risk reduction through the portfolio effect, it should make its next investment in

a. An investment that correlates negatively to the current portfolio holdings.
b. An investment that is uncorrelated to the current portfolio holdings.
c. An investment that is highly correlated to the current portfolio holdings.
d. An investment that is perfectly correlated to the current portfolio holdings.

79. During 2012, Deet Corp. experienced the following power outages:

---

* CIA adapted
** CMA adapted

Number of outages per month	Number of months
0	3
1	2
2	4
3	3
	12

Each power outage results in out-of-pocket costs of $400. For $500 per month, Deet can lease an auxiliary generator to provide power during outages. If Deet leases an auxiliary generator in 2013 the estimated savings (or additional expenditures) for 2013 would be

a. $(3,600)
b. $(1,200)
c. $1,600
d. $1,900

80. Polo Co. requires higher rates of return for projects with a life span greater than five years. Projects extending beyond five years must earn a higher specified rate of return. Which of the following capital budgeting techniques can readily accommodate this requirement?

	Internal rate of return	Net present value
a.	Yes	No
b.	No	Yes
c.	No	No
d.	Yes	Yes

81. Under frost-free conditions, Cal Cultivators expects its strawberry crop to have a $60,000 market value. An unprotected crop subject to frost has an expected market value of $40,000. If Cal protects the strawberries against frost, then the market value of the crop is still expected to be $60,000 under frost-free conditions and $90,000 if there is a frost. What must be the probability of a frost for Cal to be indifferent to spending $10,000 for frost protection?

a. .167
b. .200
c. .250
d. .333

82. Dough Distributors has decided to increase its daily muffin purchases by 100 boxes. A box of muffins costs $2 and sells for $3 through regular stores. Any boxes not sold through regular stores are sold through Dough's thrift store for $1. Dough assigns the following probabilities to selling additional boxes:

Additional sales	Probability
60	.6
100	.4

What is the expected value of Dough's decision to buy 100 additional boxes of muffins?

a. $28
b. $40
c. $52
d. $68

83. Which tool would **most** likely be used to determine the best course of action under conditions of uncertainty?

a. Cost-volume-profit analysis.
b. Expected value (EV).
c. Program evaluation and review technique (PERT).
d. Scattergraph method.

84. To assist in an investment decision, Gift Co. selected the most likely sales volume from several possible outcomes. Which of the following attributes would that selected sales volume reflect?

a. The midpoint of the range.
b. The median.
c. The greatest probability.
d. The expected value.

85. Probability (risk) analysis is

a. Used only for situations involving five or fewer possible outcomes.
b. Used only for situations in which the summation of probability weights is greater than one.
c. An extension of sensitivity analysis.
d. Incompatible with sensitivity analysis.

Multiple-Choice Answers and Explanations

Answers

1. c __ __	19. b __ __	37. d __ __	55. a __ __	73. c __ __
2. b __ __	20. d __ __	38. b __ __	56. c __ __	74. b __ __
3. b __ __	21. a __ __	39. d __ __	57. c __ __	75. c __ __
4. c __ __	22. d __ __	40. c __ __	58. c __ __	76. d __ __
5. b __ __	23. a __ __	41. d __ __	59. d __ __	77. d __ __
6. c __ __	24. d __ __	42. d __ __	60. c __ __	78. a __ __
7. b __ __	25. a __ __	43. c __ __	61. a __ __	79. c __ __
8. b __ __	26. b __ __	44. b __ __	62. c __ __	80. d __ __
9. d __ __	27. d __ __	45. c __ __	63. d __ __	81. b __ __
10. a __ __	28. c __ __	46. d __ __	64. d __ __	82. c __ __
11. c __ __	29. c __ __	47. a __ __	65. b __ __	83. b __ __
12. b __ __	30. d __ __	48. c __ __	66. a __ __	84. c __ __
13. c __ __	31. c __ __	49. a __ __	67. b __ __	85. c __ __
14. a __ __	32. c __ __	50. a __ __	68. b __ __	
15. c __ __	33. c __ __	51. a __ __	69. c __ __	
16. c __ __	34. d __ __	52. c __ __	70. b __ __	
17. b __ __	35. d __ __	53. c __ __	71. d __ __	1st: __/85 = __%
18. c __ __	36. d __ __	54. b __ __	72. a __ __	2nd: __/85 = __%

Explanations

1. (c) The requirement is to identify the preferred method of calculating the expected return for an investment that is expected to be held for a long period of time. Answer (c) is correct because the geometric average depicts the compound annual return earned by the investor. This method is preferred for evaluating long-term investments. Answer (a) is incorrect because the arithmetic average does not provide as good a measure as the geometric average especially when the returns vary through time. Answer (b) is incorrect because the median is a poor measure of return. Answer (d) is incorrect because a subjective estimate is not as good as a mathematical average.

2. (b) The requirement is to identify the relationship between risk and return. Answer (b) is correct because there is a direct (positive) relationship between risk and return. Higher returns are associated with higher degrees of risk. Answers (a) and (c) are incorrect because an inverse (negative) relationship would imply that higher returns are associated with less risk. Answer (d) is incorrect because there is a direct relationship between risk and returns.

3. (b) The requirement is to identify the measure of the expected return of a portfolio. Answer (b) is correct because the weighted-average of the expected returns of the assets in the portfolio is equal to the expected return of the portfolio. Answers (a), (c), and (d) are incorrect because they are all measures of variability.

4. (c) The requirement is to identify the proposal that has the least amount of relative risk. Relative risk is measured as the ratio of the standard deviation of the return to the expected return. Therefore, answer (c) is correct because this investment's relative risk is .550 (11%/20%). Answers (a), (b),

and (d) are incorrect because they have higher measures of relative risk.

5. (b) The requirement is to calculate the expected return of the portfolio. Answer (b) is correct because the expected return of the portfolio is the weighted-average of the individual investments. The expected return is equal to $9.68\% = [15\% \times (\$100,000 \div 700,000)] + [10\% \times (\$300,000 \div 700,000)] + (8\% \times \$200,000 \div 700,000)] + [8\% \times (\$100,000 \div 700,000)]$. Answer (a) is incorrect because this is the unweighted return for the portfolio.

6. (c) The requirement is to select the investment that should be sold. Answer (c) is correct because Investment C has a low return and the highest positive beta. The positive beta indicates that its return is highly correlated with the return of the portfolio and, therefore, it increases the risk of the portfolio. Answer (a) is incorrect because Investment A has the highest return and its beta is not as high as Investment C. Answer (b) is incorrect because it has a higher return than Investment C and its beta is negative. Therefore, Investment B reduces the overall risk of the portfolio. Answer (d) is incorrect because Investment D has a large negative beta and therefore, it reduces the overall risk of the portfolio.

7. (b) The requirement is to interpret an equity beta of 1.4. Beta is a measure of systematic risk of the investment. Answer (b) is correct because a beta of greater than 1 means the investment's systematic risk is higher than that of the market portfolio. Answer (a) is incorrect because the beta would have to be less than 1 for this relationship to exist. Answers (c) and (d) are incorrect because beta focuses on systematic risk.

8. (b) The requirement is to identify the measure of the risk of an investment relative to other investments in general. Answer (b) is correct because the beta coefficient of an individual stock is the correlation between the stock's price and the price of the overall market. As an example, if the market goes up 5% and the individual stock's price, on average, goes up 10%, the stock's beta coefficient is 2.0. Answer (a) is incorrect because the coefficient of variation compares the risk of the stock to its expected return. Answer (c) is incorrect because the standard deviation measures the dispersion of the individual stock's returns. Answer (d) is incorrect because the expected return does not measure risk.

9. (d) The requirement is to identify the riskier stock. Answer (d) is correct because the coefficient of variation for Mustang is higher. The coefficient of variation provides a measure of the relative variability of investments. It is calculated by dividing the standard deviation of the investment by its expected return. The coefficient of variation for Cornhusker is .75 (.15 ÷ .20) and the coefficient of variation for Mustang is .9 (0.09 ÷ .10). Answer (a) is incorrect because a higher return does not always mean higher risk. Answer (b) is incorrect because the higher standard deviation must be viewed relative to the expected return. Answer (c) is incorrect because Mustang's coefficient of variation is higher than Cornhusker's coefficient of variation.

10. (a) The requirement is to identify the alternative that provides the **best** risk-adjusted rate of return. The correct answer is (a) because expanding the investment into Britain would increase the portfolio return from 20% to 21%, and, at the same time, reduce risk as measured by the standard deviation. Answer (b) is incorrect because undertaking the Canadian investment would increase the return from 20% to 24% without any reduction in the risk. Answer (c) is incorrect because the investment into Britain increases portfolio return while reducing risk. Answer (d) is incorrect because the answer can be determined.

11. (c) The requirement is to identify the determinate of long-term interest rates under market segmentation theory. Market segmentation theory states that the Treasury securities market is divided into market segments by the various financial institutions investing in the market. Answer (c) is correct because life insurance companies prefer long-term securities because of the nature of their commitments to policyholders. Answer (a) is incorrect because commercial banks prefer securities with short maturities. Answer (b) is incorrect because savings institutions prefer intermediate-term maturities. Answer (d) is incorrect because individual investors do not significantly affect the market.

12. (b) The requirement is to calculate the effective annual interest rate. Answer (b) is correct because the effective interest rate (EAR) is calculated as follows:

$$EAR = \left(1 + \frac{r}{m}\right)^m - 1$$

$$= \left(1 + \frac{.08}{4}\right)^4 - 1$$

$$= 8.24\%$$

Where

r = Stated interest rate
m = Compounding frequency

Answer (a) is incorrect because it is the stated interest rate. Answer (c) is incorrect because it is the interest rate for three months.

13. (c) The requirement is to interpret the yield curve. Answer (c) is correct because the term structure of interest rates is the relationship between yield to maturity and time to maturity. This relationship is depicted by a yield curve. The normal expectation is for long-term investments to pay higher rates because of their higher interest rate risk. Answers (a) and (b) are incorrect because the yield curve does not reflect the credit risk premium of bonds. Answer (d) is incorrect because long-term interest rates are normally higher than short-term rates.

14. (a) The requirement is to identify the true statement about short-term interest rates. Answer (a) is correct because there is less risk involved in the short run and investors are willing to accept lower rates on short-term investments because of their liquidity. Short-term rates have ordinarily been lower than long-term rates. Answer (b) is incorrect because short-term rates are typically lower than long-term rates. Answer (c) is incorrect because short-term rates are more likely to be greater than long-term rates if current levels of inflation are high. Answer (d) is incorrect because long-term rates may be viewed as short-term rates adjusted by a risk factor.

15. (c) The requirement is to predict the effect of inflation on the yield curve. The correct answer is (c) because a downward sloping yield curve indicates that long-term rates are lower than short-term rates. For this to be the case investors would have to be expecting a decline in the rate of inflation. Answers (a) and (b) are incorrect because an upward sloping yield curve would mean that investors are expecting an increase in inflation. Answer (d) is incorrect because a downward sloping yield curve would imply that investors are expecting inflation to decline.

16. (c) The requirement is to describe the effect on the yield curve of an expectation of an increase in inflation. Answer (c) is correct because if inflation is expected to increase, interest rates are expected to rise and therefore, intermediate-term and long-term rates will be higher than short-term rates. Answer (a) is incorrect because a humped yield curve is not consistent with expectations theory. Answer (b) is incorrect because a downward sloping curve would imply an expectation that inflation will decrease. Answer (d) is incorrect because a flat yield curve would imply inflation is expected to remain constant.

17. (b) The requirement is to identify a graph that depicts the rate of return on the vertical axis and time on the horizontal axis. Answer (b) is correct because such a graph presents a yield curve that shows the term structure of interest rates. The term structure of interest rates refers to how interest rates vary by time to maturity. Answer (a) is incorrect because internal rate of return is the interest rate that equates the present value of the future cash flows from an investment with its initial cost. Answer (c) is incorrect because it is the definition of net present value. Answer (d) is incorrect because it defines an annuity.

18. (c) The requirement is to identify the return paid for the use of borrowed capital. Answer (c) is correct because the return paid for the use of borrowed funds is called interest. Answers (a) and (b) are incorrect because dividends are paid to equity holders. Answer (d) is incorrect because the principal payment represents the return of capital.

19. (b) The requirement is to identify the appropriate hedging strategy. Answer (b) is correct because by selling Treasury notes for delivery in the future, the company can hedge increases in short-term interest rates. If interest rates increase, the value of the Treasury notes will decline, resulting in a gain to the company. If the hedge is effective, the gain will offset the increase in the company's interest costs. Answer (a) is incorrect because buying Treasury notes would put the company at greater risk with respect to increases in interest rates. Answer (c) is incorrect because buying an option on Treasury bonds would hedge a decline in interest rates. Answer (d) is incorrect because an option allows the purchaser the option, but not the obligation, to purchase Treasury bonds. Therefore, selling options would not be effective at hedging increases in interest rates.

20. (d) The requirement is to identify the variable that is **not** used in valuing an interest rate swap. Answer (d) is correct because the underlying assets are not relevant. An interest rate swap involves an exchange of cash flows, usually the exchange of fixed cash flows for variable cash flows. Answer (a), (b), and (c) are all incorrect because they are all variables that are used in the zero-coupon method.

21. (a) The requirement is to identify the technique used to value stock options. Answer (a) is correct because the Black-Scholes option-pricing model is a commonly used option-pricing model. Answer (b) is incorrect because the zero-coupon method is used to value interest rate swaps. Answer (c) is incorrect because the weighted-average method is used to determine the expected return of a portfolio.

22. (d) The requirement is to identify the risk that relates to the possibility that a derivative might not be effective at hedging a particular asset. Answer (d) is correct because basis risk is the risk of loss from ineffective hedging activities. Answer (a) is incorrect because credit risk is the risk of loss as a result of the counterparty to the derivative agreement failing to meet its obligation. Answer (b) is incorrect because market risk is the risk of loss from adverse changes in market factors. Answer (c) is incorrect because legal risk is the risk of loss from a legal or regulatory action that invalidates the derivative agreement.

23. (a) The requirement is to identify how a company may hedge exchange risk. Answer (a) is the correct answer because by buying pounds today with a forward exchange contract, the firm protects itself against depreciation in the value of the dollar in relation to the pound. Answer (b) is incorrect because selling pounds would put the firm in greater risk with respect to appreciation of the pound. Answers (c) and (d) are incorrect because buying and selling dollars would do nothing to hedge the value of the pound.

24. (d) The requirement is to identify the strategy of matching maturities. Answer (d) is correct because the strategy of

matching asset and liability maturities is referred to as a hedging approach. The strategy helps ensure that funds are generated from the assets when the related liabilities are due. Answer (a) is incorrect because working capital management involves managing current assets and current liabilities. Answer (b) is incorrect because return maximization is a more aggressive strategy than maturity matching. Answer (c) is incorrect because financial leverage is the relationship between debt and equity financing.

25. (a) The requirement is to identify the incorrect strategy when currency values are expected to fall. Answer (a) is correct because granting credit means that Banner will be paid back with currency that has less value. Answer (b) is incorrect because investing in assets will hedge a decrease in currency value. Answer (c) is incorrect because purchasing materials and supplies will hedge a decrease in currency value. Answer (d) is incorrect because if funds are borrowed they are paid back with currency with less value.

26. (b) The requirement is to identify a means of hedging a decline in the price of stock. Answer (b) is correct because purchasing a put option on the stock allows the purchaser the option to sell the stock at the specified price in the future. Thus, if the price of the stock declines, the value of the put option will increase by an equivalent amount. Answer (a) is incorrect because purchasing a call option on the stock provides the company with an option to purchase stock at a specified price. Answer (c) is incorrect because selling a put option provides the purchaser with an option to sell stock at a specified price. Answer (d) is incorrect because a warrant provides the purchaser with the option of obtaining additional stock at a specified price.

27. (d) The requirement is to identify the risk of loss because of fluctuations in the relative value of foreign currencies. Answer (d) is correct because the risk of fluctuations in the relative value of foreign currencies is referred to as exchange rate risk. Answers (a) and (b) are incorrect because expropriation and sovereign risks relate to the possibility that a country might seize a foreign investment. Answer (c) is incorrect because multinational beta would be risk of the individual investment relative to the multinational market as a whole.

28. (c) The requirement is to identify characteristics of bonds that sell at a premium. Item I is not correct because if the bond sells at a premium the market rate is less than the coupon rate. Item III is not correct because the coupon rate is higher than the market rate. Item V is incorrect because the bond sells at a premium not a discount. Therefore, answer (c) is the only answer with two correct characteristics, II and IV.

29. (c) The requirement is to determine the annual savings needed for an investment to realize a 12% yield. The internal rate of return method of capital budgeting determines the rate of return at which the present value of the cash flows will exactly equal the investment outlay. In this problem, the desired IRR is given and the cash flows must be determined. The necessary annual savings can be computed as follows:

TVMF × Cash flows	=	PV (investment today)
3.60X + (.57 × $10,000)	=	$50,000
3.60X	=	$50,000 – (.57 × $10,000)
3.60X	=	$44,300
X	=	$12,306

If the annual savings equals $12,306, the present value of the cash inflows will exactly equal the cash outflows.

30. (d) Accounting standards state that receivables bearing an unreasonably low stated interest rate should be recorded at their present value. The Maxx receivable would be recorded at its present value, since it matures in five years. The Maxx receivable will result in a lump-sum collection of $11,593 ($10,000 × 1.1593), so its present value is $7,883 ($11,593 × .680).

31. (c) The market price of a bond issued at any amount (par, premium, or discount) is equal to the present value of all of its future cash flows, discounted at the current market (effective) interest rate. The market price of a bond issued at a discount is equal to the present value of both its principal and periodic future cash interest payments at the stated (cash) rate of interest, discounted at the current market (effective) rate.

32. (c) The requirement is to identify the stage that management is **most** likely to use present value techniques. Answer (c) is correct because present value techniques will most likely be used in the selection stage in which management evaluates various alternatives. Commonly used present value techniques include net present value and the internal rate of return. Answer (a) is incorrect because the identification stage involves determining the types of capital projects that are necessary to achieve management's strategies. Answer (b) is incorrect because in the search stage management attempts to identify capital investments that will achieve management's objectives. Answer (d) is incorrect because in the financing stage management decides on the best source of funding for projects.

33. (c) The requirement is to identify the difference between the payback method and the discounted payback method. Answer (c) is correct because the discounted payback method evaluates investments by discounting future cash flows and determining how many years it will take to recover the initial investment. Answer (a) is incorrect because the discounted payback method involves the same estimates of cash flows as the payback method. Answer (b) is incorrect because neither the payback method nor the discounted payback method considers the overall profitability of the investment. Answer (d) is incorrect because neither the payback method nor the discounted payback method considers variability of return.

34. (d) The payback period is computed by dividing the initial investment by the annual net cash inflow. Depreciation expense is not subtracted from cash inflow; only the income taxes that are affected by the depreciation deduction are subtracted. One of the weaknesses of the payback period is that it ignores the time value of money.

35. (d) The payback method is easy to understand but it is not very sophisticated. Answer (a) is incorrect because the payback method only considers cash flows until the cost is recovered. Answer (b) is incorrect because the payback method only considers net cash inflows from all sources. Answer (c) is incorrect because the payback method does not consider the time value of money.

36. (d) The payback method evaluates investments on the length of time until total dollars invested are recouped in the form of cash inflows or cash outflows avoided. It is calculated as Initial investment ÷ Annual cash inflow of a project. The payback period of the equipment under consideration by Tam is

$$\$100,000 \div \$20,000 = 5 \text{ years}$$

37. (d) The requirement is to identify the capital budgeting technique that does **not** use cash flows. Answer (d) is correct because the accounting rate of return uses accrual basis net income. Answers (a), (b), and (c) are incorrect because all of the other techniques use cash flows as the primary basis for the calculation.

38. (b) The requirement is to identify the advantage of the accounting rate of return method. Answer (b) is correct because accounting return is often used as a performance evaluation measure. Therefore, if it is also used as an evaluation technique, the consistency may lead to better decisions. Answer (a) is incorrect because the fact that results are affected by the depreciation method used is a disadvantage. Answer (c) is incorrect because the accounting rate of return method does not consider the time value of money. Answer (d) is incorrect because the accounting rate of return method does not consider the risk of the investment.

39. (d) The accounting rate of return (ARR) computes an approximate rate of return which ignores the time value of money. It is calculated as Expected increase in annual net income ÷ Initial (or Average) investment in a project. Tam's expected increase in annual income is as follows:

Annual savings in after-tax cash costs	$20,000
Annual depreciation on equipment	
($100,000 ÷ 10 years)	(10,000)
Increase in annual net income	$10,000

A $100,000 initial investment is required to purchase the equipment. Thus, the ARR of the equipment under consideration by Tam is

$$\$10,000 \div \$100,000 = 10\%$$

40. (c) The accounting rate of return method (ARR) computes an approximate rate of return which ignores the time value of money. It is computed as follows:

ARR = Expected increase in annual net income ÷ Average investment

Therefore, $40,000 (as stated in problem) is the numerator, the expected increase in annual income.

41. (d) The accounting rate of return (ARR) is based on financial statements prepared on the accrual basis. The formula to compute the ARR is

$$ARR = \frac{\text{Expected increase in annual net income}}{\text{Initial (or average) investment}}$$

Both the revenue over life of project and depreciation expense are used in the calculation of ARR. Depreciation expense over the project's life and other expenses directly associated with the project under consideration including income tax effects are subtracted from revenue over life of the project to determine net income over life of project. Net income over the project's life is then divided by the economic life to determine annual net income, the numerator of the ARR formula. This is a weakness of the ARR method because it does not consider actual cash flows or the time value of money.

42. (d) The requirement is to identify the implications of a profitability index of 1.15. Answer (d) is correct because the profitability index is the net present value of future cash flows divided by the amount of the initial investment. If the index is greater than 1.00, the net present value of the investment is positive.

43. (c) The requirement is to select the rate at which the NPV method assumes that the project's cash flows are reinvested. The correct answer is (c) because the NPV method assumes that cash flows can be reinvested at the discount rate used in the calculation. This is usually the cost of capital. Answer (a) is incorrect because the internal rate of return method assumes that cash flows are reinvested at that rate. Answer (b) is incorrect because the risk-free rate is never used to evaluate a project. Answer (d) is incorrect because the accounting rate of return is not relevant to the NPV method.

44. (b) The maximum amount that Kern Co. should invest now to obtain a 15% internal rate of return is the present value of the project's total net cash flows as computed below.

Year	Net cash flows		Present value of an ord. annuity		Present value of net cash flows
1	$50,000	×	.870	=	$43,500
2	$80,000	×	.756	=	$60,480
	Total present value				$103,980

45. (c) The requirement is to determine the present value of the future cash savings resulting from purchase of the new machine. The present value of the $30,000 savings per year for the first two years is calculated using the present value of an annuity for two periods. Since the amount of the cash savings drops to $20,000 in year three, this amount must be calculated separately. The PV of an annuity for three periods minus the PV of an annuity for two periods, equals the PV of an amount to be received three years in the future. The total present value of the cash savings is calculated as follows:

PV of $30,000 for 2 periods = $30,000 × 1.65	=	$49,500
PV of $20,000 in period 3 = $20,000 × (2.32 − 1.65)	=	13,400
Total present value of cash savings		$62,900

Alternatively, $20,000 could have been treated as an annuity for three years and an additional $10,000 for two years.

46. (d) The net present value of a project equals

$$NPV = (\text{PV future cash flows}) - (\text{Investment})$$

Since this problem involves a lease requiring only annual payments there is no initial investment in this case. Lease amortization must be subtracted from cash inflows to determine income tax expense.

$7,500	Annual cash inflow
−5,000	Tax basis lease amortization
$2,500	Taxable lease income
×40%	
$1,000	Tax expense per year

However, lease amortization is **not** a cash outflow and is thus excluded from the calculation of NPV. The after-tax present value of the lease equals:

$7,500	Annual cash inflow
=1,000	Cash outflow for taxes
$6,500	
×1.74	PV factor for two years at 10%
$11,310	

47. (a) A project's net present value is determined by considering the project's cash inflows and cash outflows discounted to their present values using the required rate of return. The initial outlay for the replacement asset is considered to be the cash outflow reduced by any proceeds from the sale of the asset to be replaced.

48. (c) The requirement is to determine when the discount rate (hurdle rate) must be determined before a capital budgeting method can be used. The payback method measures the time it will take to recoup, in the form of cash inflows from operations, the initial dollars invested in a project. The payback method does **not** consider the time value of money. The time-adjusted rate of return method is also called the internal rate of return method. This method computes the rate of interest at which the present value of expected cash inflows from a project equals the present value of expected cash outflows of the project. Here, the discount rate is not determined in advance but is the end result of the calculation. The net present value method is the correct answer because it calculates the expected net monetary gain or loss from a project by discounting all expected future cash inflows and outflows to the present using some predetermined minimum desired rate of return (hurdle rate).

49. (a) The requirement is to identify a description of the application of the internal rate of return. Answer (a) is correct because the IRR is the interest rate that equates the present value of the future cash inflows with the present value of the future cash outflows.

50. (a) The requirement is to identify the items used in the computation of the internal rate of return. Answer (a) is correct because the IRR uses the net incremental investment and the net annual cash flows. However, it does not include the incremental average operating income.

51. (a) The requirement is to compare NPV and IRR. Answer (a) is correct because NPV and IRR criteria will always lead to the same accept or reject decision. Answer (b) is incorrect because if the second project's internal rate of return is higher than the first project's, the organization would accept the second project based on IRR.

52. (c) The requirement is to calculate the net present value of Project A. Answer (c) is correct. The December 31, 2015 cash inflow is five years from the present cash outflow, and the net present value method uses the firm's cost of capital of 18%. The present value factor for 18% for 5 years is .4371, and $7,400,000 times .4371 equals $3,234,540, which is $265,460 less than the present cash outflow of $3,500,000. Answer (a) is incorrect because this answer discounts the cash inflow at the correct discount rate (18%), but for four years instead of five. Answer (b) is incorrect because this answer discounts the cash inflow at 15% (the project's internal rate of return) instead of at 18% (the cost of capital), which the net present value method uses. Answer (d) is incorrect because this answer discounts the cash inflow at the correct discount rate (18%), but for four years instead of five, and also subtracts the cash outflow from the cash inflow, instead of vice versa.

53. (c) The requirement is to estimate Project B's internal rate of return. Answer (c) is correct because 20% is the rate of return that equates the discounted cash inflows with the cash outflows. The factor related to dollars received after five years that equates the $4,000,000 initial cash outflow with present value of the future cash flow of $9,950,000 is approximately .4019 (.4019 × $9,950,000 = $3,998,905).

54. (b) The requirement is to calculate the cost of the project from its cash flow information. Answer (b) is correct. The internal rate of return is the discount rate that sets the net present value of the project to zero, so the present value of the costs equals the present value of the cash inflows. The cost of Project A can be calculated by determining the present value of the annual annuity of $10,000 cash flows discounted at 15%. Therefore, the cost of the investment is $22,832 ($10,000 × 2.2832). Answer (a) is incorrect because this solution uses the present value interest factor of 15%, one period rather than the present value interest factor for an annuity. Answer (c) is incorrect because this solution is obtained using a 10% rather than a 15% discount rate. Answer (d) is incorrect because this solution is obtained using a 5% rather than a 15% discount rate.

55. (a) The requirement is to calculate the net present value of Project B. Answer (a) is correct because the net present value is the present value of the cash inflows less the cost of the project. The net present value of the future inflows is

$24,079 [($5,000 × .9091) + ($10,000 × .8264) + ($15,000 × .7513)]. Therefore, the net present value of the project is $4,079 ($24,079 − $20,000). Answer (b) is incorrect because this solution is obtained using a 5%, rather than a 10%, discount rate. Answer (c) is incorrect because this is the net present value of Project A at a 10% discount rate. Answer (d) is incorrect because this solution is obtained using the present value interest factor for annuities.

56. (c) The requirement is to calculate the payback period of Project C. Answer (c) is correct because after two years, the cumulative cash inflows for Project C are exactly equal to the initial investment outlay, $25,000 ($15,000 + 10,000). Answer (a) is incorrect because the payback period would be zero only if a project had no cost or provided immediate cash inflows in excess of the investment outlay. Project C does not provide an immediate payback of its investment cost. Answer (b) is incorrect because after one year, the cumulative cash inflows for Project C are only $15,000 versus an initial investment outlay of $25,000. The project has not yet recovered its costs. Answer (d) is incorrect because Project C pays back its initial investment outlay in only two years.

57. (c) The requirement is to calculate the year 2 cash inflow for Project D. Answer (c) is correct. The discounted payback period is the length of time required for discounted cash flows to recover the cost of the investment. The year 2 cash inflow for Project D that is consistent with a discounted payback period of 2 years can be calculated as follows:

Investment cost = present value of year 1 and 2 cash inflows $30,000 = $20,000 × (.9524) + year 2 cash inflow × (0.9070) Year 2 cash inflow = [$30,000 − ($20,000 × .9524)] ÷ 0.9070 = $12,075.

Answer (c) is incorrect because this solution is obtained using the present value interest factor for annuities. Answer (b) is incorrect because this solution is based on the regular payback period. Since the cash inflow in year 1 is $20,000, Project D pays back its $30,000 cost in two years if the cash inflow in year 2 is $10,000. Answer (d) is incorrect because this solution is obtained using a 10%, rather than a 5%, discount rate.

58. (c) The internal rate of return (IRR) determines the rate of discount at which the present value of the future cash flows will exactly equal the investment outlay. It is computed by setting up the following equation

$$\text{Initial investment} = \text{TVMF} \times \text{Cash flows}$$

and solving for the time value of money factor (TVMF). The IRR can then be found by locating the TVMF for (n) periods in the present value of an ordinary annuity table and tracing to the top of that column to find the rate of return. The problem asks for the TVMF for the IRR of the equipment, which is calculated as follows:

$$\$100,000 = \text{TVMF} \times \$20,000$$
$$5.00 = \text{TVMF}$$

In estimating the IRR, the factors in the table of present values of an annuity should be taken from the columns closest to 5.00.

59. (d) The internal rate of return of a proposed project includes the residual sales value of a project but not the depreciation expense. This is true because the residual sales value represents a future cash flow whereas depreciation expense (ignoring income tax considerations) provides no cash inflow or outflow.

60. (c) The relationship between the NPV method and the IRR method can be summarized as follows:

NPV	IRR
NPV > 0	IRR > Discount rate
NPV = 0	IRR = Discount rate
NPV < 0	IRR < Discount rate

Since the problem states that Neu Co. has a positive net present value on the investment, then the internal rate of return would be > 12%.

61. (a) The requirement is to determine which mutually exclusive investment should be accepted. Answer (a) is correct because Project X has the higher net present value as calculated below.

$$\text{Net present value of Project X} = \$6,800$$
$$= (\$40,000 \times 3.170) - \$120,000$$

$$\text{Net present value of Project Y} = \$5,310 = [(\$10,000 \times 0.909)$$
$$+ (\$20,000 \times 0.826) + (\$60,000 \times 0.751)$$
$$+ (\$80,000 \times 0.683)] - \$120,000$$

62. (c) The requirement is to select the projects that should be undertaken assuming no budget constraints. Answer (c) is correct because the company should undertake all projects with a positive net present value. This would include Projects 2, 3, and 4. Answers (a), (b), and (d) are incorrect because Project 1 has a negative net present value and should not be undertaken.

63. (d) The requirement is to select the projects that should be undertaken assuming the company has only $600,000 available. Answer (d) is correct because Projects 3 and 4 have the highest NPV, profitability indexes, and IRRs, so they are the most profitable projects. Answer (a) is incorrect because Project 1 has a negative net present value. Answer (b) is incorrect because it violates the $600,000 restriction. Answer (c) is incorrect because the combined NPV of Projects 2 and 3 is less than the combined NPV of Projects 3 and 4.

64. (d) The requirement is to identify the project(s) that should be undertaken assuming the company has only $300,000 available. Answer (d) is correct; because Project 3 has the highest profitability index and a positive NPV, it should be undertaken. The profitability index provides a good measure for comparing investments of different amounts because it provides an indication of the NPV per dollar invested. Answer (a) is incorrect because it has a negative NPV. Answers (b) and (c) are incorrect because they violate the $300,000 constraint.

65. (b) The requirement is to define the nature of a tax shield. Answer (b) is correct because the benefit of depreciation in cash flow analysis is the resulting tax savings (reduction in

income taxes). Answers (a), (c), and (d) are incorrect because they do not describe the nature of the tax shield.

66. (a) The requirement is to identify the effects of income taxes on future cash flows. Answer (a) is correct because income taxes decrease both revenues and costs in projecting future cash flows. Answers (b), (c), and (d) are incorrect because income taxes decrease both benefits and costs.

67. (b) The requirement is to determine which costs are economically relevant to Buff Co.'s decision of whether to replace an old machine with a new machine. Costs that will not differ among alternatives are not relevant for decision-making purposes. Sunk costs are those that are not avoidable and are the result of a past decision. The original cost, accumulated depreciation, and therefore the carrying amount of Buff's old machine are not relevant to the decision because this is a past cost that cannot be changed. The costs associated with the new machine are avoidable. The disposal value of a new machine is relevant to Buff's decision because it represents a cash inflow that differs between the alternatives.

68. (b) The requirement is to calculate the after-tax cash flows in year 2. Answer (b) is correct. The after-tax cash flows are calculated by deducting tax expense from the before-tax cash flows. Since depreciation is deductible for tax purposes it provides a tax shield. Therefore, income taxes for year 2 are equal to $15,000 [($140,000 – 90,000) × 30%], and after-tax cash flows are $125,000 ($140,000 – 15,000). Answer (a) is incorrect because $140,000 is the before-tax cash flows. Answer (c) is incorrect because this solution fails to consider the deductibility of depreciation.

69. (c) The requirement is to calculate the net present value of the investment. Answer (c) is correct. The net present value is equal to the present value of the future after-tax cash flows minus the initial investment. The after-tax annual cash flows are calculated by taking the before-tax cash flows and deducting income taxes. Since depreciation is deductible for tax purposes, annual tax expense is equal to $15,000 [($140,000 – 90,000) × 30%]. Therefore, annual cash flows after taxes are $125,000 ($140,000 – 15,000). The present value of $125,000 received annually for 5 years discounted at 10% is $473,875 ($125,000 × 3.791). To properly evaluate the project, the investment in working capital ($10,000) must be considered a part of the initial investment, and its recovery at the end of year 5 must be discounted back to its present value, along with the terminal value of the investment of $50,000. The present value of $60,000 received at the end of 5 years is equal to $37,260 ($60,000 × .621). Therefore, the net present value is equal to $1,135 ($473,875 + 37,260 – 500,000 – 10,000). Answer (a) is incorrect because it is the result when amounts are not discounted. Answer (b) is incorrect because it is the result when taxes are not considered.

70. (b) The requirement is to calculate the expected contribution of a new product. Answer (b) is correct because the expected value of the contribution margin is equal to $110,000 [($700,000 × 30%) + ($200,000 × 30%) + (-$400,000 × 40%)].

71. (d) The requirement is to determine the expected value of cost of goods sold. Answer (d) is correct because the estimated cost of goods sold is calculated by multiplying the cost of goods sold percentage by the expected value of sales. The expected value of sales is $84,000 [($60,000 × 25%) + (85,000 × 40%) + ($100,000 × 35%). Therefore, cost of goods sold is estimated to be $67,200 ($84,000 × 80%).

72. (a) The requirement is to identify the technique that would allow management to justify an investment based on considerations other than expected cash flows. Answer (a) is correct because the real options technique views an investment as purchasing an option. This may allow management to justify investments that do not currently have positive cash flows. Answers (b), (c), and (d) are all techniques that require expected return to exceed the initial investment.

73. (c) The requirement is to calculate the expected return for the project. Answer (c) is correct because the expected return is calculated by summing the outcomes weighted by their probability of occurrence. Therefore, the expected return is equal to $470,000 [($200,000 × .4) + ($500,000 × .3) + ($800,000 × .3)]. Answer (a) is incorrect because it is the simple average of the three potential outcomes. Answer (b) is incorrect because it is the median return.

74. (b) The requirement is to compute the coefficient of variation of the project. Answer (b) is correct because the coefficient of variation is equal to the standard deviation of returns divided by the amount of the expected return. The coefficient of variation is equal to .3191 ($150,000 ÷ 470,000).

75. (c) The requirement is to identify the technique that recognizes the series of decisions involved in an investment. Answer (c) is correct because decision tree provides management with a technique for evaluating investments that involve a series of decisions. Answer (a) is incorrect because probability analysis involves assigning probabilities to various outcomes. Answer (b) is incorrect because the risk-adjusted discount rate technique involves assigning different discount rates based on the risk involved. Answer (d) is incorrect because sensitivity analysis involves examining the sensitivity of results to changes in significant assumptions.

76. (d) The requirement is to identify the technique that is **not** used to consider risk. Answer (d) is correct because the traditional internal rate of return method does not explicitly include consideration of risk. Answer (a) is incorrect because probability analysis involves assigning probabilities to various outcomes. Therefore, it considers risk. Answer (b) is incorrect because the risk-adjusted discount rate method adjusts discount rates for risk. Answer (c) is incorrect because simulation techniques allow management to simulate results based on expected values and levels of risk.

77. (d) The requirement is to identify the type of risk that concerns investors in a diversified company. Answer (d) is correct because a diversified company can be thought of as an investment portfolio. The relevant risk for both management and investors is the weighted average of project risk. Answer (a) is incorrect because the firm has a diversified set of projects and, therefore, a single project risk is not relevant. Answer (b) is incorrect because pure play risk relates to a single project. Answer (c) is incorrect because the standard deviation of project risk does not adequately measure the risk of the portfolio.

78. (a) The requirement is to identify the nature of the next investment in a portfolio. Answer (a) is correct because to reduce the risk of a portfolio, the investor should select investments with negatively correlated returns. In that way, when one investment decreases in value others will increase. Therefore, the company should select an investment that correlates negatively to current portfolio holdings. Answer (b) is incorrect because an investment that is uncorrelated to the current holdings does not reduce risk as much as one that is negatively correlated. Answer (c) is incorrect because an investment that is highly correlated to the current holdings increases the risk of the portfolio. Answer (d) is incorrect because an investment that is perfectly correlated to the current holdings increases the risk of the portfolio.

79. (c) The requirement is to calculate Deet's estimated savings for 2013 if it leases an auxiliary generator for use during power outages. In 2012 Deet incurred the following costs due to power outages:

Number of outages per month		Number of months		Number of outages
0	×	3	=	0
1	×	2	=	2
2	×	4	=	8
3	×	3	=	9
		12		19

19 outages × $400/outage = $7,600

The cost of leasing an auxiliary generator is only $6,000 (12 mos. × $500/mo). Therefore, Deet would be expected to save $1,600 ($7,600 – $6,000) in 2013 by leasing the generator.

80. (d) The internal rate of return method determines the rate of return at which the present value of the cash flows will exactly equal the investment outlay. It will indicate the rate of return earned over the life of the project. The net present value method determines the present value of all future cash flows at a selected discount rate. If the NPV of the cash flows is positive, the return earned by the project is higher than the selected rate. Both methods will provide the information needed to decide if a project's rate of return will meet Polo Co.'s requirement.

81. (b) The requirement is to determine what the probability of frost must be for Cal to be indifferent to spending $10,000 for frost protection. In other words, you must find the point at which the cost of the frost protection equals the expected value of the loss from frost damage. The table below summarizes the possible outcomes.

	Frost	Frost-free
Protected	$90,000 Market value	$60,000 Market value
Unprotected	$40,000 Market value	$60,000 Market value

The difference between the market value of protected and unprotected strawberries if a frost were to occur is $50,000. Since we want to determine the probability of a frost when the expected value of the loss from frost damage is $10,000, this probability can be calculated as follows:

Loss from damage	×	Probability of frost	=	Expected value of the loss
$50,000	×	P	=	$10,000
		P	=	$10,000
				$50,000
		P	=	.200

82. (c) Expected values are calculated as the weighted-average of all possible outcomes using the probabilities of the outcomes as weights. The expected number of additional muffin sales is

Additional sales		Probability		Expected value
60	×	0.6	=	36
100	×	0.4	=	40
				76

Since Dough earns $1 profit per box ($3 sales price – $2 cost), this represents $76 (76 boxes × $1 profit) of additional profit. However, the twenty-four unsold boxes would have to be sold at a $1 loss per box ($1 sales price – $2 cost) through Dough's thrift store. Therefore, the expected value of the decision to purchase the additional muffins is $52 net profit ($76 profit – $24 loss).

83. (b) Because it is not always possible to make decisions under conditions of total certainty, decision makers must have a method of determining the best estimate or course of action where uncertainty exists. One method is probability analysis. Probabilities are used to calculate the expected value of each action. The expected value of an action is the weighted-average of the payoffs for that action, where the weights are the probabilities of the various mutually exclusive events that may occur. Cost-volume-profit analysis is used to predict profits at all levels of production in the relevant range. Program evaluation and review technique (PERT) is used to estimate, schedule, and manage a network of interdependent project activities. It is useful for managing large-scale, complex projects. The scattergraph method is a graphical approach to computing the relationship between two variables.

84. (c) A probability distribution describes the possible outcomes relating to a single action and the likelihood of occurrence of each possible outcome. Gift Co. selected the most likely sales volume from several possible outcomes, which was simply the sales volume with the greatest probability of occurring. Gift Co. did not calculate the weighted-average of the outcomes (the sum of the probability of each outcome occurring times the sales volume of that outcome) to find the expected value.

85. (c) Probability analysis is an extension of sensitivity analysis. There is no specified limit on the number of possible outcomes. The summation of the probability weights should always equal one. Probability analysis and sensitivity analysis are not incompatible.

Written Communication Task

Written Communication Task 1

Written
Communication

Help

Yeager Company is considering several alternative capital investments. In evaluating the investments, management of the company has used the payback and accounting rate of return methods. Prepare a memorandum to Linda Gordon, the chief financial officer, describing the limitations of these two methods for evaluating investments and suggesting other methods that might be more appropriate.

> **REMINDER:** Your response will be graded for both technical content and writing skills. Technical content will be evaluated for information that is helpful to the intended reader and clearly relevant to the issue. Writing skills will be evaluated for development, organization, and the appropriate expression of ideas in professional correspondence. Use a standard business memo or letter format with a clear beginning, middle, and end. Do not convey information in the form of a table, bullet point list, or other abbreviated presentation.

To: Ms. Linda Gordon, CFO
        Yeager Company
From: CPA Candidate

Written Communication Task Solution

Written Communication Task 1

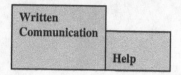

To: Ms. Linda Gordon, CFO
          Yeager Company
From: CPA Candidate

You have requested that I provide an evaluation of the two methods that Yeager Company uses for capital budgeting: the payback and the accounting rate of return methods.

As you know, the payback method evaluates investments based on the length of time it takes to recapture the initial investment. The payback method has two major limitations. First, it ignores the overall profitability of the investment. Second, it does not take into account the time value of money. These are major limitations which can result in selecting investments that are not consistent with maximization of the company's return on investment.

The accounting rate of return method evaluates investment alternatives based on their rate of accounting return. Like the payback method, the accounting rate of return method ignores the time value of money. As a result, it too can result in choosing investments that may not result in maximization of the company's return on investment.

The most effective capital budgeting techniques are those that consider the time value of money. As an example, the net present value method evaluates investment alternatives based on the present values of the future cash flows of the investments. It considers both the total profitability of the investment and the time value of money. Another technique, the internal rate of return method, evaluates investment alternatives based on their time-adjusted rates of return. This technique also considers the total profitability of the investment and adjusts for the time value of money.

I would suggest that you consider replacing your current techniques for capital budgeting with a technique or techniques that are superior, such as the present value and the internal rate of return techniques. If you have any other questions about capital budgeting, please contact me.

Module 44: Financial Management

Overview

This module describes major aspects of financial management. Financial management deals with the various types of monetary decisions that must be made by managers in a company, along with the tools and analyses used to make those decisions.

Financial management includes the following five functions:

1. **Financing function**—Raising capital to support the firm's operations and investment programs.
2. **Capital budgeting function**—Selecting the best projects in which to invest firm resources, based on a consideration of risks and return.
3. **Financial management function**—Managing the firm's internal cash flows and its capital structure (mix of debt and equity financing) to minimize the financing costs and ensure that the firm can pay its obligations when due.
4. **Corporate governance function**—Developing an ownership and corporate governance system for the firm that will ensure that managers act ethically and in the best interest of stakeholders.
5. **Risk-management function**—Managing the firm's exposure to all types of risk.

This module focuses primarily on the financing, financial management and financial risk management functions. It is divided into four sections. The first section reviews the concepts of working capital management, the second section deals with the topic of a firm's capital structure, asset and liability valuation is described in the third section, and the final section focuses on business mergers. Before beginning the reading you should review the key terms at the end of the module.

WORKING CAPITAL MANAGEMENT

A. Working capital management involves managing and financing the current assets and current liabilities of the firm. The primary focus of working capital management is managing inventories and receivables.

1. **Managing the Firm's Cash Conversion Cycle**

   The cash conversion cycle of a firm is the length of time between when the firm makes payments and when it receives cash inflows. This cycle is illustrated below.

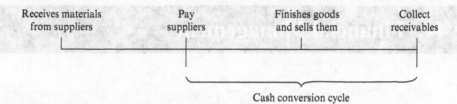

Cash conversion cycle

To enable more detailed analysis, the cash conversion cycle may be analyzed using the following three periods:

- Inventory conversion period
- Receivables collection period
- Payables deferral period

    a.   **Inventory conversion period**—The average time required to convert materials into finished goods and sell those goods.

$$\text{Inventory conversion period} = \frac{\text{Average inventory}}{\text{Cost of goods sold per day*}}$$

    * In some references this ratio is calculated using sales per day instead of cost of goods sold per day

---

EXAMPLE

Assume that average inventory is $10,000,000 and annual cost of goods sold are $40,000,000; the inventory conversion period is equal to 91 days, as calculated below.

$$\text{Inventory conversion period} \quad = \quad \frac{\$10,000,000}{\$40,000,000/365 \text{ days}}$$

$$= \quad 91 \text{ days}$$

---

    b.   **Receivables collection period (days sales outstanding)**—The average time required to collect accounts receivable.

$$\text{Receivables collection period} = \frac{\text{Average receivables}}{\text{Credit sales per day}}$$

EXAMPLE

Assume that the average receivables balance is $3,000,000 and credit sales are $40,000,000; the receivables collection period is equal to 27 days as calculated below.

$$\text{Receivables collection period} \quad = \quad \frac{\$3,000,000}{\$40,000,000/365 \text{ days}}$$

$$= \quad 27 \text{ days}$$

---

    c.   **Payables deferral period**—The average length of time between the purchase of materials and labor and the payment of cash for them.

$$\begin{aligned} \text{Payables deferral} \\ \text{period} \end{aligned} \quad = \quad \frac{\text{Average payables}}{\text{Purchases per day}}$$

$$= \quad \frac{\text{Average payables}}{\text{Cost of goods sold}/365}$$

> **EXAMPLE**
>
> Assume that the average payables balance for labor and materials is $2,500,000 and cost of goods sold is $30,000,000; the payables deferral period is 30 days as calculated below.
>
> $$\text{Payables deferral period} = \frac{\$2,500,000}{\$30,000,000/365 \text{ days}}$$
>
> $$= 30 \text{ days}$$

d.   The cash conversion cycle nets the three periods described above and, therefore, measures the time period from the time the firm pays for its materials and labor to the time it collects its cash from sales of goods. The conversion period calculated from the above examples is shown below.

Cash conversion cycle	=	Inventory conversion period	+	Receivables conversion period	−	Payables deferral period
	=	91 days	+	27 days	−	30 days
	=	88 days				

e.   Effective working capital management involves shortening the cash conversion cycle as much as possible without harming operations. This strategy improves profitability because the longer the cash conversion cycle, the greater the need for financing. We will now turn our attention to the management of each type of current asset.

2. Cash Management

A firm should attempt to minimize the amount of cash on hand while maintaining a sufficient amount to (1) take advantage of trade discounts, (2) maintain its credit rating, and (3) meet unexpected needs.

a.   Firms hold cash for two basic purposes

- *Transactions.* Cash must be held to conduct business operations.
- *Compensation to financial institution.* Financial institutions require minimum balances (1) for certain levels of service or (2) as a requirement of loan agreements. Such minimums are referred to as **compensating balances**.

b.   Firms prepare cash budgets to make sure that they have adequate cash balances to

- Take advantage of **cash discounts**. Suppliers often offer lucrative discounts for early payment of invoices.
- Assure that the firm maintains its credit rating.
- Take advantage of favorable business opportunities, such as opportunities for business acquisitions. These amounts are sometimes called **speculative balances**.
- Meet emergencies, such as funds for strikes, natural disasters, and cyclical downturns. These amounts are sometimes called **precautionary balances**.

c.   A key technique for cash management is managing float. **Float** is the time that elapses relating to mailing, processing, and clearing checks. A float exists for both the firm's payments to suppliers and the firm's receipts from customers. **Effective cash management involves extending the float for disbursements and shortening the float for cash receipts.**

d.   **Zero-balance accounts.** This cash management technique involves maintaining a regional bank account to which just enough funds are transferred daily to pay the checks presented. Regional banks typically receive the checks drawn on their customers' accounts in the morning from the Federal Reserve. The customer can then be notified as to the amount of cash needed to cover the checks and arrange to have that amount of cash transferred to the account. This arrangement has two advantages:

- Checks take longer to clear at a regional bank, providing more float for cash disbursements.
- Extra cash does not have to be deposited in the account for contingencies.

A zero-balance account is cost-effective if the amount the firm saves on interest costs from the longer float is adequate to cover any additional fees for account maintenance and cash transfers.

EXAMPLE

A firm has an opportunity to establish a zero-balance account system using three different regional banks. The total amount of the maintenance and transfer fees is estimated to be $5,000 per year. The firm believes that it will increase the float on its operating disbursements by an average of three days, and its cost of short-term funds is 4%. Assuming that the firm estimates its average daily operating disbursements to be $50,000, should the firm establish the accounts?

The solution to this problem is found by comparing the $5,000 cost in fees to the benefit in terms of reduced interest costs. If the float on the average is lengthened by three days, the firm gets the use of $150,000 of additional funds ($50,000 per day × 3 days). The annual value of the use of an extra $150,000 in funds is measured by the interest savings, or $6,000 ($150,000 × 4%). Therefore, the firm would save an estimated $1,000 ($6,000 − $5,000) by establishing the zero-balance accounts.

e. **Lockbox system.** In a lockbox system, customer payments are sent to a post office box that is maintained by a bank. Bank personnel retrieve the payments and deposit them into the firm's bank account. This technique has the following advantages:

- Increases the internal control over cash because firm personnel do not have access to cash receipts.
- Provides for more timely deposit of receipts which reduces the need for cash for contingencies.

    If management is evaluating the feasibility of establishing a lockbox system solely based on the cash flow benefit, the system is cost effective if the interest costs saved due to obtaining more timely deposits is sufficient to cover the net increase in costs of cash receipt processing (bank fees less internal costs saved from having the bank process receipts). The computation would be similar to the one illustrated above for a zero-balance account.

EXAMPLE

Assume that a firm is evaluating whether to establish a lockbox system. The following information is available to make the decision:

- The bank will charge $25,000 per year for the process and the firm will save approximately $8,000 in internal processing costs. Therefore, the estimated net additional cost of processing the receipts is $17,000 ($25,000 − $8,000).
- The float for cash receipts will be reduced by an estimated two days. Therefore, the firm will receive use of the cash receipts on the average two days earlier.
- Average daily cash receipts are equal to $300,000 and short-term interest costs are 4%.

Should the firm establish the lockbox system?

Based solely on cash flow considerations, the firm should establish the system if the interest savings is greater than the increased costs. In this case, the amount of interest savings is measured by multiplying the increase in average funds, $600,000 ($300,000 per day × 2 days), by the interest cost, 4%. The firm will save an estimated $24,000 ($600,000 × 4%) in annual interest costs. Therefore, the cost savings for the lockbox system is estimated to be $7,000, the savings in interest cost less the net increase in processing costs ($24,000 − $17,000). The real benefit may be even greater, because of the intangible value of the increase in internal control from having the bank process cash receipts. This reduces the firm's business risk.

f. **Concentration banking.** Another way to speed up collection of payments on accounts is concentration banking. Using this technique, customers in an area make payments to a local branch office rather than firm headquarters. The local branch makes deposits in an account at a local bank. Then, surplus funds are periodically transferred to the firm's primary bank. Since these offices and banks are closer to customers, the firm gets the use of the funds more quickly. The float related to cash receipts is shortened. However, transferring funds between accounts can be costly. Wire transfers generally involve a significant fee. A slower but less expensive way of transferring funds is through the use of **official bank checks** (depository transfer checks) which are preprinted checks used to make transfers.

> **EXAMPLE**
>
> Assume that a firm is considering establishing a concentration banking system and has the following information to make the decision:
>
> - The concentration banking arrangement will allow access to the firm's average $100,000 daily cash receipts from customers two days faster.
> - Bank maintenance and transfer fees are estimated at $4,000 per year.
> - The firm's short-term borrowing cost is 3.5%.
>
> Should the firm establish the concentration banking system?
>
> Again, in evaluating the decision, management must compare the interest savings, $7,000 [($100,000 per day × 2 days) × 3.5%] to the additional costs, $4,000. Thus, management would save $3,000 ($7,000 – $4,000) by establishing the concentration banking system.

g. **Electronic funds transfer.** Electronic funds transfer is a system in which funds are moved electronically between accounts without the use of a check. As an example, through a terminal at a supermarket a customer's payment is automatically charged with a "debit card" against the customer's bank account before he or she leaves the store. Electronic funds transfer systems actually take the float out of both the receipts and disbursements processes.

h. **International cash management.** Multinational firms can use various systems, including electronic systems, to manage the cash accounts they hold in various countries. Carefully managing international accounts may provide management with opportunities to increase earnings. As an example, management may be able to transfer funds to a country in which interest rates are higher, allowing increased returns on investments.

3. **Marketable Securities Management**

In most instances firms hold marketable securities for the same reasons they hold cash. Such assets can generally be converted to cash very quickly, and marketable securities have an advantage over cash in that they provide an investment return. There are many securities to choose from for short-term investment. The factors that are considered in making the choice include

- **Minimum investment required**—Some investments, such as high-yield certificates of deposit, require larger investments.
- **Safety**—The risk to principal.
- **Marketability (liquidity)**—Relates to the speed with which the investment can be liquidated.
- **Maturity**—The length of time the funds are committed.
- **Yield**—Generally, the higher the yield the better. However, additional yield comes with higher risk or longer maturity.

Because short-term investments must be available to meet the current cash needs of the firm, the most important considerations with respect to these investments are liquidity and safety. Major types of short-term investments include

a. **Treasury bills (T-bills)**—Short-term obligations of the federal government. Although treasury bills are initially offered with maturities of from 91 to 182 days, existing T-bills may be purchased on the market with virtually any maturity date up to 182 days. T-bills are popular short-term investments because the active market ensures liquidity.

b. **Treasury notes**—Government obligations with maturities from one to ten years. These securities are appropriate for the investment of short- to intermediate-term funds.

c. **Treasury Inflation Protected Securities (TIPS)**—Government obligations that pay interest that equates to a real rate of return specified by the US Treasury, plus principal at maturity that is adjusted for inflation. These are useful to a firm that wants to minimize interest rate risk.

d. **Federal agency securities**—Offerings of government agencies, such as the Federal Home Loan Bank. These securities offer security, liquidity (active market), and pay slightly higher yields than treasury issues.

e. **Certificates of deposit (CD)**—Savings deposits at financial institutions. There is actually a two-tier market for CDs—small CDs ($500 – $10,000) with lower interest rates and large ($100,000 or more) with higher interest rates. There is a secondary market for large CDs, providing some liquidity. Interest yields are higher on CDs than for government securities but CDs are not as liquid or as safe. CDs are normally insured up to $100,000 by the federal government.

f. **Commercial paper**—Large unsecured short-term promissory notes issued to the public by large creditworthy corporations. Commercial paper has a two- to nine-month maturity period and is usually held to maturity by the investor because there is no active secondary market.

g. **Banker's acceptance**—A draft drawn on a bank for payment when presented to the bank. Banker's acceptances generally arise from payments for goods by corporations in foreign countries. The corporation receiving the banker's acceptance may have to wait 30–90 days to present the acceptance for payment. As a result, a secondary market has developed for the sale of these instruments at a discount. Therefore, management may purchase banker's acceptances as short-term investments. Banker's acceptances involve slightly more risk than government securities but also offer slightly higher yields.

h. **Eurodollar certificate of deposit**—Eurodollars are US dollars held on deposit by foreign banks and in turn lent by the banks to anyone seeking dollars. To obtain dollars, foreign banks offer Eurodollar certificates of deposit. As an investment, Eurodollar certificates of deposit pay higher yields than treasury bills or certificates of deposit at large US banks.

i. **Money market funds**—Shares in a fund that purchases higher-yielding bank CDs, commercial paper, and other large-denomination, higher-yielding securities. Money market funds allow smaller investors to participate in these markets.

j. **Money market accounts**—Similar to savings accounts, individual or business investors deposit idle funds in the accounts and the funds are used to invest in higher-yielding bank CDs, commercial paper, etc.

k. **Equity and debt securities**—Management may also decide to invest in the publicly traded stocks and bonds of other corporations. Such investments have greater risk than other short-term investments, but they also offer higher average long-term returns. If management invests in such securities it should purchase a balanced portfolio to diversify away the **unsystematic risk** (e.g., default risk) of the individual investments.

4. **Inventory Management**

    Effective inventory management starts with effective forecasting of sales and coordination of purchasing and production. The two goals of inventory management are

    • To ensure adequate inventories to sustain operations, and
    • To minimize inventory costs, including carrying costs, ordering and receiving costs, and cost of running out of stock.

a. **Production pattern.** If the firm has seasonal demand for its products, management must decide whether to plan for level or seasonal production. Level production involves working at a consistent level of effort to manufacture the annual forecasted amount of inventory. Level production results in the most efficient use of labor and facilities throughout the year. However, it also results in inventory buildups during slow sales periods. This results in additional inventory holding costs. Seasonal production involves increasing production during periods of peak demand and reducing production during slow sales periods. Seasonal production often has additional operating costs for such things as overtime wages and maintenance.

EXAMPLE

A firm has projected the following data for the two alternatives of level production and seasonal production. The firm's short-term interest cost is 7%.

	Level production	Seasonal production
Average inventory	$200,000	$150,000
Production costs	$1,000,000	$1,010,000

Which alternative is preferable?

Under the level production alternative, the firm would incur an additional $3,500 (($200,000 – $150,000) × 7%) in inventory holding costs, but it would also save $10,000 ($1,010,000 – $1,000,000) in production costs. Therefore, level production would be the best production alternative. It would save the firm $6,500 ($10,000 – $3,500).

---

b. **Inventory and Inflation.** A firm's inventory policy also might be affected by inflation (deflation). As an example, if a firm uses silver as a raw material, the firm could experience significant gains or losses simply because of price fluctuations that occur in the silver market. Price instability occurs in a number of markets, such as copper, wheat, sugar, etc. The problem may be partially controlled by holding low levels of inventory. Another way would be to hedge the price movement with a futures contract to sell silver at a specified price in the future. In this manner, if the price of the silver falls, reducing the value of the inventory, the value of the future contract would rise to completely or partially offset the inventory loss.

c. **Supply chain.** The term **supply chain** describes a good's production and distribution. It illustrates the flow of goods, services, and information from acquisition of basic raw materials through the manufacturing and distribution process to delivery of the product to the consumer, regardless of whether those activities occur in one or many firms. To manage inventories and their relationships with their suppliers many firms use a process known as **supply chain management.** A key aspect of supply chain management is the sharing of key information from the point of sale to the final consumer back to the manufacturer, to the manufacturer's suppliers, and to the suppliers' suppliers. As an example, if a manufacturer/distributor shares its sales forecasts with its suppliers and they in turn share their sales forecasts with their suppliers, the need for inventories for all firms is significantly decreased. The manufacturer/distributor, for example, needs far less raw materials inventory than normally would be the case because its suppliers are aware of the manufacturer's projected needs and are prepared to have the materials available when needed. Specialized software facilitates the process of information sharing along the supply chain network.

d. **Economic order quantity**

How much to order? The amount to be ordered is known as the **economic order quantity** (EOQ). The EOQ minimizes the sum of the ordering and carrying costs. The total inventory cost function includes **carrying costs** (which increase with order size) and **ordering costs** (which decrease with order size). The EOQ formula is derived by setting the annual carrying costs equal to annual ordering cost or by differentiating the cost function with respect to order size.

$$EOQ = \sqrt{\frac{2aD}{k}}$$

Where

   a = cost of placing one order

   D = annual demand in units

   k = cost of carrying one unit of inventory for one year.

When to reorder? The objective is to order at a point in time so as to avoid **stockouts** but not so early that an excessive **safety stock** is maintained. Safety stocks may be used to guard against stockouts; they are maintained by increasing the lead time (the time that elapses from order placement until order arrival). Thus, safety stocks decrease stockout costs but increase carrying costs. Examples of these costs include

Carrying costs of safety stock (and inventory in general)	Stockout costs
1. Storage	1. Profit on lost sales
2. Interest	2. Customer ill will
3. Spoilage	3. Idle equipment
4. Insurance	4. Work stoppages
5. Property taxes	

The amount of safety stock held should minimize total stockout and carrying costs, as shown below.

The most common approach to setting the optimum safety-stock level is to examine previous lead-time periods to determine the probabilities of running out of stock (a stockout) for different assessed levels of safety stock.

e.   **Inventory Management and MRP.** Materials requirements planning (MRP) is a computerized system that manufactures finished goods based on demand forecasts. Demand forecasts are used to develop bills of materials that outline the materials, components, and subassemblies that go into the final products. Finally, a master production schedule is developed that specifies the quantity and timing of production of goods, taking into account the lead time required to purchase materials and to manufacture the various components of finished products. A key weakness of MRP is that it is a "push through" system. Once the master schedule is developed goods are pushed through the production process whether they are needed or not. Therefore, inventories may accumulate at various stages, especially if there are production slowdowns or unreliable demand forecasts. **MRP II** was developed as an extension of MRP and it features an automated closed loop system. That is, production planning drives the master schedule which drives the materials plans which is input to the capacity plan. It uses technology to integrate the functional areas of a manufacturing company.

f.   **Just-in-Time (JIT) Purchasing.** JIT is a demand-pull inventory system which may be applied to purchasing so that raw material arrives just as it is needed for production. The primary benefit of JIT is **reduction of inventories, ideally to zero**. Because of its non-value-added nature, inventory is regarded as undesirable. In a JIT system, suppliers inspect their own goods and make frequent deliveries of materials, which are placed into production immediately upon receipt. This process eliminates the need for incoming inspection and the storeroom. Suppliers all along the supply chain are informed through specialized software (e.g., enterprise resource systems) about the forecasted demand for their products allowing them to plan to supply the items when needed.

Obviously, the most important aspect of a JIT purchasing system is selection of, and relationships with, suppliers. If suppliers do not make timely delivery of defect-free materials, stockouts and customer returns will occur and they will be more pronounced. In addition, if sales forecasts are not reliable, goods ordered will vary from what is expected, causing inventories to build up somewhere along the supply chain.

g.   **JIT Production.** JIT methodology can also be applied to production. JIT production is a "demand pull" system in which each component of a finished good is produced when needed by the next production stage. The production process is driven by the demand. It begins with an order by the customer triggering the need for a finished good and works its way back through each stage of production to the beginning of the process. A JIT system strives to produce high-quality products that meet the customer's needs on a timely basis and at the lowest possible cost. Obviously, JIT production reduces inventories to a minimal level. To accomplish JIT production, management must

- **Emphasize reducing production cycle time (manufacturing lead time) and setup time.** Cycle time is the time required to complete a product from the start of its production until it is finished. Setup time is the time required to get equipment and materials ready to start working on the product. The time for both is cut to a minimum in a JIT system.
- **Emphasize production flexibility.** Plant layout is organized around **manufacturing cells** that produce a product or type of product with the workers being able to operate a number of the different machines. Machinery is purchased that can be used for multiple functions.
- **Emphasize solving production problems immediately.** If it is discovered that parts are absent or defective, production is corrected on the spot. This practice contrasts with traditional systems, in which the production of defective products often continues because defective goods are sitting in inventory—awaiting sale and thus ultimate feedback from the customer. In a JIT system, each worker is responsible for the quality of his or her own work. Thus, JIT results in reductions in scrap and rework.
- **Focus on simplifying production activities.** The goal of JIT is to identify and eliminate non-value-added activities. Less factory space is used for inventory storage and production activities, and materials handling between workstations is streamlined.

JIT purchasing and production systems offer many advantages over traditional systems, including the following:

- Lower investments in inventories and in space to store inventory.
- Lower inventory carrying and handling costs.
- Reduced risk of defective and obsolete inventory.
- Reduced manufacturing costs.
- The luxury of dealing with a reduced number (when compared with traditional systems) of reliable, quality-oriented suppliers.
- JIT allows a simplified costing system called **backflush costing**. The lack of inventories in a JIT system makes choices about cost-flow (such as LIFO and FIFO) unimportant—all manufacturing costs are simply run through cost of goods sold.

On the other hand, JIT systems can break down with disastrous results if (1) suppliers do not provide timely delivery of quality materials, (2) employers are not well trained or supervised, or (3) technology and equipment are not reliable.

h. **Enterprise Resource Planning (ERP) Systems.** ERP systems are enterprise-wide computerized information systems that connect all functional areas within an organization. By sharing information from a common database, marketing, purchasing, production, distribution, and customer relations management can be effectively coordinated. ERP systems also facilitate supply chain management by connecting the firm electronically to its suppliers and customers.

5. **Receivables Management**

Effective receivables management involves systems for deciding whether or not to grant credit and for monitoring the receivables. Obviously, management should establish consistent credit evaluation procedures that balance the costs of lost sales with the costs of credit losses (uncollectible accounts). The firm's credit policy consists of the following four variables:

- Credit period—The length of time buyers are given to pay for their purchases.
- Discounts—Percentage provided and period allowed for discount for early payment.
- Credit criteria—Required financial strength of acceptable credit customers. Firms often use a statistical technique called **credit scoring** to evaluate a potential customer.
- Collection policy—Diligence used to collect slow-paying accounts.

a. The credit period and discount policies will be the major determinant of the eventual size of the receivables balance. If a firm has $10,000 in credit sales per day and allows 30 days for payment, the firm will carry an approximate balance of $300,000 ($10,000 × 30). If the firm extends the terms to 45 days, the receivables balance will swell to approximately $450,000 ($10,000 × 45).

b. In making an individual credit decision, management must determine the level of credit risk of the customer based on prior records of payment, financial stability, current financial position, and other factors. Credit information is available from sources such as **Dun & Bradstreet Information Services** to make such decisions. Dun & Bradstreet makes available its Business Information Report (BIR) and a number of credit scoring reports.

c. To provide overall monitoring of receivables, management will often use measures such as the days sales outstanding and aging schedules. The days sales outstanding provides an overall measure of the accumulation of receivables and is calculated as follows:

$$\text{Days sales outstanding} = \frac{\text{Receivables}}{\text{Sales per day}}$$

EXAMPLE

Assume that a firm's outstanding receivables balance is $2,000,000 and annual sales is $52,000,000; the days sales outstanding is calculated below.

$$\text{Days sales outstanding} = \frac{\$2,000,000}{\$52,000,000/365 \text{ days}} = 14 \text{ days}$$

An aging schedule breaks down receivables by age, as shown below.

Age of Account (Days)	Amount	Percentage
0–10	$1,355,000	67.7
11–30	505,000	25.3
31–45	90,000	4.5
46–60	43,000	2.2
Over 60	7,000	0.3
Total	$2,000,000	100.0

By monitoring days sales outstanding and the aging schedule, management can detect adverse trends and evaluate the performance of the credit department.

---

d. Management of accounts receivable also involves determining the appropriate credit terms and criteria to maximize profit from sales after considering the cost of holding accounts receivable and losses from uncollectible accounts.

EXAMPLE

Assume that management believes that if they relax the firm's credit standards, sales will increase by $240,000. The firm's average collection period for these new customers will be 60 days and the payment period for existing customers is not expected to change. Management expects 5% losses from uncollectible accounts for these new customers. If variable costs are 75% of sales, and the cost of financing accounts receivable is 10%, should management decide to relax credit standards? The answer to this question involves comparing incremental revenues to incremental costs as shown below.

Incremental revenue	$240,000
Variable costs ($240,000 × 75%)	(180,000)
Uncollectible account expense ($240,000 × 5%)	(12,000)
Interest cost on additional average receivables ($40,000 × 10%)	(4,000)
Incremental revenue	$44,000

The interest cost is calculated by recognizing that if collection takes approximately 60 days, there will be approximately 60 days sales outstanding during the year. Average outstanding receivables is calculated as

$$
\begin{aligned}
\text{Average outstanding receivables} \quad &= \quad (\text{Sales}/360 \text{ days}) \times 60 \text{ days} \\
&= \quad (\$240,000/360) \times 60 \\
&= \quad \$40,000
\end{aligned}
$$

6. Financing Current Assets

a. Because many firms have seasonal fluctuations in the demand for their products or services, current assets tend to vary in amount from month to month. Conventional wisdom would say that such assets should be financed with current liabilities—accounts payable, commercial bank loans, commercial paper, etc. However, a certain amount of current assets are required to operate the business in even the slowest periods of the year. This amount of current assets is called the amount of **permanent current assets**. Permanent current assets are more appropriately financed with long-term financing, such as stock or bonds. Additional current assets (inventory, accounts receivable, etc.) are accumulated during periods of higher production and sales. These current assets are called **temporary current assets,** and they may be appropriately financed with short-term financing.

b. Various strategies are used to finance current assets. Since short-term debt is less expensive than long-term, firms generally attempt to finance current assets with short-term debt. However, use of extensive amounts of short-term debt is **aggressive** in that firms must pay off the debt or replace it as it comes due. A business recession may render the firm unable to meet these obligations. In addition, the amount of interest expense over time will be more volatile because the firm has not locked in an interest rate on a long-term basis. More **conservative** strategies involve financing some current assets with long-term debt which involves a more stable interest rate. However, as indicated above long-term debt tends to be more expensive, and the provisions or **covenants** of long-term debt agreements generally constrain the firm's future actions. Finally, prepayment penalties may make early repayment of long-term debt an expensive proposition.

c. Illustrated in the graph below is a conservative short-term investment strategy in which permanent current assets are financed with long-term debt.

d. The **maturity matching** or **self-liquidating approach** to financing assets involves matching asset and liability maturities. This strategy minimizes the risk that the firm will be unable to pay its maturing obligations. This method is often referred to as a hedging approach.

e. Generalizations about the cost, riskiness, and flexibility of short-term versus long-term debt depend on the type of short-term debt being used. We will now turn our attention to the different sources of short-term funds.

7. **Sources of Short-Term Funds**

a. **Accounts payable (trade credit).** Firms generally purchase goods and services from other firms on credit. Trade credit, especially for small firms, is a very significant source of short-term funds. A major advantage of trade credit is that it arises in the normal course of conducting business and bears no interest cost, providing it is paid on time.

Many firms have credit terms that allow a cash discount for early payment of the invoice. For example, a firm might sell on terms of 2/10, net 30, which means that payment is due in thirty days and a 2% discount is allowed for payment within 10 days. Generally, it is a good financial decision to take advantage of such discounts because the rate of interest realized for early payment is significant. The approximated cost of not taking the discount is calculated with the following formula:

$$\frac{\text{Discount percent}}{100\% - \text{Discount percent}} \times \frac{365 \text{ days}}{\text{Total pay period} - \text{Discount period}}$$

With our example of 2/10, net/30, the discount percentage is 2%, the total pay period is 30 days, and the discount period is 10 days. Therefore, the nominal annual cost is equal to 37.2% as calculated below.

$$\text{Nominal annual cost} = \frac{2\%}{100\% - 2\%} \times \frac{365 \text{ days}}{30 \text{ days} - 10 \text{ days}}$$
$$= 37.2\%$$

The nominal rate does not consider the effects of compounding. Therefore, the effective annual rate is significantly higher than the 37.2%.

b. **Short-term bank loans.** Notes payable to commercial banks represents the second most important source of short-term funds. We will now turn our attention to key features of bank loans.

Maturity—While banks do make long-term loans, the majority of their lending has a maturity date of one year or less. Business loans typically mature every 90 days requiring the firm to pay or renew the loan on a regular basis.

Promissory note—Notes are executed using a signed promissory note. The note specifies the terms of the agreement.

Interest—The rate for short-term bank loans fluctuates with changes in short-term interest rates as measured by such indexes as

- *Prime rate*—The rate a bank charges its most creditworthy customers. The rate increases for customers with more credit risk. As an example, a customer might have a rate of prime plus 100 basis points, which would be equal to the prime rate plus one percent. One basis point is equal to one hundredth of one percent (0.01%).

- *London Interbank Offered Rate (LIBOR)*—This rate is important because of the availability of dollars for loan on the international market. US companies can decide to borrow money in the US financial markets, London, or any other major money market center. LIBOR reflects price of funds in the international market.

Compensating balances—Loan agreements may require the borrower to maintain an average demand deposit balance equal to some percentage of the face amount of the loan. Such requirements increase the effective interest rate of the loan, because the firm does not get use of the full amount of the loan principal. As an example, if a firm gets a $100,000, 90-day loan at 6% with a 10% compensating balance arrangement, the effective interest rate on the loan would be calculated as follows:

$$\text{Principal available} = \$100,000 - (10\% \times \$100,000)$$
$$\text{Interest for 90 days} = \$100,000 \times 6\% \times (90 \text{ days}/360 \text{ days})$$
$$= \$1,500$$

$$\begin{aligned}
\text{Effective interest rate} &= \text{Interest paid/Principal available} \times (360 \text{ days}/90 \text{ days}) \\
&= \$1,500/\$90,000 \times (360 \text{ days}/90 \text{ days}) \\
&= 6.67\%
\end{aligned}$$

Informal line of credit—An informal specification of the maximum amount that the bank will lend the borrower.

Revolving credit agreements—A line of credit in which the bank is formally committed to lend the firm a specified maximum amount. The bank typically receives a commitment fee as a part of the agreement. Revolving credit arrangements are often used for intermediate-term financing.

Letter of credit—An instrument that facilitates international trade. A letter of credit, issued by the importer's bank, promises that the bank will pay for the imported merchandise when it is delivered. It is designed to reduce the risk of nonpayment by the importer.

c. **Commercial paper.** Commercial paper is a form of unsecured promissory note issued by large, creditworthy firms. It is sold primarily to other firms, insurance companies, pension funds, banks, and mutual funds. Commercial paper typically has maturity dates that vary from one day to nine months. This form of financing is very favorable for corporations with the financial strength to issue it. The rate is often 2 to 3% less than the prime rate and there are no compensating balance requirements. However, the market is less predictable than bank financing.

d. **Accounts receivable financing.**

(1) **Pledging of receivables.** Pledging accounts receivable involves committing the receivables as collateral for a loan from a financial institution. The financial institution will evaluate the receivables to see if they are of sufficient quality to serve as collateral. The interest rate will depend on the financial strength of the firm and the quality of the receivables. Typically, the financial institution will lend 60 to 80% of the value of the receivables and the outstanding balance of the loan will fluctuate with the amount of the receivables outstanding. Interest is computed based on the outstanding loan balance and tends to be quite high. However, for small or troubled companies the interest rate will be less than for unsecured loans.

(2) **Factoring.** When accounts receivable are factored, they are sold outright to a finance company. In such situations, the finance company is often directly involved in the credit decisions, and will submit the funds to the firm upon acceptance of the account. For taking the risk, the finance company is generally paid a fee of from 1 to 3% of the invoices accepted. In addition, the finance company receives the interest rate for advancing the funds.

EXAMPLE

Assume that a finance company charges a 2% fee and a 12% annual interest rate for factoring the firm's receivables which are payable in 30 days. The effective annual rate of interest on this arrangement would be calculated as follows:

> 2% Fee
> 1% Interest for 1 month (12% annual/12)
> 3% Monthly × 12 = 36% annual rate

Obviously, with the high rates associated with factoring, it is only considered by firms that have few other options.

---

(3) **Asset-backed public offerings.** Large firms recently have begun floating public offerings of debt (e.g. bonds) collateralized by the firm's accounts receivables. Because they are collateralized, such securities generally carry a high credit rating, even though the issuing firm may have a lower credit rating. Therefore, this form of accounts receivable financing can be advantageous. The creation of asset-backed securities is also called **securitization of assets**.

e. **Inventory financing.** A firm may also borrow funds using its inventory as collateral. The extent of the feasibility of this strategy depends on the marketability of the inventory. Obviously, widely traded raw materials such as lumber, metals, and grains are easily used as collateral. The methods used by lenders to control the pledged inventories include

- **Blanket Inventory Lien**—This is simply a legal document that establishes the inventory as collateral for the loan. No physical control over inventory is involved.
- **Trust Receipt**—An instrument that acknowledges that the borrower holds the inventory and that proceeds from sale will be put in trust for the lender. Each item is tagged and controlled by serial number. When the inventory is sold, the funds are transferred to the lender and the trust receipt is cancelled. This form of financing is also referred to as *floor planning* and is widely used for automobile and industrial equipment dealers.
- **Warehousing**—This is the most secure form of inventory financing. The inventory is stored in a **public warehouse** or under the control of public warehouse personnel. The goods can only be removed with the lender's permission.

f. **Hedging to reduce interest rate risk.** Firms that must borrow significant amounts of short-term variable rate funds are exposed to high levels of interest rate risk. If interest rates go up suddenly, the firm could experience a significant increase in interest costs. To mitigate this interest rate risk, management may decide to hedge the risk with derivatives purchased or sold in the **financial futures market**. Derivatives and hedging strategies are described in Module 43.

NOW REVIEW MULTIPLE-CHOICE QUESTIONS 1 THROUGH 80

CAPITAL STRUCTURE

This section focuses on determining the appropriate **capital structure** of the firm which involves a combination of debt and equity.

A. Long-Term Debt

The characteristics of the various forms of financing available to the firm help determine the funding sources that are most appropriate.

1. Public and Private Debt

Debt is increasingly a source of funds for US corporations. In issuing debt, management must first decide whether to issue the debt privately or publicly.

a. **Private debt** is of two principal types. The first type is loans from financial institutions (either an individual institution or a syndicated loan from multiple institutions). Such loans almost universally have a floating interest rate that is tied to a base rate, usually **LIBOR** (the London Interbank Offered Rate) or the US bank prime interest rate. The second type of private debt involves the **private placement** of unregistered bonds sold directly to accredited investors (often pension funds or insurance companies). Such debt is typically less expensive to issue than public debt.

b. In the United States, **public long-term debt** offerings involve selling SEC registered bonds directly to investors. The bond agreement specifies the par value, the coupon rate, and the maturity date of the debt. The par value is the face amount of the bond and most corporate bonds have a $1,000 face amount. The coupon rate is the interest rate paid on the face amount of the bond. Since most bonds pay a fixed rate of interest, the market value of the bond fluctuates with changes in the market interest rate. The maturity date is the final date on which repayment of the bond principal is due.

EXAMPLE

Baker Corporation issued $500,000 in 6% bonds, maturing in 20 years. Assuming that the bonds were issued at face value and interest is paid semiannually, the coupon rate of 6% is paid in installments of $30 (3% × $1,000) every six months for each $1,000 bond. Total annual interest for the firm every year is $30,000 ($500,000 × 6%). If the market rate of interest increases to 7% after the bonds are issued, the market value of the bonds will decline to an amount that will allow a new purchaser to realize a 7% yield to maturity. On the other hand, if the market rate of interest decreases to 5%, the market price of the bond will increase to an amount that will allow the new purchaser to earn only a 5% yield to maturity. This example illustrates the **interest rate risk** that investors assume when they purchase long-term fixed-rate bonds.

c.   A debt market with increasing importance is the market for **Eurobonds**. A Eurobond is a bond payable in the borrower's currency but sold outside the borrower's country. As an example, the bond of a US firm, payable in US dollars, might be sold in Germany, London, and Japan through an international syndicate of investment bankers. The registration and disclosure requirements for Eurobonds are less stringent than those of the SEC for US-issued bonds. Therefore, the cost of issuance is less.

2. **Debt Covenants and Provisions**

a.   **Debt covenants.** Both private and public debt agreements contain restrictions, known as **debt covenants**. Such covenants allow investors (lenders) to monitor and control the activities of the firm. Otherwise, management could make decisions that would be detrimental to the interests of the debt holders. Negative covenants specify actions the borrower cannot take, such as restrictions on

(1)   The sale of certain assets.
(2)   The incurrence of additional debt.
(3)   The payment of dividends.
(4)   The compensation of top management.

Positive covenants specify what the borrower must do and include such requirements as

(1)   Provide audited financial statements each year.
(2)   Maintain certain minimum financial ratios.
(3)   Maintain life insurance on key employees.

These covenants restrict the action of management and are an important consideration in determining the type of financing to obtain. In addition, major covenants must be disclosed in the footnotes to the firm's financial statements. Now, let's turn our attention to some typical provisions of debt agreements.

b.   **Security provisions.** Debt may be secured or unsecured. Secured debt is one in which specific assets of the firm are pledged to the bondholders in the event of default. Based on their security provisions debt may be classified as follows:

(1)   **Mortgage bond**—A bond secured with the pledge of specific property. The securing property is typically property or plant assets.
(2)   **Collateral trust bond**—A bond secured by financial assets of the firm.
(3)   **Debenture**—A bond that is not secured by the pledge of specific property. It is a general obligation of the firm. Because of the **default risk,** such bonds can only be issued by firms with the highest credit rating. Debentures typically have a higher yield than mortgage bonds and other secured debt.
(4)   **Subordinated debenture**—A bond with claims subordinated to other general creditors in the event of bankruptcy of the firm. That is, the bondholders receive distributions only after general creditors and **senior** debt holders have been paid. As you would expect, subordinated debentures have higher yields than senior unsecured debt.
(5)   **Income bond**—A bond with interest payments that are contingent on the firm's earnings. Obviously, these bonds also have a high degree of risk and carry even higher yields. These types of bonds are often associated with firms undergoing restructuring.

c.   **Methods of payment.** Bonds may be paid as a single sum at maturity, or through

(1)   **Serial payments—Serial bonds** are paid off in installments over the life of the issue. Serial bonds may be desirable to bondholders because they can choose their maturity date.
(2)   **Sinking fund provisions**—The firm makes payments into a sinking fund which is used to retire bonds by purchase.
(3)   **Conversion**—The bonds may be convertible into common stock and this may provide the method of payment.
(4)   **Redeemable**—A bondholder may have the right to redeem the bonds for cash under certain circumstances (e.g., if the firm is acquired by another firm).
(5)   **A call feature**—The bonds may have a call provision allowing the firm to force the bondholders to redeem the bonds before maturity. Call provisions typically call for payment of a 5 to 10% premium over par value to redeem the bonds. Investors generally do not like call features because they may be used to force them to liquidate their investment.

3. **Bond Yields**

a.   There are three different yields that are relevant to bonds: the **coupon rate,** the **current yield,** and **yield to maturity**.

EXAMPLE

Assume that a bond has a par value of $1,000 and pays 12% interest, $120 ($1,000 × 12%) per year for the remaining term of 10 years. The bond is currently selling for $900.

- The coupon rate (nominal yield) is equal to the 12% stated rate.
- The current yield is the stated interest payment divided by the current price of the bond.

$$\frac{\$120}{\$900} = 13.33\%$$

- The yield to maturity is the interest rate that will equate future interest payments and the maturity payment to the current market price. The future interest payments are $120 per year and the principal payment is $1,000 received at the end of 10 years. The current price of the bond is $900, and the yield to maturity can be estimated with the following formula:

$$YM = \frac{\text{Annual interest payment} + \dfrac{\text{Principal payment} - \text{Bond price}}{\text{Number of years to maturity}}}{0.6 \, (\text{Price of bond}) + 0.4 \, (\text{Principal payment})}$$

$$= \frac{\$120 + \dfrac{\$1,000 - \$900}{10}}{0.6 \, (\$900) + 0.4 \, (\$1,000)}$$

$$= 13.83\%$$

b. The price of a bond is dependent on the current **risk-free interest rate** and the **credit risk** of the particular bond. Bond rating agencies have rating systems for bonds to capture credit risk. For example, Moody's Investor Service provides the following nine categories of ranking:

Aaa	Aa	A	Baa	Ba	B	Caa	Ca	C

Lowest risk   Highest risk

Companies that invest in a significant amount of bonds may decide to share the credit risk by purchasing credit default insurance.

For additional discussion of the valuation of bonds, review the section on present value in Module 43.

4. **Other Types of Bonds**
   a. **Zero-coupon rate bonds**—These types of bonds do not pay interest. Instead they sell at a deep discount from the face or maturity value. The return to the investor is the difference between the cost and the bond's maturity value. The advantage of these bonds is that there are no interest payment requirements until the bonds mature. In addition, the amortization of interest is tax-deductible even though the firm is not making any interest payments.
   b. **Floating rate bonds**—The rate of interest paid on this type of bond floats with changes in the market rate (usually monthly or quarterly). Therefore the market price of the bond does not fluctuate as widely. **Reverse floaters** are floating rate bonds that pay a higher rate of interest when other interest rates fall and a lower rate when other rates rise. Reverse floaters are riskier than normal bonds.
   c. **Registered bonds**—These bonds are registered in the name of the bondholder. Interest payments are sent directly to the registered owners.
   d. **Junk bonds**—These bonds carry very high-risk premiums. Junk bonds often have resulted from **leveraged buyouts** or are issued by large firms that are in troubled circumstances. They may appeal to investors who feel they can diversify the risk by purchasing a portfolio of the bonds in different industries.
   e. **Foreign bonds**—These bonds are international bonds that are denominated in the currency of the nation in which they are sold. Foreign bonds might serve as an effective hedge for a firm that is heavily invested in assets in the foreign country.
   f. **Eurobonds**—As described above, these bonds are international bonds that are denominated in US dollars.

5. **Advantages and Disadvantages of Debt Financing**

    In deciding whether debt should be used as a form of financing, management must keep in mind the following advantages and disadvantages. The advantages of debt financing include

- Interest is tax-deductible.
- The obligation is generally fixed in terms of interest and principal payments.
- In periods of inflation, debt is paid back with dollars that are worth less than the ones borrowed.
- The owners (common stockholders) do not give up control of the firm.
- Debtors do not participate in excess earnings of the firm.
- Debt is less costly than equity. Therefore, the use of debt, up to some limit, will lower the firm's cost of capital. Cost of capital is discussed later in this module.

Disadvantages of debt financing include

- Interest and principal obligations must be paid regardless of the economic position of the firm.
- Interest payments are fixed in amount regardless of how poorly the firm performs.
- Debt agreements contain covenants that place restrictions of the flexibility of the firm.
- Excessive debt increases the risk of equity holders and therefore depresses share prices.

6. **Leasing as a Form of Financing**

    a.   Another potential source of intermediate or long-term financing involves leasing assets. From a financial statement standpoint, leases may be capital leases or operating leases. **Capital leases** are those that meet any one of the following four conditions as set forth in SFAS 13:

        (1)   The arrangement transfers ownership of the property to the lessee by the end of the lease.
        (2)   The lease contains a bargain purchase option at the end of the lease. The option price must be sufficiently low so exercise of the option appears reasonably certain.
        (3)   The lease term is equal to 75% or more of the estimated life of the leased property.
        (4)   The present value of the minimum lease payments equals 90% or more of the fair value of the leased property at the inception of the lease.

        If a lease meets one of these conditions, the firm must record the leased asset and related liability on its balance sheet, and account for the asset much like it would a purchased asset. The asset is recorded at the present value of the future lease payments and amortized (depreciated). A liability is recorded at the same amount and each lease payment involves payment of interest and principal on the obligation.

    b.   An **operating lease** is one that does not meet the criteria to be treated as a capital lease. Operating leases are treated as rental agreements; the asset and obligation are not recorded on the firm's balance sheet. The lease payments are expensed as rent as they are incurred.

    c.   A **sale-leaseback** is a transaction in which the owner of the property sells the property to another and simultaneously leases it back. Such arrangements often provide financing and tax advantages.

    d.   Leases have a number of advantages over purchasing the asset and financing through other means, including

- A firm may be able to lease an asset when it does not have the funds or credit capacity to purchase the asset.
- The provisions of a lease agreement may be less stringent than a bond indenture.
- There may be no down payment requirement.
- Creditor claims on certain types of leases, such as real estate, are restricted in bankruptcy.
- The cost of a lease to the lessee may be reduced because the lease may be structured such that the lessor retains the tax benefits.
- Operating leases do not require recognition of a liability on the financial statement of the lessor.

    e.   On the other hand, the dollar cost of leasing an asset is often higher than the cost of purchasing the asset.

B. Equity

This section describes the use of various forms of equity used for long-term financing.

1. **Common Stock**

    The ultimate owners of the firm are the common shareholders. They generally have control of the business and are entitled to a residual claim to income of the firm after the creditors and preferred shareholders are paid. Common stock ownership involves a high degree of risk. The investor is the last in line to receive earnings and distributions upon liquidation of the firm. On the other hand, common stockholders have the potential opportunity to receive very high returns. The return of the common stockholder includes dividends and appreciation in the value of the stock.

a. **Classes of common stock.** Most firms issue only one class of common stock. However, a firm may issue a second class of stock that differs with respect to the stockholders' right to vote or receive dividends. As an example, if the current stockholders do not wish to give up control of the firm, a class B stock might be issued that has limited voting rights. Obviously, the class B stock would sell for less than the class A stock as a result of the restriction.

b. **Stock warrants.** Stock warrants are sometimes issued with bonds to increase their marketability. A stock warrant is an option to buy common stock at a fixed price for some period of time. Once the bond is sold, the stock warrants often may be sold separately and are traded on the market.

c. **Advantages of issuing common stock**

- The firm has no firm obligation, which increases financial flexibility.
- Increased equity reduces the risk to borrowers and, therefore, will reduce the firm's cost of borrowing.
- Common stock is more attractive to many investors because of the future profit potential.

d. **Disadvantages of common stock**

- Issuance costs are greater than for debt.
- Ownership and control is given up with respect to the issuance of common stock.
- Dividends are not tax-deductible by the corporation whereas interest is tax-deductible.
- Shareholders demand a higher rate of return than lenders.
- Issuance of too much common stock may increase the firm's cost of capital.

2. **Preferred stock** is a hybrid security. Preferred shareholders are entitled to receive a stipulated dividend and, generally, must receive the stipulated amount before the payment of dividends to common shareholders. In addition preferred stockholders have a priority over common stockholders in the event of liquidation of the firm. Common features of preferred stock include

- **Cumulative dividends**—Most issues are cumulative preferred stock and have a cumulative claim to dividends. That is, if dividends are not declared in a particular year, the amount becomes in arrears and the amount must be paid in addition to current dividends before common shareholders can receive a dividend.
- **Redeemability**—Some preferred stock is redeemable at a specified date. This makes the stock very similar to debt. On the firm's balance sheet such stock is often presented between debt and equity (the so-called mezzanine).
- **Conversion**—Preferred stock may be convertible into common stock.
- **Call feature**—Preferred stock, like debt, may have a call feature.
- **Participation**—A small percentage of preferred shares are participating, which means they may share with common shareholders in dividends above the stated amount.
- **Floating rate**—A small percentage of preferred shares have a floating rather than fixed dividend rate.

a. **Advantages of issuing preferred stock**

- The firm still has no obligation to pay dividends until they are declared, which increases financial flexibility.
- Increased equity reduces the risk to borrowers and, therefore, will reduce the firm's cost of borrowing.
- Common stockholders do not give up control of the firm.
- Preferred stockholders do not generally participate in superior earnings of the firm.

b. **Disadvantages of preferred stock**

- Issuance costs are greater than for debt.
- Dividends are not tax-deductible by the corporation whereas interest is tax-deductible.
- Dividends in arrears accumulated over a number of years may create financial problems for the firm.

3. **Convertible Securities**

A convertible security is a bond or share of preferred stock that can be converted, at the option of the holder, into common stock. When the security is initially issued it has a **conversion ratio** that indicates the number of shares that the security may be converted into.

The advantage of convertible securities is the fact that investors require a lower yield because of the prospects that conversion may result in a significant gain.

The major disadvantage is that conversion dilutes the ownership of other common stockholders.

4. **Spin-Offs**

A spin-off occurs when a public diversified firm separates one of its subsidiaries, distributing the shares on a pro rata basis to the existing stockholders. Spin-offs are often part of management's strategy to turn its focus to its core businesses.

5. Tracking Stocks

A tracking stock is a specialized equity offering that is based on the operations and cash flows of a wholly owned subsidiary of a diversified firm. They are hybrid securities, because the subsidiary is not separated from the parent, legally or operationally. The stock simply is entitled to the cash flows of the subsidiary and, therefore, the trading stock trades at a valuation based on the subsidiary's expected future cash flows. Managers that issue trading stock believe that stockholder wealth will be maximized by separate valuation of two or more parts of the consolidated group.

6. Venture Capital

Venture capital is a pool of funds that is used to make actively managed direct equity investments in rapidly growing private companies. Such funds may be institutionally managed or involve ad hoc investments by wealthy individuals. In addition to capital, professional venture capitalists provide managerial oversight and business advice to the companies. Venture capitalists generally plan to exit the investment within three to seven years by selling the stock to another firm or by initiating a public offering of the stock. Venture capital provides a good source of capital for promising private companies, but it is expensive and management gives up significant control.

7. Going Public

As a private firm grows, one decision that must be made is whether and when to go public. Going public involves registering the firm's shares with the SEC. From that point on, the firm must comply with the reporting and other requirements of the SEC and the exchange on which the stock trades.

a. Advantages of going public

- An initial public offering provides the firm with access to a larger pool of equity capital.
- Publicly traded stock may be used for acquisitions of other firms. If a private company decides to acquire another company it generally must do so with cash.
- The firm can offer stock options and other stock-based compensation to attract and retain qualified managers.
- Going public provides the owners of the private company liquidity for their investments. These individuals can more easily sell portions of their stock in the firm and diversify their portfolio with other investments.

b. Disadvantages of going public

- Significant costs and management effort must be put into an initial public offering.
- There are significant costs of being public related to compliance with the securities laws and SEC and stock exchange regulations. These costs have been significantly increased by the provisions of the Sarbanes-Oxley Act of 2002.
- Being public necessarily causes management to be focused on maximizing stock price. This may or may not be in the best long-term interest of the firm.
- Management must provide a great deal of information about the firm to investors.

8. Employee Stock Ownership Plans (ESOPs)

Firms often reward management and key employees with stock or stock options as part of their compensation. These plans are designed to motivate management to focus on shareholder value. ESOPs are sometimes used as a vehicle for a **leveraged buyout**. ESOPs have certain tax advantages to the employees, and compensation expense may or may not have to be recognized by the firm.

9. Going Private

Some public corporations have decided (often to concentrate control) to go private. These transformations are sometimes executed through a **leveraged buyout** (LBO). In an LBO large amounts of debt are used to buy all or a voting majority of the shares of stock outstanding. Obviously, the firm, after the LBO, is heavily leveraged with much greater risk.

C. Evaluating the Best Source of Financing

To understand completely the considerations involved in making financing decisions, one must understand the concepts of leverage and cost of capital.

1. Leverage

The finance literature generally discusses two types of leverage: operating leverage and financial leverage.

a. Operating leverage.
Operating leverage measures the degree to which a firm builds fixed costs into its operations. If fixed costs are high a significant decrease in sales can be devastating. Therefore, all other things being equal, the greater a firm's fixed costs the greater its **business risk**. On the other hand, if sales increase for a firm with a high degree of operating leverage, there will be a larger increase in return on equity. The degree of operating leverage (DOL) may be computed using the following formula:

$$\text{DOL} = \frac{\text{Percent change in operating income}}{\text{Percent change in unit volume}}$$

Highly leveraged firms, such as Ford Motor Company, enjoy substantial increases in income when sales volume increases. Less leveraged firms enjoy only modest increases in income as sales volume increases.

b. **Financial leverage.** Financial leverage measures the extent to which the firm uses debt financing. While the use of debt can produce high returns to stockholders, it also increases their risk. Since debt generally is a less costly form of financing, a firm will generally attempt to use as much debt for financing as possible. However, as more and more debt is issued, the firm becomes more leveraged and the risk of its debt increases, causing the interest rate on additional debt to rise. Therefore, the optimal capital structure for a firm involves a mixture of debt and equity. The degree of financial leverage (DFL) for a firm may be computed using the following formula:

$$\text{DFL} = \frac{\text{Percent change in EPS}}{\text{Percent change in EBIT}}$$

Where

EPS = Earnings per share

EBIT = Earnings before interest and taxes

EXAMPLE

Let's examine two different leverage strategies. Under Plan 1 (the leveraged plan) management borrows $400,000 and sells 20,000 shares of common stock at $10 per share. Under Plan 2 (the conservative plan) the firm borrows $100,000 and issues 50,000 shares of stock at $10 per share. The debt bears interest at 10% and the firm has a 40% tax rate. These alternatives are illustrated below.

	Plan 1	Plan 2
Debt (10% interest)	$400,000	$100,000
Common stock	200,000	500,000
Total financing	$600,000	$600,000
Common stock	20,000 shares	50,000 shares

Now let's examine two sets of financial results. First, assume that the firm loses $200,000 before interest and taxes (EBIT). The financial results under the two different financing scenarios is shown below.

	Plan 1	Plan 2
EBIT	$(200,000)	$(200,000)
Interest (10% × principal)	(40,000)	(10,000)
Earnings before taxes	$(240,000)	$(210,000)
Tax benefit (40% × EBT)	96,000	84,000
Net loss	$(144,000)	$(126,000)
Loss per share	($7.20)	($2.52)

Next, assume that the firm earns $200,000 before interest and taxes. Again, the financial results under the two different financing scenarios are shown below.

	Plan 1	Plan 2
EBIT	$200,000	$200,000
Interest (10% × principal)	(40,000)	(10,000)
Earnings before taxes	$160,000	$190,000
Tax expense (40% × EBT)	(64,000)	(76,000)
Net earnings	$96,000	$114,000
Earnings per share	$4.80	$2.28

As you can see from the tables, the more leveraged strategy results in much higher earnings for common stockholders when the firm performs well. However, it results in much larger loss per share when the firm performs poorly. These examples clearly illustrate the major advantages and disadvantages of financial leverage.

2. Cost of Capital

A firm's cost of capital is an important concept in discussing financing decisions, especially those involving financing capital projects (long-term financing). If a firm can earn a return on an investment that is greater than its cost of capital, it will increase the value of the firm. The cost of capital for a firm is the weighted-average cost of its debt and equity financing components. The cost of the various components are determined as described below.

a. The **cost of debt** is equal to the interest rate of the loan adjusted for the fact that interest is deductible. Specifically, the cost is calculated as the interest rate times one minus the marginal tax rate. As an example, if a firm's interest rate on a long-term debt is 6% and its marginal tax rate is 30%, the cost of the debt is 4.2% $(0.06 \times (1.00 - .30))$. Remember in considering the cost of new debt, costs of issuing the debt (floatation costs) must be considered. For example, assume the firm issues at face value $20,000,000 of 6% coupon bonds and floatation costs are equal to $1,000,000. The maturity date of the bonds is in 10 years and interest is payable semiannually. To compute the cost of the debt, management should determine the interest rate (internal rate of return) that equates the future interest and principal payments with the present value of the debt. This is equivalent to the bond issue's yield to maturity. To get an accurate yield one would need to use a computer or programmable calculator. However, the following formula may be used to approximate the yield on bonds.

$$ YM = \frac{\text{Annual interest payment} + \dfrac{\text{Principal payment} - \text{Bond price}}{\text{Number of years to maturity}}}{0.6 \,(\text{Price of bond}) + 0.4 \,(\text{Principal payment})} $$

$$ = \frac{\$1,200,000 + \dfrac{\$20,000,000 - \$19,000,000}{10}}{0.6\,(\$19,000,000) + 0.4\,(\$20,000,000)} $$

$$ = 6.70\% $$

b. The **cost of preferred equity** is determined by dividing the preferred dividend amount by the issue price of the stock. For example, if 1,000 shares of $8.00 preferred stock is issued for $102,500, the cost of preferred stock is equal to 7.8% ($8,000/$102,500).

c. The **cost of common equity** is greater than that of debt or preferred equity because common shareholders assume more risk. Thus, they demand a higher return for their investment. Common equity is raised in two ways: (1) by retaining earnings, and (2) by issuing new common stock. Equity raised by issuing stock has a somewhat higher cost due to the flotation costs involved with new stock issues.

3. The Cost of Existing Common Equity

Firms use a number of techniques to estimate the cost of existing common equity including the Capital Asset Pricing Model, the Arbitrage Pricing Model, the Bond-Yield-Plus approach, and the Dividend-Yield-Plus-Growth-Rate approach.

a. **The Capital Asset Pricing Model (CAPM) Method.** One method of estimating the cost of common equity is by using the CAPM. The steps involved in estimating CAPM are

(1) Estimate the risk-free rate of interest, k_{RF}. Generally, firms use the either the US Treasury bond rate or the short-term Treasury bill rate.

(2) Estimate the stock's beta coefficient, b_i for use as an index of the stock's risk. The beta coefficient measures the correlation between the price volatility of the stock market and the price volatility of an individual firm's stock. If the stock price consistently rises and falls to the same extent as the overall market, the stock's beta would be equal to 1.00. Higher betas indicate more volatility and more risk. Betas are computed and reported by financial reporting services.

(3) Estimate the expected rate of return on the market, k_M. This is the expected rate of return on stock investments with similar risk. This factor is designed to capture systematic risk of the stock investment.

(4) Use the following equation to calculate the CAPM which can be used as an estimate of the cost of equity capital.

$$ k_S\,(\text{CAPM}) = k_{RF} + (k_M - k_{RF})b_i $$

> **EXAMPLE**
>
> Assume the risk-free interest rate (k_{RF}) is equal to 5%, the expected market rate of interest (k_M) is equal to 10%, and the stock's beta coefficient (b_i) is equal to 0.9 for a given stock; CAPM is calculated as follows:
>
> $$\begin{aligned} k_s &= 5\% + (10\% - 5\%)(0.9) \\ &= 5\% + (5\%)(0.9) \\ &= 5\% + 4.5\% \\ &= 9.5\% \end{aligned}$$
>
> Thus, an estimate of the cost of existing common equity is 9.5%

b. **Arbitrage pricing model.** As indicated previously, investors face two different types of risk for an investment.

- Systematic risk—Market risk that cannot be diversified away.
- Unsystematic risk—The risk of the specific investment that can be eliminated through diversification.

CAPM uses only one variable to capture systematic risk, the market rate of return or km. The arbitrage pricing model uses a series of systematic risk factors to develop a value that reflects the multiple dimensions of systematic risk. For example, systematic risk may be affected by future oil prices, exchange rates, interest rates, economic growth, etc. The formulation of the arbitrage pricing model is as follows:

$$r_p = b_1(k_1 - k_{RF}) + b_2(k_2 - k_{RF}) + b_3(k_3 - k_{RF}) \dots$$

Where

r_p = The risk premium on the particular investment. This is the amount that should be added to the risk-free rate to get an estimate of the cost of capital.

k_{rf} = The risk-free interest rate.

$b_{1,2,3}$ = The betas for the individual risk factors (e.g., exchange rate risk, oil price risk, interest rate risk, etc.).

$k_{1,2,3}$ = The market interest rate associated with each of the risk factors.

As you can see, the amounts in the parentheses are equal to the risk premium associated with each of the factors, (i.e., the market rate for each factor minus the risk-free rate).

c. **Bond-yield-plus approach.** The bond-yield-plus approach simply involves adding a risk premium of 3 to 5% to the interest rate on the firm's long-term debt.

d. **Dividend-yield-plus-growth-rate approach.** The dividend-yield-plus-growth-rate (dividend valuation) approach estimates the cost of common equity by considering the investors' expected yield on their investment. Specifically, the following formula is used:

$$k_s = \frac{D_1}{P_0} + \text{Expected } g$$

Where

D_1 = Next expected dividend

P_0 = Current stock price

g = Growth rate in earnings

EXAMPLE

Assume that a firm's stock sells for $25, its next annual dividend is estimated to be $1 and its expected growth rate is 6%. The cost of existing common equity would be calculated as follows:

$$k_s = \frac{D_1}{P_0} + \text{Expected G}$$

$$k_s = \frac{\$1}{\$25} + 6\%$$

$$= 4\% + 6\%$$

$$= 10\%$$

4. The Cost of New Common Stock

If a firm is issuing new common stock, a slightly higher return must be earned. This higher return is necessary to cover the cost of distribution of the new securities (floatation or selling costs). As an example, assume that the cost of capital for existing stockholders is 10% and the current share price of the stock is $25. Also, assume that the cost of floating the new stock issue is $2 per share, the next expected dividend is $1, and the expected growth rate in earnings for the firm is 6%. Using the dividend-yield-plus-growth-rate approach the cost of issuing new stock would be calculated using the following formula:

$$k_s = \frac{D_1}{P_0 - F} + \text{Expected G}$$

Where

D_1 = Next expected dividend
P_0 = Current stock price
G = Growth rate in earnings
F = Flotation cost per share

$$k_s = \frac{D_1}{P_0 - F} + \text{Expected G}$$

$$k_s = \frac{\$1}{\$25 - \$2} + 6\%$$

$$= 10.35\%$$

5. Evaluating the Cost of Capital—An Example

Assume that Café Roma operates a chain of coffee shops located in the Northwest. Management has decided to undertake an aggressive expansion program into California and is considering the following three financing options to obtain the $38,000,000 needed.

a. Issuance of $40,000,000 bonds with an 8% coupon rate. After floatation costs the firm would receive approximately $39,000,000, and the effective yield would equal 8.5%.

b. Issuance of $40,000,000 in 6% preferred stock that would yield approximately $38,000,000 after floatation costs.

c. Issuance of 2,000,000 shares of common stock at $20 per share that would yield approximately $38,000,000 after floatation costs.

The current market value of Café Roma's common stock is $20 per share, and the common stock dividend for the year is expected to be $1 per share. Investors are expecting a growth rate in earnings and dividends for the firm of 5%. The firm is subject to an effective tax rate of 40%.

To determine which of the alternatives is least expensive in terms of cost of capital, the cost of each alternative would be calculated as shown below.

$$\text{Cost of bond issue} = \text{Interest rate} \times (1.00 - \text{The effective rate})$$
$$= 8.5\% (1.00 - .40)$$
$$= 5.1\%$$

$$\text{Cost of preferred stock} = \text{Total dividend amount/Total issuance price}$$
$$= \text{The annual dividend amount/Issue price}$$
$$= (6\% \times \$40,000,000)/\$38,000,000$$
$$= \$2,400,000/\$38,000,000$$
$$= 6.3\%$$

$$\text{Cost of common stock} = \frac{D_1}{P_0 - F} + \text{Expected G}$$
$$= \frac{\$1}{\$20 - \$1} + 5\%$$
$$= 10.3\%$$

Because total floatation costs are $2,000,000 [(2,000,000 × $20) – $38,000,000], flotation costs per share are $1 ($2,000,000/2,000,000).

6. **Optimal Capital Structure**

   a. The optimal capital structure defines the mix of debt, preferred, and common equity that causes the firm's stock price to be maximized. The optimal or target capital structure involves a trade-off between risk and return. Incurring more debt generally leads to higher returns on equity but it also increases the risk borne by the stockholders of the firm. From a theoretical standpoint a firm's optimal capital structure is the one that minimizes the weighted-average cost of capital as shown in the graph below.

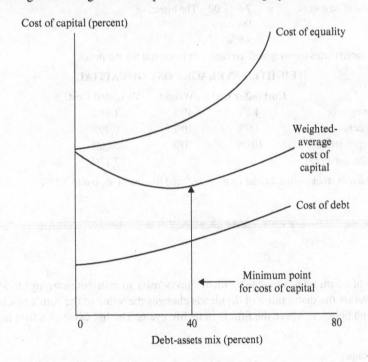

In practice, the following factors generally affect a firm's capital structure strategies:

   (1) *Business risk.* The greater the inherent risk of the business the lower the optimal debt to equity ratio.
   (2) *Tax position.* A major advantage of debt is the tax deductibility of interest payments. If the firm has a low marginal tax rate, debt becomes less advantageous as a form of financing.
   (3) *Financial flexibility.* Financial flexibility is the ability of the firm to raise capital on reasonable terms under adverse conditions. Less debt should be assumed by firms with less financial flexibility.

(4) *Management conservatism or aggressiveness.* A firm's target capital structure will be affected by the risk tolerance of management. More aggressive management may take on more debt.

b. **Weighted-average cost of capital (WACC).** In determining the optimum capital structure, management often calculates the firm's weighted-average cost of capital. This process involves taking the cost of the various types of financing (debt, preferred equity, common equity, etc.) and weighting each by the actual or proposed percentage of total capital. A computation of weighted-average cost of capital is presented below.

WEIGHTED-AVERAGE COST OF CAPITAL

	Cost (after tax)	Weight	Weighted Cost
Debt	4.2%	40%	1.68%
Preferred stock	7.8%	10%	0.78%
Common stock	10.0%	50%	<u>5.00</u>%
Weighted-average			<u>7.46</u>%

As illustrated, the weighted-average cost of capital for the firm is 7.46%. Management can now use this model to evaluate various forms of proposed financing options in terms of their effects on the firm's average cost of capital.

EXAMPLE

Assume that management, with the capital structure described in the table above, is considering calling the preferred stock and issuing 7% debentures. Assume that the costs to call the preferred shares are negligible and the firm's effective tax rate is 30%. What would be the effect on the firm's weighted-average cost of capital?

The cost of the new debentures is calculated below.

Cost of new debt = 7% (1.00 – The effective
                     tax rate)
                  = 4.9%

The following table recalculates the weighted-average cost of capital for the firm.

WEIGHTED-AVERAGE COST OF CAPITAL

	Cost (after tax)	Weight	Weighted Cost
Existing debt	4.2%	40%	1.68%
New debt	4.9%	10%	0.49%
Common stock	10.0%	50%	<u>5.00</u>%
Weighted-average			<u>7.17</u>%

By replacing the preferred stock with debt, the firm has reduced its cost of capital to 7.17%

D. Dividend Policy

1. The dividend policy of a firm relates to management's propensity to distribute earnings to stockholders. While it is unclear as to whether the distribution of dividends changes the value of the firm's stock, one of the major influences on dividend policy is where the firm is in its life cycle. The life cycle of a firm has the following four stages:

    a. Development stage
    b. Growth stage
    c. Expansion stage
    d. Maturity stage

    In its first two stages the firm needs to retain its profits to finance development and growth. If any dividends are issued, they tend to be stock dividends. When the firm hits the expansion stage, its need for investment declines and management may decide to issue small cash dividends. Finally, if the firm is successful in its maturity stage, it will tend to begin issuing regular and growing cash dividends.

2. Most people argue that the relevance of dividends is in their *information content.* Dividends **signal** to investors that management believes that the firm had a good year. Increases in dividends tend to increase share prices, while reductions tend to depress share prices. As a result, management is hesitant to decrease dividends.

3. Other factors that affect management's dividend policy include

- *Legal requirements*—Most states forbid firms to pay dividends that would impair the initial capital contributions to the firm.
- *Cash position*—Cash must be available to pay the dividends.
- *Access to capital markets*—If the firm has limited access to capital markets, management is more likely to retain the earnings of the firm.
- *Desire for control*—Retaining earnings results in less need for management to seek other forms of financing which might come with restrictions on management's actions.
- *Tax position of shareholders*—Stockholders must pay taxes on dividends and wealthier individuals pay higher taxes.
- *Clientele effect*—Some firms may have a strategy of attracting investors that require a dividend, such as retired individuals.
- *Investment opportunities*—Retained earnings should be reinvested in the firm if the firm can earn a return that exceeds what the investor can earn on another investment with similar risk.

4. **Other Types of Dividends**

   a. **Stock dividends** are payments to existing stockholders of a dividend in the form of the firm's own stock. As an example, a 10% stock dividend would involve the issuance of 10% more shares to each stockholder. Such dividends are designed to signal to investors that the firm is performing well, but it does not require the firm to distribute cash.

   b. **Stock splits** are similar to stock dividends but they are generally designed to reduce the stock's price to a target level that will attract more investors. As an example, a 2-for-1 stock split doubles the number of shares outstanding and it would be expected that the price of the stock would drop approximately in half.

E. **Share Repurchases**

Firms will often repurchase some of their shares to have them available for executive stock options or acquisitions of other firms. However, management of some firms have undertaken other repurchase programs based on the following rationales:

- It sends a positive signal to investors that management believes the stock is undervalued.
- It reduces the number of shares outstanding and thereby increasing earnings per share.
- It provides a temporary floor for the stock.

Many analysts question the validity of these rationales. As an example, the impact on earnings per share is uncertain because investing the cash in operations instead of spending it to repurchase stock might actually increase earnings per share to a greater extent.

F. **Financial Markets**

Financial markets are markets in which financial assets are traded. Such markets facilitate borrowing and lending, sale of previously issued securities, and sale of newly issued securities. Primary markets are markets in which newly issued securities are sold, and secondary markets are markets in which previously issued securities are sold. Examples of markets for stocks and debt include the New York Stock Exchange, the US government bond market, and NASDAQ. Futures and option contracts are traded on exchanges such as the Chicago Board of Trade and the Chicago Mercantile Exchange. A rising market is referred to as a **bull market,** and a declining or lethargic market is referred to as a **bear market**. The major players in markets include

1. **Brokers**—Commissioned agents of buyers or sellers.
2. **Dealers**—Similar to brokers in that they match buyers and sellers. However, dealers can and do take positions in the assets and buy and sell their own inventory.
3. **Investment banks**—Assist in the initial sale of newly issued securities by providing advice, underwriting, and sales assistance.
4. **Financial intermediaries**—Financial institutions that borrow one form of financial asset (e.g., a savings deposit) and distribute the asset in another form (e.g., a commercial loan).

NOW REVIEW MULTIPLE-CHOICE QUESTIONS 81 THROUGH 132

ASSET AND LIABILITY VALUATION

An important aspect of financial management is the valuation of assets and liabilities. Valuations are needed for a number of purposes including investment evaluation, capital budgeting, mergers and acquisitions, financial reporting, tax reporting, and litigation. The major types of valuation models include

1. Market values obtained from active markets for identical assets
2. Market values derived from active markets for similar but not identical assets
3. Valuation models

A. Using Active Markets for Identical Assets

The most straightforward method of valuing a financial instrument is using prices for identical instruments in an active market. The use of such markets is appropriate if they have sufficient volume of transactions to insure that the market price is reliable.

B. Using Markets for Similar Assets

Another method for valuing instruments involves deriving values from (1) the active market prices of similar but not identical instruments or (2) the market prices for identical items in inactive markets. The key to this method of valuation is accurate adjustment for differences that exist between the instrument being valued and the instrument that is traded in the market. For example, the price might need to be adjusted for such factors as restrictions on sales, or differences in maturity dates, exercise dates, block sizes, credit risk, etc. Financial models are often used to adjust the value of the instrument for these differences.

C. Valuation Models

A method that can be used in the absence of an active market is determining estimated fair value based on a valuation model, such as discounted cash flows. Such valuations generally rely on assumptions about future events and conditions that affect income and cash flows. These assumptions could materially affect the fair value estimate. Accordingly, they must be examined to determine whether they are reasonable and consistent with existing market information, the economic environment and past experience. For example, in determining the fair value of a rare asset for which market information is not available, consideration should be given to sales of similar assets, the general economic environment in which the asset is used, and past experiences with similar assets. As another example, discount rates for calculating discounted cash flows must reflect market expectations of future rates and be consistent with the level of risk inherent in the future cash flows.

In determining estimates of fair values it is also important that the model being used is appropriate based on the nature of the asset and current economic conditions.

D. Valuation Under US GAAP

Under US GAAP, accounting fair value is defined as the price that would be received to sell an asset or paid to transfer a liability in an orderly transaction between market participants at the measurement date. This assumes that the asset or liability is exchanged in an orderly transaction between market participants to sell the asset or transfer the liability in the principal market (or, in absence of a principal market, the most advantageous market).

1. **Market approach.** The market approach uses prices and other relevant information generated by market transactions involving identical or comparable assets or liabilities. This approach is used for such items as publicly traded commodities, stocks, bonds, and derivatives.
2. **Income approach.** The income approach uses valuation techniques to convert future benefits or sacrifices to a single present value. Examples include discounted cash flows and earnings capitalization models.
3. **Cost approach.** The cost approach is based on the amount that currently would be required to replace the service capacity of an asset (often referred to as current replacement cost). This approach is particularly appropriate for specialized facilities or equipment.

BUSINESS VALUATION

Business valuations are obtained for a number of purposes, including tax purposes, sales purposes, acquisition purposes, etc. The individual performing the valuation must also consider the premise of the valuation because the methodology used will vary depending on whether the value is for the existing assets in use or it is assumed that the business will be sold. Further, if it is to be sold the value will vary considering whether the business will be sold as a going-concern or in liquidation. Several approaches are used to value **firms**, including

A. **Market Approach**—Determines the value a nonpublic company based on the market value of comparable firms that are publicly traded. The valuation is performed by examining the relationship of the comparable company's stock price and its earnings or revenue (the multiple). This multiple is then adjusted for such factors as lack of marketability, restrictions on sale of the stock, and the portion of the company being acquired (e.g., a premium is provided for control and a discount is provided for a minority interest). The disadvantage of this approach is the difficulty in obtaining comparable companies to perform the valuation.

B. **Income Approach**—Determines the value of the firm is by estimating the present value of the future benefit stream (income or cash flow) of the firm. Net present value is determined by applying a discount or capitalization rate that reflects the risk level of the investment firm. Alternative income approaches include

   1. **Discounted cash flow analysis**—Application of capital budgeting techniques to an entire firm rather than a single investment.

      a. Two key items are needed for this valuation method:

         (1) A set of pro forma financial statements are developed that project the incremental cash flows that are expected to result from the merger.
         (2) A discount rate, or cost of capital, to apply to the projected cash flows. The appropriate discount rate is the cost of equity rather than an overall cost of capital. The discount rate used must reflect the underlying riskiness of the firm's operations (future cash flows).

      b. A risk analysis should be performed with the cash flows (e.g., sensitivity analysis, scenario analysis, etc.).

   2. **Capitalization of earnings**—Determines the value of the firm by capitalizing future earnings based on the required rate of return. For example, if the firm is expected to earn $1,000,000 per year and the required return is 10%, the firm would be valued at $10,000,000 ($1,000,000/10%). Note this example assumes no income growth or inflation.

   3. **Multiple of earnings**—Determines the value of the firm by applying a multiple to forecasted earnings. This is equivalent to the capitalization approach described above. For example, a 10% capitalization rate is equivalent to an earning multiple of 10.

C. **Asset Approach**—Determines the value of the firm by valuing the individual assets of the firm. This method is more applicable to a firm in liquidation rather than a going concern.

MERGERS

A. Business mergers involve many of the **considerations** involved in the acquisition of any asset or group of assets. However, there are additional considerations.

   1. Firms often acquire other firms due to **synergies**; the two firms can perform more effectively together than separately. Synergies arise from operating or financial economies, as well as managerial efficiency.
   2. Management may also acquire a firm for diversification or tax considerations, or to take advantage of a bargain purchase.

B. **Types of Mergers**

   1. **Horizontal merger**—When a firm combines with another in the same line of business.
   2. **Vertical merger**—When a firm combines with another firm in the same supply chain (e.g., a combination of a manufacturer with one of its suppliers).
   3. **Congeneric merger**—When the merging firms are somewhat related but not enough to make it a vertical or horizontal merger.
   4. **Conglomerate merger**—When the firms are completely unrelated. These types of mergers provide the greatest degree of diversification.

NOW REVIEW MULTIPLE-CHOICE QUESTIONS 133 THROUGH 138

KEY TERMS

Arbitrage pricing model. Uses a series of systematic risk factors to develop a value that reflects the multiple dimensions of systematic risk.

Cash discounts. Discounts for early payment of accounts.

Compensating balance. Required minimum level of deposit based on loan agreement.

Concentration banking. Payments from customers are routed to local branch offices rather than firm headquarters. This reduces collection time.

Cost of capital. The weighted-average cost of a firm's debt and equity financing components.

Debenture. A bond that is not secured by the pledge of specific property.

Economic order quantity. An inventory technique that minimizes the sum of inventory ordering and carrying costs.

Electronic funds transfer. The movement of funds electronically without the use of a check.

Factoring. The sale of receivables to a finance company.

Financial leverage. Measures the extent to which the firm uses debt financing.

Float. The time that elapses relating to mailing, processing, and clearing checks.

Inventory conversion period. The average length of time required to convert materials into finished goods and sell the goods.

Just-in-time production. A demand-pull system in which each component of a finished good is produced when needed by the next stage of production.

Just-in-time purchasing. A demand-pull inventory system in which raw materials arrive just as they are needed for production. It minimizes inventory holding costs.

Lockbox system. A system in which customer payments are sent to a post office box that is maintained by the company's bank. This reduces collection time and improves controls.

Mortgage bond. A bond secured with the pledge of specific property.

Operating leverage. Measures the degree to which a firm builds fixed costs into its operations.

Payables deferral period. The average length of time between the purchase of materials and labor and the payment of cash for them.

Precautionary balances. Cash available for emergencies.

Receivables collection period. The average length of time required to collect accounts receivable.

Speculative balances. Cash available to take advantage of favorable business opportunities.

Subordinated debenture. A bond with claims subordinated to other general creditors.

Supply chain. Describes the processes involved in a good's production and distribution.

Warehousing. Inventory financing in which the inventory is held in a public warehouse under the lender's control.

Multiple-Choice Questions (1–138)

Working Capital Management

1. Which of the following is **not** a function of financial management?

    a. Financing.
    b. Risk-management.
    c. Internal control.
    d. Capital budgeting.

2. The inventory conversion period is calculated as follows:

    a. $\dfrac{\text{Average inventory}}{\text{Cost of sales per day}}$

    b. $\dfrac{\text{Year-end inventory}}{\text{Cost of sales per day}}$

    c. $\dfrac{\text{Average inventory}}{\text{Accounts receivable}}$

    d. $\dfrac{\text{Year-end inventory}}{\text{Cost of sales}}$

3. The payables deferral period is calculated as follows:

    a. $\dfrac{\text{Average payables}}{\text{Sales per day}}$

    b. $\dfrac{\text{Beginning payables}}{\text{Sales per day}}$

    c. $\dfrac{\text{Average payables}}{\text{Purchases per day}}$

    d. $\dfrac{\text{Average payables}}{\text{Cost of goods sold}}$

4. All of the following statements in regard to working capital are correct **except:

    a. Current liabilities are an important source of financing for many small firms.
    b. Profitability varies inversely with liquidity.
    c. The hedging approach to financing involves matching maturities of debt with specific financing needs.
    d. Financing permanent inventory buildup with long-term debt is an example of an aggressive working capital policy.

**5. Determining the appropriate level of working capital for a firm requires

    a. Evaluating the risks associated with various levels of fixed assets and the types of debt used to finance these assets.
    b. Changing the capital structure and dividend policy of the firm.

    c. Maintaining short-term debt at the lowest possible level because it is generally more expensive than long-term debt.
    d. Offsetting the benefit of current assets and current liabilities against the probability of technical insolvency.

6. Which of the following actions is likely to reduce the length of a firm's cash conversion cycle?

    a. Adopting a new inventory system that reduces the inventory conversion period.
    b. Adopting a new inventory system that increases the inventory conversion period.
    c. Increasing the average days sales outstanding on its accounts receivable.
    d. Reducing the amount of time the firm takes to pay its suppliers.

7. Eagle Sporting Goods has $2.5 million in inventory and $2 million in accounts receivable. Its average daily sales are $100,000. The firm's payables deferral period is 30 days and average daily cost of sales are $50,000. What is the length of the firm's cash conversion period?

    a. 100 days.
    b. 60 days.
    c. 50 days.
    d. 40 days.

8. Jones Company has $5,000,000 of average inventory and cost of sales of $30,000,000. Using a 365-day year, calculate the firm's inventory conversion period.

    a. 30.25 days.
    b. 60.83 days.
    c. 45.00 days.
    d. 72.44 days.

9. The length of time between the acquisition of inventory and payment for it is called the

    a. Operating cycle.
    b. Inventory conversion period.
    c. Accounts receivable period.
    d. Accounts payable deferral period.

10. If everything else remains constant and a firm increases its cash conversion cycle, its profitability will likely

    a. Increase.
    b. Increase if earnings are positive.
    c. Decrease.
    d. Not be affected.

*11. An organization offers its customers credit terms of 5/10 net 20. One-third of the customers take the cash discount

---

* CIA adapted
** CMA adapted

and the remaining customers pay on day 20. On average, 20 units are sold per day, priced at $10,000 each. The rate of sales is uniform throughout the year. Using a 360-day year, the organization has days' sales outstanding in accounts receivable, to the nearest full day, of

    a. 13 days.
    b. 15 days.
    c. 17 days.
    d. 20 days.

Cash Management

**12. Troy Toys is a retailer operating in several cities. The individual store managers deposit daily collections at a local bank in a noninterest-bearing checking account. Twice per week, the local bank issues a depository transfer check (DTC) to the central bank at headquarters. The controller of the company is considering using a wire transfer instead. The additional cost of each transfer would be $25; collections would be accelerated by two days; and the annual interest rate paid by the central bank is 7.2% (0.02% per day). At what amount of dollars transferred would it be economically feasible to use a wire transfer instead of the DTC? Assume a 360-day year.

    a. It would never be economically feasible.
    b. $125,000 or above.
    c. Any amount greater than $173.
    d. Any amount greater than $62,500.

13. Which of the following is true about electronic funds transfer from a cash flow standpoint?

    a. It is always beneficial from a cash flow standpoint.
    b. It is never beneficial from a cash flow standpoint.
    c. It is beneficial from a cash receipts standpoint but not from a cash disbursements standpoint.
    d. It is beneficial from a cash disbursements standpoint but not from a cash receipts standpoint.

14. Management of Radker Corp. is considering a lockbox system. The bank will charge $10,000 annually for the service, which will save the firm approximately $5,000 in processing costs. The lockbox system will reduce the float for cash receipts by three days. Assuming that the average daily receipts are equal to $100,000, and short-term interest costs are 5%, calculate the benefit or loss from adopting the lockbox system.

    a. $5,000 loss.
    b. $10,000 loss.
    c. $10,000 benefit.
    d. $5,000 benefit.

15. Which of the following is true about a firm's float?

    a. A firm strives to minimize the float for both cash receipts and cash disbursements.
    b. A firm strives to maximize the float for both cash receipts and cash disbursements.

    c. A firm strives to maximize the float for cash receipts and minimize the float for cash disbursements.
    d. A firm strives to maximize the float for cash disbursements and minimize the float for cash receipts.

16. A firm is evaluating whether to establish a concentration banking system. The bank will charge $5,000 per year for maintenance and transfer fees. The firm estimates that the float will be reduced by two days if the concentration banking is put into place. Assuming that average daily receipts are $115,000 and short-term interest rates are 4%, what decision should the firm make regarding the concentration banking system?

    a. Do not establish the concentration banking system because the net cost is $5,000.
    b. Do not establish the concentration banking system because the net cost is $21,000.
    c. Establish the concentration banking system because the net benefit is $115,000.
    d. Establish the concentration banking system because the net benefit is $4,200.

17. A firm is evaluating whether to establish a lockbox system. The bank will charge $30,000 per year for the lockbox and the firm will save approximately $8,000 in internal processing costs. The firm estimates that the float will be reduced by three days if the lockbox system is put into place. Assuming that average daily cash receipts are $350,000 and short-term interest rates are 4%, what decision should the firm make regarding the lockbox system?

    a. Do not establish the lockbox system because the net cost is $30,000.
    b. Do not establish the lockbox system because the net cost is $22,000.
    c. Establish the lockbox system because the net benefit is $12,000.
    d. Establish the lockbox system because the net benefit is $20,000.

18. An organization has an opportunity to establish a zero balance account system using four different regional banks. The total amount of the maintenance and transfer fees is estimated to be $6,000 per annum. The organization believes that it will increase the float on its operating disbursements by an average of four days, and its cost of short-term funds is 4.5%. Assuming the organization estimates its average daily operating disbursements to be $40,000 what decision should the organization make regarding this opportunity?

    a. Do not establish the zero balance account system because it results in estimated additional net costs of $6,000.
    b. Do not establish the zero balance account system because it results in estimated additional net costs of $1,200.
    c. Establish the zero balance account system because it results in estimated net savings of $1,200.
    d. Establish the zero balance account system because it results in estimated net savings of $7,200.

**CMA adapted

**19. A working capital technique that increases the payable float and therefore delays the outflow of cash is

    a. Concentration banking.
    b. A draft.
    c. Electronic Data Interchange (EDI).
    d. A lockbox system.

**20. Newman Products has received proposals from several banks to establish a lockbox system to speed up receipts. Newman receives an average of 700 checks per day averaging $1,800 each, and its cost of short-term funds is 7% per year. Assuming that all proposals will produce equivalent processing results and using a 360-day year, which one of the following proposals is optimal for Newman?

    a. A $0.50 fee per check.
    b. A flat fee of $125,000 per year.
    c. A fee of 0.03% of the amount collected.
    d. A compensating balance of $1,750,000.

**21. A firm has daily cash receipts of $100,000. A bank has offered to reduce the collection time on the firm's deposits by two days for a monthly fee of $500. If money market rates are expected to average 6% during the year, the net annual benefit (loss) from having this service is

    a. $3,000
    b. $12,000
    c. $0
    d. $6,000

*22. A minimum checking account balance that a firm must maintain with a commercial bank is a

    a. Transaction balance.
    b. Compensating balance.
    c. Precautionary balance.
    d. Speculative balance.

**23. A firm has daily receipts of $100,000. A bank has offered to reduce the collection time on the firm's deposits by two days for a monthly fee of $500. If money market rates are expected to average 6% during the year, the net annual benefit from having this service is

    a. $0
    b. $3,000
    c. $6,000
    d. $12,000

**24. Cleveland Masks and Costumes Inc. (CMC) has a majority of its customers located in the states of California and Nevada. Keystone National Bank, a major west coast bank, has agreed to provide a lockbox system to CMC at a fixed fee of $50,000 per year and a variable fee of $.50 for each payment processed by the bank. On average, CMC receives 50 payments per day, each averaging $20,000. With the lockbox system, the company's collection float will decrease by 2 days. The annual interest rate on money market securities is 6%. If

CMC makes use of the lockbox system, what would be the net benefit to the company? Use 365 days per year.

    a. $ 51,750
    b. $ 60,875
    c. $111,750
    d. $120,875

Marketable Securities Management

25. The most important considerations with respect to short-term investments are

    a. Return and value.
    b. Risk and liquidity.
    c. Return and risk.
    d. Growth and value.

26. All of the following are alternative marketable securities suitable for investment **except:

    a. US treasury bills.
    b. Eurodollars.
    c. Commercial paper.
    d. Convertible bonds.

27. Which of the following investments generally pay the highest return?

    a. Money market accounts.
    b. Treasury bills.
    c. Treasury notes.
    d. Commercial paper.

28. Which one of the following is **not a characteristic of a negotiable certificate of deposit? Negotiable certificates of deposit

    a. Have a secondary market for investors.
    b. Are regulated by the Federal Reserve System.
    c. Are usually sold in denominations of a minimum of $100,000.
    d. Have yields considerably greater that bankers' acceptances and commercial paper.

Inventory Management

29. Which changes in costs are most conducive to switching from a traditional inventory ordering system to a just-in-time ordering system?

	Cost per purchase order	Inventory unit carrying costs
a.	Increasing	Increasing
b.	Decreasing	Increasing
c.	Decreasing	Decreasing
d.	Increasing	Decreasing

---

*CIA adapted
**CMA adapted

30. To determine the inventory reorder point, calculations normally include the

    a. Ordering cost.
    b. Carrying cost.
    c. Average daily usage.
    d. Economic order quantity.

31. Which of the following is **not a correct comparison of a just-in-time system with a traditional system?

	Traditional	Just-in-time
a.	Longer lead times	Shorter lead times
b.	Inventory is an asset	Inventory is a liability
c.	Some scrap tolerated	Zero defects desired
d.	Lot size based on immediate need	Lot size based on formulas

32. The benefits of a just-in-time system for raw materials usually include

    a. Elimination of non-value-added operations.
    b. Increase in the number of suppliers, thereby ensuring competitive bidding.
    c. Maximization of the standard delivery quantity, thereby lessening the paperwork for each delivery.
    d. Decrease in the number of deliveries required to maintain production.

33. Bell Co. changed from a traditional manufacturing philosophy to a just-in-time philosophy. What are the expected effects of this change on Bell's inventory turnover and inventory as a percentage of total assets reported on Bell's balance sheet?

	Inventory turnover	Inventory percentage
a.	Decrease	Decrease
b.	Decrease	Increase
c.	Increase	Decrease
d.	Increase	Increase

34. As a consequence of finding a more dependable supplier, Dee Co. reduced its safety stock of raw materials by 80%. What is the effect of this safety stock reduction on Dee's economic order quantity?

    a. 80% decrease.
    b. 64% decrease.
    c. 20% increase.
    d. No effect.

35. The economic order quantity formula assumes that

    a. Periodic demand for the good is known.
    b. Carrying costs per unit vary with quantity ordered.
    c. Costs of placing an order vary with quantity ordered.
    d. Purchase costs per unit differ due to quantity discounts.

36. Ral Co. sells 20,000 radios evenly throughout the year. The cost of carrying one unit in inventory for one year is

$8, and the purchase order cost per order is $32. What is the economic order quantity?

    a. 625
    b. 400
    c. 283
    d. 200

37. The following information pertains to material X that is used by Sage Co.:

Annual usage in units	20,000
Working days per year	250
Safety stock in units	800
Normal lead time in working days	30

Units of material X will be required evenly throughout the year. The order point is

    a. 800
    b. 1,600
    c. 2,400
    d. 3,200

38. Firms that maintain very low or no inventory levels

    a. Have higher ordering costs.
    b. Have higher carrying costs.
    c. Have higher ordering and carrying costs.
    d. Have lower ordering and carrying costs.

**39. An example of a carrying cost is

    a. Disruption of production schedules.
    b. Quantity discounts lost.
    c. Handling costs.
    d. Obsolescence.

*40. Which of the following is a characteristic of just-in-time (JIT) inventory management systems?

    a. JIT users determine the optimal level of safety stocks.
    b. JIT is applicable only to large companies.
    c. JIT does not really increase overall economic efficiency because it merely shifts inventory levels further up the supply chain.
    d. JIT relies heavily on good quality materials.

*41. To evaluate the efficiency of purchase transactions, management decides to calculate the economic order quantity for a sample of the company's products. To calculate the economic order quantity, management would need data for all of the following **except:**

    a. The volume of product sales.
    b. The purchase prices of the products.
    c. The fixed cost of ordering products.
    d. The volume of products in inventory.

Items 42 and 43 are based on the following information:

---

* CIA adapted
** CMA adapted

Ethan, Inc. has seasonal demand for its products and management is considering whether level production or seasonal production should be implemented. The firms' short-term interest cost is 8%, and management has developed the following information to make the decision:

	Alternative 1 Level production	Alternative 2 Seasonal production
Average inventory	$2,000,000	$1,500,000
Production costs	$6,000,000	$6,050,000

42. Which alternative should be accepted and how much is saved over the other alternative?

    a. Alternative 1 with $500,000 in savings.
    b. Alternative 2 with $50,000 in savings.
    c. Alternative 2 with $10,000 in savings.
    d. Alternative 1 with $10,000 in savings.

43. At what short-term interest rate would the two alternatives have the same cost?

    a. 6%
    b. 9%
    c. 10%
    d. 12%

**44. The amount of inventory that a company would tend to hold in stock would increase as the

    a. Sales level falls to a permanently lower level.
    b. Cost of carrying inventory decreases.
    c. Variability of sales decreases.
    d. Cost of running out of stock decreases.

*45. An appropriate technique for planning and controlling manufacturing inventories, such as raw materials, components, and subassemblies, whose demand depends on the level of production, is

    a. Materials requirements planning.
    b. Regression analysis.
    c. Capital budgeting.
    d. Linear programming.

Receivables Management

46. The procedures followed by the firm for ensuring payment of its accounts receivables are called its

    a. Discount policy.
    b. Credit policy.
    c. Collection policy.
    d. Payables policy.

Items 47 and 48 are based on the following information:

Effective September 1, a company initiates seasonal dating as a component of its credit policy, allowing wholesale customers to make purchases early but not requiring payment until the retail selling season begins. Sales occur as follows:

Date of sale	Quantity sold
September 1	300 units
October 1	100 units
November 1	100 units
December 1	150 units
January 1	50 units

- Each unit has a selling price of $10, regardless of the date of sale.
- The terms of sale are 2/10 net 30, January 1 dating.
- All sales are on credit.
- All customers take the discount and abide by the terms of the discount policy.
- All customers take advantage of the new seasonal dating policy.
- The peak selling season for all customers is mid-November to late December.

47. For the selling firm, which of the following is **not** an expected advantage to initiating seasonal dating?

    a. Reduced storage costs.
    b. Reduced credit costs.
    c. Attractive credit terms for customers.
    d. Reduced uncertainty about sales volume.

48. For sales after the initiation of the seasonal dating policy on September 1, total collections on or before January 11 will be

    a. $0
    b. $6,370
    c. $6,860
    d. $7,000

49. Which of the following describes the appropriate formula for days' sales outstanding?

    a. $\dfrac{\text{Average receivables}}{\text{Sales per day}}$

    b. $\dfrac{\text{Receivables balance}}{\text{Sales per day}}$

    c. $\dfrac{\text{Sales}}{\text{Average receivables}}$

    d. $\dfrac{\text{Receivables balance}}{\text{Total sales}}$

50. Which of the following describes a firm's credit criteria?

    a. The length of time a buyer is given to pay for his/her purchases.
    b. The percentage of discount allowed for early payment.

---

*CIA adapted
**CMA adapted

c. The diligence to collect slow-paying accounts.
d. The required financial strength of acceptable customers.

Items 51 and 52 are based on the following information:

A company plans to tighten its credit policy. The new policy will decrease the average number of days in collection from 75 to 50 days and reduce the ratio of credit sales to total revenue from 70 to 60%. The company estimates that projected sales would be 5% less if the proposed new credit policy were implemented. The firm's short-term interest cost is 10%.

**51. Projected sales for the coming year are $50 million. Calculate the dollar impact on accounts receivable of this proposed change in credit policy. Assume a 360-day year.

    a. $ 3,819,445 decrease.
    b. $ 6,500,000 decrease.
    c. $ 3,333,334 decrease.
    d. $18,749,778 increase.

**52. What effect would the implementation of this new credit policy have on income before taxes?

    a. $2,500,000 decrease.
    b. $2,166,667 decrease.
    c. $83,334 increase.
    d. $33,334 increase.

**53. The sales manager at Ryan Company feels confident that if the credit policy at Ryan's were changed, sales would increase and consequently, the company would utilize excess capacity. The two credit proposals being considered are as follows:

	Proposal A	Proposal B
Increase in sales	$500,000	$600,000
Contribution margin	20%	20%
Bad debt percentage	5%	5%
Increase in operating profits	$ 75,000	$ 90,000
Desired return on sales	15%	15%

Currently, payment terms are net 30. The proposed payment terms for Proposal A and Proposal B are net 45 and net 90, respectively. An analysis to compare these two proposals for the change in credit policy would include all of the following factors **except** the

    a. Cost of funds for Ryan.
    b. Current bad debt experience.
    c. Impact on the current customer base of extending terms to only certain customers.
    d. Bank loan covenants on days' sales outstanding.

**54. A company enters into an agreement with a firm who will factor the company's accounts receivable. The factor agrees to buy the company's receivables, which average $100,000 per month and have an average collection period of 30 days. The factor will advance up to 80% of the face value

of receivables at an annual rate of 10% and charge a fee of 2% on all receivables purchased. The controller of the company estimates that the company would save $18,000 in collection expenses over the year. Fees and interest are not deducted in advance. Assuming a 360-day year, what is the cost of engaging in this arrangement?

    a. 10.0%
    b. 14.0%
    c. 16.0%
    d. 17.5%

**55. A company with $4.8 million in credit sales per year plans to relax its credit standards, projecting that this will increase credit sales by $720,000. The company's average collection period for new customers is expected to be 75 days, and the payment behavior of the existing customers is not expected to change. Variable costs are 80% of sales. The firm's opportunity cost is 20% before taxes. Assuming a 360-day year, what is the company's benefit (loss) from the planned change in credit terms?

    a. $0
    b. $28,800
    c. $144,000
    d. $120,000

Financing Current Assets

56. Gild Company has been offered credit terms of 3/10, net 30. Using a 365-day year, what is the nominal cost of **not** taking advantage of the discount if the firm pays on the 35th day after the purchase?

    a. 14.2%
    b. 32.2%
    c. 37.6%
    d. 45.2%

57. Newton Corporation is offered trade credit terms of 3/15, net 45. The firm does not take advantage of the discount, and it pays the account after 67 days. Using a 365-day year, what is the nominal annual cost of not taking the discount?

    a. 18.2%
    b. 21.71%
    c. 23.48%
    d. 26.45%

58. Assume that Williams Corp is financed with a heavy reliance on short-term debt and short-term rates have increased. How do these facts impact the interest expense, net income, and financial risk for Williams Corp?

	Interest expense	Net income	Financial risk
a.	Decreases	Decreases	Decreases
b.	Increases	Decreases	Increase
c.	Decrease	Increases	Increases
d.	Increases	Decreases	Decreases

** CMA adapted

59. If a firm is offered credit terms of 2/10, net 30 on its purchases. Sound cash management practices would mean that the firm would pay the account on which of the following days?

    a. Day 2 and 30.
    b. Day 2 and 10.
    c. Day 10.
    d. Day 30.

**60. The following forms of short-term borrowings are available to a firm:

- Floating lien
- Factoring
- Revolving credit
- Chattel mortgages
- Bankers' acceptances
- Lines of credit
- Commercial paper

The forms of short-term borrowing that are unsecured credit are

    a. Floating lien, revolving credit, chattel mortgage, and commercial paper.
    b. Factoring, chattel mortgage, bankers' acceptances, and line of credit.
    c. Floating lien, chattel mortgage, bankers' acceptances, and line of credit.
    d. Revolving credit, bankers' acceptances, line of credit, and commercial paper.

*61. A company obtaining short-term financing with trade credit will pay a higher percentage financing cost, everything else being equal, when

    a. The discount percentage is lower.
    b. The items purchased have a higher price.
    c. The items purchased have a lower price.
    d. The supplier offers a longer discount period.

**62. If a firm borrows $500,000 at 10% and is required to maintain $50,000 as a minimum compensating balance at the bank, what is the effective interest rate on the loan?

    a. 10.0%
    b. 11.1%
    c. 9.1%
    d. 12.2%

63. If a retailer's terms of trade are 3/10, net 45 with a particular supplier, what is the cost on an annual basis of **not taking the discount? Assume a 360-day year.

    a. 24.00%
    b. 37.11%
    c. 36.00%
    d. 31.81%

64. Which of the following is **not** related to loans involving inventory?

    a. Factoring.
    b. Blanket liens.
    c. Trust receipts.
    d. Warehousing.

65. The London Interbank Offered Rate (LIBOR) represents an example of a

    a. Risk-free rate.
    b. Nominal rate.
    c. Credit risk adjusted rate.
    d. Long-term rate.

66. An advantage of the use of long-term debt as opposed to short-term debt to finance current assets is

    a. It decreases the risk of the firm.
    b. It generally is less costly than short-term debt.
    c. It generally places fewer restrictions on the firm.
    d. It is easy to repay.

67. The chief financial officer of Smith Glass Inc. follows the policy of matching the maturity of assets with the maturity of financing. The implications of this policy include all of the following **except that

    a. The seasonal expansion of cash, receivables, and inventory should be financed by short-term debt such as vendor payables and bank debt.
    b. The minimum level of cash, receivables, and inventory required to stay in business can be considered permanent, and financed with long-term debt or equity.
    c. Cash, receivables, and inventory should be financed with long-term debt or equity.
    d. Long-term assets, like plant and equipment, should be financed with long-term debt or equity.

68. Which form of asset financing involves the public offering of debt collateralized by a firm's accounts receivables?

    a. Trust receipts.
    b. Warehousing.
    c. Blanket inventory liens.
    d. Securitization of assets.

**69. Hagar Company's bank requires a compensating balance of 20% on a $100,000 loan. If the stated interest on the loan is 7%, what is the effective cost of the loan?

    a. 5.83%
    b. 7.00%
    c. 8.40%
    d. 8.75%

Items 70 and 71 are based on the following information:

CyberAge Outlet, a relatively new store, is a café that offers customers the opportunity to browse the Internet or play computer games at their tables while they drink coffee. The

---

customer pays a fee based on the amount of time spent signed on to the computer. The store also sells books, tee shirts, and computer accessories. CyberAge has been paying all of its bills on the last day of the payment period, thus forfeiting all supplier discounts. Shown below are data on CyberAge's two major vendors, including average monthly purchases and credit terms.

Vendor	Average monthly purchases	Credit terms
Web Master	$25,000	2/10, net 30
Softidee	50,000	5/10, net 90

**70. Assuming a 360-day year and that CyberAge continues paying on the last day of the credit period, the company's weighted-average annual interest rate for trade credit (ignoring the effects of compounding) for these two vendors is

   a. 27.0%
   b. 25.2%
   c. 28.0%
   d. 30.2%

**71. Should CyberAge use trade credit and continue paying at the end of the credit period?

   a. Yes, if the cost of alternative short-term financing is less.
   b. Yes, if the firm's weighted-average cost of capital is equal to its weighted-average cost of trade credit.
   c. No, if the cost of alternative long-term financing is greater.
   d. Yes, if the cost of alternative short-term financing is greater.

72. With respect to the use of commercial paper by an industrial firm, which one of the following statements is **most likely to be true?

   a. The commercial paper is issued through a bank.
   b. The commercial paper has a maturity of 60–270 days.
   c. The commercial paper is secured by the issuer's assets.
   d. The commercial paper issuer is a small company.

**73. A company obtained a short-term bank loan of $250,000 at an annual interest rate of 6%. As a condition of the loan, the company is required to maintain a compensating balance of $50,000 in its checking account. The company's checking account earns interest at an annual rate of 2%. Ordinarily, the company maintains a balance of $25,000 in its checking account for transaction purposes. What is the effective interest rate of the loan?

   a. 6.44%
   b. 7.11%
   c. 5.80%
   d. 6.66%

*74. A manufacturing firm wants to obtain a short-term loan and has approached several lending institutions. All of the potential lenders are offering the same nominal interest rate, but the terms of the loans vary. Which of the following combinations of loan terms will be most attractive for the borrowing firm?

   a. Simple interest, no compensating balance.
   b. Discount interest, no compensating balance.
   c. Simple interest, 20% compensating balance required.
   d. Discount interest, 20% compensating balance required.

**75. Elan Corporation is considering borrowing $100,000 from a bank for one year at a stated interest rate of 9%. What is the effective interest rate to Elan if this borrowing is in the form of a discount note?

   a. 8.10%
   b. 9.00%
   c. 9.81%
   d. 9.89%

**76. The Red Company has a revolving line of credit of $300,000 with a one-year maturity. The terms call for a 6% interest rate and a ½% commitment fee on the unused portion of the line of credit. The average loan balance during the year was $100,000. The annual cost of this financing arrangement is

   a. $6,000
   b. $6,500
   c. $7,000
   d. $7,500

**77. Which of the following financial instruments generally provides the largest source of short-term credit for small firms?

   a. Installment loans.
   b. Commercial paper.
   c. Trade credit.
   d. Mortgage bonds.

**78. The prime rate is the

   a. Size of the commitment fee on a commercial bank loan.
   b. Effective cost of a commercial bank loan.
   c. Rate charged on business loans to borrowers with high credit ratings.
   d. Rate at which a bank borrows from the Federal Reserve central bank.

**79. A compensating balance

   a. Compensates a financial institution for services rendered by providing it with deposits of funds.
   b. Is used to compensate for possible losses on a marketable securities portfolio.
   c. Is a level of inventory held to compensate for variations in usage rate and lead time.
   d. Is an amount paid by financial institutions to compensate large depositors.

---

* CIA adapted
** CMA adapted

**80. On January 1, Scott Corporation received a $300,000 line of credit at an interest rate of 12% from Main Street Bank and drew down the entire amount on February 1. The line of credit agreement requires that an amount equal to 15% of the loan be deposited into a compensating balance account. What is the effective annual cost of credit for this loan arrangement?

    a. 11.00%
    b. 12.00%
    c. 12.94%
    d. 14.12%

Long-Term Debt

81. Which of the following statements is correct when comparing bond-financing alternatives?

    a. A bond with a call provision typically has a lower yield to maturity than a similar bond without a call provision.
    b. A convertible bond must be converted to common stock prior to its maturity.
    c. A call provision is generally considered detrimental to the investor.
    d. A call premium requires the investor to pay an amount greater than par at the time of purchase.

82. Which of the following are characteristics of Eurobonds?

    a. They are always denominated in Eurodollars.
    b. They are always sold in some country other than the one in whose currency the bond is denominated.
    c. They are sold outside the country of the borrower but are denominated in the currency of the county in which the issue is sold.
    d. They are generally issued as registered bonds.

83. At the inception of an operating lease how should the leased asset be accounted for on the lessee financial statements?

    a. The present value of the future lease payments is recorded as an asset on the balance sheet.
    b. The total amount of the lease payments is recorded as an asset on the balance sheet.
    c. An asset is not recorded. The lease payments are expensed as rent as they are incurred.
    d. The future value of the lease payments is recorded as an asset on the balance sheet.

84. Capital and operating leases differ in that the lessee

    a. Obtains use of the asset only under a capital lease.
    b. Is using the lease as a source of financing only under an operating lease.
    c. Receives title to the asset in a capital lease.
    d. Capitalizes the net investment in the lease.

85. Which of the following is an advantage of debt financing?

    a. Interest and principal obligations must be paid regardless of the economic position of the firm.
    b. Debt agreements contain covenants.
    c. The obligation is generally fixed in terms of interest and principal payments.
    d. Excessive debt increases the risk of equity holders and therefore depresses share prices.

86. All of the following are advantages of debt financing **except**

    a. Interest is tax deductible.
    b. The use of debt will assist in lowering the firm's cost of capital.
    c. In periods of inflation, debt is paid back with dollars that are worth less than the ones borrowed.
    d. The acquisition of debt decreases stockholders' risk.

87. If an investor is concerned about interest rate risk, the investor should consider investing in

    a. Serial bonds.
    b. Sinking fund bonds.
    c. Convertible bonds.
    d. Floating rate bonds.

88. Bonds in which the principal amount is paid as a series of installments over the life of the bond issue are called

    a. Serial bonds.
    b. Sinking fund bonds.
    c. Convertible bonds.
    d. Callable bonds.

89. Wilson Corporation issued bonds two years ago. If the _____ interest rate _____, the market value of the bond will decrease.

    a. Coupon; increases.
    b. Coupon; decreases.
    c. Market; increases.
    d. Market; decreases.

**90. DQZ Telecom is considering a project for the coming year that will cost $50 million. DQZ plans to use the following combination of debt and equity to finance the investment:

- Issue $15 million of 20-year bonds at a price of 101, with a coupon rate of 8%, and flotation costs of 2% of par.
- Use $35 million of funds generated from earnings.

The equity market is expected to earn 12%. US Treasury bonds are currently yielding 5%. The beta coefficient for DQZ is estimated to be .60. DQZ is subject to an effective corporate income tax rate of 40%.

The before-tax cost of DQZ's planned debt financing, net of flotation costs, in the first year is

    a. 11.80%
    b. 8.08%
    c. 10.00%
    d. 7.92%

**CMA adapted

91. The **best reason corporations issue Eurobonds rather than domestic bonds is that

    a. These bonds are denominated in the currency of the country in which they are issued.
    b. These bonds are normally a less expensive form of financing because of the absence of government regulation.
    c. Foreign buyers more readily accept the issues of both large and small US corporations than do domestic investors.
    d. Eurobonds carry no foreign exchange risk.

92. Which of the following provisions is generally considered detrimental to the investor?

    a. Conversion.
    b. Redeemable.
    c. Callable.
    d. Serial maturity.

93. Which of the following is **not** an advantage of leasing as a form of long-term financing?

    a. Up front costs may be less.
    b. The provisions of the agreement may be less stringent than for other debt agreements.
    c. The dollar cost.
    d. The firm may be able to lease the asset when it does not have the credit capacity to purchase the asset.

94. Nerco has a bond issue that matures in fifteen years. Recently, the company's bond rating has gone from B to Baa. How would this affect the market price of the bonds?

    a. Increase.
    b. Decrease.
    c. Remain the same.
    d. The effect cannot be predicted.

Items 95 through 97 are based on the following information:

Watco, Inc. issued $1,000,000 in 8% bonds, maturing in ten years and paying interest semiannually. The bonds were issued at face value.

95. What can you assume about the interest rates at the time the bonds were issued?

    a. The market rate for this bond was about 8%.
    b. The nominal rate of interest was about 8%.
    c. The coupon rate on the bond includes no premium for credit risk.
    d. The risk-free interest rate is about 6%.

96. If the market rate of interest for this type of bond increases to 9%, which of the following is true?

    a. The market value of Watco's bond will increase.
    b. The market value of Watco's bond will decrease.
    c. The effect will depend on the change in the LIBOR rate.
    d. The effect cannot be predicted.

97. Assume that one of Watco's bonds with $1,000 face value is currently selling for $950. What is the current yield on the bond?

    a. 8.00%
    b. 9.00%
    c. 7.56%
    d. 8.42%

Equity

98. The market for outstanding, listed common stock is called the

    a. Primary market.
    b. New issue market.
    c. Over-the-counter market.
    d. Secondary market.

99. In capital markets, the primary market is concerned with

    a. New issues of bonds and stock securities.
    b. Exchanges of existing bond and stock securities.
    c. The sale of forward or future commodities contracts.
    d. New issues of bond and stock securities and exchanges of existing bond and stock securities.

*100. Which of the following is usually **not** a feature of cumulative preferred stock?

    a. Has priority over common stock with regard to earnings.
    b. Has priority over common stock with regard to assets.
    c. Has voting rights.
    d. Has the right to receive dividends in arrears before common stock dividends can be paid.

101. Which of the following is **not** an advantage of going public?

    a. Access to capital.
    b. Compliance.
    c. Use of stock options.
    d. Liquidity for owners' investments.

Items 102 and 103 are based on the following information:

The following information is available for Rothenberg, Inc.:

Balance sheet

Current assets	$ 500,000
Property, plant, and equipment	4,000,000
Total assets	$4,500,000
Current liabilities	$ 30,000
Long-term debt	2,500,000
Common stock	200,000
Retained earnings	1,770,000
Total liabilities and stockholders' equity	$4,500,000

---

* CIA adapted
** CMA adapted

Budget income information	100,000 units	105,000 units
Sales	$3,000,000	$3,150,000
Expenses	(2,800,000)	(2,850,000)
Operating income (EBIT)	$ 200,000	$ 300,000
Earnings per share (EPS)	$0.20	$1.20

Optimal Capital Structure

102. What is Rothenberg's degree of operating leverage?

   a. 1/5
   b. 10
   c. 5
   d. 2/3

103. What is the degree of financial leverage for Rothenberg, Inc.?

   a. 10
   b. 5
   c. 1/6
   d. 1/10

104. Which of the following is an advantage of equity financing in comparison to debt financing?

   a. Issuance costs are greater than for debt.
   b. Ownership is given up with respect to the issuance of common stock.
   c. Dividends are not tax deductible by the corporation whereas interest is tax deductible.
   d. The company has no firm obligation to pay dividends to common shareholders.

105. Assume that Company A and Company B are alike in all respects except that Company A utilizes more debt financing and less equity financing than does Company B. Which of the following statements is **most** likely to be true?

   a. Company A has more net earnings variability than Company B.
   b. Company A has more operating earnings variability than Company B.
   c. Company A has less operating earnings variability than Company B.
   d. Company A has less financial leverage than Company B.

106. Which of the following is **not** a source of capital used to finance long-term projects?

   a. Common stock.
   b. Long-term debt.
   c. Preferred stock.
   d. Line of credit.

107. Which of the following factors generally does **not** impact management's capital structure strategy?

   a. Business risk.
   b. Tax position.
   c. Management aggressiveness.
   d. Expected return on assets.

**108. A firm with a higher degree of operating leverage when compared to the industry average implies that the

   a. Firm has higher variable costs.
   b. Firm's profits are more sensitive to changes in sales volume.
   c. Firm is more profitable.
   d. Firm is less risky.

*109. When a company increases its degree of financial leverage

   a. The equity beta of the company falls.
   b. The systematic risk of the company falls.
   c. The unsystematic risk of the company falls.
   d. The standard deviation of returns on the equity of the company rises.

*110. A company has made the decision to finance next year's capital projects through debt rather than additional equity. The benchmark cost of capital for these projects should be

   a. The before-tax cost of new-debt financing.
   b. The after-tax cost of debt financing.
   c. The cost of equity financing.
   d. The weighted-average cost of capital.

Items 111 and 112 are based on the following information:

Management of Russell Corporation is considering the following two potential capital structures for a newly acquired business.

Alternative 1

Long-term debt, 6% interest	$3,000,000
Common equity	$3,000,000
Cost of common equity, 10%	
Marginal tax rate, 15%	

Alternative 2

Long-term debt, 7% interest	$5,000,000
Common equity	$1,000,000
Cost of common equity, 12%	
Marginal tax rate, 15%	

111. Which of the following statements is **not** true if management decides to accept Alternative 1?

   a. Alternative 1 is the more conservative capital structure.
   b. Alternative 1 provides the greatest amount of financial leverage.
   c. Net income will be less variable under Alternative 1.
   d. Total interest expense will be less under Alternative 1.

112. Which of the alternatives has the lowest weighted-average cost of capital and how much is the differential?

   a. Alternative 1 by 1.5%
   b. Alternative 2 by 0.59%
   c. Alternative 1 by 0.167%
   d. The alternatives have equal weighted-average cost of capital.

---

* CIA adapted
** CMA adapted

Cost of Capital

113. Management of Kelly, Inc. uses CAPM to calculate the estimated cost of common equity. Which of the following would reduce the firm's estimated cost of common equity?

    a. A reduction in the risk-free rate.
    b. An increase in the firm's beta.
    c. An increase in expected inflation.
    d. An increase in the risk-free interest rate.

**114. In general, it is more expensive for a company to finance with equity than with debt because

    a. Long-term bonds have a maturity date and must, therefore, be repaid in the future.
    b. Investors are exposed to greater risk with equity capital.
    c. The interest on debt is a legal obligation.
    d. Equity capital is in greater demand than debt capital.

115. Which of the following is **not** a characteristic of the capital asset pricing model for estimating the cost of equity?

    a. The model is simple to understand and implement.
    b. The model can be applied to all firms.
    c. The model does not rely on any dividend assumptions or growth of dividends.
    d. It is based upon the stock's actual market price.

116. Management of Terra Corp. is attempting to estimate the firm's cost of equity capital. Assuming that the firm has a constant growth rate of 5%, a forecasted dividend of $2.11, and a stock price of $23.12, what is the estimated cost of common equity using the dividend-yield-plus-growth approach?

    a. 9.1%
    b. 14.1%
    c. 15.6%
    d. 12.3%

117. If nominal interest rates increase substantially but expected future earnings and dividend growth for a firm over the long run are not expected to change, the firm's stock price will

    a. Increase.
    b. Decrease.
    c. Stay constant.
    d. Change, but in no determinable direction.

118. Assume that two companies, Company X and Company Y, are alike in all respects, except the market value of the outstanding common shares of Company X is greater than the market value of Company Y shares. This may indicate that

    a. Company X's investors expect higher dividend growth than Company Y's investors.
    b. Company X's investors expect lower dividend growth than Company Y's investors.

    c. Company X's investors have longer expected holding periods than Company Y's investors.
    d. Company X's investors have shorter expected holding periods than Company Y's investors.

119. Which of the following methods explicitly recognizes a firm's risk when determining the estimated cost of equity?

    a. Capital asset pricing model.
    b. Dividend-yield-plus-growth model.
    c. Bond-yield-plus model.
    d. Return on equity.

120. Assume a firm is expected to pay a dividend of $5.00 per share this year. The firm along with the dividend is expected to grow at a rate of 6%. If the current market price of the stock is $60 per share, what is the estimated cost of equity?

    a. 8.3%
    b. 6.0%
    c. 14.3%
    d. 12.0%

121. The bond-yield-plus approach to estimating the cost of common equity involves adding a risk premium of 3% to 5% to the firm's

    a. Cost of short-term debt.
    b. Cost of long-term debt.
    c. Return on assets.
    d. Return on equity.

**122. In practice, dividends

    a. Usually exhibit greater stability than earnings.
    b. Fluctuate more widely than earnings.
    c. Tend to be a lower percentage of earnings for mature firms.
    d. Are usually changed every year to reflect earnings changes.

Items 123 and 124 are based on the following information:

Martin Corporation
STATEMENT OF FINANCIAL POSITION
December 31, 2012
(**Dollars in millions**)

Assets	
Current assets	$ 75
Plant and equipment	250
Total assets	$325
Liabilities and shareholders' equity	
Current liabilities	$ 46
Long-term debt (12%)	64
Common equity:	
Common stock, $1 par	10
Additional paid in capital	100
Retained earnings	105
Total liabilities and shareholders' equity	$325

**CMA adapted

Additional data

- The long-term debt was originally issued at par ($1,000/bond) and is currently trading at $1,250 per bond.
- Martin Corporation can now issue debt at 150 basis points over US Treasury bonds.
- The current risk-free rate (US Treasury bonds) is 7%.
- Martin's common stock is currently selling at $32 per share.
- The expected market return is currently 15%.
- The beta value for Martin is 1.25.
- Martin's effective corporate income tax rate is 40%.

**123. Martin Corporation's current net cost of debt is

    a. 5.5%
    b. 7.0%
    c. 5.1%
    d. 8.5%

**124. Using the Capital Asset Pricing Model (CAPM), Martin Corporation's current cost of common equity is

    a. 8.75%
    b. 10.00%
    c. 15.00%
    d. 17.00%

*Items 125 and 126 are based on the following information:

DQZ Telecom is considering a project for the coming year that will cost $50 million. DQZ plans to use the following combination of debt and equity to finance the investment.

- Issue $15 million of 20-year bonds at a price of 101, with a coupon rate of 8%, and flotation costs of 2% of par.
- Use $35 million of funds generated from earnings.

The equity market is expected to earn 12%. US Treasury bonds are currently yielding 5%. The beta coefficient for DQZ is estimated to be .60. DQZ is subject to an effective corporate income tax rate of 40%.

**125. Assume that the after-tax costs of debt is 7% and the cost of equity is 12%. Determine the weighted-average cost of capital.

    a. 10.50%
    b. 8.50%
    c. 9.50%
    d. 6.30%

**126. The Capital Asset Pricing Model (CAPM) computes the expected return on a security by adding the risk-free rate of return to the incremental yield of the expected market return that is adjusted by the company's beta. Compute DQZ's expected rate of return.

    a. 9.20%
    b. 12.20%
    c. 7.20%
    d. 12.00%

*127. When calculating the cost of capital, the cost assigned to retained earnings should be

    a. Zero.
    b. Lower than the cost of external common equity.
    c. Equal to the cost of external common equity.
    d. Higher than the cost of external common equity.

128. According to the Capital Asset Pricing Model (CAPM), the relevant risk of a security is its

    a. Company-specific risk.
    b. Diversifiable risk.
    c. Systematic risk.
    d. Total risk.

**129. Hi-Tech Inc. has determined that it can minimize its weighted-average cost of capital (WACC) by using a debt/equity ratio of 2/3. If the firm's cost of debt is 9% before taxes, the cost of equity is estimated to be 12% before taxes, and the tax rate is 40%, what is the firm's WACC?

    a. 6.48%
    b. 7.92%
    c. 9.36%
    d. 10.80%

Items 130 through 132 are based on the following information:

A new company requires $1 million of financing and is considering two arrangements as shown in the table below.

Arrangement	Amount of equity raised	Amount of debt financing	Before-tax cost of debt
#1	$700,000	$300,000	8% per annum
#2	$300,000	$700,000	10% per annum

In the first year of operations, the company is expected to have sales revenues of $500,000, cost of sales of $200,000, and general and administrative expenses of $100,000. The tax rate is 30%, and there are no other items on the income statement. All earnings are paid out as dividends at year-end.

130. If the cost of equity were 12%, then the weighted-average cost of capital under Arrangement #1, to the nearest full percentage point, would be

    a. 8%
    b. 10%
    c. 11%
    d. 12%

131. Which of the following statements comparing the two financing arrangements is true?

    a. The company will have a higher expected gross margin under Arrangement #1.
    b. The company will have a higher degree of operating leverage under Arrangement #2.

---

* CIA adapted
** CMA adapted

c. The company will have higher interest expense under Arrangement #1.

d. The company will have higher expected tax expense under Arrangement #1.

132. The return on equity will be <List A> and the debt ratio will be <List B> under Arrangement #2, as compared with Arrangement #1.

	List A	List B
a.	Higher	Higher
b.	Higher	Lower
c.	Lower	Higher
d.	Lower	Lower

Asset and Liability Valuation

133. Which of the following methods of valuation provides the most reliable measure of fair value?

a. Use of a discounted cash flow method.

b. Market values obtained from active markets.

c. Combination of valuation models and active markets.

d. Sophisticated valuation models.

Mergers

*134. A parent company sold a subsidiary to a group of managers of the subsidiary. The purchasing group invested $1 million and borrowed $49 million against the assets of the subsidiary. This is an example of a

a. Spin-off.

b. Leveraged buyout.

c. Joint venture.

d. Liquidation.

**135. The acquisition of a retail shoe store by a shoe manufacturer is an example of

a. Vertical integration.

b. A conglomerate.

c. Market extension.

d. Horizontal integration.

**136. A horizontal merger is a merger between

a. Two or more firms from different and unrelated markets.

b. Two or more firms at different stages of the production process.

c. A producer and its supplier.

d. Two or more firms in the same market.

137. A soft drink producer acquiring a bottle manufacturer is an example of a

a. Horizontal merger.

b. Vertical merger.

c. Congeneric merger.

d. Conglomerate merger.

138. A shoe manufacturing firm acquiring a brokerage house is an example of a

a. Horizontal merger.

b. Vertical merger.

c. Congeneric merger.

d. Conglomerate merger.

---

* CIA adapted

** CMA adapted

Multiple-Choice Answers and Explanations

Answers

1.	c	__ __	30.	c	__ __	59.	c	__ __	88.	a	__ __	117.	b	__ __
2.	a	__ __	31.	d	__ __	60.	d	__ __	89.	c	__ __	118.	a	__ __
3.	c	__ __	32.	a	__ __	61.	d	__ __	90.	b	__ __	119.	a	__ __
4.	d	__ __	33.	c	__ __	62.	b	__ __	91.	b	__ __	120.	c	__ __
5.	d	__ __	34.	d	__ __	63.	d	__ __	92.	c	__ __	121.	b	__ __
6.	a	__ __	35.	a	__ __	64.	a	__ __	93.	c	__ __	122.	a	__ __
7.	d	__ __	36.	b	__ __	65.	b	__ __	94.	a	__ __	123.	c	__ __
8.	b	__ __	37.	d	__ __	66.	a	__ __	95.	a	__ __	124.	d	__ __
9.	d	__ __	38.	a	__ __	67.	c	__ __	96.	b	__ __	125.	a	__ __
10.	c	__ __	39.	d	__ __	68.	d	__ __	97.	d	__ __	126.	a	__ __
11.	c	__ __	40.	d	__ __	69.	d	__ __	98.	d	__ __	127.	b	__ __
12.	d	__ __	41.	d	__ __	70.	b	__ __	99.	a	__ __	128.	c	__ __
13.	c	__ __	42.	d	__ __	71.	d	__ __	100.	c	__ __	129.	c	__ __
14.	c	__ __	43.	c	__ __	72.	b	__ __	101.	b	__ __	130.	b	__ __
15.	d	__ __	44.	b	__ __	73.	a	__ __	102.	b	__ __	131.	d	__ __
16.	d	__ __	45.	a	__ __	74.	a	__ __	103.	a	__ __	132.	a	__ __
17.	d	__ __	46.	c	__ __	75.	d	__ __	104.	d	__ __	133.	b	__ __
18.	c	__ __	47.	b	__ __	76.	c	__ __	105.	a	__ __	134.	b	__ __
19.	b	__ __	48.	c	__ __	77.	c	__ __	106.	d	__ __	135.	a	__ __
20.	d	__ __	49.	b	__ __	78.	c	__ __	107.	d	__ __	136.	d	__ __
21.	d	__ __	50.	d	__ __	79.	a	__ __	108.	b	__ __	137.	b	__ __
22.	b	__ __	51.	c	__ __	80.	d	__ __	109.	d	__ __	138.	d	__ __
23.	c	__ __	52.	b	__ __	81.	c	__ __	110.	d	__ __			
24.	b	__ __	53.	b	__ __	82.	b	__ __	111.	b	__ __			
25.	b	__ __	54.	d	__ __	83.	c	__ __	112.	b	__ __			
26.	d	__ __	55.	d	__ __	84.	d	__ __	113.	a	__ __			
27.	d	__ __	56.	d	__ __	85.	c	__ __	114.	b	__ __			
28.	d	__ __	57.	b	__ __	86.	d	__ __	115.	d	__ __	1st:	__/138 = __%
29.	b	__ __	58.	b	__ __	87.	d	__ __	116.	b	__ __	2nd:	__/138 = __%

Explanations

1. (c) The requirement is to identify the function that is **not** related to financial management. The correct answer is (c) because internal control is a function of the controller's office. Answers (a), (b), and (d) are incorrect because the functions of financial management include: financing, capital, budgeting, financial management, corporate governance, and risk management.

2. (a) The requirement is to identify the formula for the inventory conversion period. Answer (a) is correct because the inventory conversion period describes the average time required to convert materials into finished goods and sell those goods. Answers (b), (c), and (d) are all incorrect versions of the formula.

3. (c) The requirement is to identify the formula for the calculation of the payables deferral period. Answer (c) is correct because the payables deferral period is equal to the average length of time between the purchase of materials and the payment of cash for them. Answers (a), (b), and (d) are all incorrect because they illustrate inaccurate versions of the formula.

4. (d) The requirement is to determine the false statement regarding working capital management. Answer (d) is correct because financing permanent inventory buildup with long-term debt is an example of a conservative working capital policy. Answers (a), (b), and (c) are all accurate statements about working capital management.

5. (d) The requirement is to identify the factor considered in determining the appropriate level of working capital. Answer (d) is correct because the main reason to retain working capital is to meet the firm's financial obligations.

Therefore, the amount is determined by offsetting the benefit of current assets and current liabilities against the probability of technical insolvency. Answer (a) is incorrect because it is a consideration regarding long-term financing. Answer (b) is incorrect because it is a consideration regarding capital structure. Answer (c) is incorrect because short-term debt is generally less expensive than long-term debt.

6. (a) The requirement is to identify the impact of decisions on the cash conversion cycle. The cash conversion cycle is equal to the Inventory conversion period + Receivables collection period – Payables deferral period. Answer (a) is correct because the impact of a decreased inventory conversion period is a reduction in the cash conversion cycle. Answers (b), (c), and (d) are incorrect because these actions would increase the length of a firm's cash conversion cycle.

7. (d) The requirement is to calculate the cash conversion cycle. The cash conversion period is calculated as the Inventory conversion period + Receivables collection period – Payables deferral period. Answer (d) is correct because the inventory conversion period is $2,500,000/$50,000 = 50 days, and the receivable conversion period is $2,000,000/$100,000 = 20 days. Therefore, the cash conversion cycle is equal to 50 days + 20 days – 30 days = 40 days. Answer (a) is incorrect because it erroneously adds the payable deferral period.

8. (b) The requirement is to calculate the inventory conversion period. The inventory conversion period is calculated as average inventory/(cost of sales per day). Answer (b) is correct because $5,000,000/($30,000,000/365) = 60.83 days.

9. (d) The requirement is to identify the definition of the payables deferral period. Answer (d) is correct because the payables deferral period is the average length of time between the purchase of materials and the payment of cash for them. Answer (a) is incorrect because the operating cycle is the period of time elapsing between the acquisition of goods and services involved in the manufacturing process and the final collection of cash from sale of the products. Answer (b) is incorrect because the inventory cycle is the average time required to convert materials into finished goods and sell those goods. Answer (c) is incorrect because the accounts receivable period is the length of time required to collect accounts receivable.

10. (c) The requirement is to identify the impact of the length of the cash conversion cycle on a firm's profitability. Answer (c) is correct because the longer the cash conversion cycle the greater the amount of time from when a firm pays its suppliers to the time it ultimately collects receivables. The greater the time frame the more likely the firm will have to borrow funds and incur interest expense which reduces profitability. Answers (a), (b), and (d) are incorrect because the incurrence of interest will reduce profitability.

11. (c) The requirement is to calculate the number of days' sales outstanding. Answer (c) is correct. One-third of the customers take advantage of the 5% cash discount and pay on day ten. The remaining two-thirds of the customers pay on day 20. Average days' sales outstanding is calculated as

Days' sales outstanding = (1/3) (10 days) + (2/3) (20 days) = 17 days

Answer (a) is incorrect because this inappropriately weights the two different types of customers. Answer (b) is incorrect because this uses a simple average of days rather than a weighted-average. Answer (d) is incorrect because this solution uses the 20-day collection period for customers not taking the cash discount as the days' sales outstanding, rather than the average days for payment by all customers.

12. (d) The requirement is to determine the effect of changing from using a depository transfer check to using a wire transfer. The change is feasible if the interest savings offsets the increased costs. For a fee of $25, the firm gets two extra days' interest on the average transfer amount. By dividing the $25 fee by the interest rate for two days, .04% (2 days × .02%), we get $62,500. Therefore, management should make the change if the average transfer is expected to be greater than $62,500. Answer (a) is incorrect because it is calculating assuming there is only a one-day decrease in float.

13. (c) The requirement is to consider the cash flow implications of electronic funds transfer. Answer (c) is correct because electronic funds transfer takes the float out of both the cash receipts and disbursements processes. It is beneficial to take the float out of the cash receipts process but not the cash disbursements process.

14. (c) The requirement is to determine the benefit or loss from establishing the lockbox system. The firm saves money if the interest savings is greater than the increased cost of processing cash receipts. The increased cost of processing cash receipts is equal to $5,000 ($10,000 bank charge – $5,000 cost savings). The interest savings is measured by multiplying the increase in average funds by the short-term interest rate. The firm will have use of an additional $300,000 ($100,000 × 3 days) in average funds. Therefore, the interest savings is equal to $15,000 ($300,000 × 5%), and the overall benefit is equal to $10,000 ($15,000 – $5,000). Answer (a) is incorrect because it ignores the interest savings. Answer (b) is incorrect because it only considers the bank charge.

15. (d) The requirement is to describe how firms attempt to manage float. Float is the time that elapses relating to mailing, processing, and clearing checks. A firm strives to minimize its cash receipts float to get use of the receipts as soon as possible, and to maximize its cash disbursement float to get use of the funds for as long as possible. Therefore, the correct answer is (d).

16. (d) The requirement is to calculate the financial cost/benefit of establishing a concentration banking arrangement. The cost savings in interest from establishing the arrangement is equal to $9,200 [($115,000 × 2 days) × 4%]. Therefore, answer (d) is correct because implementing the concentration banking arrangement would result in a net savings of $4,200 ($9,200 – $5,000). Answer (a) is incorrect because it only considers the $5,000 cost. Answer (c) is incorrect because it considers the $115,000 in daily cash receipts the benefit.

17. (d) The requirement is to calculate the financial cost/benefit of establishing a lockbox system. Answer (d) is correct because the solution is found by comparing the cost in fees to the benefits in terms of reduced interest costs. Since the float is reduced by three days the firm gets the use of $1,050,000 ($350,000 × 3 days) in additional funds that results in interest savings of $42,000 ($1,050,000 × 4%). Therefore, the net benefit is equal to $20,000 ($42,000 – $22,000). Answer (a) is incorrect because it only considers the bank fee. Answer (b) is incorrect because it only considers the net change in processing costs.

18. (c) The requirement is to calculate the financial costs/benefit of establishing a zero balance account system. Answer (c) is correct because the solution is found by comparing the cost in fees to the benefit in terms of reduced interest costs. Since the float is reduced by four days then the firm gets the use of $160,000 ($40,000 × 4 days) additional funds which results in interest savings of $7,200 ($160,000 × 4.5%). The $1,200 savings is the excess of the interest savings of $7,200 over the costs of $6,000. Answer (a) is incorrect because it only considerers the cost without considering the interest savings. Answer (b) is incorrect because it is calculated by considering the $7,200 interest savings as a cost and the $6,000 in maintenance and transfer fees as a benefit. Answer (d) is incorrect because it only considers the interest savings.

19. (b) The requirement is to identify the working capital technique that increases the payable float. Answer (b) is the correct answer because payment by draft (e.g., a check) is slower than other methods of payment such as electronic cash transfers. Answers (a) and (d) are incorrect because they are techniques designed to speed the processing of cash receipts. Answer (c) is incorrect because EDI involves processing transactions electronically. This would speed up the payment of payables.

20. (d) The requirement is to determine the optimal agreement for a lockbox system. The number of checks issued during the year is determined by multiplying 700 times 360 days, which results in a total of 252,000 checks. The total amount of collections is equal to $453,600,000 (252,000 checks × $1,800 per check). Answer (d) is correct because it results in the lowest cost of $122,500 ($1,750,000 × 7%), which is the cost of maintaining the compensating balance. Answer (a) is incorrect because it results in a cost of $126,000 ($.50 × 252,000 checks). Answer (b) is incorrect because it results in a cost of $125,000. Answer (c) is incorrect because it results in a fee of $136,080 (3% × $453,600,000).

21. (d) The requirement is to calculate the annual benefit from accepting the bank's proposal. Answer (d) is correct because the net benefit from the reduction of the cash receipts float is $12,000 [($100,000 × 2) × 6%] minus the annual service fee, $6,000 ($500 × 12 months), which is equal to $6,000. Answer (b) is incorrect because it ignores the bank service charge. Answer (c) is incorrect because it assumes only a one-day reduction in float.

22. (b) The requirement is to identify the term used to describe a required minimum checking account balance. Answer (b) is correct because a compensating balance is a minimum balance required by the bank to compensate the

bank for services. Answer (a) is incorrect because transactions balance is the amount of funds the firm needs on deposit to conduct day-to-day transactions. Answer (c) is incorrect because this precautionary balance represents the balance available for emergencies. Answer (d) is incorrect because this speculative balance represents the balance available for bargain purchases.

23. (c) The requirement is to calculate the net benefit from accepting the bank's proposal. The correct answer is (c) because the annual benefit is $6,000 which is equal to the interest income $12,000 ($100,000 × 2 days × 6%) – $6,000 ($500 × 12) cost.

24. (b) The requirement is to calculate the net benefit of using the lockbox system. Answer (b) is correct because the net benefit is equal to $60,875, which is equal to the interest savings of $120,000 ($20,000 average payment × 50 payments × 2 days × 6%) minus the cost of the service of $59,125 [$50,000 + (50 payments per day × 365 days × $0.50)].

25. (b) The requirement is to identify the most important consideration with respect to short-tem investments. Answer (b) is correct because short-term investments must be available to convert to cash when needed. Therefore, risk and liquidity are the most important considerations. Answers (a), (c), and (d) are incorrect because they are important considerations with respect to long-term investments.

26. (d) The requirement is to identify the security that is **not** suitable as a marketable investment. Answer (d) is correct because convertible bonds are long-term investments that have more risk than securities that are typically used for short-term investment. The primary considerations regarding short-term investments are liquidity and safety. Answers (a), (b), and (c) are all appropriate as marketable investments. They are liquid and have a low degree of risk.

27. (d) The requirement is to identify the instrument with the highest return. Answer (d) is correct because commercial paper is issued by a corporation and, therefore, has more risk than Treasury notes, Treasury bonds, or money market accounts.

28. (d) The requirement is to identify the item that is **not** a characteristic of a negotiable certificate of deposit. The correct answer is (d) because negotiable certificates of deposit have lower yields than banker's acceptances and commercial paper—they have less risk. Answer (a) is incorrect because negotiable certificates of deposit do have a secondary market. Answer (b) is incorrect because negotiable certificates of deposit are regulated by the Federal Reserve System. Answer (c) is incorrect because they are usually sold in denominations of a minimum of $100,000.

29. (b) In a just-in-time (JIT) purchasing system, orders are placed such that delivery of raw materials occurs just as they are needed for production. This system requires the placement of more frequent, smaller orders and ideally eliminates inventories. Conversely, in a traditional system large orders are placed less frequently and extra inventory is carried to avoid stockouts and the resulting production delays during order lead time. Certain cost changes would encourage managers to switch to a JIT system. One is **decreased** cost per purchase order, which would increase the attractiveness of placing the many more orders required. Another is **increased** inventory unit carrying costs, which would make the elimination of inventories desirable.

30. (c) Calculation of the reorder point includes consideration of the average daily usage, average delivery time, and stock-out costs. Answer (a) is incorrect because ordering costs are included in determining the economic order quantity but not the reorder point. Answer (b) is incorrect because carrying cost is considered in determining the economic order quantity but not the reorder point. Answer (d) is incorrect because the economic order quantity is not considered in determining the reorder point.

31. (d) The requirement is to identify the item that involves an incorrect comparison of a just-in-time system and a traditional system. Answer (d) is correct because in a just-in-time system the lot size is based on immediate need; a traditional system bases lot size on formulas. Answers (a), (b), and (c) are all incorrect because they express correct comparisons of just-in-time and traditional systems.

32. (a) The goal of a just-in-time system is to identify and eliminate all non-value-added activities. One of the major features of a just-in-time system is a decrease in the number of suppliers to build strong relations and ensure quality goods. In a just-in-time system raw material is purchased only as it is needed for production, thereby eliminating the need for costly storage. In a just-in-time system, vendors make more frequent deliveries of small quantities of materials that are placed into production immediately upon receipt.

33. (c) The purpose of a just-in-time production system is to decrease the size of production runs while increasing the number of lots processed during the year. This production philosophy requires that inventory be delivered as it is needed, rather than held in large quantities. Inventory turnover is computed as

$$\frac{\text{Cost of goods sold}}{\text{Average inventory}}$$

As average inventory decreases, inventory turnover increases. As average inventory levels decrease, inventory as a percentage of total assets will also decrease.

34. (d) The requirement is to determine the effect of a decrease in safety stock on Dee Co.'s economic order quantity (EOQ). The EOQ represents the optimal quantity of inventory to be ordered based on demand and various inventory costs. The formula for computing EOQ is

$$EOQ = \sqrt{\frac{2aD}{k}}$$

Where

D = Demand (in units) for a specified time period

a = Ordering costs per purchase order

k = Cost of carrying one unit in inventory for the specified time period

Safety stock is a buffer of excess inventory held to guard against stockouts. Safety stock is usually a multiple of demand and has no effect on a company's EOQ.

35. (a) The economic order quantity (EOQ) formula was developed on the basis of the following assumptions:

1. Demand occurs at a constant rate throughout the year and is known with certainty.
2. Lead-time on the receipt of orders is constant.
3. The entire quantity ordered is received at one time.
4. The unit costs of the items ordered are constant; thus, there can be no quantity discounts.
5. There are no limitations on the size of the inventory.

Answer (a) is correct because it is assumption 1. Answer (b) is incorrect because it contradicts assumption 5. Answers (c) and (d) are incorrect because they are the opposite of assumption 4.

36. (b) The requirement is to calculate the economic order quantity (EOQ). The EOQ formula is

$$EOQ = \sqrt{\frac{2aD}{k}}$$

In the above equation, a = cost of placing one order, D = annual demand in units, and k = cost of carrying one unit in inventory for one year. Substituting the given information, the equation becomes

$$EOQ = \sqrt{\frac{(2)(32)(20,000)}{8}} = \sqrt{160,000} = 400 \text{ units}$$

37. (d) The requirement is to determine the order point for material X. When safety stock is maintained, the order point is computed as follows:

$$\frac{\text{Daily}}{\text{Demand}} \times \frac{\text{Lead time}}{\text{in days}} + \frac{\text{Safety}}{\text{stock}}$$

Daily demand is eighty units (20,000 units ÷ 250 days). Therefore, the order point is 3,200 units [(80 × 30) + 800].

38. (a) The requirement is to identify the impact of inventory levels on costs. Maintaining a low level of inventory requires that many smaller orders of inventory be made in order to satisfy customer demand. Answer (a) is correct because each order incurs ordering cost and as the quantity of orders increases the ordering costs will also increase. Answer (b) is incorrect because carrying costs are higher with a higher level of inventory. Answer (c) is incorrect because although the ordering costs are higher the carrying costs are lower. Answer (d) is incorrect because the ordering costs would be higher.

39. (d) The requirement is to identify an inventory carrying cost. The correct answer is (d). Part of the cost of holding inventory is the cost of obsolescence. Answer (a) is an example of a stockout cost. Answer (a) is a stock-out cost. Answer (b) and (c) are examples of ordering costs.

40. (d) The requirement is to identify the characteristic of JIT inventory systems. Answer (d) is correct because JIT systems rely on quality materials; otherwise production shutdowns will occur because no extra materials are available. Answer (a) is incorrect because there are no safety stocks in JIT systems. Answer (b) is incorrect because JIT is applicable to all size corporations. Answer (c) is incorrect because JIT generally is applied all along the supply chain.

41. (d) The requirement is to identify the factor **not** used in the economic order quantity formula. Answer (d) is correct because the volume of products in inventory is not a component of the economic order quantity formula. Answers (a), (b), and (c) are incorrect because they are all components of the EOQ formula.

42. (d) The requirement is to determine the cost savings from selecting one of the production alternatives. Under the level production alternative, the firm would incur an additional $40,000 [($1,500,000 – $2,000,000) × 8%] in inventory holding costs but it would save $50,000 in production costs. Therefore, answer (d) is the correct answer. Alternative 1 results in $10,000 ($50,000 – $40,000) in savings over Alternative 2.

43. (c) The requirement is to calculate the short-term interest rate that would cause the two alternatives to have equal costs. The cost of implementing Alternative 2 is the $50,000 in additional production costs. When the inventory holding costs related to Alternative 1 equals that amount the costs are equal. By dividing the $50,000 by the $500,000 in additional average inventory, we get 10% ($50,000 ÷ $500,000). Therefore, the correct answer is (c) because at a 10% interest rate the cost of holding the additional inventory under Alternative 1 is equal to the additional production costs under Alternative 2.

44. (b) The requirement is to determine the factor that would increase inventory levels. In answering this question, you should consider the components of the EOQ formula. The correct answer is (b) because if the cost of holding inventory decreases it would enable the firm to carry more inventory. Answer (a) is incorrect because a decrease in sales would result in a decrease in the required level of inventory. Answer (c) is incorrect because a decrease in sales variability decreases the required level of inventory. Answer (d) is incorrect because a decrease in the cost of running out of stock decreases the required level of inventory.

45. (a) The requirement is to identify the technique used to plan and control manufacturing inventories. Answer (a) is correct because materials requirements planning is an inventory planning technique. Answer (b) is incorrect because regression analysis is a technique used to estimate the relationship between variables. Answer (c) is incorrect because capital budgeting is a technique used to evaluate investments in capital assets. Answer (d) is incorrect because linear programming is a technique used to determine the optimal decision when resources are constrained.

46. (c) The requirement is to identify the definition of collection policy. Answer (c) is correct because a firm's collection policy is the diligence used to collect slow paying accounts. Answer (a) is incorrect because the discount policy is the policy regarding the percentage discount given for early payment. Answer (b) is incorrect because the credit policy is a firm's requirements for customers in order to grant them

credit. Answer (d) is incorrect because the payables policy is unrelated to accounts receivable.

47. (b) The requirement is to identify which item is **not** an advantage of initiating seasonal dating. Seasonal dating is a procedure for inducing customers to buy early by not requiring payment until the customers' selling season, regardless of when the merchandise is shipped. Under seasonal dating the selling firm incurs higher credit costs, as customers take longer to pay. Therefore, answer (b) is correct because this is not an advantage of seasonal dating. Answer (a) is incorrect because under seasonal dating, customers buy earlier and the selling firm incurs lower storage costs. This is an advantage of seasonal dating. Answer (c) is incorrect because providing attractive credit terms for customers is an advantage of a seasonal dating policy. Answer (d) is incorrect because reduced uncertainty about sales volume is an advantage of a seasonal dating policy.

48. (c) The requirement is to calculate the total collections on or before January 11. Answer (c) is correct because if all customers take advantage of seasonal dating and all customers take the discount, then collections on or before January 11 will be

= (Number of units sold) (Unit selling price)
   (1 – Discount percentage)

= (700 units) × $10 × .98 (1 – .02) = $6,860

Answer (a) is incorrect because all customers take the discount and abide by the terms of the discount policy, so they will pay on or before January 11. Answer (b) is incorrect because this solution omits the collection of the January 1 sales revenue. Answer (d) is incorrect because this solution does not take the discount into account.

49. (b) The requirement is to identify the formula for days' sales in accounts receivable. Answer (b) is correct because days' sales in receivables provides an overall measure of the accumulation of receivables. It is calculated by dividing the balance of receivables by sales per day. Answers (a), (c), and (d) are incorrect because they do not accurately illustrate the formula.

50. (d) The requirement is to describe a firm's credit criteria. Answer (d) is correct because the credit criteria are the policies used to decide whether a customer should be extended credit. Answer (a) is incorrect because it describes the credit period. Answer (b) is incorrect because it describes a portion of the discount policy. Answer (c) is incorrect because it describes the collection policy.

51. (c) The requirement is to calculate impact of this change in policy on accounts receivable. Under the existing policy, sales are equal to $50,000,000, 70% of which are on credit. Therefore, the average accounts receivable balance is equal to $7,291,667 [($35,000,000 credit sales ÷ 360 days) × 75 days]. Under the new policy credit sales are estimated to be $28,500,000 [($50,000,000 × 95%) × 60%]. Accordingly, the average accounts receivable balance under the new policy is estimated to be $3,958,333 [($28,500,000 credit sales ÷ 360) × 50 days]. Answer (c) is correct because the change in accounts receivable balance is estimated to be a decrease of $3,333,334 ($7,291,667 – $3,958,333).

52. (b) The requirement is to calculate the effect of the new policy on net income before taxes. Answer (b) is correct because the decrease in operating income is equal to $2,166,667 [$2,500,000 loss in sales – ($3,333,334 × 10%) interest savings]. Answer (a) is incorrect because it only considers the loss in sales. Answer (c) is incorrect because it treats the entire $3,333,334 change in average receivables as a benefit.

53. (b) The requirement is to determine the factor that is **not** considered in determining whether to change credit policy. Answer (b) is correct because the current bad debt experience is irrelevant to the decision. Management should consider only those factors that change based upon the alternative selected. Answer (a) is incorrect because the cost of funds is relevant to the decision. Answer (c) is incorrect because if there is any impact on the current customer base, this factor should be considered. Answer (d) is incorrect because the impact on bank loan covenants is obviously relevant.

54. (d) The requirement is to calculate the cost of the financing. Answer (d) is correct because the total amount paid to the factor would be ($100,000 × 80%) × 10% + ($100,000 × 12) × 2% = $32,000. The net cost is equal to $14,000 ($32,000 – $18,000 cost savings). Therefore, the interest cost is equal to $14,000/$80,000 = 17.5%.

55. (d) The requirement is to calculate the benefit or loss from changing credit policy. Answer (d) is correct because the benefit is equal to the contribution margin received from the additional sales minus the cost of having incremental funds tied up in accounts receivable. The benefit from an increase in sales is equal to $144,000 ($720,000 sales × 20% contribution margin). The interest opportunity cost is equal to 75 days' interest on the variable portion of sales, or ($720,000 × 80%)/360 × 75 × 20% interest = $24,000. Therefore, the net benefit is equal to $120,000 ($144,000 – $24,000).

56. (d) The requirement is to calculate the cost of not taking a trade discount. The cost is calculated with the following formula:

$$\frac{\text{Discount percent}}{100\% - \text{Discount percent}} \times \frac{365 \text{ days}}{\text{Total pay period} - \text{Discount period}}$$

Answer (d) is correct because the discount percentage is 3%, the total pay period is 35 days, and the discount period is 15 days. Therefore, the nominal cost is calculated as follows:

$$\frac{3\%}{100\% - 3\%} \times \frac{365 \text{ days}}{35 \text{ days} - 10 \text{ days}} = 45.2\%$$

57. (b) The requirement is to calculate the cost of not taking a trade discount. The cost is calculated with the following formula:

$$\frac{\text{Discount percent}}{100\% - \text{Discount percent}} \times \frac{365 \text{ days}}{\text{Total pay period} - \text{Discount period}}$$

Answer (b) is correct because the discount percentage is 3%, the total pay period is 67 days, and the discount period is 15 days. Therefore, the nominal cost is calculated as follows:

$$\frac{3\%}{100\% - 3\%} \times \frac{365 \text{ days}}{67 \text{ days} - 15 \text{ days}} = 21.71\%$$

58. (b) The requirement is to analyze the impact upon a firm of rising short-term interest rates. A heavy reliance on short-term debt means that interest expense and the related net income will be variable and this increases the financial risk of the firm. Answer (b) is correct because if short-term interest rates increase then interest expense will increase which will cause a related decrease in net income.

59. (c) The requirement is to evaluate credit terms to made sound cash management decisions. Answer (c) is correct because a firm should take advantage of the cash discount and pay on the last day of the discount period, which is day 10. Answers (a) and (b) are incorrect because "2" is the amount of the percentage discount; not the discount period. Answer (d) is incorrect because if a firm pays bills on the final due date, it will not have taken advantage of cash discounts which are very lucrative.

60. (d) The requirement is to identify the forms of borrowing that are unsecured. Answer (d) is correct because revolving credit agreements, bankers' acceptances, lines of credit, and commercial paper all represent unsecured obligations. Answer (a) is incorrect because floating liens and chattel mortgages are secured. Answer (b) is incorrect because factoring agreements and chattel mortgages are secured. Answer (c) is incorrect because floating liens and chattel mortgages are secured.

61. (d) The requirement is to evaluate the cost of trade credit. Answer (d) is correct because if the discount period is longer, the days of extra credit obtained by forgoing the discount are fewer. This makes the trade credit more costly. Answer (a) is incorrect because the lower the discount percentage, the lower the opportunity cost of forgoing the discount and using the trade credit financing. Answers (b) and (c) are incorrect because percentage financing cost is unaffected by the purchase price of the items.

62. (b) The requirement is to calculate the effective interest rate on a loan with a compensating balance requirement. The interest rate is calculated with the following formula:

$$\frac{\text{Interest cost}}{\text{Funds available}} = \frac{10\% \times \$500,000}{\$500,000 - \$50,000} = 11.1\%$$

Therefore, answer (b) is correct.

63. (d) The requirement is to calculate the cost of not taking a trade discount. The formula for computing the interest is

$$\frac{\text{Discount percent}}{100\% - \text{Discount percent}} \times \frac{360 \text{ days}}{\text{Total pay period} - \text{Discount period}}$$

$$\frac{3\%}{100\% - 3\%} \times \frac{360 \text{ days}}{45 \text{ days} - 10 \text{ days}} = 31.81\%$$

Therefore, answer (d) is correct.

64. (a) The requirement is to identify the term that is **not** related to loans involving inventory. Answer (a) is correct because factoring involves the sale of accounts receivable. Answer (b) is incorrect because a blanket inventory lien involves a legal document that establishes inventory as collateral for a loan. Answer (c) is incorrect because a trust receipt is an instrument that acknowledges that the borrower holds the inventory and the proceeds from sales will be put in trust for the lender. Answer (d) is incorrect because warehousing involves storing inventory in a public warehouse under the control of the lender.

65. (b) The requirement is to identify the nature of LIBOR. Answer (b) is correct because LIBOR, like the prime rate, is an example of a nominal rate. It is adjusted for inflation risk, but not credit risk. Answer (a) is incorrect because the risk-free rate is a theoretical rate that is not quoted. Answer (c) is incorrect because LIBOR is not credit risk adjusted. Answer (d) is incorrect because LIBOR is a short-term rate.

66. (a) The requirement is to identify the advantage of using long-term debt as a source of financing current assets. Answer (a) is correct because financing with long-term as opposed to short-term debt reduces the risk of the firm. Long-term debt does not have to be repaid as soon as short-term debt. Answer (b) is incorrect because long-term debt is generally more costly than short-term debt. Answer (c) is incorrect because the debt covenants are usually more restrictive in long-term debt agreements. Answer (d) is incorrect because early payment of long-term debt can result in prepayment penalties.

67. (c) The requirement is to identify the item that is **not** an implication of the policy of matching maturity assets with the maturity of financing. Answer (c) is correct because under this policy current assets are financed with current liabilities. Answers (a), (b), and (d) are incorrect because they are all appropriate implications of the policy.

68. (d) The requirement is to identify the term used to describe asset-backed public offerings. Answer (d) is correct because securitization of assets is the offering of debt collateralized by a firm's accounts receivable. Answer (a) is incorrect because a trust receipt is an instrument that acknowledges that the borrower holds a collateralized inventory and that proceeds from the sale will be put in trust for the lender. Answer (b) is incorrect because warehousing is the storage of inventory in a public warehouse that can only be removed with the lender's permission. Answer (c) is incorrect because a blanket inventory lien is a document that establishes the inventory as collateral for the loan.

69. (d) The requirement is to calculate the effective cost of a loan with a compensating balance requirement. Answer (d) is correct because the effective interest rate is equal to the interest paid, $7,000 ($100,000 × 7%) divided by the funds that are available, $80,000 (80% × $100,000). Therefore, the effective interest rate is equal to 8.75% ($7,000 ÷ $80,000). Answer (a) is not reasonable because the amount is less than the stated interest rate. Answer (b) is incorrect because it is the stated rate. Answer (c) is incorrect because it is computed by adding 20% of the stated rate to the stated rate.

70. (b) The requirement is to calculate the weighted-average annual interest rate for trade credit. If the company does not pay Web Master within the discount period, it will incur interest costs of $500 ($25,000 × 2%). This results in an annualized interest rate of 36.7347% [($500 ÷ $24,500) × 360 days ÷ (30 − 10 days)]. If the company does not pay the Softidee account during the discount period, it will incur

interest cost of $2,500 ($50,000 × 5%). This results in an annualized interest rate of 23.6842% [($2,500 ÷ $47,500) × 360 days ÷ (90 − 10 days)]. To determine the weighted-average interest rate, we must first determine the average amount borrowed. For Web Master, this is equal to $24,500 × (20 days ÷ 360 days) = $1,361.11, and for Softidee, it is equal to $47,500 × (80 days ÷ 360 days) = $10,555.56. Therefore, the weighted-average interest rate is equal to 25.2% {[(36.7347% × $1,361.11) + (23.6842% × $10,555.56)] ÷ ($1,361.11 + $10,555.56)}. Answer (a) is incorrect because it uses weights of $25,000 and $50,000. Answer (c) is incorrect because it is based on weights of $24,500 and $47,500. Answer (d) is incorrect because it is the unweighted-average of the two rates.

71. (d) The requirement is to identify the statement that determines whether CyberAge should continue to use the trade credit. Answer (d) is correct because the company should continue to use the trade credit as long as the alternative cost of other forms of financing is higher. Answer (a) is incorrect because if alternative sources are less, the alternative should be used. Answer (b) is incorrect because in considering short-term financing alternatives, it is the marginal cost of capital that is important, not the weighted-average cost of capital. Answer (c) is incorrect because if the cost of long-term financing is greater, the trade credit should be used.

72. (b) The requirement is to identify the statement that is **most** likely true about commercial paper. Answer (b) is correct because commercial paper is normally issued with a short maturity period, usually 2 to 9 months. Answer (a) is incorrect because commercial paper is issued by the corporation. Answer (c) is incorrect because commercial paper is unsecured. Answer (d) is incorrect because commercial paper is typically issued by large corporations.

73. (a) The requirement is to calculate the effective interest on the loan. Answer (a) is correct because the effective interest is 6.44%. The effective interest rate is determined by calculating the net interest expense, which is $15,000 ($250,000 × 6%) minus the interest income from the compensating balance $500 ($25,000 × 2%) equals $14,500. Then, this amount is divided by the amount of money that the firm has available, $250,000 − $25,000 compensating balance. Thus, the effective interest rate is 6.44% ($14,500/$225,000).

74. (a) The requirement is to identify the loan with the most favorable terms. Answer (a) is correct because simple interest with no compensating balance is the most favorable terms from an effective interest basis. Answers (b), (c), and (d) are incorrect because discount interest and/or a compensating balance increase the effective interest rate on the loan.

75. (d) The requirement is to calculate the effective interest rate when a loan is in the form of a discounted note. When a note is on a discounted basis, the interest is withheld from the proceeds. Answer (d) is correct because the effective interest rate is calculated by dividing the total amount of interest by the amount of funds available. In this case, the interest is equal to $9,000 ($100,000 × 9%) and the funds available are $91,000 ($100,000 − $9,000). Thus the interest rate is 9.89% ($9,000/$91,000). Answer (b) is incorrect because it represents the stated rate, not the effective rate.

76. (c) The requirement is to calculate the annual cost of the financing arrangement. Answer (c) is correct because the annual cost of the arrangement is calculated as $7,000 (6% × $100,000) + [($300,000 – $100,000) × 1/2%)]. Answers (a), (b), and (d) are incorrect because they represent inaccurate computations of the cost of the financing.

77. (c) The requirement is to identify the largest source of short-term financing. Answer (c) is correct because trade credit is the largest source of short-term financing for most small firms. It occurs automatically with the purchase of goods and services. Answers (a) and (b) are incorrect because they are not the largest source of short-term financing for most small firms. Answer (d) is incorrect because mortgage bonds are a source of long-term financing.

78. (c) The requirement is to define the prime rate of interest. Answer (c) is correct because the prime rate of interest is the rate financial institutions charge their customers with the highest credit rating. Answer (a) is incorrect because a commitment fee is not related to the rate of interest. Answer (b) is incorrect because the effective rate on the bank loans of most firms is greater than the prime rate. Answer (d) is incorrect because the rate at which a bank borrows from the Federal Reserve central bank is the discount rate.

79. (a) The requirement is to describe the purpose of a compensating balance. Answer (a) is correct because a compensating balance provides a form of additional compensation to financial institutions. Answers (b), (c), and (d) are incorrect because they do not describe the purpose of a compensating balance.

80. (d) The requirement is to calculate the effective annual interest rate of the credit arrangement. Answer (d) is correct because the effective interest rate is equal to the interest cost divided by the available funds. The interest cost is $36,000 ($300,000 × 12%), and the available funds is equal to $255,000 [$300,000 – (15% × $300,000)]. Therefore, the effective interest rate is 14.12% ($36,000/$255,000).

81. (c) The requirement is to identify the correct statement about bond financing alternatives. Answer (c) is correct because a call provision is detrimental to the investor because he or she may be forced to redeem the bond. Answer (a) is incorrect because a bond with a call provision typically has a higher yield than a similar bond without a call provision. Answer (b) is incorrect because a convertible bond is convertible at the option of the holder. Answer (d) is incorrect because the relationship of the stated rate on the bond to the market rate determines whether or not the bond will sell for more than par value.

82. (b) The requirement is to identify the definition of Eurobonds. Answer (b) is correct because Eurobonds are always sold in some country other than the one in whose currency the bond issue is denominated. The advantage of Eurobonds is that they are less regulated than other bonds and the transaction costs are lower. Answer (a) is incorrect because Eurobonds are not always denominated in Eurodollars, which are US dollars deposited outside the US. Answer (c) is incorrect because foreign bonds are denominated in the currency of the country in which they are sold. Answer (d)

is incorrect because Eurobonds are usually issued not as registered bonds, but as bearer bonds.

83. (c) The requirement is to identify the proper accounting for an operating lease. Answer (c) is correct because an operating lease is one that does not meet the criteria to be a capital lease. Operating leases are treated as rental agreements and the payments are expensed as rent as incurred. Answer (a) is incorrect because it describes the proper accounting for a capital lease. Answers (b) and (d) are incorrect because they describe accounting that is not proper for either type of lease.

84. (d) The requirement is to identify the difference between a capital and an operating lease. Answer (d) is correct because in a capital lease, the risks and rewards of ownership are transferred to the lessee. If the risks/rewards are not transferred, the lease is a rental arrangement and is called an operating lease. In accounting for a capital lease, the lessee capitalizes the net investment in the lease. Answer (a) is incorrect because the lessee obtains use of the asset in all lease agreements. Answer (b) is incorrect because the lessee uses the lease as a source of financing under a capital lease. Answer (c) is incorrect because the lessee does not receive title to the asset in all cases.

85. (c) The requirement is to identify the advantages/disadvantages of debt versus equity financing. Answer (c) is correct because the fixed obligation of interest and principal is an advantage to debt financing. Answers (a), (b), and (d) are incorrect because they are all disadvantages of debt financing.

86. (d) The requirement is to identify the advantages/disadvantages of debt versus equity financing. Answer (d) is correct because debt actually increases stockholders' risk because the financial leverage of the firm is higher. Answers (a), (b), and (c) are incorrect because they are all advantages of debt financing.

87. (d) The requirement is to identify what type of bond has less interest rate risk. Answer (d) is correct because a floating rate bond has a rate of interest that floats with changes in the market interest rate. Therefore, the market price of the bond does not fluctuate as widely. Answer (a) is incorrect because serial bonds are those that are paid off in installments over the life of the issue. Answer (b) is incorrect because sinking fund bonds are those for which the firm makes payments into a sinking fund to be used to retire the bonds by purchase. Answer (c) is incorrect because convertible bonds are those that may be converted into common stock.

88. (a) The requirement is to identify the defining characteristic of serial bonds. Answer (a) is correct because serial bonds are those that are paid off in installments over the life of the issue. Answer (b) is incorrect because sinking fund bonds are those for which the firm makes payments into a sinking fund to be used to retire the bonds by purchase. Answer (c) is incorrect because convertible bonds are those that may be converted into common stock. Answer (d) is incorrect because callable bonds are those that have a call provision that allows the firm to force the bondholders to redeem the bonds before maturity.

89. (c) The requirement is to identify the impact of changes in the market rate of interest on bond valuation.

Answer (c) is correct because if the market rate of interest increases, the bond value will decrease (an inverse effect). Answers (a) and (b) are incorrect because the coupon rate does not change after issuance and determines the amount of the periodic interest payments, not changes in the bond valuation. Answer (d) is incorrect because if the market rate decreases, the value of the bond will increase.

90. (b) The requirement is to calculate the first-year, before-tax cost of the planned debt financing, net of floatation costs. The first year cost would be calculated by dividing the interest rate by the amount of funds received after floatation costs. Therefore, the interest cost before tax is equal to 8% ÷ (101% issue price − 2% floatation costs) = 8.08%. Therefore, the correct answer is (b).

91. (b) The requirement is to identify the reason for issuing Eurobonds rather than domestic bonds. Answer (b) is correct because Eurobonds are not subject to extensive regulation like US issued domestic bonds; therefore, they are less expensive to issue. Answer (a) is incorrect because Eurobonds are not denominated in the currency of the country in which they are issued. Answer (c) is incorrect because foreign buyers are not more readily accepting of the issues. Answer (d) is incorrect because Eurobonds do carry foreign exchange risk for the investor; they have losses if the US dollar declines relative to the country's currency.

92. (c) The requirement is to identify the bond provision that is generally considered to be detrimental to the investor. Answer (c) is correct because a callable bond is one that can be redeemed at the option of the issuer. The investor has no choice but to redeem the bond. Answer (a) is incorrect because a conversion feature means the bond can be converted to common stock at the option of the investor. This is a favorable provision for the investor. Answer (b) is incorrect because redeemable bonds are redeemable at the option of the investor. Answer (d) is incorrect because bonds with serial maturity allow the investor to select the desired maturity date.

93. (c) The requirement is to identify the statement that is not an advantage of leasing as a form of long-term financing. Answer (c) is correct because the dollar cost to lease an asset in the long term is generally greater than the cost to purchase and finance through other means. Answer (a) is incorrect because leases often do not require down payments. Answer (b) is incorrect because the provisions of lease agreements are usually less stringent than for other forms of debt. Answer (d) is incorrect because firms may be able to lease when they do not have the credit capacity to buy an asset.

94. (a) The requirement is to identify the effect of an increase in bond rating. Answer (a) is correct because going from a B rating to a Baa rating is an increase in the bond rating indicative of lower risk. Therefore, the market value of the bonds should increase. Answers (b), (c), and (d) are incorrect because the bond value should increase.

95. (a) The requirement is to identify the statement that can be assumed from the case scenario. Answer (a) is correct because if the bond sold at face value, then the coupon rate of 8% must have approximated the market rate for this bond. Answer (b) is incorrect because the nominal rate does not

include credit risk. Answer (c) is incorrect because the coupon rate, if it was about equal to the market rate, includes a credit risk premium. Answer (d) is incorrect because the risk-free interest rate is always about 1 to 2%.

96. (b) The requirement is to identify the correct statement regarding the effect of a change in the market rate. Answer (b) is correct because an increase in the market rate will cause the bond to reduce in value until it sells at a price that will result in a yield to maturity equal to the current market rate. Answer (a) is incorrect because the market rate would have to decline for the bond to increase in value. Answer (c) is incorrect because LIBOR is only indirectly related to the long-term bond rate. Answer (d) is incorrect because the change in value can be predicted.

97. (d) The requirement is to calculate the current yield on a bond. The current yield is equal to the annual interest paid divided by the bond market price. Watco's $1,000 bond pays $80 per year in interest, the $1,000 face value × the 8% coupon rate. Answer (d) is correct because the current yield is equal to 8.42% ($80 ÷ $950). Answer (a) is incorrect because 8% is the coupon rate.

98. (d) The requirement is to identify the purpose of the secondary market. Answer (d) is correct because outstanding stocks of publicly owned companies are traded among investors in the secondary market. The original issuer receives no additional capital as a result of such trades. Answers (a) and (b) are incorrect because firms raise capital by issuing new securities in the primary market, and the initial public offering market is a frequently used term for the market in which previously privately owned firms issue new securities to the public. Answer (c) is incorrect because the over-the-counter market is the network of dealers that provides for trading in unlisted securities.

99. (a) The requirement is to identify the purpose of the primary market. Answer (a) is correct because the primary market is the market for new stocks and bonds. Answer (b) is incorrect because existing securities are traded on a secondary market. Answer (c) is incorrect because the futures market is where commodities contracts are sold, not the capital market. Answer (d) is incorrect because exchanges of existing securities do not occur in the primary market.

100. (c) The requirement is to identify the characteristic that is **not** usually a feature of cumulative preferred stock. Answer (c) is correct because preferred stock usually does not have voting rights. Preferred shareholders are generally given the right to vote for directors of the company only if the company has not paid the preferred dividend for a specified period of time, such as ten quarters. Answer (a) is incorrect because preferred stock does have priority over common stock with regard to earnings, so dividends must be paid on preferred stock before they can be paid on common stock. Answer (b) is incorrect because preferred stock does have priority over common stock with regard to assets, so in the event of bankruptcy, the claims of preferred shareholders must be satisfied in full before the common shareholders receive anything. Answer (d) is incorrect because cumulative preferred stock does have the right to receive any dividends in arrears before common stock dividends are paid.

101. (b) The requirement is to identify the statement that describes an advantage of going public. Answer (b) is correct because the compliance cost of going public and complying with SEC regulations is substantial. Answer (a) is incorrect because going public does provide access to more capital. Answer (c) is incorrect because public companies can issue stock options to attract and retain management. Answer (d) is incorrect because owners obtain immediate liquidity for their investments when the firm goes public.

102. (b) The requirement is to calculate the degree of operating leverage of the company. The formula for degree of operating leverage is

$$DOL = \frac{\text{Percent change in operating income}}{\text{Percent change in unit volume}}$$

In this case, the percent change in operating income is equal to 50% [($300,000 − $200,000) ÷ $200,000], and the percent change in unit volume is equal to 5% [(105,000 − 100,000 units) ÷ 100,000 units]. Therefore, the correct answer is (b) because DOL is equal to 10 (50% ÷ 5%).

103. (a) The requirement is to calculate the degree of financial leverage for the company. The formula for degree of financial leverage is

$$DFL = \frac{\text{Percent change in EPS}}{\text{Percent change in EBIT}}$$

In this case, the percent change in EPS is equal to 500% [($1.20 − $0.20) ÷ $0.20], and the percent change in EBIT is equal to 50% [($300,000 − $200,000) ÷ $200,000]. Therefore, the DFL is equal to 10 (500% ÷ 50%), and answer (a) is correct.

104. (d) The requirement is to identify the advantages/disadvantages of equity financing. Answer (d) is correct because the lack of a firm obligation to pay dividends to common shareholders is an advantage of equity financing. Answers (a), (b), and (c) are incorrect because they are all disadvantages of equity financing.

105. (a) The requirement is to identify the impact of debt versus equity financing. Answer (a) is correct because Company A is more highly leveraged. It has greater fixed charges in the form of interest. Therefore, Company A will have more volatile net earnings than Company B. Answers (b) and (c) are incorrect because the level of fixed financing charges does not affect operating earnings variability. Operating income is computed before interest expense. Answer (d) is incorrect because Company A has greater, not less, financial leverage than Company B.

106. (d) The requirement is to identify the item that is **not** a potential long-term source of funding for a firm. Answer (d) is correct because a line of credit is a short-term financing source. Answers (a), (b), and (c) are incorrect because they are possible sources of financing for long-term projects.

107. (d) The requirement is to identify the factor that does **not** affect management's judgment about the firm's capital structure. Answer (d) is correct because the expected return on assets is not a factor that affects management's judgment about the firm's capital structure. Answer (a) is incorrect because the greater the inherent risk of a business, the lower the optimal

debt to equity ratio. Answer (b) is incorrect because a major advantage of debt is the tax deductibility of interest payments. Answer (c) is incorrect because a firm's target capital structure will be affected by the risk tolerance of management. More aggressive management may take on more debt.

108. (b) The requirement is to identify a characteristic of higher operating leverage. Higher operating leverage involves more fixed costs, which results in more operating variability and more risk. Answer (b) is correct because a firm's profits are more sensitive to changes in sales volume when the firm is more leveraged. Answer (a) is incorrect because higher leveraged firms have less variable costs. Answer (c) is incorrect because the firm may or may not be more profitable. Answer (d) is incorrect because a highly leveraged firm is more risky.

109. (d) The requirement is to identify the consequences of an increase in financial leverage. Answer (d) is correct because when the degree of financial leverage rises, fixed interest charges rise. This causes the standard deviation of returns to equity holders to increase. Answers (a) and (b) are incorrect because an increase in the degree of financial leverage is associated with an increase in equity beta and an increase in the systematic risk of the company. Equity beta is a measure of systematic risk of the company. Answer (c) is incorrect because unsystematic risk of the company does not fall.

110. (d) Answer (d) is correct because a weighted-average of the costs of all financing sources should be used, with the weights determined by the usual financing proportions. Answer (a) is incorrect because the cost of funds for a particular project does not represent the cost of capital for the firm. The cost of capital should also be calculated on an after-tax basis. Answer (b) is incorrect because the cost of capital is a composite, or weighted-average, of all financing sources in their usual proportions. Answer (c) is incorrect because the cost of capital is a composite, or weighted-average, of all financing sources in their usual proportions. It includes both the after-tax cost of debt and the cost of equity financing.

111. (b) The requirement is to identify the statement that is **not** true regarding the acceptance of Alternative 1. Answer (b) is correct because Alternative 1 involves much less financial leverage than Alternative 2. Answer (a) is incorrect because Alternative 1 is the more conservative capital structure because it involves less debt. Answer (c) is incorrect because net income will be less variable under Alternative 1. Answer (d) is incorrect because total interest expense will be less under Alternative 1.

112. (b) The requirement is to compare the weighted-average cost of capital for the two alternatives. Answer (b) is correct because the cost of debt after tax for is 5.1% [6% × (100% − 15% tax rate)] for Alternative 1 and 5.95% [7% × (100% − 15% tax rate)] for Alternative 2. The weighted-average cost of capital for Alternative 1 is 7.55% [(5.1% × $3,000,000 ÷ $6,000,000) + (10% × $3,000,000 ÷ $6,000,000)], and the weighted-average cost of capital for Alternative 2 is 6.96% [(5.95% × $5,000,000 ÷ $6,000,000) + (12% × $1,000,000 ÷ $6,000,000)]. Therefore, the differential is 0.59% (7.55% − 6.96%). Answer (a) is incorrect because it results from an unweighted computation. Answer (c) is incorrect because it is the before-tax computation.

113. (a) The requirement is to identify the factor that affects the calculation of the cost of equity using CAPM. Answer (a) is correct because a reduction in the risk-free rate would reduce the required return demanded by stockholders. Answers (b), (c), and (d) are incorrect because an increase in these items would cause the estimated cost of common equity to increase.

114. (b) The requirement is to identify the reason why it is more expensive to finance with equity than with debt. Answer (b) is correct because equity holders are subject to more risk than debt holders. Therefore, they require a higher rate of return.

115. (d) The requirement is to identify the item that does **not** describe a characteristic of the capital asset pricing model. Answer (d) is correct because CAPM does not include the stock's market price in its computation. Answers (a), (b), and (c) are incorrect because they are all characteristics of CAPM model.

116. (b) The requirement is to apply the dividend-yield-plus-growth approach to calculate the cost of common equity. The formula for estimated cost of common equity is equal to the expected dividend divided by the stock price plus the growth rate. Therefore, the correct answer is (b) because the estimated cost of equity is 14.1% $[(2.11/23.13) + 5\%]$.

117. (b) The requirement is to identify the impact of an increase in nominal interest rates on a company's share price. Answer (b) is correct because an increase in the nominal interest rate would mean that investors would expect a higher return on all investments. If the stock earnings and dividend growth is unchanged, the stock price will decrease.

118. (a) The requirement is to identify the impact of investor expectations on stock price. Answer (a) is correct because if investors expect a higher dividend growth rate, the market value of the common shares will be greater. Answer (b) is incorrect because if investors expect a lower dividend growth rate, the market value of common shares will be lower. Answers (c) and (d) are incorrect because holding periods are not related to the market value of common shares.

119. (a) The requirement is to identify the technique that explicitly considers risk in calculating the firm's estimated cost of equity. Answer (a) is correct because CAPM is the only technique that explicitly considers risk in the form of the firm's beta. Beta measures the relationship between the price volatility of the market as a whole and the price volatility of the individual stock. Answers (b) and (c) are incorrect because they do not directly incorporate the firm's risk in the calculation of the estimated cost of equity. Answer (d) is incorrect because it is not utilized to determine the estimated cost of equity.

120. (c) The requirement is to use the dividend-yield-plus-growth-rate approach to calculate the estimated cost of equity. The estimated cost of equity is equal to the dividend divided by the price of the stock + the growth rate. Accordingly, answer (c) is correct because the estimated cost of equity is equal to 14.3% $[(\$5 \div \$60) + 6\%]$.

121. (b) The requirement is to identify how the bond-yield-plus approach to estimating the cost of equity is applied. Answer (b) is correct because the bond-yield-plus approach involves adding a risk premium of 3% to 5% to the interest rate of the firm's long-term debt. Answers (a), (c), and (d) are incorrect because they involve items that are not components of the formula.

122. (a) The requirement is to identify the characteristic of typical dividend policies. Answer (a) is correct because management is hesitant to decrease dividends. Therefore, they are more stable than earnings. Answer (b) is incorrect because they do not fluctuate more widely than earnings. Answer (c) is incorrect because dividends tend to be higher for mature firms. Answer (d) is incorrect because dividends are usually not changed every year.

123. (c) The requirement is to calculate the current net cost of debt. The current cost of debt before tax is 8.5% (7% Treasury bond rate + 1.5%), and the cost of debt after tax is 5.1% $[8.5\% \times (1 - 40\% \text{ tax rate})]$. Therefore, the correct answer is (c).

124. (d) The requirement is to calculate the cost of capital using CAPM. The CAPM formula is Cost of capital = Risk-free rate + (Market rate – Risk-free rate) × Beta. In this case, the estimated cost of equity is equal to 17% $[7\% + (15\% - 7\%) \times 1.25]$. Thus, the answer is (d).

125. (a) The requirement is to calculate the weighted-average cost of capital. The weighted-average cost of capital is determined by summing the cost of each funding source weighted by its percentage of the total. In this case, the funds received from the debt are equal to 99% (101% – 2%) × $15,000,000, or $14,850,000, and the funds from equity is $35 million, the amount of retained earnings. Therefore, total funding is $49,850,000. The weighted-average cost of capital is equal to ($14,850,000/$49,850,000) × 7% + ($35,000,000/$49,850,000) × 12% = 10.50%. Thus, the answer is (a).

126. (a) The requirement is to use the capital asset pricing model to compute the cost of equity (expected return of equity holders). The CAPM formula is: Cost of equity = Risk-free interest rate + (Market rate – Risk-free interest rate) × Beta. Therefore, the expected return = 9.2% $[5\% + (12\% - 5\%) \times .60]$, or answer (a).

127. (b) The requirement is to specify the cost of capital assigned to retained earnings. Answer (b) is correct because newly issued or "external" common equity is more costly than retained earnings because the company incurs issuance costs when raising new funds. Answer (a) is incorrect because the cost of retained earnings is the rate of return stockholders require on retained equity capital. The opportunity cost of retained funds will be positive. Answer (c) is incorrect because retained earnings will always be less costly than external equity financing because earnings retention does not involve the payment of issuance costs. Answer (d) is incorrect because the cost is lower as described above.

128. (c) The requirement is to identify the relevant risk of a security according to CAPM. Answer (c) is correct because systematic risk is the component of the total risk of a security that cannot be eliminated through diversification and is relevant to valuation. Answer (a) is incorrect because "company-specific" risk can be eliminated through portfolio diversification and is not relevant to the valuation of the security. Answer (b) is incorrect because "diversifiable" risk can be eliminated through portfolio diversification and is not relevant to the valuation of the security. Answer (d) is incorrect because only the systematic component of total risk is relevant to security valuation.

129. (c) The requirement is to calculate the weighted-average cost of capital (WACC). Answer (c) is correct because the WACC is calculated as 9.36% {2/5 × [9% × (1 – 40%)]} + (3/5 × 12%). Answers (a), (b), and (d) are incorrect because they represent inaccurate computations of the cost of the financing.

130. (b) Answer (b) is correct because the weighted-average cost of capital is calculated as follows:

= (Weight of equity) × (Cost of equity) + (Weight of debt) × (Before-tax cost of debt) × (1 – Tax rate)

= (.7) × (.12) + (.3) × (.08) × (1 – .3) = .084 + .0168 = 10%

Answer (a) is incorrect because 8% is the cost of equity before tax. Answer (c) is incorrect because this solution uses the before-tax cost of debt rather than the after-tax cost of debt. Answer (d) is incorrect because 12% is the cost of equity.

131. (d) The requirement is to identify the true statement about the financing alternatives. Answer (d) is correct because taxes payable will be higher under Arrangement #1 because with lower interest expense, taxable income will be higher. Under Arrangement #1, interest expense will be $300,000 (.08) = $24,000, while under Arrangement #2, interest expense will be $700,000 (.10) = $70,000 per annum. Answer (a) is incorrect because expected gross margin is unaffected by the choice of financing arrangement. Answer (b) is incorrect because the degree of operating leverage is not affected by the method of financing. Answer (c) is incorrect because interest expense will be higher under Arrangement #2.

132. (a) The requirement is to calculate the return on equity and the debt ratio. Answer (a) is correct because return on equity is calculated as net income divided by the amount of equity invested. The debt ratio is the amount of debt financing divided by total assets. Calculations of the two ratios for both financing arrangements are as follows:

	#1	#2
Sales revenue	$500,000	$500,000
Cost of sales	200,000	200,000
General & admin. expense	100,000	100,000
Interest expense	24,000	70,000
Taxable income	$176,000	$130,000
Tax payable (30%)	52,800	39,000
Net income	$123,200	$91,000
Equity invested	700,000	300,000
Return on equity	$\frac{123,200}{700,000}$	$\frac{91,000}{300,000}$
	17.6%	30.3%
Debt ratio	$\frac{300,000}{1,000,000}$	$\frac{700,000}{1,000,000}$
	.3	.7

133. (b) The requirement is to identify the most reliable valuation method. Answer (b) is correct because the most reliable valuation comes from market values obtained from active markets. Answers (a), (c), and (d) are incorrect because these are all less reliable methods of determining fair value.

134. (b) The requirement is to identify the type of transaction described. Answer (b) is correct because a leveraged buyout is one that is financed primarily with debt using very little equity capital. Answer (a) is incorrect because a spin-off is a divestiture in which stock of a subsidiary are issued to existing shareholders of the parent. Answer (c) is incorrect because a joint venture is a project conducted jointly by two or more independent parties. Answer (d) is incorrect because liquidation involves the piecemeal sale of the assets of a firm.

135. (a) The requirement is to identify the type of merger described. Answer (a) is correct because vertical integration is a merger involving companies in the same industry, but at different levels of the supply chain. Answer (b) is incorrect because a conglomerate merger is one involving firms from different industries. Answer (c) is incorrect because market extension involves moving into new market areas. Answer (d) is incorrect because a horizontal merger involves firms that are competitors in the same market.

136. (d) The requirement is to identify a horizontal merger. Answer (d) is correct because a horizontal merger is one between competitors in the same market. Answer (a) is incorrect because it describes a conglomerate merger. Answers (b) and (c) are incorrect because they describe vertical mergers.

137. (b) The requirement is to identify the type of merger. Answer (b) is correct because a vertical merger is a merger between a firm and one of its suppliers or customers. A bottle manufacturer can supply bottles to be used by a soft drink producer. Answer (a) is incorrect because a horizontal merger is a combination of two firms producing the same type of good or service. Answer (c) is incorrect because a congeneric merger is a merger of firms in the same industry, but the two firms do not have a customer or supplier relationship (as in vertical merger). Answer (d) is incorrect because a conglomerate merger is a merger of companies in totally different industries.

138. (d) The requirement is to identify the type of merger. Answer (d) is correct because a conglomerate merger is a merger of companies in totally different industries. A shoe manufacturer and brokerage house are in totally different industries. Answer (a) is incorrect because a horizontal merger is a combination of two firms producing the same type of good or service. Answer (b) is incorrect because a vertical merger is a merger between a firm and one of its suppliers or customers. Answer (c) is incorrect because a congeneric merger is a merger of firms in the same industry, but the two firms do not have a customer or supplier relationship (as in vertical merger).

Written Communication Task

Written Communication Task 1

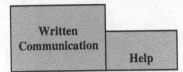

Talon, Inc. is a privately held manufacturing company. Management of the company is considering taking the company public through the issuance of common stock.

Terry Savage, the president of the company, has asked you prepare a memorandum describing the advantages and disadvantages of going public.

REMINDER: Your response will be graded for both technical content and writing skills. Technical content will be evaluated for information that is helpful to the intended reader and clearly relevant to the issue. Writing skills will be evaluated for development, organization, and the appropriate expression of ideas in professional correspondence. Use a standards business memo or letter format with a clear beginning, middle, and end. Do not convey information in the form of a table, bullet point list, or other abbreviated presentation.

To: Mr. Terry Savage, President
        Talon, Inc.
From: CPA Candidate

Written Communication Task Solution

Written Communication Task 1

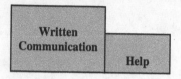

To: Mr. Terry Savage, President
        Talon, Inc.
From: CPA Candidate

As you requested, this memorandum describes the advantages and disadvantages of taking your company, Talon, Inc., public. A primary advantage of going public is that Talon will have access to a much larger pool of equity capital. The company's stock will trade on an organized market. Therefore, the company can more easily issue additional stock. Because the stock of the company is publicly traded, it can be used for business acquisitions, and the company can offer stock-based compensation to Talon's employees. Finally, the owners of Talon are afforded the opportunity to readily sell all, or a portion, of their investment in the company. Therefore, the owners' investments become liquid.

The primary disadvantage of going public is the cost. There are significant costs involved in the initial public offering of stock, and the continuing costs of compliance with SEC laws and regulations, including the Sarbanes-Oxley Act. Being a public company necessarily causes management to focus on maximizing stock price, which may not be in the best long-term interest of Talon. Finally, public companies must disclose significant amounts of information that becomes available to competitors, customers, and potential corporate raiders.

Because of these significant costs and benefits, it is important that the board of directors of Talon carefully evaluate the decision about whether or not to go public. If you need any additional information, please contact me.

Module 45: Performance Measures and Management Techniques

Overview

Organizational performance measures (including financial and nonfinancial measures) are used for a variety of purposes including: resource allocation, incentive compensation, divisional and business unit evaluation, budgeting and planning, and setting targets. Performance measures are used to manage and monitor performance in many areas of the organization including: financial, customer, internal processes, employees, and suppliers.

Organizational performance measures should be aligned to the strategy of the organization and useful in executing that strategy.

Strategy describes how an organization uses its activities and resources to achieve its objectives. For a business, the objective is to ethically maximize financial value. **Execution** includes the performance measures used (1) to ensure the strategy of the organization is being executed and (2) to monitor performance. To be successful, an organization must have an effective strategy and an effective execution system in place, including performance measures that closely link to the strategy. Before beginning the reading you should review the key terms at the end of the module.

A. Financial and Nonfinancial Performance Measures

Both financial and nonfinancial performance measures are needed to manage an organization. Financial measures gauge performance, profitability, or costs and are expressed as dollar amounts, ratios, or other forms. Nonfinancial performance measures are expressed in nonmonetary terms and include measures of customer satisfaction, customer retention, on-time delivery, quality, employee satisfaction, etc.

B. Balanced Scorecard and Performance Measures

The balanced scorecard, a performance measurement system that includes financial and nonfinancial performance measures, was developed by Kaplan and Norton.

1. What Is the Balanced Scorecard?

The **balanced scorecard** is a strategic performance measurement and management framework for implementing strategy by translating an organization's mission and strategy into a set of performance measures. These performance measures are generally in four primary perspectives: **financial, customer, internal business processes, and learning and growth.**

2. **Four Perspectives of the Balanced Scorecard**

   a. **Financial perspective.** This perspective focuses on return on investment and other supporting financial performance measures. Example performance measures include profitability, return on invested capital, and revenue growth.

   b. **Customer perspective.** This perspective focuses on performance in areas that are most critical to the customer. Example performance measures include customer satisfaction and customer retention.

   c. **Internal business processes perspective.** This perspective focuses on operating effectively and efficiently and includes performance measures on cost, quality and time for processes that are critical to the customers. It focuses on business processes, which are the structured activities of an organization that produce a product or service. Example performance measures include number of defects and cycle time.

   d. **Learning and growth perspective.** This perspective focuses on performance measures relating to employees, infrastructure, teaming and capabilities necessary for the internal processes to achieve customer and financial objectives. Example performance measures include employee satisfaction, hours of training per employee, and information technology expenditures per employee.

3. **Components of the Balanced Scorecard**

   a. **Strategic objectives.** A statement of what the strategy must achieve and what is critical to its success.
   b. **Performance measures.** Describe how success in achieving the strategy will be measured and tracked.
   c. **Baseline performance.** The current level of performance for the performance measure.
   d. **Targets.** The level of performance or rate of improvement needed in the performance measure.
   e. **Strategic initiatives.** Key action programs required to achieve strategic objectives.

   Strategic objectives focus on **what** is to be achieved. Strategic initiatives focus on **how** it will be achieved and performance measures, baseline performance and targets relate to how it will be **measured**.

   The **value chain** in the balanced scorecard framework is the sequence of business processes in which usefulness is added to the products or services of a company and includes the **innovation process, operations process**, and **post-sales process**. The value chain is one way to describe the internal process perspective in the balanced scorecard and its performance measures.

4. **Characteristics of the Balanced Scorecard**

   Characteristic of the balanced scorecard include the following:

   • **Strategy-focused.** Performance measures are driven by mission, vision and strategy. The balanced scorecard communicates the strategy to all members of the organization.

   • **Balanced.** Performance measures are "balanced" in terms of financial and nonfinancial measures, leading and lagging measures and internal (internal processes) and external (customer) measures. Accordingly, the scorecard highlights suboptimal tradeoffs that managers may make when they fail to consider operational and financial measures together.

   • **Includes both financial and nonfinancial measures.** Performance measures include traditional financial measures, as well as nonfinancial measures.

   • **Cause-and-effect linkages.** Performance measures are connected using cause-and-effect linkages. Performance measures include **performance drivers** (leading indicators) and **outcome performance measures** (lagging indicators). The focus on cause and effect linkages limits the number of measures used by identifying the most critical ones.

   • **Unique to the strategy.** Performance measures are unique and customized to an organization's strategy.

5. **Strategy Maps and Cause-and-Effect Linkages**

   Strategy maps are diagrams of the cause-and-effect relationships between strategic objectives. When looking at cause and effect linkages in the balanced scorecard framework, it is important to remember that the classification of performance measures as leading or lagging is not a dichotomy, but rather must be considered as a continuum. For example, customer satisfaction may be a leading indicator (performance driver) to return on investment (the lagging indicator or outcome measure). However, customer satisfaction may be a lagging indicator to on-time delivery (the leading indicator).

EXAMPLE

Balanced scorecard

The following is a simple example of a balanced scorecard. Within each of the four perspectives are key strategic objectives and related performance measures.

Financial perspective

Strategic objective	Performance measure
Increase return on investment (ROI)	ROI
Revenue growth	Percent growth in revenue
Increase profitability	Net income as a percentage of sales

Customer perspective

Strategic objective	Performance measure
Increase customer satisfaction	Customer satisfaction ratings
Increase customer share	Revenue per customer
Attract new customers	Number of new customers
	Revenue from new customers

Internal business processes perspective

Strategic objective	Performance measure
Improve on-time delivery	Percentage of on-time deliveries
Improve quality performance	Number of rejects

Learning and growth perspective

Strategic objective	Performance measure
Train employees on quality tools	Hours of training on quality tools
Use information systems to manage on-time delivery status	Percent of employees using information system

In this example, we see possible cause-and-effect relationships. Increasing the training in the use of quality tools may improve on-time delivery performance which may improve customer satisfaction and therefore increase return on investment. The connection between customer satisfaction and return on investment at some companies is based on the following observation: more satisfied customers pay invoices faster, therefore accounts receivable turnover (a component of return on assets) increases and return on investment increases.

6. **Performance Measures in the Balanced Scorecard**

Here are examples of performance measures that are classified within the four perspectives of the balanced scorecard.

> **Financial perspective**
>
> Return on investment
> Economic profit
> Economic value added
> Cash flow ROI
> Free cash flow
> Net income/sales ratio
> Sales/asset ratio
> Revenue growth
> Revenue from new products (existing customers)
> Revenue from new products (new customers)
> Cost of sales %

Customer perspective
Customer satisfaction
Customer retention
Customer acquisition
Percentage of highly satisfied customers
Depth of relationship
Percentage of business from customer referrals
Customer satisfaction with new product/service offerings

Internal process perspective
On-time delivery
Cost per unit
Percentage of late orders
Total cost of quality
Cycle time
Process efficiency
Capacity utilization
Inventory turnover
Lead times (order to delivery)

Internal process perspective
Percentage of on-time deliveries
Time to resolve customer complaints
Inventory obsolescence
Order backlog
Number of leads/conversion rate
Hours with customers
Time spent with target accounts
Number of new projects based on client input
Number of joint projects
Number of technology and product partners
Number of patents
Total time from concept to market
Time from pilot to full production
Manufacturing-process yield
Number of failures, defects, and customer returns
Warranty costs
Number of safety incidents

Learning and growth perspective
Employee satisfaction and engagement
Employee turnover
Employee objectives linked to the balanced scorecard
Employee awareness of the strategy
Percentage of employees trained in total quality management
Number of six-sigma black belts
Performance improvement from employees' suggestions
Percentage of ideas and best practices shared across organization
Percentage of R&D employees to total employees
R&D expenditure as a percent of sales revenue

NOW REVIEW MULTIPLE-CHOICE QUESTIONS 1 THROUGH 13

C. Value-Based Management (VBM) and Financial Performance Measures

VBM involves the use of value-based metrics (performance measures) in a strategic management system and as such may be viewed as a financial scorecard. The spectrum of value-based metrics include performance measures such as: return on investment (ROI), economic profit, economic value added (EVA), cash flow ROI, and residual income.

When is it appropriate to use economic value added measures (EVA) (or other value-based metrics) as a performance measure? EVA is particularly useful for incentive compensation, resource allocation and investor relations. Executive compensation and incentive compensation firmwide have been the most popular target of EVA. The premise is "pay for performance" where performance is defined as creating financial value (earning a return above the cost of capital). Using EVA alone can have certain disadvantages by failing to reflect all the pathways to value creation. This limitation can be minimized by integrating EVA with a balanced scorecard framework which would avoid the temptation to focus only on low-hanging fruit (cost reduction and increased asset intensity) but miss the opportunity to create additional value through growth strategies.

1. **Return on Investment (ROI)**

   Return on investment is the ratio of a measure of "return" divided by a measure of "investment." There are various ways to measure ROI including: return on assets (ROA), return on net assets (RONA) and return on equity (ROE). ROI is most often computed using net income (income after interest and taxes) but it also may be computed using operating income or operating income after taxes.

2. **DuPont ROI Analysis**

   DuPont ROI analysis looks at ROI as driven by two factors: return on sales (net income/sales) and asset turnover (sales/total assets). The calculation of DuPont ROI is as follows:

   $$\text{ROI} = \text{Net income/total assets}$$
   $$= \text{Net income/sales} \times \text{Sales/average investment}$$
   $$= \text{Return on sales} \times \text{Asset turnover ratio}$$

   The DuPont method highlights the two basic ways to improve profits: (1) increasing income per dollar of sales, and (2) using assets to generate more sales.

EXAMPLE

The following selected data pertain to the Amy Division of Cara Products, Inc. for 2012:

Sales	$20,000,000
Average invested capital (total assets)	5,000,000
Net income	1,250,000
Cost of capital	10%

ROI (based on total assets) and DuPont ROI would be calculated as follows:

$$\text{DuPont ROI} = 1,250,000/5,000,000 = 25\%$$
$$= 1,250,000/20,000,000 \times 20,000,000/5,000,000$$
$$= 6.25\% \times 4.0$$
$$= 25\%$$

The return on sales of 6.25% times the asset turnover ratio of 4.0 equals the ROI of 25%.

---

3. **Residual Income**

   Residual income is net income (or operating income after taxes) minus a cost of capital based on capital invested in a division or project.

   $$\text{Residual income} = \text{Net income} - \text{Interest on investment}$$
   $$= \text{Net income} - (\text{Required rate of return} \times \text{Invested capital})$$

EXAMPLE

Using the data from the previous example for Amy Division

Sales	$20,000,000
Average invested capital	5,000,000
Net income	1,250,000
Required rate of return	10%

$$\text{Residual income} = \$1,250,000 - (10\% \times \$5,000,000)$$
$$= \$1,250,000 - 500,000$$
$$= \$750,000$$

Remember that the ROI was 25% for this company and the required interest rate is 10%. The difference between the ROI and the required interest rate (cost of capital) is sometimes called the **spread**. In this case the spread can be computed as follows:

$$\text{Spread} = \text{ROI} - \text{Cost of capital}$$
$$= 25\% - 10\%$$
$$= 15\%$$

Notice that the residual income of $750,000 divided by the invested capital of $5,000,000 equals the spread of 15%.

4. Residual Income Profile

The **residual income profile** is a graphical way to look at the relationship between residual income and ROI. The residual income profile shows the interrelationship between residual income and ROI. The vertical axis shows residual income in dollars. The horizontal axis shows the implicit cost of capital and ROI.

The formula for the residual income profile is

$$\text{Residual income} = \text{Net income} - i \,(\text{Invested capital})$$

Where: i = Cost of capital or required rate of return for computing residual income

The formula for the residual income profile is the same as the formula for residual income with the required rate of return as the coefficient. As the required rate of return increases, residual income decreases. Where residual income is zero, the required rate of return equals the ROI.

EXAMPLE

The following information is available for Iceman, Inc. for 2012:

Net income	$ 300,000
Average invested capital	$2,000,000
Cost of capital	12%

The ROI and residual income are computed below.

$$\text{ROI} = \frac{\$300,000}{\$2,000,000} = 15\%$$

Residual income = $300,000 − (12% × 2,000,000)

= $300,000 − 240,000

= $60,000

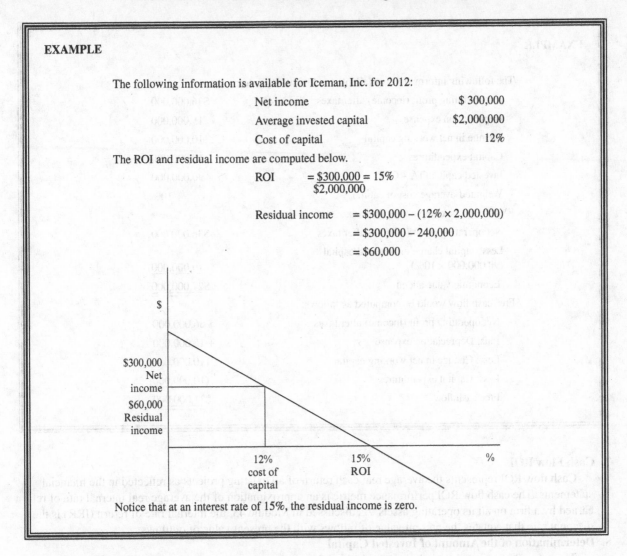

Notice that at an interest rate of 15%, the residual income is zero.

5. Economic Profit and EVA

Economic profit and economic value added measures stress the importance of making investments only when the return exceeds cost and, in the process, value to the stockholder is maximized. Economic profit is accounting profit minus the cost of capital. EVA is a variation of economic profit. Economic Value Added (EVA) is net operating profit (income) after taxes (NOPAT) minus the after-tax weighted-average cost of capital (WACC) multiplied by total assets (TA) minus current liabilities (CL) (net assets).

EVA = Net operating profit after taxes (NOPAT) − [(TA − CL) × WACC]

Market value added is the difference between the market value of a company (both equity and debt) and the capital that lenders and shareholders have entrusted to it over the years in the form of loans, retained earnings and paid-in capital. Market value added is a measure of the difference between "cash in" (what investors have contributed) and "cash out" (what they could get by selling at today's prices).

6. Free Cash Flow

Free cash flow can be computed as follows:

Free cash flow = Net operating profit after taxes (NOPAT) + Depreciation and amortization
− Capital expenditures − Change in working capital requirements

EXAMPLE

The following information is available for Armstrong Enterprises:

Net operating profit (income) after taxes	$36,000,000
Depreciation expense	15,000,000
Change in net working capital	10,000,000
Capital expenditures	10,000,000
Invested capital (TA – CL)	90,000,000
Weighted-average cost of capital	10%

EVA would be computed as follows:

Net operating profit (income) after taxes	$36,000,000
Less: capital charge on invested capital (90,000,000 × 10%)	(9,000,000)
Economic value added	$27,000,000

Free cash flow would be computed as follows:

Net operating profit (income) after taxes	$ 36,000,000
Plus: Depreciation expense	+ 15,000,000
Less: Change in net working capital	(10,000,000)
Less: Capital expenditures	(10,000,000)
Free cash flow	$31,000,000

7. **Cash Flow ROI**

Cash flow ROI represents the average real cash return of all existing projects as reflected in the financial statements. The cash flow ROI performance metric is an approximation of the average real internal rate of return earned by a firm on all its operating assets. As discussed in Module 43, the internal rate of return (IRR) is the discount rate that equates the present value of inflows with the present value of outflows.

8. **Determination of the Amount of Invested Capital**

The amount of invested capital for computation of performance measures generally is determined in two ways: current cost or historical cost. Current cost is the current replacement cost of the existing investment and provides a better measure of the economic returns from the investment. The drawback to using current cost is that the estimates of current cost may be difficult and costly to obtain. When using historical cost the firm either uses the gross book value (original cost) or the net book value (original cost less accumulated depreciation). Advocates of gross book value indicate that it results in measures that are more comparable across business units. If net book value is used, ROI increases simply due to the effects of annual depreciation.

Advocates of net book value indicate that it is consistent with the amount of assets shown on the balance sheet and with net income that is calculated after the deprecation deduction. Most firms use net book value to measure investment but may compensate by establishing target ROIs that adjust for the effects of the limitations of historical cost measures of investment.

D. **Choosing among Different Performance Measures**

1. Choosing among different performance measures involves understanding how the performance measure will be used. Is it being used for executive compensation, resource allocation or business unit performance evaluation? It also involves understanding how well the performance measure enables management to execute business strategy and monitor how well it is being executed. Here are some guidelines for choosing among different performance measures.

   a. **Strategy-focused.** How well does the performance measure reflect the strategy of the organization? This is where the balanced scorecard framework and the performance measures within the balanced scorecard framework can be useful. A well-designed balanced scorecard will include the right mix of performance measures to communicate and operationalize the strategy.

b. **Economic reality and cash flow.** How well does the performance measure reflect the economic reality that a firm must earn a return on capital invested in excess of its cost of capital in order to create financial value? Here is where value-based management and its metrics (ROI, economic profit, free cash flow, and cash flow ROI) can be useful.

c. **Quality of the performance measure.** The relevance and reliability of the performance measures also should be considered. For example, relevant and reliable manager performance measures are ones that are sensitive to factors within the control of the manager and not sensitive to factors beyond the manager's control.

2. The most common financial measures used for performance measurement include return on investment (ROI), residual income (RI), economic value added (EVA), and return on sales (ROS). It is important to distinguish between those measures that are used to evaluate the business unit and those that are used to evaluate a manager's performance.

3. Performance measures should not encourage decisions that maximize the measure in the short run but are in conflict with the long-term goals of the firm. For example, a manager could decide to postpone machine maintenance to make ROI for a particular year look better, but the decision may cause long-run profits to suffer. The focus on short-run performance may be mitigated by using measures with multiple-year time horizons or by using a combination of financial and nonfinancial measures. Compensation tied to changes in the value of the firm's stock also encourages managers to take a long-run perspective, because stock prices reflect the future value of current management decisions.

4. A focus on ROI as a performance measure may cause a lack of goal congruence. As an example, managers of very profitable business units may reject projects that from a firm-wide perspective should be accepted. In such situations, RI rather than ROI provides a performance measure that better aligns the goals of business unit managers with the goals of the overall organization.

EXAMPLE

Borke Company's cost of capital is 10%. One of Borke Company's division managers has the opportunity to invest in a project that will generate $45,000 of net income per year for eight years on an initial investment of $300,000. The division's current income is $250,000 from a total divisional asset base of $1,000,000. The manager should accept the project since it offers a 15% return and the company's cost of capital is 10%. Chances are the manager will reject the project since it will lower the division current ROI from

$$\frac{\$250,00}{\$1,000,000} = 25\% \text{ to } \frac{\$250,00 + 45,000}{\$1,000,000 + 300,000} = 22.7\%$$

In this case the use of ROI has led to an incorrect decision.

NOW REVIEW MULTIPLE-CHOICE QUESTIONS 14 THROUGH 37

E. **Traditional Financial Statement Analysis**

One type of commonly used set of financial measures is derived from traditional financial statement analysis. Financial statement analysis involves the calculation and comparison of financial statement ratios. Financial ratios used to evaluate the financial position and operations of firms typically are classified into the following five categories:

1. **Profitability ratios**

   - Gross margin
   - Operating profit margin
   - Return on assets
   - Return on equity
   - Dividend payout ratio

2. **Asset utilization ratios**

- Receivable turnover
- Average collection period
- Inventory turnover
- Fixed asset turnover
- Total asset turnover

3. **Liquidity ratios**

- Current ratio
- Quick or acid ratio

4. **Debt utilization ratios**

- Debt to total assets
- Debt to equity
- Times interest earned

5. **Market ratios**

- Price/earnings ratio
- Market/book ratio

The calculation of these ratios will be illustrated using the following financial statements from Home Depot.

The Home Depot, Inc. and Subsidiaries
CONSOLIDATED BALANCE SHEETS

Amounts in millions, except per share data	February 2, 21X3	February 3, 21X2
Assets		
Current assets:		
Cash and cash equivalents	$ 2,188	$ 2,477
Short-term investments, including current maturities of long-term investments	65	69
Receivables, net	1,072	920
Merchandise inventories	8,338	6,725
Other current assets	254	170
Total current assets	11,917	10,361
Property and equipment, at cost:		
Land	5,560	4,972
Buildings	9,197	7,698
Furniture, fixtures and equipment	4,074	3,403
Leasehold improvements	872	750
Construction in progress	724	1,049
Capital leases	306	257
	20,733	18,129
Less accumulated depreciation and amortization	3,565	2,754
Net property and equipment	17,168	15,375
Notes receivable	107	83
Cost in excess of the fair value of net assets acquired, net of accumulated amortization of $50 at February 2, 2003, and $49 at February 3, 2002	575	419
Other assets	244	156
Total assets	$30,011	$26,394
Liabilities and Stockholders' Equity		
Current liabilities:		
Accounts payable	$ 4,560	$3,436
Accrued salaries and related expenses	809	717

Sales taxes payable	307	348
Deferred revenue	998	851
Income taxes payable	227	211
Other accrued expenses	1,134	938
Total current liabilities	8,035	6,501
Long-term debt, excluding current installments	1,321	1,250
Other long-term liabilities	491	372
Deferred income taxes	362	189
Total liabilities	$10,209	8,312

Stockholders' Equity

Common stock, par value $0.05; authorized: 10,000 shares, issued and outstanding 2,362 shares at February 2, 21X3, and 2,346 shares at February 3, 21X2	118	117
Paid-in capital	5,858	5,412
Retained earnings	15,971	12,799
Accumulated other comprehensive loss	(82)	(220)
Unearned compensation	(63)	(26)
Treasury stock, at cost, 69 shares at February 2, 21X3	(2,000)	—
Total stockholders' equity	19,802	18,082
Total liabilities and stockholders' equity	$30,011	$26,394

The Home Depot, Inc. and Subsidiaries
CONSOLIDATED STATEMENTS OF EARNINGS

	Fiscal Year Ended		
	February 2,	February 3,	January 28,
Amounts in millions, except per share data	**21X3**	**21X2**	**21X1**
Net Sales	$58,247	$53,553	$45,738
Cost of merchandise sold	40,139	37,406	32,057
Gross profit	18,108	16,147	13,681
Operating expenses:			
Selling and store operating	11,180	10,163	8,513
Preopening	96	117	142
General and administrative	1,002	935	835
Total operating expenses	12,278	11,215	9,490
Operating income	5,830	4,932	4,191
Interest income (expense):			
Interest and investment income	79	53	47
Interest expense	(37)	(28)	(21)
Interest, net	42	25	26
Earnings before provision for income taxes	5,872	4,957	4,217
Provision for income taxes	2,208	1,913	1,636
Net earnings	$3,664	$3,044	$2,581
Weighted-average common shares	2,336	2,335	2,315
Basic earnings per share	$1.57	$1.30	$1.11
Diluted weighted-average common shares	2,344	2,353	2,352
Diluted earnings per share	$1.56	$1.29	$1.10

1. **Profitability Ratios**

   Profitability ratios measure how effective a firm is at generating profit from operations. They are some of the most closely watched and widely quoted financial ratios. Management attempts to maximize these ratios to maximize firm value.

   a. **Gross margin** measures the percentage of each sales dollar remaining after payment for the goods sold.

   $$\text{Gross margin} = \frac{\text{Gross profit}}{\text{Net sales}} = \frac{\$18,108}{\$58,247} = 31.09\%$$

   Remember that gross profit is equal to net sales minus cost of goods sold.

b. To find the proportion of revenue that finds its way into profits, analysts look at profit margin. Profit margin is calculated as net income divided by net sales, as shown below.

$$\text{Profit margin} = \frac{\text{Net income after interest and taxes}}{\text{Net sales}} = \frac{\$3,664}{\$58,247} = 6.29\%$$

c. **Operating profit margin** measures the percentage of each sales dollar that remains after the payment of all costs and expenses except for interest and taxes. This ratio is followed closely by analysts because it focuses on operating results. Operating profit is often referred to as earnings before interest and taxes or EBIT.

$$\text{Operating profit margin} = \frac{\text{Operating profit}}{\text{Net sales}} = \frac{\$5,830}{\$58,247} = 10.01\%$$

d. **Return on assets (return on investment)** measures the percentage return generated on the assets available (investment). This ratio may be calculated as

$$\text{Return on assets} = \frac{\text{Net income after interest and taxes}}{\text{Average total sales}} = \frac{\$3,664}{\$28,203} = 12.99\%$$

$$\text{Average total assets} = (\text{Ending total assets} + \text{Beginning total assets})/2$$
$$= (\$30,011 + \$26,394)/2$$
$$= \$28,203$$

As discussed previously, return on investment is calculated and dissected in a number of ways and is very important to value-based management.

e. **Return on equity** measures the percentage return generated to common stockholders.

$$\text{Return on equity} = \frac{\text{Net income after interest and taxes}}{\text{Average common stockholders' equity}} = \frac{\$3,664}{\$18,942} = 19.34\%$$

$$\text{Average stockholders' equity (SE)} = (\text{Ending SE} + \text{Beginning SE})/2$$
$$= (\$19,802 + \$18,082)/2$$
$$= \$18,942$$

f. **The dividend payout ratio** measures the dividend paid in relation to net earnings. If Home Depot's dividend for the year was $0.22, the dividend payout is calculated as

$$\text{Dividend payout ratio} = \frac{\text{Cash dividend per common share}}{\text{Earnings per common share}}$$

$$= \frac{\$0.22}{\$1.57}$$

$$= .14 \text{ or } 14\%$$

2. Asset Utilization (Activity) Ratios

Asset utilization ratios measure the time it takes to convert various assets to sales or cash. Asset utilization ratios are used to measure the efficiency with which assets are managed. For this reason, they are often called **asset management ratios**.

a. **Receivables turnover** measures the number of times per year the balance of receivables is collected. This is a very important measure of the efficiency with which management is managing accounts receivable.

$$\text{Receivables turnover} = \frac{\text{Net credit sales}}{\text{Average accounts receivable}}$$

This ratio cannot be computed for Home Depot since the company does not break out the amount of credit sales.

b. The **average collection period** measures the average number of days it takes to collect an account receivable. This ratio is also referred to as **the number of days of receivable** and **the number of days' sales in receivables**.

$$\text{Average collection period} = \frac{\text{Average accounts receivable}}{\text{Average sales per day}}$$

Again, this ratio cannot be calculated for Home Depot because the company does not break out the amount of credit sales.

c. **Inventory turnover** measures the efficiency with which a firm utilizes (manages) its inventory.

$$\text{Inventory turnover} = \frac{\text{Cost of goods sold}}{\text{Average inventory}} = \frac{\$40,139}{\$7,532} = 5.33 \text{ times}$$

$$\begin{aligned} \text{Average inventory} &= (\text{Ending inventory} + \text{Beginning inventory})/2 \\ &= (\$8,338 + \$6,725)/2 \\ &= \$7,532 \end{aligned}$$

d. A related measure is the number of days' sales in inventory.

$$\begin{aligned} \text{Number of days' sales in inventory} &= \frac{\text{Average inventory}}{\text{Cost of goods sold}/365} \\ &= \frac{\$7,532}{\$40,139/365} \\ &= 68.49 \text{ days} \end{aligned}$$

e. **Fixed asset turnover** measures the efficiency with which the firm uses its fixed assets.

$$\text{Fixed asset turnover} = \frac{\text{Sales}}{\text{Average net fixed assets}} = \frac{\$58,247}{\$16,272} = 3.58 \text{ times}$$

$$\begin{aligned} \text{Average fixed assets} &= (\text{Ending fixed assets} + \text{Beginning fixed assets})/2 \\ &= (\$17,168 + \$15,375)/2 \\ &= \$16,272 \end{aligned}$$

f. **Total asset turnover** measures the efficiency with which the firm uses its total assets.

$$\text{Total asset turnover} = \frac{\text{Sales}}{\text{Average total assets}} = \frac{\$58,247}{\$28,203} = 2.07 \text{ times}$$

3. Liquidity Ratios

Liquidity ratios measure the firm's ability to meet its short-term obligations as they come due.

a. The **current ratio** is the most common measure of short-term liquidity. It is sometimes referred to as the **working capital ratio** because net working capital is the difference between current assets and current liabilities.

$$\text{Current ratio} = \frac{\text{Current assets}}{\text{Current liabilities}} = \frac{\$11,917}{\$8,035} = 1.48 \text{ times}$$

- **Current assets** include cash and cash equivalents, net accounts receivable, marketable securities classified as current, inventories and prepaid expenses.
- **Current liabilities** include accounts payable, short-term notes payable, current maturities of long-term debt, unearned revenue, and other accrued liabilities.

Changes in the current ratio can be misleading. As an example, if management simply borrows money from a bank and invests the funds in marketable securities, both current assets and current liabilities go up by an identical amount. Net working capital is unaffected but the current ratio changes. Thus the current ratio is subject to "window dressing" by management.

b. The **quick (acid) ratio** provides a more conservative measure of short-term liquidity. It takes out inventory because in times of financial difficulty inventory may be saleable only at liquidation value.

$$\text{Quick ratio} = \frac{\text{Current assets} - \text{Inventory}}{\text{Current liabilities}} = \frac{\$11,917 - 8,338}{\$8,035} = .45$$

4. Debt Utilization Ratios

Debt utilization ratios measure the effectiveness with which management finances the assets of the firm. They are used to evaluate the financial leverage of the firm.

a. The **debt to total assets** measures the proportion of total assets financed with debt and, therefore, the extent of financial leverage.

$$\text{Debt to total assets} = \frac{\text{Total liabilities}}{\text{Total assets}} = \frac{\$10,209}{\$30,011} = 34.02\%$$

b. The **debt to equity ratio** also measures the extent of the firm's financial leverage.

$$\text{Debt to equity ratio} = \frac{\text{Total liabilities}}{\text{Total equity}} = \frac{\$10,209}{\$19,802} = 51.56\%$$

c. The **times interest earned** measures the firm's ability to make contractual interest payments.

$$\text{Times interest earned} = \frac{\text{Earnings before interest and taxes}}{\text{Interest expense}} = \frac{\$5,830}{\$37} = 157.57\%$$

5. Market Ratios

Market ratios involve measures that consider the market value of the firm's common stock.

a. The **price/earnings (PE) ratio** is the most commonly quoted market measure. Assuming that Home Depot's stock price is \$34.00, the price/earnings ratio would be computed as follows:

$$\text{Price/earning} = \frac{\text{Stock price per share}}{\text{Earnings per share}} = \frac{\$34}{\$1.57} = 21.66$$

b. The **market/book ratio** provides another evaluation of how investors view the firm's past and future performance. To calculate the ratio, the book value per share of the firm's stock must first be calculated.

$$\text{Book value per share} = \frac{\text{Common stock equity}}{\text{Number of shares of common stock outstanding}}$$

$$= \frac{\$19,802}{\$2,362} = \$8.38 \text{ per share}$$

Again, assuming a \$34 market price per share of common stock, the market/book ratio is calculated as follows:

$$\text{Market/book ratio} = \frac{\text{Market value per share of common stock}}{\text{Book value per share of common stock}}$$

$$= \frac{\$34.00}{\$8.38} = 4.06$$

6. Interpreting Financial Ratios

How does one decide whether a particular ratio is good or bad? To get value from ratio analysis, the measures must be compared to benchmarks. There are two basic approaches to this analysis, horizontal analysis and cross-sectional analysis. While **horizontal analysis** involves an evaluation of the firm's ratios and trends over time,

cross-sectional analysis involves benchmarking the ratios against ratios of similar firms at a point in time. Industry averages are often used for cross-sectional analysis. Averages for industries are published by the US Department of Commerce, Dun & Bradstreet, Robert Morris Associates, and others. Researching data on firms in the same industry is facilitated through the Standard Industrial Classification (SIC) system.

The figure below illustrates horizontal (trend) and cross-sectional analysis of a firm's income statement. The figure also illustrates a **common-size** income statement, in which all revenues and expenses are presented as a percentage of net sales. A common-size balance sheet presents all assets, liabilities and stockholders' equity as a percentage of total assets. The development of common-size financial statements is also known as **vertical analysis**.

CARSON CORPORATION

	Dollars (000s omitted)			Common-size statements		
	20X6	20X7	Percent change	20X6	20X7	Industry averages 20X7
Gross sales	78,428	82,212	4.8	103%	105%	104%
Less: Returns and Allowances	2,284	4,235	85.4	3%	5%	4%
Net sales	76,144	77,977	2.4	100%	100%	100%
Cost of goods sold	46,213	46,478	0.6	61%	60%	58%
Gross profit	29,931	31,499	5.2	39%	40%	42%
Selling and administrative expenses	20,105	22,487	11.8	26%	29%	28%
Income from operations	9,826	9,012	–8.3	13%	12%	14%
Interest expense	1,930	1,584	–17.9	3%	2%	3%
Net income before taxes	7,896	7,428	–5.9	10%	10%	11%
Income taxes	3,807	2,971	–22.0	5%	4%	4%
Net income	4,089	4,457	9.0	5%	6%	7%
EPS	0.78	0.84	10.5			
Ratios						
Current	1.7	1.9				2.1
Quick	1.0	1.1				1.3
Receivables turnover	5.3	5.6				5.1
Days' sales in ending receivables	68.1	64.3				65.6
Inventory turnover	4.7	3.2				3.5
Days' sales in ending inventory	76.0	75.0				74.4
Interest expense/outstanding debt	0.11	0.08				0.09

Horizontal (Trend) analysis | Vertical analysis | Cross-sectional analysis

To use ratio analysis effectively, analysts must be aware of the relationship between the items used in calculating the ratio. For example, in comparing the gross margin of a company over time, it should be remembered that this ratio may be affected by the fact that cost of goods sold is made up of fixed and variable costs or the fact that the sales mix has changed.

7. **Limitations of Financial Ratios**

While comparing the firm's ratios with those of similar firms in the same industry provides information about the performance of the firm, it does have limitations.

a. Other firms in the industry may not be comparable due to differences in size, diversification of operations, accounting principles used, different year-ends, etc.
b. Industry averages may not be reliable (e.g., based on too small a sample of firms).

c. There are variations in the way ratios are calculated.

d. Financial statements contain estimates that might distort results.

e. Ratios are only financial measures and do not provide a balanced view of performance.

F. Benchmarking and Best Practices

Benchmarking is the continuous process of comparing the levels of performance in producing products and services and executing activities against the best levels of performance. It is the search for and implementation of "best practices." There are different types of benchmarking including:

- *Internal benchmarking* compares similar operations within different units of the same organization.
- *Competitive benchmarking* targets processes and methods used by an organization's direct competitors.
- *Functional or industry benchmarking* compares similar functions within the same broad industry.
- *Generic benchmarking* compares processes that are independent of industry.

Best practices are the best ways to perform a process. Best practices represent the means by which world-class organizations have achieved superior performance. However, no practice can be considered a "best practice" for all organizations or in all situations. The advice of Dr. W. Edwards Deming applies to benchmarking: "Adapt, don't adopt."

Benchmarks are the performance metrics used in benchmarking.

NOW REVIEW MULTIPLE-CHOICE QUESTIONS 38 THROUGH 55

G. Quality Control Principles and Tools

1. **Total Quality Management (TQM)** focuses on managing the organization to excel in quality in all dimensions of products and services for customers.

2. **Six-Sigma Quality**

    What is six-sigma? A statistical measure expressing how close a product comes to its quality goal. One-sigma means 68% of products are acceptable; three-sigma means 99.7%. Six-sigma is 99.999997% perfect: 3.4 defects per million parts.

    Six-sigma black belts must attend a minimum of four months of training in statistical and other quality improvement methods. Six-sigma black belts are experts in the six-sigma methodology. They learn and demonstrate proficiency in the DMAIC methodology and statistical process control (SPC) techniques within that methodology. DMAIC is the structured methodology for process improvement within the six-sigma framework. It stands for define, measure, analyze, improve, and control.

3. **Quality Award Programs**

    There are a number of quality award programs. Here is a summary of some of the major programs.

    - **Malcolm Baldrige National Quality Award** is an award that was established in 1987 to recognize total quality management in American industry. The Baldrige award is given to businesses—manufacturing and service, small and large—and to education and health care organizations that apply and are judged to be outstanding in seven areas: leadership, strategic planning, customer and market focus, information and analysis, human resource focus, process management, and business results. Congress established the award program in 1987 to recognize US organizations for their achievements in quality and performance and to raise awareness about the importance of quality and performance excellence as a competitive edge. The award is not given for specific products or services. Three awards may be given annually in each of these categories: manufacturing, service, small business, education, and health care.
    - **The Deming Prize** is named after American statistician Dr. W. Edwards Deming, who developed the quality concepts for Japanese industry after World War II.
    - **European Quality Award.** The European Quality Award is Europe's most prestigious award for organizational excellence. It is open to every high-performing organization in Europe and focuses on recognizing excellence and providing detailed, independent feedback to all applicants to help them on their continuing journey to excellence.

4. **ISO Quality Standards**

    ISO 9000 Series is a series of standards agreed upon by the International Organization for Standardization (ISO) and adopted in 1987. ISO 9000 evolved in Europe. The ISO Series consists of five parts numbered 9000 through 9004.

ISO 14000 series was developed to control the impact of an organization's activities on the environment and focuses on reducing the cost of waste management, conserving energy and materials, and lowering distribution costs.

5. **Quality Tools and Methods**

   a. **Total quality control (TQC).** The application of quality principles to all company activities. Also known as total quality management (TQM).

   b. **Continuous improvement and Kaizen**

   Continuous improvement (CI) seeks continual improvement of machinery, materials, labor, and production methods, through various means including suggestions and ideas from employees and customers.

   Kaizen is the Japanese art of continuous improvement. A philosophy of continuous improvement of working practices that underlies total quality management and just-in-time business techniques.

   PDCA (Plan-Do-Check-Act), also called the Deming Wheel, focuses on the sequential and continual nature of the CI process.

   c. **Cause-and-effect analysis**

   Cause-and-effect (fishbone or Ishikawa) diagrams identify the potential causes of defects. Four categories of potential causes of failure are: human factors, methods and design factors, machine-related factors, and materials and components factors. Cause-and-effect diagrams are used to systematically list the different causes that can be attributed to a problem (or an effect). A cause-and-effect diagram can aid in identifying the reasons why a process goes out of control.

   A **Pareto chart** is a bar graph that ranks causes of process variations by the degree of impact on quality. The Pareto chart is a specialized version of a histogram that ranks the categories in the chart from most frequent to least frequent. A related concept, the "Pareto Principle" states that 80% of the problems come from 20% of the causes. The Pareto Principle states that: "Not all of the causes of a particular phenomenon occur with the same frequency or with the same impact."

   d. **Control charts and robust design**

   Control charts are statistical plots derived from measuring factory processes; they help detect "process drift," or deviation, before it generates defects. Control charts also help spot inherent variations in manufacturing processes that designers must account for to achieve "robust design."

   Robust design is a discipline for making designs "production-proof" by building in tolerances for manufacturing variables that are known to be unavoidable.

   e. **Poka-yoke (mistake-proofing).** Poka-yoke involves making the workplace mistake-proof. For example, a machine fitted with guide rails permits a part to be worked on in just one way.

H. Cost of Quality

Cost of quality is based on the philosophy that failures have an underlying cause, prevention is cheaper than failures, and cost of quality performance can be measured. Cost of quality consists of four components.

- Prevention cost
- Appraisal cost
- Internal failure cost
- External failure cost

1. **Prevention cost.** The cost of prevention is the cost of any quality activity designed to help do the job right the first time. Examples of prevention cost include:

   - Quality engineering
   - Quality training
   - Quality circles
   - Statistical process control activities
   - Supervision of prevention activities
   - Quality data gathering, analysis, and reporting
   - Quality improvement projects
   - Technical support provided to suppliers
   - Audits of the effectiveness of the quality system

2. **Appraisal cost.** The cost of quality control including testing and inspection. It involves any activity designed to appraise, test, or check for defective products. Examples of appraisal costs include:

   - Testing and inspection of incoming materials
   - Testing and inspection of in-process goods

- Final product testing and inspection
- Supplies used in testing and inspection
- Supervision of testing and inspection activities
- Depreciation of test equipment
- Maintenance of test equipment
- Plant utilities in the inspection area
- Field testing and appraisal at customer site

3. **Internal failure cost.** The costs incurred when substandard products are produced but discovered before shipment to the customer. Examples of internal failure costs include:

- Scrap
- Spoilage
- Rework
- Rework labor and overhead
- Reinspection of reworked products
- Retesting of reworked products
- Downtime caused by quality problems
- Disposal of defective products
- Analysis of the cause of defects in production
- Reentering data because of keying errors
- Debugging software errors

4. **External failure cost.** The cost incurred for products that do not meet requirements of the customer and have reached the customer. Examples of external failure costs include

- Cost of field servicing and handling complaints
- Warranty repairs and replacements
- Product recalls
- Liability arising from defective products
- Returns and allowances arising from quality problems
- Lost sales arising from reputation for poor quality

I. Business Process Management

Business process management focuses on continuously improving processes to align all activities with the desires and needs of the customer. As a managerial approach, business process management views processes as strategic assets that must be understood, managed, and improved. To improve processes, management focuses on both the human and technological aspect of processes, and the interaction of the two. Many organizations are finding it productive to improve processes by focusing on this human—technology interaction, as they try to develop technology that is designed for a task and the way the particular individual works.

The life cycle of business process management includes design, modeling, execution, monitoring, and optimization.

1. Design

The design phase involves identification of existing processes and design of process improvements. Good process design is critical to preventing problems over the life of the process.

2. Modeling

In the modeling phase management simulates the process in a test environment and performs "what if" analysis to try to determine how it will work under varying conditions.

3. Execution

Execution involves installing software, training personnel, and implementing the new processes. It also involves testing the new processes.

4. Monitoring

The monitoring phase is continuous after the execution phase. It involves tracking the processes with performance statistics.

5. Optimization

This phase of the life cycle involves retrieving performance statistics from modeling or monitoring and identifying potential bottlenecks or other problems for additional improvement of the process.

As processes are analyzed for improvement, it is sometime discovered that processes that were once performed by several departments should be centralized in one department. For example, employee training might become a centralized process to improve efficiency and effectiveness. Alternatively, management may decide to outsource a process to an external organization, or even outsource a process to an organization in another country (often referred to as off-shoring). There are a number of reasons that an organization may decide to outsource or off-shore, including costs saving, quality improvement, tax benefit, scalability, or to focus on core competencies. However, such strategy may present additional risks, including

- *Quality risk.* The company may have less control over the quality of outsourced or off-shored activities.
- *Language risk.* Control over activities and customer service may be affected by language issues.
- *Information security risk.* Control over confidential company or customer information may be put at risk.
- *Intellectual property risk.* Information about the company's products and processes may be put at risk.
- *Public opinion risk.* The company's reputation may be put at risk because it is off-shoring jobs.
- *Social responsibility risk.* The company's reputation may be put at risk based on the practices of the organizations used in other countries.

Obviously, the company can implement policies and controls, including requiring effective operating agreements, to mitigate these risks.

6. **Other techniques that focus on improving processes include**

   a. **Reengineering (business process reengineering)** is the fundamental rethinking and redesign of business processes to achieve improvements in critical measures of performance such as cost, quality, service speed and customer satisfaction. The scope of reengineering can affect operations and manufacturing processes, as well as financial and administrative processes such as accounts payable and procurement and can impact internal controls.

   b. **Lean manufacturing philosophy.** Lean manufacturing is an operational strategy focused on achieving the shortest possible cycle time by eliminating waste. It is based on increasing the value-added work by eliminating waste and reducing incidental work. The technique often decreases the time between a customer order and shipment, and it is designed to improve profitability, customer satisfaction, throughput time, and employee morale.

   c. **Theory of constraints (TOC)** refers to methods to maximize operating income when faced with some bottleneck operations. **Bottleneck resources** are any resource or operation where the capacity is less than the demand placed upon it. **Nonbottleneck resources** have capacity greater than demand. The objective of TOC is to increase *throughput contribution* while decreasing *investment* and *operating costs*. **Throughput contribution** is revenues minus the direct materials cost of goods sold. **Investment** is the sum of materials, cost in direct materials, work in process and finished goods inventories; research and development costs; and the costs of equipment and buildings. **Operating costs** include the salaries and wages, rental expense, utilities, and depreciation.

   d. **Workflow Analysis** examines the overall flow of work to find ways to improve the flow. It focuses on identifying non-value-added activities and interdependence among various departments. By eliminating non-value-added activities and improving the coordination among departments, efficiencies may be achieved.

NOW REVIEW MULTIPLE-CHOICE QUESTIONS 56 THROUGH 71

J. Project Management

A project is a series of activities and tasks that

- Have specific definable objectives,
- Have defined start and end dates,
- Are subject to funding constraints,
- Consume resources, people, equipment, etc., and
- Cut across various functional areas of the organization.

Projects are usually planned and executed by multidisciplinary teams, consisting of individuals from different functional areas and led by a project manager. Team members must be knowledgeable and able to work together to plan and execute work in a team setting. Some projects are assigned a project oversight or steering group which takes responsibility for the business issues related to the project. These committees are responsible for approving budgetary strategy, defining and realizing benefits, and monitoring risks, quality and timeliness.

Effective project management involves efficiently achieving the project objectives within time and cost constraints. To achieve effective project management, the project leader must manage the four basic elements of a project, including

1. Resources—people, equipment, materials, etc.
2. Time—task durations, task interdependencies, the critical path, etc.
3. Money—costs, contingencies, profit, etc.
4. Scope—project size, goals, requirements, etc.

The processes involved in project management include project initiation, project planning, project execution, project monitoring and control, and project closure.

1. Project initiation includes

   a. Selection of the best project given resource constraints.
   b. Recognizing the benefits of the project.
   c. Authorizing the project. The project must have full support of management of the organization. Since projects often cross functional lines, a commitment by top management of the organization is critical to the success of any project.
   d. Assigning the project manager (leader). The project manager should be competent and have sufficient authority to get access to needed resources and people the project manager should have planning skills, organizational skills, negotiating skills, administration skills, resource allocation skills, and entrepreneurial skills. A **project charter** authorizes the project, and sets forth the project manager's authority and responsibility.

2. Project planning involves determining the activities that need to be performed, who should perform them, and when the activities need to be completed. Planning includes

   a. Defining the work requirements.
   b. Defining the quality and quantity of the work.
   c. Indentifying the needed resources.
   d. Scheduling the activities and tasks.
   e. Indentifying and assessing risks.

   The planning process results in a number of documents. The scope of the work is often set forth in a **statement of work (SOW),** which is a narrative description of the work to be performed to complete the project, including the deliverables. One of the most common reasons for a scope change in a project is a poorly defined statement of work.

   The statement of work often includes the **project specifications,** which is a detailed listing of the man-hour, equipment, and materials requirements. The **milestone schedule** sets forth the start date, the end date and other major milestones involved in completing the project. Finally, the **work breakdown structure (WBS)** breaks the project into manageable, independent, and measureable elements that can be budgeted and for which responsibility can be assigned. The WBS provides a basis for costing, risk analysis, control, and scheduling the project.

   Many companies use a **life-cycle approach** in planning, in which project planning is divided into defined phases, such as conceptualization, feasibility study, etc. At the end of each phase an assessment is done to evaluate the success of the phase and determine whether the next phase should be undertaken.

3. Many different techniques are used to schedule and control a project, including

   a. Gantt chart—a type of bar chart that illustrates the scheduled start and finish of elements of a project over time.
   b. Milestone chart—a type of chart that illustrates the milestones for a project over time.
   c. Line of balance—a type of chart that illustrates the series of activities that are related. It is appropriate where a project has a series of repetitive activities.
   d. Network diagram—illustrates the logical representation of activities that defines the sequence of the work of a project. It illustrates the path of a project. A network diagram has advantages over other forms of techniques because it (1) illustrates the interdependencies between activities, (2) identifies critical paths in a project, (3) facilitates risk analysis for the activities in the project, and (4) enables management to evaluate the effect of an activity delay on the project completion date.
   e. Program Evaluation and Review Technique (PERT)—PERT is a network technique that formally focuses on the interdependency of activities and the time required to complete an activity to schedule and control the project. This technique focuses on the **critical path,** which is the shortest amount of time necessary to accomplish the project. Any slippage in the time of performing the activities along the critical path will result in a delay in completion of the project. Therefore, management knows which activities and events are most critical to timely completion of the project. PERT uses three time estimates (optimistic, most likely, and pessimistic) to derive

expected time to complete a particular task. In PERT analysis **slack time** is the difference between the expected time and the latest time the activity can be completed without delaying the project. PERT is probabilistic in nature which allows the calculation of the risk in completing the project. PERT is typically used where there is a high variability of completion times, such as research and development projects.

f. PERT cost—allows the addition of resource cost considerations to the schedule produced by the PERT technique. This allows the inclusion of cost uncertainty into the analysis.

g. Critical Path Method (CPM)—CPM is similar to PERT but it only uses one time estimate that represents the normal time to complete an activity. CPM is used for projects where there is less variability in time estimates. CPM includes a procedure for time/cost tradeoff to minimize the sum of direct and indirect project costs.

h. Graphical Evaluation and Review Technique (GERT)—GERT is similar to PERT but it has the advantage of allowing looping and branching based on the results of a particular activity. It is appropriate for projects that may be completed in a number of ways.

i. **Project crashing** is a term used to describe the practice of adding resources to shorten selected activity time on the critical path of a project. In effect, the manager is trading off money for time. Therefore, each activity may be viewed as having two types—a normal (planned) time and the crash time (the shortest possible time).

j. Another technique that is often used in conjunction with any of these scheduling techniques is **ABC analysis**. ABC analysis involves the categorization of tasks into groups. These groups are often marked A, B, and C— hence the name. Activities are ranked upon the following general criteria:

A—Tasks that are perceived as being urgent and important.
B—Tasks that are important but not urgent.
C—Tasks that are neither urgent nor important.

Then, each group is rank-ordered in priority. This technique is particularly applicable to project management because it focuses attention on the critical activities or tasks.

Risk management is also applicable to project management. Project risks include those related to costs overruns, time slippage, inappropriately defined scope, and dissatisfaction with the deliverables. The steps in the risk management of a project include (1) identification of risks, (2) quantifying the risks, (3) prioritizing risks, and (4) developing a risk response. Like any type of risk management the response may involve such activates as developing controls or shifting the risk to another party.

4. Project execution includes

a. Negotiating for the team members.
b. Directing the work.
c. Managing team members to improve performance.

Management of a project requires much the same skills as managing any function. However, if the project crosses functional lines, the management process becomes complicated. Problems in project management typically arise from one of the following:

- Organizational uncertainty. The working relationship between the project manager and the functional managers has not been adequately defined by senior management.
- Unusual decision pressures. Project managers must make quick decisions in uncertain situations and with incomplete information. Senior management must recognize these difficulties and support the project manager's decisions.
- Inadequate senior management support. Delays in approval, inability to resolve reporting conflicts, and delays in providing resources can significantly delay or derail projects.

5. Project monitoring and control includes

a. Tracking progress of the project.
b. Comparing actual outcomes to predicted outcomes.
c. Analyzing variances and their effects.
d. Making adjustments.

Many of the typical management techniques are used to control projects, including budgets, variance analysis, and status analysis. The scheduling techniques discussed above also facilitate control of the project by allowing management to focus its attention on critical activities.

6. Project closure includes

a. Determining that all work has been completed.
b. Closure of the contract, financial charges, and paperwork.

NOW REVIEW MULTIPLE-CHOICE QUESTIONS 72 THROUGH 76

KEY TERMS

Balanced scorecard. A strategic performance measurement system that includes financial and nonfinancial performance measures. The measures are in the four perspectives of financial, customer, internal business processes, and learning and growth.

Cash flow ROI. The average real cash return on all existing projects as reflected in the financial statements.

Continuous improvement. Seeks continual improvement of machinery, materials, labor, and production methods by soliciting suggestions and ideas from employees and customers.

Cost of quality. A technique that is based on the philosophy that failures have an underlying cause, prevention is cheaper than failures, and cost of quality performance can be measured.

Cross-sectional analysis. Involves benchmarking the firm's ratios against ratios of similar firms at a point in time.

Economic profit. Accounting profit minus the cost of capital.

Economic value added. Net operating profit after taxes minus the after-tax weighted-average cost of capital multiplied by total assets minus current liabilities.

Free cash flow. Net operating profit after taxes plus depreciation and amortization minus capital expenditures minus the change in working capital requirements.

Horizontal analysis. Involves an evaluation of the firm's ratios and trends over time.

Kaizen. The Japanese art of continuous improvement.

Pareto chart. A bar graph that ranks causes of process variations by the degree of impact on quality.

Strategy maps. Diagrams of the cause and effect relationships between strategic objectives.

Residual income. Net income minus a cost of capital based on capital invested in the project or division.

Residual income profile. A graphical way to look at the relationship between residual income and return on investment.

Total quality management. Focuses on managing the firm to excel in quality in all dimensions of products and services for customers.

Value-based management. Involves the use of value-based metrics in a strategic management system.

Multiple-Choice Questions (1–76)

Balanced Scorecard and Performance Measures

1. What is the most important purpose of a balanced scorecard?

    a. Develop strategy.
    b. Measure performance.
    c. Develop cause-and-effect linkages.
    d. Set priorities.

2. Which of the following is **not** one of the four perspectives of the balanced scorecard?

    a. Investment in resources perspective.
    b. Customer perspective.
    c. Learning and growth perspective.
    d. Financial perspective.

3. The balanced scorecard generally uses performance measures with four different perspectives. Which of the following performance measures would be part of those used for the internal business processes perspective?

    a. Cycle time.
    b. Employee satisfaction.
    c. Hours of training per employee.
    d. Customer retention.

4. The balanced scorecard has been adopted by many corporations. Which of the following **best** describes the balanced scorecard?

    a. A strategy that meets management's objectives.
    b. A diagram illustrating cause and effect relationships.
    c. A table of key actions to achieve strategic objectives.
    d. A strategic performance measurement and management framework.

5. The balanced scorecard and value-based management are techniques that are being used by a number of corporations. In comparison to the balanced scorecard, value-based management focuses on

    a. Nonfinancial measures.
    b. Financial measures.
    c. Both financial and nonfinancial measures.
    d. Quality measures.

6. Management has identified a relationship between customer satisfaction and return on investment. This relationship could be depicted in a

    a. Strategy map.
    b. Value chain.
    c. Customer perspectives chart.
    d. Strategic initiatives list.

7. Which of the following is **not** a component of the balanced scorecard?

    a. Strategic objectives.
    b. Targets.
    c. Strategy initiatives.
    d. Assessment of human resources.

8. Which of the following **best** describes a value chain in the balanced scorecard framework?

    a. The cause-and-effect linkages.
    b. The baseline level of performance.
    c. The sequence of business processes in which usefulness is added to products or services.
    d. The chain of financial and nonfinancial measures.

9. Which of the following is **not** a characteristic of the balanced scorecard?

    a. Both financial and nonfinancial performance measures are included.
    b. Cause-and-effect linkages between strategic objectives.
    c. Customer performance measures are excluded.
    d. Internal process performance measures are included.

10. In the balanced scorecard framework, employee retention is a potential measure in which of the four perspectives?

    a. Financial.
    b. Customer.
    c. Internal business processes.
    d. Learning and growth.

*11. Which of the following is an example of an efficiency measure?

    a. The rate of absenteeism.
    b. The goal of becoming a leading manufacturer.
    c. The number of insurance claims processed per day.
    d. The rate of customer complaints.

12. A strategy objective in the balanced scorecard framework is

    a. A statement of what the strategy must achieve and what is critical to its success.
    b. Key action programs required to achieve strategic objectives.
    c. Diagrams of the cause-and-effect relationships between strategic objectives.
    d. The level of performance or rate of improvement needed in the performance measure.

---

*CIA adapted

13. A target in the balanced scorecard framework is

   a. A statement of what the strategy must achieve and what is critical to its success.
   b. A key action program required to achieve strategic objectives.
   c. A diagram of the cause-and-effect relationships between strategic objectives.
   d. The level of performance or rate of improvement needed in the performance measure.

Value-Based Management: ROI and Residual Income

Items 14 through 18 are based on the following information:

The following is selected data for the Consumer Products division of Arron Corporations for 200X:

Sales	$50,000,000
Average invested capital (assets)	20,000,000
Net income	2,000,000
Cost of capital	8%

14. What is the return on sales (ROS) for the division?

   a. 8%
   b. 4%
   c. 10%
   d. 20%

15. What is the asset turnover ratio for the division?

   a. .25
   b. 10
   c. 2.5
   d. 8

16. What is the return on investment (ROI) for the division?

   a. 10%
   b. 8%
   c. 4%
   d. 2%

17. What is the amount of residual income (RI) for the division?

   a. $2,000,000
   b. $1,600,000
   c. $1,000,000
   d. $400,000

18. What is the amount of interest rate spread for the division?

   a. 8%
   b. 10%
   c. 2%
   d. 20%

Items 19 and 20 are based on the following information:

The following data is available for Cara Corp. for 2014:

Sales	$2,000,000
Average invested capital	500,000
Net income	300,000
Required rate of return	18%

19. What is the return on investment at Cara Corp.?

   a. 60%
   b. 33%
   c. 18%
   d. 15%

20. What is the residual income for Cara Corp.?

   a. $0
   b. $200,000
   c. $210,000
   d. $246,000

Items 21 and 22 are based on the following information:

On the graph below, the line (A-B-C) illustrates residual income (measured on the vertical axis in dollars) at various interest rates. Point D is the cost of capital or the required rate of return. Point E is the residual income at the cost of capital.

21. What does point B represent?

   a. Return on sales.
   b. Return on investment.
   c. Asset turnover.
   d. Operating income.

22. What does point A represent?

   a. Return on sales.
   b. Return on investment.
   c. Asset turnover.
   d. Net income.

23. On the graph below, lines A-B-C and D-E-F illustrates residual income (measured on the vertical axis in dollars) at various interest rates. Point G is the firm's cost of capital. Line ABC represents the residual income of Division X at various interest rates. Line DEF represents the residual income of Division Y at various interest rates.

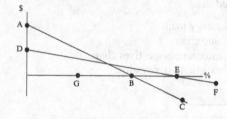

Based on the graph above, for Division X versus Division Y, is the residual income and ROI for Division X greater than or less than that of Division Y?

	Residual income of Division X is greater than the residual income for Division Y	**Return on investment of Division X is greater than the ROI for Division Y**
a.	Yes	Yes
b.	Yes	No
c.	No	Yes
d.	No	No

24. A company's rate of return on investment (ROI) is equal to the

a. Percentage of profit on sales divided by the capital employed turnover rate.
b. Percentage of profit on sales multiplied by the capital employed turnover rate.
c. Investment capital divided by the capital employed turnover rate.
d. Investment capital multiplied by the capital employed turnover rate.

25. Return on investment can be increased by

a. Increasing operating assets.
b. Decreasing operating assets.
c. Decreasing revenues.
d. Both b. and c.

26. The following information pertains to Bala Co. for the year ended December 31, 2014:

Sales	$600,000
Net income	100,000
Capital investment	400,000

Which of the following equations should be used to compute Bala's return on investment?

a. $(4/6) \times (6/1) = ROI$
b. $(6/4) \times (1/6) = ROI$
c. $(4/6) \times (1/6) = ROI$
d. $(6/4) \times (6/1) = ROI$

27. Select Co. had the following 2014 financial statement relationships:

Asset turnover	5
Profit margin on sales	0.02

What was Select's 2014 percentage return on assets?

a. 0.1%
b. 0.4%
c. 2.5%
d. 10.0%

28. The following selected data pertain to the Darwin Division of Beagle Co. for 2014:

Sales	$400,000
Net income	40,000
Capital turnover	4
Imputed interest rate	10%

What was Darwin's 2014 residual income?

a. $0
b. $ 4,000
c. $10,000
d. $30,000

29. Division A is considering a project that will earn a rate of return which is greater than the imputed interest charge for invested capital, but less than the division's historical return on invested capital. Division B is considering a project that will earn a rate of return that is greater than the division's historical return on invested capital, but less than the imputed interest charge for invested capital. If the objective is to maximize residual income, should these divisions accept or reject their projects?

	A	**B**
a.	Accept	Accept
b.	Reject	Accept
c.	Reject	Reject
d.	Accept	Reject

30. Which combination of changes in asset turnover and income as a percentage of sales will maximize the return on investment?

	Asset turnover	**Income as a percentage of sales**
a.	Increase	Decrease
b.	Increase	Increase
c.	Decrease	Increase
d.	Decrease	Decrease

*31. Residual income is often preferred over return on investment (ROI) as a performance evaluation because

a. Residual income is a measure over time while ROI represents the results for a single time period.
b. Residual income concentrates on maximizing absolute dollars of income rather than a percentage return as with ROI.
c. The imputed interest rate used in calculating residual income is more easily derived than the target rate that is compared to the calculated ROI.
d. Average investment is employed with residual income while year-end investment is employed with ROI.

---

*CIA adapted

Value-Based Management: EVA

32. What is a major disadvantage of using economic value added (EVA) alone as a performance measure?

    a. It fails to focus on creating shareholder value.
    b. It promotes the acceptance of unprofitable projects.
    c. It fails to reflect all of the ways that value may be created.
    d. It discourages cost cutting.

Items 33 and 34 are based on the following information:

The following are selected data for Walkin Corporation for the year ended 20X1:

Net operating profit before taxes	$31,250,000
Inventory	5,000,000
Long-term debt	40,000,000
Depreciation expense	9,000,000
Change in net working capital	5,000,000
Capital expenditures	8,000,000
Invested capital (net assets)	80,000,000
Weighted average cost of capital	10%
Tax rate	20%

33. Which of the following measures economic value added for Walkin Corporation for the year?

    a. $3,000,000
    b. $7,000,000
    c. $15,000,000
    d. $17,000,000

34. Which of the following measures the amount of free cash flow for Walkin Corporation for the year?

    a. $7,000,000
    b. $8,000,000
    c. $21,000,000
    d. $25,000,000

35. The following information is available for the wholesale products division of Watco:

Net operating profit before interest and taxes	$30,000,000
Depreciation expense	10,000,000
Change in net working capital	5,000,000
Capital expenditures	4,000,000
Invested capital (total assets – current liabilities)	50,000,000
Weighted-average cost of capital	10%
Tax rate	40%

What is the amount of economic value added (EVA) for the division?

    a. $30,000,000
    b. $13,000,000
    c. $25,000,000
    d. $ 5,000,000

Items 36 and 37 are based on the following information:

The following information is available for Armstrong Enterprises for 2014:

Net operating profit (income) after taxes	$36,000,000
Depreciation expense	15,000,000
Change in net working capital	10,000,000
Capital expenditures	12,000,000
Invested capital (total assets – current liabilities)	100,000,000
Weighted-average cost of capital	10%

36. What is the amount of the economic value added (EVA)?

    a. $20,000,000
    b. $26,000,000
    c. $15,000,000
    d. $36,000,000

37. What is the free cash flow for 2014?

    a. $36,000,000
    b. $30,000,000
    c. $29,000,000
    d. $26,000,000

Traditional Financial Statement Analysis

38. Which of the following is **not** a measure of asset utilization?

    a. Inventory turnover.
    b. Average accounts receivable collection period.
    c. Fixed asset turnover.
    d. Debt to total assets.

39. What financial analysis technique would imply benchmarking with other firms?

    a. Horizontal analysis.
    b. Vertical analysis.
    c. Cross-sectional analysis.
    d. Ratio analysis.

Items 40 and 41 are based on the following information:

The Dawson Corporation projects the following for the year 2014:

Earnings before interest and taxes	$35 million
Interest expense	5 million
Preferred stock dividends	4 million
Common stock dividend payout ratio	30%
Common shares outstanding	2 million
Effective corporate income tax rate	40%

**40. The expected common stock dividend per share for Dawson Corporation for 2014 is

    a. $2.34
    b. $2.70
    c. $3.90
    d. $2.10

** CMA adapted

**41. If Dawson Corporation's common stock is expected to trade at a price/earnings ratio of eight, the market price per share (to the nearest dollar) would be

   a. $125
   b. $56
   c. $72
   d. $68

Items 42 through 46 are based on the following information:

The data presented below show actual figures for selected accounts of McKeon Company for the fiscal year ended December 31, 2014. McKeon's controller is in the process of reviewing the 2014 results. McKeon Company monitors yield or return ratios using the average financial position of the company. (Round all calculations to three decimal places if necessary.)

	12/31/14	12/31/13
Current assets	$210,000	$180,000
Noncurrent assets	275,000	255,000
Current liabilities	78,000	85,000
Long-term debt	75,000	30,000
Common stock ($30 par value)	300,000	300,000
Retained earnings	32,000	20,000

2014 Operations

Sales*		$350,000
Cost of goods sold		160,000
Interest expense		3,000
Income taxes (40% rate)		48,000
Dividends declared and paid in 2014		60,000
Administrative expense		67,000

* All sales are credit sales.

Current Assets

	12/31/14	12/31/13
Cash	$ 20,000	$10,000
Accounts receivable	100,000	70,000
Inventory	70,000	80,000
Other	20,000	20,000

**42. McKeon Company's debt-to-total-asset ratio at 12/31/14 is

   a. 0.352
   b. 0.315
   c. 0.264
   d. 0.237

**43. The 2014 accounts receivable turnover for McKeon company is

   a. 1.882
   b. 3.500
   c. 5.000
   d. 4.118

**44. Using a 365-day year, McKeon's inventory turnover is

   a. 2.133
   b. 2.281
   c. 1.995
   d. 4.615

**45. McKeon Company's total asset turnover for 2014 is

   a. 0.805
   b. 0.761
   c. 0.722
   d. 0.348

**46. The 2014 return on assets for McKeon Company is

   a. 0.261
   b. 0.148
   c. 0.157
   d. 0.166

Items 47 through 53 are based on the following information:

Depoole Company is a manufacturer of industrial products and employs a calendar year for financial reporting purposes. Assume that Depoole's total quick assets exceeded total current liabilities both before and after the transaction. Further assume that Depoole has positive profits during the year and a credit balance throughout the year in its retained earnings account.

**47. Payment of a trade account payable of $64,500 would

   a. Increase the current ratio but the quick ratio would not be affected.
   b. Increase the quick ratio but the current ratio would not be affected.
   c. Increase both the current and quick ratios.
   d. Decrease both the current and quick ratios.

**48. The purchase of raw materials for $85,000 on open account would

   a. Increase the current ratio.
   b. Decrease the current ratio.
   c. Increase net working capital.
   d. Decrease net working capital.

**49. The collection of a current accounts receivable of $29,000 would

   a. Increase the current ratio.
   b. Decrease the current ratio and the quick ratio.
   c. Increase the quick ratio.
   d. Not affect the current or quick ratios.

**50. Obsolete inventory of $125,000 was written off during the year. This transaction

   a. Decreased the quick ratio.
   b. Increased the quick ratio.
   c. Increased net working capital.
   d. Decreased the current ratio.

** CMA adapted

**51. The issuance of new shares in a five-for-one split of common stock

    a. Decreases the book value per share of common stock.
    b. Increases the book value per share of common stock.
    c. Increases total shareholders' equity.
    d. Decreases total shareholders' equity.

**52. The issuance of serial bonds in exchange for an office building, with the first installment of the bonds due late this year,

    a. Decreases net working capital.
    b. Decreases the current ratio.
    c. Decreases the quick ratio.
    d. Affects all of the answers as indicated.

**53. The early liquidation of a long-term note with cash affects the

    a. Current ratio to a greater degree than the quick ratio.
    b. Quick ratio to a greater degree than the current ratio.
    c. Current and quick ratio to the same degree.
    d. Current ratio but not the quick ratio.

Benchmarking and Best Practices

54. Southwest Airlines benchmarked the process of turning around an airplane with the pit stop process for formula racecars. This is an example of

    a. Internal benchmarking.
    b. Generic benchmarking.
    c. Competitor benchmarking.
    d. Functional benchmarking.

55. Which measures would be useful in evaluating the performance of a manufacturing system?

  I. Throughput time.
  II. Total setup time for machines/Total production time.
  III. Number of rework units/Total number of units completed.

    a. I and II only.
    b. II and III only.
    c. I and III only.
    d. I, II, and III.

Quality Control Principles

56. A tool which indicates how frequently each type of defect occurs is a

    a. Control chart.
    b. Pareto diagram.
    c. Cause-and-effect diagram.
    d. Fishbone diagram.

57. A tool which identifies potential causes for failures or defects is

    a. Control chart.
    b. Pareto diagram.
    c. Cause-and-effect diagram.
    d. Strategy map.

58. Which of the statements **best** describes the concept of six-sigma quality?

    a. 10 defects per million.
    b. 3.4 defects per million.
    c. 6.0 defects per million.
    d. 100 defects per million.

59. Which of the following quality tools is another term for continuous improvement?

    a. Theory of constraints.
    b. Kaizen.
    c. Six-sigma.
    d. Lean manufacturing.

Cost of Quality

60. In considering cost of quality methodology, quality circles are associated with

    a. Prevention.
    b. Appraisal.
    c. Internal failure.
    d. External failure.

61. In the cost of quality, which of the following is an example of an "internal failure"?

    a. Cost of inspecting products on the production line by quality inspectors.
    b. Labor cost of product designers whose task is to design components that will not break under extreme temperature conditions.
    c. Cost of reworking defective parts detected by the quality assurance group.
    d. Cost of parts returned by customers.

62. In the cost of quality, which of the following is an example of a "prevention cost"?

    a. Cost of inspecting products on the production line by quality inspectors.
    b. Labor cost of product designers whose task is to design components that will not break under extreme temperature conditions.
    c. Cost of reworking defective parts detected by the quality assurance group.
    d. Cost of parts returned by customers.

63. Delta Manufacturing Co. has had a problem with its product quality. The company has had a large amount of costs related to product recalls. In considering cost of quality methodology, if the company wants to reduce these costs, the **most** likely place to incur costs would be for

    a. Prevention.
    b. Appraisal.
    c. Internal failure.
    d. External failure.

** CMA adapted

64. In the cost of quality, costs incurred in detecting individual units of product that do **not** conform to specifications are

    a. Prevention costs.
    b. Appraisal costs.
    c. Internal failure costs.
    d. External failure costs.

Business Process Management

65. In an attempt to improve operations, companies often go through analyses and redesign of the way processes are performed. Which of the following is **not** considered to be an aspect of a business process that may be focused on to achieve improvement?

    a. Technology.
    b. Human performance.
    c. The interaction between technology and human performance.
    d. Strategic goals.

66. Management of organizations that engage in business process management view business processes as

    a. Requirements for good control over the organization.
    b. Systems that provide information for good management.
    c. Strategic assets that must be understood, managed and improved.
    d. Mechanisms that keep employees from shirking.

67. At which phase in the business process management life-cycle does management simulate performance of the process in a test environment?

    a. Design.
    b. Modeling.
    c. Execution.
    d. Optimization.

68. In the theory of constraints, an operation or resource where the work performed approaches or exceeds the available time is referred to as

    a. A bottleneck.
    b. A time driver.
    c. Customer-response time.
    d. Manufacturing lead time.

**69. Antlers, Inc. produces a single product that sells for $150 per unit. The product is processed through the Cutting and Finishing departments. Additional data for these departments are as follows:

	Cutting	Finishing
Annual capacity (36,000 direct labor hours available in each department)	180,000 units	135,000 units
Current production rate (annualized)	108,000 units	108,000 units
Fixed manufacturing overhead	$1,296,000	$1,944,000

Fixed selling and administrative expense	$864,000	$1,296,000
Direct materials cost per unit	$ 45	$ 15

The current production rate is the budgeted rate for the entire year. Direct labor employees earn $20 per hour and the company has a "no layoff" policy in effect. What is the amount of the throughput contribution per unit as computed using the theory of constraints?

    a. $90.00
    b. $76.67
    c. $46.67
    d. $26.67

**70. Three of the basic measurements used by the Theory of Constraints (TOC) are

    a. Gross margin (or gross profit), return on assets, and total sales.
    b. Number of constraints (or subordinates), number of nonconstraints, and operating leverage.
    c. Throughput (or throughput contribution), inventory (or investments), and operational expense.
    d. Fixed manufacturing overhead per unit, fixed general overhead per unit, and unit gross margin (or gross profit).

71. Which statement **best** describes the objective of the theory of constraints?

	Throughput contribution	Investment	Operating costs
a.	Increase	Decrease	Decrease
b.	Increase	Increase	Increase
c.	Decrease	Increase	Decrease
d.	Increase	Increase	Decrease

Project Management

72. Which of the following involves comparing measures of actual progress of a project to planned progress?

    a. Project planning.
    b. Project scheduling.
    c. Project control.
    d. Project closure.

73. Which of the following is a detailed listing of the man-hour, equipment, and materials requirements for a project?

    a. Statement of work.
    b. Work breakdown structure.
    c. Project specifications.
    d. Milestone schedule.

74. Which of the following is used to describe the practice of adding resources to shorten selected activity time on the critical path of a project?

    a. Making adjustments.
    b. Project crashing.
    c. Slack time.
    d. Reengineering.

** CMA adapted

75. When a project can be completed in a number of completely different ways that might involve branching after performing activities, the **best** schedule and control technique would be

    a. Program Evaluation and Review Technique.
    b. Gant chart.
    c. Critical Path Method.
    d. Graphical Evaluation and Review Technique.

76. A technique that is often used in project management to identify tasks where attention should be focused because they are the most critical or valuable is referred to as

    a. ABC Analysis.
    b. Milestone analysis.
    c. Work breakdown analysis.
    d. Tasking.

Multiple-Choice Answers and Explanations

Answers

1.	b	__ __	17.	d	__ __	33.	d	__ __	49.	d	__ __	65.	d	__ __
2.	a	__ __	18.	c	__ __	34.	c	__ __	50.	d	__ __	66.	c	__ __
3.	a	__ __	19.	a	__ __	35.	b	__ __	51.	a	__ __	67.	b	__ __
4.	d	__ __	20.	c	__ __	36.	b	__ __	52.	d	__ __	68.	a	__ __
5.	b	__ __	21.	b	__ __	37.	c	__ __	53.	b	__ __	69.	a	__ __
6.	a	__ __	22.	d	__ __	38.	d	__ __	54.	b	__ __	70.	c	__ __
7.	d	__ __	23.	b	__ __	39.	c	__ __	55.	d	__ __	71.	a	__ __
8.	c	__ __	24.	b	__ __	40.	d	__ __	56.	b	__ __	72.	c	__ __
9.	c	__ __	25.	b	__ __	41.	b	__ __	57.	c	__ __	73.	c	__ __
10.	d	__ __	26.	b	__ __	42.	b	__ __	58.	b	__ __	74.	b	__ __
11.	c	__ __	27.	d	__ __	43.	d	__ __	59.	b	__ __	75.	d	__ __
12.	a	__ __	28.	d	__ __	44.	a	__ __	60.	a	__ __	76.	a	__ __
13.	d	__ __	29.	d	__ __	45.	b	__ __	61.	c	__ __			
14.	b	__ __	30.	b	__ __	46.	c	__ __	62.	b	__ __			
15.	c	__ __	31.	b	__ __	47.	c	__ __	63.	a	__ __	1st:	__/76 = __%
16.	a	__ __	32.	c	__ __	48.	b	__ __	64.	b	__ __	2nd:	__/76 = __%

Explanations

1. (b) The requirement is to identify the purpose of a balanced scorecard. Answer (b) is correct because the balanced scorecard uses financial and nonfinancial measures to measure performance. Answer (a) is incorrect because strategic planning is designed to develop strategy. Answer (c) is incorrect because developing cause-and-effect linkages is an important part of developing a balanced scorecard. Answer (d) is incorrect because setting priorities is a part of strategic planning.

2. (a) The requirement is to identify the item that is **not** one of the four perspectives of the balanced scorecard. Answer (a) is correct because investment in resources is not a perspective of the balanced scorecard. The balanced scorecard deals with performance measurement. Answer (b) is incorrect because customer perspective is used in the balanced scorecard. Answer (c) is incorrect because learning and growth perspective is used in the balanced scorecard. Answer (d) is incorrect because financial perspective is used in the balanced scorecard.

3. (a) The requirement is to identify the measure that is related to internal business processes. Answer (a) is correct because cycle time is the time it takes to manufacture a product and, therefore, is an important part of the business processes perspective. Answers (b) and (c) are incorrect because they are part of the learning and growth perspective. Answer (d) is incorrect because it is part of the customer perspective.

4. (d) The requirement is to define the balanced scorecard. Answer (d) is correct because the balanced scorecard is a strategic performance measurement and management framework. Answer (b) is incorrect because it is the definition of a strategy map. Answer (c) is incorrect because it is the definition of a list of strategic initiatives.

5. (b) The requirement is to identify the focus of value-based management. Answer (b) is correct because value-based management focuses on financial measures to measure performance. The balanced scorecard uses both financial and nonfinancial measures to measure performance.

6. (a) The requirement is to identify what illustrates cause-and-effect relationships. Answer (a) is correct because a strategy map displays cause-and-effect relationships within the balanced scorecard framework. Answer (b) is incorrect because the value chain is the sequence of business processes that add value to a good or service.

7. (d) The requirement is to identify the item that is **not** a component of the balanced scorecard. Answer (d) is correct because an assessment of human resources is not a component of a balanced scorecard. Answer (a) is incorrect because a statement of strategic objectives is a component of a balanced scorecard. Answer (b) is incorrect because targets for performance are part of a balanced scorecard. Answer (c) is incorrect because strategy initiatives are part of a balanced scorecard.

8. (c) The requirement is to identify the description of the value chain. Answer (c) is correct because the value chain is the sequence of business processes in which usefulness is added to the product or service. Answer (a) is incorrect because cause-and-effect linkages are used to develop the balanced scorecard. Answer (b) is incorrect because the baseline level of performance is the current level of performance. Answer (d) is incorrect because there is no chain of financial and nonfinancial measures.

9. (c) The requirement is to identify which item is **not** a characteristic of the balanced scorecard. Answer (c) is correct because customer performance is one of the four primary components of the balanced scorecard framework; therefore, it is not excluded. Answers (a), (b), and (d) are incorrect because they are all characteristics of the balanced scorecard.

10. (d) The requirement is to identify where, in the balanced scorecard framework, employee retention is a potential measure. Answer (d) is correct because employee retention would appear in the learning and growth perspective which includes various employee measures including employee turnover. Answer (a) is incorrect because the financial perspective includes measures such as profitability and return on investment. Answer (b) is incorrect because the customer perspective includes measures like customer satisfaction. Answer (c) is incorrect because the internal business processes perspective includes measures related to cost, quality, and time.

11. (c) The requirement is to identify the efficiency measure. Answer (c) is correct because an efficiency measure relates output to a measure of input. Answer (a) is incorrect because it does not relate output to input. Answer (b) is incorrect because it is an effectiveness measure. Answer (d) is incorrect because it does not relate output to input.

12. (a) The requirement is to identify the definition of a strategy objective. Answer (a) is correct because it is the definition of a strategy objective in the balanced scorecard framework. Answer (b) is incorrect because it describes a strategic initiative. Answer (c) is incorrect because it is the definition of a strategy map. Answer (d) is incorrect because it is the definition of a target.

13. (d) The requirement is to identify the definition of a target. Answer (d) is correct because it is the definition of a target in the balanced scorecard framework. Answer (a) is incorrect because it is the definition of a strategic objective. Answer (b) is incorrect because it is the definition of strategy initiatives. Answer (c) is incorrect because it is the definition of a strategy map.

14. (b) The requirement is to calculate the return on sales for the division. Answer (b) is correct because return on sales is calculated as net income/sales which is equal to 4% ($2,000,000/$50,000,000).

15. (c) The requirement is to calculate the asset turnover ratio for the division. Answer (c) is correct because the asset turnover ratio is calculated by dividing sales by the average investment amount. Therefore, it is equal to 2.5 ($50,000,000/$20,000,000).

16. (a) The requirement is to calculate ROI for the division. Answer (a) is correct because ROI is calculated by dividing net income by the amount of the average investment. Therefore, ROI is equal to 10% ($2,000,000/ $20,000,000).

17. (d) The requirement is to calculate RI for the division. Answer (d) is correct because RI is equal to net income minus interest on the investment. Therefore, RI is equal to $400,000 [$2,000,000 − ($20,000,000 × 8%)].

18. (c) The requirement is to calculate the interest rate spread for the division. Answer (c) is correct because the interest rate spread is the difference between the return on investment and the required rate of return (cost of capital). In this case, the spread is equal to 2% [($2,000,000/ $20,000,000) − 8%].

19. (a) The requirement is to calculate the return on investment. Answer (a) is correct because the return on investment would be computed by dividing net income by average invested capital ($300,000/$500,000 = 60%).

20. (c) The requirement is to calculate the residual income. Answer (c) is correct because the residual income would be computed as follows: Net income ($300,000) minus the interest on invested capital $90,000 (18% × $500,000) is equal to $210,000.

21. (b) The requirement is to identify the graphical representation of ROI. Answer (b) is correct because point B is equal to ROI. Answer (a) is incorrect because return on sales (net income/sales) is not represented on this graph. Answer (c) is incorrect because asset turnover (sales/total assets) is not represented on this graph. Answer (d) is incorrect because operating income is located at point A.

22. (d) The requirement is to identify the graphical representation of net income. Answer (d) is correct because point A is equal to net income. Answer (a) is incorrect because return on sales (net income/sales) is not represented on this graph. Answer (b) is incorrect because ROI is represented at point B. Answer (c) is incorrect because asset turnover (sales/total assets) is not represented on the graph.

23. (b) The requirement is to identify the graphical representation of the relationship between residual income and ROI. Division X's residual income is located at point A and Division Y's residual income is located at point D. Division X has a larger residual income. Division X's ROI is located at point B and Division Y's ROI is located at point E. Thus Division Y's ROI is greater than Division X's ROI.

24. (b) The requirement is to identify the formula for ROI. Answer (b) is correct because it describes the DuPont ROI analysis: ROI = Return on sales multiplied by the capital employed turnover rate (which can be measured as total asset turnover).

25. (b) The requirement is to identify how ROI might be increased. One way of measuring ROI is return on assets (ROA). The formula is net income/total assets. Answer (b) is correct since if operating assets decrease (the denominator in ROI), then ROI would decrease. Answer (a) is incorrect because increasing operating assets would cause ROI to decrease. Answer (c) is incorrect because decreasing revenue would cause net income (the numerator) to decrease. A reduction in operating income would cause ROA to decrease.

26. (b) Return on investment (ROI) may be calculated using the following equation:

$$\frac{\text{Sales}}{\text{Investment}} \times \frac{\text{Net income}}{\text{Sales}} = \text{ROI}$$

Thus, the equation that should be used to compute Bala's return on investment is $(6/4) \times (1/6) = \text{ROI}$.

27. (d) Return on assets, also referred to as return on investment (ROI), is calculated as follows:

$$\text{ROI} = \text{Profit margin} \times \text{Asset turnover}$$
$$\text{ROI} = 0.02 \times 5$$
$$\text{ROI} = 0.10, \text{ or } 10\%$$

28. (d) Residual income equals the net income of a division minus imputed interest on the division's assets. In this question, we are given Darwin's operating income and imputed interest rate, but Darwin's assets must be derived using sales and capital turnover, as shown below.

$$\text{Capital turnover} = \frac{\text{Sales of division}}{\text{Invested capital of division}}$$

$$4 = \frac{\$400,000}{x}$$

$$x = \frac{\$400,000}{4} = \$100,000$$

Since Darwin's invested capital is $100,000, its operating income is $40,000, and interest is imputed at 10%, residual income is calculated as follows:

$$\text{RI} = \frac{\text{Division}}{\text{net income}} - \frac{\text{Imputed interest on}}{\text{investment}}$$
$$\text{RI} = \$40,000 - (\$100,000 \times 10\%)$$
$$\text{RI} = \$30,000$$

29. (d) Residual income is income minus an imputed interest charge for invested capital. Residual income will be maximized as long as the division earns a rate of return that exceeds the imputed charge. Division A's project will earn a rate of return **greater** than the imputed interest charge, so this project should be accepted. Division B's project will earn a rate of return **less** than the imputed interest charge, so this project should not be accepted.

30. (b) The DuPont formula is used to calculate return on investment.

$$\frac{\text{Asset}}{\text{turnover}} \times \frac{\text{Income as a}}{\text{percentage of}} = \frac{\text{Return on}}{\text{investment}}$$
$$\text{sales} \qquad (\text{ROI})$$

$$\frac{\text{Revenue}}{\text{Invested capital}} \times \frac{\text{Income}}{\text{Revenue}} = \frac{\text{Income}}{\text{Invested capital}}$$

The combination of changes which will maximize return on investment are to increase both asset turnover and income as a percentage of sales, since multiplying two larger numbers will result in a larger product.

31. (b) The requirement is to identify why residual income is preferred over return on investment as a performance evaluation technique. Answer (b) is correct because the focus on return on investment can cause high-performing divisions not to invest in projects that are in the best interest of the overall organization. Answer (a) is incorrect because both techniques can measure results for a single period. Answer (c) is incorrect because the imputed interest rate and the target rate should be the same. Answer (d) is incorrect because the investment level should be computed on the same basis.

32. (c) The requirement is to identify the major disadvantage of using EVA alone. Answer (c) is correct because many times value creation activities do not immediately increase return, and EVA (in the short run) does not reflect the value of these activities. Answer (a) is incorrect because a major advantage of EVA is its focus on creating shareholder value. Answer (b) is incorrect because EVA does not promote the acceptance of unprofitable projects. Answer (d) is incorrect because EVA encourages cost cutting activities.

33. (d) The requirement is to calculate EVA. Answer (d) is correct because EVA is equal to Operating profit after taxes – Cost of invested capital. Net operating profit after taxes is equal to Net operating profit before taxes multiplied by one minus the tax rate, or $25,000,000 [$31,250,000 × (1 – .20)]. Accordingly, EVA is equal to $17,000,000 [$25,000,000 – ($80,000,000 × 10%)].

34. (c) The requirement is to calculate free cash flow. Answer (c) is correct because free cash flow is equal to Net operating profit after taxes + Depreciation expense – Change in net working capital – Capital expenditures. Therefore, free cash flow is equal to $21,000,000 ($25,000,000 + $9,000,000 – $5,000,000 – $8,000,000).

35. (b) The requirement is to calculate EVA for the division. Answer (b) is correct because EVA is calculated as net operating profit after taxes (NOPAT) minus the capital charge on invested capital. In this case, NOPAT is equal to net operating profit before interest and taxes ($30,000,000) minus taxes ($30,000,000 × 40%), which is equal to $18,000,000. EVA is then equal to $13,000,000 [$18,000,000 – ($50,000,000 × 10%)].

36. (b) The requirement is to calculate economic value added. The formula for EVA is Net operating profit after taxes – Cost of invested capital. EVA would be computed as follows:

Net operating profit after taxes	$ 36,000,000
– Capital charge on invested capital ($100,000,000 × 10%)	(10,000,000)
= Economic value added	$ 26,000,000

37. (c) The requirement is to calculate free cash flow. Free cash flow would be computed as follows:

Net operating profit after taxes	$ 36,000,000
+ Depreciation expense	15,000,000
– Change in net working capital	(10,000,000)
– Capital expenditures	(12,000,000)
Free cash flow	$ 29,000,000

38. (d) The requirement is to identify the ratio that does **not** measure asset utilization. Answer (d) is correct because the debt to total assets ratio is a debt utilization (financial leverage) ratio. Answers (a), (b), and (c) are incorrect because they are asset utilization ratios.

39. (c) The requirement is to identify the nature of benchmarking with other firms. Answer (c) is correct because cross-sectional analysis involves comparing results and ratios to those of other firms in the same industry. Answer (a) is incorrect because horizontal analysis involves comparisons of results and ratios for the same firm over time. Answer (b) is incorrect because vertical analysis involves comparisons of relationships in a firm's financial statements for a single year. Answer (d) is incorrect because ratio analysis does not imply any particular comparison.

40. (d) The requirement is to calculate the expected dividend per share. Earnings after interest is equal to $30 million ($35 million – $5 million). Net earnings after taxes is equal to $18 million [$30 million × 1 – Tax rate (40%)]. The net earnings after dividends to preferred shareholders is equal to $14 million ($18 million – $4 million), and the dividend for common stockholders is equal to $4,200,000 ($14 million × 30%). The dividend per share is equal to $4,200,000/$2 million shares = $2.10. Therefore, the correct answer is (d).

41. (b) The requirement is to calculate the market price from the earnings per share and price/earnings ratio. Net earnings is equal to $18 million ($35 million – $5 million) × (1 – 40%). Net earnings available to common stockholders is equal to $14 million ($18 million – $4 million). Earnings per share is equal to $14 million/2 million shares, or $7.00. Therefore, the estimated market price would be $7.00 × 8 = $56, or answer (b).

42. (b) The requirement is to calculate the debt-to-total-asset ratio. Answer (b) is correct. The debt-to-total-asset ratio is calculated by dividing total debt by total assets. Therefore, the debt-to-total-asset ratio is equal to 0.315 ($78,000 current liabilities + $75,000 long-term debt) ÷ ($210,000 current assets + $275,000 noncurrent assets). Answers (a), (c), and (d) are incorrect because the computations are not correct.

43. (d) The requirement is to calculate accounts receivable turnover. Answer (d) is correct. Accounts receivable turnover is calculated by dividing total credit sales by the average balance of accounts receivable. The average balance of accounts receivable is $85,000 [($100,000 + $70,000) ÷ 2]. Therefore, accounts receivable turnover is equal to 4.118 ($350,000 credit sales ÷ $85,000 average accounts receivable).

44. (a) The requirement is to calculate inventory turnover. Answer (d) is correct. Inventory turnover is calculated by dividing cost of goods sold by average inventory. Average inventory is equal to $75,000 [($70,000 + $80,0000) ÷ 2]. Therefore, inventory turnover is equal to 2.133 ($160,000 ÷ $75,000).

45. (b) The requirement is to calculate total asset turnover. Answer (b) is correct. Total asset turnover is calculated by dividing sales by average total assets. Average total assets is equal to $460,000 = [($210,000 + $275,000) + ($180,000 +

$255,000)] ÷ 2. Therefore, total asset turnover is equal to 0.761 ($350,000 ÷ $460,000).

46. (c) The requirement is to calculate return on total assets. Answer (c) is correct. Return on assets is calculated by dividing net income by average total assets. As determined in the previous question, average total assets is equal to $460,000. Net income is equal to $72,000 ($350,000 sales – $160,000 cost of goods sold – $3,000 interest expense – $48,000 income taxes – $67,000 administrative expense). Therefore, return on assets is equal to 0.157 ($72,000 ÷ $460,000), or 15.7%.

47. (c) The requirement is to determine the effect of payment of an account payable. Answer (c) is correct. The quick ratio is equal to quick assets divided by current liabilities and the current ratio is equal to current assets divided by current liabilities. Since we are told that quick assets exceed current liabilities, both ratios are greater than one. With a ratio greater than one if you reduce the numerator and denominator by an equal amount, the ratio will increase.

48. (b) The requirement is to determine the effect of a purchase of raw materials on account. The correct answer is (b). Since we know that the current ratio is greater than one, an increase in the numerator and the denominator by an equal amount will decrease the ratio. Answers (c) and (d) are incorrect because working capital will not change.

49. (d) The requirement is to determine the effect of the collection of accounts receivable. Answer (d) is correct. Collection of accounts receivable has no effect on the quick or current ratio because both cash and accounts receivable are part of the numerator of both ratios.

50. (d) The requirement is to determine the effect of writing off inventory. Answer (d) is correct because a write-off of inventory will decrease the current ratio. Answers (a) and (b) are incorrect because inventory is not used in computing the quick ratio. Answer (c) is incorrect because working capital will be decreased.

51. (a) The requirement is to determine the effect of a five-for-one stock split. Answer (a) is correct because a stock split increases the number of shares outstanding and, therefore, reduces the book value per share. Answers (c) and (d) are incorrect because the transaction does not affect total stockholders' equity.

52. (d) The requirement is to determine the effect of issuing serial bonds in exchange for an office building. Answer (d) is correct because the first installment is a current liability which affects the quick ratio, the current ratio, and working capital.

53. (b) The requirement is to determine the effect of liquidating a long-term note with cash. Answer (b) is correct. Cash is included in the numerator of both the quick and current ratios. However, a reduction in cash affects the quick ratio more than the current ratio because it is smaller.

54. (b) The requirement is to identify the definition of benchmarking outside of the firm's industry. Answer (b) is correct because generic benchmarking involves benchmarking to the best practices regardless of the industry. Answer (a) is incorrect because internal benchmarking involves benchmarking within the firm. Answer (c) is incorrect because competitor benchmarking involves benchmarking against direct competitors. Answer (d) is incorrect because functional benchmarking involves benchmarking within the same broad industry.

55. (d) Answer (d) in correct because of these nonfinancial measures would be useful in evaluating the performance of a manufacturing system. Throughput (cycle) time measures the total amount of production time required per unit. This measure is important to assess the timeliness of the production process, which is required for on-time delivery of goods. The proportion of total production time consumed by setup activities reflects one aspect of production efficiency. Setup time represents money spent on a non-value-adding activity, and thus should be minimized as much as possible. The proportion of total units completed which require rework is a useful measure of product quality. An excessive rate of rework alerts management that it needs to examine its quality control procedures.

56. (b) The requirement is to identify which tool is used to identify frequency of defects. Answer (b) is correct because a Pareto chart ranks the causes of process variations by the degree of impact on quality. Answer (a) is incorrect because a control chart is a statistical plot that helps to detect deviations before they generate defects. Answer (c) is incorrect because a cause-and-effect diagram is used to identify the potential causes of defects. Answer (d) is incorrect because a fishbone diagram is an alternative name for cause-and-effect diagrams.

57. (c) The requirement is to select which tool identifies causes of failures or defects. Answer (c) is correct because cause-and-effect diagrams identify causes of failures/defects and can be used to identify the reasons why a process goes out of control. Answer (a) is incorrect because a control chart is a statistical plot that helps to detect deviations before they generate defects. Answer (b) is incorrect because a Pareto diagram indicates how frequently a type of defect may occur. Answer (d) is incorrect because a strategy map is a statement of what the strategy must achieve and what is critical to its success.

58. (b) The requirement is to identify the concept of six-sigma quality. Answer (b) is correct because six-sigma is a statistical measure expressing how close a product comes to its quality goal. Six-sigma is 99.999997% perfect with 3.4 defects per million parts.

59. (b) The requirement is to identify the terms used to identify continuous improvement. Answer (b), Kaizen, is correct because it is the Japanese art of continuous improvement. It underlies the total quality management and JIT business techniques. Answer (a) is incorrect because the theory of constraints is a method to maximize operating income when faced with some bottleneck operations. Answer (c) is incorrect because six-sigma is a statistical measure expressing how close a product comes to its quality goal. Six-sigma is 3.4 defects per million parts. Answer (d) is incorrect because lean manufacturing is an operational strategy focused on achieving the shortest possible cycle time by eliminating waste.

60. (a) The requirement is to identify the nature of quality circles. Answer (a) is correct because quality circles are designed to develop ways to prevent defects. Answer (b) is incorrect because appraisal costs are related to inspecting and testing to ensure product acceptability. Answer (c) is incorrect because internal failure involves the costs of finding defective units before they are shipped to customers. Answer (d) is incorrect because external failure is the cost of defects that reach the customer.

61. (c) The requirement is to identify the item which reflects the internal failure component. An internal failure cost is a cost incurred when substandard products are produced but discovered before shipment to the customer. Reworking defective parts is an example of an internal failure. Answer (a) is incorrect because it is an example of an appraisal cost. Answer (b) is incorrect because it is an example of a prevention cost. Answer (d) is incorrect because it is an example of an external failure cost.

62. (b) The requirement is to identify the item which reflects the prevention cost component. A prevention cost is a cost incurred to prevent defects. These costs include the cost to identify the cause of the defect, take corrective action to eliminate the cause, train people, and redesign the product or the production process. Answer (b) is correct because it is an example of a quality activity designed to do the job right the first time. Answer (a) is incorrect because it is an example of an appraisal cost. Answer (c) is incorrect because it is an example of an internal failure cost. Answer (d) is incorrect because it is an example of an external failure cost.

63. (a) The requirement is to identify where to incur costs to prevent product recalls. Answer (a) is correct because spending funds to prevent defects is generally most cost effective.

64. (b) The requirement is to identify how costs incurred to detect nonconforming units are classified. Answer (b) is correct because appraisal costs are costs associated with quality control and include testing and inspection. Answer (a) is incorrect because prevention costs involve any quality activity designed to do the job right the first time. Answer (c) is incorrect because internal failures occur when substandard products are produced but discovered before shipment to the customer. Answer (d) is incorrect because external failure costs are incurred for products that do not meet requirements of the customer and have been shipped to the customer.

65. (d) The requirement is to identify the aspect of business process improvement that is **not** generally a focus. Answer (d) is correct because examination of strategic goals is part of strategic planning, not part of business process management. Answers (a), (b) and (c) are incorrect because they all represent ways to improve business processes.

66. (c) The requirement is to identify how business process managers view business processes. Answer (c) is correct because business process managers view processes as strategic assets that can create value and competitive advantage. Answers (a), (b) and (d) are incorrect because they all describe very limited views of business processes.

67. (b) The requirement is to identify the phase that involves simulation of performance of the process in a test environment. Answer (b) is correct because this describes the modeling phase. Answer (a) is incorrect because the design phase involves design of the new process. Answer (c) is incorrect because the execution phase involves implementing the process. Answer (d) is incorrect because optimization involves identifying additional improvements in the process after it is implemented.

68. (a) The requirement is to identify a component of the theory of constraints. Answer (a) is correct because a bottleneck is any resource or operation where the capacity is less than the demand placed upon it. Answers (b), (c), and (d) are incorrect because they are not components of the theory of constraints.

69. (a) The requirement is to compute throughput contribution per unit. Answer (a) is correct because through put contribution per unit is equal to revenue minus direct materials. Thus, throughput contribution per unit is equal to $150 (revenue per unit) – $45 (Cutting direct materials) – $15 (Finishing direct materials) = $90. Answers (b), (c), and (d) are incorrect because they represent incorrect computations of throughput contribution per unit.

70. (c) The requirement is to identify the three basic measurements used by the Theory of Constraints. Answer (c) is correct because the Theory of Constraints focuses on throughput contribution, investment (or inventory), and operational expense (operating costs). Answers (a), (b), and (d) are incorrect because they represent other types of performance measures.

71. (a) The requirement is to describe the objectives of the theory of constraints (TOC). The objective of TOC is to increase *throughput contribution* while decreasing *investment* and *operating costs*. Throughput contribution is revenues minus the direct materials cost of goods sold. Investment is the sum of materials cost in direct materials; work in process and finished goods inventories; research and development costs; and the costs of equipment and buildings. Operating costs include salaries and wages, rental expense, utilities, and depreciation.

72. (c) The requirement is to identify the stage that involves comparing measures of actual progress to planned progress. Answer (c) is correct because this describes an aspect of project control. Answers (a), (b), and (d) are incorrect because they represent other stages of the project management lifecycle.

73. (c) The requirement is to identify which of the items is a detailed listing of the man-hour, equipment, and materials requirements for a project. Answer (c) is correct because this is a description of the project specifications. Answer (a) is incorrect because the statement of work is a narrative description of the work to be performed. Answer (b) is incorrect because the work breakdown structure breaks the project into manageable, independent, and measureable elements that can be budgeted and assigned. Answer (d) is incorrect because the milestone schedule sets forth the start date, the end date, and other major milestones involved in completing the project.

74. (b) The requirement is to identify the term used to describe the practice of adding resources to shorten selected activity time on the critical path of a project. Answer (b) is correct because this describes project crashing. Answers (a), (c), and (d) are incorrect because they are not terms used to describe this process.

75. (d) The requirement is to identify the scheduling and control technique that would be most appropriate when a project can be completed in a number of completely different ways. Answer (d) is correct because the Graphical Evaluation and Review Technique is appropriate for these types of projects. Answers (a), (b), and (c) are incorrect because these scheduling and control techniques do not perform as well under these circumstances.

76. (a) The requirement is to identify the technique used to identify critical or valuable tasks. Answer (a) is correct because ABC Analysis involves categorizing tasks into groups from those that are urgent and important to those that are neither urgent nor important. Answers (b), (c), and (d) are incorrect because they are not terms used to describe a technique to identify critical or valuable tasks.

Written Communication Tasks

Written Communication Task 1

Written
Communication
Help

The management of Hewitt Company is considering adopting a balanced scorecard to measure performance. Karen Wells, the chief financial officer for the company, has asked you to prepare a memorandum describing a balanced scorecard and the advantages of adopting such a system.

> **REMINDER:** Your response will be graded for both technical content and writing skills. Technical content will be evaluated for information that is helpful to the intended reader and clearly relevant to the issue. Writing skills will be evaluated for development, organization, and the appropriate expression of ideas in professional correspondence. Use a standard business memo or letter format with a clear beginning, middle, and end. Do not convey information in the form of a table, bullet point list, or other abbreviated presentation.

To: Ms. Karen Wells, CFO
         Hewitt Company
From: CPA Candidate

Written Communication Task 2

Written
Communication
Help

The management of Taylor Corporation is attempting to adopt new performance measures. Henry Warren, the chief executive officer, has asked you to prepare a memorandum describing how management should choose between alternative measures.

> **REMINDER:** Your response will be graded for both technical content and writing skills. Technical content will be evaluated for information that is helpful to the intended reader and clearly relevant to the issue. Writing skills will be evaluated for development, organization, and the appropriate expression of ideas in professional correspondence. Use a standard business memo or letter format with a clear beginning, middle, and end. Do not convey information in the form of a table, bullet point list, or other abbreviated presentation.

To: Mr. Henry Warren, CEO
         Taylor Corporation
From: CPA Candidate

Written Communication Task 3

Written Communication	
	Help

Assume that you are a consultant providing services for Webster Corp. Webster is performing a significant project-based implementation of a new enterprise resource system. The company is concerned about the difficulties in performing the project. Compose a memorandum to management describing the risks involved in executing a project that is cross-functional in nature.

> **REMINDER:** Your response will be graded for both technical content and writing skills. Technical content will be evaluated for information that is helpful to the intended user and clearly relevant to the issue. Writing skills will be evaluated for development, organization, and the appropriate expression of ideas in professional correspondence. Use a standard business memorandum or letter format with a clear beginning, middle, and end. Do not convey the information in the form of a table, bullet point list, or other abbreviated presentation.

To: Webster Corp. President
Re: ERP project management
From: CPA Candidate

Written Communication Task Solutions

Written Communication Task 1

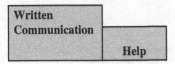

To: Ms. Karen Wells, CFO
        Hewitt Company
From: CPA Candidate

I understand that you are considering implementing a balanced scorecard performance measurement system at Hewitt Company. This memorandum explains the nature and benefits of such a system.

The balanced scorecard is a performance measurement system that includes both financial and nonfinancial measures. It includes measures in the four perspectives of financial, customer, internal business processes, and learning and growth. By measuring performance with multiple measures across these four perspectives, a balanced scorecard is more strategic than other systems that rely primarily on financial measures. It aids in communicating the company's strategy to all members of the organization and helps insure that they work to achieve the organization's strategic goals.

I suggest that you continue with your plan to implement a balanced scorecard system because I believe that it is superior to other single-dimensional systems.

If you have any questions, please contact me.

Written Communication Task 2

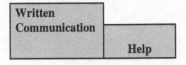

To: Mr. Henry Warren, CEO
        Taylor Corporation
From: CPA Candidate

This memorandum is designed to assist you in deciding how to select among different performance measures for Taylor Corporation.

Selecting among different performance measures requires an understanding how the measures will be used. Possible uses include for compensation, resource allocation, and business unit performance. Different measures are more appropriate for different purposes.

It is important that all performance measures reflect the strategy of the company. Measures that are strategic communicate the goals of the organization and motivate management to pursue those goals. Performance measures must also represent economic reality. They should provide a clear and accurate measure of relative performance. Finally, if the measures are used to evaluate and compensate managers, they should be sensitive to factors that are in the manager's control and not sensitive to factors beyond the manager's control. The measures should be clearly controllable by the manager being evaluated.

As you can see, selection of appropriate performance measures is a complex process. If you would like to discuss your selection of measures in more detail, please contact me.

Written Communication Task 3

Written Communication	
	Help

To: Webster Corp. President
Re: ERP project management
From: CPA Candidate

You have requested that we provide information about the issues involved in executing a project to implement an enterprise resource management system. In particular, you are concerned that the cross-functional nature of the project will be difficult to manage.

You should understand that the cross-functional nature of this project creates additional risk of failure that must be controlled. The most important requirement for success of a cross-functional project is full support by top management. The team must have this support to get adequate cooperation from the various functional managers of the organization. This also means that the relationships between the project manager and various functional managers must be clearly defined to avoid conflict. Finally, senior management must support the project manager's decisions, recognizing that these decisions must be made quickly and with limited information to ensure that the project remains on schedule. If senior management recognizes and resolves these issues, the risk of failure will be significantly reduced.

If you have any additional questions about the issues regarding completing the project, please contact me.

Module 46: Cost Measurement and Assignment

Overview

A primary purpose of cost measurement is to allocate the costs of production (direct materials, direct manufacturing labor, and manufacturing overhead) to the units produced. It also provides important information for management decisions, such as product pricing decisions. Cost measurement is achieved through a costing system (job-order, process, activity-based) as described in this module. Before you begin the reading, you should review the key terms at the end of the module.

A. Cost of Goods Manufactured

Regardless of which costing system is used, a cost of goods manufactured (CGM) statement is prepared to summarize the manufacturing activity of the period. CGM for a manufacturing firm is equivalent to purchases for a merchandising firm. Although it may take different forms, essentially the CGM statement is a summary of the direct materials and work in process (WIP) accounts.

$$BWIP + DM + DML + MOH - EWIP = CGM$$

A typical CGM statement is presented below.

Uddin Company
COST OF GOODS MANUFACTURED
Year Ended December 31, 2014

Direct materials		
Inventory, Jan. 1	$ 23,000	
Purchases	98,000	
Materials available for use	121,000	
Inventory, Dec. 31	16,000	
Direct materials used		$105,000
Direct manufacturing labor		72,000
Factory overhead		
Indirect labor	$ 14,000	
Supplies	4,000	
Utilities	8,000	

Depreciation	13,000	
Other	3,000	42,000
Manufacturing costs incurred, 2014		219,000
Add work in process inventory, Jan. 1		25,000
Manufacturing costs to account for		244,000
Deduct work in process inventory, Dec. 31		30,000
Cost of goods manufactured (completed)		$ 214,000

The result of the CGM statement is used in the cost of goods sold (CGS) statement or cost of goods sold section of the income statement, as indicated below.

Uddin Company
COST OF GOODS SOLD
Year Ended December 31, 2014

Finished goods, Jan. 1	$ 40,000
Add cost of goods manufactured (completed) per statement above	214,000
Cost of goods available for sale	254,000
Deduct finished goods, Dec. 31	53,000
Cost of goods sold	$201,000

B. Cost Flows

Before discussing any particular costing system, it is important to understand the flow of costs through the accounts, as summarized in the diagram below.

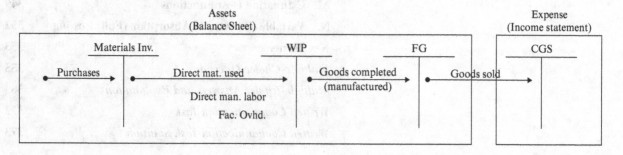

Analyze the diagram carefully before proceeding. The details will be explained further in the next few pages.

C. Job-Order Costing

Job-order costing is a system for allocating costs to groups of unique products. It is applicable to the production of customer-specified products such as the manufacture of special machines and even to cost a particular service (e.g., providing legal services for the client of a law firm). Each job becomes a cost center for which costs are accumulated. A subsidiary record (job-order cost sheet) is needed to keep track of all unfinished jobs (work in process) and finished jobs (finished goods). Note that the total of unfinished job cost sheets will equal the work in process balance.

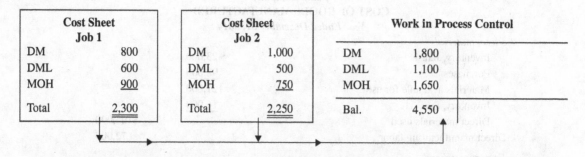

NOTE: Whenever work in process is debited or credited in the above entries, the amount of the entry is the sum of the postings on the job-order cost sheets.

The balances on the job-order cost sheets are also the basis for the entries transferring completed goods to finished goods inventory and transferring the cost of goods shipped to customers to cost of goods sold. The work in process account is analyzed below.

Work in Process Control

1. Beginning balance	
2. Direct materials used	
3. Direct labor used	
4. Overhead applied	**5.** Cost of goods manufactured (CGM)
6. Ending balance	

A similar analysis can be performed on the finished goods account.

Finished Goods Control

1. Beginning balance	
2. Cost of goods manufactured	**3.** Cost of goods sold (CGS)
4. Ending balance	

D. Accounting for Overhead

Accounting for manufacturing overhead is an important part of job-order costing and any other costing system. Overhead consists of all manufacturing costs other than direct materials and direct manufacturing labor. The distinguishing feature of manufacturing overhead is that while it must be incurred in order to produce goods, **it cannot be directly traced to the final product** as can direct materials and direct manufacturing labor. Therefore, overhead must be **applied,** rather than directly charged, to goods produced. The overhead application process is described below.

1. Overhead items are grouped by cost behavior (e.g., fixed and variable).
2. The fixed and variable overhead costs are estimated for the forthcoming period (e.g., $200,000 for variable overhead and $400,000 for fixed overhead).
3. A denominator (activity) base is chosen (see discussion below). A common choice is direct labor hours or machine hours.
4. The actual activity level is estimated for the forthcoming year (e.g., 80,000 hours).
5. Determine the normal capacity of the facility (e.g., 100,000 hours).
6. Determine the predetermined overhead rates:

   a. For variable overhead use actual activity level

   $$\frac{\text{Estimated variable overhead costs}}{\text{Estimated actual activity level}} = \frac{\$200,000}{80,000 \text{ hours}} = \$2.50/\text{hour}$$

   b. For fixed overhead use normal capacity

   $$\frac{\text{Estimated fixed overhead costs}}{\text{Normal capacity}} = \frac{\$400,000}{100,000 \text{ hours}} = \$4.00/\text{hour}$$

   NOTE: Alternatively, the variable overhead may simply be estimated on a per unit basis based on past history (e.g., $2.50 per unit).

7. As actual overhead costs are incurred, they are debited to the factory overhead accounts.

Variable factory overhead (actual)	900	
Various accounts		900
Fixed factory overhead (actual)	1,000	
Various accounts		1,000

8. As jobs are completed, the predetermined overhead rate(s) is used to apply overhead to these jobs.

EXAMPLE

Assume job 17 used 52 direct labor hours, $338 [$130 (52 × $2.50)] for variable overhead and $208 (52 × $4) for fixed overhead] of overhead would be charged to work in process and entered on the job cost sheet.

Work in process control	338	
Variable factory overhead (applied)		130
Fixed factory overhead (applied)		208

US financial reporting standards require the allocation of fixed production overhead to inventory based on the normal capacity of the production facilities. Normal capacity is the production expected to be achieved over a number of periods or seasons under normal circumstances. The actual level of production may be used if it approximates normal capacity. Therefore, for financial reporting purposes companies must use normal capacity to allocate fixed overhead but the actual activity level is used to allocate variable overhead.

To allocate the costs of overhead to units produced, an **activity base** must be chosen for use in the computation of a predetermined overhead rate. This activity base should bear a causal relationship to the incurrence of overhead costs. Examples of activity bases are

1. Direct manufacturing labor hours
2. Direct manufacturing labor cost
3. Machine hours

For example, overhead may result from (be a function of) hours worked regardless of who works, which would mean that direct manufacturing labor hours should be the activity base. If, on the other hand, more overhead costs were incurred because of heavily automated operations, machine hours might be a more appropriate activity base.

However, for internal purposes, management may use a number of approaches to determine the activity level, as shown below.

Approach	Definition
Theoretical capacity	Output is produced efficiently 100% of the time.
Practical capacity	ADJUSTED FOR: factors such as days off, down-time, etc. Output is produced maximum percentage of time practical (75–85%).
Normal capacity	ADJUSTED FOR: long-run product demand. Average annual output necessary to meet sales and inventory fluctuations over 4-to-5-year period.
Expected annual capacity	ADJUSTED FOR: current year fluctuations. Expected output for current year.

Note that theoretical capacity is larger than practical capacity, which is larger than normal volume. Expected annual capacity fluctuates above and below normal volume.

At year-end fixed overhead may be

1. **Overapplied**—More is applied than incurred because
   a. Overhead costs were overestimated,
   b. Actual activity was greater than normal capacity, and/or
   c. Actual overhead costs were less than expected.

2. **Underapplied**—Less overhead is applied than incurred because
   a. Overhead costs were underestimated,
   b. Actual activity was less than normal capacity, and/or
   c. Actual overhead costs were more than expected.

E. Disposition of Under- and Overapplied Overhead

1. If the under- or overapplied overhead is immaterial, it is frequently written off to cost of goods sold on grounds of expediency.

Cost of goods sold (debit or credit)	xx	
Factory overhead (debit or credit)		xx

2. If the amount of under- or overapplied variable overhead is significant, then an adjustment must be made to all goods which were costed at the erroneous application rate during the current period. The goods with the incorrect costs will be in three accounts: Work in Process Control, Finished Goods Control, and Cost of Goods Sold.

    Proration may be made based upon total ending balance (before proration) of the three accounts or on some other equitable basis. The exam will normally give specific directions on what allocation base should be used.

    The amount of under- or overapplied fixed overhead should always be charged to cost of goods sold.

F. Service Department Cost Allocation

A large firm will have several production departments, each of which may compute a separate predetermined overhead rate. A problem arises when a **service** (support) department (maintenance, receiving, etc.) incurs costs and benefits multiple production departments.

Costs of these service departments must be allocated to production departments because all manufacturing costs must ultimately be traced to products. For example, the costs of the materials-handling cost center may need to be allocated to the production departments (and possibly other service departments). Apportionment of service department costs should be based on meaningful criteria such as

1. Services provided
2. Services available
3. Benefits received
4. Equity

Examples of apportionment bases are

1. Square feet for building costs
2. Usage for electricity
3. Employees for cafeteria, personnel, and first aid
4. Usage for materials handling, maintenance, etc.

Service department costs can be allocated by

1. Direct method
2. Step method
3. Reciprocal method

1. Direct Method

The direct method simply allocates the costs of each service department to each of the producing departments based on a relative level of the apportionment base. For example, if a service department had costs of $140,000, and producing departments X and Y used 80% and 20% of the apportionment base, X and Y would be assigned $112,000 and $28,000 respectively. Note that the direct method ignores use of services by other service departments. For example, the direct method would ignore the fact that service department A uses the services of service department B. The essence of the direct method is shown in the following diagram.

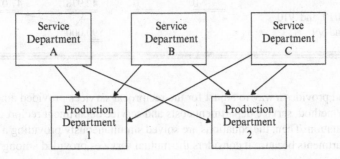

2. Step Method

The step method allocates service department costs to other service departments as well as production departments. The allocation process is

a. Select the service department serving the most other service departments

   (1) When more than one service department services an equal number of service departments, select the department with the highest costs

b. Allocate the costs of the service department selected in step a. to the production departments and other service departments based on a relative level of the apportionment base as in the direct method.

c. Allocate the costs of each remaining service department selected in the same manner as described in step a.

d. Costs of service departments are never allocated back to departments whose costs have already been allocated.

NOTE: The step method ignores the fact that reciprocal services are used between some service departments.

EXAMPLE

			DEPARTMENTS		
	Service		**Production**		
	A	**B**	**1**	**2**	**Totals**
Costs	$4,000	$6,000	$38,000	$42,000	$90,000
Use of A		10%	40%	50%	100%
Use of B	30%		40%	30%	100%

Direct Method—Allocate A's and B's costs directly to production departments 1 and 2.

	A	**B**	**1**	**2**
Costs prior to allocation	4,000	6,000	38,000	42,000
Allocation of A's costs*	(4,000)		1,778	2,222
Allocation of B's costs**		(6,000)	3,429	2,571
	0	0	43,207	46,793

*4/9 and 5/9
**4/7 and 3/7

$90,000

Step Method—Allocate B's costs (B has more costs than A) to departments A, 1, and 2. Next allocate A's costs to departments 1 and 2; you cannot allocate A's costs back to B, as B's costs have already been allocated.

	A	**B**	**1**	**2**
Costs prior to allocation	4,000	6,000	38,000	42,000
Allocation of B's costs*	1,800	(6,000)	2,400	1,800
Allocation of A's costs ($4,000 + $1,800)**	(5,800)		2,578	3,222
	0	0	42,978	47,022

*3/10, 4/10, and 3/10
**4/9 and 5/9

$90,000

---

3. Reciprocal Method

The reciprocal method provides a way to adjust for the reciprocal services provided among the service departments. Using this method, service department costs and service department reciprocal service relationships are described by a linear equation. Then, the equations are solved simultaneously providing a more precise allocation of costs to production departments because it considers the mutual services provided among the service departments.

G. Process Costing

Process costing, in contrast to job-order costing, is applicable to a continuous process of production of the same or similar goods, for example, oil refining and chemical production. Since the product is uniform, there is no need to determine the costs of different groups of products and each processing department becomes a cost center.

Process costing computations can be broken down into five steps:

1. Visualize the **physical flow of units**
2. Compute the **equivalent units of production**
3. Determine **costs to allocate**
4. Compute **unit costs**
5. **Allocate total costs** to

    a. Goods completed
    b. Ending work in process

Note that the five steps above can be memorized using the acronym: PECUA (**P**hysical Flow, **E**quivalent Units of Production, **C**osts to Allocate, **U**nit Costs, **A**llocate Costs).

1. Flow of Units

The cost flow diagram shown under Section B in this module is the same for process costing except there will typically be several WIP accounts (i.e., one for every department). When solving a process costing problem, it is helpful to visualize the physical flow of units, as illustrated in the diagram below.

The units in BWIP are either completed or become spoiled. Units started during the period but not completed become EWIP.

2. Equivalent Units of Production (EUP)

An EUP is the amount of work equivalent to completing one unit from start to finish. In a process costing system, products are assigned costs periodically (usually monthly). At any one moment some units are incomplete which makes the EUP calculations necessary to allocate manufacturing costs between

    a. Goods finished during the period (cost of goods manufactured)
    b. Ending work in process

The two primary EUP methods used for process costing are first-in, first-out (FIFO) and weighted-average (WA). Past questions on the exam have emphasized the weighted-average method. Under the weighted-average approach, current costs are combined with prior period costs, and all units are carried at an average cost of production. Importantly, the method assumes that all units completed during a period are started and completed during that period. As a result, the **percentage** of work done last period on the beginning work in process inventory is ignored.

3. Simple Process Costing Example

The BW Toy Company uses a weighted-average process cost system to collect costs. Data relevant to 2014 production is given below. Assume we begin with 800 units 25% complete for labor and overhead (conversion costs), and 100% complete for materials because they are introduced at the start of the process. We start 4,200 units. 4,000 units are completed, while 1,000 remain in EWIP (20% complete for labor and overhead and 100% complete for materials). No spoilage exists. The costs are summarized in the following T-account:

Work in Process Control				
BWIP				
materials	900			
labor + OH	532	1,432	???	Goods finished
Current				
materials	4,200			
labor + OH	14,000	18,200		
EWIP		???		

Step 1: The physical flow of units is accounted for.

BWIP	800
Started	4,200
To account for	5,000
Units completed	4,000
EWIP	1,000
Accounted for	5,000

Step 2: The units completed and ending work in process are converted to equivalent units.

		Equivalent units	
Description	**Total**	**Direct mtls.**	**Conv.**
Physical units to account for			
Beginning inventory	800		
Units started	4,200		
Units to be accounted for	5,000		
Equivalent units of production			
Good units completed and transferred out	4,000	4,000*	4,000**
Ending WIP	1,000	1,000*	200
Units accounted for	5,000	5,000	4,200

*These units are 100% complete with respect to materials because materials are introduced at the start of the process.
These units are 100% complete with respect to conversion because all units completed are **assumed to be started and completed during the period.

Steps 3 and 4: Determine costs to allocate and equivalent unit costs.

Manufacturing costs			
Beginning inventory	$ 1,432	$ 900	$ 532
Current costs	18,200	4,200	14,000
Total costs to account for	$19,632	$5,100	$14,532
Cost per equivalent unit		$ 1.02*	$ 3.46**

*Notice the resulting costs are averages: $5,100 ÷ 5,000 equivalent units = $1.02.
**$14,532 ÷ 4,200 equivalent units = $3.46.

Step 5: Allocate total costs to goods completed and ending work in process.

Units completed [4,000 × ($1.02 + $3.46)]		$17,920
Ending WIP:		
Mat. (1,000 × $1.02)	$1,020	
Conv. (200 × $3.46)	692	1,712
Total costs accounted for		$19,632

The allocation is accomplished by multiplying the individual equivalent unit figures by the unit costs.

4. EUP for Material

In the above example, material was assumed to be added at the beginning of the production process. Material can also be added at different points in the process (e.g., 10%, 70%) or gradually during the process.

5. FIFO Work in Process Assumption

The FIFO approach is not as popular as the weighted-average approach on the exam. Thus, we will focus solely on the calculation of equivalent units. With FIFO, the first batch into production (i.e., the beginning work in process inventory) is assumed to be the first batch completed. This batch is treated as a separate, distinct layer—separate from goods that are started and completed during the period.

The weighted-average assumption (all goods are assumed to be started and completed during the period) no longer holds for FIFO. Thus, any work done last period on the beginning work in process inventory must be taken into consideration. After all is said and done, the equivalent unit figures reflect the work done during the current accounting period. Also, the only difference between the two methods is the treatment of the beginning work in process inventory.

The equivalent-unit calculations for BW Toy follow.

Description	Total	Direct mtls.	Conv.
Physical units to account for			
Beginning inventory	800		
Units started	4,200		
Units to be accounted for	5,000		
Equivalent units of production			
Good units completed and transferred out:			
From beg. WIP	800	0*	600**
Started and completed	3,200	3,200***	3,200***
Ending WIP	1,000	1,000	200
Units accounted for	5,000	4,200	4,000

*All material was introduced last period.
**75% of the work was necessary this period to complete the units.
***100% of the materials and conversions were introduced this period.

6. Spoilage (Scrap) in Process Costing

The following terms are commonly used:

- **Spoilage (scrap)**—Inferior goods either discarded or sold for disposal value
- **Defective units**—Inferior goods reworked and sold as normal product

A major distinction is made between normal and abnormal spoilage.

a. Normal spoilage is the cost of spoiled units caused by the nature of the manufacturing process (i.e., which occur under efficient operating conditions).

   (1) Normal spoilage is a necessary cost in the production process and is, therefore, a **product cost**.

b. Abnormal spoilage is the cost of spoiled units which were spoiled through some unnecessary act, event, or condition.

   (1) Abnormal spoilage is a **period cost** (e.g., "loss on abnormal spoilage").
   (2) Abnormal spoilage costs should not be included in cost of goods sold.

Spoilage must be considered in EUP calculations. For example, if spoilage is discovered at the 60% point in processing and 100 units of abnormal spoilage are discovered, 60 EUP have occurred. The amount of abnormal loss would be the cost of 60 EUP (processing) plus the materials added to 100 units of production up to the 60% point. In contrast, if the spoilage was considered normal in nature, the spoilage cost would be treated as a product cost and simply added to the cost of the good units completed.

7. Spoilage in Job Costing

In a job-order costing system, the costs of normal spoilage and defective units can be handled in two different ways. When spoilage is attributable to general factory conditions, net spoilage costs are allocated to all jobs through overhead application (i.e., estimated spoilage costs are included with other overhead in the computation of the overhead application rate). Alternatively, when spoilage is attributable to exacting job specifications, net spoilage costs are charged to specific jobs. With this approach, spoilage is **not** reflected in the predetermined overhead rate. Under both methods, the proceeds from the sale of spoiled goods should be offset against the cost of spoiled goods produced. Net spoilage cost would be charged to factory overhead in the first case and left in work in process in the second case.

Costs of abnormal spoilage should **not** be charged to jobs but should be written off as a loss of the period.

H. Hybrid-Costing System

Because of the nature of their operations certain manufacturers use costing systems that blend characteristics of both the job-order and process costing systems. Such so-called hybrid-costing systems are often used by firms that manufacture a relatively large number of closely related standardized parts (e.g., automobile manufacturers and clothing manufacturers). An example of a hybrid-costing system is the **operation-costing system** that applies costs to batches of similar, but not identical, products. Direct materials are traced directly to each batch, similar to job costing. Conversion costs are traced to each operation and allocated to products that pass through the operation.

I. Backflush Costing

When a firm uses a **just-in-time (JIT)** production system, as described in Module 44, management may decide to use backflush costing for their products. Instead of using accounting records to track costs of goods as they are purchased and go through the production process, backflush costing uses normal or standard costs to work backward to "flush out" the costs of the goods finished or sold. Backflush costing does not strictly adhere to generally accepted accounting principles. However, because of the negligible amount of inventories that is characteristic of JIT production systems, the difference is often not material.

NOW REVIEW MULTIPLE-CHOICE QUESTIONS 1 THROUGH 37

J. Activity-Based Costing

Activity-based costing (ABC) is based upon two principles. First, activities consume resources. Second, these resources are consumed by products, services, or other cost objectives (output). ABC allocates overhead costs to products on the basis of the resources consumed by each activity involved in the design, production, and distribution of a particular good. This is accomplished through the assignment of costs to homogeneous cost pools that represent specific activities and then the allocation of these costs, using appropriate cost drivers, to the product. ABC may be used in conjunction with either job order or process costing systems.

Central to ABC are the activities performed to fulfill organizational objectives (producing products or services for customers). Activities may be value-added or non-value-added. **Value-added activities** are those which customers perceive as increasing the worth of a product or service and for which customers are willing to pay. They include only production activities. **Nonvalue-added activities** increase the cost of a product but do not increase its value to customers. Examples include materials handling and rework. Packaging is required for some products such as milk or potting soil, but it may be non-value-added for other products such as books (it is also costly and takes up huge amounts of landfill space). Thus, these activities may be eliminated and/or restructured without customers perceiving a decline in the value of the product/service. An activity (process) map is a flowchart which indicates all activities involved in the production process and identifies both value-added and non-value-added activities.

Cost drivers are those activities which have a direct cause and effect relationship to the incurrence of a particular cost. Traditional costing uses only variable and fixed or total overhead cost pools and views cost drivers at the output unit level, wherein costs are allocated based on labor hours, machine hours, etc. Some costs though, such as setup costs, vary at the batch level (batch-level costs) and should be spread over the units in the batch to which they relate (**not** machine hours). Product-sustaining (process-level) costs such as engineering change orders should be assigned to the products for which the orders were issued. Facility-sustaining costs incurred at the organizational level support operations and can only be arbitrarily assigned to products. As shown by the following table, ABC uses both transaction-related (e.g., purchase orders) and volume-related (e.g., machine hours) cost drivers. Traditional product costing tends to use only volume-related cost drivers.

Activity	Cost driver
Purchase of materials	Number of purchase transactions
Receiving	Number of shipments received
Disbursing	Number of checks issued
Setup costs	Number of setups or setup hours
Machining	Number of machine hours
Repair costs	Number of machine hours
Engineering changes to products	Number of engineering change notices

The activities listed above are all examples of direct activities which can be traced to an output or service. In contrast, indirect activities such as human resources are not directly attributable to output. The cost of indirect activities may be allocated or simply labeled as nontraceable.

To illustrate, ABC traces the costs of setup activities to the production batch that caused the setup costs to be incurred. The cost of each setup is then spread over the units in that batch. On the other hand, a traditional costing system would typically allocate setup costs as overhead on the basis of a volume-related cost driver such as direct manufacturing labor hours. Assume that product A and product B incur setup costs as follows:

	A	B	Total
Production volume	7,500	10,000	
Batch size	250	1,000	
Number of setups	30	10	
Total setup costs incurred	$60,000	$20,000	$80,000
Total cost per setup	$ 2,000	$ 2,000	
Direct manuf. labor hours/unit	3	3	
Total direct manuf. labor hours	22,500	30,000	52,500
Setup cost per DMLH ($80,000 ÷ 52,500)			$ 1.52
Traditional setup cost/unit			
A ($1.52 × 3 DMLH required)	$ 4.56		
B ($1.52 × 3 DMLH required)		$ 4.56	
ABC setup cost/unit			
A ($2,000/setup ÷ 250 units/batch)	$ 8.00		
B ($2,000/setup ÷ 1,000 units/batch)		$ 2.00	

In this case, products A and B are assigned different total setup costs. However, because they require the same number of direct manufacturing labor hours per unit, traditional costing allocates equal setup costs per unit to both products. In effect, one product picks up cost that was caused by another product (cross-subsidization), which distorts product costing information. ABC assigns different setup costs per unit to each product because **each unit** of product A demands more resources for setup activity than does **each unit** of product B. Note that the **total** setup cost remains the same under either method.

Activity-based management (ABM) integrates ABC with other concepts such as Total Quality Management (TQM) and target costing to produce a management system that strives for excellence through cost reduction, continuous process improvement, and productivity gains.

K. Joint Products

Joint products are two or more products produced together up to a split-off point where they become separately identifiable. They cannot be produced by themselves. For example, a steak cannot be produced without also producing roasts, ribs, liver, hamburger, etc. Other industries which produce joint products include

1. Chemicals
2. Lumber
3. Mining
4. Petroleum

Joint products incur common, or joint costs, before the split-off point. The split-off point is the point of production at which the joint products can be individually identified and removed from the joint, or common, process. The joint products can then be sold or processed further. Costs incurred after the split-off point for any one of the joint products are called separable costs.

Common costs are allocated to the joint products at the split-off point, usually on the basis of sales value at the split-off point, estimated net realizable value (NRV) at split-off point, or some physical measure. The estimated net realizable value method allocates joint costs using the estimated sales values of the joint products after further processing less the separable processing costs. Of the first two methods listed, the sales value at split-off method **must** be used if a sales value at split-off point exists. The following example illustrates the sales value at split-off and estimated net realizable value methods.

SALES VALUE AT SPLIT-OFF

Product	Sales value @ split-off	Ratio	×	Joint costs	=	Allocated joint costs
X_1	$4,000	$\dfrac{\$4,000}{\$5,000}$	×	$3,000	=	$2,400
Y_1	$1,000	$\dfrac{\$1,000}{\$5,000}$	×	$3,000	=	$ 600
Total	$5,000					$3,000

If the sales value at split-off is not available or one did not exist, we would use the estimated net realizable value method (NRV).

ESTIMATED NET REALIZABLE VALUE METHOD (NRV)

Product	Final sales value	–	Separable costs	=	Estimated net realizable value	Ratio	×	Joint costs	=	Allocated joint costs
X2	$6,700	–	$2,000	=	$4,700	$\dfrac{\$4,700}{\$6,000}$	×	$3,000	=	$2,350
Y2	$1,700	–	$ 400	=	$1,300	$\dfrac{\$1,300}{\$6,000}$	×	$3,000	=	$650
Total					$6,000					$3,000

Physical measures (units, pounds, etc.) generally are not used because of the misleading income statement effect. With an allocation based on pounds, steak would show a big profit while ground beef would be a consistent loser; each pound would carry the same cost although steak sells for much more per pound.

Joint cost allocation is performed for the purpose of inventory valuation and income determination. However, joint costs should be **ignored** for any internal decisions including the decision on whether to process a joint product beyond the split-off point. Such costs are not relevant to the sell or process further decision. The **sell or process further** decision should be based on incremental revenues and costs beyond the split-off point. If incremental revenue from further processing exceeds incremental costs, then process further. If incremental costs exceed incremental revenues, then sell at the split-off point. In the previous example in which we assumed a sales value at the split-off point, both X_1 and Y_1 should be further processed.

	Incremental revenue		Incremental cost		Advantage of further processing
X_1:	$6,700 – $4,000 = $2,700	–	$2,000	=	$700
Y_1:	$1,700 – $1,000 = $700	–	$400	=	$300

If X_1 could have sold for only $5,500 after further processing, the incremental revenue ($1,500) would not cover the incremental cost ($2,000), and X1 should not be further processed.

L. By-Products

By-products, in contrast to joint products, have little market value relative to the overall value of the product(s) being produced. Joint (common) costs are usually not allocated to a by-product. Instead, by-products are frequently valued at market or net realizable value (NRV) and accounted for as a contra production cost, that is, a reduction in the joint costs that will be allocated to the joint products.

Rather than recognizing by-product market value as a reduction of production cost, it is sometimes recognized when sold and disclosed as

1. Ordinary sales
2. Other income
3. Contra to cost of sales

Given the variety of approaches, the exam will normally specify the method that is to be followed.

NOW REVIEW MULTIPLE-CHOICE QUESTIONS 38 THROUGH 53

M. Estimating Cost Functions

A **cost function** is a mathematical expression of how a cost changes with changes in the level of activity. Cost functions may be illustrated on a graph with the x-axis measuring the level of activity and the y-axis measuring the corresponding total cost. Underlying cost functions is the belief that the level of activity explains the total costs, and that the relationship is linear (expressed as a straight line) within the relevant range. The relevant range is the range of costs for which the relationships are predictable. The following three types of cost functions may be observed:

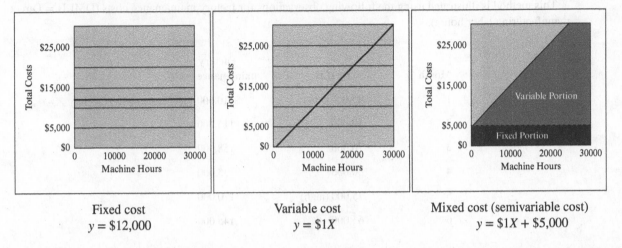

Fixed cost	Variable cost	Mixed cost (semivariable cost)
$y = \$12,000$	$y = \$1X$	$y = \$1X + \$5,000$

As illustrated, the fixed cost is a constant amount of $12,000 over the relevant range, and the variable cost is equal to $1 per machine hour over the relevant range. The mixed cost is made up of $5,000 in fixed cost and $1 per unit of variable cost.

As indicated previously, one of the most important aspects of estimating a cost function is determining whether there is a causal relationship between the level of activity (the cost driver) and the cost. A causal relationship is necessary to developing reliable cost predictions.

There are four different basic approaches to cost estimation.

1. **Industrial engineering (work-measurement) method**—Estimates of cost functions are derived from analyzing the physical relationships between inputs (e.g., direct labor hours) and outputs. As an example, a time and motion study might be used to determine how many hours it takes to assemble a table. This method of developing cost functions is time-consuming and costly.

2. **Conference method**—Estimates of cost functions are derived from analysis and opinions about cost relationships by individuals from various departments. This method can be done quickly but may not be as reliable as those that are based on quantitative methods.

3. **Account analysis method**—Estimates of cost functions are derived by analyzing ledger accounts and designating them as containing fixed costs, variable costs, or mixed costs. This is a widely used method but to be reliable it must be performed by individuals who understand operations.

4. **Quantitative methods**—Estimates of cost functions are derived using formal mathematical models. Using quantitative methods, management identifies a cost and one or more cost drivers to be used to predict the cost. Then they collect historical data to estimate the cost function. A number of quantitative methods are used, including

   a. **Scattergraph method.** The scattergraph method is a graphical approach to computing the relationship between two variables. The dependent variable is plotted on the vertical axis and the independent variable on the horizontal axis. A straight line is then drawn through the observation points which best describes the relationship between the two variables. In the graph below, the broken line illustrates the relationship. This method lacks precision, because by freely drawing the line through the points, it is possible to obtain a line that does not minimize the deviations of the points from the line.

b. **High-low method.** The high-low method computes the slope for the variable rate based on the highest and lowest observations.

$$\text{Slope} = \frac{\text{Change in cost between high and low points}}{\text{Change in activity between high and low points}}$$

This method is illustrated using the following observations for factory maintenance costs (DMLH = Direct manufacturing labor hours).

Month	DMLH	Factory maintenance cost
1	45,000 (low)	$110,000
2	50,000	115,000
3	70,000	158,000
4	60,000	135,000
5	75,000 (high)	170,000
6	65,000	145,000

The difference in cost is divided by the difference in activity to obtain the variable cost. The fixed cost can then be computed by using either the high observation or the low observation. The same result will be obtained with either one. The computation for separating factory maintenance cost is detailed below.

Variable rate computation	**Fixed rate computation**
$\dfrac{\$170,000 - \$110,000}{75,000 - 45,000} = \$2/\text{DMLH}$	$\$170,000 - (75,000 \times \$2) = \$20,000$ or $\$110,000 - (45,000 \times \$2) = \$20,000$

The high-low method is a rather crude technique compared to regression analysis. For example, this method may be inaccurate if the high and low points are not representative (i.e., are outliers) as illustrated by the solid line in the chart included with the discussion of the scattergraph method.

c. **Regression analysis.** Regression (least squares) analysis determines the functional relationship between variables with a measure of probable error. For example, you may wish to determine the relationship of electricity cost to level of activity. Based on activity levels and electricity charges of past months, the following chart (scattergraph) might be prepared.

As production increases, electric costs increase. The relationship appears linear. Linearity is an assumption underlying regression. If the power costs begin to fall after 3,000 units of production, the relationship between electricity and production would not be linear, and linear regression would not be appropriate.

The method of least squares fits a regression line between the observation points such that the sum of the squared vertical differences between the regression line and the individual observations is minimized. The simple regression equation for a linear cost function is

$$y = a + bx$$

Where

> y = estimated total cost
> a = constant, the portion of the cost that is fixed over the relevant range
> b = the slope, the amount by which the cost changes based on changes in the level of activity over the relevant range
> x = the level of activity as measured by the cost driver

The goodness of the least squares fit (i.e., how well the regression line fits the observed data) is measured by the coefficient of determination (R^2). The better the line fits the observed data points (i.e., the closer the observed data points are to the line), the closer R^2 will be to 1.00 — R^2s of 90–99% are considered very good. However, you must remember that a high R^2 does not prove that there is a cause-and-effect relationship between the two variables.

If only one independent variable exists, the analysis is known as simple regression (as in the above example). **Multiple regression** consists of a functional relationship with multiple independent variables (e.g., cost may be a function of several cost drivers). Multiple regression is described in detail in the next module.

d. **Correlation analysis.** Correlation is the relationship between variables. If the variables move with each other, they have a direct relationship (positive correlation) as in A. If the variables move in opposite directions, they have an inverse relationship (negative correlation) as in B.

  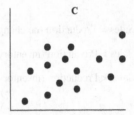

The degree and direction of correlation is measured from –1 to 1. The sign (negative or positive) describes whether the relationship is inverse or direct. The coefficient of correlation is measured by

$$\sqrt{\frac{\text{Amount of Variation explained}}{\text{Total variation}}}$$

If all of the observations were in a straight line, all of the variation would be explained and the coefficient of correlation would be 1 or –1 depending upon whether the relationship is positive or negative. If there is no correlation, as in C above, the coefficient of correlation is 0.

> **NOTE:** The coefficient of correlation is similar in concept to the coefficient of determination discussed above in "method of least squares." The coefficient of determination cannot have a negative value, as can the coefficient of correlation, because the coefficient of determination is based on squared deviations (i.e., if you square a negative number, the result is positive).

Management often has a choice of cost drivers to use in estimating a particular cost. In evaluating the best driver to use, management should consider

- Economic plausibility—Does the relationship between the cost and the cost driver make intuitive economic sense?
- Goodness of fit—Historically how well do changes in the cost driver explain total costs?
- Slope of the regression line—A steep regression line indicates a stronger relationship than a flatter line.

Cost functions may also be nonlinear. For example, **step functions** are often encountered in which the cost increases in discrete amounts periodically as the level of activity increases. Nonlinear functions also occur due to **learning curves**. As an example, labor hours per unit to assemble a new product may decline as production increases due to workers getting better at doing their jobs. Two models that attempt to capture the effect of learning are

- **Cumulative average-time model**—The cumulative average time per unit declines by a constant percentage each time the quantity of units produced doubles.
- **Incremental unit-time learning model**—The incremental unit time needed to produce the last unit declines by a constant percentage each time the cumulative quantity of units produced doubles.

N. Variable (Direct) and Absorption (Full) Costing

Variable (direct) costing is a form of inventory costing. Variable costing considers fixed manufacturing costs as period rather than product costs. It is advocated because, for internal reporting, it presents a clear picture of performance when there is a significant change in inventory. However, remember that variable costing is not acceptable as GAAP for external reporting.

Variable and absorption costing methods of accounting for fixed manufacturing overhead differ: under variable costing, fixed manufacturing overhead is expensed whereas under absorption costing, such amounts are treated as a product cost and inventoried. The treatment of fixed manufacturing overhead often results in different levels of net income between the absorption and variable costing methods. The differences are timing differences, which result from recognizing the fixed manufacturing overhead as an expense.

1. In the period incurred—variable costing
2. In the period in which the units to which fixed overhead has been applied are sold—absorption costing

The relationship between variable costing (VC) income and absorption costing (AC) income follows:

Sales = Production (no change in inventory)	No difference in income
Sales > Production (inventory decreases)	VC income greater than AC income
Sales < Production (inventory increases)	VC income less than AC income

---

EXAMPLE

Production begins in period A with 5,000 units. Fixed manufacturing costs equal $5,000 and variable manufacturing costs are $1/unit. Sales were 4,000 units at $3/unit. In period B, units produced and production costs were the same as in period A. Sales were 6,000 units at $3/unit.

	Variable costing		Absorption costing	
	Period A	**Period B**	**Period A**	**Period B**
Sales	$12,000	$18,000	$12,000	$18,000
Less costs	9,000	11,000	8,000	12,000
Profit	$3,000	$7,000	$4,000	$6,000

With absorption costing, $1 of fixed manufacturing overhead is attached to each unit produced ($5,000 ÷ 5,000 units). Notice that both variable and absorption costing recognized $10,000 profit in periods A + B. Variable costing income in period A was less than absorption income, because production exceeded sales which resulted in $1,000 of fixed costs being **inventoried** under AC that were **expensed** under VC.

	Fixed costs expensed		Variable costs expensed		Total costs expensed	
	Period A	**Period B**	**Period A**	**Period B**	**Period A**	**Period B**
Variable	$5,000*	$5,000*	$4,000	$6,000	$9,000	$11,000
Absorption	4,000**	6,000**	4,000	6,000	8,000	12,000

* The same every period.
**$1 per unit × number of units sold.

The yearly income difference between the two methods can normally be reconciled as follows:

Change in inventory units × Fixed overhead per unit (e.g., 1,000 units × $1)

If the example above included either variable or fixed selling costs, they would be handled the same under either method—deducted in total on the income statement in the period in which they were incurred.

Note that the format of the income statement changes under variable costing to reflect the alternate treatment given to the fixed manufacturing costs and to emphasize the contribution margin. The recommended format under variable costing follows:

Sales
- <u>Variable manufacturing costs</u>
= Manufacturing contribution margin
- <u>Variable selling and administrative expenses</u>
= Contribution margin
- <u>Fixed manufacturing, selling, and administrative expenses</u>
= <u>Net income</u>

NOW REVIEW MULTIPLE-CHOICE QUESTIONS 54 THROUGH 62

KEY TERMS

Absorption (full) costing. Considers fixed manufacturing overhead to be a product cost.

Activity-based costing (ABC). A cost system that focuses on activities, determines their costs, and then uses appropriate cost drivers to trace costs to the products based on the activities.

Activity-based management (ABM). Integrates ABC with other concepts such as Total Quality Management (TQM) and target costing to produce a management system that strives for excellence through cost reduction, continuous process improvement, and productivity gains.

Actual activity level. The level of production actually occurring for the period.

Backflush costing. A costing system that omits recording some or all of the journal entries to track the purchase and production of goods. Goods are costed after they have been completed.

Computer-integrated manufacturing (CIM). A highly automated and integrated production process that is controlled by computers.

Conversion costs. These include direct manufacturing labor and manufacturing overhead. They are the costs of converting direct materials into finished products.

Cost assignment. This encompasses both **cost tracing** (assignment of direct costs to a cost object) and **cost allocation** (assignment of indirect costs to the cost object). A **cost object** is the item (product, department, process, etc.) for which cost is being determined.

Cost driver. A factor that causes a cost to be incurred. Cost drivers may be volume-related (e.g., repair costs may depend on the volume of machine hours) and transaction-related (purchasing costs may depend on the number of purchase transactions).

Cost estimation. The examination of past relationships of costs and level of activity to develop predictions of future costs.

Cost management system (CMS). A planning and control system that measures the cost of significant activities, identifies non-value-added costs, and identifies activities that will improve organizational performance.

Cost pools. Groupings of related costs accumulated together to be allocated to a product or some other cost object.

Cycle time (or throughput time). The time required to complete a good from the start of the production process until the product is finished.

Direct costs. Costs easily traced to a specific business segment (e.g., product, division, department).

Direct manufacturing labor. The cost of labor directly transforming a product. This theoretically should include fringe benefits, but frequently does not. This is contrasted with **indirect manufacturing labor,** which is the cost of supporting labor (e.g., material-handling labor, factory supervisors).

Direct materials inventory. This includes the cost of materials awaiting entry into the production system.

Direct materials. The cost of materials directly and conveniently traceable to a product. Minor material items (nails, glue) are not deemed conveniently traceable. These items are treated as **indirect materials** along with production supplies.

Engineered costs. Determined from industrial engineering studies that examine how activities are performed and if/how performance can be improved.

Factory (manufacturing) overhead. Normally includes indirect manufacturing labor costs, supplies cost, and other production facility costs such as plant depreciation, taxes, etc. It is comprised of all manufacturing costs that are not direct materials or direct manufacturing labor.

Finished goods inventory. Includes the cost of units completed but unsold.

Fixed costs. Costs that do not vary with the level of activity within the relevant range for a given period of time (usually one year), for example, plant depreciation.

Flexible manufacturing system (FMS). A series of computer-controlled manufacturing processes that can be **easily** changed to make a variety of products.

Hybrid-costing. A system that blends the characteristics of both the job order and process costing systems. Firms using this system typically produce large numbers of closely related products.

Indirect costs. Costs that are not easily traceable to specific segments and include factory overhead.

Job order costing. A system for allocating costs to groups of unique products made to customer specifications.

Joint costs. Costs common to multiple products that emerge at a split-off point.

Joint costing. A system of assigning joint costs to **joint products** whose overall sales values are relatively significant.

Learning curve. A function that demonstrates how productivity improves as workers become more proficient at producing the product.

Mixed costs (semivariable). Costs that have a fixed component and a variable component. These components are separated by using the scattergraph, high-low, or linear regression methods.

Nonlinear cost function. A cost function that is not described by a straight line over the relevant range.

Non-value-added costs. The cost of activities that can be eliminated without the customer perceiving a decline in product quality or performance.

Normal activity level. The production level expected to be achieved over a number of periods or seasons under normal circumstances.

Period costs. Costs that cannot be associated (or matched) with manufactured goods (e.g., advertising expenditures). Period costs become expenses when incurred.

Prime costs. Costs easily traceable to specific units of production and include direct manufacturing labor and direct materials.

Process costing. A system for allocating costs to homogeneous units of a mass-produced product.

Product costs. Costs that can be associated with the production of specific goods. Product costs attach to a physical unit and become an expense in the period in which the unit to which they attach is sold. Product costs normally include direct manufacturing labor, direct materials, and factory overhead.

Product life-cycle costing. Tracks the accumulation of costs that occur starting with the research and development for a product and ending with the time at which sales and customer support are withdrawn.

Relevant range. The operating range of activity in which cost behavior patterns are valid. It is the production range for which fixed costs remain constant (e.g., if production doubles, an additional shift of salaried foremen would be added and fixed costs would increase).

Stepped costs (or semifixed costs) are fixed over relatively short ranges of production levels (e.g., supervisors' salaries). Fixed, variable, and semifixed costs are diagrammed below.

Value chain. The sequence of business functions in which value is added to a firm's products or services. This sequence includes research and development, product design, manufacturing, marketing, distribution, and customer service.

Value-added cost. The cost of activities that *cannot* be eliminated without the customer perceiving a decline in product quality or performance.

Variable (direct) costing. Costing that considers all fixed manufacturing overhead as a period cost rather than as a product cost.

Work in process inventory. Includes the cost of units being produced but not yet completed.

A. Cost of Goods Manufactured

1. The following information was taken from Kay Company's accounting records for the year ended December 31, 2014:

Increase in raw materials inventory	$ 15,000
Decrease in finished goods inventory	35,000
Raw materials purchased	430,000
Direct manufacturing labor payroll	200,000
Factory overhead	300,000
Freight-out	45,000

There was no work in process inventory at the beginning or end of the year. Kay's 2014 cost of goods sold is

a. 950,000
b. 965,000
c. 975,000
d. 995,000

Items 2 through 4 are based on the following information pertaining to Arp Co.'s manufacturing operations:

Inventories	3/1/14	3/31/14
Direct materials	$36,000	$30,000
Work in process	18,000	12,000
Finished goods	54,000	72,000

Additional information for the month of March 2014:

Direct materials purchased	$84,000
Direct manufacturing labor payroll	60,000
Direct manufacturing labor rate per hour	7.50
Factory overhead rate per direct labor hour	10.00

2. For the month of March 2014, prime cost was

a. 90,000
b. 120,000
c. 144,000
d. 150,000

3. For the month of March 2014, conversion cost was

a. 90,000
b. 140,000
c. 144,000
d. 170,000

4. For the month of March 2014, cost of goods manufactured was

a. 218,000
b. 224,000
c. 230,000
d. 236,000

5. During the month of March 2014, Nale Co. used $300,000 of direct material. At March 31, 2014, Nale's direct materials inventory was $50,000 more than it was at March 1, 2014. Direct material purchases during the month of March 2014 amounted to

a. 0
b. 250,000
c. 300,000
d. 350,000

6. Fab Co. manufactures textiles. Among Fab's 2014 manufacturing costs were the following salaries and wages:

Loom operators	$120,000
Factory foreman	45,000
Machine mechanics	30,000

What was the amount of Fab's 2014 direct manufacturing labor?

a. 195,000
b. 165,000
c. 150,000
d. 120,000

7. The fixed portion of the semivariable cost of electricity for a manufacturing plant is a

	Period cost	Product cost
a.	Yes	No
b.	Yes	Yes
c.	No	Yes
d.	No	No

8. Gram Co. develops computer programs to meet customers' special requirements. How should Gram categorize payments to employees who develop these programs?

	Direct costs	Value-added costs
a.	Yes	Yes
b.	Yes	No
c.	No	No
d.	No	Yes

9. In a job-costing system, issuing indirect materials to production increases which account?

a. Materials control.
b. Work in process control.
c. Manufacturing overhead control.
d. Manufacturing overhead allocated.

by responsibility center for control

355

o order costing	Process costing
Yes	Yes
Yes	No
No	No
d. No	Yes

C. Job-Order Costing

11. Birk Co. uses a job order cost system. The following debits (credit) appeared in Birk's work in process account for the month of April 2014:

April	Description	Amount
1	Balance	$ 4,000
30	Direct materials	24,000
30	Direct manufacturing labor	16,000
30	Factory overhead	12,800
30	To finished goods	(48,000)

Birk applies overhead to production at a predetermined rate of 80% of direct manufacturing labor costs. Job No. 5, the only job still in process on April 30, 2014, has been charged with direct manufacturing labor of $2,000. What was the amount of direct materials charged to Job No. 5?

a. 3,000
b. 5,200
c. 8,800
d. 24,000

12. In a job cost system, manufacturing overhead is

	An indirect cost of jobs	A necessary element in production
a.	No	Yes
b.	No	No
c.	Yes	Yes
d.	Yes	No

13. Under Pick Co.'s job order costing system manufacturing overhead is applied to work in process using a predetermined annual overhead rate. During January 2014, Pick's transactions included the following:

Direct materials issued to production	$ 90,000
Indirect materials issued to production	8,000
Manufacturing overhead incurred	125,000
Manufacturing overhead applied	113,000
Direct labor costs	107,000

Pick had neither beginning nor ending work in process inventory. What was the cost of jobs completed in January 2014?

a. 302,000
b. 310,000
c. 322,000
d. 330,000

14. A direct manufacturing labor overtime premium should be charged to a specific job when the overtime is caused by the

a. Increased overall level of activity.
b. Customer's requirement for early completion of job.
c. Management's failure to include the job in the production schedule.
d. Management's requirement that the job be completed before the annual factory vacation closure.

*15. A company services office equipment. Some customers bring their equipment to the company's service shop; other customers prefer to have the company's service personnel come to their offices to repair their equipment. The most appropriate costing method for the company is

a. A job order costing system.
b. An activity-based costing system.
c. A process costing system.
d. An operations costing system.

D. Accounting for Overhead

16. In developing a predetermined variable factory overhead application rate for use in a process costing system, which of the following could be used in the numerator and denominator?

	Numerator	Denominator
a.	Actual variable factory overhead	Actual machine hours
b.	Actual variable factory overhead	Estimated machine hours
c.	Estimated variable factory overhead	Actual machine hours
d.	Estimated variable factory overhead	Estimated machine hours

17. A job order cost system uses a predetermined fixed factory overhead rate based on normal activity and expected fixed cost. At the end of the year, underapplied fixed overhead might be explained by which of the following situations?

	Actual volume	Actual fixed costs
a.	Greater than normal	Greater than expected
b.	Greater than normal	Less than expected
c.	Less than normal	Greater than expected
d.	Less than normal	Less than expected

---

* CIA adapted

E. Disposition of Under- and Overapplied Overhead

18. Worley Company has underapplied variable overhead of $45,000 for the year ended December 31, 2014. Before disposition of the underapplied overhead, selected December 31, 2014 balances from Worley's accounting records are as follows:

Sales	$1,200,000
Cost of goods sold	720,000
Inventories:	
Direct materials	36,000
Work in process	54,000
Finished goods	90,000

Under Worley's cost accounting system, over- or underapplied variable overhead is allocated to appropriate inventories and cost of goods sold based on year-end balances. There are no amounts of under or overapplied fixed overhead. In its 2014 income statement, Worley should report cost of goods sold of

- a. 682,500
- b. 684,000
- c. 756,000
- d. 757,500

F. Service Department Cost Allocation

19. Parat College allocates support department costs to its individual schools using the step method. Information for May 2014 is as follows:

	Support departments	
	Maintenance	Power
Costs incurred	$99,000	$54,000
Service percentages provided to:		
Maintenance	–	10%
Power	20%	–
School of Education	30%	20%
School of Technology	50%	70%
	100%	100%

What is the amount of May 2014 support department costs allocated to the School of Education?

- a. 40,500
- b. 42,120
- c. 46,100
- d. 49,125

G. Process Costing

20. Kerner Manufacturing uses a process cost system to manufacture laptop computers. The following information summarizes operations relating to laptop computer model #KJK20 during the quarter ending March 31:

	Units	Direct Materials
Work in process inventory, January 1	100	$70,000
Started during the quarter	500	
Completed during the quarter	400	
Work-in-process inventory, March 31	200	
Costs added during the quarter		$750,000

Beginning work in process inventory was 50% complete for direct materials. Ending work in process inventory was 75% complete for direct materials. What were the equivalent units of production with regard to materials for March using the FIFO unit cost, inventory valuation method?

- a. 450
- b. 500
- c. 550
- d. 600

21. Kerner Manufacturing uses a process cost system to manufacture laptop computers. The following information summarizes operations relating to laptop computer model #KJK20 during the quarter ending March 31:

	Units	Direct Materials
Work in process inventory, January 1	100	$50,000
Started during the quarter	500	
Completed during the quarter	400	
Work in process inventory, March 31	200	
Costs added during the quarter		$720,000

Beginning work in process inventory was 50% complete for direct materials. Ending work in process inventory was 75% complete for direct materials. What is the total value of material costs in ending work in process inventory using the FIFO unit cost, inventory valuation method?

- a. 183,000
- b. 194,000
- c. 210,000
- d. 216,000

22. In a process cost system, the application of factory overhead usually would be recorded as an increase in

- a. Finished goods inventory control.
- b. Factory overhead control.
- c. Cost of goods sold.
- d. Work in process inventory control.

23. The following information pertains to Lap Co.'s Palo Division for the month of April:

	Number of units	Cost of materials
Beginning work in process	15,000	$ 5,500
Started in April	40,000	18,000
Units completed	42,500	
Ending work in process	12,500	

All materials are added at the beginning of the process. Using the weighted-average method, the cost per equivalent unit for materials is

a. 0.59
b. 0.55
c. 0.45
d. 0.43

24. The Forming Department is the first of a two-stage production process. Spoilage is identified when the units have completed the Forming process. Costs of spoiled units are assigned to units completed and transferred to the second department in the period spoilage is identified. The following information concerns Forming's conversion costs in May 2014:

	Units	Conversion costs
Beginning work in process (50% complete)	2,000	$10,000
Units started during May	8,000	75,500
Spoilage—normal	500	
Units completed and transferred	7,000	
Ending work in process (80% complete)	2,500	

Using the weighted-average method, what was Forming's conversion cost transferred to the second production department?

a. 59,850
b. 64,125
c. 67,500
d. 71,250

25. In computing the current period's manufacturing cost per equivalent unit, the FIFO method of process costing considers current period costs

a. Only.
b. Plus cost of beginning work in process inventory.
c. Less cost of beginning work in process inventory.
d. Plus cost of ending work in process inventory.

26. In process 2, material G is added when a batch is 60% complete. Ending work in process units, which are 50% complete, would be included in the computation of equivalent units for

	Conversion costs	Material G
a.	Yes	No
b.	No	Yes
c.	No	No
d.	Yes	Yes

27. A process costing system was used for a department that began operations in January 2014. Approximately the same number of physical units, at the same degree of completion, were in work in process at the end of both January and February. Monthly conversion costs are allocated between

ending work in process and units completed. Compared to the FIFO method, would the weighted-average method use the same or a greater number of equivalent units to calculate the monthly allocations?

	Equivalent units for weighted-average compared to FIFO	
	January	**February**
a.	Same	Same
b.	Greater number	Greater number
c.	Greater number	Same
d.	Same	Greater number

28. A department adds material at the beginning of a process and identifies defective units when the process is 40% complete. At the beginning of the period, there was no work in process. At the end of the period, the number of work in process units equaled the number of units transferred to finished goods. If all units in ending work in process were 66 2/3% complete, then ending work in process should be allocated

a. 50% of all normal defective unit costs.
b. 40% of all normal defective unit costs.
c. 50% of the material costs and 40% of the conversion costs of all normal defective unit costs.
d. None of the normal defective unit costs.

29. In its April 2014 production, Hern Corp., which does not use a standard cost system, incurred total production costs of $900,000, of which Hern attributed $60,000 to normal spoilage and $30,000 to abnormal spoilage. Hern should account for this spoilage as

a. Period cost of $90,000.
b. Inventoriable cost of $90,000.
c. Period cost of $60,000 and inventoriable cost of $30,000.
d. Inventoriable cost of $60,000 and period cost of $30,000.

Items 30 through 37 are based on the following:

Kimbeth Manufacturing uses a process cost system to manufacture Dust Density Sensors for the mining industry. The following information pertains to operations for the month of May 2014:

	Units
Beginning work in process inventory, May 1	16,000
Started in production during May	100,000
Completed production during May	92,000
Ending work in process inventory, May 31	24,000

The beginning inventory was 60% complete for materials and 20% complete for conversion costs. The ending inventory was 90% complete for materials and 40% complete for conversion costs.

Costs pertaining to the month of May are as follows:

- The beginning inventory costs are: materials, $54,560; direct labor, $20,320; and factory overhead, $15,240.

- Costs incurred during May are: materials used, $468,000; direct labor, $182,880; and factory overhead, $391,160.

**30. Using the first-in, first-out (FIFO) method, the equivalent units of production for materials are

    a. 97,600 units.
    b. 104,000 units.
    c. 107,200 units.
    d. 108,000 units.

**31. Using the FIFO method, the equivalent units of production for conversion costs are

    a. 85,600 units.
    b. 88,800 units.
    c. 95,200 units.
    d. 98,400 units.

**32. Using the FIFO method, the equivalent unit cost of materials for May is

    a. 4.12
    b. 4.50
    c. 4.60
    d. 4.80

**33. Using the FIFO method, the equivalent unit conversion cost for May is

    a. 5.65
    b. 5.83
    c. 6.00
    d. 6.20

**34. Using the FIFO method, the total cost of units in the ending work in process inventory at May 31 is

    a. 153,168
    b. 145,800
    c. 155,328
    d. 156,960

**35. Using the weighted-average method, the equivalent unit cost of materials for May is

    a. 4.12
    b. 4.50
    c. 4.60
    d. 5.03

**36. Using the weighted-average method, the equivalent unit conversion cost for May is

    a. 5.65
    b. 5.83
    c. 6.00
    d. 6.41

**37. Using the weighted-average method, the total cost of the units in the ending work in process inventory at May 31 is

    a. 86,400
    b. 154,800
    c. 155,328
    d. 156,960

---

* CIA adapted
** CMA adapted

J. Activity-Based Costing

*38. Which of the following would be a reasonable basis for allocating the material handling costs to the units produced in an activity-based costing system?

    a. Number of production runs per year.
    b. Number of components per completed unit.
    c. Amount of time required to produce one unit.
    d. Amount of overhead applied to each completed unit.

*39. An assembly plant accumulates its variable and fixed manufacturing overhead costs in a single cost pool which are then applied to work in process using a single application base. The assembly plant management wants to estimate the magnitude of the total manufacturing overhead costs for different volume levels of the application activity base using a flexible budget formula. If there is an increase in the application activity base that is within the relevant range of activity for the assembly plant, which one of the following relationships regarding variable and fixed costs is correct?

    a. The variable cost per unit is constant, and the total fixed costs decrease.
    b. The variable cost per unit is constant, and the total fixed costs increase.
    c. The variable cost per unit and the total fixed costs remain constant.
    d. The variable cost per unit increases, and the total fixed costs remain constant.

*40. In Belk Co.'s just-in-time production system, costs per setup were reduced from $28 to $2. In the process of reducing inventory levels, Belk found that there were fixed facility and administrative costs that previously had not been included in the carrying cost calculation. The result was an increase from $8 to $32 per unit per year. What were the effects of these changes on Belk's economic lot size and relevant costs?

	Lot size	Relevant costs
a.	Decrease	Increase
b.	Increase	Decrease
c.	Increase	Increase
d.	Decrease	Decrease

41. What is the normal effect on the numbers of cost pools and allocation bases when an activity-based cost (ABC) system replaces a traditional cost system?

	Cost pools	Allocation bases
a.	No effect	No effect
b.	Increase	No effect
c.	No effect	Increase
d.	Increase	Increase

42. Which of the following is true about activity-based costing?

    a. It should not be used with process or job costing.
    b. It can be used only with process costing.
    c. It can be used only with job costing.
    d. It can be used with either process or job costing.

43. In an activity-based costing system, what should be used to assign a department's manufacturing overhead costs to products produced in varying lot sizes?

  a. A single cause-and-effect relationship.
  b. Multiple cause-and-effect relationships.
  c. Relative net sales values of the products.
  d. A product's ability to bear cost allocations.

44. In an activity-based costing system, cost reduction is accomplished by identifying and eliminating

	All cost drivers	Non-value-adding activities
a.	No	No
b.	Yes	Yes
c.	No	Yes
d.	Yes	No

45. Nile Co.'s cost allocation and product costing procedures follow activity-based costing principles. Activities have been identified and classified as being either value-adding or non-value-adding as to each product. Which of the following activities, used in Nile's production process, is non-value-adding?

  a. Design engineering activity.
  b. Heat treatment activity.
  c. Drill press activity.
  d. Raw materials storage activity.

46. Hoger Corporation accumulated the following cost information for its two products, A and B:

	A	B	Total
Production volume	2,000	1,000	
Total direct man. labor hrs.	5,000	20,000	25,000
Setup cost per batch	$1,000	$2,000	
Batch size	100	50	
Total setup costs incurred	$20,000	$40,000	$60,000
DMLH per unit	2	1	

A traditional costing system would allocate setup costs on the basis of DMLH. An ABC system would trace costs by spreading the costs per batch over the units in a batch. What is the setup cost per unit of product A under each costing system?

	Traditional	ABC
a.	$ 4.80	$ 10.00
b.	$ 2.40	$ 10.00
c.	$40.00	$200.00
d.	$ 4.80	$ 20.00

K. Joint Products

47. Lane Co. produces main products Kul and Wu. The process also yields by-product Zef. Net realizable value of by-product Zef is subtracted from joint production cost of Kul

and Wu. The following information pertains to production in July 2014 at a joint cost of $54,000:

Product	Units produced	Market value	Additional cost after split-off
Kul	1,000	$40,000	$ 0
Wu	1,500	35,000	0
Zef	500	7,000	3,000

If Lane uses the net realizable value method for allocating joint cost, how much of the joint cost should be allocated to product Kul?

  a. 18,800
  b. 20,000
  c. 26,667
  d. 27,342

48. The diagram below represents the production and sales relationships of joint products P and Q. Joint costs are incurred until split-off, then separable costs are incurred in refining each product. Market values of P and Q at split-off are used to allocate joint costs.

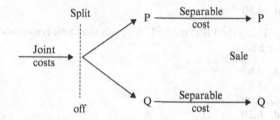

If the market value of P at split-off increases and all other costs and selling prices remain unchanged, then the gross margin of

	P	Q
a.	Increases	Decreases
b.	Increases	Increases
c.	Decreases	Decreases
d.	Decreases	Increases

49. For purposes of allocating joint costs to joint products, the sales price at point of sale, reduced by cost to complete after split-off, is assumed to be equal to the

  a. Joint costs.
  b. Total costs.
  c. Net sales value at split-off.
  d. Sales price less a normal profit margin at point of sale.

L. By-Products

50. Mig Co., which began operations in 2014, produces gasoline and a gasoline by-product. The following information is available pertaining to 2014 sales and production:

Total production costs to split-off point	$120,000
Gasoline sales	270,000
By-product sales	30,000
Gasoline inventory, 12/31/14	15,000
Additional by-product costs:	
Marketing	10,000
Production	15,000

Mig accounts for the by-product at the time of production. What are Mig's 2014 cost of sales for gasoline and the by-product?

	Gasoline	By-product
a.	$105,000	$25,000
b.	$115,000	$0
c.	$108,000	$37,000
d.	$100,000	$0

51. The following information pertains to a by-product called Moy:

Sales in 2014	5,000 units
Selling price per unit	$6
Selling costs per unit	2
Processing costs	0

Inventory of Moy was recorded at net realizable value when produced in 2013. No units of Moy were produced in 2014. What amount should be recognized as profit on Moy's 2014 sales?

a. 0
b. 10,000
c. 20,000
d. 30,000

52. Kode Co. manufactures a major product that gives rise to a by-product called May. May's only separable cost is a $1 selling cost when a unit is sold for $4. Kode accounts for May's sales by deducting the $3 net amount from the cost of goods sold of the major product. There are no inventories. If Kode were to change its method of accounting for May from a by-product to a joint product, what would be the effect on Kode's overall gross margin?

a. No effect.
b. Gross margin increases by $1 for each unit of May sold.
c. Gross margin increases by $3 for each unit of May sold.
d. Gross margin increases by $4 for each unit of May sold.

53. In accounting for by-products, the value of the by-product may be recognized at the time of

	Production	Sale
a.	Yes	Yes
b.	Yes	No
c.	No	No
d.	No	Yes

M. Estimating Cost Functions

54. Day Mail Order Co. applied the high-low method of cost estimation to customer order data for the first four months of 2014. What is the estimated variable order filling cost component per order?

Month	Orders	Cost
January	1,200	$ 3,120
February	1,300	3,185
March	1,800	4,320
April	1,700	3,895
	6,000	$14,520

a. 2.00
b. 2.42
c. 2.48
d. 2.50

55. Sender, Inc. estimates parcel mailing costs using data shown on the chart below.

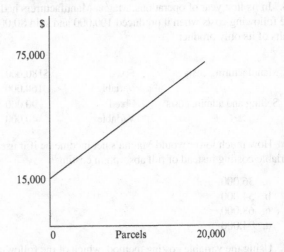

What is Sender's estimated cost for mailing 12,000 parcels?

a. 36,000
b. 45,000
c. 51,000
d. 60,000

56. Which of the following may be used to estimate how inventory warehouse costs are affected by both the number of shipments and the weight of materials handled?

a. Economic order quantity analysis.
b. Probability analysis.
c. Correlation analysis.
d. Multiple regression analysis.

57. Sago Co. uses regression analysis to develop a model for predicting overhead costs. Two different cost drivers (machine hours and direct materials weight) are under consideration as the independent variable. Relevant data were run on a computer using one of the standard regression programs, with the following results:

Machine hours	Coefficient
Y Intercept	2,500
B	5.0
$R^2 = .70$	
Direct materials weight	
Y Intercept	4,600
B	2.6
$R^2 = .50$	

What regression equation should be used?

a. $Y = 2,500 + 5.0X$
b. $Y = 2,500 + 3.5X$
c. $Y = 4,600 + 2.6X$
d. $Y = 4,600 + 1.3X$

N. Variable (Direct) and Absorption (Full) Costing

58. In its first year of operations, Magna Manufacturers had the following costs when it produced 100,000 and sold 80,000 units of its only product:

Manufacturing costs	Fixed	$180,000
	Variable	160,000
Selling and admin. costs	Fixed	90,000
	Variable	40,000

How much lower would Magna's net income be if it used variable costing instead of full absorption costing?

a. 36,000
b. 54,000
c. 68,000
d. 94,000

59. Using the variable costing method, which of the following costs are assigned to inventory?

	Variable selling and administrative costs	Variable factory overhead costs
a.	Yes	Yes
b.	Yes	No
c.	No	No
d.	No	Yes

60. At the end of Killo Co.'s first year of operations, 1,000 units of inventory remained on hand. Variable and fixed manufacturing costs per unit were $90 and $20, respectively. If Killo uses absorption costing rather than variable (direct) costing, the result would be a higher pretax income of

a. 0
b. 20,000
c. 70,000
d. 90,000

61. A manufacturing company prepares income statements using both absorption and variable costing methods. At the end of a period actual sales revenues, total gross profit, and total contribution margin approximated budgeted figures, whereas net income was substantially greater than the budgeted amount. There were no beginning or ending inventories. The **most** likely explanation of the net income increase is that, compared to budget, actual

a. Manufacturing fixed costs had increased.
b. Selling and administrative fixed expenses had decreased.
c. Sales prices and variable costs had increased proportionately.
d. Sales prices had declined proportionately less than variable costs.

62. A single-product company prepares income statements using both absorption and variable costing methods. Manufacturing overhead cost applied per unit produced in 2014 was the same as in 2013. The 2014 variable costing statement reported a profit whereas the 2014 absorption costing statement reported a loss. The difference in reported income could be explained by units produced in 2014 being

a. Less than units sold in 2014.
b. Less than the activity level used for allocating overhead to the product.
c. In excess of the activity level used for allocating overhead to the product.
d. In excess of units sold in 2014.

Multiple-Choice Answers and Explanations

Answers

1. a	_ _	14. b	_ _	27. d	_ _	40. d	_ _	53. a	_ _
2. d	_ _	15. a	_ _	28. a	_ _	41. d	_ _	54. a	_ _
3. b	_ _	16. d	_ _	29. d	_ _	42. d	_ _	55. c	_ _
4. d	_ _	17. c	_ _	30. b	_ _	43. b	_ _	56. d	_ _
5. d	_ _	18. d	_ _	31. d	_ _	44. c	_ _	57. a	_ _
6. d	_ _	19. c	_ _	32. b	_ _	45. c	_ _	58. a	_ _
7. c	_ _	20. b	_ _	33. b	_ _	46. a	_ _	59. d	_ _
8. a	_ _	21. d	_ _	34. a	_ _	47. c	_ _	60. b	_ _
9. c	_ _	22. d	_ _	35. c	_ _	48. d	_ _	61. b	_ _
10. a	_ _	23. d	_ _	36. c	_ _	49. c	_ _	62. a	_ _
11. b	_ _	24. c	_ _	37. d	_ _	50. d	_ _		
12. c	_ _	25. a	_ _	38. b	_ _	51. a	_ _	1st: __/62 = __%
13. b	_ _	26. a	_ _	39. c	_ _	52. b	_ _	2nd: __/62 = __%

Explanations

1. (a) Three computations must be performed: raw materials used, cost of goods manufactured, and cost of goods sold.

(1)	Raw materials purchased	$430,000
	Less: Increase in raw materials inventory	15,000
	Raw materials used	$415,000
(2)	Beginning WIP	–
	Raw materials used (from above)	415,000
	Direct manufacturing labor	200,000
	Factory overhead	300,000
	Cost to account for	$915,000
	Less: Ending WIP	–
	Cost of goods manufactured	$915,000
(3)	Cost of goods manufactured	$915,000
	Add: Decrease in finished goods inventory	35,000
	Cost of goods sold	$950,000

The increase in raw materials inventory represents the amount of inventory that was purchased but was not used. Therefore, this increase must be subtracted from raw materials purchased to determine the amount of raw materials used. Work in process inventory is an adjustment in arriving at cost of goods manufactured (as shown above). For this question no adjustment is necessary because Kay has no work in process inventory. The decrease in finished goods inventory represents the amount of inventory that was sold in excess of the inventory manufactured during the current period. Therefore,

this amount must be added to cost of goods manufactured to determine cost of goods sold. The freight-out of $45,000 is irrelevant for this question because freight-out is a selling expense and thus, would not be used in computing cost of goods sold.

2. (d) Prime cost is the sum of direct materials and direct manufacturing labor. Direct manufacturing labor is $60,000. Direct materials used must be computed. The solutions approach is to enter the information given into the materials T-account and solve for the unknown:

Direct Materials Control

3/1/14 bal.	36,000		
Purchases	84,000	?	Materials used
3/30/14	30,000		

Using the T-account above, direct materials used are easily computed as $90,000. Thus, prime cost incurred was $150,000 ($90,000 + $60,000).

3. (b) Conversion cost is the sum of direct manufacturing labor ($60,000, as given) and applied factory overhead. The factory overhead rate per direct manufacturing labor hour is $10.00. To compute the number of direct manufacturing labor hours worked, the direct manufacturing labor payroll ($60,000) is divided by the direct manufacturing labor rate per hour ($7.50), resulting in 8,000 direct manufacturing labor hours. Factory overhead applied is 8,000 hours at $10 per hour, or $80,000. Thus, conversion cost incurred was $140,000 ($60,000 of direct manufacturing labor plus $80,000 of applied factory overhead).

4. (d) Cost of goods manufactured (CGM) is the cost of goods completed **and** transferred to finished goods. It is the sum of direct materials used, direct manufacturing labor used, applied factory overhead, and any adjustment for work in process inventories. Direct manufacturing labor used ($60,000) is given. Direct materials used ($90,000) and applied factory overhead ($80,000) were computed in the answers to the two previous questions. Beginning work in process ($18,000) and ending work in process ($12,000) are given. Using this data, CGM can be computed as follows:

BWIP	$ 18,000
DM used	90,000
DML	60,000
OH applied	80,000
Costs to account for	$248,000
EWIP	(12,000)
CGM	$236,000

5. (d) To determine Nale's direct materials purchases for the month of March, trace the flow of costs through the direct materials account.

Direct materials

Beg. bal.	x	
Purchased		$300,000 Used
End. bal.	x + $50,000	

The beginning balance was not given, but the problem states that the ending balance was $50,000 greater. Thus, we can label the beginning balance X and the ending balance X + $50,000. Purchases may be determined as follows:

$$(x + \$50,000) + \$300,000 - x = \$350,000$$

6. (d) Direct manufacturing labor costs include all labor costs which can be directly traced to the product in an economically feasible way. All other factory labor is considered indirect manufacturing labor. For Fab Co., the wages of loom operators can be directly traced to the textiles produced. However, the labor cost of factory foremen and machine mechanics are **not** direct manufacturing labor since these workers do not work directly on the product. Thus, answer (d) is correct because the amount of Fab's direct manufacturing labor is the loom operator cost of $120,000.

7. (c) Product costs are costs that can be associated with the production of specific revenues. These costs attach to a physical unit and become expenses in the period in which the

unit to which they attach is sold. Product costs include direct labor, direct material, and factory overhead. Period costs, on the other hand, cannot be associated with specific revenues and, therefore, become expenses as time passes. Answer (c) is correct because the cost of electricity for a manufacturing plant, whether fixed or variable, is included in factory overhead and, therefore, is a product cost.

8. (a) The labor cost incurred to develop computer programs for sale to customers represents both a direct cost and a value-adding cost. The software is the cost object, and direct costs include any costs that are both related to it and which are easily traceable to specific units of production. Value-adding costs are those that cannot be eliminated without the customer perceiving a decline in product quality or performance. Obviously, the computer programmers cannot be eliminated from the software development process, so these payroll costs add value to the product.

9. (c) The requirement is to identify the account that is increased when indirect materials are issued to production. Answer (c) is correct because the cost of indirect materials used increases the Manufacturing Overhead Control account and decreases Materials Control. Answer (a) is incorrect because Materials Control is decreased with the transfer. Answer (b) is incorrect because Work in Process Control is increased by costs of direct materials and direct labor and the allocation of manufacturing overhead. Manufacturing Overhead Allocated is credited when overhead is allocated to work in process and debited when it is closed out at the end of the period.

10. (a) A responsibility center is any point within an organization where control exists over cost incurrence, revenue generation, and/or the use of investment funds. A responsibility center can be an operation, a department, a division, or even an individual. The key point to note for this question is that no matter what product costing method is used, the responsibility center is always used for control purposes. In job order costing, costs are accumulated by responsibility center and then assigned to specific jobs or orders through the use of a job cost sheet. Even though the job cost sheet will usually reflect the efforts of a number of responsibility centers, it will not be used for control purposes. Any needed cost control will be handled on the responsibility center level. In process costing, costs are accumulated by the responsibility center and recorded on a production cost report that will be used to develop a product's cost. Since the production cost report shows the efforts of only one responsibility center, it is used for both product costing and control purposes. Thus, for control purposes, costs are accumulated by responsibility center for both job-order and process costing.

11. (b) The requirement is to determine the amount of direct materials charged to Job No. 5. The problem states that Job 5 is the only job still in process on April 30, so the total costs charged to this job must equal the ending balance in work in process.

Work in Process Control

Beg. bal.	4,000		
DM	24,000		
DML	16,000		
O/H	12,800	48,000	To FG
End. bal.	8,800		

The total costs charged to Job 5 are $8,800. Direct manufacturing labor accounts for $2,000 of this figure and overhead accounts for $1,600 ($2,000 DL × 80% O/H rate).

Direct manufacturing labor	$2,000
Factory overhead	1,600
Direct materials	–
Total cost of Job 5	$8,800

The remaining cost of $5,200 [$8,800 – ($2,000 + $1,600)] must be the amount of direct materials.

12. (c) Manufacturing overhead is considered an indirect cost because it is not directly traceable to specific jobs, although overhead is a necessary (inevitable) cost of production.

13. (b) The requirement is to determine the cost of jobs completed in January 2014. In a job order costing system, manufacturing overhead cannot be traced to specific jobs. Instead, overhead is accumulated in an overhead control account and applied to work performed based on some predetermined overhead rate. The difference between actual and applied overhead is normally either allocated to work in process, finished goods, and cost of goods sold or written off to cost of goods sold. In this case the cost of jobs completed is being determined for January only. Under- or overapplied overhead is not usually considered on a monthly basis. Therefore, the cost of jobs completed should include allocated overhead only. The amount of indirect materials issued to production has already been included in overhead applied. These costs do not need to be considered again in determining the cost of jobs completed. The cost of jobs completed can be computed as follows:

Direct materials issued to production	$ 90,000
Manufacturing overhead applied	113,000
Direct labor costs	107,000
Cost of jobs completed	$310,000

14. (b) The requirement is to determine which situation would cause a direct manufacturing labor overtime premium to be charged directly to a specific job. Answer (b) is correct because overtime resulting from a customer's requirement of early completion of a job would result in overtime directly traceable to that job. Answer (a) is incorrect because overtime incurred due to an overall high level of activity should be prorated over all jobs. Since production scheduling is generally at random, a specific job should not be penalized simply because it happened to be scheduled during overtime hours. Answers (c) and (d) are incorrect because the overtime is a result of management inefficiency.

15. (a) The requirement is to identify the appropriate type of costing system. Answer (a) is correct because job-order costing systems are designed to accumulate costs for tasks or projects that are unique and nonrepetitive. Service organizations are interested in identifying the costs applicable to each customer and/or each service call. Answer (b) is incorrect because the primary purpose of activity-based costing systems focuses on generating more accurate cost information by costing activities using cost drivers. Answer (c) is incorrect because process costing systems are designed for homogeneous products that are mass produced in continuous production runs. Answer (d) is incorrect because operations costing systems are designed for batches of homogeneous products; operations costing is a hybrid costing method between job-order and process costing.

16. (d) A variable overhead application rate is commonly called a predetermined variable overhead rate and is computed as follows:

$$\frac{\text{Estimated variable overhead costs}}{\text{Estimated activity level}} = \frac{\text{Predetermined}}{\text{variable rate}}$$

Estimated figures are used because actual figures are not known at the beginning of a period. Estimated variable overhead (the numerator) is estimated variable overhead costs, and estimated machine hours (the denominator) is an estimated activity level. Actual figures (either overhead costs or activity levels) are not known until the end of the period.

17. (c) A predetermined factory overhead rate is developed by dividing estimated fixed overhead costs by the normal capacity based on a selected cost driver (DML, cost, machine hours, etc.). Overhead costs are then applied by multiplying the predetermined rate by the actual volume of the cost driver during the period. Overhead costs will be underapplied if (1) overhead costs are underestimated, making the application rate too small (actual costs are larger than expected), or (2) normal capacity is greater than actual activity, making the application rate too small (actual volume is less than normal).

18. (d) The requirement is to determine the amount of costs of goods sold to be reported on the 2014 income statement. The balance in the cost of goods sold account is $720,000. This amount must be increased by the portion of underapplied variable overhead allocated to cost of goods sold. The underapplied overhead is appropriately allocated to work in process, finished goods, and cost of goods sold. No overhead is allocated to direct materials inventory, since this account contains only the cost of unused materials. The other three accounts contain the cost of materials, labor, and overhead. The amounts to be allocated to work in process, finished goods, and cost of goods sold are determined by each account's relative balance as compared to the total balance in the accounts. The total balance of the three accounts is $864,000 ($720,000 + $54,000 + $90,000). Therefore, the amount allocable to cost of goods sold is [$720,000/ $864,000 × ($45,000)] or $37,500. Since variable overhead was underapplied, not enough costs were applied to production during the year. Thus, cost of goods sold is increased to $757,500 ($720,000 + $37,500).

19. **(c)** The step method of allocating support department costs uses a sequence of allocations which result in partial recognition of services rendered by one support department to another. Total costs of the support department that provides the greatest proportion of its services to other support departments are allocated first, followed by the department with the next highest proportion, and so forth. As each "step" is allocated, each succeeding step involves one less department. Parat College's support department cost allocation is

	Support Departments		Operating Departments	
	Maintenance	Power	School of Education	School of Technology
Costs before allocation	$99,000	$54,000		
Allocation of maintenance $\left(\frac{2}{10},\frac{3}{10},\frac{5}{10}\right)$	(99,000)	19,800	$29,700	$49,500
	$ 0			
Allocation of power $\left(\frac{2}{9},\frac{7}{9}\right)$		(73,800)	16,400	57,400
		$ 0	$46,100	$106,900

Therefore, $46,100 of May 2014 support department costs are allocated to the School of Education.

20. **(b)** Equivalent units of production are calculated as follows:

Completed units	400
Plus: Equivalent units in ending inventory (200 × 75%)	150
Less: Equivalent units in beginning inventory (100 × 50%)	(50)
Equivalent units of production	500

21. **(d)** Material costs in ending work in process inventory is calculated as $216,000 = 150 (equivalent units in ending inventory) × $1,440 ($720,000/500) per equivalent unit. Equivalent units of production are calculated as: 500 = 400 completed units + 150 (200 × 75%) equivalent units in ending inventory − 50 (100 × 50%) equivalent units in beginning inventory.

22. **(d)** The application of factory overhead would increase the work in process inventory control account. In addition, the work in process account would be increased for other product costs (direct manufacturing labor and direct material). Only costs of completed products increase finished goods inventory control. Factory overhead control is increased by actual factory overhead costs incurred. Cost of goods sold is increased by the product costs of the finished units sold.

23. **(d)** The requirement is to determine the cost per equivalent unit for materials using the weighted-average method. Under the weighted-average method, equivalent units of production and cost per unit are based on **all** work (this period's and last period's) done on units completed plus all work done to date on the units in ending work in process. Since materials are added at the beginning of the production process, both the units completed and the ending work in process are 100% complete with respect to materials. The cost per equivalent unit can be computed as follows:

Units completed	42,500
Ending WIP	12,500
Total equivalent units	55,000
Cost of materials:	
Beginning WIP	$ 5,500
Units started	18,000
Total costs incurred	$23,500
Divide by EUP	÷ 55,000
Cost per equivalent unit	$ .43

24. **(c)** The requirement is to calculate the amount of conversion cost transferred by Forming to the next production department. First, the physical flow of units must be determined.

Next, equivalent units of production (EUP) must be calculated, in this case using the weighted-average (WA) method. The WA computations of EUP and cost per equivalent unit include both work done **last** period on the current period's BWIP and all work done in the current period on units completed and on EWIP. Forming's EWIP is 80% complete.

Spoiled units must be accounted for separately because Forming adds their cost only to the cost of units transferred. To ignore spoiled units would result in the same total cost being allocated to 500 fewer units, thus spreading spoilage costs over all work done during the period, including EWIP.

	Total units	Equivalent units
Started and completed	7,000	7,000
Spoilage—normal	500	500
EWIP (80% complete)	2,500	2,000*
	10,000	9,500

*2,500 units × 80% completion

Since conversion costs total $85,500 for the period ($10,000 for BWIP + $75,500 for units started), Forming's conversion cost per equivalent unit is $9.00 ($85,500 ÷ 9,500 EUP). These costs are assigned as follows:

Good units completed (7,000 × $9)	$63,000
Spoiled units (500 × $9)	4,500
Conversion cost transferred	$67,500
EWIP (2,000 × $9)	18,000
Total costs accounted for	$85,500

Therefore, $67,500 was transferred to the second department.

25. (a) The FIFO method determines equivalent units of production (EUP) based on the work done in the current period only. The work done in the current period can be dichotomized as (1) the work necessary to complete beginning work in process (BWIP), and (2) the work performed on the units started in the current period.

26. (a) Conversion costs consist of direct manufacturing labor and factory overhead. Because the EWIP units are 50% in process 2, some conversion costs have been incurred. These units would be included in the computation of equivalent units for conversion costs. However, because material G is added only when a batch is 60% complete, this material has not yet been added to this batch. These units would not be included in the computation of equivalent units for material G.

27. (d) The requirement is to compare the number of equivalent units of production (EUP) computed using the weighted-average method to the EUP computed using the FIFO method for two months. The weighted-average method determines EUP based on the work done on the units in all periods, while the FIFO method uses only the work done in the current period. Because the system began in January, there was no beginning inventory for the first month of the comparison. Both methods would compute the same number of EUP for January because the only work done on these units was done in the period under consideration. Because there was ending inventory in January, however, February would have a beginning inventory. The weighted-average method would therefore compute a greater number of EUP than FIFO for February because it would include the work done in January while FIFO would not.

28. (a) The requirement is to determine the proper allocation of **normal** defective unit costs to the ending work in process. **Normal** defective unit costs are spread over the units of **good** output because the attaining of good units necessitates the appearance of normal spoiled units. The cost of the normal defective units is included in the total costs of the **good** equivalent units of output. Ending inventory comprised one-half of the total units of good output produced during the year; therefore, it will bear 50% of the normal defective unit costs incurred during the year.

29. (d) Normal spoilage is the cost of spoiled units which results due to the nature of the manufacturing process. Normal spoilage may be unavoidable under efficient operating conditions and is thus a necessary cost in the production process. Since it is treated as a product cost, the $60,000 normal spoilage should be inventoried. Conversely, units become abnormally spoiled as a result of some unnecessary

act, event, or condition. Therefore, the $30,000 abnormal spoilage is treated as a period cost.

30. (b) The requirement is to calculate the equivalent units of production for materials using the FIFO method. Equivalent units of production are calculated as follows:

Completed units	92,000
Plus: Equivalent units in ending inventory (24,000 × 90%)	21,600
Less: Equivalent units in beginning inventory (16,000 × 60%)	(9,600)
Equivalent units of production	104,000

31. (d) The requirement is to calculate the equivalent units of production for conversion costs using the FIFO method. Equivalent units of production are calculated as follows:

Completed units	92,000
Plus: Equivalent units in ending inventory (24,000 × 40%)	9,600
Less: Equivalent units in beginning inventory (16,000 × 20%)	(3,200)
Equivalent units of production	98,400

32. (b) The requirement is to calculate the equivalent unit cost of materials using the FIFO method. The amount is determined by dividing the cost of materials used during the month by the number of equivalent units of production, which is equal to $4.50 ($468,000 ÷ 104,000).

33. (b) The requirement is to calculate the equivalent unit cost of conversion using the FIFO method. The amount is determined by dividing the conversion costs incurred during the month by the number of equivalent units of production, which is equal to $5.83 [($182,880 + $391,160) ÷ 98,400].

34. (a) The requirement is to calculate the cost of units in ending work in process inventory using the FIFO method. The amount is determined as follows:

Ending WIP:	
Material costs (24,000 units × 90%) × $4.50	$ 97,200
Conversion costs (24,000 units × 40%) × $5.83	55,968
Total	$153,168

35. (c) The requirement is to calculate the equivalent unit cost of materials for the month using the weighted-average method. This amount is calculated as follows:

Units completed	92,000
Ending WIP (24,000 × 90%)	21,600
Total equivalent units	113,600
Cost of materials:	
Beginning WIP	$ 54,560
Units started	468,000
Total costs incurred	$522,560
Divide by EUP	÷ 113,600
Costs per equivalent unit	$4.60

36. (c) The requirement is to calculate the equivalent unit conversion cost for the month using the weighted-average method. This amount is calculated as follows:

Units completed	92,000
Ending WIP (24,000 × 40%)	9,600
Total equivalent units	101,600
Conversion costs:	
Beginning WIP	$ 35,560
Units started	574,040
Total costs incurred	$609,600
Divide by EUP	÷ 101,600
Costs per equivalent unit	$6.00

37. (d) The requirement is to calculate the total cost of the units in the ending work in process inventory using the weighted-average method. The amount is calculated as follows:

Ending WIP	
Material costs (24,000 units × 90%) × $4.60	$ 99,360
Conversion costs (24,000 units × 40%) × $6.00	57,600
Total	$156,960

38. (b) The requirement is to indicate the reasonable basis for allocating costs. Answer (b) is correct because there is a direct causal relationship between the number of components in a finished product and the amount of material handling costs incurred. Answer (a) is incorrect because this allocation basis is related to "batch" costs and not to individual unit costs. Answer (c) is incorrect because this allocation basis is the traditional basis for allocating overhead costs to the units produced when the production process is labor-intensive. Answer (d) is incorrect because this is not an allocation basis but rather the result of the allocation process when determining production costs.

39. (c) The requirement is to identify the valid cost relationship. Answer (c) is correct because both parts of the solution are stated correctly. Within the relevant range for the application activity base, the variable cost per unit and the total fixed cost would be constant. Answer (a) is incorrect because the second part of the solution is stated incorrectly. The fixed cost per unit of activity would decrease (cost is spread over more units), but total fixed cost in the flexible budget would be constant within the relevant range for the application activity base. The first part of the solution (variable cost per unit is constant) is correctly stated resulting in the total variable cost increasing with an increase in volume. Answer (b) is incorrect because the second part of the solution is stated incorrectly. The fixed cost per unit of activity would decrease (cost is spread over more units), but total fixed costs in the flexible budget would be constant within the relevant range for the application activity base. The first part of the solution (variable cost per unit is constant) is correctly stated resulting in the total variable cost increasing with an increase in volume. Answer (d) is incorrect because the first part of the solution is stated incorrectly. The variable cost per unit does not increase (it is constant); rather, total variable cost would increase. The second part (the total fixed costs remain constant) of the solution is correctly stated because the total fixed costs in the flexible budget would be constant within the relevant range for the application activity base.

40. (d) The purpose of the just-in-time (JIT) production system is to decrease the size of production runs (and therefore inventory levels) by decreasing setup costs. Lot **sizes** would decrease as the **number** of lots processed during the year increases. Since inventory levels would decrease with JIT, relevant costs would also drop (i.e., capital invested in inventory could be invested in other assets—a cost savings). The **fixed** facility and administrative costs are irrelevant as fixed costs would remain the same regardless of changes for JIT. The unit costs will increase because fixed costs will be spread over fewer inventory units produced from JIT's eliminating effect on excess inventory production.

41. (d) An activity-based costing system allocates costs to products by determining which activities being performed by the entity are driving the costs. An activity-based costing approach differs from traditional costing methods that accumulate costs by department or function. Activity-based costing accumulates and allocates costs by the specific activities being performed. Since most entities perform a variety of activities, the number of cost pools and allocation bases greatly increases under activity-based costing.

42. (d) Activity-based costing can be used in conjunction with either process or job costing. Answer (a) is incorrect because activity-based costing can be used in conjunction with either process or job costing. Answer (b) is incorrect because activity-based costing can be used in conjunction with job costing. Answer (c) is incorrect because activity-based costing can be used in conjunction with process costing.

43. (b) In an activity-based costing (ABC) system, the activities which drive the manufacturing department's overhead costs would be analyzed. Overhead would then be allocated to products based on the resources consumed in their production. The effect of producing different products in different lot sizes is that some products incur more setup costs than others; products produced in small batches must be produced more often, and thus require more setups to achieve a given level of output. Therefore, setup costs bear a cause-and-effect relationship with and should be assigned to each production **batch** (and then spread over the units in the batch). However, setups are not the only activities driving overhead costs. Other overhead cost drivers identifiable in production systems may include materials handling, engineering changes to products, and rework costs. Therefore, manufacturing overhead should be assigned to products based on **multiple** cause-and-effect relationships [answer (b) is correct and answer (a) is incorrect]. Answers (c) and (d) are incorrect because allocation via these methods would wholly defeat the purpose of ABC, which is founded upon cause and effect allocation of costs to products.

44. (c) Activity-based costing (ABC) involves the allocation of overhead costs to products based on the cost driver that actually **caused** those costs to be incurred. In contrast to traditional costing methods which accumulate costs by department or function, ABC accumulates costs by the specific activity being performed. For example, costs related to the purchase of materials may be allocated according to the number of purchase transactions which occurred. Therefore, cost drivers comprise a necessary part of any ABC system. On the other hand, non-value-added activities represent expenditures for which no value is added to the product. Hence, costs can be reduced by eliminating non-value-added activities without affecting the salability of the product.

45. (d) Activity-based costing focuses on incorporating into product costs only those activities that provide value to the product. Design engineering is a fundamental activity needed to design a good product. Heat treatment activities would strengthen and protect the product being produced. A drill press activity alters the physical product as it moves on toward becoming a finished good. Raw materials storage activity does nothing to alter or improve the value of a product. It is a non-value-adding activity.

46. (a) Under a traditional costing system, setup costs are allocated using a cost driver, in this case, direct manufacturing labor hours. The first step is to calculate the setup costs per direct manufacturing labor hour ($60,000 incurred ÷ 25,000 total DMLH) of $2.40. Since two DMLH are needed to produce one unit of product A, the total setup cost per unit of A is ($2.40 × 2 DMLH) $4.80. Under ABC, one **batch** of product A creates the demand for setup activities that produce value. The setup cost per unit of A under ABC is calculated as the setup cost **per batch** of A ($1,000) divided by the number of units per batch (100), or, $10.00.

47. (c) The requirement is to determine how to allocate joint cost using the net realizable value (NRV) method when a by-product is involved. NRV is the predicted selling price in the ordinary course of business less reasonably predictable costs of completion and disposal. The joint cost of $54,000 is reduced by the NRV of the by-product ($4,000) to get the allocable joint cost ($50,000). The computation is

	Sales value at split-off	Weighting	Joint costs allocated
Kul	$40,000	40,000/75,000 × 50,000	$26,667
Wu	35,000	35,000/75,000 × 50,000	23,333
	$75,000		$50,000

Therefore, $26,667 of the joint cost should be allocated to product Kul.

48. (d) When using the relative sales value at split-off method for joint products, joint costs are allocated based on the ratio of each product's sales value at split-off to total sales value at split-off for all joint products. If the market value at split-off (sales value) of joint product P increases, then a larger proportion of the total joint costs will be allocated to that product. Because all other costs and selling prices remain unchanged, the gross margin of product P will, therefore, decrease. Product Q's gross margin will, however, increase because a smaller proportion of the total joint costs will be allocated to it.

49. (c) Joint costs may be allocated to joint products based on either sales price or some physical measure. Methods which use estimated sales price include relative sales value at split-off, estimated net realizable value (NRV), and constant gross margin percentage NRV. Under the sales value at split-off method, joint costs are allocated based on the ratio of each product's sales value at split-off to total sales value at split-off for all joint products. The estimated NRV method allocates joint costs at the split-off point based on net sales value (Estimated sales value of the joint products – Separable processing costs). Under the constant gross margin percentage NRV method, the overall gross margin (GM) percentage for all joint products combined (after deducting both joint and separable costs) is used to determine the GM for each joint product. This GM is deducted from the sales price of each joint product to determine total costs, and separable costs are then deducted from total costs to determine the joint cost allocation. However, this is not the same as answer (d), which uses a predetermined profit margin and ignores actual costs. The constant GM percentage NRV method does not use a preset GM, it uses the actual overall GM and spreads it uniformly among products so that all joint products yield the same GM percentage. The sales price cannot be based solely on costs. Conversely, costs must be based on sales price (or some physical measure) because joint costs can only be allocated arbitrarily.

50. (d) The requirement is to find the cost of sales for both gasoline and the gasoline by-product. The value of the by-products may be recognized at two points in time: (1) at the time of production, or (2) at the time of sale. Under the production method (as given in the problem), the net realizable value of the by-products **produced** is deducted from the cost of the major products **produced**. The net realizable value of the by-product is as follows:

Sales value of by-product	$30,000	
Less: separable costs	25,000	(10,000 + 15,000)
	$ 5,000	

Therefore, cost of sales for gasoline is calculated as follows:

Total production (joint) costs	$120,000
Less: net realizable value of by-product	5,000
Net Production Cost	115,000
Less: costs in 12/31/14 inventory	15,000
	$100,000

Therefore, total cost of gasoline sales is $100,000, and no cost of sales is reported for the by-product.

51. (a) Because the inventory of by-product Moy was recorded at its net realizable value of $20,000 [($6 – $2) × 5,000] when produced in 2013, no profit will be recognized in 2014. When the units of Moy were sold in 2014, the proceeds equaled the inventory cost plus disposal costs, resulting in $0 profit for 2014. The following journal entries help to illustrate the situation:

2013	Main product(s) inventory	xxxx	
	By-product inventory	20,000	
	Work in process control		xxxx
2014	Cash or accounts receivable	30,000	
	Inventory		20,000
	Selling expenses		10,000

52. (b) The difference between treating the product named "May" as a joint product versus a by-product would be that under by-product treatment, the selling cost is netted against May's selling price thus reducing gross margin whereas under joint-product accounting, the selling cost would be deducting below the gross margin line as a selling expense. Thus, if the change to joint-product accounting were made, gross margin would increase.

53. (a) The value of the by-products may be recognized at two points in time: (1) at the time of production, or (2) at the time of sale. Under the production method, the net realizable value of the by-products **produced** is deducted from the cost of the major products **produced**. Under the sale method, net revenue from by-products **sold** (gross revenue from by-product sales minus separable costs incurred) is deducted from the cost of the major products **sold**.

54. (a) The requirement is to determine the variable component of order filling cost per order. The high-low method of analysis should be used to separate the mixed cost into its fixed and variable components. The formula used in developing the variable rate is

$$\frac{\text{Cost at high point} - \text{Cost at low point}}{\text{High activity point} - \text{Low activity point}} = \text{Variable rate}$$

In this problem, order filling costs are given at four levels of activity because the number of orders was different in each month. Substituting the highest and lowest cost ($4,320 and $3,120) and activity (1,800 and 1,200) figures into the formula yields the variable cost of order filling per order.

$$\frac{\$4,320 - \$3,120}{1,800 - 1,200} = \$2.00/\text{order}$$

55. (c) The graph depicts Sender's fixed and variable parcel mailing costs. Fixed costs total $15,000, since this amount of cost is incurred even when zero parcels are mailed. Variable costs at a mailing volume of 20,000 parcels is $60,000 ($75,000 total cost − $15,000 fixed cost), resulting in a per unit variable cost of $3.00 ($60,000 VC / 20,000 units). Therefore, Sender's estimated cost of mailing 12,000 parcels is $51,000 [$15,000 FC + ($3 VC × 12,000 units)].

56. (d) Regression analysis determines the functional relationship between variables and provides a measure of probable error. Multiple regression analysis involves the use of two or more independent variables (such as the number of shipments and the weight of materials handled) to predict one dependent variable (inventory warehouse costs). Economic

order quantity analysis determines the amount to be ordered while minimizing the sum of ordering and carrying costs. Probability analysis is an application of statistical decision theory that, under conditions of uncertainty, leads to more reliable decisions. Correlation analysis determines the relationship between only two variables.

57. (a) The determination that needs to be made is which of the cost drivers would be the best predictor of overhead costs (machine hours or direct materials weight). The information given regarding the coefficient of determination (R^2) measures the correlation between the cost driver and overhead costs. The higher the R^2, the better the correlation. Therefore, machine hours would be the more accurate cost driver.

58. (a) The difference between net income under variable costing and net income under full absorption costing is $36,000, which is equal to 20,000 × $180,000/100,000. The difference between the two methods is the fixed cost of manufacturing in the ending inventory that would be capitalized under the full absorption costing method and expensed under the variable costing method. Answer (b) is incorrect because the fixed selling and administration costs would be expensed under either method.

59. (d) Under variable costing, both variable direct and variable indirect manufacturing costs are assigned to inventory. All fixed costs are considered sunk costs and thus are written off as an expense of the period. Additionally, variable selling and administrative costs are also treated as period costs and thus not assigned to inventory.

60. (b) The requirement is to determine the different results obtained using absorption and variable costing. Under absorption costing, fixed costs are applied to units produced and are inventoried as product costs. Variable costing considers fixed costs to be period rather than product costs. Killo Co.'s inventoried costs under both methods are as follows:

	Absorption	Variable
Variable costs	1,000 × $90 = $90,000	1,000 × $90 = $90,000
Fixed costs	1,000 × $20 = 20,000	———
Total cost of inventory	$110,000	$90,000

Under the variable method, the $20,000 of fixed cost was charged to income, whereas with absorption costing the fixed costs were absorbed into inventory. Therefore, absorption costing results in a pretax income that is higher by $20,000.

61. (b) The solutions approach is to visualize each income statement as shown below.

Absorption costing is

	Sales
−	Cost of goods sold
	Gross profit (margin)
−	Selling & Admin. Expenses
	Operating income

Variable costing is

> Sales
> — Variable expenses
> Contribution margin
> — Fixed expenses
> Operating income

Because the question states that actual sales revenue, total gross profit, and total contribution margin approximated budgeted figures, CGS and variable expenses must have also approximated budgeted figures. Net income is substantially greater, therefore, because selling and administrative fixed expenses had decreased. If manufacturing fixed costs had increased, gross margin would have decreased. If sales prices and variable costs had increased proportionately, the contribution margin would have increased by the same percentage. If sales prices had declined proportionately less than variable costs, the contribution margin would have again increased.

62. (a) The requirement is to determine what situation would cause variable costing net income to be higher than absorption costing net income. Answer (a) is correct because this difference in reported income is explained if units produced in 2014 are less than units sold in 2014. This is true because under variable costing, the amount of overhead included in cost of goods sold is the amount applied in 2014 (since all units produced were sold), whereas under absorption costing the overhead released to cost of goods sold includes that applied in 2014 as well as overhead included in the 2013 year-end inventory. Answer (b) is incorrect since a level of production lower than the activity level used to allocate overhead would result in underapplied overhead. Answer (c) is incorrect because the opposite situation results in overapplied overhead. Answer (d) is incorrect because production in excess of units sold would produce a higher absorption costing income than the variable costing income.

Written Communication Task

Written Communication Task 1

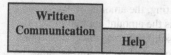

The controller of Tennyson, Inc., Howard Lester, is concerned that the company's costing system is not providing good information about product costs. As a result, he fears that the company is not making good sales or production decisions. Currently, the company uses a simple job order costing system and allocates service department costs on the direct method. Prepare a memorandum to Mr. Lester describing the importance of having good cost information and ways in which the existing system may be improved.

> **REMINDER:** Your response will be graded for both technical content and writing skills. Technical content will be evaluated for information that is helpful to the intended reader and clearly relevant to the issue. Writing skills will be evaluated for development, organization, and the appropriate expression of ideas in professional correspondence. Use a standard business memo or letter format with a clear beginning, middle, and end. Do not convey information in the form of a table, bullet point list, or other abbreviated presentation.

To: Mr. Howard Lester, Controller
        Tennyson, Inc.
From: CPA Candidate

Written Communication Task Solution

Written Communication Task 1

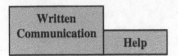

To: Mr. Howard Lester, Controller
         Tennyson, Inc.

From: CPA Candidate

At your request, this memorandum provides information about the importance of a good cost system and the manner in which Tennyson's system may be improved.

It is essential that a company's cost system reflect accurately the costs of production. Product cost information is a very important input into a number of business decisions, including those involving product pricing, inventory levels, and allocation of productive resources. Historically, the company has allocated service department costs on the direct method. This method simply allocates the costs of each service department to production departments based on the relative level of use. The direct method can result in inaccurate costing when service departments provide significant amounts of services to other service departments.

Two methods of cost allocation are superior to the direct method: the step method and the reciprocal method. The step method allocates service department costs to other service departments as well as the production departments, starting with the service departments that provide the most services to other service departments. The reciprocal method uses simultaneous equations to allocate costs to production departments, resulting in the most accurate allocation of costs when service departments provide services to other service departments.

Because of the importance of developing accurate cost information, I encourage you to evaluate your current system of costing. As described, the step and the reciprocal methods of allocation of service department costs are superior to the direct method which is currently being used by the firm.

Module 47: Planning, Control, and Analysis

Overview

This module discusses a number of tools used internally for financial planning, control, and analysis. In the area of financial planning, the module focuses on cost-volume-profit analysis. An understanding of the behavior of costs is essential to effective management of an organization. The module also examines the tools managers use to make effective financial decisions, including forecasting, budgeting, and regression analysis.

In the area of control, the module focuses on the establishment of standards and variance analysis. Finally, the module reviews the techniques used to perform specific tasks or make particular types of decisions, including project management, product and service pricing, transfer pricing, and short-term differential cost analysis. Before beginning the reading you should review the key terms at the end of the module.

A. Cost-Volume-Profit (CVP) Analysis

1. Overview

Cost-volume-profit (CVP) analysis provides management with profitability estimates at all levels of production in the relevant range (the normal operating range). CVP (or breakeven) analysis is based on the firm's profit function. Profit is a function of sales, variable costs, and fixed costs.

$$\text{Profit (NI)} = \text{Sales (S)} - \text{Fixed Costs (FC)} - \text{Variable Costs (VC)}$$
When profit is zero $\quad 0 = S - FC - VC$
$$S = FC + VC$$

Fixed costs are constant in the relevant range, but both sales and variable costs are a function of the level of activity, and vary with respect to a single, output-related driver (e.g., units manufactured or sold). For example, if widgets are sold at $2.00/unit, variable costs are $.40/unit, and fixed costs are $20,000, breakeven is 12,500 units.

$$
\begin{aligned}
X &= \text{Units of production and sales to breakeven} \\
\$2.00X &= \$.40X + \$20,000 \\
\$1.60X &= \$20,000 \\
X &= 12,500 \text{ units (breakeven point)}
\end{aligned}
$$

The cost-volume-profit relationship is diagrammed below.

375

The breakeven point can be thought of as the amount of contribution margin (sales minus variable costs) required to cover the fixed costs, or the point of zero profit. In the previous example, the unit contribution margin (CM) is $1.60 ($2.00 – $.40). Thus, sales of 12,500 units are required to cover the $20,000 of fixed costs. This illustrates the possibility of two shortcut approaches.

Shortcut 1

$$\text{Units to break even} = \frac{\text{Fixed costs}}{\text{Unit CM}} = \frac{\$20,000}{\$1.60} = 12,500 \text{ units}$$

Shortcut 2ww

$$\text{Dollars to break even} = \frac{\text{Fixed costs}}{\text{CM percentage (ratio)}} = \frac{\dfrac{\text{Fixed costs}}{\text{CM per unit}}}{\text{Selling price per unit}} = \frac{\$20,000}{\dfrac{\$1.60}{\$2.00}} = \frac{\$20,000}{80\%} = \$25,000 \text{ sales dollars}$$

A number of variations on the basic CVP calculation are found on the CPA exam. These are illustrated in the following paragraphs:

a. **Target net income.** Selling price is $2, variable cost per unit is $.40, fixed costs are $20,000, and desired net income is $5,000. What is the level of sales in units?

Equation ⟶   Sales = VC + FC + NI
                $2X = $.4X + $20,000 + $5,000

Shortcut ⟶ $\dfrac{\text{FC + NI}}{\text{CM}} = \dfrac{\$20,000 + \$5,000}{\$1.60}$

Solution ⟶   15,625 units

b. **Target net income-percentage of sales.** Same facts, except desired net income is 30% of sales. What is the level of sales in units?

Equation ⟶   Sales = VC + FC + NI
                $2X = $.4X + $20,000 + .30($2X)

Solution ⟶   20,000 units

c. **No per-unit information given.** Fixed costs are $20,000, and variable expenses are 20% of sales. What is the breakeven level of sales in dollars?

Equation ⟶   Sales = VC + FC
                S = .2(S) + $20,000

Shortcut ⟶ $\dfrac{\text{FC}}{\text{CM\%}} = \dfrac{20,000}{80\%}$

Solution ⟶ $25,000 sales dollars

d. **Decision making.** Selling price is $2, variable cost per unit is $.40, and fixed costs are $20,000. Purchasing a new machine will increase fixed costs by $5,000, but variable costs will be cut by 20%. If the selling price is cut by 10%, what is the breakeven point in units?

Equation ⟶   Sales = VC + FC
                $1.8X = $.32X + $25,000

Shortcut ⟶ $\dfrac{\text{FC}}{\text{CM}} = \dfrac{\$25,000}{\$1.48}$

Solution ⟶   16,892 units

2. **Breakeven: Multiproduct Firm**

If a firm makes more than one product, it is necessary to use composite units to find the number of units of each product to breakeven. A composite unit consists of the proportionate number of units which make up the firm's sales mix. For example, assume that a firm has two products with the following selling prices and variable costs.

Product	Selling price	Variable costs	Contribution margin
A	$.60	$.20	$.40
B	$.40	$.15	$.25

Also assume that the sales mix consists of 3 units of A for every 2 units of B (3:2) and fixed costs are $34,000. The **first** step is to find the composite contribution margin.

$$\text{Composite contribution margin} = 3(\$.40) + 2(\$.25) = \$1.70$$

Next compute the number of composite units to breakeven.

$$\frac{\$34,000 \text{ fixed costs}}{\$1.70 \text{ composite contribution margin}} = 20,000 \text{ composite units}$$

Finally, determine the number of units of A and B at the breakeven point by multiplying the composite units by the number of units of A (i.e., 3) and the number of units of B (i.e., 2) in the mix.

$$A: 20,000 \times 3 = \underline{\underline{60,000}} \text{ units}$$
$$B: 20,000 \times 2 = \underline{\underline{40,000}} \text{ units}$$

3. **Assumptions of CVP Analysis**

When applying CVP to a specific case and in interpreting the results therefrom, it is important to keep in mind the assumptions underlying CVP which are listed below.

- a.   Selling price does not change with the activity level
- b.   The sales mix remains constant
- c.   Costs can be separated into fixed and variable elements
- d.   Variable costs per unit are constant
- e.   Total fixed costs are constant over the relevant range
- f.   Productivity and efficiency are constant
- g.   Units produced = Units sold

NOW REVIEW MULTIPLE-CHOICE QUESTIONS 1 THROUGH 14

B. **Financial Planning**

1. **Financial planning is the process of:**

- a.   Analyzing the investment and financing alternatives available to a firm
- b.   Forecasting the future consequences of the alternatives
- c.   Deciding which alternatives to undertake
- d.   Measuring subsequent performance against established goals

2. Financial planning must be tied to the strategic plans of top management. Good financial planning can help managers ensure that their financing strategies are consistent with their capital budgets. It also highlights the investing and financing decisions necessary to support management's strategic plans.

3. Management often uses a **financial planning model** to help assess the consequences of alternative operating and financial strategies. Such models range from those that are fairly simple to those that incorporate hundreds of variables and equations, using specialized software. The input to the models generally consists of current financial statements and expectations about future conditions.

4. In developing the financial plan, management generally will prepare a series of pro forma financial statements, one of which will represent the forecast. The forecast depicts the firm's most- likely future financial results. However, effective financial planning generally requires the development of a series of possible scenarios to allow management to plan for various contingencies. Sensitivity analysis may be used with the model to explore the effects of changes in significant variables on the firm's performance. In addition, financial planning can be used to explore the implications of the various decision alternatives.

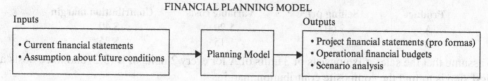

FINANCIAL PLANNING MODEL

Inputs

- Current financial statements
- Assumption about future conditions

Planning Model

Outputs

- Project financial statements (pro formas)
- Operational financial budgets
- Scenario analysis

As shown in the exhibit above, the outputs of the financial planning process are pro forma financial statements, operating and financial budgets for the firm, and scenario analysis that explores other possible outcomes.

C. Budgeting

1. To be most effective, the firm's budget should be an integral part of the strategic plan. It must reflect management's objectives and plans. A master budget summarizes the results of all of the firm's individual budgets into a set of projected financial statements and schedules. Specifically the master budget summarizes the results of the following two major budgets:

   a. **The operating budget**—The budgeted income statement and supporting schedules.
   b. **The financial budget**—The capital budget, cash budget, and the budgeted balance sheet and statement of cash flows.

2. Budgets are prepared for some set period of time, usually one year. However, some budgets must be broken down into shorter time frames. For example, a cash budget is usually prepared monthly to allow management to plan for the firm's cash needs. Many firms use **rolling budgets** which are continually updated as time passes. As an example, a 12-month rolling budget adds a future month and drops the current month as it ends.

3. Budgets may be constructed in a number of ways.

   a. Top-down mandated approach—Upper-level management establishes the budget parameters and it is passed down through the organization to each operating unit.

      (1) Advantages include quick preparation time and clear communication of management's objectives.
      (2) Disadvantage is that lower-level management and employees may view it to be dictatorial and not fully embrace and accept the budget.

   b. Participative (bottom-up) is driven by involving lower-level management and employees.

      (1) Advantages are that employees may more readily accept the budget, morale may be improved, and budget input is provided by a larger number of individuals.
      (2) Disadvantages are that the process is time-consuming, and managers may try to pad their budgets.

   c. Many budgets are prepared using a blended approach that combines aspects of the top-down and bottom-up methods.

4. A budget displays a plan of action for future operations. The most important functions of a budget are to coordinate the various functional activities of the firm and to provide a basis for control of the activities. Budgets may be prepared for all elements of the value chain, which includes R&D, design, production, marketing, distribution, customer service, and administration. The budgets process begins with an estimate of sales and then proceeds systematically as outlined below.

   a. Develop a sales forecast
   b. Develop a production schedule to calculate production costs and costs of goods sold
   c. Estimate other expenses and revenues
   d. Complete the pro forma financial statements and budgets

Pictorially, this process is shown below.

5. The basic formats of some of the key budgets are presented below.

Production budget		**DM budget**
Budgeted sales		Production needs
+ Desired end. FG inventory	× DM	± Desired end. DM inventory
Total needs	per	Total needs
− Beg. FG inventory	unit	− Beg. DM inventory
Units to be produced		DM to be purchased (units)
		× Price per unit
		DM purchases in dollars

Note that before proceeding to the cash budget, DM purchases would have to be converted to **payments** for DM purchases, based on some payment schedule (e.g., 70% in month of purchase, 30% in month following). On the CPA exam you may be given questions that require you to calculate cash inflows from sales or cash outflows for expenses.

EXAMPLE

Assume that a firm sells all of its products on credit and collects 40% of the receivables in the month of sale, 50% in the following month, and 9% in the month after that. If the firm had the following monthly sales, how much is the estimated collections in June?

January	February	March	April	May	June
$20,000	$25,000	$30,000	$10,000	$20,000	$30,000

June's collections would consist of 40% of June's sales, 50% of May's sales, and 9% of April's sales. Therefore, June's collections would be estimated to be $22,900 [($30,000 × 40%) + ($20,000 × 50%) + ($10,000 × 9%)].

---

6. Remember it is cash collections and cash payments that go into the cash budget, as shown below. Also remember that depreciation is not a cash expense.

Cash budget

    Beginning cash balance
 + Receipts (collections from customers, etc.)
    Cash available

- <u>Payments</u> (materials, expenses, payroll, etc.)
  Estimated cash balance before financing
+/- <u>Financing</u> (planned borrowing or short-term investing to bring cash to desired balance)
= <u>Ending cash balance</u>

To illustrate, Adams Company prepared the following cash budget for 2014.

Adams Company
CASH BUDGET
For Year Ending December 31, 2014

Cash balance, beginning		$ 15,000
Add receipts		
Collections from customers		723,000
Total cash available		$738,000
Less payments		
Direct materials	$184,000	
Other costs and expenses	126,000	
Payroll	395,000	
Income taxes	13,000	
Total cash needed		718,000
Estimated cash balance before financing		$ 20,000
Financing		
Borrowings	$25,000	
Repayments	(17,000)	
Interest payments	(1,600)	
Total effects of financing		6,400
Cash balance, ending		$ 26,400

7. The **capital (capital expenditures) budget** displays the financial effects of purchases and retirements of long-lived assets. This information is needed to budget the cash and financing needs of the firm. Because of the need to plan for purchases of long-lived assets, capital budgets tend to span several years.

8. **Kaizen budgeting** projects costs on the basis of improvements yet to be implemented rather than upon current conditions. The budget will not be achieved unless the improvements are actually made.

9. **Activity-based budgeting (ABB)** complements activity-based costing (ABC) by focusing on the costs of activities necessary for production and sales. When ABB is used, operating budgets are formulated for each activity in the activity management system. An activity-based budget is developed by multiplying the budgeted level of the cost driver for each activity by the budgeted cost rate and summing the costs by functional or spending categories. ABB budgeting estimates the costs of performing various activities, in contrast to traditional budgeting which directly budgets costs for functional or spending categories. Management is provided with more insight into what causes costs and is in a much better position to control them.

10. **Developing an Operating Budget—An Example**

    This example is designed to provide an overview of the process of developing an operating budget. On the CPA exam, you can expect multiple-choice questions that will deal with particular aspects of the process. As an example, you might be given manufacturing costs and inventory levels and be asked to compute cost of goods manufactured.

    In our example, Snyder Corporation is developing a financial plan for the year ending December 31, 2014. The company has two primary products, Product A and Product B. Based on an assessment of the projected economic conditions, management has developed forecasted sales of Product A of 25,000 units at a sales price of $100, and forecasted sales of Product B of 30,000 units at a sales price of $120. Therefore, total forecasted sales is $6,100,000.

    Assume that management wants an inventory of 1,200 units of Product A and 1,000 units of Product B at year-end. The beginning inventory is shown in the following schedule.

Schedule 1—Beginning Finished Goods Inventory

	Product A	Product B	Total
Units	1,200	1,200	
Cost per unit	$ 70	$ 80	
Total cost	$84,000	$96,000	$180,000

There was no work-in-process beginning inventory and none is anticipated at the end of the year. This information can then be used to prepare the production schedule shown below.

Schedule 2—Production Schedule

	Product A	Product B
Projected unit sales	25,000	30,000
Desired ending inventory	1,200	1,000
Beginning inventory	(1,200)	(1,200)
Units to be produced	25,000	29,800

Once the production schedule is developed, management can develop the raw materials usage budget and budgets for labor and overhead. Information to develop these schedules can be obtained from the following product specifications schedule.

Schedule 3—Product Specifications

	Product A	Product B	Estimated Cost
Materials			
Silver	7 oz.	6 oz.	$5.15 per oz.
Red Oak	1 b.f.		$3.95 per b.f.
Teak		1 b.f.	$6.10 per b.f.
Direct Labor	½ hour	¾ hour	$ 40 per hour

Schedule 4—Direct Materials Usage Budget

Physical Units	Silver oz.	Red Oak b.f.	Teak b.f.	Total
Product A				
Silver	175,000			
Red Oak		25,000		
Product B				
Silver	178,800			
Teak			29,800	
To be used in production	353,800	25,000	29,800	
Cost Budget				
Available from beginning inventory				
Silver 4,000 oz. @ $5.00 per oz.	$ 20,000			
Red Oak 1,000 b.f. @ $4.00 per b.f.		$ 4,000		
Teak 1,000 b.f. @ $6.00 per b.f.			$ 6,000	
From purchases				
Silver $5.15 × (353,800 – 4,000)	1,801,470			
Red Oak $3.95 × (25,000 – 1,000)		94,800		
Teak $6.10 × (29,800 – 1,000)			175,680	
Cost of direct materials to be used	$1,821,470	$98,800	$181,680	$2,101,950

Schedule 5—Direct Manufacturing Labor Budget

Product A
(25,000 × ½ hour × $40 per hour) $ 500,000
Product B
(29,800 × ¾ hour × $40 per hour)   894,000
                                                    $1,394,000

Schedule 6—Manufacturing Overhead Budget (at 34,850 budgeted direct labor hours)

Variable overhead costs:
    Supplies $ 60,000
    Indirect labor   135,000
    Maintenance   50,000
    Electricity   100,000
    Miscellaneous   30,000
Fixed overhead costs:
    Depreciation $306,400
    Insurance   40,000
    Plant supervision   90,000
    Miscellaneous   25,000
Total manufacturing overhead $836,400
Overhead application rate:
Direct labor hours
    Product A (25,000 × ½ hour)   12,500
    Product B (29,800 × ¾ hour)   22,350
        Total direct labor hours   34,850
Application rate ($836,400 / 34,850) $ 24 per hour

Based on the budgeted amounts of materials, labor, and overhead, management can now determine the unit production cots, and the ending inventories and costs of goods sold budgets as shown below.

Schedule 7—Unit Production Costs

	Product A	Product B
Materials	$40	$37
Direct labor	20	30
Manufacturing overhead ($24 per DLH)	12	18
	$72	$85

Schedule 8—Cost of Goods Sold Budget

	Schedule		
Beginning finished goods inventory	1		$ 180,000
Direct materials used	4	$2,101,950	
Direct labor	5	1,394,000	
Manufacturing overhead	6	836,400	
Cost of goods manufactured			4,332,350
Cost of goods available for sale			4,512,350
Deduct ending finished goods inventory			171,400
Cost of goods sold			$4,340,950

With estimates of sales and general and administrative expenses and the tax rate, management can now prepare the pro forma income statement for next period as shown below.

Snyder Corporation
PRO FORMA INCOME STATEMENT
For the Year Ending December 31, 2014

Sales	$6,100,000
Cost of goods sold	4,340,950
Gross profit	1,759,050
General & administrative expenses	1,020,000
Operating income (EBIT)	739,050
Interest expense	260,000
Earnings before taxes	479,050
Taxes (30%)	143,715
Net income	$ 335,335

D. Forecasting Methods

1. Management may choose from a number of methods for forecasting the firm's sales. Such methods are generally classified as qualitative or quantitative techniques. Qualitative approaches base the forecast on management judgment. Examples of qualitative techniques include

   a. Executive opinions
   b. Sales-force polling
   c. Customer surveys

2. Structured approaches, such as the **Delphi technique,** may be used to assist in developing qualitative forecasts. This technique develops consensus among a group about the future through a series of structured questionnaires and an iterative process. The results of prior questionnaires are used to develop subsequent questionnaires until consensus is achieved.

3. Quantitative approaches to the development of forecasts may be broken down into three major types:
   (1) approaches based on historical data, (2) approaches based on observed associations, (3) approaches based on forecasts of consumer behavior. Examples include the following:

   a. Approaches based on historical data:

      (1) **Naive models**—These models are based exclusively on historical observation of sales or other variables. As an example, management might examine historical data on sales by product line and make a subjective estimate of the next period's sales.

      (2) **Moving average**—This technique simply uses the average of sales for the most recent periods to predict the next period's sales.

      (3) **Exponential smoothing**—This technique is similar to moving average but the more recent sales data are weighted more heavily than older data in computing the forecast. Underlying the technique is the belief that more recent data are more relevant to predictions of future sales.

      (4) **Decomposition of time series**—This technique is especially appropriate when sales are seasonal or cyclical in nature. The technique examines prior sales data and estimates seasonal and cyclical effects. When these effects are extracted from the prior data, historical trends may be observed and projected into the future. Once the trends are used to develop initial forecasts, seasonal and cyclical effects are reintroduced to develop the final forecast.

   b. Approaches based on observed associations:

      (1) **Regression analysis**—This technique estimates sales based on an observed relationship between sales (the dependent variable) and one or more predictors of sales (independent variables).

      (2) **Econometric models**—Involve the use of regression analysis to model the firm's sales based on economic data. For example, forecasts of personal disposable income, interest rates, etc. might be used to develop an estimate of future sales.

   c. Approaches based on forecasts of consumer behavior:

      (1) **Markov techniques**—These techniques attempt to forecast consumer purchasing by considering factors such as brand loyalty and brand switching behavior. These data are used to predict changes in the firm's market share, which is then used to develop the sales forecast.

4. Regression Analysis

As described in Module 46, regression is a technique for estimating mathematically the average relationship between a dependent variable (y) and one or more independent variables (x). Simple regression involves only one independent variable and the estimation equation is shown below.

$$y = a + bx + e$$

Where

y = the dependent variable
x = the independent variable
a = the y-intercept or constant value
b = the slope of the regression line
e = an error term that is assumed to be normally distributed with a mean of 0

Since the random error term (e) is assumed to have a zero mean, it is ignored and the equation becomes simply

$$y = a + bx$$

a. Major assumptions underlying regression analysis include

(1) The relationship is linear within the relevant range.
(2) The variance of the error (residual) term is constant. A violation of this assumption is referred to as **heteroscedasticity**. While it does not affect the accuracy of the regression estimates (*a* and *b*), heteroscedasticity does reduce the reliability of the estimates of standard errors and therefore affects the precision of any estimates developed from the equation.
(3) The error (residual) values are independent.
(4) The error values are normally distributed around the regression line.

b. Trend Analysis

Regression might be used as a tool in performing trend analysis. In this case regression analysis is used to fit a trend line to a time series of data. As an example, assume that management believes that sales for the next period might be estimated based on the trend of prior sales. The following data have been collected:

Period	Sales	Period	Sales
1	$60,000	6	$67,500
2	$62,000	7	$69,000
3	$62,500	8	$71,000
4	$65,000	9	$71,500
5	$66,500	10	$72,500

The output of regression analysis of this data using a spreadsheet program is illustrated below.

Summary Output

Regression Statistics

Multiple R	0.994088
R Square	0.988211
Adjusted R Square	0.986738
Standard Error	498.4825
Observations	10

	Df	SS	MS	F	Significance F
Regression	1	1.67E+08	1.67E+08	670.6128	5.31E–09
Residual	8	1987879	248484.8		
Total	9	1.69E+08			

	Coefficients	Standard error	t-Stat	P-value	Lower 95%	Upper 95%
Intercept	58933.33	340.5284	173.0644	1.39E–15	58148.07	59718.59
Period	1421.212	54.88112	25.89619	5.31E–09	1294.656	1547.768

c. **Goodness of fit** measures how well the predicted values of the dependent variable match the actual amounts. Regression analysis computes a measure of goodness of fit, the **coefficient of determination**. The coefficient of determination (adjusted R Squared) in this case indicates that 98.6738% of the variance in sales is explained by the time series (period).

d. The significance of the relationship is measured by the *t*-Statistic. In this case, the *t*-Statistic for Period is 25.89619 which is very significant. The P-value of 5.31E–09 (0.00000000531) indicates that there is an extremely low probability (0.000000531%) that this relationship occurred by chance.

e. From the coefficients section we see that the equation to predict sales is as follows:

$$\text{Sales} = 58933.33 + (1421.212 \times \text{Period})$$

If we wanted to predict sales for Period 11, we would simply substitute 11 for the period and calculate the estimate as shown below.

$$\begin{aligned} \text{Sales} &= 58933.33 + (1421.212 \times 11) \\ &= \$74,566.66 \end{aligned}$$

5. Multiple Regression

Multiple regression is used when management wishes to forecast sales using two or more associated variables. As an example, assume that management of a growing toy manufacturer believes that an accurate estimate of sales can be obtained with two variables—expenditures for advertising and the number of newly introduced toys. Management has collected the following data:

Period	Sales	Advertising expenditures	Number of new toys	Period	Sales	Advertising expenditures	Number of new toys
1	$40,000,000	$1,000,000	5	6	$49,000,000	$1,000,000	12
2	$45,000,000	$1,250,000	7	7	$54,000,000	$1,600,000	12
3	$44,000,000	$ 900,000	9	8	$52,000,000	$1,500,000	4
4	$48,000,000	$1,500,000	9	9	$55,000,000	$1,500,000	13
5	$50,000,000	$1,200,000	14	10	$57,000,000	$1,500,000	15

a. The output of regression analysis of this data using a spreadsheet program is illustrated below.

SUMMARY OUTPUT

Regression Statistics

Multiple R	0.910234
R Square	0.828526
Adjusted R Square	0.779534
Standard Error	2506160
Observations	10

	Df	SS	MS	F	Significance F
Regression	2	2.12E+14	1.06E+14	16.91129	0.002088
Residual	7	4.4E+13	6.28E+12		
Total	9	2.56E+14			

	Coefficients	Standard error	*t*-Stat	P-value	Lower 95%	Upper 95%
Intercept	24678459	4466529	5.525199	0.000883	14116805	35240114
Advertising	13.63897	3.302376	4.130049	0.004404	5.830102	21.44785
New Toys	705906.9	224772.5	3.140539	0.016367	174404.7	1237409

b. The **coefficient of determination** (Adjusted R Squared) is .779534. As discussed above, this is a measure of goodness of fit. In this case 77.9534% of the variation in sales is explained by advertising expenditures and the number of new toys introduced.

c. The equation for predicting sales is shown below.

$$\text{Estimated sales} = \$24,678,459 + (13.63897 \times \text{Ad. Exp.}) + (705,906.9 \times \text{No. New Toys})$$

d. For the next period, assume that management estimates that $1,600,000 will be spent on advertising and 10 new toys will be introduced. The estimated sales for the period would be calculated as follows:

Estimated sales   = $24,678,459 + (13.63897 × $1,600,000) + (705,906.9 × 10)

Estimated sales   = $53,559,880

e. Other important regression statistics to consider include

(1) **The Standard Error of the Estimate and Confidence Level**—The standard error of the estimate, in this case 2,506,160, is the standard deviation of the regression. This number can be used to establish confidence intervals around the estimate of sales. If the manager wants a prediction to be 95% confident, the confidence interval would be the estimated value from the equation ± $2,506,160 × 2.3436. The 2.3436 is derived from a normal curve area table that shows the relative area under a normal curve from one standard deviation to another. For a normal distribution, 95% of the values fall within 2.3436 standard deviations from the mean. Using the estimated sales number calculated above, $53,559,880, management can be 95% confident that sales for the next period will fall within the range calculated below.

95% Confidence Interval   = $53,559,880 ± $2,506,160 × 2.3436
                           = $47,686,443 to $59,433,317

(2) **The F-Statistic**—This statistic provides an overall measure of the significance of the regression equation. In the above case the F-Statistic is 16.91129 and is significant at the .002088 level. This means that there is only about a two-tenths of one percent chance (0.2088%) that the relationship occurred by chance.

(3) **The t-Statistics**—Each independent variable will have a t-Statistic which indicates its significance. In the above case, the t-Statistics are 4.130049 and 3.140539 with P-values of .004404 and .016367, respectively. The P-values measure the level of significance of each variable to the equation. In this case both are significant at less than the .05 (5%) level, which means that there is less than a 5% probability that the relationship occurred by chance.

f. Previously, we described the assumptions underlying regression. In evaluating the results, consideration should be given to two related issues.

(1) **Multicollinearity**—When using more than one independent variable there may be a high correlation between the independent variables. This will cause the equation to be in error and may produce spurious forecasts. Indicators of multicollinearity include low t-Statistics for variables that should be important, or variables with coefficients with illogical signs (e.g., a negative relationship between advertising and sales).

(2) **Autocorrelation**—Remember from the discussion above regression analysis assumes that the error term is randomly distributed and independent. If the errors are serially correlated this can again distort the results. Autocorrelation may indicate that a major independent variable is not included in the model. The Durbin-Watson statistic provides a test for autocorrelation.

E. Flexible Budgets

A flexible budget is a budget adjusted for changes in volume. In the planning phase, a flexible budget is used to compare the effects of various activity levels on costs and revenues. In the controlling phase, the flexible budget is used to help analyze actual results by comparing actual results with a flexible budget for the level of activity achieved in the period. Standard costing naturally complements flexible budgeting. However, even without standard costing, flexible budgeting can be used based upon actual costs and quantities of outputs (although lack of input data precludes computation of price and efficiency variances).

Presented below is a sample flexible budget for overhead costs.

FACTORY OVERHEAD

FLEXIBLE BUDGET

Direct manufacturing labor hours	18,000	20,000	22,000
Variable factory overhead			
Supplies	$ 18,000	$ 20,000	$ 22,000
Power	99,000	110,000	121,000
Idle time	3,600	4,000	4,400
Overtime premium	1,800	2,000	2,200
Total ($6.80 per DMLH)	$122,400	$136,000	$149,600
Fixed factory overhead			
Supervision	$ 15,000	$ 15,000	$ 15,000
Depreciation	32,000	32,000	32,000
Power	8,000	8,000	8,000
Property taxes	5,000	5,000	5,000
Insurance	1,500	1,500	1,500
Total	$ 61,500	$ 61,500	$ 61,500
Total overhead	$183,900	$197,500	$211,100

> **NOW REVIEW MULTIPLE-CHOICE QUESTIONS 15 THROUGH 43**

F. Responsibility Accounting

Responsibility accounting allocates those revenues and/or assets which a manager can control to that manager's responsibility center and holds the manager accountable for operating results. If a manager is only responsible for costs, his/her area of responsibility is called a **cost center**. Cost centers represent the most basic activities or responsibilities. Nonrevenue generating departments (purchasing and billing, for example) are usually organized as cost centers.

If the manager is responsible for both revenues and costs, his/her area of responsibility is called a **profit center**. A contribution income statement similar to the one shown below would be prepared for each profit center. Finally, if the manager is responsible for revenues, costs, and asset investment, his/her area of responsibility is called an **investment center**.

G. Segmented Reporting and Controllability

Variable (Direct) and Absorption (Full) Costing reports (as described in Section B) can be broken into further detail to emphasize controllability.

1. Variable manufacturing costs are deducted from sales to obtain **manufacturing contribution margin**.
2. Variable selling and administrative expenses are deducted from manufacturing contribution margin to obtain **contribution margin**.
3. Fixed costs controllable by segment managers at various levels (e.g., division, department) are deducted from contribution margin to obtain the **controllable contribution** at that level.
4. Fixed costs controllable by others at various levels are deducted from controllable contribution to obtain the **segment contribution** at that level.
5. Costs common to all operations are finally deducted to obtain **income before taxes**.

EXAMPLE CONTRIBUTION APPROACH INCOME STATEMENT

	Total	Segment 1	Segment 2
Sales	$600	$350	$250
−Variable manufacturing costs	220	115	105
Manufacturing contribution margin	380	235	145
−Variable selling and admin. exp.	100	70	30
Contribution margin	280	165	115
−Controllable, traceable fixed costs	80	35	45

	Total	Segment 1	Segment 2
Controllable contribution	200	130	70
−Uncontrollable, traceable fixed costs	90	60	30
Segment contribution	$110	$70	$40
−Unallocable common costs	60*		
Income before taxes	$50		

* Not allocated to any segment of the firm. Examples include corporate office salaries and advertising for firm name.

Costs not controllable by a subdivision (cost or profit center) of a firm should not be allocated to the subdivision for evaluation or decision making purposes (see Section F. Responsibility Accounting).

Contribution margin data can be used in a variety of situations, including planning (CVP analysis) and decision making (which products to emphasize, which products should be retained and which should be eliminated, and so forth).

H. Standards and Variances

Standard costs are predetermined target costs which should be attainable under efficient conditions. The tightness, or attainment difficulty, of standard costs should be determined by the principles of motivation (e.g., excessively tight standards may result in employees feeling that the standards are impossible to achieve; consequently, they may ignore them). Standard costs are used to aid in the budget process, pinpoint trouble areas, and evaluate performance.

The tightness of standards is generally described by one of two terms. **Ideal** standards reflect the absolute minimum costs which could be achieved under perfect operating conditions. **Currently attainable** standards should be . achieved under efficient operating conditions. Generally, currently attainable standards are set so they will be difficult, but not impossible, to achieve. Currently attainable standards are most often used since they are more realistic for budgeting purposes and are a better motivational tool than ideal standards.

Variances are differences between actual and standard costs. The total variance is generally broken down into subvariances to further pinpoint the causes of the variance.

1. Variance Analysis

In calculating the variances for direct material and direct manufacturing labor the following symbols will be employed as defined:

AP: Actual price paid per unit of input (e.g., price per foot of lumber, per hour of labor, per ton of steel, etc.)
SP: Standard price per unit of input
AQ: The actual quantity of input (feet, hours, tons, etc.) used in production
SQ: The standard quantity of input that should have been used for the good units produced
Variances can be computed using the diagram approach that follows.

2. Material Variances

The diagram for computing material variances is

The price variance is unfavorable if AP > SP; the quantity variance is unfavorable if AQ > SQ. Favorable variances arise when actual amounts are less than standard amounts.

The only alternative allowed on the variances above concerns the material price variance. The price variance can be recognized when material is placed in production (as assumed in the previous discussion) or when material is purchased (which is desirable for early identification and control). If the price variance is to be recognized at the time of purchase, AQ (for the price variance **only**) becomes quantity **purchased** rather than quantity **used**.

The materials price variance is generally considered to be the responsibility of the purchasing department, while the materials quantity variance is the responsibility of the production department or production design engineers.

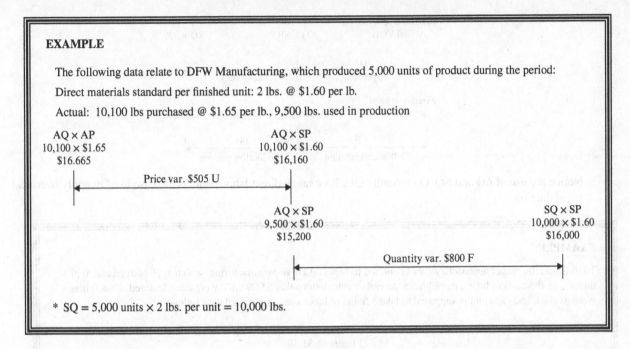

EXAMPLE

The following data relate to DFW Manufacturing, which produced 5,000 units of product during the period:

Direct materials standard per finished unit: 2 lbs. @ $1.60 per lb.

Actual: 10,100 lbs purchased @ $1.65 per lb., 9,500 lbs. used in production

AQ × AP
10,100 × $1.65
$16.665

AQ × SP
10,100 × $1.60
$16,160

Price var. $505 U

AQ × SP
9,500 × $1.60
$15,200

SQ × SP
10,000 × $1.60
$16,000

Quantity var. $800 F

* SQ = 5,000 units × 2 lbs. per unit = 10,000 lbs.

3. **Labor Variances**

The computational form of the labor variances is similar to the calculation of material variances—except that the price being used changes from price per pound of material to price (rate) per hour of labor, and the quantity changes from pounds, yards, etc., to hours. Therefore, the diagrams are the same, although the terminology differs.

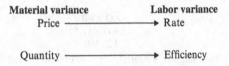

Material variance   Labor variance
Price ───────────────→ Rate

Quantity ─────────────→ Efficiency

Both labor variances are usually considered to be the responsibility of the production department or production design engineers.

EXAMPLE

The following data relate to DFW Manufacturing. Recall that the company produced 5,000 units of product during the period:

Direct labor standard per finished unit: 3 hours @ $2.50 per hour

Actual: 15,400 hours worked @ $2.60 per hour

AH × AR
15,400 × $2.60
$40,040

AH × SR
15,400 × $2.50
$38,500

SH* × SR
15,000 × $2.50
$37,500

Rate var. $1,540U   Efficiency var.$1.000U

* SH = 5,000 units × 3 hours = 15,000 hours

4. **Overhead Variances**

Overhead variances tend to be more complicated than those computed for direct materials and direct labor, primarily because of the different computation methods that are available. The easier approach to master is a parallel of the variance grids shown earlier, with overhead being subdivided into fixed and variable elements. Variable overhead parallels the calculation of direct labor variances; fixed overhead, in contrast, requires a minor modification. The general setup approach follows:

Variable overhead
Actual VOH   AQ × SR   SQ × SR
      (1)   (2)
    spending   Efficiency

Fixed overhead
Actual FOH   Budget   SQ × SR
      (3)   (4)
  Budget/spending   Production volume

Notice the use of AQ and SQ. On virtually all CPA exams, direct labor hours is the base used to apply overhead to production.

EXAMPLE

To illustrate the proper approach, we will continue to focus on DFW Manufacturing, which applies overhead to production on the basis of hours. Recall from the earlier calculations that 5,000 units were manufactured. 15,400 hours were worked, and each unit is supposed to take 3 hours of labor time. Additional data follow.

Estimated (standard) factory overhead based on a "normal capacity" of 16,000 labor hours:

Variable	3 hours @ $1.50
Fixed	3 hours @ $0.50*

Actual overhead cost for the period

Variable	$22,800
Fixed	$ 8,100

* $8,000 budgeted fixed overhead costs ÷ 16,000 direct labor hours

Variable Overhead

	AQ × SR	SQ × SR
Actual	15,400 × $1.50	15,000 × $1.50
$22,800	$23,100	$22,500

Spending var. $ 300F   Efficiency var. $ 600U

Fixed Overhead

		SQ × SR
		15,000 × $0.50
Actual	Budget	$7,500
$8,100	$8,000	

Spending budget var. $ 100U   Production volume var. $ 500U

This example illustrates several key points.

According to the information presented, DFW has a capacity to work 16,000 hours, which is the equivalent of 5,334 units (16,000 ÷ 3 hours per unit). Since the firm produced only 5,000 units, the production volume variance is unfavorable.

Overhead in the SQ × SR column ($22,500 + $7,500 = $30,000) is the amount applied to production. Since actual overhead was $30,900 ($22,800 + $8,100), overhead is $900 underapplied. This latter amount will always coincide with the combination of all four variances ($300F – $600U – $100U – $500U = $900U).

The 3-variance approach. The 3-variance method results in the calculation of three variances rather than the four just illustrated. The **only** difference between these two approaches is in the calculation of the spending variance, which is a combination of (1) and (3) to create a total spending variance as shown below.

(1) + (3)   (2)   (4)
Total spending   Efficiency   Production volume

For DFW, the total spending variance is $200F ($300F – $100U).

The 2-variance approach. The 2-variance approach results in the calculation of only two variances: the production volume variance shown earlier and a combined spending/efficiency variance (see the following diagram).

This latter variance for DFW is $400U ($300F – $100U – $600U).

Some computational hints. These variance approaches are fairly straightforward if you start with the 4-variance method and then work backwards to arrive at the 3-variance approach and then work that backwards to arrive at the last method. Occasionally, the exam may not give you enough data to perform all calculations to do this. The following hints have proven to be extremely helpful:

- The production volume variance is the same no matter what approach is used.
- The efficiency variance is the same for the 3- and 4-variance approach.
- When in doubt, you can calculate the total variance (the difference between actual total overhead and applied overhead [SQ × SR]), subtract the variances that you can compute, and the result, a forced figure, will often be the variance that is requested by the examiners.

Miscellaneous. The budget variance (also called the controllable variance) arises when the amount spent on both fixed and variable overhead differs from the amount budgeted for the actual hours worked.

The production volume variance is solely a **fixed** overhead variance. It is caused by under- or overutilization of capacity. If actual output is less than (more than) capacity activity, an unfavorable (favorable) output level variance results. The capacity volume is the activity level used to set the predetermined fixed overhead rate for product costing purposes (see Module 46).

5. **Disposition of Variances**

If insignificant, variances are frequently written off to cost of goods sold on the grounds of expediency. (ARB 43 states that you may report inventories using standard costs if they are based on currently attainable standards.) If significant, the variances must be allocated among the inventories and cost of goods sold, usually in proportion to the ending balances. Remember, SFAS 151 requires that fixed overhead costs be allocated based on normal capacity and variances related to fixed overhead volume should be allocated only to cost of goods sold (treated as a period cost).

NOW REVIEW MULTIPLE-CHOICE QUESTIONS 44 THROUGH 64

I. Product and Service Pricing

Product pricing requires the use of judgment by the cost accountant and management to maximize the entity's profits and to increase shareholder wealth. To find the combination of sales price and volume yielding the greatest profits, management must make many assumptions regarding customer preferences, competitors' reactions, economic conditions, cost structures, etc. In maximizing shareholders' wealth, management must consider not only product costs but must also react to external changes, for example, a competitor's price on a relatively undifferentiated product. Additionally, management must consider the company's cost of capital in determining a desired **rate of return**. This rate of return represents the desired minimum markup on the cost of goods.

Costs are usually the starting point in determining prices. In the long run, all costs, including fixed costs, must be considered. However, decisions involving short-range pricing, such as a special order, may be evaluated on the basis of contribution margin. The **contribution margin approach** considers all relevant variable costs plus any additional fixed costs needed to sustain the new production level. Which costs are relevant is determined by analyzing how total costs of each component of the value chain will change if the order is accepted.

Cost-plus pricing is one model for the pricing decision; prices are set at variable costs plus a percentage markup, at full manufacturing or service cost plus a percentage markup, or at target ROI per unit. The percentage markup must cover fixed costs and profit (variable approach), operating expenses and a profit (full cost approach), or invested capital (target ROI approach). Consider the following example:

Annual sales—10,000 units		Invested capital—$100,000		Target ROI—15%
Manufacturing costs:			Operating costs:	
Fixed	$20,000		Fixed	$10,000
Variable	$3/unit		Variable	$2.50/unit

If price is set at total variable cost plus 60% ($5.50 × 160%), or full manufacturing cost plus 76% ($5.00 × 176%), the selling price would be $8.80. The selling price under the target ROI approach is calculated as follows:

	Invested capital	$100,000
×	Target ROI	× 15%
	Total target ROI	15,000
÷	Annual sales	÷ 10,000
	Target oper. inc. per unit	1.50
+	Cost base (total cost)	+ 8.50
	Selling price	$ 10.00

Note that the rate of markup ($1.50/$8.50 = 17.65%) has nothing to do with target ROI (15%), which expresses operating income as a percentage of **investment**.

Another alternative is **target pricing**, which sets prices at the amount that consumers are willing to pay based on their perceived value of the product or service. Based on targeted prices and income, a target cost is determined; the targeted cost is the estimated cost of the product or service that yields the targeted income at the target price. To meet target costs, a company must often improve its products or increase efficiency. **Value engineering** examines all components of the value chain to find opportunities for improvements and cost reduction. Activity-based costing helps to identify opportunities for cost reduction by improving specific activities.

A number of other pricing strategies may be used by companies, some of which are not legal in many countries, including:

1. **Dual pricing** is the practice of pricing goods or services at a different price depending on the currency used or the country in which it is sold. Dual pricing may be used for a variety of purposes, such as to gain entry into a foreign market, or as a method of price discrimination. It may be illegal if it is used as a method of product **dumping**.
2. **Collusive pricing** is a secret agreement between two or more companies to control or influence the price of a product or service. Collusive pricing is illegal in many countries.
3. **Predatory pricing** is the practice of selling a product or service at a very low price to drive competitors out of the market, or create barriers to entry into the market. Predatory pricing is illegal in many countries.

J. Transfer Pricing

Decentralization of profit or investment centers requires pricing policies for optional internal transfers of intermediate goods or services between those centers. The transfer price represents revenue to the selling subunit and cost to the purchasing subunit, which are included in the operating income of the divisions. The goal of transfer pricing is to provide autonomous segment managers with incentive to maximize profits of the company as a whole, not just the performance of their own divisions.

In theory, outlay cost plus opportunity cost should determine the transfer price. However, opportunity cost may be difficult or impossible to measure. Therefore, three transfer pricing alternatives exist: cost-based price, market price, and negotiated price. Transfer prices based on cost may consider variable manufacturing costs, total manufacturing (absorption) costs, or full product costs. Actual costs are unstable (vary seasonally, etc.) and allow the producing division to pass its inefficiencies to the buyer; thus, standard costs should be used. Any variances from standard affect the operating income of the selling division (cannot be passed on).

A transfer price based on **full cost** includes the transferring division's fixed costs (absorption costing). A problem with full cost transfer pricing is that special orders at below full cost but above variable cost may be rejected because they result in losses for the selling division even though the contribution to fixed costs benefits the company as a whole (suboptimization). Thus, the use of full cost for transfer pricing could lead to poor motivation and dysfunctional decision making.

A **full product cost** transfer price includes absorption manufacturing cost plus a share of other costs of the value chain, such as R&D or other administrative, selling, or general expenses.

A transfer price based on the **market price** of similar products or services is justified if a competitive market exists for the product/service. A market transfer price may also be based on the transferring division's price to outside customers. However, if any costs can be avoided by selling internally rather than externally (e.g., commissions, advertising) then the market price should be reduced by these cost savings. Market transfer prices are useful because they are objective, they avoid the need to define cost, and because they show each division's contribution to company profit.

Alternatively, two divisions may establish a **negotiated transfer price**. Cost and market price information may be useful in the bargaining process, but it is not required that the transfer price be specifically related to either. However the resulting transfer price should fall within a range limited by a ceiling and a floor. The ceiling, which is the lowest external market price, helps the purchasing subunit keep costs down. The floor equals the transferring division's outlay plus opportunity costs, so the seller can cover costs. The transfer price serves to divide this amount between the divisions involved, which affects divisional operating income and thus performance measurement and responsibility accounting.

To enhance cooperation between divisions, prevent suboptimization by managers, encourage the transferring division to maximize income, and provide the purchasing division with cost information relevant for short-term decision making, a **dual transfer pricing** system may be established. Here, transfers are recorded by the selling subunit at one price while the purchaser records the transfer at a different transfer price.

K. Short-Term Differential Cost Analysis
Differential cost decisions include:

1. Sell or process further (see also Section L, Module 46)
2. Special order
3. Outsourcing (make or buy)
4. Closing a department or segment
5. Sale of obsolete inventory
6. Scarce resources

These decisions would better be described as differential cost and **revenue** decisions, since basically the decision maker must consider differences in costs and revenues over various alternatives. All other things being equal, the alternative providing the greatest profit (or cost savings) should be chosen.

Three concepts relate to most differential cost decisions.

1. **The only relevant costs or revenues are those expected future costs and revenues that differ across alternatives.** If an alternative leads to increased revenues (costs) as compared to the present method used or other alternative considered, then these revenues (costs) are **relevant** (i.e., a differential cash flow).
2. **All costs incurred in the past (sunk costs) are irrelevant, unless they have future tax ramifications.** Past costs include joint costs, the cost of obsolete inventory, and fixed costs (in the short run).
3. **Opportunity cost, the income obtainable from an alternative use of a resource, must be considered.** If an alternative is profitable and that alternative is rejected in favor of others, the benefits forgone become a "cost" to be evaluated in the decision-making process.

To work a relevant cost problem, you must first identify the type of decision that is involved. Once you have identified the decision, you can determine which costs and revenues are relevant for accepting or rejecting an alternative and in reaching a decision. For example, in a decision to sell at split-off or process further, joint costs are irrelevant and a decision to process further is made if incremental revenue exceeds incremental cost. Finally, a decision is made based on the benefit or loss that would be derived from each alternative.

The table presented below summarizes various differential cost decisions and includes only **quantitative** factors.

Decision	Description	Decision guideline
1. Sell or process further	Should joint products be sold at split-off or processed further?	Ignore joint costs. Process further if incremental revenue exceeds incremental cost.
2. Special order	Should a discount-priced order be accepted when there is idle capacity?	If regular sales are not affected, accept order when the revenue from the order exceeds the incremental cost. Fixed production costs are usually irrelevant—they remain the same no matter what the company does.
3. Outsourcing (make or buy)	Should a part be manufactured or bought from a supplier?	Choose lower cost option. Fixed costs usually are irrelevant. Often opportunity costs are present.

4. Closing a department or segment	Should a segment of the company, such as a product line, be terminated?	Compare existing contribution margin with alternative. Consider any changes in future fixed costs.

Decision	Description	Decision guideline
5. Sale of obsolete inventory	Should obsolete inventory be reworked or junked?	Cost of inventory is sunk and ignored. Choose alternative with greatest excess of future revenue over future cost.
6. Scarce resources	Which products should be emphasized when capacity is limited?	Determine scarce resource (e.g., machine hours). Emphasize products with greatest contribution margin per unit of scarce resource.

Qualitative factors may be equally important in nonroutine decisions. For example, in the outsourcing decision, qualitative factors include

1. Quality of purchased part compared to manufactured part
2. Relationships with suppliers
3. Quickness in obtaining needed parts

Uncertainty also affects decision making. See the probability section at the end of this module for further discussion.

An example of a differential cost decision (special order) is presented below, comparing the simpler, more efficient **incremental** approach with the equally effective but more cumbersome **total** approach. Unless a problem requires the total approach, use of the incremental approach will save valuable exam time.

EXAMPLE

Potts Co. manufactures cookware. Expected annual volume of 100,000 sets per year is well below full capacity of 150,000. Normal selling price is $40/set. Manufacturing cost is $30/set ($20 variable and $10 fixed). Total fixed manufacturing cost is $1,000,000. Selling and administrative expenses are expected to be $500,000 ($300,000 fixed and $200,000 variable). A catalog company offers to buy 25,000 sets for $27/set. No extra selling and administrative costs would be caused by the order, and acceptance will not affect regular sales. Should the offer be accepted?

INCREMENTAL APPROACH

Incremental revenue (25,000 × $27)	$ 675,000
Incremental cost (25,000 × $20)	(500,000)
Benefit of accepting order (contribution margin)	$ 175,000

TOTAL APPROACH

		Without order		With order
Sales (100,000 × $40) less variable costs:		$ 4,000,000	[+(25,000 × $27)]	$ 4,675,000
Manufacturing	(100,000 × $20)	(2,000,000)	[+(25,000 × $20)]	(2,500,000)
Sell. and admin.	(100,000 × $2)	(200,000)		(200,000)
		1,800,000		1,975,000
Contribution margin less fixed costs:				
Manufacturing		$(1,000,000)		(1,000,000)
Sell. and admin.		(300,000)		(300,000)
Operating income		$ 500,000		$ 675,000

At first glance, it may appear that the order should not be accepted because the selling price of $27 is less than the $30 manufacturing cost per set. However, fixed costs do not increase if the order is accepted and are therefore irrelevant to this decision. The result is that, with either the incremental or the total approach, operating income is increased by $175,000. Therefore, Potts Company should accept the order.

NOW REVIEW MULTIPLE-CHOICE QUESTIONS 65 THROUGH 77

KEY TERMS

Activity-based budgeting. A budgeting approach that focuses on the cost of activities required to produce and sell products. It is an extension of activity-based costing.

Avoidable costs. Costs that will **not** continue to be incurred if a department or product is terminated.

Benchmarking. Requires that products, services, and activities be continually measured against the best levels of performance either inside or outside the organization.

Budget. A quantification of the plan for operations. A **flexible budget** is a budget that is adjusted for changes in volume. **Performance reports** compare budgeted and actual performance.

Budgetary slack. The practice of underestimating revenues and overestimating expenses to make budgeted targets more easily achievable.

Committed costs. Arise from a company's basic commitment to open its doors and engage in business (e.g., depreciation, property taxes, management salaries, etc.).

Contribution margin. Equals revenue less **all** variable costs.

Controllable costs. Can be affected by a manager during the current period (e.g., amount of direct manufacturing labor per unit of production is usually under the control of a production supervisor). Uncontrollable costs are those that cannot be affected by the individual in question (e.g., depreciation is not usually controllable by the production supervisor).

Cost management. Refers to the approaches and activities used by management to make planning and control decisions for the firm.

Cost-volume-profit (CVP) analysis. A planning tool used to analyze the effects of changes in volume, sales mix, selling price, variable expense, fixed expense, and profit.

Differential (incremental) cost. The difference in cost between two alternatives.

Discretionary costs. Fixed costs whose level is set by current management decisions (e.g., advertising, research and development, etc.).

Financial planning models. Support the financial planning process by making it easier to construct projected financial scenarios. These models incorporate the interrelationships among operating activities, financial activities, and other factors that affect the business, and range from simple models to those that incorporate hundreds of equations.

Financial budget. The cash budget, the capital budget, the budgeted balance sheet, and the budgeted statement of cash flows.

Fixed costs. Costs that do not vary with the level of activity within the relevant range for a given period of time (usually one year), for example, plant depreciation.

Incremental budgeting. Involves developing budgets that require only justification for increases in the funding over the prior period.

Life-cycle budgeting. Involves estimating the revenues and costs attributable to each product from initial research and development to its final customer and support.

Management by exception. Focuses attention on material deviations from plans (e.g., variances in a performance report) while allowing areas operating as expected to continue to operate without interference.

Master budget. A comprehensive expression of management's operating and financial plans for a future period that is summarized as budgeted financial statements. It consists of the operating and financial budgets.

Mixed costs (semivariable). Costs that have a fixed component and a variable component. These components are separated by using the scattergraph, high-low, or linear regression methods.

Multiple regression. A model that estimates the relationship between a dependent variable and two or more independent variables. It may be used to develop sales forecasts.

Operating budget. The budgeted income statement and related schedules.

Opportunity cost. The maximum income or savings (benefit) forgone by rejecting an alternative.

Outlay (out-of-pocket) costs. The cash disbursement associated with a specific project.

Planning. Involves selecting goals and choosing methods to attain those goals. **Control** is the implementation of the plans and evaluation of their effectiveness in attaining goals.

Relevant costs. Future costs that will change as a result of a specific decision.

Relevant range. The operating range of activity in which cost behavior patterns are valid. Thus, it is the production range for which fixed costs remain constant (e.g., if production doubles, an additional shift of salaried foremen would be added and fixed costs would increase).

Responsibility accounting. Measures subunit performance based on the costs and/or revenues assigned to responsibility centers.

Standard costs. Predetermined target costs.

Sunk, past, or unavoidable costs. Committed costs which are not avoidable and are therefore irrelevant to the decision process.

Tactical profit plan. A defined short-term financial plan that includes assigned responsibilities at all levels.

Target costing. Identifies the estimated cost of a new product that must be achieved for that product to be priced competitively and still produce an acceptable profit. Often the product is redesigned and the production process simplified several times before the target cost can be met.

Transfer pricing. The determination of the price at which goods and services will be "sold" to profit or investment centers via internal company transfers.

Variable costs. Costs that vary proportionately **in total** with the activity level throughout the relevant range (e.g., direct materials).

Variances. Differences between standards and actual results.

Zero-based budgeting. Involves developing budgets from the ground up by requiring each program or department to justify its level of funding.

Multiple-Choice Questions (1–77)

A. Cost-Volume-Profit (CVP) Analysis

1. At the breakeven point, the contribution margin equals total

   a. Variable costs.
   b. Sales revenues.
   c. Selling and administrative costs.
   d. Fixed costs.

2. The **most** likely strategy to reduce the breakeven point would be to

   a. Increase both the fixed costs and the contribution margin.
   b. Decrease both the fixed costs and the contribution margin.
   c. Decrease the fixed costs and increase the contribution margin.
   d. Increase the fixed costs and decrease the contribution margin.

3. Del Co. has fixed costs of $100,000 and breakeven sales of $800,000. What is its projected profit at $1,200,000 sales?

   a. $ 50,000
   b. $150,000
   c. $200,000
   d. $400,000

**4. Associated Supply, Inc. is considering introducing a new product that will require a $250,000 investment of capital. The necessary funds would be raised through a bank loan at an interest rate of 8%. The fixed operating costs associated with the product would be $122,500 while the contribution margin percentage would be 42%. Assuming a selling price of $15 per unit, determine the number of units (rounded to the nearest whole unit) Associated would have to sell to generate earnings before interest and taxes (EBIT) of 32% of the amount of capital invested in the new product.

   a. 35,318 units.
   b. 32,143 units.
   c. 25,575 units.
   d. 23,276 units.

5. During 2013, Thor Lab supplied hospitals with a comprehensive diagnostic kit for $120. At a volume of 80,000 kits, Thor had fixed costs of $1,000,000 and a profit before income taxes of $200,000. Due to an adverse legal decision, Thor's 2014 liability insurance increased by $1,200,000 over 2013. Assuming the volume and other costs are unchanged, what should the 2014 price be if Thor is to make the same $200,000 profit before income taxes?

   a. $120.00
   b. $135.00

   c. $150.00
   d. $240.00

6. Breakeven analysis assumes that over the relevant range

   a. Unit revenues are nonlinear.
   b. Unit variable costs are unchanged.
   c. Total costs are unchanged.
   d. Total fixed costs are nonlinear.

7. Product Cott has sales of $200,000, a contribution margin of 20%, and a margin of safety of $80,000. What is Cott's fixed cost?

   a. $16,000
   b. $24,000
   c. $80,000
   d. $96,000

8. On January 1, 2014, Lake Co. increased its direct manufacturing labor wage rates. All other budgeted costs and revenues were unchanged. How did this increase affect Lake's budgeted breakeven point and budgeted margin of safety?

	Budgeted breakeven point	Budgeted margin of safety
a.	Increase	Increase
b.	Increase	Decrease
c.	Decrease	Decrease
d.	Decrease	Increase

Item 9 is based on the following:

The diagram below is a cost-volume-profit chart.

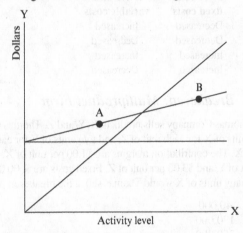

9. At point A compared to point B, as a percentage of sales revenues

	Variable costs are	Fixed costs are
a.	Greater	Greater
b.	Greater	The same
c.	The same	The same
d.	The same	Greater

**CMA adapted

10. Which one of the following is an advantage of using variable costing?

    a. Variable costing complies with the US Internal Revenue Code.

    b. Variable costing complies with generally accepted accounting principles.

    c. Variable costing makes cost-volume relationships more easily apparent.

    d. Variable costing is most relevant to long-run pricing strategies.

11. In the profit-volume chart below, EF and GH represent the profit-volume graphs of a single-product company for 20X1 and 20X2, respectively.

If 20X1 and 20X2 unit sales prices are identical, how did total fixed costs and unit variable costs of 20X2 change compared to 20X1?

	20X2 total fixed costs	20X2 unit variable costs
a.	Decreased	Increased
b.	Decreased	Decreased
c.	Increased	Increased
d.	Increased	Decreased

A.2. Breakeven: Multiproduct Firm

12. Thomas Company sells products X, Y, and Z. Thomas sells three units of X for each unit of Z, and two units of Y for each unit of X. The contribution margins are $1.00 per unit of X, $1.50 per unit of Y, and $3.00 per unit of Z. Fixed costs are $600,000. How many units of X would Thomas sell at the breakeven point?

    a. 40,000

    b. 120,000

    c. 360,000

    d. 400,000

13. In calculating the breakeven point for a multiproduct company, which of the following assumptions are commonly made?

    I. Sales volume equals production volume.

    II. Variable costs are constant per unit.

    III. A given sales mix is maintained for all volume changes.

    a. I and II.

    b. I and III.

    c. II and III.

    d. I, II, and III.

14. In the budgeted profit/volume chart below, EG represents a two-product company's profit path. EH and HG represent the profit paths of products #1 and #2, respectively.

Budget profit/volume chart

Sales prices and cost behavior were as budgeted, actual total sales equaled budgeted sales, and there were no inventories. Actual profit was greater than budgeted profit. Which product had actual sales in excess of budget, and what margin does OE divided by OF represent?

	Product with excess sales	OE/OF
a.	#1	Contribution margin
b.	#1	Gross margin
c.	#2	Contribution margin
d.	#2	Gross margin

B. Financial Planning

15. Which of the following is an output of a financial planning model?

    a. Strategic plan.

    b. Actual financial results.

    c. Projected financial statements.

    d. Variance analysis.

C. Budgeting

16. Mien Co. is budgeting sales of 53,000 units of product Nous for October 2014. The manufacture of one unit of Nous requires four kilos of chemical Loire. During October 2014, Mien plans to reduce the inventory of Loire by 50,000 kilos and increase the finished goods inventory of Nous by 6,000 units. There is no Nous work in process inventory. How many kilos of Loire is Mien budgeting to purchase in October 2014?

    a. 138,000

    b. 162,000

    c. 186,000

    d. 238,000

** CMA adapted

17. The master budget

    a. Shows forecasted and actual results.
    b. Reflects controllable costs only.
    c. Can be used to determine manufacturing cost variances.
    d. Contains the operating budget.

Items 18 and 19 are based on the following information:

Operational budgets are used by a retail company for planning and controlling its business activities. Data regarding the company's monthly sales for the last 6 months of the year and its projected collection patterns are shown below.

    The cost of merchandise averages 40% of its selling price. The company's policy is to maintain an inventory equal to 25% of the next month's forecasted sales. The inventory balance at cost is $80,000 as of June 30.

Forecasted Sales

July	$775,000
August	750,000
September	825,000
October	800,000
November	850,000
December	900,000

Types of Sales

Cash sales	20%
Credit sales	80%

Collection Pattern for Credit Sales

In the month of sale	40%
In the first month following the sale	57%
Uncollectible	3%

*18. The budgeted cost of the company's purchases for the month of August would be

    a. $302,500
    b. $305,000
    c. $307,500
    d. $318,750

*19. The company's total cash receipts from sales and collections on account that would be budgeted for the month of September would be

    a. $757,500
    b. $771,000
    c. $793,800
    d. $856,500

20. Which of the following **best** describes tactical profit plans?

    a. Detailed, short-term, broad responsibilities, qualitative.
    b. Broad, short-term, responsibilities at all levels, quantitative.
    c. Detailed, short-term, responsibilities at all levels, quantitative.
    d. Broad, long-term, broad responsibilities, qualitative.

21. Which of the following budgeting systems focuses on improving operations?

    a. Responsibility budgeting.
    b. Activity-based budgeting.
    c. Operational budgeting.
    d. Kaizen budgeting.

22. Which of the following is included in a firm's financial budget?

    a. Budgeted income statement.
    b. Capital budget.
    c. Production schedule.
    d. Cost of goods sold budget.

23. Rolling Wheels purchases bicycle components in the month prior to assembling them into bicycles. Assembly is scheduled one month prior to budgeted sales. Rolling pays 75% of component costs in the month of purchase and 25% of the costs in the following month. Component cost included in budgeted cost of sales are

April	May	June	July	August
$5,000	$6,000	$7,000	$8,000	$8,000

What is Rolling's budgeted cash payment for components in May?

    a. $5,750
    b. $6,750
    c. $7,750
    d. $8,000

24. A 2014 cash budget is being prepared for the purchase of Toyi, a merchandise item. Budgeted data are

Cost of goods sold for 2014	$300,000
Accounts payable 1/1/14	20,000
Inventory—1/1/14	30,000
12/31/14	42,000

Purchases will be made in twelve equal monthly amounts and paid for in the following month. What is the 2014 budgeted cash payment for purchases of Toyi?

    a. $295,000
    b. $300,000
    c. $306,000
    d. $312,000

25. Trumbull Company budgeted sales on account of $120,000 for July, $211,000 for August, and $198,000 for September. Collection experience indicates that 60% of the budgeted sales will be collected the month after the sale,

---

*CIA adapted
**CMA adapted

36% the second month, and 4% will be uncollectible. The cash from accounts receivable that should be budgeted for September would be

    a. $169,800
    b. $194,760
    c. $197,880
    d. $198,600

26. Cook Co.'s total costs of operating five sales offices last year were $500,000, of which $70,000 represented fixed costs. Cook has determined that total costs are significantly influenced by the number of sales offices operated. Last year's costs and number of sales offices can be used as the bases for predicting annual costs. What would be the budgeted costs for the coming year if Cook were to operate seven sales offices?

    a. $700,000
    b. $672,000
    c. $614,000
    d. $586,000

D. Forecasting Methods

*27. In regression analysis, which of the following correlation coefficients represents the strongest relationship between the independent and dependent variables?

    a. 1.03
    b. −.02
    c. −.89
    d. .75

*28. The internal auditor of a bank has developed a multiple regression model which has been used for a number of years to estimate the amount of interest income from commercial loans. During the current year, the auditor applies the model and discovers that the R^2 value has decreased dramatically, but the model otherwise seems to be working okay. Which of the following conclusions are justified by the change?

    a. Changing to a cross-sectional regression analysis should cause R^2 to increase.
    b. Regression analysis is no longer an appropriate technique to estimate interest income.
    c. Some new factors, not included in the model, are causing interest income to change.
    d. A linear regression analysis would increase the model's reliability.

*29. All of the following are useful for forecasting the needed level of inventory **except:**

    a. Knowledge of the behavior of business cycles.
    b. Internal accounting allocations of costs to different segments of the company.
    c. Information about seasonal variations in demand.
    d. Econometric modeling.

---

*CIA adapted

Items 30 thru 32 are based on the following information:

In preparing the annual profit plan for the coming year, Wilkens Company wants to determine the cost behavior pattern of the maintenance costs. Wilkens has decided to use linear regression by employing the equation $y = a + bx$ for maintenance costs. The prior year's data regarding maintenance hours and costs, and the result of the regression analysis are given below.

Average cost per hour	$9.00
A	684.65
B	7.2884
Standard error of a	49.515
Standard error of b	.12126
Standard error of the estimate	34.469
R^2	.99724

	Hours of activity	Maintenance costs
January	480	$ 4,200
February	320	3,000
March	400	3,600
April	300	2,820
May	500	4,350
June	310	2,960
July	320	3,030
August	520	4,470
September	490	4,260
October	470	4,050
November	350	3,300
December	340	3,160
Sum	4,800	$43,200
Average	400	$ 3,600

*30. In the standard regression equation $y = a + bx$, the letter b is **best** described as a(n)

    a. Independent variable.
    b. Dependent variable.
    c. Constant coefficient.
    d. Variable coefficient.

*31. The letter x in the standard regression equation is best described as a(n)

    a. Independent variable.
    b. Dependent variable.
    c. Constant coefficient.
    d. Coefficient of determination.

*32. Based upon the data derived from the regression analysis, 420 maintenance hours in a month would mean the maintenance costs (rounded to the nearest dollar) would be budgeted at

    a. $3,780
    b. $3,600
    c. $3,790
    d. $3,746

Items 33 thru 36 are based on the following information:

Lackland Ski Resort uses multiple regression to predict ski lift revenue for the next week based on the forecasted number of dates with temperatures above 10 degrees and predicted number of inches of snow. The following function has been developed:

Sales = 10,902 + (255 × no. of days predicted above 10 degrees) + (300 × no. of inches of snow predicted)

Other information generated from the analysis include

Coefficient of determination	
(Adjusted R squared)	.6789
Standard error	1,879
F-Statistic	6.279 with a significance of .049

33. Which variables(s) in this function is (are) the dependent variable(s)?

a. Predicted number of days above 10 degrees.
b. Predicted number of inches of snow.
c. Revenue.
d. Predicted number of days above 10 degrees and predicted number of inches of snow.

34. Assume that management predicts the number of days above 10 degrees for the next week to be 6 and the number of inches of snow to be 12. Calculate the predicted amount of revenue for the next week.

a. $10,902
b. $11,362
c. $16,032
d. $20,547

35. Which of the following represents an accurate interpretation of the results of Lackland's regression analysis?

a. 6.279% of the variation in revenue is explained by the predicted number of days above 10 degrees and the number of inches of snow.
b. The relationships are not significant.
c. Predicted number of days above 10 degrees is a more significant variable than number of inches of snow.
d. 67.89% of the variation in revenue is explained by the predicted number of days above 10 degrees and the number of inches of snow.

36. Assume that Lackland's model predicts revenue for a week to be $13,400. Calculate the 95% confidence interval for the amount of revenue for the week. (The 95% confidence interval corresponds to the area representing 2.3436 deviations from the mean.)

a. $13,400 ± 6,279
b. $13,400 ± 4,404
c. $13,400 ± 6,786
d. $13,400 ± 8,564

37. Which of the following is a quantitative approach used to develop sales forecasts based on analysis of consumer behavior?

a. Markov techniques.
b. Regression analysis.

c. Econometric models.
d. Exponential smoothing.

38. Which of the following is a quantitative approach to developing a sales forecast?

a. Delphi technique.
b. Customer surveys.
c. Moving average.
d. Executive opinions.

**39. A forecasting technique that is a combination of the last forecast and the last observed value is called

a. Delphi.
b. Least squares.
c. Regression.
d. Exponential smoothing.

40. Using regression analysis, Fairfield Co. graphed the following relationship of its cheapest product line's sales with its customers' income levels:

If there is a strong statistical relationship between the sales and customers' income levels, which of the following numbers **best** represents the correlation coefficient for this relationship?

a. −9.00
b. −0.93
c. +0.93
d. +9.00

E.   *Flexible Budgets*

41. The basic difference between a master budget and a flexible budget is that a master budget is

a. Only used before and during the budget period and a flexible budget is only used after the budget period.
b. For an entire production facility and a flexible budget is applicable to single departments only.
c. Based on one specific level of production and a flexible budget can be prepared for any production level within a relevant range.
d. Based on a fixed standard and a flexible budget allows management latitude in meeting goals.

42. A flexible budget is appropriate for a

	Marketing budget	Direct material usage budget
a.	No	No
b.	No	Yes
c.	Yes	Yes
d.	Yes	No

43. When production levels are expected to increase within a relevant range, and a flexible budget is used, what effect would be anticipated with respect to each of the following costs?

	Fixed costs per unit	Variable costs per unit
a.	Decrease	Decrease
b.	No change	No change
c.	No change	Decrease
d.	Decrease	No change

F. Responsibility Accounting

44. Controllable revenue would be included in a performance report for a

	Profit center	Cost center
a.	No	No
b.	No	Yes
c.	Yes	No
d.	Yes	Yes

45. The following is a summarized income statement of Carr Co.'s profit center No. 43 for March 2014:

Contribution margin		$70,000
Period expenses:		
Manager's salary	$20,000	
Facility depreciation	8,000	
Corporate expense allocation	5,000	33,000
Profit center income		$37,000

Which of the following amounts would **most** likely be subject to the control of the profit center's manager?

- a. $70,000
- b. $50,000
- c. $37,000
- d. $33,000

46. Wages earned by machine operators in producing the firm's product should be categorized as

	Direct labor	Controllable by the machine operators' foreman
a.	Yes	Yes
b.	Yes	No
c.	No	Yes
d.	No	No

H. Standards and Variances

47. Companies in what type of industry may use a standard cost system for cost control?

	Mass production industry	Service industry
a.	Yes	Yes
b.	Yes	No
c.	No	No
d.	No	Yes

48. In connection with a standard cost system being developed by Flint Co., the following information is being considered with regard to standard hours allowed for output of one unit of product:

	Hours
Average historical performance for the past three years	1.85
Production level to satisfy average consumer demand over a seasonal time span	1.60
Engineering estimates based on attainable performance	1.50
Engineering estimates based on ideal performance	1.25

To measure controllable production inefficiencies, what is the **best** basis for Flint to use in establishing standard hours allowed?

- a. 1.25
- b. 1.50
- c. 1.60
- d. 1.85

49. Which of the following standard costing variances would be **least** controllable by a production supervisor?

- a. Overhead volume.
- b. Overhead efficiency.
- c. Labor efficiency.
- d. Material usage.

50. The standard direct material cost to produce a unit of Lem is four meters of material at $2.50 per meter. During May 2014, 4,200 meters of material costing $10,080 were purchased and used to produce 1,000 units of Lem. What was the material price variance for May 2014?

- a. $400 favorable.
- b. $420 favorable.
- c. $ 80 unfavorable.
- d. $480 unfavorable.

51. Dahl Co. uses a standard costing system in connection with the manufacture of a "one size fits all" article of clothing. Each unit of finished product contains two yards of direct material. However, a 20% direct material spoilage calculated on input quantities occurs during the manufacturing process. The cost of the direct material is $3 per yard. The standard direct material cost per unit of finished product is

- a. $4.80
- b. $6.00
- c. $7.20
- d. $7.50

52. Carr Co. had an unfavorable materials usage variance of $900. What amounts of this variance should be charged to each department?

	Purchasing	Warehousing	Manufacturing
a.	$0	$0	$900
b.	$0	$900	$0
c.	$300	$300	$300
d.	$900	$0	$0

53. Yola Co. manufactures one product with a standard direct manufacturing labor cost of four hours at $12.00 per hour. During June, 1,000 units were produced using 4,100 hours at $12.20 per hour. The unfavorable direct labor efficiency variance was

    a. $1,220
    b. $1,200
    c. $ 820
    d. $ 400

54. The following direct manufacturing labor information pertains to the manufacture of product Glu:

Time required to make one unit	2 direct labor hours
Number of direct workers	50
Number of productive hours per week, per worker	40
Weekly wages per worker	$500
Workers' benefits treated as direct manufacturing labor costs	20% of wages

What is the standard direct manufacturing labor cost per unit of product Glu?

    a. $30
    b. $24
    c. $15
    d. $12

55. On the diagram below, the line OW represents the standard labor cost at any output volume expressed in direct labor hours. Point S indicates the actual output at standard cost, and Point A indicates the actual hours and actual cost required to produce S.

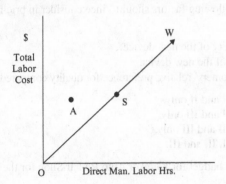

Which of the following variances are favorable or unfavorable?

	Rate variance	Efficiency variance
a.	Favorable	Unfavorable
b.	Favorable	Favorable
c.	Unfavorable	Unfavorable
d.	Unfavorable	Favorable

56. The following were among Gage Co.'s 2014 costs:

Normal spoilage	$ 5,000
Freight out	10,000
Excess of actual manufacturing costs over standard costs	20,000

Standard manufacturing costs	100,000
Actual prime manufacturing costs	80,000

Gage's 2014 actual manufacturing overhead was

    a. $ 40,000
    b. $ 45,000
    c. $ 55,000
    d. $120,000

57. Baby Frames, Inc. evaluates manufacturing overhead in its factory by using variance analysis. The following information applies to the month of May:

	Actual	Budgeted
Number of frames manufactured	19,000	20,000
Variable overhead costs	$4,100	$2 per direct labor hour
Fixed overhead costs	$22,000	$20,000
Direct labor hours	2,100	0.1 hour per frame

What is the fixed overhead spending variance?

    a. $1,000 favorable.
    b. $1,000 unfavorable.
    c. $2,000 favorable.
    d. $2,000 unfavorable.

58. Under the 2-variance method for analyzing overhead, which of the following variances consists of both variable and fixed overhead elements?

	Controllable (budget) variance	Volume variance
a.	Yes	Yes
b.	Yes	No
c.	No	No
d.	No	Yes

59. During 2014, a department's 3-variance overhead standard costing system reported unfavorable spending and volume variances. The activity level selected for allocating overhead to the product was based on 80% of practical capacity. If 100% of practical capacity had been selected instead, how would the reported unfavorable spending and volume variances be affected?

	Spending variance	Volume variance
a.	Increased	Unchanged
b.	Increased	Increased
c.	Unchanged	Increased
d.	Unchanged	Unchanged

60. The following information pertains to Roe Co.'s 2014 manufacturing operations:

Standard direct manufacturing labor hours per unit	2
Actual direct manufacturing labor hours	10,500
Number of units produced	5,000
Standard variable overhead per standard direct manufacturing labor hour	$3
Actual variable overhead	$28,000

Roe's 2014 unfavorable variable overhead efficiency variance was

    a. $0
    b. $1,500
    c. $2,000
    d. $3,500

61. Which of the following variances would be useful in calling attention to a possible short-term problem in the control of overhead costs?

	Spending variance	Volume variance
a.	No	No
b.	No	Yes
c.	Yes	No
d.	Yes	Yes

Items 62 and 63 are based on the following:

The diagram below depicts a factory overhead flexible budget line DB and standard overhead application line OA. Activity is expressed in machine hours with Point V indicating the standard hours required for the actual output in September 2014. Point S indicates the actual machine hours (inputs) and actual costs in September 2014.

62. Are the following overhead variances favorable or unfavorable?

	Volume (capacity) variance	Efficiency variance
a.	Favorable	Favorable
b.	Favorable	Unfavorable
c.	Unfavorable	Favorable
d.	Unfavorable	Unfavorable

63. The budgeted total variable overhead cost for C machine hours is

    a. AB.
    b. BC.
    c. AC minus DO.
    d. BC minus DO.

64. Lanta Restaurant compares monthly operating results with a static budget. When actual sales are less than budget, would Lanta usually report favorable variances on variable food costs and fixed supervisory salaries?

	Variable food costs	Fixed supervisory salaries
a.	Yes	Yes
b.	Yes	No
c.	No	Yes
d.	No	No

I. Product and Service Pricing

65. Cuff Caterers quotes a price of $60 per person for a dinner party. This price includes the 6% sales tax and the 15% service charge. Sales tax is computed on the food plus the service charge. The service charge is computed on the food only. At what amount does Cuff price the food?

    a. $56.40
    b. $51.00
    c. $49.22
    d. $47.40

66. Based on potential sales of 500 units per year, a new product has estimated traceable costs of $990,000. What is the target price to obtain a 15% profit margin on sales?

    a. $2,329
    b. $2,277
    c. $1,980
    d. $1,935

67. Briar Co. signed a government construction contract providing for a formula price of actual cost plus 10%. In addition, Briar was to receive one-half of any savings resulting from the formula price being less than the target price of $2,200,000. Briar's actual costs incurred were $1,920,000. How much should Briar receive from the contract?

    a. $2,060,000
    b. $2,112,000
    c. $2,156,000
    d. $2,200,000

68. Vince, Inc. has developed and patented a new laser disc reading device that will be marketed internationally. Which of the following factors should Vince consider in pricing the device?

    I. Quality of the new device.
    II. Life of the new device.
    III. Customers' relative preference for quality compared to price.

    a. I and II only.
    b. I and III only.
    c. II and III only.
    d. I, II, and III.

69. The budget for Klunker Auto Repair Shop for the year is as follows:

Direct labor per hour	$ 30
Total labor hours	10,000
Overhead costs:	
Materials handling and storage	$ 10,000
Other (rent, utilities, depreciation, insurance)	$120,000
Direct materials cost	$500,000

Klunker allocates materials handling and storage costs per dollar of direct materials cost. Other overhead is allocated based on total labor hours. In addition, Klunker adds a charge of $8 per labor hour to cover profit margin. Tardy Trucking Co. has brought one of its trucks to Klunker for an engine overhaul. If the overhaul requires twelve labor hours and $800 parts, what price should Klunker charge Tardy for these repair services?

a. $1,160
b. $1,256
c. $1,416
d. $1,472

J. Transfer Pricing

70. Ajax Division of Carlyle Corporation produces electric motors, 20% of which are sold to Bradley Division of Carlyle and the remainder to outside customers. Carlyle treats its divisions as profit centers and allows division managers to choose their sources of sale and supply. Corporate policy requires that all interdivisional sales and purchases be recorded at variable cost as a transfer price. Ajax Division's estimated sales and standard cost data for the year ending December 31, 2014, based on the full capacity of 100,000 units, are as follows:

	Bradley	Outsiders
Sales	$ 900,000	$ 8,000,000
Variable costs	(900,000)	(3,600,000)
Fixed costs	(300,000)	(1,200,000)
Gross margin	$(300,000)	$ 3,200,000
Unit sales	20,000	80,000

Ajax has an opportunity to sell the above 20,000 units to an outside customer at a price of $75 per unit during 2013 on a continuing basis. Bradley can purchase its requirements from an outside supplier at a price of $85 per unit.

Assuming that Ajax Division desires to maximize its gross margin, should Ajax take on the new customer and drop its sales to Bradley for 2014, and why?

a. No, because the gross margin of the corporation as a whole would decrease by $200,000.
b. Yes, because Ajax Division's gross margin would increase by $300,000.
c. Yes, because Ajax Division's gross margin would increase by $600,000.
d. No, because Bradley Division's gross margin would decrease by $800,000.

71. The management of James Corporation has decided to implement a transfer pricing system. James' MIS department is currently negotiating a transfer price for its services with the four producing divisions of the company as well as the marketing department. Charges will be assessed based on number of reports (assume that all reports require the same amount of time and resources to produce). The cost to operate the MIS department at its full capacity of 1,000 reports per year is budgeted at $45,000. The user subunits expect to request 250 reports each this year. The cost of temporary labor and additional facilities used to produce reports beyond capacity is budgeted at $48.00 per report. James could purchase the same services from an external Information Services firm for $70,000. What amounts should be used as the ceiling and the floor in determining the negotiated transfer price?

a. Floor, $36.00; Ceiling $56.00.
b. Floor, $45.60; Ceiling $56.00.
c. Floor, $48.00; Ceiling $70.00.
d. Floor, $57.00; Ceiling $82.00.

**72. Systematic evaluation of the trade-offs between product functionality and product cost while still satisfying customer needs is the definition of

a. Activity-based management.
b. Theory of constraints.
c. Total quality management.
d. Value engineering.

73. Which of the following statements regarding transfer pricing is **false**?

a. When idle capacity exists, there is no opportunity cost to producing intermediate products for another division.
b. Market-based transfer prices should be reduced by any costs avoided by selling internally rather than externally.
c. No contribution margin is generated by the transferring division when variable cost-based transfer prices are used.
d. The goal of transfer pricing is to provide segment managers with incentive to maximize the profits of their divisions.

K. Short-Term Differential Cost Analysis

74. Clay Co. has considerable excess manufacturing capacity. A special job order's cost sheet includes the following applied manufacturing overhead costs:

Fixed costs	$21.000
Variable costs	33.000

The fixed costs include a normal $3,700 allocation for in-house design costs, although no in-house design will be done. Instead the job will require the use of external designers costing $7,750. What is the total amount to be included in the calculation to determine the minimum acceptable price for the job?

a. $36,700
b. $40,750
c. $54,000
d. $58,050

75. For the year ended December 31, 2014, Abel Co. incurred direct costs of $500,000 based on a particular course of action during the year. If a different course of action had been taken, direct costs would have been $400,000. In addition, Abel's 2014 fixed costs were $90,000. The incremental cost was

a. $ 10,000
b. $ 90,000
c. $100,000
d. $190,000

76. Mili Co. plans to discontinue a division with a $20,000 contribution margin. Overhead allocated to the division is

$50,000, of which $5,000 cannot be eliminated. The effect of this discontinuance on Mili's pretax income would be an increase of

    a. $ 5,000
    b. $20,000
    c. $25,000
    d. $30,000

77. Following are the operating results of the two segments of Parklin Corporation:

	Segment A	Segment B	Total
Sales	$10,000	$15,000	$25,000
Variable cost of goods sold	4,000	8,500	12,500
Fixed cost of goods sold	1,500	2,500	4,000
Gross margin	4,500	4,000	8,500

Variable selling and administrative	2,000	3,000	5,000
Fixed selling and administrative	1,500	1,500	3,000
Operating income (loss)	$ 1,000	$ (500)	$ 500

Fixed costs of goods sold are allocated to each segment based on the number of employees. Fixed selling and administrative expenses are allocated equally. If Segment B is eliminated, $1,500 of fixed costs of goods sold would be eliminated. Assuming Segment B is closed, the effect on operating income would be

    a. An increase of $500.
    b. An increase of $2,000.
    c. A decrease of $2,000.
    d. A decrease of $2,500.

Multiple-Choice Answers and Explanations

Answers

1.	d __ __	17.	d __ __	33.	c __ __	49.	a __ __	65. c __ __
2.	c __ __	18.	c __ __	34.	c __ __	50.	b __ __	66. a __ __
3.	a __ __	19.	b __ __	35.	d __ __	51.	d __ __	67. c __ __
4.	b __ __	20.	c __ __	36.	b __ __	52.	a __ __	68. d __ __
5.	b __ __	21.	d __ __	37.	a __ __	53.	b __ __	69. c __ __
6.	b __ __	22.	b __ __	38.	c __ __	54.	a __ __	70. c __ __
7.	b __ __	23.	c __ __	39.	d __ __	55.	d __ __	71. b __ __
8.	b __ __	24.	c __ __	40.	b __ __	56.	a __ __	72. d __ __
9.	d __ __	25.	a __ __	41.	c __ __	57.	d __ __	73. d __ __
10.	c __ __	26.	b __ __	42.	c __ __	58.	b __ __	74. b __ __
11.	a __ __	27.	c __ __	43.	d __ __	69.	c __ __	75. c __ __
12.	b __ __	28.	c __ __	44.	c __ __	60.	b __ __	76. c __ __
13.	c __ __	29.	b __ __	45.	a __ __	61.	c __ __	77. c __ __
14.	a __ __	30.	d __ __	46.	a __ __	62.	b __ __	
15.	c __ __	31.	a __ __	47.	a __ __	63.	d __ __	1st: __/77 = __%
16.	c __ __	32.	d __ __	48.	b __ __	64.	b __ __	2nd: __/77 = __%

Explanations

1. **(d)** Any income statement can be expressed as

Sales – Variable costs – Fixed costs = Operating income

At the breakeven point, operating income = $0. In addition, the Contribution margin = Sales – Variable costs. Therefore, the above equation may be restated as

Sales – Variable costs – Fixed costs = 0
Sales – Variable costs = Fixed costs
Contribution margin = Fixed costs

This makes sense because, by definition, the breakeven point is the point at which revenues equal expenses; after variable costs are subtracted from sales, the contribution margin remaining will be just enough to cover fixed costs.

2. **(c)** The short-cut breakeven point formula is calculated as follows:

$$\text{Breakeven (units)} = \frac{\text{Fixed costs}}{\text{Contribution margin}}$$

Thus, by decreasing the numerator (fixed costs) and increasing the denominator (contribution margin), the breakeven point will be reduced.

3. **(a)** The solutions approach is to work backward from breakeven sales to determine the contribution margin (CM) ratio. The CM ratio can then be used to determine Del's projected profit at $1,200,000 sales. This is accomplished by plugging fixed costs and breakeven sales into the breakeven equation.

$$\text{Breakeven sales} = \frac{\text{Fixed costs}}{\text{CM ratio}}$$

$$\$800,000 = \frac{\$100,000}{\text{CM ratio}}$$

$$\text{CM ratio} = 0.125, \text{ or } 12.5\%$$

Therefore, projected total contribution margin from $1,200,000 sales is $150,000 ($1,200,000 × 12.5%), and projected profit is $50,000 ($150,000 CM – $100,000 fixed costs).

4. **(b)** The requirement is to calculate the number of units that must be sold to generate earnings before interest and taxes (EBIT) in an amount equal to 32% of the amount of capital invested. Answer (b) is correct because the number of units is 32,143 as calculated below.

Desired return (EBIT)	=	32% × $250,000 (investment)
	=	$80,000
Required number of units	=	(Fixed costs + desired EBIT)/ Contribution margin
	=	($122,500 + $80,000)/($15 × 42%)
	=	32,143

5. **(b)** The requirement is to determine the price that Thor Lab should charge to make the same profit with increased fixed costs. The first step in solving this problem is to calculate the variable cost per unit. The variable cost component is determined as follows:

Sales	–	VC	–	FC	=	Profit
(80,000 × $120)	–	(80,000x)	–	$1,000,000	=	$200,000
$9,600,000	–	80,000x	–	$1,000,000	=	$200,000
				$8,400,000	=	80,000x
				$105	=	x

The next step is to substitute the variable cost component and the increased fixed cost amount into the above equation to determine the necessary price. The price can be computed as follows:

80,000x – (80,000 × $105) – $2,200,000	=	$	200,000
80,000x	=		$10,800,000
x	=	$	135

6. (b) Breakeven analysis is based on several simplified assumptions. One assumption is that, over the relevant range, variable costs **per unit** remain unchanged. It is assumed that over the relevant range, selling price per unit remains constant. Thus, unit revenues are linear. Total variable costs increase with increases in production; therefore, total costs also increase. Over the relevant range, total fixed costs are always linear since they do not change.

7. (b) The requirement is to determine Cott's fixed cost using only sales, contribution margin, and margin of safety. First, Cott's breakeven sales should be determined. Since the margin of safety defines how far revenues can fall before the breakeven point is reached, breakeven sales equal $120,000 ($200,000 sales – $80,000 margin of safety). We also know that Cott's contribution margin is 20% of sales. Contribution margin (CM) equals sales minus all related variable costs (VC), and the contribution margin percentage is calculated as

$$CM\% = \frac{Total\ CM}{Revenues}$$

Or, in this case,

$$20\% = \frac{Total\ CM}{\$120,000}$$

Total CM at breakeven = ($120,000) (20%) = $24,000

At the breakeven point, no profit exists and Sales – VC = FC. Therefore, the CM at the breakeven point equals fixed costs, and Cott's fixed costs total $24,000.

8. (b) The budgeted breakeven point is the volume at which total revenues equal total expenses. An increase in direct manufacturing labor wage rates would result in higher variable expenses and a lower contribution per unit. Accordingly, this **increases** the volume of sales necessary to breakeven. The budgeted margin of safety is the excess of budgeted total revenues minus total revenues at the breakeven point. As discussed above, the increase in direct manufacturing labor wages increased the breakeven point. This higher breakeven point **decreases** the budgeted margin of safety.

9. (d) To answer this question, an understanding of cost behavior patterns and CVP charts is needed. The CVP chart presented in the problem can be interpreted as follows:

Within a relevant range, **total** variable costs vary directly with the number of units produced and sold. Because these costs remain constant per unit, the variable costs associated with point A and point B will be the same percentage of total sales associated with each point. Total fixed costs remain constant in total at any activity level. Because these costs are allocated evenly to units produced and sold, they represent a higher percentage of lower sales than of higher sales. Point A is to the left of point B, indicating a lower sales level for point A. The fixed costs will, therefore, be a greater percentage of sales at point A than at point B.

10. (c) The requirement is to identify an advantage of using variable costing. Answer (c) is correct because a major advantage of the use of variable costing is that it makes cost-volume relationships more apparent. Answer (a) is incorrect because variable costing does not comply with the US Internal Revenue Code. Answer (b) is incorrect because variable costing does not comply with generally accepted accounting principles. Answer (d) is incorrect because variable costing is not most relevant to long-run pricing strategies. In the long run all costs must be recovered.

11. (a) The profit-volume (P/V) chart provides a quick condensed comparison of how alternatives for pricing, variable costs, and/or fixed costs may affect net income as volume levels change. In this problem, sales prices remain constant and, therefore, are not relevant. In a P/V chart, the vertical (Y) axis represents net income/loss in dollars. The horizontal (X) axis represents volume in units or dollars. Points on the Y axis above the intersection with the X axis represent profits while points below the intersection represent losses. Total fixed costs are represented by the point at which a specific P/V line intersects the Y axis. This point is always below zero on the Y axis. Because point G (where the P/V line for 20X2 intersects the Y axis) is closer to zero than point E (where the P/V line for 20X1 intersects the Y axis), point G is less negative; therefore, total fixed costs decreased from 20X1 levels. The effect of total variable costs on net income is represented by the positive slope of a P/V line. Variable costs stay the same per unit but change in total as volume levels change. Therefore, a higher per unit amount of variable costs causes a lower per unit amount of net income across various volume levels. Because the graph represents changes in levels of totals, a steeper P/V line slope indicates more profit per unit. Because the slope of line GH (the P/V line for 20X2) is **less** steep than the slope of line EF (the P/V line for 20X1), net income per unit is less in 20X2 than in 20X1. Variable costs, therefore, rose between 20X1 and 20X2.

12. (b) The requirement is to determine how many units of product X (one of three products) Thomas would sell at the breakeven point. The solutions approach is first to find the number of composite units to breakeven; a composite unit consists of the number of units of each of the three products in the mix. Since Thomas sells three units of X for each unit of Z and two units of Y for each unit of X, they are selling six units of Y for each unit of Z; therefore, a composite unit consists of 3X, 6Y, and 1Z. The total contribution margin for one composite unit is

$$\begin{array}{lll} \text{X (3) (\$1.00)} & = & \$\,3 \\ \text{Y (6) (\$1.50)} & = & \$\,9 \\ \text{Z (1) (\$3.00)} & = & \underline{\$\,3} \\ & & \$15 \end{array}$$

The breakeven point in terms of units of the product mix group is

$$\$600,000 \div \$15 = 40,000 \text{ composite units}$$

Since there are three units of X in each composite unit, (40,000) (3) or 120,000 units of X are sold at breakeven.

13. (c) Breakeven analysis is based upon several simplified assumptions. Included in these assumptions is that variable costs are constant per unit and, for a multiproduct company, that a given sales mix is maintained for all volume changes. When absorption costing is used, operating income is a function of **both** production volume and sales volume. This is because an increase in inventory levels causes fixed costs to be held in inventory while a decrease in inventory levels causes fixed costs to be charged to cost of goods sold. These fluctuations can dramatically affect income and the breakeven point. On the other hand, when variable costing is used the same amount of fixed costs will be deducted from income whether or not inventory levels fluctuate. As a result, the breakeven point will be the same even if production does not equal sales. Hence, operating income under variable costing is a function **only** of sales, and assumption I. is incorrect.

14. (a) If sales prices, cost behavior, and actual **total** sales were as budgeted, then the excess profit must have resulted from a departure from budget by the **individual** products. Since the slope of line EH is greater than that of line HG (the slope representing profit per unit), Product 1 had the excess sales. Line OE represents fixed costs and line OF represents quantity sold up to the breakeven point. OE/OF is the contribution margin that may offset fixed costs until the breakeven point, F, is reached.

15. (c) The requirement is to identify the item that is an output from a strategic plan. Answer (c) is correct. A financial planning model is a mathematical model that attempts to forecast future financial results. Sets of projected financial statements are a major output from the model. Answer (a) is incorrect because strategic plans drive the financial planning process and must be developed before employing the financial planning model. Answers (b) and (d) are incorrect because the planning model does not provide outputs related to actual results.

16. (c) The requirement is to determine the number of kilos of chemical Loire that Mien is planning to purchase in October. The first step is to prepare a production budget for product Nous.

Sales	53,000
Increase in ending inventory	6,000
Total units needed	59,000

Next, a purchases budget for raw material Loire should be prepared.

Production needs (59,000 × 4)	236,000
Decrease in ending inventory	(50,000)
Total kilos needed	186,000

Note that the production needs for Loire equal the number of units of Nous to be produced times the number of kilos of Loire needed per unit (4).

17. (d) The requirement is to identify a characteristic of the master budget. Answer (d) is correct because the master budget is a comprehensive budget that includes both the operating and financial budgets. Answer (a) is incorrect because the master budget does not show actual results. Answer (b) is incorrect because the master budget shows all costs, controllable and uncontrollable. Answer (c) is incorrect because the master budget is not structured for the computation of variances.

18. (c) The requirement is to calculate the budgeted cost of purchases for the month of August. The cost of inventory needed to meet August forecasted sales is equal to $300,000 ($750,000 × 40%). The required ending inventory for August is equal to $82,500 ($825,000 September sales × 40% × 25%). The ending inventory for July is equal to $75,000 ($750,000 August sales × 40% × 25%). Budgeted cost of purchases for August would equal to $307,500 ($300,000 cost of goods sold + $82,500 required ending inventory – $75,000 beginning inventory). Therefore, answer (c) is correct. Answer (a) is incorrect because the June 30 inventory is deducted. Answer (b) is incorrect because it deducts what should be the ending inventory for June. Answer (d) is incorrect because it results from using sales prices for the beginning and ending inventories.

19. (b) The requirement is to calculate the budgeted amount of cash receipts from sales and collection for September. Forecasted sales for September are $825,000 of which $165,000 (20%) are cash sales. In addition, 40% of credit sales are collected in the month of sale, which is equal to $264,000 ($825,000) × 80% × 40%). Collections of August sales in September are equal to $342,000 ($750,000 × 80% × 57%). Accordingly, the projected collections for September are $771,000 ($165,00 + $264,000 + $342,000), and answer (b) is correct. Answer (a) is incorrect because $757,000 ignores cash sales. Answer (c) is incorrect because $793,800 assumes 57% of October sales are collected in September. Answer (d) is incorrect because $856,500 assumes the collections in September for August sales are 57% of total sales.

20. (c) The requirement is to define a tactical profit plan. Answer (c) is correct because tactical profit plans have the characteristics of being quantified, detailed and short-term, and assigning responsibilities at all levels. Answer (a) is incorrect because tactical profit plans are quantitative with detailed assigned responsibilities. Answer (b) is incorrect because tactical profit plans are detailed. Answer (d) is incorrect because tactical profit plans are detailed, short-term, quantitative, and include assigned responsibilities at all levels.

21. (d) The requirement is to identify the budgeting technique that focuses on improving operations. Answer (d) is correct because Kaizen budgeting projects costs on the basis of improvements to be implemented. Answer (a) is incorrect because responsibility budgeting focuses on the ability of the manager to control the cost. Answer (b) is incorrect because activity-based budgeting uses cost drivers to determine budgeted costs. Answer (c) is incorrect because operational budgeting focuses on budgeting operating costs.

22. (b) The requirement is to identify the item that is part of a financial budget. Answer (b) is correct. The financial budget includes the capital budget, cash budget, and the budgeted statement of cash flows. The operating budget includes the budgeted income statement and supporting budgets. Answers (a), (c), and (d) are incorrect because they are part of the operating budget.

23. (c) Calculation of the cash payments for components in May is shown below.

Payments for June sales	$1,750 ($7,000 × 25%)
Payment for July sales	$6,000 ($8,000 × 75%)
Total cash payments	$7,750

Answer (a) is incorrect because parts are ordered two months prior to sales. Therefore, costs of components for sales of June and July should be considered. Answer (b) is incorrect because parts are ordered two months prior to sales. Therefore, costs of components for sales of June and July should be considered. Answer (d) is incorrect because parts are ordered two months prior to sales. Therefore, costs of components for sales of June and July should be considered.

24. (c) The requirement is to determine budgeted cash disbursements for purchases for 2014. The solutions approach is to use T-accounts to trace the flow of budgeted costs through the accounts.

Inventory			
Bal. 1/1/14	30,000		
Purchases	?	300,000	CGS
Bal. 12/31/14	42,000		

T-account analysis reveals that total purchases of inventory for the year must be $312,000.

Goods sold or on hand at 12/31	−	Beginning inventory	=	Purchases
($300,000 + $42,000)	−	$30,000	=	$312,000

Payments for purchases are made in the month following purchase. Thus, accounts payable at 1/1/14 will be paid in January

2014 and 1/12 of 2014 purchases (since Toyi is purchased in equal amounts each month) will be paid for in January 2014.

Accounts payable is depicted as follows:

	Accounts Payable		
Cash disbursements	306,000*	20,000	Bal. 1/1/14
		312,000	Purchases
		26,000**	Bal. 12/31/14

* ($312,000 purchases × 11/12) + $20,000 beg. AP
** $312,000 purchases × 1/12

Therefore, budgeted cash payments for Toyi for 2014 is $306,000.

25. (a) The requirement is to calculate the budgeted cash from collection of accounts receivable. Answer (a) is correct because the amount is equal to July's collections in September plus August's collections in September. This amount is $169,800 (36% × $120,000 + 60% × $211,000).

26. (b) The requirement is to find the total budgeted costs for the seven stores in the coming year. Fixed costs last year were $70,000, and therefore variable costs totaled $430,000. The key is to find the variable costs per store. This is calculated by dividing variable costs ($430,000) by the number of stores last year (five), or, $86,000. Therefore, total costs budgeted in the new year is calculated as follows:

Variable cost per store	$ 86,000
Number of stores	× 7
Total budgeted variable costs	602,000
Add: fixed costs	70,000
Total budgeted costs	$672,000

27. (c) The requirement is to identify the correlation coefficient that represents the strongest relationship between the independent and dependent variables. Regression coefficients can range from −1.00 (perfect negative correlation to 1.00 (perfect positive correlation, and the closer to −1.00 or 1.00 the stronger the relationship. Answer (c) is correct because it is the coefficient closest to −1.00 or 1.00. Answer (a) is incorrect because it is not possible to have a correlation coefficient greater than 1.00. Answers (b) and (d) are incorrect because they are both further from −1.00 or 1.00.

28. (c) The requirement is to provide an explanation for a drop in R^2. The coefficient of determination (R^2) provides a measure of amount of variation in the dependent variable (interest income) explained by the independent variables. If there is a dramatic decrease in the coefficient of determination, the implication is that there are some new factors that are causing interest income to change. Therefore, answer (c) is correct. Answer (a) is incorrect because cross-sectional regression is not appropriate. Management is attempting to estimate interest income over time. Answer (b) is incorrect because regression analysis may still be appropriate. Answer (d) is incorrect because multiple regression is a linear model. Management may want to try other models such as nonlinear multiple regression.

29. (b) The requirement is to identify the factor that is not relevant to forecasting the needed level of inventory. Answer (b) is correct because knowledge of the internal accounting allocations is not relevant to determining the demand for the product. Answers (a), (c), and (d) are incorrect because they are all relevant to determining demand for the product and, therefore, the needed level of inventory.

30. (d) The requirement is to identify the meaning the of the letter *b* in the regression equation. Answer (d) is correct because *b* is the coefficient for the independent variable. The variable coefficient that describes the slope of the regression function. Answer (a) is incorrect because *x* is the independent variable. Answer (b) is incorrect because *y* is the dependent variable. Answer (c) is incorrect because *a* is the constant coefficient.

31. (a) The requirement is to identify the meaning of the letter *x* in the regression equation. Answer (a) is correct because *x* is the independent variable, the variable that is being used to predict the dependent variable. Answer (b) is incorrect because *y* is the dependent variable. Answer (c) is incorrect because *a* is the constant variable. Answer (d) is incorrect because R^2 is the coefficient of determination.

32. (d) The requirement is to use the regression equation to determine the amount of predicted maintenance costs. Substituting 420 maintenance hours into the equation results in a budgeted cost of $3,746.

$$y = a + bx$$
$$y = 684.65 + 7.2884 (420)$$
$$y = \$3,746$$

Therefore, (d) is the correct answer.

33. (c) The requirement is to identify the dependent variable. Answer (c) is correct because the dependent variable is the one being predicted, in this case revenue. Answers (a), (b), and (d) are incorrect because predicted number of days above 10 degrees and predicted number of inches of snow are both independent variables.

34. (c) The requirement is to calculate the predicted revenue for the next week. Answer (c) is correct because revenue is equal to $10,902 + (255 \times 6) + (300 \times 12) = 16,032$. Answers (a), (b), and (d) are all incorrect computations of the prediction.

35. (d) The requirement is to identify the appropriate conclusion. Answer (d) is correct because the coefficient of determination indicates that 67.89% of revenue is explained by the predicted number of days above 10 degrees and the number of inches of snow. Answer (a) is incorrect because the *F*-Statistic measures the significance of the relationship. Answer (b) is incorrect because the *F*-Statistic indicates that the regression is significant. Answer (c) is incorrect because there is no information provided to make this determination.

36. (b) The requirement is to calculate the 95% confidence interval for the prediction of revenue. Answer (b) is correct because the 95% confidence interval is calculated by multiplying

the standard error of the regression by 2.3436. Therefore, it is equal to 4,404 ($1,879 \times 2.3436$).

37. (a) The requirement is to identify the sales forecasting technique that involves estimating sales based on analysis of consumer behavior. Answer (a) is correct because Markov techniques attempt to forecast consumer purchasing by considering factors such as brand loyalty and brand switching behavior. Answer (b) is incorrect because regression analysis forecasts sales based on the relationship between sales and one or more predictors. Answer (c) is incorrect because econometric models forecast sales based on the relationship between sales and economic data. Answer (d) is incorrect because exponential smoothing is used to forecast sales based on historical data.

38. (c) The requirement is to identify the quantitative technique to developing a sales forecast. Answer (c) is correct because the moving average technique uses the average of sales for the most recent periods to predict next period's sales. Answer (a) is incorrect because the Delphi technique is simply a structured approach to developing a subjective estimate from a group of people. Answers (b) and (d) are incorrect because they involve qualitative approaches to developing a sales forecast.

39. (d) The requirement is to identify the forecasting technique that is determined by a combination of the last forecast and the last observed value. Answer (d) is correct because exponential smoothing is a quantitative technique that forecasts sales based on prior data with the most recent observation being weighted more heavily. Answer (a) is incorrect because the Delphi technique forecasts with a consensus of opinion. Answers (b) and (d) are incorrect because least squares and regression forecast sales based on the correlation of sales with one or more independent variables.

40. (b) The correlation coefficient is a relative measure of the relationship between two variables. The range of the correlation coefficient is from –1 (perfect negative correlation) to +1 (perfect positive correlation). A correlation coefficient of zero means that there is **no** correlation between the two variables. Since the level of sales **increases** as the level of income **decreases,** this relationship represents a strong **negative** correlation. Answer (c) is incorrect because it represents a **positive** correlation. Answers (a) and (d) are incorrect because they lie outside of the range for correlation coefficients.

41. (c) A flexible budget is simply a static budget adjusted for various possible volume levels within the relevant range. A master budget or a flexible budget may be used during both the planning phase, when the budget is prepared, and the controlling phase, when actual results are compared to the budget. A flexible budget may be prepared for any unit for which costs vary with changes in activity level. Flexible budgets provide as much cost control as do master budgets because they are based on costs **allowable** at different activity levels. In fact, flexible budgets may offer an even greater degree of control because valid guidelines are available to managers even if output deviates from expectations, whereas static budgets supply information regarding only the planned volume.

42. (c) The requirement is to determine whether a flexible budget is appropriate for a marketing and/or a direct material usage budget. Flexible budgets are used to analyze changes in costs and revenues as changes in activity levels take place. If no changes are expected to occur and thus all amounts in the flexible budget remain constant throughout the relevant range (i.e., all costs are fixed), there is no need for a flexible budget. A marketing budget includes expenses incurred for promotion and sales. Some of these items, such as sales commissions or sample promotional products change with activity level. Direct material usage is directly dependent on activity level. Since a flexible budget would be appropriate for both a marketing and a direct materials usage budget, answer (c) is correct.

43. (d) Within the relevant range, **total** fixed costs remain constant. As production levels increase, the same amount of fixed cost is spread over a greater number of units, and fixed costs **per unit** decrease. In contrast, variable costs **per unit** do not change within the relevant range.

44. (c) Responsibility accounting allocates to responsibility centers those costs, revenues, and/or assets which a manager can control. If a manager is responsible only for costs, the area of responsibility under his/her control is called a cost center. If the manager is responsible for both revenues and costs, his/her area of control is called a profit center. Thus, controllable revenue pertains to the profit center but not the cost center.

45. (a) A manager of a profit center is responsible for both the revenues and the costs of that center. Costs charged directly to a profit center, excluding fixed costs, are subject to the control of the profit center manager. As a result, the profit center's contribution margin (Sales – All variable costs) is controllable by the center manager. In this case, the manager of Carr Co.'s center No. 43 would be most likely to control the center's contribution margin of $70,000. The period expenses shown in the problem would not be subject to the manager's control and thus are irrelevant items.

46. (a) Direct manufacturing labor costs are labor costs that can be easily traced to the manufacture of a product. Wages earned by machine operators producing a firm's product are, therefore, direct manufacturing labor costs. Controllable costs are those which can be directly influenced by a given manager within a given time span. Wages earned by machine operators are controllable by the machine operators' foreman.

47. (a) Many service firms, nonprofit organizations, and governmental units, in addition to manufacturing firms, use standard cost systems. For example, a trucking company may set standards for fuel costs.

48. (b) Standard costs are predetermined target costs which should be attainable under **efficient** conditions. Currently attainable standards should be achieved under efficient operating conditions. Therefore, engineering estimates based on attainable performance would provide the best basis for Flint in establishing standard hours allowed.

49. (a) The requirement is to determine the standard costing variance which would be **least** controllable by a production supervisor. The overhead output level (volume) variance arises because the **actual** production volume level achieved usually does not coincide with the production level used as a denominator volume for calculating a budgeted overhead **application** rate. The overhead output level variance results from treating a **fixed cost** as if it were a **variable cost**.

Answers (b), (c), and (d) are incorrect because all of these variances arise when the quantity of actual inputs used differs from the quantity of inputs that should have been used. A production manager would have more control over inputs to production than over the determination of the denominator volume.

50. (b) The requirement is to determine Lem's material price variance for May. The direct materials price variance is the difference between actual unit prices and standard unit prices multiplied by the actual quantity, as shown below.

AQ × AP	AQ × SP
$10,080	$10,500
	(4,200m × $2.50/m)

Material price variance, $420F

The $420 price variance is favorable because the actual purchase price of the material was lower than the standard price. Since the material was purchased for only $2.40 per meter ($10,080 cost ÷ 4,200m), Lem saved $.10 per meter compared to the standard price, for a total price savings of $420 (4,200m × $.10/m). Note that the standard quantity of materials is ignored in order to isolate these price differences; differences in quantity are addressed by the materials usage variance.

51. (d) Each unit of finished product contains two yards of direct material. However, the problem states that the 20% direct material spoilage is calculated on the quantity of direct material **input**. Although not mentioned, the facts in this question infer that the spoilage is normal and should be part of the product's standard cost. The solutions approach would be to set up the following formula:

Input quantity	–	Spoilage	=	Output amount
X	–	.2X	=	2 yds.
		.8X	=	2 yds.
		X	=	2.5 yds.

Thus, the standard direct material cost per unit of finished product is $7.50 (2.5 yds. × $3).

52. (a) The materials usage variance measures the **actual** amount of materials **used** versus the standard amount that should have been used given the level of output. Normally the only department with controls over usage of materials is the manufacturing department. The purchasing department normally controls the cost of materials **purchased,** and not the amounts used (materials price variance). The warehouse department has little or no control over the materials used.

53. (b) The solutions approach to compute the direct manufacturing labor efficiency variance is to set up a diagram as follows:

AH × SR	SH × SR
(4,100 × $12)	(4,000 × $12)
$49,200	$48,000

?

Efficiency variance
$1,200 unfavorable

NOTE: To compute the Standard Hours (SH), multiply the Standard Hours allowed per unit produced (4) by the number of units produced (1,000).

54. (a) Standard costs are predetermined target costs which should be attainable under efficient conditions. The standard direct manufacturing labor cost per unit of product Glu is calculated as follows:

Weekly wages per worker	$500
Benefits treated as DML cost	100
Total DML per week per worker	$600
Hours per week	÷ 40
DML cost per hour	$ 15
Hours required for each unit	× 2
Standard DML cost per unit	$ 30

55. (d) A labor rate variance is the difference between budgeted wage rates and the wage rates actually paid. The problem states that line OW represents the standard labor cost at any output volume. Because point A is **above** the line, the actual cost was higher than the standard. The rate variance is, therefore, unfavorable. A labor efficiency variance is the difference between actual hours worked and standard hours allowed for output. On the diagram, point S is further on the X axis (Direct manufacturing labor hours) than point A indicating that the standard hours allowed are higher than the actual hours worked. Because actual hours are less than standard hours, this variance would be favorable.

56. (a) To determine Gage's actual manufacturing overhead from the information given, total actual manufacturing costs must first be computed.

Standard manufacturing cost	$100,000
Excess of actual manufacturing cost over standard costs	20,000
Total actual costs	$120,000

Since prime costs consist of direct materials and direct manufacturing labor, these costs are deducted from total actual costs to derive the portion that are overhead costs. Ordinarily, normal spoilage is not added to actual manufacturing overhead. The cost of normal spoilage should be added to the cost of good units produced. Freight out is also excluded because it is a selling expense.

Total actual costs	$120,000
Prime costs	(80,000)
Actual manufacturing overhead	$ 40,000

57. (d) The fixed overhead spending variance is calculated as follows:

Budgeted fixed overhead	$20,000
Actual fixed overhead	22,000
Unfavorable fixed overhead spending variance	$ 2,000

58. (b) The requirement is to determine which of the variances given consist of both variable and fixed overhead elements under a two-variance method. As shown in the diagram below, the controllable or budget variance includes both variable and fixed overhead elements, because the actual overhead amount, the first vertical line, includes both elements as does the budgeted overhead amount, the middle vertical line.

	Budget for outputs achieved	Applied
Actual	FOH + (SQ × SVR)	SQ × STR*
	Budget var.	Volume var.

* STR = Standard variable rate (SVR) + Standard fixed rate (SFR)

The output level (volume) variance includes only the variance of fixed overhead, because the SQ × SVR is common to both amounts (i.e., it is included in the STR) used to determine the output level variance. The difference in the two amounts is the output level variance. It arises because the middle vertical line includes the total amount of budgeted fixed overhead, whereas the third vertical line includes the amount of fixed overhead applied using a per unit amount based on normal volume or level of activity. Whenever the standard activity level based on good output (SQ) is different than the normal activity level, a volume variance will arise. Therefore, both variable and fixed overhead elements are included in the controllable variance but not in the output level variance.

59. (c) The requirement is to determine how unfavorable spending and output level (volume) variances computed using the three-variance method would be affected if the estimated activity level were increased. An increase in the activity level used to allocate overhead to the product will lower the standard fixed application rate (SFR). The formula for computing the SFR is

$$\text{Predetermined overhead rate} = \frac{\text{Estimated fixed overhead cost}}{\text{Estimated activity level}}$$

If the denominator in this formula is raised, the SFR is lowered. However, an increase in activity level used to allocate overhead will not affect the standard variable application rate (SVR). This rate is computed using the high-low method or regression analysis. The diagram for the 3-variance method is

	Budget for actual inputs	Budget for outputs achieved	Applied
Actual	FOH + (AQ × SVR)	FOH + (SQ × SVR)	(SQ × STR)*
	Spending var.	Efficiency var.	Output level var.

:————————Net (overall) overhead variance————————:

* STR = Standard variable rate (SVR) + Standard fixed rate (SFR)

When computing the standard variance, the SVR is used but the SFR is not. Therefore, this variance will not change with a change in activity level. The output level variance is computed by comparing the budgeted amount of total overhead costs for outputs achieved with the total amount of overhead applied.

Both computations use SVR, but only the applied figure uses the SFR. In this problem, the output level variance is unfavorable indicating that the budgeted amount is more than the applied amount. When the SFR is lowered with the increase in activity level, less cost will be applied for every unit produced. The output level variance will therefore be increased and become more unfavorable.

60. (b) The solutions approach to compute the variable overhead efficiency variance is to set up a diagram as follows:

AH × SR   SH × SR
(10,500 × $3)   ((2 × 5,000) × $3)
$31,500 $30,000
              ?

Variable overhead efficiency variance
$1,500 unfavorable

61. (c) A spending variance is caused by differences between the actual amount spent on fixed and variable overhead items and the amounts budgeted based on actual inputs. An output level variance is the difference between budgeted fixed overhead and applied fixed overhead. It is caused by under- or overutilization of plant capacity. Differences between actual and budgeted amounts (spending variances) occur often and can be corrected by changing the accounting estimates used in the budgeting process or the purchasing policies used. A difference in under- or over-utilization of plant capacity is a complex problem not easily corrected. Spending variances indicate short-term problems dealing with amounts spent on overhead while output level variances indicate long-term problems dealing with plant capacity.

62. (b) The output level variance is solely a **fixed** overhead variance and is caused by under-/overutilization of capacity. This variance is computed by comparing the amount of fixed overhead budgeted with the amount of fixed overhead applied.

On the graph, line DB represents the flexible budget line for various outputs achieved and line OA represents the standard application line for various outputs achieved. Point V represents the standard quantity allowed for the output achieved. The dashed line extended vertically from V indicates the amount of overhead applied (where dashed line crosses OA) and the flexible budget amount (where dashed line crosses DB). Because the point on DB is below the point on OA, a larger amount was applied than the flexible budget amount. The output level variance is, therefore, favorable.

An overhead efficiency variance is solely a **variable** overhead variance and is caused by more (less) variable overhead being incurred due to inefficient (efficient) use of inputs. This variance is computed by comparing the flexible budget amount for actual inputs (Actual quantity of inputs × Standard variable application rate) with the amount applied (Standard quantity allowed for achieved output × Standard variable application rate). On the graph, Point S indicates the actual hours (inputs) used. Point V indicates the standard quantity allowed for the achieved outputs. Point S falls on the X axis further from zero than does Point V. Therefore, more hours were actually used than budgeted for the output achieved. The efficiency variance is unfavorable.

63. (d) On the graph, line DB represents the total factory overhead flexible budget line for various outputs achieved. Point D (the Y intercept) indicates the amount of fixed overhead included in the flexible budget. Line BC represents the total flexible budget amount estimated for the level of inputs used at Point C. Budgeted total variable overhead cost for C machine hours is total overhead budget (BC) less fixed overhead budgeted (DO).

64. (b) The requirement is to determine if favorable variances for variable food costs and fixed supervisory salaries would be reported by comparing actual results to amounts in a static budget. A static budget has only one planned volume level. The budget is not adjusted or altered to reflect changes in volume or other conditions during the budget period. In this problem, the actual level of sales was lower than the level used to make the static budget. Because variable costs remain the same per unit but change with levels of activity within the relevant range, actual variable costs would be lower than those in the budget. The variance reported for these costs would therefore be favorable. Fixed costs, however, are assumed to remain the same in total at all activity levels within the relevant range unless a change is specifically indicated. Because no such change is indicated in this problem concerning the fixed supervisory salaries, the actual amount for this cost would be the same as the amount in the static budget. There would be no variance reported for this fixed cost.

65. (c) The solutions approach is to algebraically reconstruct how Cuff Caterers determined the total price per person. Three components comprise the total price: the cost of the food, the service charge, and the sales tax. The 15% service charge is computed on the food (F) only. The 6% sales tax is computed on the food plus the service charge. The following equation is used to compute the price:

$$F + .15F + .06 (F + .15F) = \$60.00$$

Where

$$F = \text{the cost of the food alone}$$
$$.15F = \text{the service charge}$$
$$.06 (F + .15F) = \text{the sales tax}$$

Solving algebraically

$$1.219F = \$60.00$$
$$F = \$49.22$$

66. (a) The target price is to be set at a budgeted ratio of operating income to revenue, or a profit margin on sales of 15%. This problem may be solved using the following equation:

$$\text{Let } x = \text{Target price}$$
$$\text{Revenue} - \text{Cost} = \text{Profit}$$
$$500x - \$990,000 = .15(500x)$$
$$.85(500x) = \$990,000$$
$$425x = \$990,000$$
$$x = \$2,329$$

67. (c) The requirement is to determine the amount that Briar should receive from the contract. This amount can be computed as follows:

Actual costs incurred $1,920,000
Multiply by 110% (cost + 10%) × 1.10
Formula price $2,112,000

The target price of $2,200,000 exceeds the formula price of $2,112,000 by $88,000. Briar is to receive 50% of this amount, or $44,000, in addition to the formula price. Therefore, Briar is to receive a total of $2,156,000 ($2,112,000 + $44,000).

68. (d) To determine the price at which expected product sales will yield the greatest profits, many factors such as customer preferences, competitors' reactions, cost structures, etc. must be considered. A customer's perception of the quality and durability (life) of a product affects how much s/he is willing to pay for that product. However, in some cases a customer may prefer to pay less money and receive a product of lesser quality. Therefore, Vince should consider the quality and life of the new device as well as customers' relative preference for quality compared to price.

69. (c) Klunker is using a "time and material" pricing approach. The charges for each are calculated below.

$$\text{Time: } \frac{\text{Labor}}{\text{cost per}} + \frac{\text{Other overhead}}{\text{Total labor hours}} + \frac{\text{Profit}}{\text{margin}}$$
$$\text{hour} \qquad\qquad\qquad\qquad \text{per hour}$$

$$\$30 + \frac{\$120,000}{10,000} + \$8 = \$50 \text{ per labor hour}$$

$$\text{Materials} \left(\begin{array}{c}\text{Materials} \\ \text{cost for job}\end{array}\right) + \left(\begin{array}{c}\text{Materials} \\ \text{cost of job}\end{array} \times \dfrac{\begin{array}{c}\text{Materials} \\ \text{Handling \& Storage}\end{array}}{\begin{array}{c}\text{Total materials} \\ \text{cost for year}\end{array}}\right)$$

$$\$800 + \left(\$800 \times \frac{\$10,0000}{\$500,000}\right) = \$816$$

The total price for the overhaul should therefore be $1,416 [($50/hr. × 12 hrs) + $816)]. Note that materials handling and storage costs are allocated at $0.02 per dollar of materials, and other overhead is allocated at $12 per labor hour.

70. (c) The requirement is to determine whether Ajax should take on a new customer and end its sales to the Bradley division and why. As a profit center, Ajax will make the decision independent of the effects on the corporation as a whole. If Ajax sells to the new customer, its revenues will increase to $1,500,000 ($75 × 20,000), but its costs will remain the same at $1,200,000 ($900,000 + $300,000). This results in a positive gross margin of $300,000 ($1,500,000 – $1,200,000). The new gross margin is $600,000 [$300,000 – (–$300,000)] greater than the original gross margin. The shortcut (incremental) approach is to multiply 20,000 units times the $30 increase ($75 – $45) in Ajax's unit selling (transfer) price.

71. (b) Negotiated transfer prices should fall within a range limited by a ceiling and a floor. The ceiling is the lowest market price that could be obtained from an external supplier, and the floor equals the outlay costs plus opportunity cost of the transferring division. Since James' MIS department does not have to option to sell services to external customers, its opportunity cost is $0. Since all costs of service departments must be covered by the revenue-producing departments, the MIS department's outlay cost equals its total costs. The

department's full capacity level is 1,000 reports per year. However, the user departments will be requesting 1,250 reports (5 user subunits × 250 reports each). Thus, the MIS department will incur costs of $12,000 [$48 × (1,250 – 1,000)] for the 250 reports above capacity, in addition to the $45,000 budgeted costs for full capacity. The total cost of $57,000 ($45,000 + $12,000) is used to calculate the floor. The ceiling is based on the $70,000 that would be incurred to purchase MIS services externally. Since the MIS department will be producing 1,250 reports, the floor is $45.60 ($57,000 ÷ 1,250), and the ceiling is $56.00 ($70,000 ÷ 1,250). At full capacity, any differential costs of additional production are added to the floor. $48.00 represents only the differential cost of producing each report above full capacity, not cost per report for total production. Budgeted costs are based on production of 1,250 reports, not 1,000.

72. (d) The requirement is to identify the process that involves a systematic evaluation of the trade-offs between product functionality and product cost while still satisfying customer needs. Answer (d) is correct because this process is defined as value engineering. Answer (a) is incorrect because activity-based management is a system that strives for excellence through cost reduction, process improvement, and productivity gains. Answer (b) is incorrect because the theory of constraints refers to methods to maximize operating income when faced with some bottleneck operations. Answer (c) is incorrect because total quality management involves the application of quality principles to all company activities.

73. (d) The goal of transfer pricing is to encourage managers to make transfer decisions which maximize profits of the company as a **whole**. Some transfers may not be profitable to a particular division, but would effect a cost savings to the company by avoiding costs of purchasing externally. For example, when a division is already operating at full capacity and uses variable cost transfer prices, additional production for internal transfer would result in a loss for the transferring division because no contribution margin is earned to cover the differential fixed costs incurred. Conversely, internal production may be cheaper to the corporate entity than purchasing the product, in which case the division should accept the order. However, the division manager is likely to engage in suboptimization by rejecting the order to enhance the division's performance, while adversely affecting overall company performance.

74. (b) When determining a price for a special order when there is idle capacity, only the differential manufacturing costs are considered. The underlying assumption is that acceptance of the order will not affect regular sales. In the short run, fixed costs are sunk costs and are irrelevant. Since regular sales will not be affected by the special order, fixed and variable costs incurred during normal operations are not considered. Clay Company should consider only the variable costs associated with the order and the differential cost of using the external designers. The costs to be considered total $40,750 ($33,000 + $7,750). The order is accepted if revenue from the order exceeds the differential costs.

75. (c) When deciding between alternatives, the only relevant costs or revenues are those expected future costs and revenues that differ across alternatives. In the short run, fixed costs are sunk costs and are irrelevant. Thus, Abel's 2014 fixed costs are ignored for purposes of short-term differential cost analysis. The incremental cost was $100,000 ($500,000 − $400,000).

76. (c) The requirement is to evaluate the effect on pretax profit if a department is discontinued. The solutions approach is to isolate those revenues and costs that would differ if the department is discontinued. If the department is discontinued, $20,000 of contribution margin would be lost. The $5,000 of allocated overhead will continue regardless of the decision made. Thus, $45,000 ($50,000 − $5,000) of allocated overhead

cost would be eliminated or avoided. The net effect on pretax profit would be an increase of $25,000 ($45,000 of cost avoided less $20,000 of contribution margin lost).

77. (c) The requirement is to determine the effect on operating income of closing Segment B. Answer (c) is correct because if Segment B is closed overall sales will be reduced by $15,000, variable costs of goods sold will be reduced by $8,500, fixed costs of goods sold will be reduced by $1,500, and variable selling and administrative expenses will be reduced by $3,000, resulting in a $2,000 ($15,000 − 8,500 − 1,500 − 3,000) decrease in operating income.

Written Communication Task

Written Communication Task 1

Written
Communication

Help

Tom Miller, the controller of Winston Corporation, is considering establishing a responsibility accounting system for the corporation. Tom would like you to prepare a memorandum describing a responsibility accounting system and its advantages over a typical budgeting and reporting systems.

REMINDER: Your response will be graded for both technical content and writing skills. Technical content will be evaluated for information that is helpful to the intended user and clearly relevant to the issue. Writing skills will be evaluated for development, organization, and the appropriate expression of ideas in professional correspondence. Use a standard business memorandum or letter format with a clear beginning, middle, and end. Do not convey the information in the form of a table, bullet point list, or other abbreviated presentation.

To: Mr. Tom Miller, Controller
         Winston Corporation
From: CPA Candidate

Written Communication Task Solution

Written Communication Task 1

Written Communication	
	Help

To: Mr. Tom Miller, Controller
            Winston Corporation
From: CPA Candidate

As we discussed, Winston Corporation is considering implementing a responsibility accounting system. A responsibility accounting system is one that evaluates center managers based on reports that include only revenues and costs that a particular manager can control. If the manager is responsible for both revenues and costs, the center is referred to as a profit center. A cost center is one in which the manager is only responsible for costs.

The primary advantage of a responsibility accounting system is that managers are rewarded based on factors that are within their control, creating a direct relationship between their performance and their performance evaluation. When being evaluated with a responsibility accounting system, managers are not frustrated by receiving performance evaluations that are influenced significantly by external factors. Also they are not rewarded for performance that results from factors outside of their control. Therefore, from a management evaluation standpoint, a responsibility accounting system has a significant advantage over traditional accounting systems.

If you need any additional information about such systems, please contact me.

APPENDICES

The following appendices provide you with additional practice for the exam.

Appendix A: Business Environment and Concepts Sample Examination

Testlet 1

1. Which of the following is **not** a component of internal control as set forth by the COSO internal control framework?

    a. Control environment.
    b. Control activities.
    c. Risk assessment.
    d. Segregation of duties.

2. Which of the following is **not** a monitoring device for effective corporate governance?

    a. The audit committee.
    b. The chief financial officer.
    c. The SEC.
    d. External auditors.

3. Which of the following is a compensation system that may result in shirking on the part of management?

    a. A fixed salary.
    b. A fixed salary plus a bonus based on accounting income.
    c. A fixed salary plus stock options.
    d. A fixed salary plus stock grants.

4. Effective enterprise risk management will provide the following benefits for a company **except:**

    a. Fewer financial surprises.
    b. Ability to seize opportunities.
    c. Avoidance of all significant risks.
    d. Alignment of risk with risk appetite.

5. Which of the following is **not** an appropriate response to an identified enterprise risk?

    a. Acceptance.
    b. Avoidance.
    c. Sharing.
    d. Assessing.

6. Which of the following is a part of the central processing unit?

    a. Analog translator converter.
    b. Arithmetic/logic unit.
    c. Optical disk.
    d. Printer unit.

7. A data model developed specifically for use in designing accounting information databases is

    a. REA data model.
    b. Data definition language.
    c. Entity-relationship model.
    d. Networked model.

8. The type of system **most** likely to be used to initially record the daily processing of transactions is

    a. Transaction processing system.
    b. Management information system.
    c. Decision support system.
    d. Executive information system.

9. Which of the following is correct concerning the Internet?

    a. All communications are processed using URL— Uniform Resource Language.
    b. It is composed of an international collection of networks of independently owned computers.
    c. It requires the use of viruses, which invariably escape their proper primary use and infect user computers.
    d. The operating center of the Internet is headquartered in the New York World Wide Web Center.

10. A method to originally capture data to multiple magnetic disks is referred to as

    a. Analog approach.
    b. Parallel magnetic drums.
    c. RAID.
    d. Zip drive approach.

11. A system that stores transactions in a single database, but processes them at various sites is referred to as

    a. Centralized system.
    b. Database management normalization system.
    c. Decentralized system.
    d. Distributed system.

Items 12 and 13 are based on the following information:

Total production costs of prior periods for a company are listed below. Assume that the same cost behavior patterns can be extended linearly over the range of 3,000 to 35,000 units and that the cost driver for each cost is the number of units produced.

Production in units per month	3,000	9,000	16,000	35,000
Cost X	$23,700	$52,680	$86,490	$178,260
Cost Y	47,280	141,840	252,160	551,600

12. What is the average cost per unit at a production level of 8,000 units for cost X?

    a. $5.98
    b. $5.85
    c. $7.90
    d. $4.83

13. Identify the cost curve for the average cost per unit for cost Y.

Curve 1   Curve 2

Quantity   Quantity

Curve 3   Curve 4

Quantity   Quantity

   a. Curve 1.
   b. Curve 2.
   c. Curve 3.
   d. Curve 4.

14. Layton Co. has an average accounts payable balance of $850,000 and its cost of goods sold for the year is $8,750,000. Using a 365-day year, calculate the firm's payables deferral period.

   a. 25.50 days.
   b. 30.50 days.
   c. 35.46 days.
   d. 42.33 days.

15. A strategy map in the balanced scorecard framework is

   a. A statement of what the strategy must achieve and what is critical to its success.
   b. Key action programs required to achieve strategic objectives.
   c. Diagrams of the cause-and-effect relationships between strategic objectives.
   d. The level of performance or rate of improvement needed in the performance measure.

Items 16 and 17 are based on the following information:

The following are selected data for Lenley Manufacturing Company for the year ended 20X1.

Sales	$30,000,000
Average invested capital (total assets)	10,000,000
Total fixed assets	6,000,000
Net income	3,000,000
Net cash flow	5,000,000
Imputed interest rate	10%

16. Which of the following measures the return on investments for Lenley Manufacturing Company for the year?

   a. 2%
   b. 8%
   c. 10%
   d. 30%

17. Which of the following measures residual income for Lenley Manufacturing Company for the year?

   a. $1,000,000
   b. $2,000,000
   c. $3,000,000
   d. $6,000,000

18. Which type of economic market structure is characterized by many firms selling a differentiated product with no significant barriers to entry?

   a. Monopoly.
   b. Oligopoly.
   c. Perfect competition.
   d. Monopolistic competition.

Items 19 and 20 are based on the following information:

The operating results in summarized form for a retail computer store for 2008 are

Revenue:	
Hardware sales	$4,800,000
Software sales	2,000,000
Maintenance contracts	1,200,00
Total revenue	$8,000,000
Costs and expenses	
Cost of hardware sales	$3,360,000
Cost of software sales	1,200,000
Marketing expenses	600,000
Customer maintenance costs	640,000
Administrative expenses	1,120,000
Total costs and expenses	$6,920,000
Operating income	$1,080,000

The computer store is in the process of formulating its operating budget for 2009 and has made the following assumptions:

- The selling prices of hardware are expected to increase 10% but there will be no selling price increases for software and maintenance contracts.
- Hardware unit sales are expected to increase 5% with a corresponding 5% growth in the number of maintenance contracts; growth in unit software sales is estimated at 8%.
- The cost of hardware and software is expected to increase 4%.
- Marketing expenses will be increased 5% in the coming year.
- Three technicians will be added to the customer maintenance operations in the coming year, increasing the customer maintenance costs by $120,000.
- Administrative costs will be held at the same level.

19. The retail computer store's budgeted total revenue for 2009 would be

   a. $8,804,000
   b. $8,460,000
   c. $8,904,000
   d. $8,964,000

20. The retail computer store's budgeted total costs and expenses for the coming year would be

a. $7,252,400
b. $7,526,960
c. $7,558,960
d. $7,893,872

21. The marginal cost of capital (MCC) curve for a company rises twice, first when the company has raised $75 million and again when $175 million of new funds have been raised. These increases in the MCC are caused by

a. Increases in the returns on the additional investments undertaken.
b. Decreases in the returns on the additional investments undertaken.
c. Decreases in the cost of at least one of the financing sources.
d. Increases in the cost of at least one of the financing sources.

22. Inventory turnover is calculated as follows:

a. $$\frac{\text{Net sales}}{\text{Year-end inventory}}$$

b. $$\frac{\text{Year-end inventory}}{\text{Net sales}}$$

c. $$\frac{\text{Cost of goods sold}}{\text{Average inventory}}$$

d. $$\frac{\text{Net sales}}{\text{Average inventory}}$$

23. Which one of the following is **not** a determinant in valuing a call option?

a. Exercise price.
b. Expiration date.
c. Forward contract price.
d. Interest rate.

24. A company obtaining short-term financing with trade credit will pay a higher percentage financing cost, everything else being equal, when

a. The discount percentage is lower.
b. The items purchased have a higher price.
c. The items purchased have a lower price.
d. The supplier offers a longer discount period.

Hints for Testlet 1

1. No trick here.

2. Top management is monitored by corporate governance devices.

3. Management shirking is caused by a lack of incentives.

4. Companies must accept some risk.

5. No trick here.

6. Think of the type of processing the computer itself often performs.

7. One of these is less familiar terminology in general IT, but more familiar in the area of accounting information systems.

8. Nothing difficult here; "transactions" is the key.

9. Most of these replies are nonsense.

10. RAID means redundant array of independent (previously, inexpensive) disks.

11. Two of the replies would suggest various sites. One of those ordinarily includes a single database.

12. Cost X is a mixed cost.

13. Use the high-low method.

14. Deferral period is equal to payables divided by cost of goods sold per day.

15. Strategy maps associate strategies with measures.

16. ROI is equal to operating income divided by total fixed assets.

17. RI is equal to operating income minus a charge for the cost of capital.

18. No tricks here.

19. Be sure to consider all the changes in the variables.

20. Be sure to consider all the changes in the variables.

21. The marginal cost of capital is the weighted-average of the costs of different financing sources.

22. Inventory turnover is equal to cost of goods sold divided by average inventory.

23. Value is based on price, time, and interest rate.

24. Recall the formula for trade credit interest rate.

Answers to Testlet 1

1.	d	**5.**	d	**9.**	b	**13.**	d	**17.**	b	**21.**	d
2.	b	**6.**	b	**10.**	c	**14.**	c	**18.**	d	**22.**	c
3.	a	**7.**	a	**11.**	d	**15.**	c	**19.**	d	**23.**	c
4.	c	**8.**	a	**12.**	a	**16.**	d	**20.**	b	**24.**	d

Explanations to Testlet 1

1. **(d)** Segregation of duties is **not** a separate component of internal control. It is an aspect of control activities.

2. **(b)** The chief financial officer is **not** a monitoring device for corporate governance. Monitoring devices control top management of the firm.

3. **(a)** A fixed salary provides no incentive for management to take risks which may lead to significant profits.

4. **(c)** Businesses must assume some risk to achieve returns.

5. **(d)** Risk assessing is the step before deciding on the risk response.

6. **(b)** The central processing unit is made up of an arithmetic/logic unit, primary memory, and a control unit.

7. **(a)** An REA data model is designed for use in designing accounting information databases.

8. **(a)** A transaction processing system is used to process transactions.

9. **(b)** The internet is an international collection of networks made up of independently owned computers.

10. **(c)** RAID (redundant array of independent disks) is a way of storing the same data redundantly on multiple magnetic disks.

11. **(d)** In a distributed system, transactions for a single database are processed at various sites.

12. **(a)** Using the high-low method: ($178,260 – 23,700)/ (35,000 – 3,000) = $4.83 variable cost. Fixed cost equals $23,700 – (3,000 × 4.83) = $9,210. Fixed cost per unit at 8,000 units is $1.15 (9,210/8,000). Average cost per unit is equal to $5.98 ($4.83 + $1.15).

13. **(d)** The average cost is constant because there are no fixed costs.

14. **(c)** The payables deferral period is equal to 35.46 [$850,000/($8,750,000/365)].

15. **(c)** Strategy maps are diagrams of the cause-and-effect relationships between strategic objectives.

16. **(d)** Return on investments is equal to 30% ($3,000,000 net income / $10,000,000 average investment).

17. **(b)** Residual income is equal to $2,000,000 [$3,000,000 net income – ($10,000,000 invested capital × 10% imputed interest rate)].

18. **(d)** Monopolistic competition is characterized by many firms selling a differentiated product with no significant barriers to entry.

19. **(d)** Budgeted revenue is equal to $8,964,000 [($4,800,000 × 1.05 × 1.10) + ($2,000,000 × 1.08) + ($1,200,000 × 1.05)].

20. **(b)** Budgeted total costs and expenses is equal to $7,526,960 [($3,360,000 × 1.05 (increase in unit sales) × 1.04 (increase in cost)] + [$1,200,000 × 1.08 (increase in unit sales) × 1.04 (increase in cost)] + [($600,000 × 1.05) + ($640,000 + $120,000) + $1,120,000].

21. **(d)** An increase in the cost of a financing source increases the marginal cost of capital.

22. **(c)** Inventory turnover is calculated as cost of goods sold divided by average inventory.

23. **(c)** A call option is valued by using the exercise price, the exercise date, and the interest rate.

24. **(d)** The cost of trade credit is measured by the [discount percent/(100% – discount percent) × 365 days/(total pay period – discount period)]. Therefore, if the discount period is increased, the interest rate increases.

Testlet 2

1. The component of COSO's Framework for internal control that deals with ensuring that employees have timely information to make decisions is referred to as

   a. The control environment.
   b. Information and communication.
   c. Knowledge management.
   d. Business knowledge.

2. Proper segregation of duties for control purposes involves segregation of authorization, approval, execution, and

   a. Custody of assets.
   b. Recordkeeping.
   c. Budgeting.
   d. Review.

3. A framework for enterprise risk management was developed by

   a. The American Institute of CPAs (AICPA).
   b. The Committee of Sponsoring Organizations (COSO).
   c. The Governmental Accountability Office (GAO).
   d. The Securities and Exchange Commission (SEC).

4. In project management, a technique that involves classifying tasks into categories based on how urgent they are is referred to as

   a. ABC Analysis.
   b. Project crashing.
   c. Critical path analysis.
   d. Sensitivity analysis.

5. A common input device is a(n)

   a. Compiler.
   b. Printer.
   c. Expert system.
   d. Point-of-sale recorder.

6. Which of the following is **most** likely to be considered an advantage of a sophisticated multiuser database?

   a. It may be operated and maintained without particular computer expertise.
   b. Information may be retrieved quickly.
   c. Conversion of traditional files to such a format is ordinarily extremely simple.
   d. It is easy to distribute information to every possible user.

7. Which of the following is **not** a widely used disaster recovery approach?

   a. Hot site.
   b. Firewall.
   c. Regular backups.
   d. Cold site.

8. Using sophisticated techniques from statistics, artificial intelligence, and computer graphics to explain, confirm, or explore relationships among data is referred to as

   a. Data mining.
   b. Data warehousing.
   c. Decision support.
   d. Distributed analysis.

9. The network most frequently used for private operations designed to link computers within a building in a research park is referred to as a(n)

   a. Bulletin board service.
   b. Local area network.
   c. Wide area network.
   d. Zero base network.

10. As used in information technology, a protocol is a set of rules for

   a. Exchanging data between two computers.
   b. Operating an operating system.
   c. Identifying proper computer technology needs.
   d. Measuring IT transmission speed.

Items 11 and 12 are based on the following information:

The power and maintenance departments of a manufacturing company are service departments that provide support to each other as well as to the organization's two production departments, plating and assembly. The manufacturing company employs separate departmental manufacturing overhead rates for the two production departments requiring the allocation of the service department costs to the two manufacturing departments. Square footage of area served is used to allocate the maintenance department costs while percentage of power usage is used to allocate the power department costs. Department costs and operation data are as follows:

Costs:	Service Departments		Production Departments	
	Power	Maintenance	Plating	Assembly
Labor	$60,000	$180,000		
Overhead	1,440,000	540,000		
Total costs	$1,500,000	$720,000		
Operating Data:				
Square feet	6,000	1,500	6,000	24,000
Percent of Usage:				
Long-run capacity	–	5%	60%	35%
Expected actual use	–	4%	70%	26%

11. The allocation method that would provide this manufacturer with the theoretically **best** allocation of service department costs would be

   a. A dual-rate allocation method allocating variable cost on expected actual usage and fixed costs on long-run capacity usage.
   b. The step-down allocation method.
   c. The direct allocation method.
   d. The reciprocal (or linear algebra) allocation method.

12. Without prejudice to your answer in 11, assume that the manufacturing company employs the step-down allocation method to allocate service department costs. If it allocates the cost of the maintenance department first, then the amount of the maintenance department's costs that are directly allocated to the plating department would be

    a. $144,000
    b. $120,000
    c. $115,200
    d. $90,000

13. Economists generally agree that business cycles are caused by changes in

    a. Aggregate expenditures resulting from technological changes, political events, or government monetary policy.
    b. Stock prices resulting from the need for market corrections, inflation, or government intervention.
    c. Public expectations about the future direction of prices resulting from government policies.
    d. Federal government fiscal policy, particularly changes in effective income tax rates.

14. In the cost of quality, liability claims are examples of

    a. Prevention costs.
    b. Appraisal costs.
    c. Internal failure costs.
    d. External failure costs.

15. If the economy is facing demand-pull inflation, which of the following would be a logical action by the government?

    a. Decrease income taxes.
    b. Sell government securities.
    c. Lower the discount rate.
    d. Increase government spending.

Items 16 and 17 are based on the following information:

The following information is available for Lopinsky, Inc.:

Balance Sheet

Current assets	$ 500,000
Property, plant, & equipment	4,000,000
Total assets	$4,500,000
Current liabilities	$ 30,000
Long-term debt	2,500,000
Common stock	200,000
Retained earnings	1,770,000
Total liabilities and stockholders' equity	$4,500,000

Cost of debt before tax	7%
Cost of equity	12%
Tax rate	25%

16. What is Lopinsky's weighted-average cost of capital?

    a. 9.50%
    b. 8.75%
    c. 8.22%
    d. 6.10%

17. What is Lopinsky's debt-to-equity ratio?

    a. 1.28
    b. 0.56
    c. 1.20
    d. 2.10

18. What is the **best** measure of risk for a well-diversified portfolio?

    a. Beta.
    b. Standard deviation.
    c. Variance.
    d. Expected value.

19. An organization has an opportunity to establish a zero balance account system using four different regional banks. The total amount of the maintenance and transfer fees is estimated to be $8,000 per annum. The organization believes that it will increase the float on its operating disbursements by an average of two days, and its cost of short-term funds is 4%. Assuming the organization estimates its average daily operating disbursements to be $80,000, what decision should the organization make regarding this opportunity?

    a. Do not open the zero balance accounts due to the additional cost of $8,000.
    b. Do not open the zero balance accounts due to an excess of costs over benefits of $1,600.
    c. Open the zero balance accounts due to an estimated savings of $1,200.
    d. Open the zero balance accounts due to an estimated savings of $6,200.

20. The formula for calculating the times-interest-earned ratio is

    a. $\dfrac{\text{Earnings before interest and taxes}}{\text{Interest expense}}$

    b. $\dfrac{\text{Earnings before taxes}}{\text{Interest expense}}$

    c. $\dfrac{\text{Interest expense}}{\text{Earnings before interest and taxes}}$

    d. $\dfrac{\text{Interest expense}}{\text{Earnings before taxes}}$

21. A company expects to produce 100,000 units of a product at a total cost of $500,000. The selling price of the product that will provide the company with a 15% before-tax return, to the nearest cent, is

    a. $0.75
    b. $1.15
    c. $5.75
    d. $7.67

22. The economic order quantity for inventory is higher for an organization that has

    a. Lower annual unit sales.
    b. Higher fixed inventory ordering costs.
    c. Higher annual carrying costs as a percentage of inventory value.
    d. A higher purchase price per unit of inventory.

23. X and Y are complementary products. If the price of product Y increases, the immediate impact on product X is that its

a. Price will decrease.
b. Quantity demanded will decrease.
c. Quantity supplied will decrease.
d. Price, quantity demanded, and supplies will remain unchanged.

24. A consultant recommends that a company hold funds for the following two reasons.

Reason 1: Cash needs can fluctuate substantially throughout the year.

Reason 2: Opportunities for buying at a discount may appear during the year.

The cash balances used to address the reasons given above are correctly classified as

	Reason 1	Reason 2
a.	Speculative balances	Speculative balances
b.	Speculative balances	Precautionary balances
c.	Precautionary balances	Speculative balances
d.	Precautionary balances	Precautionary balances

Hints for Testlet 2

1. No trick here.

2. Think about how a transaction is processed.

3. The same organization developed an internal control framework.

4. No trick here.

5. Think carefully about ways you know that data may be input into a computer.

6. This is a "sophisticated, multiuser database"—**not** a database ordinarily used by one or two individuals.

7. One reply involves attempting to avoid a disaster, rather than help in the event of a disaster.

8. Exploring is the key.

9. This is within one building.

10. IT protocols ordinarily involve multiple computers.

11. Which method theoretically results in the **best** answer?

12. Plating has 6,000 square feet of the total allocation base of 36,000 square feet.

13. Business cycles are caused by changes in aggregate demand.

14. Liability claims result from defective products that are distributed to customers.

15. What action decreases demand?

16. Remember cost of debt is after tax.

17. Debt-to-equity is equal to total debt divided by total equity.

18. It is the covariance that is important.

19. Compare cost to interest savings.

20. No trick here.

21. Sales must equal 115% of cost.

22. Economic order quantity balances order costs against holding costs.

23. Complementary products are used together.

24. Speculative balances are for investing.

Answers to Testlet 2

1.	b	5.	d	9.	b	13.	a	17.	a	21.	c
2.	b	6.	b	10.	a	14.	d	18.	a	22.	b
3.	b	7.	b	11.	d	15.	b	19.	b	23.	b
4.	a	8.	a	12.	b	16.	c	20.	a	24.	c

Explanations to Testlet 2

1. (b) Information and communication is the component that deals with information processing and availability.

2. (b) Segregation of duties involves segregation of authorization, approval, execution, and recordkeeping.

3. (b) COSO has developed a framework for enterprise risk management.

4. (a) ABC Analysis involves categorizing based on their urgency.

5. (d) A point-of-sale recorder is a common input device used by businesses that sell items over the counter.

6. (b) In a sophisticated multiuser database, information may be retrieved quickly by the users. Databases require expertise, security, and data is not necessarily easy to convert.

7. (b) A firewall is designed to protect a system from unauthorized users, and is **not** a disaster recovery approach.

8. (a) Data mining involves using sophisticated techniques to explain, confirm, or explore relationships among data.

9. (b) A local area network is a privately owned network within a single building or campus of up to a few miles in size.

10. (a) A protocol is a set of rules for exchanging data between two or more computers.

11. (d) The reciprocal method provides the **best** answer when service departments provide services to each other.

12. (b) Cost allocated to the plating department is $120,000 {$720 × [$6,000/($6,000 + $6,000 + $24,000)]}.

13. (a) It is generally agreed that business cycles are caused by changes in aggregate economic output (or expenditures).

14. (d) Liability claims result when defective products get shipped and fail in use.

15. (b) Selling government securities would decrease funds available to purchase other items. All of the other items listed would make demand-pull inflation worse.

16. (c) The cost of capital is equal to 8.22% [(12% × $1,970,000/$4,470,000) + 7% × (1 − 25%) × $2,500,000/$4,470,000)]. The current liabilities are not included in the calculation.

17. (a) The debt-to-equity ratio is equal to 1.28 ($2,530,000/$1,970,000).

18. (a) Beta is a standardized measure that has been developed to estimate investment risk.

19. (b) The cost of maintaining the zero balance accounts is $1,600 in excess of the benefits {$8,000 − [.04 × ($80,000 × 2)]}.

20. (a) The formula for calculating the times-interest-earned ratio is earnings before interest and taxes divided by the amount of interest expense.

21. (c) The selling price is equal to $5.75 {[$500,000 + (15% × $500,000)]/100,000}.

22. (b) If a firm has higher fixed inventory ordering costs they should order less often and larger amounts.

23. (b) Complementary products move together in terms of demand. Therefore, if the price of Y increases, demand will decrease. The demand for X will also decrease.

24. (c) The first reason is precautionary (cash may be needed to pay bills), and the second is speculative (cash may be used to take advantage of a discount).

Testlet 3

1. All of the following represent particular risks of outsourcing a process to foreign operations **except:**

    a. Quality risk.
    b. Language risk.
    c. Core competency risk.
    d. Public opinion risk.

2. Which of the following committees of a board of directors is most critical to corporate governance?

    a. The audit committee.
    b. The finance committee.
    c. The investment committee.
    d. The executive committee.

3. Which of the following **best** describes the New York Stock Exchange rules regarding the independence of directors?

    a. All directors must be independent.
    b. Two-thirds of all directors must be independent.
    c. More than one-half of all directors must be independent.
    d. There are no requirements regarding director independence.

4. Which of the following is **not** a component of the COSO's integrated enterprise risk management framework?

    a. Objective setting.
    b. Risk response.
    c. Risk assessment.
    d. Strategy mapping.

5. Which of the following is **not** a control for limiting access to particular electronic information within the IT system?

    a. Database replication.
    b. Views.
    c. Passwords.
    d. Restricting privileges.

6. A combination of hardware and software that links to different types of networks is referred to as a

    a. Bridge.
    b. Gateway.
    c. Switch.
    d. Router.

7. In encryption, a value that must be placed into the algorithm to decode an encrypted message is referred to as a(n)

    a. Key.
    b. Algoret.
    c. Router.
    d. Alphanumeric.

8. One would **most** frequently expect a "help desk" to be a responsibility of

    a. Applications programming.
    b. Data library.
    c. Operations.
    d. Systems programming.

9. When using a "join" operation with SQL, one would **most** likely be

    a. Adding a new computed column to a table.
    b. Combining some or all of the information in two tables.
    c. Extending computer memory capability by combining two or more CPUs.
    d. Encrypting data.

10. A commercial disaster recovery service that allows a business to continue computer operations in the event of a computer disaster is a

    a. Hot site.
    b. Checkpoint.
    c. Rollback.
    d. DOS (Disaster Operating System).

11. In forecasting purchases of inventory for a firm, all of the following are useful **except:**

    a. Knowledge of the behavior of business cycles.
    b. Internal allocations of costs to different segments of the firm.
    c. Information on the seasonal variations in demand.
    d. Econometric modeling.

Items 12 and 13 are based on the following information:

	Total Cost	Unit Cost
Sales (40,000 units)	$1,000,000	$25
Raw materials	160,000	4
Direct labor	280,000	7
Factory overhead:		
Variable	80,000	2
Fixed	360,000	
Selling and general expenses:		
Variable	120,000	3
Fixed	225,000	

12. How many units does the company need to produce and sell to make a before-tax profit of 10% of sales?

    a. 65,000 units.
    b. 36,562 units.
    c. 90,000 units.
    d. 29,250 units.

13. Assuming that the company sells 80,000 units, what is the maximum that can be paid for an advertising campaign while still breaking even?

    a. $135,000
    b. $1,015,000
    c. $535,000
    d. $695,000

14. A reduction in economic activity will be displayed by all of the following **except:**

    a. Decreased housing starts.
    b. Increase in the quantity of unemployment claims.
    c. Reduction in the amount of luxury purchases.
    d. Increase in personal travel.

15. The **primary** reason for adopting TQM is to achieve

    a. Greater customer satisfaction.
    b. Reduced delivery time.
    c. Reduced delivery charges.
    d. Greater employee participation.

16. Deming Corporation utilizes the capital asset pricing model (CAPM) to estimate the cost of its common stockholder equity. Calculate CAPM given the following: the risk-free rate of return is 5%, the expected rate of return is 10%, and the firm's beta is 1.

    a. 11%
    b. 10%
    c. 5%
    d. 15%

17. The **best** reason corporations issue Eurobonds rather than domestic bonds is that

    a. These bonds are denominated in the currency of the country in which they are issued.
    b. These bonds are normally a less expensive form of financing because of the absence of government regulation.
    c. Foreign buyers more readily accept the issue of both large and small US corporations than do domestic investors.
    d. Eurobonds carry no foreign exchange risk.

18. From an investor's viewpoint, the **least** risky type of bond in which to invest is a(n)

    a. Debenture bond.
    b. Deep discount bond.
    c. Income bond.
    d. Secured bond.

19. If a movie theater increases ticket prices for the matinee shows by 10% and the quantity of tickets demanded decreases by 5% then the demand for matinee movie tickets is

    a. Inelastic.
    b. Elastic.
    c. Unitary.
    d. Not related to the change in price.

Items 20 and 21 are based on the following information:

The standard direct labor cost to produce one pound of output for a company is presented below. Related data regarding the planned and actual production activities for the current month for the company are also given next.

> **NOTE:** DLH = Direct Labor Hours.

Direct Labor Standard:	
.4 DLH @ $12.00 per DLH = $4.80	
Planned production	15,000 pounds
Actual production	15,500 pounds
Actual direct labor costs (6,250 DLH)	$75,250

20. The company's direct labor rate variance for the current month would be

    a. $10 unfavorable.
    b. $240 unfavorable.
    c. $248 unfavorable.
    d. $250 unfavorable.

21. The company's direct labor efficiency variance for the current month would be

    a. $600 unfavorable.
    b. $602 unfavorable.
    c. $2,400 unfavorable.
    d. $3,000 unfavorable.

22. Davis Corp. is considering establishing a lockbox system. The bank will charge $30,000 annually for the service, which will save the firm approximately $15,000 in processing costs. The lockbox system will reduce the float for cash receipts by 2 days. Assuming that the average daily cash receipts are equal to $400,000, and short-term interest costs are 4%, calculate the benefit or loss from adopting the lockbox system.

    a. $30,000 loss.
    b. $15,000 loss.
    c. $12,000 benefit.
    d. $17,000 benefit.

23. A call option on a share of common stock is more valuable when there is lower

    a. Market value of the underlying share.
    b. Exercise price on the option.
    c. Time to maturity on the option.
    d. Variability of market price on the underlying share.

Item 24 is based on the following information:

The financial management team of a company is assessing an investment proposal involving a $100,000 outlay today. Manager number one expects the project to provide cash inflows of $20,000 at the end of each year for six years. She considers the project to be of low risk, requiring only a 10% rate of return. Manager number two expects the project to provide cash inflows of $5,000 at the end of the first year, followed by $23,000 at the end of each year in years two through six. He considers the project to be of medium risk, requiring a 14% rate of return. Manager number three expects the project to be of high risk, providing one large cash inflow of $135,000 at the end of the sixth year. She proposes a 15% rate of return for the project.

Additional information

Number of years	Discount rate (percent)	Present value of $1 due at the end of n periods (PVIF)	Present value of an annuity of $1 per period for n periods (PVIFA)
1	10	.9091	.9091
1	14	.8772	.8772
1	15	.8696	.8696
5	10	.6209	3.7908
5	14	.5194	3.4331
5	15	.4972	3.3522
6	10	.5645	4.3553
6	14	.4556	3.8887
6	15	.4323	3.7845

24. According to the net present value criterion, which of the following is true?

a. Manager one will recommend that the project be accepted.

b. Manger two will recommend that the project be accepted.

c. All three managers will recommend acceptance of the project.

d. All three managers will recommend rejection of the project.

Hints for Testlet 3

1. Which one is **not** affected by foreign operations?

2. Which committee deals with other corporate monitoring devices?

3. No trick here.

4. Which one does **not** deal with risk?

5. One of these replies suggests "more," rather than less.

6. For this one you need to understand the computer term.

7. To decode is similar to "unlocking" the code.

8. Which department deals with keeping the system functional on an hour-to-hour basis?

9. Which is most similar to joining a group?

10. Recovery operations often take place at another location.

11. Which item is arbitrary?

12. Calculate the contribution margin.

13. Calculate profit at 80,000 units.

14. Which item indicates improving conditions?

15. What is the ultimate value proposition for high-quality products?

16. CAPM = Risk-free rate + (Market rate – Risk-free rate) × Beta.

17. Eurobonds are denominated in US dollars.

18. What makes a bond less risky?

19. Elasticity of demand is equal to percentage of change in quantity divided by the percentage change in price.

20. Direct labor rate variance is equal to direct labor hours times the difference between the standard rate and the actual rate.

21. Direct labor efficiency variance is equal to the standard direct labor rate times the difference between the direct labor hours allowed and the actual hours worked.

22. The additional processing costs versus the interest savings.

23. An option value depends on option price, stock price, stock price variability, and maturity.

24. Calculate the net present value for each manager.

Answers to Testlet 3

1. c	5. a	9. b	13. a	17. b	21. a
2. a	6. b	10. a	14. d	18. d	22. d
3. c	7. a	11. b	15. a	19. a	23. b
4. d	8. c	12. c	16. b	20. d	24. d

Explanations to Testlet 3

1. **(c)** Core competency risk is **not** a risk related to foreign outsourcing.

2. **(a)** The audit committee of the board of directors is critical to effective corporate governance.

3. **(c)** The New York Stock Exchange rules require a majority of the directors to be independent.

4. **(d)** Strategy mapping is **not** a component of the ERM framework.

5. **(a)** Database replication is a backup procedure. All of the others are controls for limiting access.

6. **(b)** A gateway is a combination of hardware and software that links different networks.

7. **(a)** The key is the value that is used to decode the message.

8. **(c)** The operations department would normally have responsibility for the "help desk."

9. **(b)** The "join" operation in SQL is used to combine information in two different tables.

10. **(a)** A "hot site" is a disaster recovery service that allows a business to continue computer operations in the event of a disaster.

11. **(b)** Internal allocations of costs to different segments of the firm are irrelevant to forecasting purchases.

12. **(c)** The number of units that must be sold is 90,000 calculated as follows:

$$\text{Sales} = VC + FC + NI$$
$$\$25X = \$16X + \$585,000 + .10(\$25X)$$
$$\$6.5X = \$585,000$$
$$X = 90,000$$

13. **(a)** The amount can be calculated as follows:

$$\text{Sales} = VC + FC + NI$$
$$(\$25 \times 80,000) = (\$16 \times 80,000) + (\$585,000 + \text{Advertising}) + \$0$$
$$\$2,000,000 = \$1,280,000 + \$585,000 + \text{Advertising}$$
$$\text{Advertising} = \$135,000$$

14. **(d)** A reduction in economic activity will **not** be displayed by an increase in personal travel.

15. **(a)** The **primary** reason to adopt TQM is to achieve greater customer satisfaction with higher quality products.

16. **(b)** CAPM is equal to 10% [5% risk free rate + (10% expected return – 5% risk free rate) /1].

17. **(b)** The registration and disclosure requirements for Eurobonds are less stringent. Therefore, the cost of issuance is less.

18. **(d)** Secured bonds are less risky because they include collateral.

19. **(a)** The demand is inelastic because the demand does not fall as much as the price increase.

20. **(d)** The direct labor rate variance is equal to $250 [$75,250 – ($12 per hour × 6,250 actual hours)].

21. **(a)** The direct labor efficiency variance is equal to $600 unfavorable [(6,250 actual hours × $12 standard rate) – (15,500 actual production × .4 standard hours × $12 standard rate)].

22. **(d)** The result is a $17,000 benefit [$15,000 reduction in processing costs + (4% × $400,000 × 2 days) – $30,000 bank charge].

23. **(b)** The option is more valuable when there is a lower exercise price on the option.

24. **(d)** The net present value is negative in all three cases.

Testlet 4

Written Communication Task 1

Written Communication	Help

Guider Corporation is in need of long-term financing. Management is trying to decide whether to issue common stock or issue bonds. Laura Martin, the corporation's chief financial officer, has asked you to prepare a memorandum explaining the advantages and disadvantages of equity versus debt financing.

> **REMINDER:** Your response will be graded for both technical content and writing skills. Technical content will be evaluated for information that is helpful to the intended reader and clearly relevant to the issue. Writing skills will be evaluated for development, organization, and the appropriate expression of ideas in professional correspondence. Use a standard business memo or letter format with a clear beginning, middle, and end. Do not convey information in the form of a table, bullet point list, or other abbreviated presentation.

To: Ms. Laura Miller, CFO
        Guider Corporation
From: CPA Candidate

Written Communication Task 2

Written Communication	Help

Management of Howard Corp. is considering taking the corporation public. Timothy Wilson, the chief financial officer, has asked you to prepare a memorandum describing how the corporation would be affected by the compliance requirements of the SEC and the NASDAQ.

> **REMINDER:** Your response will be graded for both technical content and writing skills. Technical content will be evaluated for information that is helpful to the intended reader and clearly relevant to the issue. Writing skills will be evaluated for development, organization, and the appropriate expression of ideas in professional correspondence. Use a standard business memo or letter format with a clear beginning, middle, and end. Do not convey information in the form of a table, bullet point list, or other abbreviated presentation.

To: Mr. Timothy Wilson, CFO
        Howard Corp.
From: CPA Candidate

Written Communication Task 3

Written Communication	
	Help

Nagle, Inc. is considering implementing an activity-based cost system. The controller of the corporation, Michele Wu, has asked you to prepare a memorandum describing an activity-based cost system and the advantages of establishing such a system.

> **REMINDER:** Your response will be graded for both technical content and writing skills. Technical content will be evaluated for information that is helpful to the intended reader and clearly relevant to the issue. Writing skills will be evaluated for development, organization, and the appropriate expression of ideas in professional correspondence. Use a standard business memo or letter format with a clear beginning, middle, and end. Do not convey information in the form of a table, bullet point list, or other abbreviated presentation.

To: Mr. Michele Wu, Controller
               Nagle, Inc.
From: CPA Candidate

Grading Guidance for Communication Task-Based Simulations

Use the following guidelines to assign 0 to 5 points to your communication simulations.

- Is the communication responsive to the requirement and helpful to the reader? If not, give yourself a zero on the simulation, as it would not be graded.
- Is the communication appropriately organized with a beginning, middle, and end?
- Are the ideas clearly communicated in a form consistent with professional correspondence and with no tables, bullet lists, or other abbreviations?
- How many grammatical errors are there in the communication?

Total points _____

1. In which of the following situations would there be inelastic demand?

a. A 5% price increase results in a 3% decrease in the quantity demanded.
b. A 4% price increase results in a 6% decrease in the quantity demanded.
c. A 4% price increase results in a 4% decrease in the quantity demanded.
d. A 3% decrease results in a 5% increase in the quantity demanded.

2. A project should be accepted if the present value of cash flows from the project is

a. Equal to the initial investment.
b. Less than the initial investment.
c. Greater than the initial investment.
d. Equal to zero.

3. Which of the following cash management techniques focuses on cash disbursements?

a. Lockbox system.
b. Zero-balance account.
c. Preauthorized checks.
d. Depository transfer checks.

4. A customer intended to order 100 units of product Z96014, but incorrectly ordered nonexistent product Z96015. Which of the following controls would detect this error?

a. Check digit verification.
b. Record count.
c. Hash total.
d. Redundant data check.

1. (a) The requirement is to identify the situation in which there is inelastic demand. Demand elasticity is measured by the change in the quantity demanded divided by the change in the price. If the ratio is greater than one, demand is said to be elastic. If the ratio is less than one, demand is inelastic, and if the ratio is equal to one, demand is unitary. Accordingly, answer (a) is correct because it is the only situation that results in a ratio less than one, 3/5 = 0.60. Answer (b) is incorrect because it indicates elastic demand, 6/4 = 1.5. Answer (c) is incorrect because it indicates unitary demand, 4/4 = 1. Answer (d) is incorrect because it indicates elastic demand, 5/3 = 1.67.

2. (c) The requirement is to identify the decision rule for acceptance of a project. Answer (c) is correct because if a project's present value of cash flows is greater than the initial investment, the investment is expected to cover the cost of capital plus provide some additional return. Answer (a) is incorrect because it is not as desirable as answer (c). Answer (b) is incorrect because if management invests using this rule it will not cover the firm's cost of capital. Answer (d) is incorrect because acceptance of this project would result in losses.

3. (b) The requirement is to identify the cash management technique that focuses on cash disbursements. Answer (b) is correct because the zero-balance account technique involves establishing regional bank accounts to which just enough funds are transferred daily to pay the checks presented. It is a cash management technique for cash disbursements. Answer (a) is incorrect because a lockbox system is one in which customer payments are sent to a post office box that is maintained by the bank. Therefore, it involves cash receipts. Answer (c) is incorrect because use of preauthorized checks is not a cash management technique. Answer (d) is incorrect because depository transfer checks are used in conjunction with concentration banking which is a cash receipts management technique.

4. (a) The requirement is to identify the control that would detect the error. Answer (a) is correct because check digit verification involves use of an extra (redundant) digit added to an identification number to detect errors in inputting or processing a transaction. The check digit allows the computer to detect and reject items that are not valid. Answer (b) is incorrect because a record count is simply a control total of the number of records processed. It would not detect an invalid part number. Answer (c) is incorrect because a hash total is a control total with a total that is meaningless. It would not detect an invalid part number. Answer (d) is incorrect because a redundant data check uses two identifiers in each transaction record (e.g., customer account number and the first five letters of the customer's name). While this control might be established to detect the error, it would not be as effective as a check digit.

5. The greatest financial threat to an organization that implemented the financial accounting module of an enterprise resource planning (ERP) system from a major vendor exists from errors detected during which of the following times?

    a. Project initiation.
    b. Requirements determination.
    c. Table configuration.
    d. Implementation.

6. Which of the following procedures would an entity **most** likely include in its disaster recovery plan?

    a. Convert all data from EDI format to an internal company format.
    b. Maintain a Trojan horse program to prevent illicit activity.
    c. Develop an auxiliary power supply to provide uninterrupted electricity.
    d. Store duplicate copies of files in a location away from the computer center.

7. Which of the following definitions **best** characterizes benchmarking?

    a. A technique that examines product and process attributes to identify areas for improvements.
    b. The comparison of existing activities with the best levels of performance in other, similar organizations.
    c. The development of the most effective methods of completing tasks in a particular industry.
    d. The complete redesign of a process within an organization.

8. Which of the following is true about activity-based costing?

    a. It should not be used with process or job costing.
    b. It can be used only with process costing.
    c. It can be used only with job costing.
    d. It can be used with either process or job costing.

5. (d) The requirement is to identify the phase in which there is the greatest financial threat to an organization that implemented an ERP system. Answer (d) is correct because in the implementation phase the system is operating with real data that could be corrupted by operation of the new system. Answers (a), (b), and (c) are incorrect because they all involve development phases where real data is not being used.

6. (d) The requirement is to identify the item most likely included in a disaster recovery plan. A disaster recovery plan should include priorities, insurance, backup approaches, specific assignments, periodic testing and updating, and documentation. As a part of backup approaches the plan would include procedures for storing backup files. Therefore, answer (d) is correct. Answer (a) is incorrect because conversion of data is not a part of disaster recovery. Answer (b) is incorrect because Trojan horses are not part of disaster recovery. Answer (c) is incorrect because developing an auxiliary power supply is not part of disaster recovery. Normal power interruption is not considered a disaster.

7. (b) The requirement is to identify the **best** characterization of benchmarking. Answer (b) is correct because benchmarking involves comparison of existing activities with the best levels of performance in other or similar organizations. Answer (a) is incorrect because it describes continuous improvement. Answer (c) is incorrect because it describes best practices. Answer (d) is incorrect because it describes process reengineering.

8. (d) The requirement is to identify the true statement about activity-based costing. Activity-based costing involves assigning costs to products or cost centers based on activities and cost drivers. Answer (d) is correct because it can be used in conjunction with either process or job order costing. Answer (a), (b), and (c) are incorrect because they can be used in conjunction with either process or job order costing.

Appendix C: 2015 Released AICPA Questions for Business Environment and Concepts

1. According to COSO, the four categories of entity objectives in the enterprise risk management framework include each of the following **except**

   a. Effective and efficient use of the entity's resources.
   b. Compliance with applicable laws and regulations.
   c. Implementation of internal controls.
   d. Reliability of reporting.

2. According to COSO, the proper tone at the top helps a company to do each of the following **except**

   a. Create a compliance-supporting culture that is committed to enterprise risk management.
   b. Navigate gray areas where no specific compliance rules or guidelines exist.
   c. Adhere to fiscal budgets and goals as outlined by the internal audit committee and board of directors.
   d. Promote a willingness to seek assistance and report problems before it is too late for corrective action.

3. According to COSO, each of the following is an example of an appropriate ongoing monitoring activity **except**

   a. Follow-up of customer and vendor complaints regarding amounts due and owed.
   b. Periodic analysis of variances between expectations and actual results.
   c. Comparisons of information from various sources within the company.
   d. Approval of high-dollar transactions by supervisors.

4. Which of the following methods may the Federal Reserve use to reduce inflationary pressures?

   a. Decrease reserve requirements.
   b. Increase margin requirements.
   c. Increase the money supply.
   d. Decrease the target interest rate.

5. Product demand increases and product supply decreases. Which of the following statements is correct regarding resulting market changes?

Price	Quantity
a. Decreases	Increases
b. Uncertain	Increases
c. Increases	Decreases
d. Increases	Uncertain

1. (c) The requirement is to identify the category of objectives that is not part of the enterprise risk management framework. Answer (c) is correct because implementation of internal controls is not a category of objectives in the enterprise risk management framework. Answers (a), (b), and (d) are incorrect because they are all categories of objectives in the enterprise risk management framework.

2. (c) The requirement is to identify the item that is not an objective of a proper tone at the top. Answer (c) is correct because a proper tone at the top is not designed to cause personnel to adhere to fiscal budgets and goals as outlined by the internal audit committee and board of directors. Tone at the top is focused on ethical and compliant behavior. Answers (a), (b), and (d) are incorrect because they are all objectives of a proper tone at the top.

3. (d) The requirement is to identify the item that is not an example of an ongoing monitoring activity. Answer (d) is correct because approval of high-dollar transactions by supervisors is an example of a control activity. Answers (a), (b), and (c) are incorrect because they are all examples of ongoing monitoring activities.

4. (b) The requirement is to identify the action that would reduce inflationary pressures. Answer (b) is correct because increasing the margin requirements would reduce the supply of money and increase the cost of capital. This would reduce inflationary pressures. Answers (a) and (c) are incorrect because they would increase the money supply and decrease the cost of capital. This would fuel inflation. Answer (d) is incorrect because this would reduce the cost of capital and fuel inflation.

5. (d) The requirement is to indicate the effect on price and quantity in the market if demand increases and supply decreases. Answer (d) is correct because with an increase in price, the quantity demanded is uncertain. Answers (a), (b), and (c) are incorrect because price would increase and quantity demanded would be uncertain.

6. An importing partnership has experienced a dramatic surge in its exporting business and is looking for ways to minimize its risks from foreign currency fluctuations. The partnership's imports and exports to European Union countries are at similar levels. Which of the following methods most effectively minimizes risk?

    a. Purchase futures of the currency in which the payables will be paid.

    b. Hold payables and receivables due in the same currency and amount.

    c. Enter into an interest rate swap to mitigate the effects of exchange rate fluctuations.

    d. Conduct all foreign transactions in U.S. dollars.

7. A company invests $100,000 in property. The company has a contract to sell it for $120,000 in one year. The bank has a guaranteed interest rate of 10%. What is the net present value of the company's investment in the property?

    a. $9,091

    b. $10,000

    c. $109,091

    d. $110,000

8. Which of the following terms refers to a performance measurement that is calculated as an investment center's after-tax operating income minus the product of its total assets multiplied by the company's weighted-average cost of capital (WACC)?

    a. Economic value added

    b. Return on investment

    c. Net realizable value

    d. Profitability index

9. Which of the following observations regarding the valuation of bonds is correct?

    a. The market value of a discount bond is greater than its face value during a period of rising interest rates.

    b. When the market rate of return is less than the stated coupon rate, the market value of the bond will be more than its face value, and the bond will be selling at a premium.

    c. When interest rates rise so that the required rate of return increases, the market value of the bond will increase.

    d. For a given change in the required return, the shorter a bond's maturity, the greater the change in the market value of the bond.

6. (b) The requirement is to indicate the most effective way to minimize the risks from foreign currency fluctuations. Answer (b) is correct because holding payables and receivables due in the same currency and amount would effectively manage currency risks. Answer (a) is incorrect because it describes a strategy that reduces only a portion of the foreign currency risk. Answer (c) is incorrect because interest rate swaps are designed to mitigate the risks of interest rate fluctuations. Answer (d) is incorrect because it is not usually practical and is not a technique used to manage currency risks.

7. (a) The requirement is to determine the net present value of the investment. Answer (a) is correct because the present value of $120,000 received in one year discounted at 10% is equal to $109,091 ($120,000 × .90909). Therefore, the net present value of the investment is equal to $9,091 ($109,091 − $100,000 original investment). Answer (b) is incorrect because the net present value is equal to $9,091. Answer (c) is incorrect because $109,091 is the net present value of the sales price and does not factor in the $100,000 purchase price. Answer (d) is incorrect because the net present value is equal to $9,091.

8. (a) The requirement is to identify the performance measurement that is calculated as an investment center's after-tax operating income minus the product of its total assets multiplied by the company's weighted-average cost of capital. Answer (a) is correct because economic value added is measured as the investment center's after-tax operating income minus the product of its total assets multiplied by the company's weighted-average cost of capital. Answer (b) is incorrect because return on investment is measured as net income divided by average equity. Answer (c) is incorrect because net realizable value is equal to an asset's sales price less the costs to complete and sell the asset. Answer (d) is incorrect because the profitability index is equal to the ratio of the present value of future cash flows from an investment to the initial cost of the investment.

9. (b) The requirement is to identify the correct statement regarding the valuation of bonds. Answer (b) is correct because when the market rate of return is less than the stated coupon rate, the bond will sell at a premium above its face value. Answer (a) is incorrect because a discount bond is issued below face value and will go down in value during a period of rising interest rates. Answer (c) is incorrect because when interest rates rise, the market value of a bond will decrease. Answer (d) is incorrect because the shorter a bond's maturity, the less change in the market value of the bond.

10. An individual holds a 10-year fixed-rate bond as an investment. Three years of its life remain. When the bond was issued, interest rates were much higher than they are now. Interest rates are expected to be stable for the next three years. Which of the following statements is correct regarding the bond?

    a. The bond will become more sensitive to changes in interest rates during the next three years.

    b. The bond is currently selling at a discount.

    c. The bond will increase in value during the next three years.

    d. The bond is currently selling at a premium.

11. What is the relationship between the allowance for doubtful accounts and working capital?

    a. When bad debt expense is recorded for the period, working capital decreases.

    b. When bad debt expense is recorded for the period, cash increases.

    c. When an account is written off against the allowance, working capital decreases.

    d. When an account is written off against the allowance, cash decreases.

12. A systems engineer is developing the input routines for a payroll system. Which of the following methods validates the proper entry of hours worked for each employee?

    a. Check digit

    b. Sequence check

    c. Capacity check

    d. Reasonableness check

13. Passenger 1 and passenger 2 are booking separately on an airline Web site for the last available seat on a flight. Passenger 1 presses the enter key a few seconds before passenger 2, thus locking out passenger 2 and obtaining the last seat. This locking is a form of which of the following types of control?

    a. Concurrent update control

    b. Compensating control

    c. Data-entry control

    d. Operational data control

14. Cloud computing can best be defined as a model that

    a. Streamlines business processes onto a well-secured and highly available in-house e-commerce platform to optimize customers' online experience.

    b. Is designed for rapid application deployment by making several virtual servers run on one physical host.

    c. Allows users to access network resources from remote locations through a virtual private network.

    d. Allows organizations to use the Internet to access and use services and applications that run on remote third-party technology infrastructure.

10. (d) The requirement is to identify the correct statement regarding a 10-year fixed-rate bond. Answer (d) is correct because the bond will be selling at a premium because interest rates have decreased. Therefore, the bond is paying a higher-than-market interest rate. Answer (a) is incorrect because the bond will be less sensitive to changes in interest rates as it approaches maturity. Answer (b) is incorrect because the bond interest rate is higher than the market rate. Therefore, the bond would be selling at a premium. Answer (c) is incorrect because the bond will be selling at a premium, which will decrease as the bond approaches maturity.

11. (a) The requirement is to identify the relationship between the allowance for doubtful accounts and working capital. Answer (a) is correct because when bad debts expense is recorded, the allowance account is increased, and since it is a contra account to accounts receivable, this reduces working capital. Answer (b) is incorrect because when bad debts expense is recorded, cash is not affected. Answer (c) is incorrect because when an account is written off against the allowance, working capital does not change. Answer (d) is incorrect because when an account is written off against the allowance, cash does not change.

12. (d) The requirement is to identify the method that validates the proper entry of hours worked for each employee. Answer (d) is correct because a reasonableness check compares the number of hours input to a reasonable expectation of number of hours worked. Answer (a) is incorrect because a check digit helps ensure the accuracy of the input of a serial number or product number. Answer (b) is incorrect because a sequence check is a check of the correct sequence of a series of numbers. Answer (c) is incorrect because a capacity check is a check of the capacity of a particular storage bin.

13. (a) The requirement is to identify the control that locks out the second passenger. Answer (a) is correct because a concurrent update control helps ensure the proper results from concurrent activities. Answer (b) is incorrect because a compensating control is a control that compensates for the lack of another control. Answer (c) is incorrect because a data-entry control helps ensure the accuracy of input. Answer (d) is incorrect because an operational data control helps control the accuracy of operation data.

14. (d) The requirement is to identify the best definition of cloud computing. Answer (d) is correct because cloud computing allows organizations to use the Internet to access and use services and applications that run on remote third-party technology infrastructure. Answers (a), (b), and (c) are incorrect because cloud computing allows organizations to use the Internet to access and use services and applications that run on remote third-party technology infrastructure.

15. In a lean accounting environment, a company accepts a special order to make 200 units of a product each month for the next two months for $130 per unit. The company normally sells the unit for $170 per unit with variable costs per unit at $80. The company plans to use excess capacity. By what amount would this special order increase profit?

    a. $16,000
    b. $20,000
    c. $36,000
    d. $52,000

16. A company uses a standard costing system. The production budget for year 1 was based on 200,000 units of output. Each unit requires 2 standard hours of manufacturing labor for completion. Total overhead was budgeted at $900,000 for the year, and the budgeted fixed overhead rate was $1.50 per direct manufacturing labor hour. Both variable and fixed overheads are allocated to the product based on direct manufacturing labor hours. The actual data for year 1 are as follows:

Actual production in units	198,000
Actual direct manufacturing labor hours	425,000
Actual variable overhead	$352,000
Actual fixed overhead	$575,000

What is the amount of unfavorable variable overhead efficiency variance?

    a. $21,750
    b. $33,250
    c. $43,500
    d. $55,000

17. In year 1, a company's cash is 15% of sales, accounts receivable is 10% of sales, inventory is 20% of sales, accounts payable is 30% of sales, and long-term debt is 5% of sales. The company is preparing its forecasts and anticipates that sales will increase from $50,000 in year 1 to $55,000 in year 2. The company uses the percentage-of-sales method. What amount would be the required net working capital in year 2?

    a. ($2,750)
    b. $5,500
    c. $7,500
    d. $8,250

18. At the start of its fiscal year, a company anticipated producing 300,000 units throughout the year. The annual budgeted manufacturing overhead was $150,000 for variable costs and $600,000 for fixed costs. In April, when there was a beginning inventory for finished goods of 5,000 units, the company showed an income of $40,000 using absorption costing. That same month, ending inventory for finished goods was 7,000 units. What amount would the company recognize as income for April using variable costing?

    a. $35,000
    b. $36,000
    c. $44,000
    d. $45,000

15. (b) The requirement is to identify the amount of increase in profit that will come from accepting the special order. Answer (b) is correct because the special order will increase profit by $50 per unit ($130 – $80). Since the company will sell 400 units over two months, profit will increase by $20,000 ($50 × 400). Answers (a), (c), and (d) are incorrect because profit will increase by $20,000.

16. (a) The requirement is to calculate the amount of the unfavorable variable overhead efficiency variance. Answer (a) is correct because the variable overhead efficiency variance is equal to the actual quantity (AQ) times the standard rate (SR) minus the standard quantity (SQ) times the standard rate (SR). Since fixed overhead is budgeted at $1.50 per direct labor hour and budgeted direct labor hours is equal to 40,000 hours (20,000 units × 2 hours each), fixed overhead must be budgeted at $600,000 ($1.50 × 40,000). Therefore, variable overhead is budgeted at $300,000 ($900,000 total overhead – $600,000 fixed overhead), or $0.75 per direct labor hour ($300,000/40,000 hours). Standard quantity is equal to 198,000 units times 2 hours, or 396,000 hours. Therefore, the unfavorable variable overhead efficiency variance is equal to $21,750 (425,000 AQ × $0.75 SR – 396,000 SQ × $0.75 SR). Answers (b), (c), and (d) are incorrect because the variable overhead efficiency variance is equal to $21,750.

17. (d) The requirement is to calculate the amount of required net working capital. Answer (d) is correct because required net working capital is 15% of sales (15% cash + 10% accounts receivable + 20% inventory – 30% accounts payable). Therefore, the required net working capital is equal to $8,250 (15% × $55,000). Answers (a), (b), and (c) are incorrect because required net working capital will be equal to 15% of sales, or $8,250.

18. (b) The requirement is to compute the amount of income using variable costing. Answer (b) is correct because when using absorption costing, fixed overhead is included in inventory costs, and when using variable costing, fixed costs are expensed in the period they are incurred. Since inventory increased by 2,000 units (from 5,000 to 7,000), income using absorption costing is more than income using variable costing by $4,000 (2,000 units × $2.00 ($600,000 fixed costs / 300,000 units)). Therefore, variable costing income would be equal to $36,000 ($40,000 – $4,000). Answers (a), (c), and (d) are incorrect because variable costing income is equal to $36,000.

19. Colter Corp. is conducting an analysis of a potential capital investment. The project is expected to increase sales by $100,000 and reduce costs by $50,000 annually. Depreciation expense is $30,000 per year. Colter's marginal tax rate is 40%. What is the annual operating cash flow for the project?

    a. $42,000
    b. $72,000
    c. $90,000
    d. $102,000

20. A company is conducting a risk analysis on a project. One task has a risk probability estimated to be 0.15. The task has a budget of $35,000. If the risk occurs, it will cost $6,000 to correct the problem caused by the risk event. What is the expected monetary value of the risk event?

    a. $900
    b. $4,350
    c. $5,250
    d. $6,150

21. A company officer who is not a director is authorized to perform which of the following duties?

    a. Terminate the company's external audit firm.
    b. Remove a director for failure to exercise reasonable supervision.
    c. Declare dividends to shareholders.
    d. Enter into a contract with a vendor of computers for the company.

22. According to COSO, an executive's deliberate misrepresentation to a banker who is considering whether to make a loan to an enterprise is an example of which of the following internal control limitations?

    a. Costs versus benefits
    b. Management override
    c. Breakdown
    d. Collusion

23. Internal controls are likely to fail for any of the following reasons **except**

    a. They are not designed and implemented properly at the outset.
    b. They are designed and implemented properly as static controls, but the environment in which they operate changes.
    c. They are designed and implemented properly, but their operation changes in some way.
    d. They are designed and implemented properly, and their design changes as processes change.

19. (d) The requirement is to calculate the annual operating cash flow for the project. Answer (d) is correct because the cash flow is equal to $100,000 (increase in sales) + $50,000 (decrease in costs) − $48,000 taxes (40% × ($100,000 + $50,000 − $30,000)), or $102,000. Answers (a), (b), and (c) are incorrect because the annual operating cash flow is equal to $102,000.

20. (a) The requirement is to determine the expected monetary value of the risk event. Answer (a) is correct because the expected monetary value is equal to $6,000 (cost to correct) times 0.15 (probability of occurrence), or $900. Answer (b), (c), and (d) are incorrect because the expected monetary value is equal to $900.

21. (d) The requirement is to indicate the action that a company officer (nondirector) is authorized to perform. Answer (d) is correct because an officer is authorized to enter into a contract with a vendor of computers for the company. Answer (a) is incorrect because only the audit committee of the board of directors is authorized to terminate the external audit firm. Answer (b) is incorrect because an officer is not authorized to remove a director. Answer (c) is incorrect because only the board of directors can declare a dividend.

22. (b) The requirement is to identify the limitation of internal control that is illustrated by an executive's deliberate misrepresentation to a banker. Answer (b) is correct because this is an example of management override of internal control. Answer (a) is incorrect because costs versus benefits involves a consideration of the costs of controls versus their value to the organization. Answer (c) is incorrect because a breakdown occurs when personnel do not follow prescribed procedures. Answer (d) is incorrect because collusion involves two or more individuals conspiring to circumvent internal controls.

23. (d) The requirement is to identify the description that would not indicate control failure. Answer (d) is correct because controls should change as processes change. Answer (a) is incorrect because if controls are not designed and implemented properly, they will fail. Answer (b) is incorrect because if controls are static and the environment changes, they will fail. Answer (c) is incorrect because if the operation of controls changes, they will fail, assuming that they are not changing in response to a change in the environment.

24. Which of the following would indicate that the economy is in an expansionary phase?

a. Businesses increase capital investment.
b. The economy's resources are underused.
c. Potential national income will exceed actual national income.
d. Building up of inventories is in excess of consumer demand.

24. (a) The requirement is to identify the item that indicates the economy is in an expansionary phase. Answer (a) is correct because an increase in capital investment is indicative of an expanding economy. Answer (b) is incorrect because underuse of resources is not indicative of an expansionary economy. Answer (c) is incorrect because actual national income that is less than potential is not indicative of an expansionary economy. Answer (d) is incorrect because building of inventories is not indicative of an expansionary economy.

25. The price elasticity of demand for a good is 2.0, and the quantity demanded is 5,000 units. The price increases by 10%. What is the new quantity demanded?

a. 1,000
b. 4,000
c. 4,500
d. 6,000

25. (b) The requirement is to compute the new quantity demanded. Answer (b) is correct because price elasticity is equal to the percentage change in quantity demanded divided by the percentage change in price. Therefore, if price elasticity is equal to 2.0, a change in price of 10% produces a 20% change in quantity demanded: 2.0 = 20% ÷ 10%. If demand changes by 20% with a change in price of 10%, the quantity demanded would be reduced by 1,000 units (5,000 × 20%), and the new quantity demanded would be 4,000 units (5,000 units − 1,000 units). Answers (a), (c), and (d) are incorrect because the new quantity demanded is 4,000 units.

26. An auto parts store must maintain inventory of a wide variety of parts to satisfy its diverse customer base. As a result, the store's inventory has a high risk of obsolescence. Which of the following features would be most desirable to the store's creditors during a financial review of the auto parts store?

a. A high quick ratio
a. A high debt ratio
a. A high number of days sales outstanding in ending trade receivables
a. A low inventory turnover ratio

26. (a) The requirement is to identify the feature that would be most desirable to creditors. Answer (a) is correct because a high quick ratio means the company has a large amount of liquid assets available to pay debts. Answer (b) is incorrect because a high debt ratio indicates the company has a relatively large amount of debt. Answer (c) is incorrect because a high number of days sales outstanding in ending receivables means the company's customers are not paying quickly. Answer (d) is incorrect because a low inventory turnover ratio indicates that inventories are not being sold on a timely basis.

27. In capital budgeting, which of the following items is included in the payback model calculation?

a. The total amount of the initial outlay for the project
b. The present value of the future cash flows of the project
c. The present value of the estimated salvage value of the project
d. The amount of depreciation over the life of the project

27. (a) The requirement is to identify the item that is included in the payback model calculation. Answer (a) is correct because the payback model calculates the number of years necessary to recover the total amount of the initial outlay for the project. Answer (b) is incorrect because the payback model does not consider present value. Answer (c) is incorrect because the payback model does not consider present value. Answer (d) is incorrect because the payback method does not consider the amount of depreciation.

28. Each of the following will affect a company's return on investment **except**

a. Raising prices as demand remains unchanged.
b. Maintaining the company's cost of capital at current levels.
c. Decreasing expenses.
d. Decreasing investment in assets.

28. (b) The requirement is to determine the item that will not affect the company's return on investment. Answer (b) is correct because maintaining the company's cost of capital at current levels does not affect return on investment. Answer (a) is incorrect because increasing prices as demand remains unchanged will increase revenue and increase return on investment. Answer (c) is incorrect because decreasing expenses will increase return on investment. Answer (d) is incorrect because decreasing investment in assets will increase return on investment assuming that return from the investment is not affected.

29. In year 1, a large domestic manufacturer produces all of its motors domestically and sells them internationally. The company's management team is in the process of developing its year 2 budget, and copper costs represent a significant line item in the budget. In year 1, the company spent $1,000,000 in purchasing 250,000 pounds of copper. Economic data indicate that in year 1, copper costs had a price index of 120.0, and expectations are that the index will increase to 126.0 in year 2. Management anticipates a 5% increase in copper usage for year 2. What amount represents the year 2 budget for copper purchases?

   a. $1,000,000
   b. $1,050,000
   c. $1,102,500
   d. $1,300,000

30. A company has budgeted sales for January and February of 20,000 and 25,000 units, respectively. The selling price is $5 per unit, and the purchase price is $3 per unit. Budgeted ending inventory is 10% of the next month's sales. What is the budgeted cost of purchases for January?

   a. $54,000
   b. $60,000
   c. $61,500
   d. $75,000

31. In a business combination, the valuation of goodwill is a calculation

   a. To offset the bargain purchase cost.
   b. Of all of the unlimited life intangible assets.
   c. Of the residual paid above the fair value of the identifiable net assets.
   d. Of all of the increases in market valuation of the intangible assets acquired.

32. Which of the following classifications of security controls includes smoke detectors, generators, security guards, and ID badges?

   a. Technical
   b. Physical
   c. Administrative
   d. Logical

29. (c) The requirement is to calculate the year 2 budget for copper purchases. Answer (c) is correct because the budget is equal to $1,102,500 ($1,000,000 × 126/120 price increase × 1.05 increased usage). Answer (a) is incorrect because this is the year 1 budgeted amount. Answer (b) is incorrect because this is the year 1 amount only increase by anticipated additional usage. Answer (d) is incorrect because the correct amount is $1,102,500.

30. (c) The requirement is to calculate the amount of purchases in January. Answer (c) is correct because purchases are equal to 20,500 units (20,000 units + 2,000 beginning inventory (20,000 January sales × 10%) – 2,500 ending inventory (25,000 February sales × 10%)), which is equal to $61,500 (20,500 × $3.00). Answers (a), (b), and (d) are incorrect because purchases are equal to $61,500.

31. (c) The requirement is to identify the definition of the goodwill calculation. Answer (c) is correct because goodwill is calculated as the residual paid above the fair value of the identifiable net assets. Answers (a), (b), and (d) are incorrect because goodwill is calculated as the residual paid above the fair value of the identifiable net assets of the business.

32. (b) The requirement is to identify the type of controls that include smoke detectors, generators, security guards, and ID badges. Answer (b) is correct because these controls are physical controls. Answers (a), (c), and (d) are incorrect because the controls are examples of physical controls.

33. In an effort to recognize improvement opportunities, a company is reviewing its in-house systems. The best reason for the company to consider switching to cloud computing as a solution is that it

    a. Is the best way to secure sensitive corporate information.

    b. Is accessible only from within the company on its Intranet.

    c. Usually has lower up-front costs for equipment and maintenance.

    d. Provides better program modification options.

34. Which of the following types of business planning focuses on how a company can most effectively restore business operations following a disaster?

    a. Capacity planning

    b. Budget planning

    c. Strategy planning

    d. Continuity planning

35. Falser Co. increases all of its input factors by 100%, resulting in increased output of 90%. Which of the following statements identifies the effect of this change?

    a. Marginal returns rise.

    b. Marginal costs decrease.

    c. Returns to scale increase.

    d. Returns to scale decrease.

36. A company's standard costs for direct labor are as follows:

Direct labor

Standard quantity	Standard price
1 hour per unit	$15 per hour

Last month, the company produced and sold 100 units of its product, using 110 direct labor hours at a rate of $16 per hour. What amount is the company's direct labor efficiency variance for last month?

    a. $260

    b. $160

    c. $150

    d. $110

37. Which of the following changes would cause a company's break-even point in sales to increase?

    a. The company's contribution-margin rate increases.

    b. The company's variable cost per unit decreases.

    c. The company's total fixed costs increases.

    d. The company's selling price per unit increases.

33. (c) The requirement is to identify the best reason for a company to consider switching to cloud computing. Answer (c) is correct because cloud computing involves using third-party servers. Therefore, up-front costs for equipment and maintenance are lower. Answer (a) is incorrect because cloud computing is not the best way to secure information. Answer (b) is incorrect because cloud information is available on the Internet. Answer (d) is incorrect because cloud computing uses standard software.

34. (d) The requirement is to identify the planning that focuses on how a company can restore business operations following a disaster. Answer (d) is correct because continuity planning involves planning for disasters that could affect continuity. Answer (a) is incorrect because capacity planning involves estimating the infrastructure and software a company will need over time. Answer (b) is incorrect because budget planning involves developing expectations for future results. Answer (c) is incorrect because strategy planning involves developing a company's strategy or direction.

35. (d) The requirement is to identify the statement that identifies a situation in which input factors increase by 100%, resulting in increased output of 90%. Answer (d) is correct because this statement describes a situation in which returns to scale are decreasing. Answers (a), (b), and (c) are incorrect because the statement describes a situation in which returns to scale are decreasing.

36. (c) The requirement is to calculate the labor efficiency variance. Answer (c) is correct because the labor efficiency variance is equal to $150 (110 actual quantity × $15 standard rate) minus (100 standard quantify × $15 standard rate). Answers (a), (b), and (d) are incorrect because the labor efficiency variance is equal to $150.

37. (c) The requirement is to identify the factor that would cause break-even point in sales to increase. Answer (c) is correct because break-even point in sales is equal to fixed costs divided by the contribution margin. Answers (a), (b), and (d) are incorrect because break-even point in sales is equal to fixed costs divided by the contribution margin.

38. Which of the following costs is deducted from revenues of a manufacturing company in order to determine gross margin but not deducted from revenues to determine contribution margin?

   a. Fixed manufacturing
   b. Variable manufacturing
   c. Fixed selling and administrative
   d. Variable selling and administrative

39. A newly formed company uses a process costing system to record inventory costs. Data at the end of the first month of operations are as follows:

	Units	Direct materials (% complete)	Conversion cost (% complete)
Work-in-process inventory	100	100%	80%
Finished goods produced and sold	900	100%	100%

The company uses the weighted-average method to compute the costs. Its total costs for the month are $10,000 for direct materials and $19,600 for conversion costs. What is the total conversion cost per equivalent unit?

   a. $19.60
   b. $20.00
   c. $24.50
   d. $30.00

40. Last year a consulting company that solves computer network problems instituted a total quality management (TQM) program and produced the following summary cost-of- quality report:

	Year 1	Year 2	Change
Prevention costs	$ 200,000	$ 300,000	+50%
Appraisal costs	210,000	315,000	+50%
Internal failure costs	190,000	114,000	–40%
External failure costs	1,200,000	621,000	–48%
Total quality costs	$1,800,000	$1,350,000	–25%

Which of the following statements regarding the report is most likely correct?

   a. An increase in inspection costs was solely responsible for the decrease in quality costs.
   b. An increase in conformance costs resulted in a decrease in nonconformance costs.
   c. The increase in conformance costs indicated that the TQM program was **not** working.
   d. In the long run, increased conformance costs would cause total quality costs to increase.

38. (a) The requirement is to identify the item that is deducted from revenues to determine gross margin but not deducted from revenues to determine contribution margin. Answer (a) is correct because gross margin is equal to revenues minus fixed and variable manufacturing costs, and contribution margin is revenues minus variable manufacturing costs. Answers (b), (c), and (d) are incorrect because gross margin is equal to revenues minus fixed and variable manufacturing costs, and contribution margin is revenues minus variable manufacturing costs.

39. (b) The requirement is to compute the total conversion cost per equivalent unit. Answer (b) is correct because the conversion cost per equivalent unit is equal to $19,600 divided by 980 (900 + (100 work in process × 80%)), or $20.00. Answers (a), (c), and (d) are incorrect because the conversion cost per equivalent unit is equal to $20.00.

40. (b) The requirement is to determine the correct statement about the report. Answer (b) is correct because conformance costs (prevention and appraisal) resulted in a decrease in nonconformance costs (internal and external failure). Answer (a) is incorrect because there is no evidence that inspection costs were solely responsible for the decrease in quality costs. Answer (c) is incorrect because the increase in conformance costs (prevention and appraisal) does not indicate that the TQM program was not working because internal and external failure costs decreased more than the increase in conformance costs. Answer (d) is incorrect because there is no indication that, in the long run, increased conformance costs would cause total quality costs to increase.

Written Communication Task 1

Situation

The human resource manager of Revive Co. is considering allowing more employees to work from home for one or two days a week. Some of the department managers are eagerly encouraging the idea.

Write a memo to the department managers explaining the advantages and disadvantages of telecommuting.

Type your communication in the response area below the horizontal line using the word processor provided.

REMINDER: Your response will be graded for both technical content and writing skills. Technical content will be evaluated for information that is helpful to the intended reader and clearly relevant to the issue. Writing skills will be evaluated for development, organization, and the appropriate expression of ideas in professional correspondence. Use a standard business memo or letter format with a clear beginning, middle, and end. Do not convey information in the form of a table, bullet point list, or other abbreviated presentation.

Memorandum

To: Department managers

Re: Advantages and disadvantages to telecommuting

Solution to Written Communication Task 1

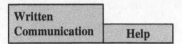

Memorandum

To: Department managers
Re: Advantages and disadvantages to telecommuting

Many of you have been considering implementing telecommuting in your divisions. This memorandum is designed to describe the advantages and disadvantages of telecommuting by employees.

Telecommuting has a number of significant advantages. First, allowing employees the flexibility to work at home can improve employee satisfaction. This may increase loyalty and reduce the turnover of valued employees. In addition, telecommuting may allow employees to be more productive as there may be fewer home distractions than at the office, including drop-ins and informal meetings. Finally, a systematic program of telecommuting may allow savings from reducing the required office and parking space.

There are also some potential disadvantages of telecommuting. There is less oversight of home workers, and some of these workers may find it difficult to be productive at home because of mind set or increased distractions. Another potential issue is security of company information. Telecommuting employees often need to use computers in their homes to access sensitive data. Strong internal controls must be established to mitigate the information security risks.

There are also potential behavioral issues. Telecommuting by employees may affect your division's culture or morale. With reduced personal contact, employees may feel isolated. There may be a feeling on the part of the employees that telecommuting may damage their careers because there is less opportunities to develop relationships. Also, the reduced interaction between employees may reduce the number of ideas that arise from employee brainstorming. To mitigate these behavioral issues it is imperative that you implement programs that encourage effective interactions.

Telecommuting can be significant employee benefit that may result in improvements in productivity. However, it is important for you to consider the implications of telecommuting, and implement controls and policies that mitigate the potential risks.

Written Communication Task 2

Written Communication	Help

Situation

The owner of a new business is consulting with you about the financial records the business will need to maintain. Specifically, the owner wants to know about balance sheets and income statements. Describe these two financial statements and compare them. Note timing, components of each, and some of the ways in which the owner will be able to use the statements.

Type your communication in the response area below.

> **REMINDER:** Your response will be graded for both technical content and writing skills. Technical content will be evaluated for information that is helpful to the intended reader and clearly relevant to the issue. Writing skills will be evaluated for development, organization, and the appropriate expression of ideas in professional correspondence. Use a standard business memo or letter format with a clear beginning, middle, and end. Do not convey information in the form of a table, bullet point list, or other abbreviated presentation.

Memorandum

To: Owner
Re: Financial Statements—purpose and use of

Solution to Written Communication Task 2

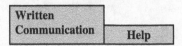

Memorandum

To: Owner
Re: Financial Statements—purpose and use of

As we discussed, this memorandum is design to provide a summary of essential financial records for a small business, with emphasis on the income statement and the balance sheet. Accurate financial records are essential to the effective management of any business. It is important that your business maintain a financial accounting system to enable the preparation of financial statements, including balance sheets and income statements.

The balance sheet for the company displays all of the assets and liabilities of the business, along with your ownership equity in the business. Accordingly, this statement displays the financial position of the company at a point in time. In the statement, assets are classified based on their liquidity and liabilities are classified based on their maturity. This allows you to assess, the company's ability to meet its short-term and long-term obligations. It also enables the company to strive to match the maturity date of debt used to finance assets with the date cash will be available from the assets. This allows the company to better meet obligations as they become due. Finally, the balance sheet allows an assessment of the extent of investment in various types of assets, which may allow the company to operate the business in a more efficient manner.

The income statement presents revenue and expenses to arrive at the net income of the business. This statement is important to understanding profitability of the business. The income statement presents the gross profit that the company achieves on the sales of its products, which allows the company to make better pricing decisions. The statement is also useful for identifying areas where costs should be better controlled. Lastly, the profitability of the business is important to determining the value of the company. This may also be very important information for you.

An effective financial accounting system is essential to the effective operations of a business. It allows the preparation of financial statements, including the balance sheet and the income statements, which can improve the quality of business decisions.

Index